T0304286

The Cost of Capital

This book provides an answer to the question 'what does the finance and economics literature say about the determination and estimation of a project's cost of capital?' Uniquely, it reviews both the theory of asset pricing in discrete time and a range of more applied topics that relate to project valuation, including the effects of corporate and personal taxes, the international dimension, estimation of the cost of equity in practice, and the cost of capital for regulated utilities. It seeks to explain models and arguments in a way that does justice to the reasoning whilst minimising the prior knowledge of finance and maths expected of the reader. It acts as a bridge between a general undergraduate or MBA text in finance, accounting or economics and the modern theoretical literature on the cost of capital.

SETH ARMITAGE is a Reader in Finance and head of the Finance Group at Heriot-Watt University, Edinburgh. His current and recent research centres on the financing of companies and has included work on rights issues and open offers, the role of banks in funding companies, sources of finance in developing countries and mutual financial institutions. He is the author of *Syndicated Lending in Europe* (1998).

The Cost of Capital

Intermediate Theory

Seth Armitage
Heriot-Watt University, Edinburgh

CAMBRIDGE
UNIVERSITY PRESS

CAMBRIDGE
UNIVERSITY PRESS

University Printing House, Cambridge CB2 8BS, United Kingdom

Cambridge University Press is part of the University of Cambridge.

It furthers the University's mission by disseminating knowledge in the pursuit of education, learning and research at the highest international levels of excellence.

www.cambridge.org
Information on this title: www.cambridge.org/9780521000444

First published 2005

A catalogue record for this publication is available from the British Library

Library of Congress Cataloguing in Publication data
Armitage, S. (Seth)
The cost of capital: intermediate theory / Seth Armitage.
    p.   cm.
Includes bibliographical references and index.
ISBN 0-521-80195-8 (hb: alk. paper) – ISBN 0-521-00044-0 (pb: alk. paper)
1. Capital investments.   2. Corporations – Finance.   I. Title.
HG4028.C4 A68   2005
332'.041'01 – dc22   2004054235

ISBN 978-0-521-80195-9 Hardback
ISBN 978-0-521-00044-4 Paperback

Contents

List of figures   *page* xi
List of tables   xii
Preface   xiii

Part I   Expected Returns on Financial Assets

1   The cost of capital under certainty   3
    1.1   Concepts   3
          1.1.1   Capital and investment   3
          1.1.2   A project and its cost of capital   4
          1.1.3   Capital budgeting and valuation   5
    1.2   The interest rate under certainty   7
          1.2.1   Choice in a timeless world   7
          1.2.2   Choice in a two-date world   9
          1.2.3   Equilibrium interest rate   13
          1.2.4   Introducing companies   13
          1.2.5   Equilibrium interest rate with companies   15
          1.2.6   Extension to multiple periods   18
    1.3   Summary   18

2   Allowing for uncertainty: contingent states   20
    2.1   Valuation   20
    2.2   Expected utility   22
    2.3   Choice and asset prices   24
          2.3.1   Choice in a two-date world   24
          2.3.2   Asset prices   28
          2.3.3   Companies   31
          2.3.4   Multiple periods   32
          2.3.5   Stochastic discount factor   32
    2.4   Some comments   33
          2.4.1   Evidence on expected utility   33

	2.4.2 Implications of market incompleteness and investor heterogeneity	34
	2.4.3 Monetary policy	36
2.5	Summary	36

3 The capital asset pricing model and multifactor models 38
3.1 The capital asset pricing model 38
    3.1.1 Assumptions 38
    3.1.2 The standard CAPM 41
    3.1.3 The CAPM without risk-free lending and borrowing 47
    3.1.4 Roll's critique 49
    3.1.5 Multiperiod setting 52
3.2 Multifactor models 52
    3.2.1 Arbitrage pricing theory 53
    3.2.2 The three-factor model 57
3.3 Note on conditional models 59
3.4 Evidence 60
3.5 Summary 63
    Appendix 3.1: Choice of risky portfolio 63
    Appendix 3.2: The expected return on an asset in an efficient portfolio 66

4 The consumption-based model 68
4.1 The stochastic discount factor 68
    4.1.1 Concept 68
    4.1.2 Determination and interpretation 70
4.2 The consumption CAPM 72
    4.2.1 Quadratic utility function 72
    4.2.2 Constant relative risk aversion and lognormal consumption 73
4.3 Multiperiod setting 78
    4.3.1 From one period to many 78
    4.3.2 An endowment or 'fruit tree' model 79
    4.3.3 Merton's intertemporal model 82
4.4 Note on evidence 85
4.5 Summary 85

5 The equity risk premium 87
5.1 Use of a historic mean premium as a forecast 88
5.2 Evidence on historic premiums 90
5.3 *Ex ante* expectations 96
    5.3.1 Inferring the expected premium 96
    5.3.2 *Ex ante* expectations in the past 98
5.4 Predictions from consumption-based theory 105
    5.4.1 The standard model 105

	5.4.2	Modified utility functions	109
	5.4.3	Market frictions	116
5.5	Summary		119

Part II   A Project's Cost of Capital

6   Project valuation   123
  6.1   The valuation model   124
    6.1.1   Multiperiod discounting   124
    6.1.2   Application of the CAPM   126
    6.1.3   Risk premium and time horizon   127
    6.1.4   Valuation using certainty equivalents   128
    6.1.5   Negative cash flows   131
    6.1.6   Bias caused by uncertainty about the discount rate   132
    6.1.7   Note on real options   132
  6.2   Capital: equity and debt   132
    6.2.1   Equity   133
    6.2.2   Debt   135
  6.3   Financing and taxes   137
    6.3.1   Definition of cash flows to discount   137
    6.3.2   Further issues   140
  6.4   *Ex ante* determinants of project beta   143
    6.4.1   Decomposition of risk based on factors affecting profit   143
    6.4.2   Decomposition of risk based on factors affecting value   145
  6.5   Notes on the user cost of capital and investment   147
  6.6   Summary   149
         Appendix 6.1: The Myers–Turnbull model   150

7   Corporation tax, leverage and the weighted average cost of capital   153
  7.1   Preliminaries   153
    7.1.1   Rates of return and levels of tax   153
    7.1.2   Financial assets compared with projects   154
    7.1.3   Corporation tax, cash flows and investment   155
  7.2   The weighted average cost of capital   157
    7.2.1   Without corporation tax   157
    7.2.2   With corporation tax   160
    7.2.3   The WACC and the CAPM   163
    7.2.4   Risky debt   165
  7.3   Expected cash flows that are not a constant perpetuity   168
    7.3.1   Without corporation tax   168
    7.3.2   With corporation tax   169
  7.4   Use of the formulas   172
  7.5   Issues concerning the WACC   174
    7.5.1   Circularity   174

	7.5.2	WACC and value additivity	175
	7.5.3	WACC and value maximisation	176
	7.5.4	Three alternative cash flow/cost-of-capital methods	178
	7.5.5	Changes in tax rates	179
7.6	Summary		180

8 Personal tax and the cost of equity: the old and the new views — 181

8.1	Extension of the Modigliani–Miller analysis		182
8.2	The 'new view': the cost of equity and the source of equity		185
	8.2.1	Introduction to the new view	185
	8.2.2	Cost of equity from retained earnings	187
	8.2.3	Cost of equity and the q-ratio	188
	8.2.4	Comparison of old and new views	192
	8.2.5	Tax irrelevance and dividend clienteles	196
8.3	Evidence		197
8.4	Summary		198
	Appendix 8.1: Personal tax and the CAPM		198
	Appendix 8.2: The Stiglitz model		201

9 Personal tax, leverage and multiple tax rates — 205

9.1	Leverage allowing for personal tax		205
	9.1.1	The Miller model	205
	9.1.2	Redundant tax shields	207
	9.1.3	Firm-specific capital gains tax	208
	9.1.4	Leverage clienteles	209
	9.1.5	Dammon's analysis	210
	9.1.6	Discussion	211
9.2	The cost of capital under the before- and after-tax views		212
9.3	Imputation systems		215
9.4	A certainty-equivalent approach		217
9.5	Evidence on leverage and tax		219
9.6	Asset pricing with multiple personal tax rates		220
9.7	Summary		224

10 Inflation and risk premiums — 225

10.1	Relations between real and nominal rates of return		225
	10.1.1	Certain inflation	225
	10.1.2	Uncertain inflation	226
10.2	Inflation and effective rates of tax on real returns		229
10.3	Risk premiums		232
10.4	Summary		235

11 The international dimension — 236

| 11.1 | The cost of equity | | 236 |
| | 11.1.1 | An integrated world capital market, and PPP holds | 236 |

11.1.2 An integrated world capital market, and PPP does
not hold   238
11.1.3 Segmented capital markets   241
11.1.4 Evidence on segmentation   244
11.2 The cost of equity for a foreign project   248
11.2.1 Two methods of valuation   248
11.2.2 More on the cost of equity   250
11.2.3 Further issues   252
11.3 Summary   254
Appendix 11.1: Errunza and Losq's model   255
Appendix 11.2: Testing the conditional CAPM   257

Part III   Estimating the Cost of Capital

12 The cost of equity: inference from present value   261
12.1 Estimation of the cost of equity in practice   262
12.2 The dividend discount model   264
12.2.1 Method   264
12.2.2 Elaboration   266
12.3 The abnormal earnings method   272
12.4 Inference from options prices   276
12.5 Summary   277

13 The cost of equity: applying the CAPM and multifactor models   278
13.1 Choice of risk-free rate   278
13.2 Choice of equity premium   281
13.3 Estimating beta from historic data   282
13.3.1 OLS estimation   282
13.3.2 Reversion to the mean   283
13.3.3 Thin trading   285
13.3.4 Measurement interval, company size and trading
frequency   289
13.3.5 Length of estimation period   290
13.3.6 Fat-tailed return distributions   291
13.3.7 Commercial estimates   291
13.3.8 Discussion   292
13.4 A Bayesian approach to estimating the CAPM   293
13.5 Multifactor models   294
13.5.1 A macrofactor model   295
13.5.2 The three-factor model   297
13.5.3 Use of the abnormal earnings method to estimate a
multifactor model   297
13.6 Summary   299

14 Estimating a project's cost of capital   300
  14.1 Estimating a project's cost of equity   300
        14.1.1 Cost of equity from pure-play companies   300
        14.1.2 Adjustment for difference in leverage   302
        14.1.3 Projects without a pure play   308
        14.1.4 Thoughts about total risk   308
  14.2 Estimating a project's WACC   310
        14.2.1 The effect of leverage   310
        14.2.2 Estimating the cost of debt   312
        14.2.3 Other issues   313
  14.3 Evidence regarding practice   315
  14.4 Estimation: what matters and what does not matter   317
  14.5 The relation between theory and practice   320
  14.6 Summary   321

15 Regulated utilities   323
  15.1 Price setting in the United States   323
  15.2 Estimation of the cost of equity   327
  15.3 Regulatory policy, risk and the allowed rate of return   328
  15.4 Price setting in the United Kingdom   331
  15.5 A note on public/private projects   333
  15.6 Summary   334

References   335
Index   347

Figures

1.1	An indifference curve	*page* 8
1.2	Consumption across two dates	10
1.3	The separation of production and the owner's consumption	14
1.4	The supply and demand for consumption units at date 1	16
2.1	Diminishing marginal utility	26
3.1	Choice of risky portfolio	42
3.2	The capital market line	45
5.1	The distribution of US equity premiums, 1926–97	95

Tables

5.1 Arithmetic mean real returns on US shares, government bonds
(or proxies) and treasury bills (or proxies), 1802–1997   *page* 92

5.2 Mean annual real returns on equity and government bonds in
sixteen countries, 1900–2000   93

7.1 The cost of capital and leverage: formula summary   173

Preface

All companies and investment projects need capital (money tied up in the business), and capital is not a free resource. A project's cost of capital is the minimum expected rate of return the project needs to offer to attract the money required. But where does the minimum expected rate come from? This book provides an answer. It sets out to explain what the finance and economics literature says about how a project's cost of capital is determined and estimated. It is written primarily for people who have already done some academic finance, accounting or economics but who are not necessarily well versed in the topics covered. In other words, it acts as a bridge between a general undergraduate or MBA text in finance, accounting or economics and the body of knowledge that relates to the cost of capital. It is suitable for students at honours, M.Sc. or MBA level who will have encountered the concept and who wish to know more.

Ease of comprehension is a high priority. Much of the book consists of explanations of theories, and many of the theories are demanding. I have done my best to present each model or argument in a way in which it can most easily be understood, whilst giving enough detail for the reader to see how a conclusion has been arrived at. The text includes plenty of discussion, supported by numerical examples. The exposition is in discrete time and uses (almost) no matrix notation. The level of mathematics is only slightly higher than that found in a typical undergraduate text in finance; the techniques most frequently used are algebra and differentiation. A basic knowledge of statistics and accounting is also assumed.

The flow of the book is from abstract models of expected returns, to less abstract models, concerned with particular features of the world that affect the cost of capital, and – finally – to methods of estimation. This seems to me to be the natural way to 'tell the story' about the cost of capital. I start by assuming a relatively simple world, and then make it more realistic. Part I, *Expected Returns on Financial Assets*, is an introduction to the theory of how expected rates of return on assets are determined. This is also known as the theory of asset pricing. There are no real-world complications in Part I, such as taxes or inflation. The theory is relevant because a project's cost of capital is the same thing as the expected rate of return on the project's capital at its market value – i.e. the capital viewed as a financial asset. So the theory of expected returns on financial assets constitutes the fundamental theory of the cost of capital.

It would have been possible to write the book, and it is more or less possible to read it, starting at Part II, which begins with project valuation and moves on to the weighted average cost of capital and tax. But this would have been to start the story halfway through. The theories discussed in Part II cannot themselves provide a satisfactory answer to the question of how the cost of capital is determined. This is because they do not attempt to explain how the expected rates of return on financial assets are determined. They *start* with an assumed required rate of return without tax, or with a model for such a rate, and then proceed.

The other motive for writing Part I was that there seemed to be a need for a treatment of asset pricing that was slightly above the level of a general undergraduate text in finance. Asset pricing is a huge and difficult area. There are now several very impressive books on the subject, but they are more advanced and detailed than Part I of this book. There have been few recent attempts to present asset pricing theory at a genuinely introductory or intermediate level, a valuable exception being by Danthine and Donaldson (2002). In fact, the same point can be made regarding most of the other topics in the book. A great deal of thinking has been done by researchers, and many absorbing lines of enquiry have been pursued. But there is surprisingly little to help the student take the steps to the research literature.

Part II is entitled *A Project's Cost of Capital*. It reviews a number of issues in the determination of a discount rate to value a project, often using the capital asset pricing model (CAPM) as the theory that explains the cost of equity. It starts with the framework for project valuation and then considers, in turn, the effects of corporation tax, personal taxes, inflation, and the existence of more than one country and currency. By the end of Part II the reader will have covered the central elements of the theory pertaining to a project's cost of equity and the weighted average cost of capital.

Part III, *Estimating the Cost of Capital*, is a discussion of the main methods of estimation used in practice, and of research on these methods. It first considers estimation of the cost of equity of a listed company – i.e. estimation of the expected rate of return on the company's shares. It then turns to what can be done to estimate the weighted average cost of capital of a project or unlisted company. The final chapter is devoted to the important special case of the cost of equity for regulated utility companies.

The book is about theory and estimation. There are summaries of the empirical evidence on the theories at various points, but there is little discussion of the empirical methods of testing them, or of debated findings, except as regards the equity risk premium. In general, I have paid more attention to the cost of equity than to the cost of debt. The models in the research reviewed are models constructed in discrete time, with a handful of exceptions. There is nothing on monetary policy, nor on models of the term structure of interest rates. Throughout, given the scale and complexity of the relevant literature, and given my own limitations, I have had to be selective both in what to review and in how to review it.

The most similar recent books specifically on the cost of capital are those by Ehrhardt (1994) and Patterson (1995). Ehrhardt provides a clear introductory account, written primarily for practitioners. Patterson offers a comprehensive review of a wide range of applied theory and evidence. The present book covers some of the same ground but, nevertheless, differs considerably from these predecessors in terms both of exposition and of content.

It is much more concerned with the explanation of theoretical arguments, and it contains more, in particular, on asset pricing theory, the equity premium and the effects of taxes. It is similar in approach and style to the book by Copeland and Weston (1988).

I hope that this book gives the reader some perspective on how the diverse topics of research it discusses relate to each other. However, many readers will not be interested in all of these topics, so individual chapters are designed, as far as possible, to be read on a stand-alone basis. They can serve as supplementary references for a variety of courses. Subjects in which the cost of capital features prominently include project and company valuation, capital budgeting, asset pricing, the assessment of company performance and the effects of taxes on corporate debt policy and dividend policy.

In summary, the book is a mixture of a monograph and a textbook. Its orientation around a single topic is in the nature of a monograph; its style of exposition is more like that of a textbook.

Acknowledgements

It is a pleasure to acknowledge the help and support I have received. I am grateful to the Leverhulme Trust, and to my referees, for the award of a Research Fellowship for the academic year 2002/03. The uninterrupted time bought by the award has helped me enormously. I wish to thank Andy Adams, Alastair Byrne, Adrian Fitzgerald, Graham Partington and John Sawkins for their comments on certain chapters and for their interest in the project. Andy Snell of the University of Edinburgh read and discussed with me a large part of the manuscript, and Paul Hare of Heriot-Watt University read all of it. Special thanks go to both of them for their time and for many thought-provoking comments. I am responsible for the shortcomings and errors that remain. I am grateful to Cambridge University Press for their commitment to the book from an early stage, to an anonymous reviewer for his or her constructive comments, and to the editors, Ashwin Rattan and later Chris Harrison, for their advice and patience. Finally, my thanks and love go to my parents, who have been characteristically enthusiastic, and most of all to Jenny Bennison and our young children. They have lived with the book for several years, and they have kept it in perspective.

SETH ARMITAGE
Edinburgh, UK
April 2004

Part I
Expected Returns on Financial Assets

1   The cost of capital under certainty

The purpose of Part I is to examine how the expected returns on financial assets are determined in simple theoretical settings. We explain in Section 1.1 that a project can be thought of as a financial asset, and that its cost of capital is the expected return on the asset at market value. So we are really looking at how the cost of capital is determined. The settings are rather abstract, and may seem odd at first sight. The reason for the abstraction is to help in understanding the economic processes that determine a project's cost of capital in the real world.

The current chapter begins with a brief account of what the terms 'capital' and 'cost of capital' mean. It then considers the interest rate in a world in which the future is known with certainty. The assumption of certainty, though unrealistic, provides a relatively easy starting point. The analysis serves to establish several ideas that will be useful when uncertainty about the future is introduced in Chapter 2.

1.1   Concepts

1.1.1   Capital and investment

It is not as easy as one might expect to say what is meant by 'capital', and by the related terms 'investment', 'saving', 'income' and the 'cost of capital'. In fact, there is a sizable literature in economics on these questions (e.g. Parker and Harcourt, 1969; Hirshleifer, 1970). We offer a brief discussion based on everyday usage.

There are at least three meanings of *capital* in common use.

(i) Many readers will think first of capital in the context of personal finance, in which it means the same as savings. Most people would consider the value of their savings (their wealth or non-human capital) to be the value of their financial assets, such as money in a bank account or shares in a mutual fund, plus the value of their house, net of their personal borrowing.

(ii) In the context of company finance, capital means money tied up in the company in the form of equity and debt. Equity and debt are financial assets that have been issued by the company at some time in exchange for cash. There are two ways of measuring the amount of money tied up that are in general use. The value of the equity and debt on the balance sheet – the accounting or book value of the capital – measures the amount of cash raised by the company and yet to be repaid, including retained cash flow, net of depreciation. At least, this is what book value measures under the pure historic-cost convention of preparing accounts, under which the cost of an asset is adjusted only for depreciation. In contrast, the market value of the money tied up measures the amount of cash that could be raised by the current holders of the equity and debt if they chose to sell their holdings.

It is normal to speak of projects or operations or divisions as having capital, regardless of whether they are actually constituted as companies. Such business units are implicitly being thought of as discrete entities, which might – in principle – exist as companies, able to issue equity and debt.

(iii) In economics, the central meaning of capital is probably assets used in the production process: tangible assets such as machinery, and intangible assets such as know-how. Such real (as opposed to financial) assets are used to provide goods and services consumed by individuals, or to produce real assets used as inputs in further production processes. Thus, capital in the economist's sense refers to resources created or nurtured as a means to an end, the ultimate end being consumption by people. The resources exist in physical form, or in the form of knowledge and skills possessed by individuals and organisations.

The common thread across the three meanings is that capital is money tied up or invested in something that provides income in the future. The 'something' is a financial asset, or property, in the context of personal finance; it is a company or project in corporate finance; and it is any real asset in economics.

The term *investment* means, in general, addition to capital. In personal finance, investment means the same as saving – that is, addition to one's financial assets or property. In company finance, investment is the injection of new cash in a company through an increase in the cash tied up as equity, via the retention of net cash flow or the issue of shares, or through an increase in the amount of debt outstanding. Investment is also the commitment of cash to a project. In economics, investment is expenditure to create or purchase real assets, which therefore increases the owner's stock of real assets.

1.1.2   *A project and its cost of capital*

We are concerned with the cost of capital for projects. We shall leave aside the distinction between equity and debt until Part II, and shall assume that all capital is in the form of equity. *A project* is a discrete undertaking that requires capital, in the corporate finance sense of cash tied up as equity, and that is expected to provide a positive real rate of return on its capital, net of operating costs (otherwise it would not be undertaken). A project's *cost of capital* is the minimum expected rate of return needed to attract the required capital. The minimum expected rate is an opportunity cost, not a cash cost. It is the rate that could be obtained by investing the cash in the next-best alternative. We shall see that the next-best alternative is to invest in other projects, or in financial assets, of the same risk as the project in question. If the asset market is efficient, assets of the same risk will offer the same expected rate of return, so there will be one expected rate for each level of risk. Any project that offers an expected rate above the market rate for its level of risk is a project that will increase the wealth of the owner. Hence, the cost of capital can also be thought of as the project's *hurdle rate*, the minimum expected rate of return that leaves investors (the providers of capital) at least as well off as they would have been had they invested in another asset of the same risk. These ideas will become clearer in the context of a model of project valuation (below and Section 2.1).

We have, in talking about an *expected* rate of return, implicitly assumed that the future is uncertain. If the future is assumed to be certain, there is no risk, and the minimum rate of return needed to attract the required capital will be the same for all projects. The cost of capital can then be called the *interest rate*. We shall assume certainty for the rest of the present chapter.

A word on terminology

A return is a percentage gain or loss in a single period. A rate of return or interest rate is a percentage gain or loss per period. They mean the same thing given a single period, or given identical returns per period. But some care is needed if there are $T > 1$ periods and the returns per period differ. A return over a particular single period will be different from the rate of return over the T periods. For the moment, we assume either a single period or identical returns per period.

1.1.3   Capital budgeting and valuation

The core application of the cost of capital is in capital budgeting, which is the process by which a company decides which projects to undertake. Capital budgeting involves the estimation of the market value of projects that have yet to be undertaken, and that do not have an observable market value. This is because there is no market for would-be projects, and financial assets are not issued that provide claims to the future net cash flows from would-be projects. The estimated market value of a project is then compared with the initial cash cost. If the value exceeds the cost, then the project adds value and should be undertaken, assuming that the aim of the investment is to increase shareholder wealth. The estimated market value of an untraded asset, whether it is a project (a real asset) or a financial asset, is an estimate of the price that investors would pay for it were it tradable. A valuation model is a model that provides an estimate of the market value; it explains the price that investors would pay for an asset.

Single-period setting

A project is something that provides one or more net cash flows or pay-offs in the future. Consider a project that will provide a single pay-off of Y_1 in real terms after one period, at date 1. The present date is date 0. Let the capital, or cash investment, required at date 0 to undertake the project be I_0. The percentage real return on the cash investment, R_{inv}, is

$$R_{inv} = Y_1/I_0 - 1 \qquad (1.1)$$

The market value V_0 of the shares issued to raise I_0 is determined by Y_1 and by the interest rate R:

$$V_0 = Y_1/(1 + R)$$

or

$$V_0(1 + R) = Y_1 \qquad (1.2)$$

Equation 1.2 is a model of the market value of the project, given Y_1 and R. Investors are willing to pay for the project because ownership gives entitlement to the future pay-off. Equation 1.2 says that the price in equilibrium that investors would be willing to pay, V_0, is such that, given the future pay-off, the return on the purchase is R. At this price, investors are indifferent between investing in the shares in the project and investing in the next-best alternative, which is another asset that provides a percentage return of R.

The project will increase shareholder wealth only if $V_0 > I_0$ (i.e. if the *net present value* (NPV)) is positive, and it will attract the required capital only if $V_0 \geq I_0$. It can be seen by comparing equations (1.1) and (1.2) that $V_0 \geq I_0$ if $R_{inv} \geq R$, since Y_1 is given. Since the cost of capital is defined as the minimum return on the cash needed to attract the amount I_0, and no one will invest unless $V_0 \geq I_0$, the cost of capital is given by the interest rate R.

Example

Suppose the investment required to undertake a project is £100 and the pay-off at date 1 is £120. The interest rate is 5 per cent. The market value of the project is then

$$V_0 = \pounds120/1.05 = \pounds114$$

from equation (1.2). Someone buying the project at this price obtains a return of 5 per cent. The net present value is positive, at £114 − £100 = £14, and the return on the cash investment of £100, which is 20 per cent, exceeds the cost of capital, which is 5 per cent.

Multiperiod setting

Things are a little more complicated with more than one period, even assuming certainty. The normal measure of the return on investment over more than one period is the *internal rate of return* (IRR). This is defined as the discount rate at which the present value of the cash flows is equal to the cash investment required at date 0. That is, we solve

$$-I_0 = Y_1/(1 + x) + Y_2/(1 + x)^2 + \cdots Y_T/(1 + x)^T \qquad (1.3)$$

for x, given V_0 and the cash flows for the T periods; and the value found for x is the IRR. The virtue of the IRR is that, if it exceeds the interest rate, then the NPV will be positive. Thus, for the purpose of working out whether the NPV is positive, the IRR can be compared with the interest rate, assuming that the interest rate is the same in all periods.

Despite this, there are several familiar problems with using the IRR in capital budgeting. IRR takes no account of the size of the project. If one or more of the cash flows is negative, there will be more than one value of x, or no value of x, that satisfies equation (1.3). It is debatable whether IRR is the best measure of the rate of return on the cash invested in the project. The amount of cash invested changes over time. The IRR is the rate of return that will be received assuming that all the cash received before the end of the project (date T) is invested until T at the IRR. It would, arguably, be more sensible to assume that cash received can be invested at the interest rate.

The problems with IRR can be avoided by using the rule that says: accept projects with positive NPV. The important point for our purposes is that the positive-NPV rule involves the concept of the cost of capital. It is equivalent to saying: accept projects with a rate of return on investment that exceeds the interest rate. We can see this by thinking of the claim to each (positive) cash flow in equation (1.3) as a separate asset or 'mini-project', each of which provides the cash flow in question. The next-best alternative to a claim to Y_t is another asset providing the same pay-off at the same date t periods from date 0. The rate of return on this asset at market value must be R per period, so its price must be $Y_t/(1 + R)^t$. Thus the market value of the package of claims to $Y_1, Y_2 \ldots Y_T$ is

$$V_0 = Y_1/(1 + R) + Y_2/(1 + R)^2 + \cdots Y_T/(1 + R)^T$$

If $V_0 > I_0$, it must be the case that the rate of return on the package – i.e. the project – exceeds the interest rate R.

1.2 The interest rate under certainty

1.2.1 Choice in a timeless world

The question to which we turn in the rest of the chapter is how the interest rate is determined assuming certainty. The model we present originates with Fisher (1930), and our presentation is based on Hirshleifer (1970) and Fama and Miller (1972).

The 'classical' microeconomic theory of interest is an extension of the traditional theory of demand for goods in a timeless world of perfect markets. We start with a sketch of this theory. The main assumptions are as follows.

(i) A perfect market is one in which there are no transactions costs, there is no taxation or other interference from outside the market, information is freely available and all the participants are price takers, unable to affect the market price by their trades.

(ii) Goods and services are traded in units that are 'small' in relation to the budgets of individuals. This ensures that marginal utility per pound spent can be equated across goods. We abstract from the facts that some goods are much more expensive than others and that goods are not 'infinitely divisible'.

(iii) Individuals are assumed to be rational and to seek to maximise their utility, or material welfare. Utility derives from the consumption of goods and services by individuals.

The following assumptions are normally made about the rationality and utility functions of individuals.

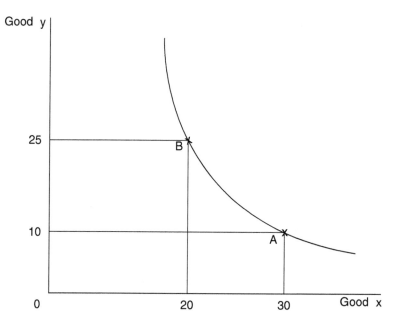

Figure 1.1   An indifference curve

1. *Comparability between goods*, or *completeness of preferences*. For any two bundles of goods A and B, the individual either prefers A to B or B to A, or is indifferent between them.
2. *Transitivity of preferences*, or *consistency*. If the individual prefers A to B and prefers B to a third bundle C, he or she prefers A to C. If he/she is indifferent between A and B and between B and C, he/she is indifferent between A and C.
3. *Non-satiation*. The individual prefers or is indifferent to having more of a given good, assuming that this does not mean having less of any other good.
4. *Diminishing marginal utility*. Starting from any combination of two individual goods, x and y, for each extra unit of one good given up the individual requires an increasing amount of the other in order to maintain the same level of total utility.

   Diminishing marginal utility implies that indifference curves are convex to the origin (the curve lies below a straight line between any two points), as illustrated in Figure 1.1 for the case of two goods. Imagine two points, A and B, that lie on the same indifference curve. These points represent different bundles of the two goods for a given individual. At point A the individual has thirty units of x and ten units of y, and he requires one unit of y for every one unit of x given up. In other words, the slope of the curve at that point, or *marginal rate of substitution* of y for x, is −1. At point B the individual has twenty units of x and twenty-five units of y and requires two units of y for every one of x given up, so the slope at this point is −2. The individual has more of y at B than A, so his marginal utility from y — his utility from an extra unit of y — is smaller at B. The total utility from each of these combinations is the same, which is why they are on the same indifference curve.

It can easily be shown that individuals maximise their utility by allocating their budget in such a way that the marginal utility, the utility from spending an extra £1 on any good, is the same. This means that, for any two goods x and y, a given individual will buy amounts of each such that the ratio of the marginal utilities for each good, and hence the marginal rate of substitution between the two, is equal to the ratio of their prices:

$$MU_x/MU_y = P_x/P_y \qquad (1.4)$$

where MU_x is the marginal utility of good x and P_x is the price of one unit of x. The market for goods and services is in equilibrium if equation (1.4) holds across all goods and all individuals. It is not necessary for individuals to have the same preferences (utility functions) for equilibrium to arise; two people with the same budget but different preferences will maximise their respective utilities by buying goods in different amounts. Also, the analysis does not require that explicit numerical (cardinal) values be assigned to different levels of utility. An ordinal utility function is sufficient. This means that the individual can rank combinations of goods in consistent orders of preference (assumptions 1 and 2 above). This is enough for different levels of utility to be identified, for indifference curves not to cross and for an individual to say how much of a good he wants in exchange for one unit of another good, so that the marginal rates of substitution are known.

1.2.2 Choice in a two-date world

There is, obviously, no role for an interest rate, or for capital, unless the analytical framework is extended to incorporate time. A simple way of introducing time is to suppose that there are just two dates, the present and a future date, with a period of time in between. The individual decides how to allocate his current budget between consumption today and saving, which enables him to consume more at the future date. At the heart of the theory of interest under certainty is the view that the utility from a unit of consumption today is not necessarily the same as the utility today from a unit of consumption in the future. The individual chooses between 'bundles' of differing amounts of present and future consumption in a way that is analogous to the choice between bundles of goods in a timeless world.

Under certainty, there is no chance that the individual will face an unforeseen shortfall in income or an unforeseen requirement for expenditure, so there is no precautionary motive for saving. There is also no opportunity to seek a higher return by taking risk. The sole reason for saving is to have more to spend in the future. We shall see that utility is maximised when the loss in utility from forgoing one unit of consumption today equals the gain in utility from being able to spend $(1 + R)$ units more in the future, where R is the real rate of interest.

Suppose for the moment that all an individual can do with his money saved is to put it under the mattress. Then £1 not spent today provides £1 more to spend at date 1. Let c_t be one unit of consumption, or bundle of goods and services, at date t. The price per unit of current consumption is $P_0 = £1$. c_1 is exactly the same unit except that it will be consumed at date 1, and its price is P_1. The real value of £1 saved – the value in terms of the consumption units that £1 buys – depends on P_1.

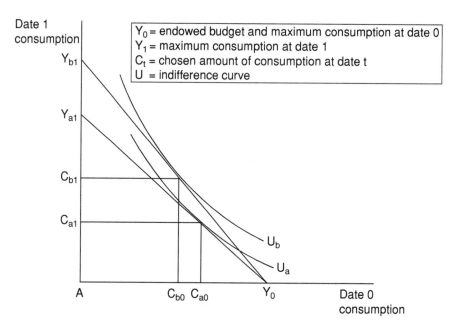

Figure 1.2   Consumption across two dates

In Figure 1.2 an individual has funds (or income or endowment) of Y_0 pounds at date 0. His budget constraint says that the total amount he can spend on consumption at dates 0 and 1 cannot exceed Y_0. It can be written

$$P_1 C_1 = Y_0 - P_0 C_0$$

where C_t is the number of units consumed at date t. The line between Y_{a1} and Y_0 represents the budget constraint assuming the price $P_{a1} = P_0 = £1$, so its slope is -1. The interest rate is zero; the real value of the funds saved stays the same.

U_a is an indifference curve showing combinations of units consumed at the two dates between which the individual is indifferent. It is convex because diminishing marginal utility of consumption at each date is assumed. Curves further away from the origin represent higher levels of 'lifetime utility' – that is, utility at date 0 from consumption at date 0 and from consumption-to-come at date 1. The shape of the individual's indifference curves depends upon his *time preference*. Greater time preference means greater utility from a given amount of consumption now in relation to utility from the same amount of consumption in the future; the indifference curves have a steeper slope, so the point of tangency occurs nearer to point Y_0, and the individual saves less. The indifference curve tangential to the budget constraint represents the highest level of lifetime utility the individual can attain, given his budget. At the point of tangency, the slope of the indifference curve equals the slope of the budget constraint, so the loss in utility from forgoing one unit of consumption at date 0 equals the gain in utility from spending the extra £1 at date 1. The individual consumes AC_{a0} and saves $C_{a0}Y_0$ at date 0, and consumes AC_{a1} at date 1.

Now suppose we have $P_{b1} < £1$, which means that £1 buys more units at date 1 than at date 0 (there is price deflation). This is the same as saying that the real value of funds saved increases at the rate R_b:

$$1/(1 + R_b) = P_{b1}/P_0$$

therefore

$$R_b = P_0/P_{b1} - 1 = £1/P_{b1} - 1$$

For example, if $P_{b1} = £0.95$, $R_b = 5.26$ per cent. Each £1 saved still sits under the mattress until it is spent; the interest rate is determined entirely by the price of c_1 in relation to the price of c_0. A positive interest rate enables an individual with a given endowment at date 0 to consume more in total, across both dates, and to reach an indifference curve U_b representing greater utility than is possible with an interest rate of zero.

In Figure 1.2 the lower price of c_1 is shown as resulting not only in an increase in the quantity demanded of c_1 but also in the proportion of the budget spent on c_1. This is not an inevitable outcome. An individual could choose to spend less on future units as their price falls. For such a person, the income effect, caused by the rise in real income considered across both dates, is negative for consumption at date 1 and outweighs the positive substitution effect, caused by the fact that date 1 units have become cheaper in relation to date 0 units. However, it is plausible to assume that individuals in aggregate (society) will save more as the real interest rate rises.

More formal exposition

The preceding discussion includes the notion of the maximisation of lifetime utility by an individual. Since this is an important notion, it is worthwhile to provide a more formal exposition. Each individual seeks to maximise his lifetime utility subject to his budget constraint. In the single-period setting, his lifetime utility at date 0, U, is a function of the amounts he consumes at dates 0 and 1:

$$U = U(C_0, C_1) \tag{1.5}$$

where $U(.)$ indicates an unspecified function that expresses the relation between the variables in the brackets and the amount of lifetime utility. The budget constraint assuming no endowment at date 1 is

$$P_1 C_1 = Y_0 - P_0 C_0 \tag{1.6}$$

where Y_0 is the individual's initial endowment at date 0 and P_0 and P_1 are given. The problem is to maximise (1.5), by choosing the appropriate amounts C_0 and C_1, subject to (1.6). This is the same as finding the point of tangency of the indifference curves with the budget constraint. The problem can be solved using the Lagrangian multiplier technique. We form a Lagrangian expression to be maximised:

$$L(C_0, C_1, \lambda) = U(C_0, C_1) - \lambda[P_0 C_0 + P_1 C_1 - Y_0]$$

where λ is the Lagrangian multiplier. The choice the individual makes is how much to consume at each date, subject to his budget constraint. The first-order conditions for maximising L with respect to C_0 and C_1 are

$$\partial L/\partial C_0 = \partial U(C_0, C_1)/\partial C_0 - \lambda P_0 = 0 \qquad (1.7)$$
$$\partial L/\partial C_1 = \partial U(C_0, C_1)/\partial C_1 - \lambda P_1 = 0 \qquad (1.8)$$
$$\partial L/\partial \lambda = P_0 C_0 + P_1 C_1 - Y_0 = 0$$

The first two conditions specify the relation that must obtain between the marginal utility from date-specific consumption units and the prices of such units. The third condition states that the budget constraint must be satisfied.

The second-order conditions for a maximum will be satisfied by virtue of the assumption of positive, diminishing marginal utility from consumption at a given date. The assumption means that the signs of $\partial U(C_0, C_1)/\partial C_0$ and $\partial U(C_0, C_1)/\partial C_1$ are positive. Given this, the second-order conditions require that $\partial^2 L/\partial C_0^2$ and $\partial^2 L/\partial C_1^2$ be negative. Differentiating equations (1.7) and (1.8) shows that the second-order conditions require that $\partial^2 U(C_0, C_1)/\partial C_0^2$ and $\partial^2 U(C_0, C_1)/\partial C_1^2$ be negative, which will be the case if diminishing marginal utility is assumed. We omit the explicit calculation that the second-order conditions for a maximum are satisfied (see, for example, Hoy, Livernois, McKenna, Rees and Stengos, 1996, chap. 13).

To find the optimum relation between marginal utility and price, we solve the simultaneous equations (1.7) and (1.8) by eliminating λ, to give

$$\frac{\partial U(C_0, C_1)/\partial C_0}{\partial U(C_0, C_1)/\partial C_1} = \frac{MU_0}{MU_1} = \frac{P_0}{P_1} = 1 + R \qquad (1.9)$$

where MU_t is the marginal utility at date 0 from consumption at date t. Equation (1.9) says that the condition for the achievement of maximum utility is that the ratio of the marginal utility from c_0 to the marginal utility from c_1 must be equal to the ratio of the price of c_0 to the price of c_1. The ratio MU_0/MU_1 is the negative of the slope of the indifference curve representing maximised utility. The slope of an indifference curve representing a given level of utility is found by setting the total differential of equation (1.5) to zero:

$$0 = MU_0 dC_0 + MU_1 dC_1$$

or

$$dC_1/dC_0 = -MU_0/MU_1 \qquad (1.10)$$

This slope is the rate of exchange at the margin between the consumption at date 0 and at date 1 that the individual requires to maintain a given level of utility. The negative of the slope, MU_0/MU_1, is the marginal rate of substitution between consumption at date 0 and at date 1, or the marginal rate of time preference. Thus, equation (1.9) says that the individual allocates his/her budget in such a way that his/her marginal rate of time preference is equal to one plus the interest rate. It is analogous to equation (1.4) in the timeless world. It says that the ratio of the prices of a unit of consumption now and a unit at date 1 is equal to the ratio of the marginal utilities from consumption now and from consumption-to-come at date 1.

1.2.3 Equilibrium interest rate

How would the (real) interest rate be determined in this world? If the only alternative to consuming units is to store them, and endowed consumption units are available only at date 0, there will be no trade in current and future units, and so there will be no market prices for these units. Individuals will simply use their endowments to buy units now and consume some at date 0 and the rest at date 1, according to their time preferences for consumption. Some people may wish to consume more of their endowment today than others, but there would be no advantage for anyone to lend what they saved to someone else. However, if endowed units are available at date 1 as well as at date 0, then trade in c_0 and c_1 may occur. Assuming that the cost of storage is zero, individuals who would have stored some c_0 units will lend rather than store them if there are individuals endowed with c_1 units willing to offer qc_1 for each c_0, where $q > 1$. This implies that $P_1 < P_0$. In other words, some people will lend if there are others willing to pay a positive real interest rate. Individuals will trade until equation (1.9) is satisfied for each of them.

The demand curve for c_1 will slope downwards with respect to its price, $P_1 = \frac{1}{1+R}$, assuming that the substitution effect for lenders, who demand c_1, outweighs any negative income effect. We can also envisage a supply curve for c_1 that slopes upwards, assuming that more is borrowed (c_1 provided in exchange for c_0) as P_1 rises (the interest rate falls). The equilibrium interest rate is the rate at which the supply equals the demand.

This is a simple model of the interest rate. It predicts that an increase in society's time preference will result in a higher interest rate, as will an increase in endowments at date 1 in relation to endowments at date 0. If the cost of storage is zero, as assumed, the interest rate will not be negative. This is because those wishing to save can earn a minimum interest rate of zero by storing consumption units. But if storage is costly or is not feasible (consumption units are perishable), it would be possible for the equilibrium interest rate to be negative – i.e. for $P_1 > P_0$ to hold.

1.2.4 Introducing companies

The above framework is, clearly, very artificial. It is designed to abstract from everything except the individual's, and society's, choice between consumption now and consumption in the future. The model can be extended somewhat to allow for the possibility of highly stylised production. We now assume that funds saved can be invested in productive activity, which creates units of the homogeneous consumption good at date 1. It is assumed that the role of a company is to organise production and to make a return for those who have provided its capital. A company does not consume and does not have an initial endowment. It raises funds at date 0 and repays them with interest at date 1. Its production opportunities consist of a number of potential projects that provide various returns on capital. Alternatively, a company can be thought of as having one productive activity with diminishing marginal

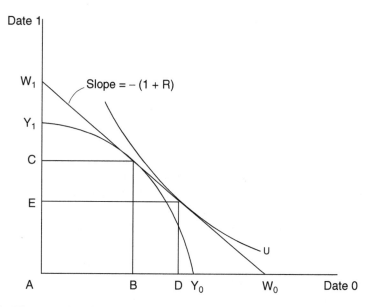

Figure 1.3   The separation of production and the owner's consumption

productivity as more funds are invested in it. It is worth investing more in a company until the point is reached at which its return on capital is equal to the prevailing interest rate. In other words, the company will undertake all projects or productive activity with positive net present value.

This is illustrated in Figure 1.3. The curve between Y_0 and Y_1 is a production possibility curve, showing the pay-off at date 1 in relation to the amount invested in the company at date 0. The slope diminishes due to diminishing marginal productivity. The slope of the line between W_0 and W_1 is $-(1 + R)$, where R is the prevailing rate of interest. The company raises funds at date 0 and invests an amount BY_0, at which point one plus the return on the marginal project, the slope at this point of the curve between Y_0 and Y_1, is equal to one plus the rate of interest, the slope of the line W_0 to W_1. At date 1 the company's investments provide a pay-off of AC.

The amount invested in a company is not affected by the utility function regarding the current and future consumption of any particular individual who has financed the company. This important proposition is often called the *separation theorem*. Individuals maximise their utility by saving the amount they wish at the given rate of interest, as in Figure 1.2. Companies maximise the wealth they create by investing in available projects until the marginal rate of return on capital is equal to the rate of interest, as in Figure 1.3. The sole factors affecting the company's investment decisions are the rates of return on potential projects and the interest rate. Suppose that the company in Figure 1.3 is owned by one individual, whose endowment is Y_0. The individual maximises his utility by a two-stage procedure. First, he invests BY_0 in the company, as explained above. His budget constraint is now W_0 to W_1; he can obtain any combination of C_0 and C_1 on this line by appropriate lending or borrowing. Second, he borrows BD, using CE of what the company provides at date 1 to repay the loan. This moves him to the point on his budget constraint that provides the highest level of utility, represented by the indifference curve U tangential to W_0 to W_1 After taking into account the individual's opportunities for investing in productive activity and for transacting in the capital market (i.e. borrowing or lending at the market rate of interest), his wealth in terms of possible consumption at date 0 is W_0 rather than his endowment Y_0, and the wealth created by the company is $W_0 - Y_0$. At date 0 he chooses to consume AD and to save DW_0, which enables him to consume AE at date 1. If the individual's time preference changes, he moves to another point on his budget constraint, but this does not affect the amount he invests in the company or the amount it produces. If he wishes to consume more at date 1, for example, he will do better to save more at the market rate of interest than to invest more in the company and persuade it to undertake the next-best project with a rate of return marginally below the rate of interest.

From a company perspective, the rate of interest is the cost of capital, and, under certainty, it is the same for all companies. We can see from Figure 1.3 that the wealth a company creates is a function of both the cost of capital and the nature of its investment opportunities. For a given production possibility curve, if the interest rate were to rise the point of tangency would roll downwards; the amount invested in it and the volume of consumption units it produced at date 1 would fall, as would the amount of wealth it would create.

1.2.5   Equilibrium interest rate with companies

The market interest rate is the result of the interplay between the time preferences of individuals in society and the productivity of companies. The analysis is presented informally, by means of a traditional supply-and-demand diagram and a numerical example. Figure 1.4 shows the supply and demand for units of consumption at date 1 in relation to their price $£1/(1 + R)$. The position and shape of the demand curve depend on the utility that individuals derive at the margin from consuming at date 1 compared with consuming at date 0. The position and shape of the supply curve now depend on the nature of productive possibilities, as well as on the endowments received by individuals.

A change in demand is caused by a change in the preference of society. For example, if there is an increase in the utility of current compared with future consumption, the demand curve for c_1 units will shift to the left. P_1 falls and R rises, with an upward-sloping supply curve. Saving and investment fall at date 0, which means that fewer projects are financed, so that supply at date 1 diminishes and the return on the marginal project is higher.

A change in supply is caused by a change in production possibilities or in endowments. For example, an increase in the return on productive investment shifts the supply curve of c_1 units to the right. There are new projects with a rate of return that exceeds the prevailing interest rate. This attracts more saving and investment at date 0, but, with diminishing marginal utility of consumption at date 1 in relation to consumption at date 0, the cost of c_1 units has to fall to attract extra demand for c_1 units, which means that the interest rate must rise.

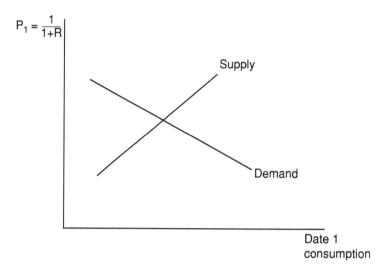

Figure 1.4   The supply and demand for consumption units at date 1

Strictly speaking, a change in tastes or production possibilities or endowments implies a new equilibrium, and a new interest rate. This is clear from the following explanation of how equilibrium is arrived at (from Fama and Miller, 1972, pp. 149–50).

Equilibrium at the beginning of period 1 [our date 0] is assumed to be reached through a process of tâtonnement with recontracting; that is, investors come to the market with their resources, tastes, and expectations on market values for period 2 [our date 1], and firms bring their production opportunity sets. Firms announce tentative production and financing decisions, investors offer their labor to firms and begin bidding for consumption goods and securities, and a tentative set of prices for consumption goods, labor and securities is established. Prices and decisions are tentative because it is agreed that no decisions will be executed until an equilibrium set of prices, that is, a set of prices at which all markets can clear at period 1, has been determined.

The interest rate is determined at the same time as net present values are worked out and projects are selected. However, the effect on the interest rate of undertaking a new project will be negligible if the project is small in relation to the market. This assumption is made implicitly when valuing individual projects using the prevailing, pre-project interest rate.

Example

The following example illustrates how the interest rate results from the utility functions of individuals, their endowments and the production possibilities. We assume for simplicity that all individuals have the same utility function and all firms have the same production function. This enables the interest rate to be derived by considering the behaviour of a representative individual and a representative firm.

$$
\begin{aligned}
\text{Utility function:} \quad & U = \ln C_0 + 0.95 \ln C_1 \\
\text{Production function:} \quad & C_1 = 100 - C_0^2/100 \\
\text{Endowment:} \quad & Y_0 = 100c_0
\end{aligned}
$$

All production is consumed at date 1.

Step 1. Set production at its optimum amount, which is the point of tangency between the production function and the line with slope of $-(1+R)$:

$$dC_1/dC_0 = -2C_0/100 = -(1+R)$$

therefore at this point

$$C_0 = 50(1+R)$$

and by substituting in the production function,

$$C_1 = 100 - 25(1+R)^2$$

This equation gives the supply curve of C_1, the number of c_1 units produced, as a function of the interest rate. A higher interest rate means that fewer projects are undertaken, which entails a smaller supply.

Step 2. Set consumption at the optimum for the individual. At this point the slope of the indifference curve between C_0 and C_1, $-MU_0/MU_1$ (equation (1.10)), is equal to the line with slope of $-(1+R)$.

$$-MU_0/MU_1 = -C_1/0.95C_0 = -(1+R)$$

therefore at this point

$$C_1 = 0.95C_0(1+R)$$

Step 3. The equilibrium interest rate and optimum C_0 and C_1 are determined by the point of tangency between the production function and the indifference map. At this point the conditions for optimum production and optimum consumption are satisfied. We have established that the condition for optimum production is

$$C_0 = 50(1+R)$$
$$C_1 = 100 - 25(1+R)^2$$

and that the condition for optimum consumption is

$$C_1 = 0.95C_0(1+R)$$

Solving for R,

$$47.5(1+R)^2 = 100 - 25(1+R)^2$$
$$R = 17.44\%$$

At this interest rate,

$$C_0 = 50(1+R) = 58.72$$
$$C_1 = 100 - 25(1+R)^2 = 65.52$$

maximised utility $= \ln 58.72 + 0.95 \ln 65.52 = 8.05$ 'units of utility'.

1.2.6   Extension to multiple periods

If there is more than one future period, the individual is conceived of as maximising his lifetime utility from consumption at each date:

$$U = U(C_0, C_1 \ldots C_T)$$

where T is the last date in the person's planning horizon, which is often interpreted as the date he will die. He may attach utility to funds that he has not spent by this date but plans to leave as a bequest. Correspondingly, firms provide consumption at different dates. Under certainty, it must be the case that

$$
\begin{aligned}
_0P_t &= {}_0P_1 \times {}_1P_2 \cdots \times {}_{t-1}P_t \\
&= \Pi_{t=1}^{T} {}_{t-1}P_t \\
&= \Pi_{t=1}^{T} 1/(1 + R_t)
\end{aligned}
\tag{1.11}
$$

where $_\tau P_t$ is the price at date τ of one unit to be received at date t and R_t is the interest rate during period t, between dates $t-1$ and t. Equation (1.11) must hold because, if it did not, people would be able to achieve risk-free gains from arbitrage. Suppose the interest rate is 5 per cent in periods 1 and 2. Then $_0P_2$ must be 0.91; at the margin you can obtain $1.00c_2$ by investing $0.91c_0$ in a firm that produces c_2. If $_0P_2$ were, say, 0.93, then you could invest $0.91c_0$ in the firm and sell the resulting claim to $1.00c_2$ for $0.93c_0$, thus making a risk-free gain of $0.02c_0$.

It can be shown, by an argument analogous to the argument in Section 1.2.1, that the individual will maximise his utility by holding claims to future units such that the marginal utility per pound spent is equal across all claims, given the prevailing market prices. For a claim to a consumption unit at any date T periods in the future,

$$MU_T/MU_0 = {}_0P_T/{}_0P_0 = \Pi_{t=1}^{T} 1/(1 + R_t)$$

The single-period spot interest rate is R_1 and each single-period forward interest rate is given by R_t, for $t = 2 \ldots T$. The single-period rates that emerge in equilibrium will not be the same for every period if time preferences or production possibilities, though certain, are not the same at every future date.

1.3   Summary

A project's cost of capital is the minimum expected rate of return needed to attract the required capital. It is an opportunity cost – i.e. the rate of return on investing in the next-best alternative to the project. Under certainty there will be a single interest rate in the economy, which is the cost of capital for all projects.

This chapter has presented an elementary model of the interest rate under certainty. The economy we have been considering might be thought to be excessively simple. However, it enables us to articulate some of the key ideas regarding the cost of capital without much complexity. Allowance for uncertainty in the next chapter will create a setting that calls for a more sophisticated analysis, but that is recognisably an extension of the setting presented here.

In particular, we have seen that the interest rate is a market price, like the price of a good, and is the result of choices made by individuals. People maximise lifetime utility by choosing between consumption now and consumption in the future. The real interest rate is a way of expressing the price of the marginal unit of consumption in the future in relation to the price of the marginal unit today. Utility is maximised by choosing the amounts of consumption at each date such that

$$MU_0/MU_1 = P_0/P_1$$

i.e. the marginal utility per pound spent on consumption today is equal to the marginal utility per pound spent on a claim to future consumption. This condition is central to the analysis assuming uncertainty. as we shall see.

We have also encountered the argument why corporate investment decisions should be made by comparing the return on an investment with the interest rate (the cost of capital), whoever the owners of the company are and whatever their choices are between consumption now and in the future (the separation theorem). This argument supports the very concept of the cost of capital, as well as the rule in capital budgeting that companies should undertake all projects with positive NPV.

2 Allowing for uncertainty: contingent states

This chapter presents a theory of choice between consumption now and claims to future consumption. It is similar in essence to the theory of intertemporal choice under certainty presented in Chapter 1. Assets provide claims to future consumption. Their prices, and the expected returns on them, are explained as the outcomes of choices made by utility-maximising individuals. The chapter aims to give an idea of how the analysis 'works', and to point to some of the worries about it. It sets the scene for the explicit models of the expected returns on assets that will be developed in Chapters 3 and 4.

Uncertainty about the future will be represented using the concept of contingent states. An individual in the present (date 0) is assumed to be able to envisage more than one contingent state, or state of the world that might come about at a given future date. Only one of the states envisaged actually will come about. The individual is assumed to be able to attach a probability to the occurrence of each state and to know in advance what will happen in each contingent state – i.e. the outcome or outcomes relevant to the analysis. There is no vagueness about the outcomes in any state; the uncertainty is entirely about which state will actually materialise. In effect, each contingent state is defined by a particular outcome of a single variable, or a combination of outcomes of more than one variable. The sources for most of the chapter are Hirshleifer (1970, chaps. 8 & 9), Hirshleifer and Riley (1992, chaps. 1–4), Danthine and Donaldson (2002, chaps. 2 & 7) and Myers (1968). For more detail, and extensions, the reader is referred to Gollier (2001).

2.1 Valuation

We start by stating the standard model for valuing a project in the contingent-states setting. This is the analogue of the model presented under certainty in Section 1.1.3.

A project provides one or more uncertain pay-offs in the future. We consider, for simplicity, a project that will provide a single pay-off at date 1. Let Y_s be the pay-off if state s arises and π_s be the probability that s will occur. There are n possible states at date 1, so $s = s_1 \ldots s_n$, and $\sum_{s=s1}^{sn} \pi_s = 1$. Henceforth we shall abbreviate $\sum_{s=s1}^{sn}$ to $\sum_s$. The expected value of the pay-off can now be written as

$$E(Y_s) = \sum_s \pi_s Y_s$$

The expected value is estimated *ex ante*, at date 0. The actual value that arises at date 1 will be one of the possible outcomes for Y_s, and is unlikely be the same as the expected value.

The capital or investment required to undertake the project is I_0 and the return on the capital in state s is $R_{inv, s}$. The expected return on the capital is

$$E(R_{inv,s}) = \Sigma_s \pi_s Y_s / I_0 - 1$$
$$= E(Y_s)/I_0 - 1 \qquad (2.1)$$

We assume that the equilibrium expected return on an asset or project is positively related to risk, and that risk is the reason why expected returns differ across assets. This assumption is justified later in the chapter. We can then say that the market value V_0 of the equity issued to raise I_0 is determined by the expected pay-off $E(Y_s)$ and by the expected return on assets of the same risk as the project, denoted $E(R_s)$. The value is determined as follows. In buying a project, an investor is buying a set of possible future pay-offs, each with a specific probability. The distribution of possible pay-offs determines the project's risk, and we assume that the risk can be quantified. The price an investor pays for the project, or for a share of the equity, determines the expected return on the price, given the expected value of the pay-off. The equilibrium price V_0 investors are willing to pay will be such that the expected return on the price is equal to the expected return on the next-best investment. The next-best investment is an asset of the same risk. Let the expected return on such an asset be $E(R_s)^*$, where R_s is the contingent return if state s arises. $E(R_s)^*$ is an expected rate that is set by investors in the capital market and that includes expected compensation for risk. Hence the equilibrium market value of the project will be the value at which the expected return on the value, $E(Y_s)/V_0 - 1$, is equal to $E(R_s)^*$, so that

$$E(Y_s)/V_0 - 1 = E(R_s)^*$$

or

$$V_0[1 + E(R_s)^*] = E(Y_s)$$

or

$$V_0 = E(Y_s)/[1 + E(R_s)^*] \qquad (2.2)$$

The project will increase shareholder wealth only if $V_0 > I_0$ and it will attract the required capital only if $V_0 \geq I_0$. It can be seen by comparing equations (2.1) and (2.2) that $V_0 \geq I_0$ if $E(R_{inv,s}) \geq E(R_s)^*$. Since the cost of capital is the minimum expected return on the cash needed to attract the required amount of cash, and no one will invest unless $V_0 \geq I_0$, the cost of capital is given by $E(R_s)^*$, the expected return on a financial asset of the same risk as the project. Hence the subject matter of Part I: how the expected returns on financial assets are determined, assuming no 'market imperfections' such as taxes. This is the same as asking how the market prices of assets are determined, given the contingent pay-offs that they provide.

Example

Suppose the investment required to undertake a project is £100 and there are two possible pay-offs at date 1, £141 and £90. These pay-offs are equally likely, so their expected value is £115.5. The expected return on a financial asset of the same risk is 10 per cent. The market value of the project is then

$$V_0 = £115.5/1.10 = £105$$

from equation (2.2). Someone buying the project for £105 obtains an expected return of 10 per cent. The expected return on the cash invested is

$$E(R_{\text{inv},s}) = 0.5(£141/£100) + 0.5(£90/£100) - 1$$
$$= 15.5\%$$

from equation (2.1). The net present value is positive, at £105 − £100 = £5, and the expected return on the investment exceeds the cost of capital.

2.2   Expected utility

The analysis under uncertainty assumes that individuals maximise lifetime expected utility. According to the expected utility theory, the utility U_j of an asset j is given by the sum of the utilities from each contingent pay-off, with each utility weighted by the probability that the relevant state will arise:

$$U_j = E(U_{js}) = \Sigma_s \pi_s U(C_{js})$$

where C_{js} is the pay-off (in consumption units) from asset j in state s and $U(C_{js})$ is an explicit numerical (cardinal) value that measures the utility of C_{js} if state s were to arise. The notion of expected utility is straightforward enough, but we should show that it is reasonable to assume that an individual behaves as though he/she assigns numerical values to the utilities of contingent pay-offs.

Claims to contingent pay-offs are similar to lotteries, in which you win something only if a particular number is drawn (equivalent to the occurrence of a particular state). It is possible to postulate an explicit numerical measure of the utility an individual derives from a lottery, given certain assumptions about the individual's behaviour. These assumptions are the rules or axioms that rational individuals are assumed to follow in making choices between lotteries. The first three rules are those of *comparability* and *transitivity* across lotteries, and of *non-satiation*. Individuals were assumed to follow the same rules in choosing between goods in the present or between certain amounts of consumption at different dates (Section 1.2.1). The expected utility theory requires that individuals behave as though they follow three additional rules.

1. *Certainty equivalence*: for any lottery, the individual is able to specify a certain payment, which is such that he is indifferent between receiving this payment and receiving the opportunity to play the lottery once. The certain payment must lie between the maximum

and minimum possible payment (prize) from the lottery, and is known as the certainty-equivalent value of the lottery.

2. *Independence*: the utility from a particular pay-off is independent of the lottery in which this pay-off is one of the possible outcomes. Imagine two lotteries. Lottery 1 pays £1 if a coin is spun and it is heads, and £2 if it is tails. Lottery 2 pays £1 for heads and £3 for tails. The independence axiom says that the individual's utility from the pay-off of £1 will be the same whether the individual receives £1 as a result of playing lottery 1 or of playing lottery 2. The argument is that only one outcome will actually arise, so the utility from that outcome is not affected by the other possible outcomes in the lottery that might have been. In terms of states of the world, the independence axiom implies that the utility from consumption in one possible state is not affected by the utility from consumption in another possible state.

3. *Uniqueness*: the certainty-equivalent value of a lottery depends uniquely on the pay-offs and on their attached probabilities. In other words, the utility from winning a given amount £Y is not dependent on the workings of chance via which the individual has ended up with £Y. Suppose that lottery 1 offers a 30 per cent chance of winning £1, and a 70 per cent chance of winning nothing. Lottery 2 offers a 20 per cent chance of winning £1 and an 80 per cent chance of playing lottery 2a, which offers a 12.5 per cent chance of winning £1 and an 87.5 per cent chance of winning nothing. The chance of winning £1 is the same for lotteries 1 and 2, and the uniqueness axiom says that both will have the same certainty-equivalent value. In terms of states of the world, the uniqueness axiom implies that the utility function (not utility itself) is the same across states.

Given these assumptions, we can show that the individual will behave as though he assigns a numerical measure of utility to each pay-off. The utility of a gamble can then be measured by the expected value of the utilities of the pay-offs. This was proved by von Neumann and Morgenstern (1947). We explain the argument via an example.

Example

Let us consider lotteries in which the prizes lie between £0 and £100. We assign an arbitrary utility of 0 to receipt of £0 for certain and a utility of 1 to receipt of £100 for certain. The utility values do not have to be 0 and 1, but it is easy to use these numbers. What, in terms of this utility scaling, is the utility ascribable to the receipt of, say, £10 for certain? Given the certainty-equivalence axiom, we can say that £10 is the certainty-equivalent value of a lottery with a probability p of winning £100 and $1 - p$ of winning £0. For example, if p is 0.2, the individual is indifferent between receiving £10 for certain and a lottery with a 20 per cent chance of winning £100 and an 80 per cent chance of winning £0. Since we have specified that the utility of £100 is 1 and the utility of £0 is 0, p is a measure of the utility gained by this individual from receiving £10 for certain. Given the axioms, the individual will assign a different p-value to every certain payment between £0 and £100, increasing from 0 to 1 as the payments increase.

Under the above scheme, the utility of a pay-off £Y received for certain is measured by its p-value, p_Y. Given the uniqueness axiom, the utility of an uncertain pay-off can be measured by its expected utility – i.e. by p_Y times the probability that the pay-off will occur. Suppose that $p_{£10} = 0.2$, as above, and that $p_{£50} = 0.8$. The individual is offered a gamble g that pays £50 with a 0.4 probability and £10 with a 0.6 probability. The expected (weighted average) utility of the gamble is found simply by substituting the appropriate p-values for the pay-offs, given the independence axiom:

$$U_g = E[U(Y_g)] = 0.4(p_{£50}) + 0.6(p_{£10})$$
$$= 0.4(0.8) + 0.6(0.2) = 0.44$$

where $E[U(Y_g)]$ is the utility of a given pay-off from gamble g.

Similarly, the utility from a given amount of consumption in a given contingent state can be assigned a numerical value. We assign a utility as of, say, 0 to $C = 0$ and 1 to $C = 100c$, being an arbitrary maximum possible outcome. If a given state has arisen, the individual's utility from a pay-off of C units is then measured by the probability p_C in a gamble such that the individual is indifferent between receiving C for certain and receiving the gamble with pay-offs of $100c$ with probability p_C and 0 with probability $1 - p_C$. If the axioms are reasonable, it is reasonable to measure the utility of an asset by the expected utility of its pay-offs.

The actual numerical values of utility depend on the chosen scale of measurement for utility and on the utility function assumed. The chosen function, whatever it is, will 'translate' numerical values of consumption or money into numerical values of utility. In the terminology of this section, the utility function specifies the relation between C and p_C.

2.3   Choice and asset prices

2.3.1   Choice in a two-date world

We shall consider the simplest possible contingent-states world: there is a single future date at which one of two possible states will occur, state s_1 or state s_2. Each individual seeks to maximise his lifetime expected utility. This means that, for a given utility function $U = U(C_s)$, the expected utility from a given total amount of consumption in state s, C_s, is determined by the amount C and the probability π_s only. The utility function is the same across states (uniqueness axiom). But the expected utility of a given total amount C will be state-specific, as it depends on the relevant state's probability. Were the individual's utility function to differ across states, it would mean that his utility from a given total amount C would differ across states that have the same probability. This would complicate the analysis, as there would be an additional variable, the utility function, which would affect the individual's utility in each state.

It is customary to assume that utility at date 1 is discounted at a 'subjective discount rate', which reflects the individual's time preference and which does not vary across states. Positive time preference means that the individual derives greater utility from C_0 than from C_1, for a given C. The same assumption of positive time preference was made in the analysis under certainty in Chapter 1.

Having made these assumptions, we can say that the utility from total consumption of C in state s is given by the discounted expected utility

$$U_s = \delta \pi_s U(C_s)$$

where δ is the subjective discount factor, the reciprocal of one plus the subjective discount rate. Lifetime utility is given by

$$U = U(C_0) + \delta \pi_{s1} U(C_{s1}) + \delta \pi_{s2} U(C_{s2})$$
$$= U(C_0) + \delta E[U(C_s)] \qquad (2.3)$$

We now introduce assets. Let us define an *elementary claim* as an asset that provides one consumption unit in a specified state, and nothing in any other state. Such a claim is also called an Arrow–Debreu security or a state claim. We assume for the moment that the only assets available are elementary claims. The utility of a marginal claim to c_s – the utility from the purchase of an additional claim to c_s – is the discounted marginal utility of consumption in state s:

$$\delta M U_s = \delta \pi_s M U(C_s)$$

The marginal utility of consumption in state s is a function of the existing amount of consumption in s. If we assume diminishing marginal utility, larger C_s implies lower marginal utility and hence less utility from an additional claim to c_s. Marginal utility will vary across states if the individual's total consumption varies across states – i.e. if the individual is bearing risk. This is a key point.

The individual has an endowment of current funds of Y_0 and he/she maximises his/her utility function, equation (2.3), subject to the budget constraint

$$P_{s1} C_{s1} + P_{s2} C_{s2} = Y_0 - P_0 C_0$$

where P_s is the price of an elementary claim to c_s and P_0 is the price of a unit of consumption at date 0. The conditions to be satisfied for maximising utility can be found using the Lagrangian method (Section 1.2.2). The first-order conditions are

$$\delta M U_{s1} / M U_0 = P_{s1} / P_0$$
$$\delta M U_{s2} / M U_0 = P_{s2} / P_0$$

or

$$M U_0 / P_0 = \delta M U_{s1} / P_{s1} = \delta M U_{s2} / P_{s2} \qquad (2.4)$$

Equation (2.4) says that the individual allocates his/her budget across current consumption and elementary claims to future consumption in such a way that the marginal utilities per pound spent on consumption today and on each elementary claim are equal. His/her budget allocation determines the amounts of present consumption and of state-contingent consumption.

Let us consider the individual's choice about consumption in terms of taking risk. An individual chooses to take risk if he/she is uncertain about his/her future consumption. This

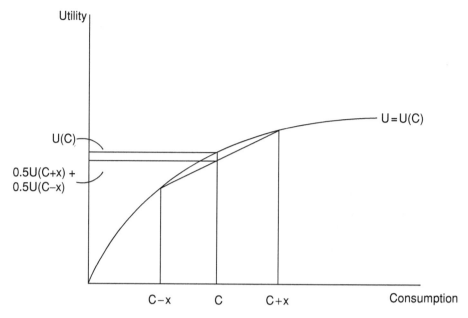

Figure 2.1   Diminishing marginal utility

means that he/she holds claims to unequal amounts of consumption across contingent states. How much risk the individual chooses to take, if any, depends on the prices of elementary claims and on his/her degree of risk aversion. It is normal to assume that individuals are averse to risk. This implies that, given the choice between receiving C for certain and undertaking a gamble with pay-offs with an expected value of C, the individual would choose C for certain. Someone who is indifferent to risk, or risk-neutral, would be indifferent between C and the gamble. Risk aversion implies diminishing marginal utility from consumption. This means that the individual's utility function is concave, as illustrated in Figure 2.1. Risk neutrality implies constant marginal utility, so the utility function is linear.

Consider someone facing contingent consumption at date 1 of $C_{s1} = C_1 + x$ or $C_{s2} = C_1 - x$, where x is a constant. Each state is equally likely, so $E(C_s) = C_1$. Assume that $\delta = 1$. With diminishing marginal utility, we have

$$U(C_1) = U[E(C_s)] > E[U(C_s)] = E[U(C_1 + x) + U(C_1 - x)]$$

which is a case of a property known as Jensen's inequality. The equation says that the utility from C_1 for certain exceeds the utility from the prospect of a 50 per cent chance of $C_1 + x$ and a 50 per cent chance of $C_1 - x$, even though the expected value of the pay-off is the same as C_1. The risk-averse individual would accept the uncertain prospect only if it offered a positive expected gain or *risk premium*, so that $E(C_s) > C_1$. The risk premium on a risky asset is defined as the expected return on the asset less the return on a risk-free asset. For example, consider an elementary claim to c_{s1}, with $\pi_{s1} = 0.30$ and $P_{s1} = £0.25 \ (= 0.25c_0)$. The expected return on this asset is $\pi_{s1} c_{s1}/P_{s1} - 1 = 20.0\%$. An elementary risk-free claim pays c_1 with 100 per cent probability. Its price is, say, £0.95, so the risk-free return is 5.3%. The risk premium is then 20.0% − 5.3% = 14.7%. The premium is an expected return. The actual premium on the elementary claim will either be 300% − 5.3% = 294.7% if state s_1 arises or −100% − 5.3% = −105.3% if s_2 arises.

Different utility functions specify different rates at which marginal utility diminishes, and thus different degrees of curvature of the function in Figure 2.1. Greater risk aversion implies a higher rate of diminution of marginal utility. A few specific examples of utility functions crop up in later chapters. All that we assume for now is that marginal utility is positive but diminishes as consumption grows.

If the price of each elementary claim equals the probability that the relevant state will occur, we have $P_{s1} = \pi_{s1}$ and $P_{s2} = \pi_{s2}$. Given these prices, it can be seen from equation (2.4) that the maximisation of utility requires that $MU_{s1} = MU_{s2}$. Since we are assuming that the utility function is the same across states, $MU_{s1} = MU_{s2}$ requires that $C_{s1} = C_{s2}$. Hence, if the prices of elementary claims mirror the probabilities that the relevant states will occur, individuals will take no risk; they will hold claims to the same quantity of consumption units in each state.

However, we would not expect the prices of elementary claims to match their probabilities, because of differences in endowment or production outcomes across states. If $P_s \neq \pi_s$, an individual may choose to hold a risky portfolio of claims – that is, a portfolio that does not guarantee the same amount of consumption in every possible state. For a risk-averse individual to buy more state-s_1 claims than state-s_2 claims, it must be that $P_{s1} < \pi_{s1}$ and $P_{s2} > \pi_{s2}$. The inducement to take risk is that the individual can thereby obtain a higher expected amount of consumption at date 1 than he/she could if he/she bought claims such that his/her consumption would be equal across all possible states. An example will help to clarify these points.

Example
Suppose we have

$$\pi_{s1} = 0.6, \ \pi_{s1} = 0.4$$
$$P_0 = £1.0, \ P_{s1} = £0.5, \ P_{s2} = £0.5$$

or

$$P_{s1} = 0.5c_0, \ P_{s2} = 0.5c_0$$

so $P_{s1} < \pi_{s1}$ and $P_{s2} > \pi_{s2}$. The individual has no endowment at date 1 and has allocated £100 to spend on elementary claims to provide consumption at date 1. He/she could avoid risk by buying 100 each of the elementary s_1 and s_2 claims, in which case he/she would receive $C_1 = 100c_1$ for certain. But suppose that he/she buys instead 120 s_1 claims and 80 s_2 claims, in which case his/her expected consumption at date 1 is

$$E(C_1) = 120c_{s1}(0.6) + 80c_{s2}(0.4)$$
$$= 104c_1$$

We can say that this individual requires a risk premium of $4c_1$ to accept the risk of having only $80c_1$ in state s_2. The expected pay-off on the chosen risky portfolio exceeds by $4c_1$ the pay-off on a risk-free portfolio costing the same ($100c_0$) as the risky portfolio. A more risk-averse individual would not accept a risk premium of $4c_1$ in exchange for living with a 0.4 probability of having only 80 units in state s_2, and so would choose a combination of claims nearer to 100 units in each state. To induce the more risk-averse person to hold only 80 of the state-s_2 claims, the ratio P_{s1}/P_{s2} would have to fall.

If the individual is bearing risk, his/her marginal utility of consumption will differ across states. In the above example, the utility from an extra unit will be smaller in state s_1, in which the individual already has 120 units, than in s_2, in which he/she has 80. However, his/her marginal expected utility per pound spent on elementary claims will be equal across claims. These statements are consistent with each other because the ratio of the prices of the claims differs from the ratio of the state probabilities. In fact, if prices do not mirror probabilities even a very risk-averse person will choose to take *some* risk, because otherwise his/her marginal expected utility across elementary claims cannot be equal.

2.3.2   Asset prices

It should be clear that financial assets and real projects can be modelled as packages of elementary claims, assuming that the asset market is complete. Consider an asset or project j that provides contingent pay-offs C_{js}. Its price P_j must be

$$P_j = \Sigma_s P_s C_{js} \tag{2.5}$$

The principle at work here is that of *no arbitrage*. Given the prices of the elementary claims, and the contingent pay-offs provided by j, the price has to be $P_s C_{js}$, otherwise larger contingent pay-offs can be obtained at no extra cost today. The example later in this section provides an illustration.

The market is complete if there are as many elementary claims as there are possible states. Alternatively, if some or all elementary claims do not exist, the market is complete if all the missing prices can be inferred from the prices of non-elementary assets that do exist. Market incompleteness implies that the prices of some claims and assets cannot be determined exactly.

Since a non-elementary asset is the same thing as a package of elementary claims, the marginal utility of asset j is given by the sum of the marginal utilities of the constituent elementary claims:

$$\delta M U_j = \delta \Sigma_s M U_s C_{js}$$

C_{js} is implicitly assumed to be small enough that it does not affect $M U_s$ in any state. We have seen that utility-maximising individuals will hold elementary claims in amounts such that, given their prices, the marginal utility per pound is equal across claims (equation (2.4)). Similarly, individuals will hold all assets in amounts such that, given their prices, the marginal utility per pound invested is equal:

$$MU_0/P_0 = \delta MU_j/P_j = \delta MU_k/P_k = \ldots \delta MU_n/P_n \tag{2.6}$$

for assets $j, k \ldots n$.

A risk-free elementary claim F is one that provides a consumption unit in every possible state at date 1. It follows from equation (2.6) that individuals will hold risk-free claims in amounts such that

$$MU_0/P_0 = MU_F/P_F$$

and therefore

$$MU_0/\delta MU_F = P_0/P_F = 1 + R_F \tag{2.7}$$

where $MU_F = \Sigma_s \pi_s MU_s$, the marginal utility from a unit of consumption for certain at date 1; P_F is the price of an asset providing one unit at date 1; and R_F is the (real) risk-free return.

Equation (2.6) is a condition for the maximisation of an individual's utility, taking asset prices as given. For this equation to hold for each investor, it is not necessary to assume that they all assign the same probabilities to the possible future states, or that they share the same utility functions or that they have the same wealth. There is, however, the question of how the prices are determined, which calls for an analysis of equilibrium. A standard simplifying device is to assume that individuals are identical, in which case the price-setting process within the asset market can be modelled by the choices made by a *representative individual*. Allowing for individual heterogeneity makes the analysis of equilibrium much more difficult. Equation (2.6) becomes the condition for maximising the utility of the representative individual, and can be treated as an equation that explains or determines asset prices. It tells us what asset prices must be, given the supply of each asset, its contingent pay-offs, the amounts of any endowed contingent consumption and the representative individual's utility function. Prices must adjust to make the equation hold, as everything else is given.

Viewed as an explanation of prices, equation (2.6) says that the market price of an asset depends on the marginal utility of the contingent pay-offs it provides. Assuming that the representative individual is risk averse, an asset's price will be such that the expected return exceeds the risk-free return if the asset's pay-offs differ across states in a way that increases the risk the individual faces. Risk is the prospect of less total consumption in some states than in others. So the purchase of an asset increases risk if its pay-off is positively correlated with existing contingent consumption, which means that the pay-off is high in states in which consumption is already high, and low in states in which consumption is already low (we are assuming that all pay-offs are consumed at date 1). A negative correlation between pay-off and contingent consumption implies that the purchase of the asset will reduce the individual's risk, and so the asset will be priced such that its expected return is less than the risk-free. Thus an uncertain pay-off is a necessary but not sufficient condition for an asset to be priced to provide a positive risk premium. The premium will be negative for some patterns of contingent pay-off.

Example

Let us consider another example with two contingent states. Suppose that

$$\pi_{s1} = 0.75, \ \pi_{s1} = 0.25$$
$$P_0 = £1.00, \ P_{s1} = £0.61, \ P_{s2} = £0.30$$

or

$$P_{s1} = 0.61c_0, \ P_{s2} = 0.30c_0$$

The price of a unit in state s_2 is much higher in relation to its probability than is the price of a unit in s_1. Therefore, the marginal utility of consumption must be higher in s_2 and existing consumption must be lower. So we could label s_1 as a 'feast' state and s_2 as a 'famine' state.

The purchase of one of each type of elementary claim costs £0.61 + £0.30 = £0.91 = $0.91c_0$, and provides a certain income of one unit at date 1. So the risk-free return is

$$R_F = 1.00c_1/0.91c_0 - 1 \approx 10\%$$

Now consider an asset j that provides six units in state s_1 or two units in s_2. The expected pay-off is

$$E(C_{js}) = 6c_{s1}(0.75) + 2c_{s2}(0.25) = 5.00c_1$$

and the price must be

$$P_j = 6P_{s1} + 2P_{s2} = 4.26c_0$$

because only at this price is no gain from arbitrage possible. If j were to cost less than $4.26c_0$, for example, one could obtain increased pay-offs in both states by short-selling elementary c_{s1} and c_{s2} claims in the ratio three to one, and using the proceeds to buy units of j. No wealth would be required for this 'arbitrage portfolio'.

The expected return on j is

$$E(R_j) = E(C_{js})/P_j - 1$$
$$= 5.00c_1/4.26c_0 - 1 \approx 17\%$$

So the risk premium on this asset is 17% − 10% = 7%. The reason why the premium is positive is not merely because the returns on the asset are uncertain but because the asset provides a higher pay-off in the feast state, in which existing consumption is relatively high, than in the famine state, in which existing consumption is relatively low. Asset j adds to the risk that the individual already faces.

Now consider asset k, which provides the opposite pattern of returns to asset j: $2c_{s1}$ in state s_1 or $6c_{s1}$ in state s_2. Asset k reduces risk, so it should have a negative risk premium. Its expected pay-off is

$$E(C_{ks}) = 2c_{s1}(0.75) + 6c_{s2}(0.25) = 3.00c_1$$

and its price must be

$$P_k = 2P_{s1} + 6P_{s2} = 3.02c_0$$

So its expected return is

$$E(R_k) = 3.00c_1/3.02c_0 - 1 \approx 0\%$$

and the risk premium on k is $0\% - 10\% = -10\%$, which is negative, as expected.

It is straightforward to value projects in the contingent-states framework if the prices of elementary claims are known. If elementary claims are not traded, the no-arbitrage principle enables their notional prices to be inferred from the prices of non-elementary assets, assuming that the asset market is complete. A project can be treated as an asset, providing contingent pay-offs that can be valued separately using the prices of elementary claims, as we have seen. Alternatively, the project can be valued given its expected return and given the expected return on an asset of the same risk, as explained in Section 2.1. But we can now say more precisely what 'of the same risk' means, in the contingent-states setting with a representative individual. Any two assets or projects that provide the same distribution of returns or pay-offs across states will have the same risk and will be valued, in equilibrium, to provide the same expected return. In the preceding example, all assets providing returns or pay-offs in the ratio of three in state s_1 to one in s_2 make the same (marginal) contribution to risk and must be priced to give an expected return of 17 per cent. The latter statement is the case because, given the state probabilities and the prices of the elementary claims, possession of three claims to c_{s1} and one claim to c_{s1} provides an expected return of 17 per cent, so any asset that represents a multiple of this combination of claims will have an expected return of 17 per cent. Likewise, all assets providing returns in the ratio of one in s_1 to three in state in state s_2 will have an expected return of 0 per cent.

Whilst the no-arbitrage principle enables assets to be priced *given* the prices of elementary claims, it does not in itself explain where the prices come from. To do this, one needs to go back to the fundamental determinants of equilibrium: the utility functions; beliefs; the wealth and incomes of individuals; and the production possibilities.

2.3.3   Companies

The framework can be extended to allow for production, in which companies produce contingent consumption units. Wealth is maximised if companies accept all projects with an expected return on the required investment that is at least equal to the project's cost of capital, the expected return on an asset of the same risk. The principle is the same as under certainty, in which companies invest to the point at which the marginal return on capital is equal to the interest rate (Section 1.2.4). The productive possibilities available are a determinant of the interest rate under certainty, and of expected returns (or asset prices) under uncertainty.

Investors will agree that the objective of a firm or project should be to maximise its market value, if the market for contingent claims is complete and if investors have identical beliefs about state probabilities and project cash flows. The argument is that a claim to any contingent pay-off can be bought at a fair (no-arbitrage) price. So a project's cash flows can be replicated by purchasing elementary claims. We continue to assume that the project is 'small' enough that the market prices of the relevant elementary claims will not be affected by whether or not the project is undertaken. The value of the project is then its cost of replication, which is observable from market prices.

The objective of maximising market value continues to apply if investors have differing preferences. For example, suppose a firm is ranking two projects: project j will provide $C_j = C_{s1}$, and project k will provide $C_k = C_{s2}$. Shareholder A would prefer to receive (a share of) C_{s1}, but the market value of project k is greater. Then shareholder A will support the choice of k before j. The reason is that, in a complete market, he/she can realise the additional market value by selling shares and exchanging the proceeds for claims to state-s_1 consumption. Since the value of j is less than the value of k, the choice of k enables the shareholder to buy claims to more state-s_1 consumption than he/she would have obtained had the firm chosen j. This is the contingent-states version of the separation theorem (Section 1.2.4): the firm's investment policy does not depend on the preferences of its shareholders.

2.3.4   Multiple periods

The contingent-states framework can also be extended to allow for more than one future date. Possible states now become possible states at a particular date. However, the extension is straightforward only if the model is static, with all trading done at date 0. Then the individual will hold assets such that the marginal utilities are equal per pound spent on current consumption and on each claim to a consumption unit at a particular date. In this case the equilibrium relation between price and utility is

$$P_{s(t)}/P_0 = \delta^t M U_{s(t)}/M U_0$$

where $P_{s(t)}$ is the price at date 0 of an elementary claim to a unit in state s at date t and $M U_{s(t)}$ is the marginal utility from holding the claim. This is the multiperiod version of equation (2.4). It assumes that δ, the discount factor for future utility, is the same for every future period. Assets with pay-offs at more than one future date can be modelled as packages of the appropriate elementary claims, as in the setting with one future period.

Although there can be multiple future dates, the static nature of this multiperiod construct means that, arguably, it offers little insight beyond what the single-period version offers. The possibility of future trading, the resolution of uncertainty, and other changes in circumstance that might enrich the setting are ruled out. It is more revealing, but also more difficult, to conduct analysis in the context of a dynamic future. We say a little more about this in Section 4.2.

2.3.5   Stochastic discount factor

We have been thinking of the price of an asset in terms of the prices of elementary claims. An alternative is to think of asset prices in terms of the stochastic discount factor. This representation is more convenient for some purposes. Starting from equation (2.5),

$$P_j = \Sigma_s P_s C_{js}$$
$$= \Sigma_s \pi_s (P_s/\pi_s) C_{js}$$
$$= E(m_s C_{js}) \tag{2.8}$$

where $m_s = P_s/\pi_s$ is the stochastic discount factor. The values of the stochastic discount factor are the prices of each elementary claim per unit of state probability. The higher P_s is in relation to π_s, the more expensive a claim to additional consumption in state s is in relation to the probability of s. Equation (2.8) says that the price of an asset is given by the expected value of the product, for each state, of the stochastic discount factor and the contingent pay-off.

The equation that explains the price of an elementary claim, assuming there is a representative individual, also explains the value of the stochastic discount factor for a given state. Substituting $m_s = P_s/\pi_s$ in equation (2.4), which with $P_0 = £1$ is

$$P_s = \delta MU_s/MU_0 = \delta \pi_s MU(C_s)/MU_0$$

gives

$$m_s = \delta MU(C_s)/MU_0$$

the ratio of marginal utility in state s to marginal utility today, times the discount factor on future utility. So the stochastic discount factor varies across states with the marginal utility of consumption across states. Its expected value can be inferred from the price P_F of a risk-free asset paying one unit at date 1:

$$P_F = 1/(1 + R_F) = \Sigma_s P_s$$
$$= \Sigma_s \pi_s P_s/\pi_s$$
$$= E(m_s)$$

If the real risk-free return is a few percent, $E(m_s)$ will be a number close to one. We shall return to the stochastic discount factor representation in Chapter 4.

2.4   Some comments

2.4.1   *Evidence on expected utility*

Many writers have noted that people do not, in fact, behave as though they maximise expected utility; the model is not a good proxy for reality. Machina (1987) reviews the evidence. People seem to make various categories of 'mistake' in choice and valuation across gambles. That is, their responses do not tally with the responses predicted if they behave as though they maximise expected utility. To take one example from many, people have been asked to compare pairs of gambles. In each pair, the first gamble has a higher probability of winning, but the second has a higher expected value. A majority of people both assign a higher certainty-equivalent value to the second gamble (the one with the higher expected value) and yet, asked to choose one or the other, they opt for the first gamble – the one with the higher probability of winning. (The certainty-equivalent value of a gamble is the amount someone would accept, or pay, for certain instead of the gamble.)

Recently, Rabin and Thaler (2001) have pointed out that aversion to taking small bets cannot be used to extrapolate the utility function that applies when considering large bets, because it implies absurdly high risk aversion. The reverse also applies: moderate risk aversion towards large bets implies risk neutrality towards small bets – but people usually turn down small, fair bets.

The evidence against the expected utility theory is part of the motivation for the 'behavioural finance' view of investor behaviour. The implications for asset pricing theory are a topic for ongoing research (discussed, for example, in Campbell, 2000).

2.4.2   *Implications of market incompleteness and investor heterogeneity*

Our discussion of the determination of asset prices has assumed that the asset market is complete and that investors are identical. Relaxing these assumptions makes the model more realistic, but it complicates the analysis of equilibrium, and we do not pursue the implications very far. Our purpose here is merely to revisit the basic valuation model and the concept of the cost of capital (Section 2.1). We do consider investor heterogeneity with respect to personal taxes and ability to invest internationally later in the book.

Suppose, first, that the asset market is incomplete. This means that no exact market price can be inferred for elementary claims to pay-offs in some states from the prices of existing assets. The contingent pay-offs cannot be replicated by holdings of the relevant elementary claims, which *ex hypothesi* do not exist, nor by combinations of long and short positions in other assets. The value of projects with contingent pay-offs for which there is no exact market price cannot be determined exactly from the prices of existing assets. In reality, all shares and projects provide unique sequences of pay-off that cannot be replicated. In this case it can be shown that investors will not necessarily agree on a firm's investment policy, especially if its equity is not traded (Haley and Schall, 1979, chap. 17). It can also be shown that the Modigliani–Miller theory, that financing arrangements do not affect value, will not hold. The nature of the securities that a firm issues will affect its market value (Danthine and Donaldson, 2002, chap. 13).

We illustrate these points by considering the case of a small business owned by two shareholders. *A* is wealthy and his/her lifestyle would not be affected if the business failed; *B* is dependent on the business for his/her income. There is no existing market for the shares, and selling shares to outsiders would be very expensive due to transactions costs related to finding buyers, providing them with credible information, and so on. There will be no market price of the business that can be observed or inferred exactly from the prices of other assets, so *B* may be unable to sell his/her shares to *A* at an agreed price. (*B* may also be unwilling to sell to *A* because of the loss of voting rights, though this is to bring in new considerations that do not directly flow from the assumption of an incomplete market.) In addition, *B* may be unable to buy insurance against failure of the business. In the circumstances, *B* will probably be more anxious to avoid failure of the business than *A*, in which case *B* will wish the business to pursue a more cautious investment policy than *A*. In addition, it is possible that both *A* and *B* would be better off if the firm were to issue relatively safe, debt-type securities. *B* could hold the debt, and *A* the levered equity (though this ignores the voting rights issue).

Now let us suppose that the asset market is complete but that investors have different beliefs. In this case the firm's shareholders will not agree on the value of a given project, and they may not agree that a firm's objective should be to maximise market value. To illustrate, suppose that the market value of project *j* is greater than that of project *k*, but that shareholder *A* assigns *k* the higher value because he/she believes that *k*'s contingent pay-offs are higher than the pay-offs implied by its market value. In this case *k* is not worth enough for him/her to be able to replicate what he/she believes to be the pay-offs by selling the project and buying elementary claims to the amounts of his/her forecasts of the pay-offs. *A* believes that 'the market' is making a mistake in assigning a higher value to *j*, and would rank *k* before *j*, despite the fact that *j* has the higher market value.

It can be argued that, since market incompleteness and heterogeneity across individuals characterise the real world, it is unrealistic to assume that firms will, or even should, seek to maximise their market value, especially if they are not listed on a stock market. For example, King (1977, p. 143) writes that

given the existence of even a limited degree of set-up costs it is not surprising that we observe a finite number of firms, and these firms will have some degree of monopoly power. The very nature of business risk is that the firm has open to it projects which have a unique pattern of returns across states of the world, and it is the role of the entrepreneur or of management to take such risks in the knowledge that no insurance market can offer them complete protection against failure.

King notes that wealth means power, in that individuals who are personally wealthy, or who control companies with large retained profits, can pursue projects that are worthwhile to them, regardless of whether they are as worthwhile to others. Rich people are not dependent on external finance, and so their investment decisions are not contingent on approval by capital market investors.

If an entrepreneur assigns a higher value to a project than the market does, and is able to finance the project, does this mean that its cost of capital is less than it would have been using external finance? This is a tricky question, which does not appear to have been given a definitive answer. Suppose we agree that the cost of capital differs across projects only because of differences in project risk (i.e. the distribution of contingent returns). Then we can say that the entrepreneur assigns a higher value than the market, either because he thinks the contingent pay-offs are higher or because he thinks project risk is lower, or both. It is only disagreement about risk that implies disagreement about the cost of capital. Let us suppose for the sake of argument that the disagreement about value is due to differing beliefs about risk only.

Consider first a project with shares freely traded on the capital market. If investors have differing beliefs about risk, a project's expected return is determined by those investors in the pool who have the most favourable assessment of the project's risk. It is they who are willing to pay the most for the shares. This implies that a project's cost of capital is given by the expected return on another asset of the same risk, as assessed by the group of investors who hold the shares. There will not be market-wide agreement on an asset's risk or cost of capital, but we can still think of the cost of capital as implying 'with risk as assessed by the project's shareholders'. This does not seem to be an undue stretch of the concept.

Now let us return to the case of a project that is privately funded by a single entrepreneur, who assigns it a higher value (lower level of risk) than its market value would be were the shares traded. This implies that the entrepreneur has a *more* optimistic belief about the project's risk than the beliefs of the most optimistic of market investors – those who would hold the shares were they traded. Why would the entrepreneur be more optimistic than any investor in the market? The obvious possibilities are that he/she has better information, or that he/she would derive private benefits from the project, or that he/she is making a mistake – he/she is not making a reasonable assessment of the risk. If the entrepreneur's estimate of the cost of capital were based on superior information, this would lend credence to his/her estimate. The 'true' cost of capital is less than market investors think, on the basis of their inferior information. But if one believed the estimate to be biased by private benefits from the project, or simply not to be reasonable, it would be hard to accept the entrepreneur's estimate of the cost of capital as a 'proper' estimate, even though it is the entrepreneur who provides the capital. It seems essential to the concept that the pay-offs on a project are pay-offs measured in cash (or consumption units), not in investor-specific private utility, and that the assessment of risk by the providers of finance is reasonable.

The above line of argument suggests a somewhat qualified meaning of the 'cost of capital' in the context of the real world, namely the 'minimum expected rate of return necessary to attract funds from a group of rational outside investors'. The term 'outside investors' is meant to distinguish the providers of finance from the insider(s) who are organising the project.

2.4.3   Monetary policy

Any model is a simplification of the real world. Our primary interest in the contingent-states model is as the setting for theories of expected returns on assets. From this perspective, one simplification that makes the model seem rather remote is the absence of a government. This absence arises because prices in the model are determined in a completely free asset market, and because all prices and returns are in real terms, since wealth and pay-offs are expressed in consumption units. There is no analytical role for money and so no possibility of 'money illusion'. In later chapters, wealth and pay-offs are expressed in money values but inflation is assumed to be zero (or inflation can be non-zero, but all prices and returns are assumed to have been converted to real terms). This applies throughout the book, except in Chapter 10, which deals with inflation.

There is no doubt that, in reality, governments and central banks can and do exercise some control over real interest rates. For example, Allsopp and Glyn (1999, p. 8) remark that 'discussions on interest rate policy, for example in the United States, in the Euro zone, or the UK, nowadays simply take the authorities' control over interest rates for granted'. Yet monetary policy is scarcely mentioned in research on the cost of capital or on asset pricing (at least, this is true about the references in this book). One explanation is that the one-period risk-free return is treated as an exogenous variable in the standard CAPM and in arbitrage pricing theory. But the return on a risk-free asset, if there is one, is an endogenous variable in the analysis of equilibrium in the contingent-states world (see equation (2.7)).

2.5   Summary

We have allowed for uncertainty in this chapter by imagining that there could be more than one contingent state (possible state of the world) at a given future date, and that people can assign to each state a probability that it will be the one to come about. We have presented the model for the value of a project in a one-period setting with contingent states, in which the cost of capital is the expected return on a project or asset of the same risk.

We then considered how asset prices, and thus expected returns, are determined in this setting. It was assumed that a representative individual maximises lifetime expected utility. The individual does this by allocating his/her budget in such a way that the marginal utility per pound spent is equal across current consumption and claims to future consumption. He/she is exposed to risk if there are differences in total consumption across the contingent states. For a given expected (weighted average) amount of pay-off, an asset that pays off most in relatively high-consumption states will add to risk, whilst an asset that pays off most in relatively low-consumption states will reduce risk. The (marginal) utility of the risk-increasing asset is less than the utility of the risk-reducing asset. So in equilibrium, with marginal utility per pound equal across assets, the riskier asset must have a lower price and a higher expected return than the less risky asset, assuming each provides the same expected amount of pay-off. This is the key insight from the discussion. Some of the doubts and limitations regarding the model were discussed in the final section.

The analysis in this chapter did not progress to the derivation of a specific measure of risk, nor of a function that specifies the equilibrium expected return on an asset with a given level of risk. In other words, we did not present an explicit asset pricing model. This is the task of the next two chapters.

3   The capital asset pricing model and multifactor models

The previous chapter introduced the contingent-states framework and discussed in a general way how asset prices are determined. We now turn to the major topic of models of expected returns. These are models that result in equations in which the expected return on an asset is a function of one or more variables that measure the risk of the asset. At least three approaches to modelling expected returns have been developed: the CAPM; the arbitrage pricing theory (APT) and multifactor models; and the consumption CAPM. The current chapter starts with a derivation of the standard CAPM, which assumes that there is a risk-free asset. The standard CAPM is important for this book because it is widely used in practice to estimate the cost of equity, and because much of the applied analysis in Part II assumes that the cost of equity is modelled by the standard CAPM. The Black version of the CAPM, which does not assume that there is a risk-free asset, is also described. There are shorter sections on arbitrage pricing theory and multifactor models, and the chapter ends with a brief summary of relevant evidence. The consumption CAPM is considered in Chapter 4.

3.1   The capital asset pricing model

There are several ways of deriving the standard CAPM. It can be seen as a special case of APT, as shown in Section 3.2.1, and of the consumption CAPM, as shown in Chapter 4. This section presents a traditional derivation, which results from the portfolio theory of Markowitz (1959). A derivation provides a theoretical justification for a model or result; it enables one to understand why a result is what it is. The nature of the justification is a demonstration that, *if* we make a particular list of assumptions, *then* it must be the case, as a matter of logic, that a certain model – in the sense of a specific relation between variables – is true. The term 'model' can also mean a theoretical setting, a list of assumptions. A relation between variables would then be described as a result or conclusion, in the context of a given model. In our case, we are explaining the expected return on an asset of a given risk.

3.1.1   Assumptions

The contingent-states setting of Chapter 2 is assumed. There are two dates, now ($t = 0$) and a future date ($t = 1$), with one time period in between. Each investor seeks to maximise his lifetime expected utility subject to the value of his/her wealth, which is taken to be a fixed endowment at date 0. His/her utility derives from consumption at the two dates, and he/she decides how much of his/her wealth to consume now and how much to save. Under uncertainty he/she also chooses his/her portfolio. Investors are price takers and face a capital market in which many assets are traded (in principle, the relevant market consists of all tradable assets). Asset holdings can be constrained to be non-negative; it is not necessary to allow short-selling to derive the standard CAPM. All investors are assumed to have the same beliefs about contingent returns.

The supply of assets, and the contingent returns on each asset, are taken as given. Each asset j has a market price at date 0 of P_{j0}. The asset will provide an uncertain cash pay-off at date 1, which will be consumed. The pay-off is the market value P_{js} plus any dividend Div_{js}.

The return on j in state s is

$$R_{js} = (P_{js} + Div_{js} - P_{j0})/P_{j0}$$

and the expected return is

$$E(R_{js}) = \Sigma_s \pi_s R_{js}$$

where π_s is the probability of state s; $\Sigma_s \pi_s = 1$. Henceforth in this chapter we shall suppress the s subscript. The worst outcome is a pay-off of zero, or return of -100 per cent, ensured by limited liability.

The investor chooses a portfolio H. Any portfolio is defined by the proportions in which the n constituent assets are held. The proportion or weight of each asset j in the portfolio is w_j, and the sum of the weights must equal one. It is assumed in portfolio theory that an investor's utility per pound spent on a portfolio H, $U(H)$, can be calculated from its expected return and risk, measured by the variance of the return on the portfolio:

$$U(H) = U\left[E(R_H), \sigma_H^2\right]$$

where utility increases in expected return $E(R_H)$ and decreases in variance of the return σ_H^2 ('mean-variance utility'). The expected return on the portfolio is the weighted average of the expected returns on its constituent assets:

$$E(R_H) = \Sigma_{j=1}^n w_j E(R_j)$$

or henceforth

$$[\Sigma_j w_j E(R_j)]$$

The expected variance of the portfolio's return is

$$\begin{aligned} \sigma_H^2 &= \mathrm{var}(R_H) \\ &= E[R_H - E(R_H)]^2 \\ &= \Sigma_j \Sigma_k w_j w_k \sigma_{jk} \end{aligned} \tag{3.1}$$

where σ_{jk} is the expected covariance of the returns on j and k, $\mathrm{cov}(R_j, R_k)$. For $j = k$, $\sigma_{jj} = \sigma_j^2$ is the expected variance of the returns on j, $\mathrm{var}(R_j)$.

Markowitz (1959) was concerned to establish that the assumption of mean-variance utility can be consistent with the assumption that investors maximise expected utility. The calculation of the expected utility of a portfolio per pound spent involves two steps. First, a numerical measure of utility is assigned to each possible portfolio return. Second, the assigned utility value of each return is multiplied by its probability. The expected utility is the sum of the probability-weighted utilities of the returns across the possible states:

$$U(H) = E[U(R_H)] \qquad (3.2)$$

The expected utility is affected both by the expected return and by the distribution of possible returns.

For the maximisation of mean-variance utility to result in the maximisation of expected utility requires that the expected utility from a portfolio is a function of the expected return and variance of return only. But this is not generally the case, which is one reason why the setting for portfolio theory is less general than the contingent-states setting described in Chapter 2. Either of two additional assumptions is needed to make maximisation of mean-variance utility equivalent to maximisation of expected utility. One is the assumption that the returns on individual assets are normally distributed, and that the joint distribution of the returns is normal, in which case the returns on portfolios selected from these assets are also normally distributed. If a variable is normally distributed, the probability distribution is completely described by its mean (expected return) and variance. Hence, given the mean and variance, we could list all the possible future returns, together with their probabilities, and we could therefore work out the expected utility from the portfolio, as shown in equation (3.2). We do not require any further information. (In fact, the formula for the normal distribution assumes that the variable of interest is continuous, so in the case of a discrete variable we are dealing with an approximation to the normal distribution.)

The second assumption that could be made to justify mean-variance utility is that investors have a quadratic utility function, which is a function of the form

$$U(H) = a + bR_H + cR_H^2$$

for a given value of R_H, where a, b and c are positive or negative constants. Assuming diminishing marginal utility, c will be negative. The expected utility of (the contingent returns on) H assuming a quadratic utility function is

$$\begin{aligned} E[U(H)] &= a + bE(R_H) - cE(R_H^2) \\ &= a + bE(R_H) - c[E(R_H)^2 + \text{var}(R_H)] \end{aligned}$$

The second line follows because, for a variable x, $\text{var}(x) = E(x^2) - E(x)^2$. With a utility function of this form, it is clear that the utility of a portfolio is determined by its expected return and variance of return only, because these are the only two statistics describing the distribution of returns that enter the utility function, regardless of whether the distribution is normal. Thus portfolio returns need not be normally distributed for mean-variance utility to result in utility maximisation, if investors have quadratic utility functions.

Unfortunately, neither of these additional assumptions is entirely satisfactory. Returns on assets are not normally distributed. The distribution is curtailed at -100 per cent, so it is skewed to the right, and the skewness is more pronounced the longer the interval is over which returns are measured. The distribution has also been found to be 'leptokurtic'; there are more extreme positive and negative observations, beyond two standard deviations from the mean, than there would be in a normal distribution. A quadratic utility function has the problem that the investor's aversion to risk increases if his initial wealth increases, which is implausible. It is also the case that there is a portfolio return above which marginal utility becomes negative. Markowitz (1959, pp. 282–85) is aware of this and observes, in mitigation, that a quadratic function in the range before marginal utility turns negative is a close approximation to several non-quadratic functions, such as $U = \ln(1 + R)$, that are concave and do not turn negative.

Let us assume, as an approximation, that asset returns are normally distributed. Then the positive relation of utility with expected return and negative relation with variance are obtained by assuming positive but diminishing marginal utility from consumption, as in Chapter 2 (see Figure 2.1). The utility function need not be specified further. Since the pay-off from the portfolio is spent on consumption, we have diminishing marginal utility from portfolio pay-offs or returns. This implies that the indifference curves plotted in expected return, variance space are convex, as shown in Figure 3.1. Investors derive more utility (are on a higher indifference curve) from a higher expected return for a given variance, or from a smaller variance for a given expected return. Also, the indifference curves are convex; for each extra unit of variance, investors require increasing compensation in terms of expected return.

The reason why a diminishing marginal utility function implies an indifference map of the form in Figure 3.1 can be explained as follows, for the case of normally distributed returns. Consider a return R^+ that is x standard deviations above the mean. Given the normal distribution, the return R^-, which is x standard deviations below the mean, is equally probable, and $E(R) - R^- = R^+ - E(R)$. With diminishing marginal utility it is the case that $U[R^+ - E(R)] < U[E(R) - R^-]$, and, further, that as the absolute amount $E(R) - R$ increases the difference $U[R^+ - E(R)] - U[E(R) - R^-]$ becomes more negative. An increase in the variance of the distribution means that the amount $E(R) - R$ increases for any given value of x standard deviations. Since the expected return $E(R)$ stays the same, it follows that expected utility falls as the variance of return rises, and because the utility function is concave utility falls increasingly rapidly as variance rises. Hence increasing expected return is required per unit of extra variance to maintain a given level of utility, which means that indifference curves are convex.

3.1.2 The standard CAPM

Choice of risky portfolio

The decision regarding the proportion of wealth to save rather than consume at date 0 is a matter of finding the proportion that maximises the total utility from consumption at date 0 and from the portfolio acquired by saving. This is a problem of the same form as the

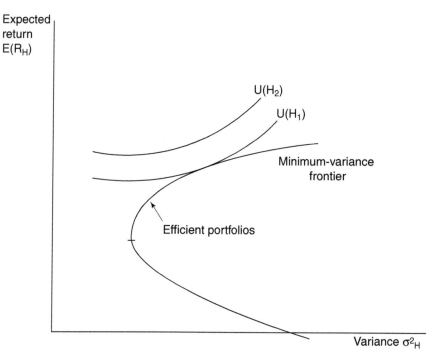

Figure 3.1   Choice of risky portfolio

allocation of a budget between two goods, as discussed in Section 1.2. Our concern here is with the other decision at date 0: the choice of portfolio given the amount to be saved.

The investor buys amounts of assets $j = 1, 2 \ldots n$ to form his/her portfolio H, subject to the budget constraint that the market value of the portfolio does not exceed the amount he/she has saved. The budget constraint can be ignored since, whatever the size of the portfolio, the utility from it is, by assumption, solely a function of its expected return $E(R_H)$ and variance of return σ_H^2, which in turn depend on the proportion of the portfolio held in each asset. So the composition of the optimum portfolio will be independent of its size. Thus, the investor's goal is

$$\text{maximise } U\left[E(R_H), \sigma_H^2\right] \text{ with respect to } w_j$$
$$\text{subject to the constraint } \Sigma_j w_j = 1$$

We assume for the moment that there is no feasible portfolio that has zero variance, which implies that there is no risk-free asset and that there is no pair of assets that are perfectly negatively correlated. The solution to the maximisation is detailed in Appendix 3.1. The solution is that each investor will choose an efficient portfolio, and this is the main conclusion of portfolio theory. A portfolio is *efficient* if, for a given pool of assets from which portfolios can be constructed, no portfolio is feasible that has the same or a higher expected return and a lower variance.

The *minimum-variance frontier* for risky assets shows, for any expected return, the minimum possible variance of a portfolio that provides that expected return. We assume that the correlation coefficients r_{jk} between all risky assets $j, k \ldots$ are in the range $-1 < r_{jk} < 1$. It can be then shown that the frontier is a parabola (Merton, 1972), the efficient section of which is concave to the horizontal (variance) axis, as in Figure 3.1. The assumption that all $r_{jk} > -1$ implies that all portfolios have some risk (variance > 0); the assumption that all $r_{jk} < 1$ implies that no assets or portfolios will be perfectly correlated, and therefore that the frontier will not be a straight line. Most investment texts provide an informal explanation of the shape of the minimum-variance frontier.

Perhaps the most familiar route from here to the standard CAPM is to continue by showing that, if there is risk-free lending and borrowing, all efficient portfolios are combinations of risk-free lending or borrowing and a single efficient portfolio, the market portfolio M. The risk-free rate R_F has zero variance, and the correlation of the risk-free rate with the return on any risky asset or portfolio is zero. The investor now has the opportunity to hold a proportion $1 - \alpha$ of his/her portfolio as a risk-free loan, combined with α, in any efficient portfolio of risky assets, labelled H^*, with expected return $E(R_{H^*})$ and variance $\sigma_{H^*}^2$. Therefore $\alpha > 1$ is possible, at least to an extent, and this means that the investor has borrowed a certain amount to invest in the risky portfolio. If the investor's portfolio H includes lending or borrowing, its expected return and variance are, respectively,

$$E(R_H) = (1 - \alpha)R_F + \alpha E(R_{H^*})$$

and

$$\sigma_H^2 = \alpha \sigma_{H^*}^2$$

Solving the second equation for α and substituting the result in the first equation, we find that, as α varies, $E(R_H)$ varies with σ_H^2 according to the equation

$$E(R_H) = R_F + \sigma_H^2[E(R_{H^*}) - R_F]/\sigma_{H^*}^2 \tag{3.3}$$

which plots on a straight line in expected return, variance space. The equation of any straight line is of the form $y = a + bx$; in equation (3.3) the constant $a = R_F$ and the slope $b = dE(R_H)/d\sigma_H^2 = [E(R_{H^*}) - R_F]/\sigma_{H^*}^2$. Since we are assuming that investors are risk averse, we know that the slope must be positive; equilibrium asset prices must be such that the expected return on a risky asset or portfolio must exceed the risk-free rate, since otherwise there will be no demand for risky assets.

An investor choosing amongst portfolios that include lending or borrowing would always prefer the slope in equation (3.3) to be steeper. For any given variance σ_H^2, a steeper slope implies a higher expected return $E(R_H)$. This means that the investor will choose the efficient risky portfolio that results in the steepest slope in equation (3.3). Due to the concavity of the efficient frontier of risky portfolios, there will be a unique risky efficient portfolio H^{**} that results in the steepest slope, for all investors. The line in equation (3.3), with $H^* = H^{**}$, will lie at a tangent to the frontier at H^{**}, and the expected return-variance combinations available on this line will dominate the combinations on the efficient frontier of risky assets.

Thus the efficient frontier with risk-free lending and borrowing is given by equation (3.3), with $H^* = H^{**}$. This is sometimes known as the mutual fund or single fund theorem.

A more formal proof requires matrix algebra (see, e.g., Huang and Litzenberger, 1988, pp. 76–80). The essence is that the investor is maximising

$$w_j^\top[\mathrm{E}(R_j) - R_F\mathbf{1}] - (\gamma_i/2)(w_j^\top V w_j)$$

with respect to asset weights w_j, for risky assets $j, k \ldots n$. Bold face for w_j and R_j indicates a vector (ordered list) of asset weights and returns, $^\top$ stands for transpose, $\mathbf{1}$ is a vector of n 1's, γ_i is a measure of investor i's risk aversion and V is the variance-covariance matrix: $\sigma_{H^*}^2 = \Sigma_j\Sigma_k w_j w_k \sigma_{jk} = w_j^\top V w_j$. The asset returns, the risk-free rate and V are given. The solution to the maximisation problem is

$$w_j = (1/\gamma_i)V[\mathrm{E}(R_j) - R_F\mathbf{1}]$$

The optimum weights vary across investors with the fraction $1/\gamma_i$. The point is that $1/\gamma_i$ affects the proportion of investor i's wealth allocated to risky assets but does not affect the composition of i's risky portfolio – the list of risky assets and the proportions in which they are held. Therefore, all investors hold the same risky portfolio, though not in the same amounts. This was first shown by Tobin (1958).

Equilibrium expected returns

To proceed further, we move from the perspective of an individual to consideration of the capital market, in which asset prices are determined. The supply of each asset is taken as exogenous. The argument above shows that all investors will hold the same efficient portfolio of risky assets, which we have labelled H^{**} so far. Since all investors own positive amounts of the same list of assets (unless they hold only the risk-free asset), any asset not on the list has zero demand and will not be held. Therefore, the assets in H^{**} must be all the assets that exist, so H^{**} must be the market portfolio M, defined as all the traded assets at their equilibrium market values. This is a condition for the clearing of the market: if an asset's market price is the equilibrium (market-clearing) price, the demand equals the supply.

The proportion of each asset in M is the total value of the asset (the number of units in supply times the price per unit) divided by the total value of M. Since all investors hold M, and since the efficient frontier consists of combinations of risk-free lending or borrowing with M, the trade-off for all investors between expected return and variance is given by substituting M for the efficient portfolio of risky assets H^* in equation (3.3) to give

$$\begin{aligned}
\mathrm{E}(R_H) &= R_F + \sigma_H^2[\mathrm{E}(R_M) - R_F]/\sigma_M^2 \\
&= R_F + \alpha[\mathrm{E}(R_M) - R_F]
\end{aligned} \tag{3.4}$$

where $\mathrm{E}(R_M)$ and σ_M^2 are the expected return and variance on the market portfolio and α is the proportion of H invested in the market portfolio. Equation (3.4) is known as the *capital market line* (Figure 3.2).

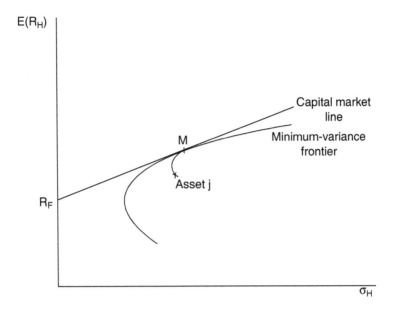

Figure 3.2   The capital market line

The assumption of homogeneous beliefs (Section 3.1.1) is necessary for the conclusion that all investors will hold the same portfolio of risky assets. Without agreement amongst investors about the possible pay-offs to be provided by each asset, investors would differ in their beliefs about the expected return and variance of the asset, given the market price, and they would differ in their assessment of the set of efficient portfolios, including the tangency portfolio H^{**}.

We have now established that the portfolio H of an investor with mean-variance utility and homogeneous beliefs will be an efficient portfolio consisting of the market portfolio M in combination with risk-free lending or borrowing. Each investor faces a linear relation between the expected return and variance of efficient portfolios given by equation (3.4), once asset prices at date 0 have been set. The variance of an efficient portfolio is determined by the variance of M and by the exposure of H to the variance of M, determined by the proportion of H invested in M: $\sigma_H^2 = \alpha \sigma_M^2$. The CAPM itself states that, in equilibrium, asset prices must be such that each risky asset offers the same linear relation between expected return and exposure to the variance of the market portfolio. One way of showing this is as follows (Sharpe, 1964).

Consider an individual asset or portfolio j in Figure 3.2 that is below the efficient frontier of risky portfolios (a portfolio could equally well be on this frontier). We can imagine a portfolio H with $1 - \theta$ in asset j and θ in the market portfolio M. As θ varies between zero and one, portfolio H moves along the curve between j and M in Figure 3.2. The slope of this curve is the trade-off between the expected return and risk of H, which will change with a change in θ. We are interested in the slope at the point where θ approaches one and the curve is tangent to the capital market line, since the slope at this point gives the marginal change in expected return for a marginal change in portfolio risk required by investors in aggregate to hold asset j at its market price. It is convenient at this point to measure portfolio risk in terms of the standard deviation of returns rather than the variance. The slope $dE(R_H)/d\sigma_H$ can be found from the change in expected return of H with respect to a change in θ, $dE(R_H)/d\theta$, and the change in the standard deviation of the return with respect to a change in θ, $d\sigma_H/d\theta$. The expected return $E(R_H)$ is

$$E(R_H) = (1 - \theta)E(R_j) + \theta E(R_M)$$

and therefore

$$dE(R_H)/d\theta = E(R_M) - E(R_j)$$

The standard deviation σ_H is

$$\sigma_H = \sqrt{[(1 - \theta)^2\sigma_j^2 + \theta^2\sigma_M^2 + 2\theta(1 - \theta)r_{jM}\sigma_j\sigma_M]}$$

using equation (3.1), and the fact that $\sigma_{jM} = r_{jM}\sigma_j\sigma_M$, where r_{jM} is the correlation coefficient. Therefore

$$\frac{d\sigma_H}{d\theta} = \frac{-2\sigma_j^2 + 2\theta\sigma_j^2 + 2\theta\sigma_M^2 + 2(1 - 2\theta)r_{jM}\sigma_j\sigma_M}{2\sigma_H} \tag{3.5}$$

With $\theta = 1$, $\sigma_H = \sigma_M$ and equation (3.5) becomes

$$d\sigma_H/d\theta|_{\theta=1} = \sigma_M - r_{jM}\sigma_j$$

Thus we can now see that

$$\frac{dE(R_H)}{d\sigma_H}\bigg|_{\theta=1} = \frac{dE(R_H)/d\theta}{d\sigma_H/d\theta} = \frac{E(R_M) - E(R_j)}{\sigma_M - r_{jM}\sigma_j} \tag{3.6}$$

Since the slope of the capital market line is $[E(R_M) - R_F]/\sigma_M$, from equation (3.4), and equation (3.6) is the slope of the curve between j and M at the point of tangency with the capital market line, we have

$$\frac{E(R_M) - E(R_j)}{\sigma_M - r_{jM}\sigma_j} = \frac{E(R_M) - R_F}{\sigma_M}$$

therefore

$$\begin{aligned} E(R_j) &= R_F[1 - r_{jM}\sigma_j/\sigma_M] + E(R_M)r_{jM}\sigma_j/\sigma_M \\ &= R_F + \beta_j[E(R_M) - R_F] \end{aligned} \tag{3.7}$$

where $\beta_j = r_{jM}\sigma_j/\sigma_M = r_{jM}\sigma_j\sigma_M/\sigma_M^2 = \sigma_{jM}/\sigma_M^2$. Equation (3.7) is the standard CAPM.

It may help to rehearse the final steps in the argument. (i) The risk of an efficient portfolio (on the capital market line) is measured by its exposure to the variance of the market portfolio. (ii) The marginal rate of compensation for risk required by investors in aggregate to hold an asset at its market price must be the same as the relation between expected return and risk across efficient portfolios – i.e. the slope of the capital market line. This is a condition for capital market equilibrium. (iii) Points (i) and (ii) imply that the risk of an asset relevant to its price and expected return is its exposure to market variance, which we have just shown to be measured by its covariance with the market returns, σ_{jM}, or by β_j. A cross-section of assets with expected returns given by equation (3.7) offers the same linear relation between expected return and exposure to market variance as does a cross-section of portfolios on the capital market line. To confirm this, we can note that the beta of a portfolio H on the line is

$$\beta_H = \text{cov}[(1 - \alpha)R_F + \alpha R_M, R_M]/\sigma_M^2 = \alpha$$

where α is the proportion of H invested in the market.

Discussion

The standard CAPM is a partial explanation of the expected returns on assets. It tells us that, in equilibrium, there is a linear relation between the risk premium on an asset and its 'systematic risk' measured by beta, or by the covariance of the returns with the returns on the market. The risk-free rate and the market risk premium $E(R_M) - R_F$ are exogenously given (not explained by the model). They are determined by the nature of the general contingent-states equilibrium, which we introduced in Chapter 2 and will discuss further in Chapter 4. As Danthine and Donaldson (2002, p. 104) put it, 'we may view the CAPM as informing us, via modern Portfolio Theory, as to what asset return interrelationships must be in order for equilibrium asset prices to coincide with the observed asset prices'.

The model is set in the contingent-states world; it is assumed that investors at date 0 know the contingent returns on each asset at date 1 and their probabilities. This is why they know the variance of the return of each asset and all the covariances between them. The assumption seems hopelessly unrealistic. Yet the model does combine practicality with a rigorous theoretical basis, and this helps explain its great prominence in finance. If one is willing to assume that the model holds at least approximately then the assumptions required for its derivation can be put aside. It can be applied in the real world, because the three ingredients required to estimate the expected return on an asset – the risk-free rate, the market risk premium and the asset's beta – can all be estimated.

3.1.3   The CAPM without risk-free lending and borrowing

The argument in Section 3.1.2 first established that all investors would hold the market portfolio, on the assumption of risk-free lending and borrowing, and then showed the relation between expected return and variance that obtains in equilibrium for all assets in the market portfolio. An alternative way of proceeding is first to show that the relation between expected return and risk can be found from *any* portfolio of risky assets that is efficient *ex ante*, and then to argue that, in equilibrium, the market portfolio is an efficient portfolio. It is worth following this alternative route, originated by Black (1972), as it helps in understanding the CAPM.

Appendix 3.2 shows that the expected return on any asset j in an efficient portfolio of risky assets portfolio, H^*, can be expressed as

$$E(R_j) = E(R_{H^*}) - S_{H^*}\sigma_{H^*} + S_{H^*}\text{cov}(R_j, R_{H^*})/\sigma_{H^*} \tag{3.8}$$

where S_{H^*} is the slope of H^* in expected return, standard deviation space: $S_{H^*} = d\text{E}(R_{H^*})/d\sigma_{H^*}$. From equation (3.8), an asset or portfolio Z_{H^*} with zero covariance with portfolio H^* will have an expected return equal to $E(R_{H^*}) - S_{H^*}\sigma_{H^*}$. Call this expected return $E(R_{ZH^*})$. We therefore have an expression for S_{H^*}:

$$S_{H^*} = [E(R_{H^*}) - E(R_{ZH^*})]/\sigma_{H^*}$$

Substituting for S_{H^*} in equation (3.8) gives

$$E(R_j) = E(R_{ZH^*}) + [E(R_{H^*}) - E(R_{ZH^*})]\text{cov}(R_j, R_{H^*})/\sigma_{H^*}^2$$

or

$$E(R_j) = E(R_{ZH^*}) + \beta_{j,H^*}[E(R_{H^*}) - E(R_{ZH^*})] \tag{3.9}$$

where $\beta_{j,H^*} = \text{cov}(R_j, R_{H^*})/\sigma_{H^*}^2$, the beta of asset j with respect to portfolio H^*. So the conclusion is that the expected return on an asset in any efficient portfolio is given by equation (3.9). Put another way, if equation (3.9) holds, portfolio H^* is efficient.

An asset can be a constituent of different efficient portfolios, and so it does not have a single beta; β_{j,H^*} is jointly specific to the asset and to the efficient portfolio with respect to which the beta is calculated. There is nothing special about the market portfolio as yet; an equation of the form of (3.9) holds for any efficient portfolio.

The relation between expected returns and betas in equation (3.9) results entirely from the mathematics of the minimum-variance frontier, for a given set of assets and their possible returns. The prices of the assets may or may not be equilibrium prices. For betas to help explain expected returns (i.e. to interpret beta as a measure of risk), the relation between the expected return and beta needs to be a consequence of equilibrium in the asset market. Thus we need to add the assumption that the prices are equilibrium prices. The same assumption is required in the derivation of the standard CAPM, to make the step that all investors hold the market portfolio. Then the analysis will have extracted the risk/return relation that is implicit in the equilibrium. The feature that distinguishes the standard CAPM from the Black version is the assumption that there is risk-free lending and borrowing, from which it follows in the standard CAPM that all investors will hold the market portfolio.

If there is no risk-free asset, we cannot argue that all investors will hold the market portfolio. Rather, the investors will choose different risky portfolios on the efficient section of the minimum-variance frontier, depending on their utility functions. Any efficient portfolio H^* can be paired with a minimum-variance but inefficient portfolio Z_{H^*}, on the negatively sloping section of the minimum-variance frontier, with zero covariance between H^* and Z_{H^*} (except for the case of the least-variance portfolio, at the turning point of the frontier). The construction of such a minimum-variance Z-portfolio is likely to require Z_{H^*} to include short positions, and so unrestricted short-selling must be allowed in the Black version. The reason Z_{H^*} will exist, for a given efficient portfolio H^*, is as follows. Equation (3.9) establishes that any portfolio with expected return of $E(R_{ZH^*})$ must have $\beta_{j,H^*} = 0$, and the shape of the minimum-variance frontier, which is a parabola, implies that a minimum-variance portfolio does exist with a given expected return of $E(R_{ZH^*})$. The inefficiency of Z_{H^*} follows from the facts that $E(R_{H^*}) - E(R_{ZH^*})$ is positive (because $S_{H^*} > 0$) and that, for uncorrelated portfolios, there must be combinations of H^* and Z_{H^*} with lower variance than either H^* or Z_{H^*}.

The final step to the Black version of the CAPM is to assume that the asset market is in equilibrium, in which case it can be established that the market portfolio is efficient. It can be shown that any position on the minimum-variance frontier can be reached by assigning appropriate weights to any two other minimum-variance portfolios (Black, 1972; Fama, 1976, pp. 279–84). (This property of frontier portfolios is sometimes called two-fund separation.) It follows that any combination of efficient (and thus minimum-variance) portfolios is itself an efficient portfolio. If utility is quadratic or if returns are normally distributed, all investors with mean-variance utility hold efficient portfolios in equilibrium, as shown in Appendix 3.1. Therefore, the sum of the holdings of all investors, which is the market portfolio, must itself be efficient.

Having established the efficiency of the market portfolio in equilibrium, it can be used in equation (3.9) with its paired Z-portfolio Z_M, known as the zero-beta portfolio. The result is the Black version of the CAPM:

$$E(R_j) = E(R_{ZM}) + \beta_j[E(R_M) - E(R_{ZM})] \tag{3.10}$$

where β_j is asset j's beta with respect to the market portfolio, as in the standard CAPM, and $E(R_{ZM})$ is the expected return on the zero-beta portfolio – the minimum-variance portfolio that has zero covariance with the market portfolio. If there is no risk-free asset, there is no argument that all investors will hold the market portfolio. But equation (3.10) says that, even so, expected returns across assets are linearly related to their betas in equilibrium, as in the standard CAPM.

A risk-free asset has zero covariance with any risky portfolio, so R_F can be substituted for $E(R_{ZH^*})$ in equation (3.9), and the argument in Section 3.1.2 can be used that the efficient frontier will lie on a line in expected return, variance space connecting the risk-free asset and the market portfolio. Then $H^* = M$ for all investors, and equation (3.9) becomes the standard CAPM, with R_F substituted for $E(R_{ZM})$.

3.1.4   Roll's critique

Roll (1977) has pointed out that, given any sample of *ex post* asset returns, there must be an exact linear relation between the betas of their assets and their observed mean returns over several periods, if the betas are measured against a portfolio that is efficient *ex post*. The argument is as follows. We start with a sample of T returns for periods $1, 2 \ldots T$ for n shares. We have to move to a multiperiod setting since an asset's *ex post* beta cannot be estimated from one observed return. An *ex post* minimum-variance frontier can be calculated from this sample. An *ex post* efficient portfolio H^* provides the highest arithmetic mean return for a given portfolio variance, and is defined by the list of proportions of the portfolio held in each asset at date 0. It can be proved that, for any efficient portfolio H^*, on the upward-sloping part of the frontier, there is a unique portfolio Z_{H^*} that has zero covariance with H^* and that is located on the downward-sloping part of the frontier. We showed this in Section 3.1.3 working with a sample of *ex ante* uncertain returns. The mean return on Z_{H^*}, $\mu(R_{ZH^*})$, is therefore lower than the mean return on portfolio H^*, $\mu(R_{H^*})$, and the beta of Z_{H^*} with respect to H^* is zero.

Roll also proves that, for the assets in an efficient portfolio, there is always an exact cross-sectional linear relation between the sample mean return of each asset and its beta calculated with respect to that efficient portfolio. If asset j is in portfolio H^*, the beta of j with respect to H^*, β_{j,H^*}, is calculated from the time-series regression

$$R_{jt} = \alpha_{j,H^*} + \beta_{j,H^*} R_{H^*t} + e_{jt}$$

He shows that the sample arithmetic mean return on share j over the T periods, $\mu(R_{jt})$, is given exactly by

$$\mu(R_{jt}) = (1 - \beta_{j,H^*})\mu(R_{ZH^*t}) + \beta_{j,H^*}\mu(R_{H^*t})$$
$$= \mu(R_{ZH^*t}) + \beta_{j,H^*}[\mu(R_{H^*t}) - \mu(R_{ZH^*t})]$$

Therefore, there is an exact cross-sectional linear relation between mean returns and β_{j,H^*} in the sample of shares. In other words, the cross-sectional relation

$$\mu(R_{jt}) - \mu(R_{ZH^*t}) = \gamma_0 + \gamma_1 \beta_{j,H^*} + e_j \qquad (3.11)$$

must hold with $\gamma_0 = 0, \gamma_1 = \mu(R_{H^*t}) - \mu(R_{ZH^*t})$ and $e_j = 0$ for all j. The same result holds for betas calculated with respect to any other efficient portfolio. The result does not hold for a portfolio that is not efficient. Also, the relation will be exact for an efficient portfolio only if mean return and beta are calculated using the same sample of returns; many empirical studies calculate betas using one estimation period and relate these betas to mean returns calculated over a subsequent period.

The analysis has shown that, if a portfolio is efficient, there will be an exact linear relation between mean returns of constituent assets and the betas calculated with respect to that portfolio. Thus a test of the relation between mean return and beta is effectively a test of whether the portfolio with respect to which betas are calculated is an efficient portfolio. If there is an exact linear relation, the portfolio is efficient; otherwise the portfolio is not efficient.

Roll argues that the only potentially testable prediction of the Black version of the CAPM is that the market portfolio is efficient *ex ante*. If it is, there must be an exact linear relation between the expected return and expected beta with respect to the market portfolio; this is not a separate prediction. The market portfolio, if *ex ante* efficient, may not turn out to be exactly on the *ex post* efficient frontier, but it should be close, so the relation between *ex post* mean return and beta calculated with respect to the market portfolio should be close to linear. The standard version of the CAPM adds the assumption that risk-free lending and borrowing are possible, in which case the prediction is that the market portfolio is the *ex ante* efficient portfolio at the tangency of the line between the risk-free asset and the efficient frontier of risky assets (Figure 3.2).

The trouble is that evidence on the *ex post*, empirical relation between mean return and beta cannot prove or disprove either version of the CAPM. There will always be a linear relation if beta is calculated with respect to a portfolio that is efficient *ex post*, regardless of whether investors hold portfolios that are efficient *ex ante*. Conversely, if the *ex post* relation is found not to be exact or not to be linear, this does not disprove the CAPM. Rather, it proves that the market-proxy portfolio used to estimate the betas is not on the *ex post* efficient frontier. Such a finding could arise for two reasons. It could be that the proxy is not efficient because the unknown market portfolio is not efficient *ex post*, in which case the CAPM is not supported. Alternatively, it could be that the market portfolio is efficient but that the proxy used is not efficient. Roll demonstrates that equation (3.11) will be rejected (e.g. $\gamma_0 >$ 0) if a proxy is used that is inefficient *ex post* but that is very highly correlated with an efficient portfolio *ex post*. In the CAPM theory, the market portfolio is 'the value-weighted combination of all [risky] assets' held by investors (Roll, 1977, p. 136), not just shares. Thus, a proxy such as a value-weighted stock market index may be highly correlated with the unknown portfolio of all assets, but still indicate rejection of the CAPM.

This argument has sown a seed of doubt about empirical tests of the CAPM, but the feeling amongst researchers seems to have been that, if the model is true, there ought to be a roughly linear and positive empirical relation between return and beta even using a proxy for the market portfolio, such as a stock market index.

Roll's insight is difficult to grasp and is worth restating. Efficient portfolios can always be calculated in the context of a given sample of share returns. To say that a portfolio is efficient *ex post* means the same thing as saying that there is an exact linear relation, unique to that particular efficient portfolio and given by equation (3.11), between *ex post* mean asset returns and the betas calculated with respect to the portfolio. This is a mathematical truth. It says nothing about the economic process that determines expected returns. The economic content of the CAPM (either version) is the prediction that expected return is a linear function of expected beta measured against the market portfolio, 'the value-weighted combination of all assets'. But efficient portfolios can always be calculated from a sample of observed returns, regardless of whether the CAPM prediction is true. Thus a linear relation between the observed return and beta does not support the model unless the portfolio with respect to which the beta is calculated is known to be the value-weighted combination of all assets. On the other hand, if there turns out to be little or no relation between the mean return and beta *ex post* in a sample of share returns, and the mean return and beta are both calculated over the same period, all we can infer for sure is that the market-proxy portfolio with respect to which the beta is calculated is not efficient *ex post*. To infer that the CAPM is wrong requires a leap of faith that the market-proxy returns are extremely close to the unknown returns of the value-weighted combination of all assets. It is *this* unknown, comprehensive, market portfolio that would be efficient, *ex ante* and (approximately) *ex post*, if the CAPM were true.

Roll's critique concerns the testability of the CAPM, but it also highlights a worry about the CAPM *ex ante*, as a theory. Suppose the market portfolio of all assets is efficient *ex ante*, as predicted, and suppose we are able somehow to measure the cross-sectional relation between the expected returns and betas calculated from *possible* returns. If we could do this (which we can't), the CAPM would be exactly right, by virtue of the mathematical relation between the expected return and beta measured against an efficient portfolio. But suppose we make a slight mistake and calculate the *ex ante* betas using a proxy for the market portfolio that happens to be slightly inefficient *ex ante*. Then there may be *no* relation between the expected return and beta as calculated, and we would infer that the CAPM is completely wrong. It is strange that an apparently small difference in the choice of market proxy can make such a complete difference to the relation between the expected return and beta. The suspicion is that the beta is not a robust theoretical measure of risk. The mathematics of the *ex ante* relation between expected returns and betas continues to be explored (e.g. Roll and Ross, 1994).

3.1.5   Multiperiod setting

The CAPM is a single-period model; the derivations of both versions have assumed that there is a single future period. This raises the question of how it should be interpreted in a multiperiod context. The pragmatic response when using the CAPM in valuation is to assume that the expected return on an asset of given risk (beta) is constant in future periods, in which case the estimate of the expected return in the next period serves for every future period. A project's cost of equity is assumed to stay the same, at least if the project's risk can be assumed to stay the same.

But, if the theoretical setting includes more than one future period, the standard CAPM is not a correct model for the expected return on an asset over the next period, unless further assumptions are made (Cochrane, 2001, pp. 155–60). It is necessary to assume that investment opportunities remain constant – i.e. that the risk-free rate is constant and that risky returns each period are independently and identically distributed. It is also necessary to assume that each investor has no labour income or that labour income is certain, and that an investor's utility each period is a quadratic function of his consumption. Given these assumptions, it can be shown that an investor's lifetime utility from saving can be written as a quadratic function of his wealth at the next date. The investor can be 'myopic'; he can make optimal investment decisions by considering returns over the next period only. In this case, the one-period portfolio theory of Section 3.1.2 applies, and the expected return on an asset for the next period will be given by the standard CAPM. However, the additional assumptions required to reach this conclusion in the multiperiod setting presumably reduce one's confidence that the one-period model is a correct analysis of the relation between expected return and risk.

3.2   Multifactor models

A multifactor model of expected returns is one in which asset returns are correlated with more than one risk factor. The CAPM is a single-factor model, although it is worth noting that it can be re-expressed as a multifactor model if it is assumed that market returns are themselves sensitive to several factors, as in Sharpe (1977). He first shows that the standard beta of asset j measured against the market portfolio, $\beta_{j,M}$, can be expressed as a weighted average of its beta values measured against a number n of sub-portfolios that together sum to form the market portfolio:

$$\beta_{j,M} = \Sigma_{H=1}^{n} w_H \text{var}(R_H)\beta_{j,H}/\text{var}(R_M) \qquad (3.12)$$

where w_H is the proportion of market value invested in sub-portfolio H, and $\beta_{j,H}$ is the beta of asset j measured against H. Sharpe now assumes that the market return, R_M, is sensitive to a number of factors $F = F_1, \ldots F_n$,

$$R_M = \beta_{M,F1} F_1 + \beta_{M,F2} F_2 + \cdots \beta_{M,Fn} F_n + e_M \qquad (3.13)$$

where $\beta_{M,F}$ is the beta of the market measured against factor F (analogous to the beta of a share measured against the market). He also assumes that the variation in the errors e_M is sufficiently small that the covariance of returns on asset j with returns on the market is approximately the same as the covariance of j with the returns on the market as predicted by the factor model, equation (3.13):

$$\text{cov}(R_j, R_M) \approx \text{cov}\left(R_j, \Sigma_{F=F1}^{Fn} \beta_{M,F} F\right)$$

If this is the case, a factor F can be treated in the same way as a sub-portfolio H in equation (3.12), with the sensitivity of the market to the factor, $\beta_{M,F}$, being equivalent to the weight w_H:

$$\beta_{j,M} \approx \Sigma_{F=F1}^{Fn} \beta_{M,F} \text{var}(R_H)\beta_{j,F}/\text{var}(R_M)$$

where $\beta_{j,F}$ is the beta of j measured against the risk factor F. A multifactor model for an asset's beta of this nature is but an elaboration of the CAPM, because the common factors are together assumed not to explain a higher proportion of the cross-sectional variance in observed returns than the standard CAPM.

3.2.1   Arbitrage pricing theory

We have derived the CAPM as a relation that holds when the asset market is in equilibrium. The expected returns in equilibrium are the result of choices by investors that maximise their utilities. The APT uses a different approach to arrive at the relation between expected return and risk. The reasoning shows the relations between expected returns that result from an absence of arbitrage opportunities, rather than from the maximisation of investor utility. The two approaches are consistent with each other because the maximisation of utility implies an absence of arbitrage opportunities, so long as the utility of investors increases with consumption. The reason is that, if an arbitrage opportunity is available, the investor can increase his/her future consumption in at least one possible state of the world without reducing present consumption. The APT is due to Ross (1976; 1977) and is presented accessibly in Ross (1977) and Roll and Ross (1980).

It is *assumed* that there are one or more common factors that affect returns across assets. More precisely, the returns are assumed to be linearly related to one or more unrelated common factors. It is natural to think of these factors as macroeconomic variables, such as GDP growth or a change in forecast inflation, but the argument abstracts from which common factors, if any, actually do affect asset returns. Suppose for now there is just one common factor, F. The uncertain return R_j on asset j can therefore be analysed as

$$R_j = E(R_j) + \beta_{j,F}\Delta F + e_j \tag{3.14}$$

where $E(R_j)$ is the *ex ante* expected return, ΔF is the deviation of the value of the factor from its expected value, $\beta_{j,F} = \sigma_{jF}/\sigma_F^2$ (the sensitivity of the returns of j to values of F), and e_j is 'noise', the part of the return unexplained by the expected return and $\beta_{j,F}\Delta F$. The expected value of e_j is zero, and e_j is assumed to be uncorrelated with F and with the noise terms for other assets. Correlation across e_j, e_k ... would imply that there was at least one other common factor affecting returns, or affecting some subset of returns. Assuming zero cross-correlation in the errors means that equation (3.14) is a 'strict factor model'. If some cross-correlation is allowed, the model is an 'approximate factor model'.

From an *ex ante* perspective, equation (3.14) describes the assumed process by which returns on the asset are generated. From an *ex post* perspective, the relation between observed realisations of R_j and F is described by the regression equation

$$R_{jt} = \alpha_j + \beta_{j,F}\Delta F_t + e_{jt}$$

for a sample $t = 1, \ldots T$. Such an *ex post* or empirical model is a way of explaining observed returns. For example, we could have $\Delta F_t = \Delta R_{Mt} = [R_{Mt} - E(R_M)]$ in the above equation. The point of the APT is to establish the *ex ante* relation between expected returns and the common factors that affect actual returns, assuming some exist.

If there are no restrictions on short-selling, it will be possible to form an *arbitrage portfolio*, A, that (i) uses no wealth, (ii) has no systematic risk and (iii) is well diversified. (i) 'No wealth invested' means that the sum of the weights w_j of each asset in the portfolio must be zero:

$$\Sigma w_j = 0$$

So, if there are long positions in some assets (w_j positive), others must be sold short (w_j negative). (ii) 'No systematic risk' means that the realised value of the common factor F does not affect the returns on the portfolio, which requires that

$$\Sigma w_j \beta_{j,F} = 0$$

So A is a zero-beta portfolio. (iii) 'Good diversification' means that the unsystematic risk of the portfolio is negligible. As the number n of different assets held long or short in the portfolio increases, the e_j terms tend to 'cancel out'; the variance of the portfolio return unexplained by factor F approaches zero, and we can write

$$\Sigma w_j e_j \rightarrow 0 \quad \text{as} \quad n \rightarrow \infty$$

Let us assume for clarity that $\Sigma w_j e_j = 0$.

If the arbitrage portfolio A satisfies criteria (ii) and (iii), we know that its return R_A will be certain, because

$$R_A = \Sigma w_j R_j = \Sigma w_j E(R_j) + \Sigma w_j \beta_{j,F} F + \Sigma w_j e_j$$
$$= \Sigma w_j E(R_j)$$

which is certain – known in advance. But, since R_A is certain, it must be equal to zero, otherwise risk-free gain would be possible since the arbitrage portfolio can be created at no cost. So we have

$$\Sigma w_j = 0$$
$$\Sigma w_j \beta_{j,F} = 0$$
$$\Sigma w_j E(R_j) = 0$$

It is the case that, for these three equalities to be satisfied, there must be a linear relation between $E(R_j)$ and $\beta_{j,F}$:

$$E(R_j) = \lambda_0 + \lambda_1 \beta_{j,F} \tag{3.15}$$

where λ_0 and λ_1 are constants (Ross, 1977, p. 197). Equation (3.15) is the equation of a straight line. An asset with $\beta_{j,F} = 0$ is a risk-free asset, so the constant λ_0 can be interpreted as the risk-free return. The number λ_1 can then be interpreted as the expected return, in excess of the risk-free return, required for exposure to the common risk factor F, the (asset-specific) exposure being measured by $\beta_{j,F}$. In other words, λ_1 is the risk premium on the common factor. If we now assume that there are $1, 2 \ldots m$ common factors unrelated to each other, the above argument can be generalised to give the conclusion

$$E(R_j) = \lambda_0 + \lambda_1 \beta_{j,1} + \lambda_2 \beta_{j,2} + \cdots \lambda_m \beta_{j,m} \tag{3.16}$$

However, the number of factors must be small in relation to the number of assets. As the ratio of common factors to assets increases, fewer arbitrage portfolios are possible, and beyond a certain point it will not be possible to form any arbitrage portfolio.

If equation (3.16) holds for all assets, it is not possible to form a zero-cost arbitrage portfolio that will provide a positive return. If equation (3.16) does not hold for a certain asset, it is mis-priced and an investor could make a risk-free gain, as illustrated in the following example.

Example
Suppose the risk-free return is 2 per cent and the premium on the single risk factor F is 4 per cent. Consider two assets k and l, with $\beta_{k,F} = 2$ and $\beta_{l,F} = 0.5$. According to the APT, the no-arbitrage returns on the assets are given by equation (3.15):

$$R_j = 2\% + \beta_{j,F}(\text{premium on } F)$$

We continue to assume for simplicity that this equation holds precisely. The assets must be priced so that $E(R_k) = 10\%$ and $E(R_l) = 4\%$. We now check that, with the assets priced to provide returns given by the above equation, there is no possibility of arbitrage – i.e. that the return on an arbitrage portfolio formed from assets k, l and the risk-free asset is zero for certain. We first confirm that it is possible to form an arbitrage portfolio A that satisfies the three equalities

$$\Sigma w_j = 0$$
$$\Sigma w_j \beta_j = 0$$
$$\Sigma w_j E(R_j) = 0$$

A solution is $A = 3R_F + k - 4l$: hold three units of the risk-free asset and one unit of k, and short-sell four units of l.

We now check that the return on A is zero. Suppose there are four equally likely possible returns for F: -2 per cent, 0 per cent, 8 per cent, 18 per cent (so the possible premiums are -4 per cent, -2 per cent, 6 per cent and 16 per cent). The possible returns on the assets and on the arbitrage portfolio are:

		Returns (%)			
		Factor	Asset	Asset	Arbitrage portfolio
	R_F	F	k	l	$3R_F + k - 4l$
Probability					
0.25	2	-2	-6	0	0
0.25	2	0	-2	1	0
0.25	2	8	14	5	0
0.25	2	18	34	10	0
Expected return	2	6	10	4	0

The return on A is zero whatever the outcome for the risk factor (but the expected return on the risk factor has to be 6 per cent, to give an expected premium of 4 per cent). An example of mis-pricing (disequilibrium) would be if k were priced such that the expected return on k were greater than 10 per cent. The arbitrage portfolio would then make a certain gain, and the three equalities could not be satisfied.

The crucial step in the argument is that the arbitrage portfolio must have a return of zero. It is natural to suspect that there must be something wrong with this. One imagines trying to set up an arbitrage portfolio, and thinking: 'It won't work. No matter how hard I try, I won't be able to construct a portfolio that includes risky assets, that costs nothing and that will provide a guaranteed return of zero, even if I include positions in thousands of assets so that the portfolio is extremely well diversified.' No doubt this is true. But we have moved from the world of the theory to the real world. In the real world, we do not know for sure what the risk factors are, nor what the sensitivities of assets are to the risk factors. The point is that, if we did know these things, we would be able to construct an arbitrage portfolio, and we do know these things in the world of the theory.

Suppose that there is a single risk factor, and that it is assumed to be the market portfolio. More accurately, we are assuming that returns on the market portfolio are the only proxy for, or index of, the reasons that cause returns across to move together. Then λ_1 is the risk premium on the market and equation (3.15) becomes the standard CAPM. Thus, APT provides a separate derivation of the standard CAPM. The derivation via APT starts with the assumption that the only risk factor, or the only proxy for the reasons for commonality across asset returns, is the market portfolio. If more than one risk factor is assumed, then APT results in a multifactor model (equation (3.16)). The normal derivation of the CAPM, in Section 3.1, does not start with the notion that the market portfolio is a risk factor. Rather, it is a conclusion of the derivation that risk can be measured by covariance with the market portfolio.

APT is, like the CAPM, a partial explanation of expected returns. It explains the differences in expected returns across assets. It does not explain the value of the risk-free return, nor the sizes of the premiums on the risk factors.

3.2.2   The three-factor model

In the last two decades researchers have uncovered a number of macroeconomic and company-specific variables, other than beta in the standard CAPM, that have some power to explain cross-sectional differences in observed returns. These variables can be used to create an ad hoc model of expected returns; that is, a model that has been found to work using past data, rather than a model derived from a theory. The most prominent example is the three-factor model of Fama and French, presented and discussed in a series of papers by these authors. Fama and French (1992) evaluate the joint role of beta, firm size, earnings yield, leverage and the book-to-market (B/M) ratio in explaining cross-sectional differences in average historic monthly returns during 1963 to 1990. They confirm earlier evidence of an absence of relation between returns and betas, and find (p. 428) that the 'combination of size and book-to-market equity seems to absorb the roles of leverage and E/P in average stock returns'. The relation between excess returns and the three factors is estimated by running a cross-sectional regression of the following form in each month t:

$$R_{jt} - R_{Ft} = \alpha_{0t} + \alpha_{1t}\beta_{jt} + \alpha_{2t}M_{jt} + \alpha_{3t}(B_{jt}/M_{jt}) + e_{jt} \qquad (3.17)$$

for shares $j = 1, \ldots n$. β_{jt} is an estimate of the share's market beta from a regression of the excess returns on share j on market excess returns using data from a rolling estimation period that precedes month t; M_{jt} is the prevailing market value of the firm's equity in month t; B_{jt}/M_{jt} is the prevailing book value divided by the market value. Equation (3.17) is estimated for a large number of months and shares, and the average α_1, α_2 and α_3 coefficients from these regressions provide estimates of, respectively, the arithmetic mean monthly observed premium on the market ($R_{Mt} - R_{Ft}$), the premium on small companies and the premium on high B/M companies. The average coefficients (premiums) on the size and B/M variables are positive and significant; the average coefficient on beta is not significantly different from zero.

Fama and French (1993) test these findings using time-series regressions and then propose the three-factor model. They run regressions in which the dependent variable is the monthly excess return on one of twenty-five portfolios of stocks; portfolios are formed from all New York Stock Exchange, Amex and (from 1972) NASDAQ stocks. The twenty-five portfolios are formed according to the average size and B/M ratio of the constituent companies. Size is measured by the market capitalisation on 30 June of each year y and the B/M ratio is measured by shareholders' funds in the balance sheet for the financial year ending in calendar year $y - 1$, divided by the market capitalisation on 31 December of year $y - 1$. Each year companies are ranked independently by size and B/M, grouped into quintiles by each variable, then sorted into the twenty-five portfolios to give all the possible combinations. For example, the portfolio of the smallest companies with the largest B/M values consists of companies that are in both the smallest size quintile and the largest B/M quintile. The number of companies in each portfolio H varies. The time-series regression equation is

$$R_{Ht} - R_{Ft} = \alpha_H + \beta_{1H}(R_{Mt} - R_{Ft}) + \beta_{2H}(SMB_t) + \beta_{3H}(HML_t) + e_{Ht} \qquad (3.18)$$

for portfolio H in months $t = 1, \dots T$. $R_{Ht} - R_{Ft}$ is the value-weighted mean excess return on portfolio H for month t during 1963–91, and R_{Ft} is the return on one-month treasury bills. SMB_t stands for 'small minus big': the equally weighted mean return on companies with market capitalisation smaller than that of the median New York Stock Exchange company, minus the mean return on companies larger than the median. HML_t stands for 'high minus low': the equally weighted mean monthly return on companies in the top third of New York Stock Exchange companies ranked by B/M ratio, minus the mean return on the companies in the bottom third.

Fama and French test the explanatory power of equation (3.18) by examining the intercepts in the twenty-five time-series regressions. If the model is well specified, the intercepts should be zero. With only the excess return on the market as an explanatory variable, the intercepts are related to size and the B/M ratio. For example, portfolios consisting of small companies have positive intercepts. Also, there is no relation between mean excess return and market beta. With size and the B/M ratio included, the intercepts across portfolios are close to zero. With excess return on the market excluded, the intercepts are significantly positive. These findings suggest that, whilst the market return has no role in explaining cross-sectional difference in returns, it is needed to explain the average difference between returns on the market and risk-free returns.

Fama and French interpret the market portfolio, company size and B/M ratio as proxies for common risk factors. The three-factor model applied to estimate the cost of equity for company or industry j is

$$E(R_{jt}) = R_{Ft} + \beta_{j,M}[E(R_{Mt}) - R_{Ft}] + \beta_{j,SMB}E(SMB_t) + \beta_{j,HML}E(HML_t)$$

(Fama and French, 1997). The first factor is the market portfolio: the risk premium is the expected premium on the stock market, and $\beta_{j,M}$ is the share's beta measured against the market, as in the standard CAPM. The second factor is an additional source of risk associated with small size: 'small minus big' is the expected premium on small companies, and $\beta_{j,SMB}$ measures the sensitivity of R_{jt} to SMB_t. A small company would be expected to have a positive $\beta_{j,SMB}$ and a large company to have a $\beta_{j,SMB}$ that is zero or negative, since a large company could provide a hedge against the risk associated with small companies. The third factor is an additional source of risk associated with a high B/M ratio: 'high minus low' is the expected premium on companies with a relatively high B/M ratio, and $\beta_{j,HML}$ measures the sensitivity of R_{jt} to HML_t. Again, one would expect a company with a high B/M ratio to have a positive $\beta_{j,HML}$ and a company with a low B/M ratio to have a $\beta_{j,HML}$ that is zero or negative. Average historic values of $R_{Mt} - R_{Ft}$, SMB_t and HML_t are used to estimate the expected values of the three risk premiums (just as the equity premium in the standard CAPM is often estimated by a historic average; see Chapter 5). The three betas are estimated using historic data in a multivariate regression. Both the risk premiums and the betas vary through time.

Fama and French (1996) present further tests of the model and note that it cannot explain short-term persistence in returns ('momentum'). This paper also includes a general discussion of why the three-factor model works empirically. There is no doubt that the model explains more of the historic differences in company returns over time than the standard CAPM, at least using data from the early 1960s to the 1990s; that is its *raison d'être*. The question is why returns are associated with size and B/M ratio. Fama and French (1996) consider three possible explanations: (i) asset pricing is rational and conforms to the three-factor model; (ii) asset pricing is irrational, and the success of the two additional factors is explained by behavioural finance; (iii) the CAPM holds but is spuriously rejected because of survivor bias in the data, or because of data mining, or because of the use of poor proxies for the true market portfolio of all assets. Fama and French favour (i) but can make only part of a case. In a multiperiod context, investors are concerned with fluctuations in wealth or consumption over time. If such fluctuations are related to common risk factors or 'state variables' – sources of uncertainty (Section 4.3.2) – then the relation over time between an asset's returns and a state variable will affect the asset's price. Fama and French concentrate on the B/M ratio and suggest that it is a proxy for financial distress. But it is a further step to establish that distress is related to a state variable, exposure to which should attract a risk premium. They admit that they do not identify the 'state variables of special hedging concern to investors that lead to three-factor asset pricing' (Fama and French, 1996, p. 76).

3.3   Note on conditional models

The CAPM and multifactor models we have considered explain differences in expected returns across assets, at a given time. We have not yet thought about variation of the expected return on a given asset over time. This is partly because we have assumed, for much of the chapter, a static theoretical setting with one future period and no 'past'. The introduction of past and future time creates a setting in which expected returns can vary over time and can be related to the arrival of new information. In this case, the expected return on an asset at a given time is said to be conditional on the information available at that time. As time passes new information arrives and the expected return changes.

Obviously, actual returns on assets vary over time. This does not in itself prove that *expected* returns vary, but it is generally accepted that they do. Consider the application of the standard CAPM to estimate the expected return on a share. In countries with stable governments, the real risk-free rate is taken to be the prevailing real rate on government bills or bonds, and the real rates on such assets change over time. The share's beta is estimated from a recent sample of the share's returns and the returns on the market (Chapter 13). The estimate changes over time as it is updated using more recent data; in other words, the estimate is conditional on the data.

How to estimate the market premium is a matter of debate at the time of writing (2004), and is discussed in Chapter 5. It is now widely believed that the *ex ante* market premium varies, at least if the forecasting horizon is taken to be a few years. Evidence for this started to appear in the early 1980s. There is also evidence that the market premium can be forecast, to an extent. For example, it has been found that a relatively high dividend yield for the stock market is followed by relatively high observed premiums. So dividend yield on the market can be used to estimate the *ex ante* premium at a given time. In other words, it can be used in a conditional model of the premium. There are several other variables that are candidates as explanatory variables in a conditional model.

The position is similar for the case of a multifactor model. Each risk factor or proxy for a risk factor has a risk premium that can vary over time, and an asset's beta with respect to the factor can also vary. There is the possibility that the premium on a risk factor can be forecast. Examples of papers that develop and test conditional versions of the CAPM and multifactor models are those by Ferson and Harvey (1991), Harvey (1991) and Jagannathan and Wang (1996).

3.4   Evidence

There is a huge empirical and econometric literature on the testing of asset pricing models and of stock market efficiency. The current section gives a very brief introduction to tests of the CAPM and APT. Campbell (2000), Cochrane (2001, chaps. 20 and 21) and Fama (1991) are good general reviews of the evidence. Test procedures and problems in testing are reviewed in Campbell, Lo and McKinlay (1997, chaps. 5 and 6) and Cochrane (2001, part II).

The abstract contingent-states world that gives rise to the CAPM, APT and consumption CAPM assumes that markets are efficient – i.e. that prices reflect publicly available information. Empirical studies of asset pricing models therefore test a joint hypothesis that the stock market is efficient and that a particular asset pricing model is true, and more than one interpretation of the findings can usually be sustained. Consider, for example, the small companies effect: the finding that small listed companies have produced higher returns than large companies after controlling for risk as measured by beta. One explanation is that the CAPM is inadequate; there is at least one additional risk factor, exposure to which is proxied by company size, which affects expected returns. A second explanation is that the market is less efficient for small than for large companies, perhaps, in this case, because there are larger transactions costs or information costs for the shares of smaller companies. Of course, researchers try to control for the extra costs, but the extent to which the extra rate of return on small companies is compensation for the extra transactions costs remains uncertain.

The CAPM predicts a relation between *ex ante* expected return and *ex ante* beta times the expected equity premium, none of which is observable in the *ex post* data available to researchers. The normal response in a situation with unobservable variables is to argue that, if the theory has some truth, the observable proxies for the unobservable variables should provide some support for the theory. It would be natural to assume that there is some positive correlation between expected and observed betas and between expected and observed returns, in which case, if the CAPM is true, there should be a positive correlation between observed betas and returns in a large sample. The Roll critique implies that such a rationale for tests of the CAPM, while natural, is ill-founded, because the *ex post* relation to be found between returns and betas is too sensitive to the market proxy chosen to estimate betas. But this has certainly not stopped people trying to test the CAPM. Another issue is that the model assumes that there is a single future period, but it is tested using returns from many periods. This means that the researcher has to make assumptions about the predictions of the model in a multiperiod context.

The standard methods of testing the CAPM were established by Black, Jensen and Scholes (1972) and Fama and MacBeth (1973). The basic test in the Black–Jensen–Scholes method is to compare portfolio excess returns with portfolio betas, both averaged over time. Fama and French (1993) use a version of the Black–Jensen–Scholes method, as outlined in Section 3.2.2. The steps in the Fama–MacBeth cross-sectional method are as follows. (i) The betas of individual shares are estimated using historic returns – for example, monthly returns during the five years preceding the date with respect to which the share's beta is being estimated. The betas are updated every twelve months. (ii) Shares are ranked by beta and the list is split into a number of portfolios, each with an equal number of shares. (iii) The betas of the portfolios are estimated over the same period as was used to estimate the betas of the constituents. The portfolios are updated every twelve months. (iv) The relation between observed returns and betas is tested by running the following cross-sectional regression every month t:

$$R_{Ht} - R_{Ft} = \alpha_{0t} + \alpha_{1t}\beta_{Ht} + e_{Ht}$$

for $H = 1, \ldots n$ portfolios. Over a large sample of months, the standard CAPM predicts that the arithmetic mean α_{0t} is equal to the mean risk-free rate and that the mean α_{1t} is equal to the mean equity premium $R_M - R_F$.

Studies in the 1970s using US data from 1926 to the 1960s found support for the CAPM, though the slope of the empirical line of best fit relating the cross-section of betas and returns was flatter than the slope predicted by the model, $R_M - R_F$. However, the bulk of more recent evidence is not favourable. First, there appears to be little or no relation between betas and realised returns in data from the 1960s onwards. This is so for tests both with and without additional explanatory variables. But there is more support for a positive relation between beta and *ex ante* expected returns (see, e.g., Harris et al., 2003). Second, there is evidence that factors other than beta have some power to predict asset returns, and that, since these factors vary over time, predicted returns vary over time. It was established by the late 1980s that future returns for shares and equity portfolios are positively related to dividend yield and earnings yield. In addition, changes in measures of the bond default spread (the yield on high-risk long-term corporate bonds minus the yield on AAA-rated corporate bonds) and in measures of the term spread (the long-term AAA yield minus the yield on one-month treasury bills) predict future changes in stock and bond market returns. These four variables have low forecasting power for returns measured over short intervals, but each can explain in the region of 25 per cent to 40 per cent of the intertemporal variation in returns measured over intervals of between two and five years. Cochrane (1999) compares the forecastability of longer-term returns with that of the weather; the time of year provides a poor forecast of the change in temperature from today to tomorrow, but provides a much better forecast of the change in average temperature from the previous month to the next.

Fama and French (1989) argue that the variables are linked to the business cycle: expected returns on shares and risky long-term bonds are higher during a recession, due to higher risk aversion. Market prices fall, so dividend yield, earnings yield and the default and term spreads tend to be relatively high during recession. But they go on to present evidence that the factors that predict returns – dividend yield, term spread, default spread and short-term interest rates – are subsumed in their three-factor model for shares (Fama and French, 1992; 1993). For example, dividend yield et al. do not predict the residuals e_{Ht} in equation (3.18).

The evidence that there are a handful of macroeconomic variables that are correlated with share returns can be interpreted as evidence in support of arbitrage pricing theory. The exact list of variables, and how they are related to returns, vary somewhat from study to study. In a practical context, the APT is indistinguishable from an ad hoc multifactor model; the key issue is the selection of the proxies for the risk factors. For example, Elton, Gruber and Mei (1994) describe how to apply the APT to estimate the cost of equity. The variables Elton et al. select are: yield on long-term government bonds less yield on treasury bills; change in yield on treasury bills; change in exchange rate; change in forecast of real GNP; change in forecast inflation; and a 'residual market factor', calculated as the difference between the return on the market and the return explained by the other five factors.

Empirical research on the APT is reviewed thoroughly by Connor and Korajczyk (1995). Some of the questions that researchers have examined are these.

- How many common factors are there? This can be answered by the analysis of a set of returns data, by the technique of factor analysis, which identifies the existence of factors 'in the numbers' but not what they are.
- What are the common factors, in economic terms?
- How well do multifactor models with pre-specified common factors or proxies for them explain the cross-section and time series of observed returns? A well-specified factor model has testable implications. In particular, if the n factors with explanatory power have been identified, other variables should have no explanatory power. Also, the implied risk premiums on the factors should be the same across different subsets of assets.
- How do multifactor models compare with the CAPM?

The evidence indicates that multifactor models explain, or at least can account for, a higher proportion of the distribution of observed asset returns than the CAPM does. This is the case both for the three-factor model and for models in which the factors or their proxies are macro-variables, the latter being more closely identified with the APT. The finding that multifactor models perform better than the CAPM is not surprising, since the choice of which explanatory variables to retain is determined in large part by which variables are found to be related to observed returns.

From the practical point of view, the weakness of the CAPM is the doubt in recent years about whether expected returns are related to betas calculated against a market index. The weaknesses of APT/multifactor models are the added complexity and data requirements arising from the additional explanatory variables, and doubt about exactly which variables to include. For example, should one use the three-factor model, or a model with macro-variables of the type described by Elton, Gruber and Mei (1994), to estimate a company's cost of equity?

3.5   Summary

This chapter has derived the standard CAPM and the Black variant (no risk-free asset) starting from the contingent-states framework with one future period. The CAPM emerges as an implication of equilibrium in the capital market. It specifies the *ex ante* relation between the expected real return on a risky asset and the risk of the asset. Risk is measured by the covariance of the asset's returns with returns on the market portfolio of risky assets.

The chapter has also outlined the arbitrage pricing theory. The theory assumes that there are one or more common factors that affect returns across assets, and that are known as risk factors. A linear relation between expected returns and sensitivity to the risk factors emerges as an implication of the absence of arbitrage in the capital market. The APT itself does not specify what the risk factors are; it is left to the researcher to identify them or proxies for them.

The best-known example of a multifactor model is the three-factor model of Fama and French. This is a model that is designed to fit the data rather than being the result of a theoretical derivation. It was developed in the late 1980s, when evidence against the CAPM was accumulating. Not surprisingly, the empirical evidence provides stronger support for the model than it does for the CAPM. In addition, it is feasible to use the three-factor model to estimate the cost of equity. But other usable multifactor models have been suggested, and it remains debatable exactly which explanatory variables to include to estimate expected returns.

All the models in this chapter offer incomplete explanations of expected returns, because they take as given the risk-free return and the expected premium on the market (in the CAPM) or the expected premiums on the risk factors (in a multifactor model). They are models that specify differences in expected returns across assets, conditional on the available information at the time in question.

Appendix 3.1: Choice of risky portfolio

The investor's goal is:

$$\text{maximise } U\left[\text{E}(R_H), \sigma_H^2\right] = U[\Sigma_j w_j E(R_j), \Sigma_j \Sigma_k w_j w_k \sigma_{jk}]$$

with respect to w_j, subject to the constraint

$$\Sigma_j w_j = 1$$

There is no risk-free asset, so R_j is uncertain for all assets. If we assume there is no short-selling, the further constraints are required that $w_j \geq 1$ for all assets. This does not affect the solution (Fama, 1976, chap. 8). The analysis below is based on Fama and Miller (1972, pp. 243–50).

The solution starts with the Lagrangian expression

$$L = U\big[E(R_H), \sigma_H^2\big] + \lambda(1 - \Sigma_j w_j)$$

where λ is a Lagrangian multiplier. We maximise L with respect to the proportions w_j, which involves taking partial derivatives of L with respect to each w_j and with respect to λ, and setting them equal to zero:

$$\frac{\partial L}{\partial w_j} = \frac{\partial U}{\partial E(R_H)}\frac{\partial E(R_H)}{\partial w_j} + \frac{\partial U}{\partial \sigma_H^2}\frac{\partial \sigma_H^2}{\partial w_j} - \lambda = 0$$

for $j = 1, 2 \ldots n$, and

$$\partial L/\partial \lambda = 1 - \Sigma_j w_j = 0$$

Since λ is the same for all assets,

$$\frac{\partial U}{\partial E(R_H)}\frac{\partial E(R_H)}{\partial w_j} + \frac{\partial U}{\partial \sigma_H^2}\frac{\partial \sigma_H^2}{\partial w_j} = \frac{\partial U}{\partial E(R_H)}\frac{\partial E(R_H)}{\partial w_k} + \frac{\partial U}{\partial \sigma_H^2}\frac{\partial \sigma_H^2}{\partial w_k}$$

for any two assets j and k. This can be rearranged to provide an expression for $[-\partial U/\partial \sigma_H^2] \div [\partial U/\partial E(R_H)]$:

$$-\frac{\partial U/\partial \sigma_H^2}{\partial U/\partial E(R_H)} = -\frac{\partial E(R_H)/\partial w_j - \partial E(R_H)/\partial w_k}{\partial \sigma_H^2/\partial w_j - \partial \sigma_H^2/\partial w_k} \tag{A3.1}$$

The purpose of this rearrangement is to enable the nature of the optimums for w_j, w_k ... to be interpreted. The first step is to show that the left-hand side of equation (A3.1) is the slope of an indifference curve in expected return, variance space representing a given level of utility $U_{fixed} = U[E(R_H), \sigma_H^2)]$. Setting the total differential of $U[E(R_H), \sigma_H^2)]$ to zero, we have

$$\frac{\partial U}{\partial E(R_H)}dE(R_H) + \frac{\partial U}{\partial \sigma_H^2}d\sigma_H^2 = 0$$

So the slope of the indifference curve is

$$\frac{dE(R_H)}{d\sigma_H^2} = -\frac{\partial U/\partial \sigma_H^2}{\partial U/\partial E(R_H)} \tag{A3.2}$$

which is the same as the left-hand side of equation (A3.1).

The second step is to show that the right-hand side of equation (A3.1) is the slope of the efficient frontier for a given expected return $E(R_{H^*}) = x$. We will then have shown that H^* is an efficient portfolio, so that the utility-maximising choice of w_j, w_k ... is one that results in an efficient portfolio for the investor. Geometrically, the optimum is the point of tangency of an indifference curve with the efficient frontier, the set of feasible efficient portfolios plotted in expected return, variance space, illustrated in Figure 3.1. The position of the efficient frontier is a given as far as the investor is concerned, and is determined by the nature of the equilibrium in the capital market. The position of the indifference curve depends on the investor's preferences regarding expected return and variance.

To show that the right-hand side of equation (A3.1) is the slope of the efficient frontier for expected return x, we need to derive this slope. If portfolio H^*, with $E(R_{H^*}) = x$, is efficient, there must be no other portfolio with expected return of at least x and a smaller variance. One method of selecting the efficient portfolio with a given expected return is to solve the problem

$$\text{minimise } \sigma_{H^*}^2 = \Sigma_j \Sigma_k w_j w_k \sigma_{jk}$$

subject to the constraints

$$E(R_{H^*}) = x$$

and

$$\sigma_j w_j = 1$$

First form the Lagrangian expression

$$L = \sigma_{H^*}^2 + 2\lambda_1[x - E(R_{H^*})] + 2\lambda_2(1 - \Sigma w_j)$$

(The use of Lagrangian multipliers of $2\lambda_1$ and $2\lambda_2$ rather than λ_1 and λ_2 will simplify the analysis later.) Taking partial derivatives of L with respect to w_j, $2\lambda_1$ and $2\lambda_2$, and setting the derivatives equal to zero, gives

$$\frac{\partial L}{\partial w_j} = \frac{\partial \sigma_{H^*}^2}{\partial w_j} - 2\lambda_1 \frac{\partial E(R_{H^*})}{\partial w_j} - 2\lambda_2 = 0 \quad \text{for } j = 1, 2 \ldots n$$

$$\partial L/\partial 2\lambda_1 = x - E(R_{H^*}) = 0$$

$$\partial L/\partial 2\lambda_2 = 1 - \Sigma w_j = 0$$

It can be shown that $\partial^2 L/\partial w_j^2 > 0$, so that L will be a minimum. For any two assets j and k,

$$\frac{\partial \sigma_{H^*}^2}{\partial w_j} - 2\lambda_1 \frac{\partial E(R_{H^*})}{\partial w_j} = \frac{\partial \sigma_{H^*}^2}{\partial w_k} - 2\lambda_1 \frac{\partial E(R_{H^*})}{\partial w_k}$$

Rearranging,

$$\frac{1}{2\lambda_1} = -\frac{\partial E(R_{H^*})/\partial w_j - \partial E(R_{H^*})/\partial w_k}{\partial \sigma_{H^*}^2/\partial w_j - \partial \sigma_{H^*}^2/\partial w_k} \tag{A3.3}$$

This is a condition for H^* to be an efficient portfolio. Here, the Lagrangian multiplier $2\lambda_1$ pertains to the constraint $E(R_{H^*}) = x$, so it represents the increase in portfolio variance that would result from a small increase in the given expected return for the efficient portfolio H^* – i.e. $2\lambda_1 = d\sigma_{H^*}^2/dE(R_{H^*})$. Thus, $1/2\lambda_1 = dE(R_{H^*})/d\sigma_{H^*}^2$, the slope of the efficient frontier at portfolio H^*. The right-hand side of equation (A3.3) is the same as that of equation (A3.1), showing the slope of portfolio H chosen to maximise utility. So we have shown that the slope of a portfolio H chosen to maximise utility, given an expected return equal to x, is equal to the slope of an efficient portfolio H^* with the same expected return. We can conclude that a portfolio that maximises utility, assuming mean-variance utility, will be an efficient portfolio.

Appendix 3.2: The expected return on an asset in an efficient portfolio

We have already found an expression for the slope of an efficient portfolio of risky assets H^* – i.e. equation (A3.3). The next step is to analyse the partial differentials in equation (A3.3) that express the effect on portfolio expected return and variance of a small change in w_j, holding the other weights constant. The analysis is adapted from Fama (1976, pp. 258–70). We have

$$\partial E(R_{H^*})/\partial w_j = \partial \Sigma_j w_j E(R_j)/\partial w_j$$
$$= E(R_j) \tag{A3.4}$$

and

$$\partial \sigma_{H^*}^2/\partial w_j = \partial \Sigma_j \Sigma_i w_j w_i \sigma_{ji}/\partial w_j$$
$$= 2\Sigma_i w_i \sigma_{ji} \tag{A3.5}$$

where i = assets $1, 2 \ldots n$ in H^*. Equation (A3.5) follows because, in the variance-covariance matrix indicated by the double summation, each covariance term $w_j w_i \sigma_{ji}$ appears twice, and for the one $w_j w_i \sigma_j^2$ term we have $\partial w_j^2 \sigma_j^2/\partial w_j = 2w_j \sigma_j^2$. Substituting equations (A3.4) and (A3.5) for j and the same equations for k into equation (A3.3), and rearranging, gives

$$\Sigma_i w_i \sigma_{ji} - \lambda_1 E(R_j) = \Sigma_i w_i \sigma_{ki} - \lambda_1 E(R_k) \tag{A3.6}$$

The above relationship between expected return and risk holds between any two assets in an efficient portfolio, and between the portfolio itself and any constituent asset. This can be shown by multiplying both sides of equation (A3.6) by w_k and summing over the assets $k = 1, 2 \ldots n$ of portfolio H^*:

$$\Sigma_k w_k[\Sigma_i w_i \sigma_{ji} - \lambda_1 E(R_j)] = \Sigma_k w_k \Sigma_i w_i \sigma_{ki} - \lambda_1 \Sigma_k w_k E(R_k) \tag{A3.7}$$

This procedure transforms the right-hand side into the variance of H^* less λ_1 times the expected return. The left-hand side is unchanged; σ_{ji} and R_j do not relate to asset k, so multiplying the expression in square brackets by w_k and taking the sum over $k = 1, 2 \ldots n$ leaves the expression unchanged, since $\Sigma_k w_k = 1$. Thus, equation (A3.7) can be rewritten as

$$\Sigma_i w_i \sigma_{ji} - \lambda_1 E(R_j) = \sigma_{H^*}^2 - \lambda_1 E(R_{H^*})$$

or, after rearranging,

$$E(R_j) - E(R_{H^*}) = (1/\lambda_1)\left[\Sigma_i w_i \sigma_{ji} - \sigma_{H^*}^2\right] \tag{A3.8}$$

The next step is to note that $\Sigma_i w_i \sigma_{ji} = \text{cov}(R_j, R_{H^*})$. This follows from the fact that

$$\text{cov}(R_j, R_{H^*}) = \text{cov}(R_j, \Sigma_i w_i R_i)$$
$$= \Sigma_i w_i E\{[R_j - E(R_j)][R_i - E(R_i)]\}$$
$$= \Sigma_i w_i \sigma_{ji}$$

Now let S_{H^*} be the slope of H^* in expected return, standard deviation space: $S_{H^*} = dE(R_{H^*})/d\sigma_{H^*}$. Since H^* is efficient, $S_{H^*} > 0$ (H^* lies on the positively sloping section of the minimum-variance frontier). The relationship between S_{H^*} and $1/\lambda_1$ is as follows:

$$1/S_{H^*} = d\sigma_{H^*}/dE(R_{H^*})$$
$$= (d\sigma_{H^*}/d\sigma_{H^*}^2)[d\sigma_{H^*}^2/dE(R_{H^*})]$$
$$= \{[d(\sigma_{H^*}^2)^{0.5}]/d\sigma_{H^*}^2\}2\lambda_1$$
$$= 2\lambda_1/2\sigma_{H^*}$$

therefore

$$1/\lambda_1 = S_{H^*}/\sigma_{H^*}$$

The third line follows because $2\lambda_1 = d\sigma_{H^*}^2/dE(R_{H^*})$. Substituting for $\Sigma_i w_i \sigma_{ji}$ and $1/\lambda_1$ in equation (A3.8) gives

$$E(R_j) - E(R_{H^*}) = (S_{H^*}/\sigma_{H^*})[\text{cov}(R_j, R_{H^*}) - \sigma_{H^*}^2]$$

or

$$E(R_j) = E(R_{H^*}) - S_{H^*}\sigma_{H^*} + S_{H^*}\text{cov}(R_j, R_{H^*})/\sigma_{H^*}$$

This is equation (3.8) in the main text.

4   The consumption-based model

This chapter presents a model of asset valuation that emerges naturally in the contingent-states framework. The model, or class of models, answers the question: given the possible future pay-offs on an asset, how is the market price determined? This is the same as answering how the expected return on the asset is determined. As we have seen, the expected return on an asset of the same risk as a given project is the project's cost of capital. Thus, the consumption-based models of asset pricing are models of the cost of capital.

But, unlike the CAPM and some multifactor models, consumption-based models are not used to estimate the cost of capital in practice. Their interest for us lies in the fact that a consumption-based model offers a whole story regarding the expected return on an asset, given the possible pay-offs on the asset. In particular, it delivers predictions about the size of the risk-free rate and the size of the equity risk premium, whereas the risk-free rate and the equity premium are inputs, given exogenously, in the standard CAPM. Similarly, a multifactor model does not explain the risk-free rate nor the sizes of the premiums on the risk factors in the model. The CAPM and multifactor models answer the question: what is the relation between expected return and risk? This is only part of an answer to the question of how the expected return on an asset is determined.

This chapter starts by providing further background on asset pricing in the contingent-states setting, and especially on the concept of the stochastic discount factor. The chapter then concentrates on the derivation of equations that explain expected returns, first assuming a single future period and then assuming multiple periods.

4.1   The stochastic discount factor

4.1.1   *Concept*

We return to the states-of-the-world framework introduced in Chapter 2, and recapitulate a little. There are no transactions costs, short-sales are allowed and the market is complete (an elementary contingent claim exists for every possible state). There is a single future period. Let Y_{js} be the pay-off to asset j in state s at date 1 and let P_s be the price at date 0 of an elementary claim, which pays £1 in state s only. The production side is in the background, as in the CAPM and multifactor models; the possible pay-offs on assets are given exogenously.

It might be mentioned in passing that the main results of consumption-based analysis do not depend on the assumptions, made here, of a discrete time period and discrete possible states. They can be derived assuming continuous time or assuming discrete time with continuous distributions for consumption outcomes and pay-offs on assets, as in Section 4.2.2.

If the state-contingent pay-offs of any two assets or portfolios are the same their price today must be the same, since, otherwise, risk-free arbitrage would be possible. It follows that the price of j, a claim to possible pay-offs across the n differing states, is

$$P_j = \Sigma_{s=s1}^{sn} Y_{js} P_s$$

The price of an elementary claim, a claim to £1 in a given state s, is the probability π_s that the relevant state will occur, times a contingent discount factor that we shall label m_s:

$$P_s = \pi_s m_s$$

therefore

$$m_s = P_s / \pi_s$$

This discount factor can be thought of as the value today of a claim to £1 in state s at date 1, valued as though state s were certain to arise. It is, therefore, the intertemporal marginal rate of substitution between consumption now and consumption in state s. Each possible state s has its own discount factor m_s, which is known at date 0 and is applied in valuing any claim to a payment in that state. Hence, in the contingent-states setting, the law of one price implies the existence of a set of contingent discount factors (Rubinstein, 1976). Since it is not known which state will arise, and since the value of m_s differs across states, m_s is known as the *stochastic discount factor*. If asset prices are viewed as being set by a representative individual, the reason for differences in m_s across states is differences in the outcomes across states for the individual's consumption. m_s is higher for a 'famine' state than for a 'feast' state, as explained in the next section.

The price of a non-elementary asset j, P_j, can now be written as

$$P_j = \Sigma_{s=s1}^{sn} \pi_s m_s Y_{js}$$
$$= E(m_s Y_{js}) \qquad (4.1)$$

Dividing through by P_j gives

$$1 = E[m_s(1 + R_{js})]$$

where R_{js} is the state-contingent single-period return if state s arises. Equation (4.1) does *not* say that the price is the discounted expected value of the pay-off, as one might expect it to say from familiarity with conventional discounted cash flow procedure. What equation (4.1) says is that the price is the expected value of the contingent pay-offs multiplied by their contingent discount factors. This is a very general valuation model; each possible pay-off has its own discount factor. In conventional discounting the discount factor is assumed to be fixed across possible pay-offs.

Using the fact that, for any two variables x and y, $E(xy) = E(x)E(y) + \text{cov}(x, y)$, equation (4.1) can be rewritten as

$$P_j = E(m_s)E(Y_{js}) + \text{cov}(m_s, Y_{js}) \tag{4.2}$$

This elaboration of equation (4.1) says that the price is the sum of the expected value of the discount factor times the expected value of the pay-off, plus the covariance between discount factor and pay-off. Positive covariance implies a higher asset price, and thus a lower expected return, for a given expected value of the pay-off. Negative covariance implies a lower asset price and thus a higher expected return. In the case of a risk-free asset, with price P_F, Y_s is a fixed amount Y_F, so $\text{cov}(m_s, Y_F) = 0$ and we have an expression for the expected value of the stochastic discount factor:

$$E(m_s) = P_F/Y_F = 1/(1 + R_F) \tag{4.3}$$

i.e. the discount factor using the risk-free rate. Dividing equation (4.2) by P_j and using equation (4.3), equation (4.1) can be written in terms of returns:

$$E(1 + R_{js}) = 1/E(m_s) - \text{cov}[m_s, (1 + R_{js})]/E(m_s)$$
$$E(R_{js}) = R_F - \text{cov}(m_s, R_{js})(1 + R_F)$$
$$= R_F - \beta_{j,m}\lambda_m \tag{4.4}$$

where $\beta_{j,m} = \text{cov}(m_s, R_{js})/\text{var}(m_s)$, the asset's beta with respect to the stochastic discount factor, and $\lambda_m = \text{var}(m_s)(1 + R_F)$, the risk premium or price of risk. Negative covariance with the stochastic discount factor implies that the expected return carries a positive premium above the risk-free rate.

4.1.2   Determination and interpretation

Individuals differ in terms of preferences, beliefs and wealth. But, to avoid the resulting complications, it is customary to assume that all individuals are identical, so that their collective behaviour can be modelled by the behaviour of a *representative individual* (e.g. Rubinstein, 1976). Once this step is taken, the individual-level analysis of Chapter 2 applies to the whole market, as though the market were a single person. With a single period, all pay-offs are consumed at date 1 and utility at date 1 is derived entirely from contingent consumption. The individual's utility function (but not utility) is assumed to be the same across all states. It then follows readily that contingent discount factors are determined by the representative individual's marginal rate of time preference and by his contingent consumption, which determines his contingent marginal utility.

The utility from an asset is measured by the expected utility of the contingent pay-offs. A pay-off is assumed to provide marginal consumption. So the utility from a pay-off in state s is the amount of the pay-off times the individual's marginal utility in state s, which is determined by the individual's level of consumption in that state, net of the pay-off.

Under certainty, we established that the individual maximises utility at date 0 by saving to the point at which the marginal utility from saving (i.e. from consumption at date 1) is the same as the marginal utility from consumption at date 0. This condition is satisfied if equation (1.9) holds, which can be written as

$$P = \frac{\partial U_0/\partial C_1}{\partial U_0/\partial C_0} = \frac{MU_0(1)}{MU_0(0)} = \delta$$

where P is the price of a claim to one consumption unit at date 1, C_t is the individual's consumption at date t, $U_0 = U(C_0, C_1)$ is the individual's 'lifetime utility' and $MU_0(t)$ is the marginal utility at date 0 of consumption at date t. The discount factor $\delta = 1/(1 + R)$, and the rate of interest R is equal to the individual's marginal rate of time preference.

Under uncertainty, equation (2.4) holds in equilibrium, which says that the individual will allocate his budget between current consumption and elementary claims to state-contingent consumption at date 1 in such a way that the marginal utilities per pound spent on consumption today and on each elementary claim are equal. Equation (2.4) can be written as

$$m_s = P_s/\pi_s = \delta MU(C_s)/MU_0 \qquad (4.5)$$

for states $s = s_1, \ldots s_n$, where $MU(C_s)$ is undiscounted marginal utility in state s. Equation (4.5) says that the discount factor for state s is equal to the marginal rate of time preference times the ratio of the marginal utility of consumption in s to the marginal utility of current consumption. Suppose for simplicity that the state probabilities π_s are equal to each other. Relatively high marginal utility in state s suggests that the individual should attach a relatively high value to a claim to consumption in that state, and a relatively high discount factor m_s means that such a claim does have a high value, and thus has a relatively low expected return.

Equation (4.4) can now be interpreted as follows. In the consumption-based model, risk depends on the covariance of the uncertain pay-off with the stochastic discount factor. Since the marginal rate of time preference, which determines δ, is constant across possible states, and marginal utility at date 0 is known, covariance with the discount factor means covariance with contingent marginal utility at date 1, which means covariance with contingent consumption at date 1. Relatively high $MU(C_s)$ implies relatively high m_s, and relatively high $MU(C_s)$ is due to relatively low contingent consumption – a 'recession' or 'famine' state. Positive $\text{cov}(m_s, R_{js})$ and thus positive $\beta_{j,m}$ imply that asset j's possible pay-offs will be relatively high in recession states. Thus, an asset with positive covariance with marginal utility tends to pay most when income is most desirable. Positive covariance with marginal utility augments expected utility relative to the zero covariance associated with the risk-free return, which means that the expected return on the asset will be less than the risk-free return. Negative $\text{cov}(m_s, R_{js})$ and $\beta_{j,m}$ imply that the pay-off is relatively low in recession. An asset with negative covariance with contingent marginal utility tends to pay least when income is most desirable. This reduces the asset's expected utility, and means that the expected return on such an asset will have to be higher than the risk-free return for the asset to be held in equilibrium.

A variance of pay-off that is uncorrelated with m_s, and hence uncorrelated with marginal utility, does not affect the asset's value, because such variance does not increase or reduce expected utility. So, in the consumption-based model, systematic risk means negative covariance of pay-off with marginal utility, or positive covariance with consumption, and unsystematic risk means variance of pay-off uncorrelated with consumption. Risk does not mean uncertainty about pay-off per se, but the belief that the asset will pay least in recession.

4.2   The consumption CAPM

4.2.1   Quadratic utility function

The term 'consumption CAPM' means a model of expected returns that specifies a linear relation between an asset's expected return and the covariance of its returns with consumption. To derive such a model requires making further assumptions. We shall present two derivations. The first proceeds by assuming that the investor's utility function is quadratic (e.g. Danthine and Donaldson, 2002, chap. 10). In this case we can write

$$U_s = aC_s - (b/2)C_s^2$$

therefore

$$MU_s = a - bC_s$$

and

$$m_s = \delta(a - bC_s)/(a - bC_0)$$

from equation (4.5). Substituting this in equation (4.4), which is

$$E(R_{js}) = R_F - (1 + R_F)\text{cov}(m_s, R_{js})$$

and letting $\phi = \delta b(1 + R_F)/(a - bC_0)$ gives

$$E(R_{js}) = R_F - \text{cov}(R_{js}, -\phi C_s)$$

or

$$E(R_{js}) - R_F = \phi\text{cov}(R_{js}, C_s) \tag{4.6}$$

which specifies a linear relation between the expected returns on asset j and the covariance of its returns with consumption. To write equation (4.6) in the familiar CAPM format, suppose that there is a portfolio H_C with a 'consumption beta' equal to one – i.e. $\beta_{HC,C} = \text{cov}(R_{HCs}, C_s)/\text{var}(C_s) = 1$. Such a portfolio would have returns that track changes in consumption per head. Equation (4.6) holds for H_C:

$$E(R_{HCs}) - R_F = \phi\text{cov}(R_{HCs}, C_s)$$

and we can write

$$\frac{E(R_{js}) - R_F}{E(R_{HCs}) - R_F} = \frac{\phi\text{cov}(R_{js}, C_s)/\text{var}(C_s)}{\phi\text{cov}(R_{HCs}, C_s)/\text{var}(C_s)}$$

Since $\text{cov}(R_{\text{HCs}}, C_s)/\text{var}(C_s) = 1$

$$E(R_{js}) = R_F + \beta_{j,C}[E(R_{\text{HCs}}) - R_F] \tag{4.7}$$

where $\beta_{j,C}$ is the consumption beta of asset j, $\text{cov}(R_{js}, C_s)/\text{var}(C_s)$. Equation (4.6) is the version of the consumption CAPM that looks most like the standard CAPM. It says that the risk premium on an asset is the asset's consumption beta multiplied by the expected percentage change in consumption less the risk-free return. The consumption CAPM could, in principle, be used to estimate the cost of equity.

Suppose that all consumption at date 1 comes from the pay-off from saving. Then the value of the market portfolio M is the same as total consumption, so $M_s = C_s$. In this case $E(R_M)$ and $\beta_{j,M}$ can be substituted for, respectively, $E(R_{\text{HC}})$ and in $\beta_{j,C}$ equation (4.7), and the consumption CAPM becomes the same as the standard CAPM. But now R_F and $E(R_M)$ are endogenous, given by equations (4.3) and (4.4) respectively, instead of being exogenous.

4.2.2   Constant relative risk aversion and lognormal consumption

The consumption CAPM can be also be derived under the assumption that the individual displays constant relative risk aversion (CRRA), together with the assumption that returns and consumption are jointly lognormally distributed. The CRRA utility function implies that absolute risk aversion decreases as wealth increases. The quadratic function implies that absolute risk aversion and relative risk aversion increase as wealth increases, and that the marginal utility of wealth eventually becomes negative. CRRA utility is therefore more plausible than quadratic utility. The CRRA-lognormal returns route also reveals more about the determinants of the risk-free rate and of risk premiums. First, we need to understand more about the CRRA utility function.

CRRA
The CRRA utility function is of the form

$$U(C_s) = \delta C_s^{1-\gamma}/(1 - \gamma)$$

so

$$MU(C_s) = \delta C_s^{-\gamma} \tag{4.8}$$

where γ is the individual's coefficient of relative risk aversion. This measure of risk aversion is related to the curvature of the individual's utility function as follows. Consider a fair gamble in which $E(x)$ is zero, where x stands for possible pay-offs. The certainty equivalent value of the gamble is the certain amount the individual would accept in lieu of the gamble. For a risk-averse individual, the certainty equivalent value must be negative, if $E(x) = 0$, and equal to a risk premium that is the amount such that, given his/her current consumption, the individual would be indifferent between accepting the gamble and paying the premium to avoid it:

$$E[U(C + x)] = U(C - premium). \tag{4.9}$$

Equation (4.9) can be analysed using Taylor's expansion. Given a function of the form $y = f(z)$, Taylor's expansion shows the approximate impact of a non-infinitesimal change of z on y. Suppose the original value of z is z_0 and the changed value is z_1. The Taylor expression for $f(z_1)$ is

$$f(z_1) = f(z_0) + f'(z_0)(z_1 - z_0)/1! + f''(z_0)(z_1 - z_0)^2/2!$$
$$+ f'''(z_0)(z_1 - z_0)^3/3! + \text{higher-order terms}$$

where $f'(z_0) = df(z_0)/dz_0$, $f''(z_0) = d^2 f(z_0)/dz_0^2$, and so on. It can be seen that the value of derivative functions of $f(z)$ at the point $z = z_0$ is used to estimate the value of $f(z_1)$. For the left-hand side of equation (4.9), we have $C_0 = C$ (the original value of consumption) and $C_1 = C + x$ (the changed value). Using the Taylor expansion of $U(C + x)$ around $x = 0$,

$$E[U(C + x)] = E[U(C) + U'(C)(x) + U''(C)(x)^2/2 + \text{higher-order terms}]$$
$$= U(C) + E(x)U'(C) + E(x)^2 U''(C)/2$$
$$= U(C) + \text{var}(x)U''(C)/2 \qquad (4.10)$$

omitting the higher-order terms. $E[U(C)] = U(C)$ because current consumption C is certain; $E(x) = 0$ by assumption; and $E(x)^2$ is the variance of x because the mean of x is zero. For the right-hand side of equation (4.9), the expansion of $U(C - premium)$ around $premium = 0$ is

$$U(C - premium) = U(C) - U'(C)(premium) \qquad (4.11)$$

omitting the higher-order terms because $premium$ is a small amount. Setting equation (4.10) equal to equation (4.11),

$$U(C) + \text{var}(x)U''(C)/2 \approx U(C) - U'(C)(premium)$$
$$premium \approx -0.5\text{var}(x)U''(C)/U'(C)$$

The variance of x is always positive; $U'(C)$ is also positive (assuming non-satiation); whilst $U''(C)$ is negative (assuming a diminishing marginal utility of consumption). So the risk premium is a positive amount. The actual measure of risk aversion is $-U''(C)/U'(C)$, since $0.5\text{var}(x)$ is determined by the variance of the gamble, not by the individual's attitude to risk.

This measure shows explicitly how an individual's degree of risk aversion is a function of his existing consumption C, and it enables one to see whether a particular utility function incorporates increasing, constant or diminishing aversion to risk as wealth increases. The expression $-U''(C)/U'(C)$ measures absolute risk aversion, and determines the size of the premium required to accept a given gamble with variance equal to $\text{var}(x)$. The expression $-U''(C)/U'(C)$ measures relative risk aversion, and determines the size of the premium required to accept a gamble in which the uncertain pay-offs and the premium are proportions of current consumption rather than absolute amounts – i.e. $\text{var}(x) = C\text{var}(x^*)$, where the possible pay-offs x^* are percentages of C.

It can now be seen that γ in the CRRA formula, equation (4.8), measures relative risk aversion, since evaluation of $U'(C_s)$ and $U''(C_s)$, as given by equation (4.8), shows that

$$\gamma = -CU''(C_s)/U'(C_s)$$

The larger the value of γ, the greater the risk aversion that is being assumed. If $\gamma = 0$, utility is linear in consumption and the individual is risk neutral, indifferent between receiving C for certain and an uncertain C_s with expected value of C. If $\gamma > 0$, the utility function is concave and the consumer is risk averse. If $\gamma = 1$, the CRRA function is

$$U(C_s) = \ln(C_s)$$

Constant relative risk aversion means that the absolute change in utility from a given percentage change in consumption is constant. In other words, an individual's risk aversion with respect to a given percentage change in consumption is constant in relation to consumption. The individual's absolute risk aversion diminishes as consumption rises. For example, suppose that $\gamma = 1$ and $\delta = 1$, so $U(C) = \ln C$. The individual faces a rise or fall in consumption of 10 per cent with equal probability. A 10 per cent increase in C from 20 to 22 means that utility increases by 0.0953, from 2.9957 to 3.0910. A 10 per cent increase in C from 100 to 110 results in the same increase of 0.0953, from 4.6052 to 4.7005. An individual with certain future consumption of 20 has utility of 2.9957 and expected utility from uncertain future consumption of $0.5(3.0910) + 0.5(2.8904) = 2.9907$, which is 0.005 less. So the certainty equivalent of the uncertain consumption is 19.90, which means that the individual would pay up to 0.10 or 0.5 per cent of his consumption to avoid the uncertainty. The same calculation for a person with consumption of 100 gives a certainty equivalent of 99.50; this richer person would also pay 0.5 per cent of his consumption to avoid the uncertainty. If the possible rise or fall in consumption were 50 per cent rather than 10 per cent, the individual with log utility would pay 14.4 per cent of his consumption to avoid this larger uncertainty.

Consumption-based model

We now proceed with the derivation of the model, based on Aiyagari (1993) and Campbell, Lo and McKinlay (1997, pp. 304–07). Using equation (4.8), the stochastic discount factor becomes

$$m_s = \delta(C_s/C_0)^{-\gamma} \tag{4.12}$$

Substituting equation (4.12) into equation (4.1),

$$1 = E[(1 + R_{js})m_s]$$

and letting ΔC stand for C_s/C_0 gives

$$1 = E[(1 + R_{js})\delta\Delta C^{-\gamma}] \tag{4.13}$$

If $R_{js} = R_F$, we have from equation (4.3)

$$1 + R_F = (1 + \rho)/E(\Delta C^{-\gamma}) \tag{4.14}$$

where ρ = the marginal rate of time preference; $\delta = 1/(1+\rho)$.

We now assume that ΔC is a continuous variable that is lognormally distributed – that is, $\ln\Delta C$ is normally distributed with mean $E(\ln\Delta C)$ and variance $\text{var}(\ln\Delta C)$. It is the case that, for any variable x that is lognormally distributed,

$$\ln E(x) = E(\ln x) + 0.5\text{var}(\ln x) \tag{4.15}$$

or

$$E(x) = \exp[E(\ln x) + 0.5\text{var}(\ln x)]$$

where exp stands for exponent or e. Using this relation,

$$E(\Delta C^{-\gamma}) = \exp[-\gamma E(\ln\Delta C) + 0.5\gamma^2\text{var}(\ln\Delta C)] \tag{4.16}$$

and

$$1/E(\Delta C^{-\gamma}) = \exp[\gamma E(\ln\Delta C) - 0.5\gamma^2\text{var}(\ln\Delta C)]$$

Equation (4.14) can now be written

$$1 + R_F = (1 + \rho)\exp[\gamma E(\ln\Delta C) - 0.5\gamma^2\text{var}(\ln\Delta C)]$$

or

$$\ln(1 + R_F) = \ln(1 + \rho) + \gamma E(\ln\Delta C) - 0.5\gamma^2\text{var}(\ln\Delta C)$$

or, since $\ln(1 + x) \approx x$ for small x (less than, say, 0.2),

$$R_F \approx \rho + \gamma E(\ln\Delta C) - 0.5\gamma^2\text{var}(\ln\Delta C) \tag{4.17}$$

Equation (4.17) reveals that, under uncertainty, and with constant relative risk aversion, the risk-free rate is not equivalent to the marginal rate of time preference. It is positively related to the expected change in consumption and negatively related to the variance of consumption.

These points can be interpreted as follows. For a given level of current consumption, higher expected consumption implies lower future marginal utility from risk-free saving, which implies a lower value for the stochastic discount factor (equation (4.12)) – i.e. higher R_F. Higher variance of consumption implies higher expected marginal utility from risk-free saving. The reason is that, for a given expected value of future consumption, discrepancies in the individual's consumption across possible states reduce expected utility, due to Jensen's inequality (Section 2.3.1). The larger the variance in possible levels of consumption, the larger the variance of contingent marginal utility and of the stochastic discount factor, $\text{var}(m_s)$. The concavity of the utility function means that $E(MU_s)$ and hence $E(m_s)$ rises, and R_F falls, as variance of consumption rises. Finally, it can be seen that the effect of γ, the coefficient of relative risk aversion, is ambiguous in equation (4.17).

The risk premium can be established as follows. We assume that R_j is a continuous variable and that R_j and $(1 + R_{js})\Delta C^{-\gamma}$ are lognormally distributed. We know from equations (4.13) and (4.14) that

$$(1 + R_F)E(\Delta C^{-\gamma}) = E[(1 + R_{js})\Delta C^{-\gamma}] \tag{4.18}$$

We know from equation (4.15) that, if variable xy is lognormally distributed,

$$\begin{aligned} \ln E(xy) &= E(\ln xy) + 0.5\text{var}(\ln xy) \\ &= E(\ln x) + E(\ln y) + 0.5[\text{var}(\ln x) + \text{var}(\ln y) + 2\text{cov}(\ln x, \ln y)] \end{aligned} \tag{4.19}$$

since $\text{var}(x + y) = \text{var}(x) + \text{var}(y) + 2\text{cov}(x, y)$. Using equation (4.19) with $xy = (1 + R_{js})\Delta C^{-\gamma}$, using equation (4.16) to substitute for $E(\Delta C^{-\gamma})$, and taking logs, equation (4.18) can be rewritten

$$\begin{aligned} \ln(1 + R_F) &- \gamma E(\ln \Delta C) + 0.5\gamma^2 \text{var}(\ln \Delta C) \\ &= E[\ln(1 + R_{js})] - \gamma E(\ln \Delta C) + 0.5\text{var}[\ln(1 + R_{js})] \\ &\quad + 0.5\gamma^2 \text{var}(\ln \Delta C) - \gamma \text{cov}[\ln(1 + R_{js}), \ln \Delta C] \end{aligned}$$

therefore

$$E[\ln(1 + R_{js})] - \ln(1 + R_F) = \gamma \text{cov}[\ln(1 + R_{js}), \ln \Delta C] - 0.5\text{var}[\ln(1 + R_{js})] \tag{4.20}$$

Equation (4.20) can be written in approximate form as

$$E(R_{js}) - R_F \approx \gamma \text{cov}[\ln(1 + R_{js}), \ln \Delta C] \tag{4.21}$$

Equation (4.21) shows that the risk premium on an asset is positively and linearly related to the coefficient of risk aversion and to the covariance of the log of returns with consumption. For an asset with returns perfectly correlated with consumption growth, the risk premium is $\gamma \text{var}(\ln \Delta C)$. If the value of the market portfolio is the same as total consumption, the market risk premium is $\gamma \text{var}(\ln \Delta M)$.

Equation (4.21) is easy to relate to the general framework of asset pricing outlined in Chapter 2 and Section 4.1. It says that an asset with returns that covary positively with changes in consumption will be priced to give a positive risk premium. This is what we would expect for an asset that tends to pay off most in states in which marginal utility is lowest. The risk premium is positively related to γ, the measure of risk aversion, and this is also what we would expect. The higher γ is, the more rapidly marginal utility diminishes as consumption increases.

4.3   Multiperiod setting

4.3.1   From one period to many

So far we have assumed that there is a single future period. To introduce the impact of many periods, let us first review the assumptions being made if there is one period. Consider the setting for the standard CAPM. It is assumed that the utility from an asset is a function of the expected return and variance of return only. To justify this assumption, it is supposed that the utility from a portfolio is a function solely of the amounts of consumption it will provide. The latter point implies either that all consumption at date 1 comes from wealth, or that, if investors have another way of providing for consumption at date 1 (e.g. wage income), the amount of income not from wealth is certain. Otherwise marginal utility will depend on the amounts of non-wealth income as well as on the value of the portfolio. This would mean that the utility from an asset would be a function not only of the expected return and variance but also of the covariance of the return with income not from wealth.

Now consider the one-period consumption-based model. Again, all wealth is consumed at date 1. We have seen that the expected premium on an asset is determined by the covariance of its return with the stochastic discount factor (equation (4.4)) – i.e. with state-contingent marginal utility at date 1. Utility at date 1 is a function of consumption only. For this model to differ from the standard CAPM, the individual must have uncertain income not from wealth, the possible outcomes of which determine contingent marginal utility at date 1. If all consumption at date 1 comes from wealth, the model becomes merely another way of expressing the standard CAPM, as noted in Section 4.2.1.

The analysis of investment and price determination potentially becomes much more complicated in the multiperiod setting. At each date there can be changes of income not derived from wealth, changes of beliefs, trading of assets, the introduction of new assets, and maybe other changes. Not all wealth is consumed at each date; the individual has to decide how to allocate his/her resources between consumption and saving, and he/she has to decide on the composition of his/her portfolio.

With one period, the utility from holding an asset at date 0 is simply the expected utility from the contingent consumption it will provide at date 1. It is not so clear how to analyse the utility from holding an asset that exists for more than one period. The asset will have a price at each date before it expires, and the possible changes in the price over time will potentially affect the utility from holding the asset, as well as the possible cash pay-off or pay-offs.

In general, investors cannot maximise lifetime utility from information about one-period returns only. They can do so only under certain simplifications. We have noted in Section 3.1.5 that one-period 'myopic' analysis is legitimate if (i) investment opportunities do not change – i.e. the risk-free rate is constant and returns each period are independently and identically distributed; (ii) income not from wealth is nil or certain; and (iii) utility is a quadratic function of consumption. Samuelson (1969) shows in discrete time that one-period analysis is also legitimate given assumptions (i) and (ii), together with (iii) a CRRA utility function, and (iv) a risk-free asset and a single risky asset. A CRRA function means that risk aversion does not depend upon the level of consumption. A single risky asset means that investment decisions at each date reduce to the proportion of the amount saved that is invested in the risky asset. Samuelson's result is that, whilst the amount saved will vary at each date, the proportion of saving invested in the risky asset will always be the same. Also, if it is assumed that $U = \ln(C)$, it is not necessary to make assumption (i) that investment opportunities do not change.

One approach to multiperiod analysis is to assume that the individual's consumption per period is an endowment that follows a known statistical process. This simplifies the problem. Possible consumption outcomes and their probabilities can then be assumed to be known, and the value of a given asset can be inferred, given the consumption process. As Cochrane (2001, p. 43) observes, 'to solve a consumption-portfolio problem we have to model the investor's entire environment: we have to specify *all* the assets to which he has access, what his labor income looks like (or wage rate process, and include a labor supply decision). Once we model consumption directly, we can look at each asset in isolation . . .' We now present an example of the endowment approach.

4.3.2   An endowment or 'fruit tree' model

This section presents the multiperiod model given by Mehra and Prescott (1985), which is based on Lucas (1978). The model is a relatively simple example of how expressions for the expected rate of return on equity and the risk-free rate can be derived if there are many time periods. It is also a well-known model, because the Mehra–Prescott paper was the first to draw attention to the fact that a consumption-based model cannot explain the size of the historic equity premium.

There is one representative consumer and one representative company. The consumer has a CRRA utility function and maximises lifetime expected utility from consumption. The company produces an uncertain but growing amount, Y_t, of the single perishable consumption good each period, paid as a 'dividend' on its equity. This is all consumed, so $C_t = Y_t$. The growth rate of Y_t is assumed to follow a Markov process. This means that, at each date, one of a fixed number n of types of state s can arise. The probability that a given type of state will arise at date $t + 1$ is determined by the type of state that has arisen at date t. Each type of state is defined in terms of a rate of change in consumption. So, for a given type of state s at any date t, expected consumption at the next date is

$$E_t(C_{s(t+1)}) = \Sigma_{s=s1(t+1)}^{sn(t+1)} \pi_{s(t),s(t+1)} C_t g_s$$
$$= C_t E_t(g_s)$$

where $\pi_{s(t),s(t+1)}$ is the probability that state type s occurs at date $t + 1$, given that state type s has arisen at date t. g_s is one plus the expected growth rate for state type $s(t + 1)$, and, if consumption is assumed to grow on average over the long term, the unconditional expectation $E(g_s)$ exceeds one. The summation is over state types at date $t + 1$, since state $s(t)$ is given.

For example, suppose there are two types of state, s_1 and s_2. If s_1 arises, the growth rate for the period just ended was 2 per cent and the possible growth rates next period are $g_1 = 2\%$ with probability $\pi_{s1(t),s1(t+1)} = 0.4$ and $g_2 = -1\%$ with probability $\pi_{s1(t),s2(t+1)} = 0.6$. If s_2 arises, the growth rate for the period just ended was -1 per cent and the possible growth rates next period are $g_1 = 2\%$, $\pi_{s2(t),s1(t+1)} = 0.6$, and $g_2 = -1\%$, probability $\pi_{s2(t),s2(t+1)} = 0.4$.

The price per share P_t of the company's equity will be set such that the marginal utility from the sacrifice of current consumption necessary to buy the share is equal to the marginal utility of the future stream of consumption it generates. If the number of shares is normalised to one, and the next dividend is due at the next date, we have in equilibrium

$$P_t[dU(C_t)/dC_t] = E_t\{\Sigma_{\tau=1}^{\infty}\delta^{\tau} Y_{s(t+\tau)}[dU(Y_{s(t+\tau)})/dY_{s(t+\tau)}]\}$$

where $\tau = 1, 2 \ldots \infty$. Since, from equation (4.8), $dU(C_{s(t)})/dC_{s(t)} = C_{s(t)}^{-\gamma}$ and $C_{s(t)} = Y_{s(t)}$, this can be rewritten as

$$P_t = E_t\left[\Sigma_{\tau=1}^{\infty}\delta^{\tau} C_{s(t+\tau)}(C_{s(t+\tau)}/C_t)^{-\gamma}\right]$$

It follows that the expected contingent price at the next date, $P_{s(t+1)}$, is

$$E_t(P_{s(t+1)}) = E_t\left[\Sigma_{\tau=2}^{\infty}\delta^{\tau} C_{s(t+\tau)}(C_{s(t+\tau)}/C_t)^{-\gamma}\right]$$

so we can write

$$P_t = E_t\left[\delta(C_{s(t+1)} + P_{s(t+1)})(C_{s(t+1)}/C_t)^{-\gamma}\right]$$
$$= \delta\Sigma_{s=s1(t+1)}^{sn(t+1)}\pi_{s(t),s(t+1)}(C_t g_s + P_{s(t+1)})g_s^{-\gamma} \qquad (4.22)$$

since $(C_{s(t+1)}/C_t)^{-\gamma} = g_s^{-\gamma}$. Given the expected real growth rates for each state type, g_s, the linking probabilities $\pi_{s(t),s(t+1)}$ and the state type realised at date t, the expected values of consumption growth in each future period can be calculated. This implies that the price of the equity can be expressed as current consumption multiplied by a constant, denoted $w_{s(t)}$:

$$P_t = w_{s(t)}C_t \qquad (4.23)$$

We also have

$$P_{s(t+1)} = w_{s(t+1)}C_t g_s \qquad (4.24)$$

Substituting equations (4.23) and (4.24) in equation (4.22) gives an expression for the constant:

$$w_{s(t)} = \delta\Sigma_{s=s1(t+1)}^{sn(t+1)}\pi_{s(t),s(t+1)}g_s^{1-\gamma}(1 + w_{s(t+1)})$$

for each of the $s = s_1, \ldots s_n$ possible state types that could have arisen at date t. The possible state types and the linking probabilities $\pi_{s(t),s(t+1)}$ are the same at every date t, so the values of $w_{s(t)}$ are the same at every date. There is one equation for each w_s, so the n simultaneous equations can be solved given the variables δ, $\pi_{s(t),s(t+1)}$, g_s and γ.

Using equations (4.23) and (4.24), the return on the share if state type $s(t+1)$ occurs, conditional on state type $s(t)$ having occurred, is

$$R_{s(t+1)}, \text{ or } R_s \text{ for short} = \left(C_{s(t+1)} + P_{s(t+1)} - P_t\right)/P_t$$
$$= \left(C_t g_s + C_t g_s w_{s(t+1)} - C_t w_{s(t)}\right)/C_t w_{s(t)}$$
$$= g_s\left(1 + w_{s(t+1)}\right)/w_{s(t)} - 1$$

The conditional expected return is

$$E_t(R_s) = \Sigma_{s=s1}^{sn} \pi_{s(t),s(t+1)} R_s$$

and the unconditional expected rate of return is

$$E(R_s) = \Sigma_{s=s1}^{sn} \pi_s R_s \tag{4.25}$$

where π_s is the probability that state s occurs, observed over many dates.

The risk-free asset is assumed to pay one unit of the consumption good after one period, and then another risk-free asset is created. Its price P_{Ft} is given by equation (4.22), with $C_{t+1} + P_{t+1} = 1 + 0 = 1$:

$$P_{ft} = \delta\Sigma_{s=s1(t+1)}^{sn(t+1)} \pi_{s(t),s(t+1)} g_s^{-\gamma}$$

The risk-free rate is, of course, certain given the price of the risk-free asset, but the price will not be the same in every type of state. The unconditional expectation of the risk-free rate is

$$E(R_{Fs}) = E(1/P_{Fs}) - 1$$
$$= \Sigma_{s=s1}^{sn} 1/\delta\pi_s g_s^{-\gamma} - 1 \tag{4.26}$$

Equations (4.25) and (4.26) predict values for the expected rate of return on 'equity' $E(R_s)$ and the expected risk-free rate $E(R_{Fs})$, given the preference parameters γ and δ, and given the Markov process for g. In other words, the above multiperiod consumption-based model is capable of predicting the expected rates of return over time on a risky asset that provides a claim on production, and on one-period risk-free assets, given assumptions about aggregate risk aversion and about the variance of production. The model can therefore be used to predict the equity risk premium over time (Section 5.4).

What the model does is to set up a process that specifies the individual's uncertain consumption over time. The growth of consumption and the extent of its variation are determined by the values of growth (which can be negative) in each type of state, and by the linking probabilities. Given the type of state that arises at each date, the individual knows the contingent outcomes for consumption growth and their probabilities at the next date. So the values of the stochastic discount factor are determined, given the CRRA utility function and the value of γ. The value of the stochastic discount factor for a possible state s is $\delta MU_{s(t+1)}/MU_{s(t)} = \delta(C_{s(t+1)}/C_t)^{-\gamma} = \delta g_s^{-\gamma}$. The contingent pay-offs on the risky asset, being themselves total consumption, are also known in advance. So the contingent prices of the risky asset can be worked out. The risky asset will be priced to give a positive expected risk premium, for the same reason as in the single-period model (Section 4.2). The larger the pre-set variation in contingent consumption, the larger the risk premium.

4.3.3   Merton's intertemporal model

An elaboration of the consumption-based model in a multiperiod context can be achieved by introducing the concept of a *state variable*, which means a major source of uncertainty that affects the individual's consumption plan. The result is a multifactor model in which an asset's risk premium is determined by its sensitivity to the state variables. Merton (1977) argues that, if a source of uncertainty affects enough people, and a financial asset can be found with a price that is correlated with that source, then such an asset is likely to exist, as its existence provides a valuable service by enabling people better to manage risks over time. He gives as examples of state variables individuals' wage income, the relative prices of consumption goods, and the one-period rate of interest, as well as the return on the market portfolio. He postulates the existence of an asset with returns correlated with next period's change in wage income, a second asset with returns correlated with the change in price of a particular good, and a two-period bond, which will have a one-period return that is negatively correlated with the change in the one-period interest rate. Each asset can be used to hedge against the uncertain outcome of the state variable with which it is correlated.

The key to the state variable concept is that the contingent outcome of a state variable affects the individual's optimal contingent consumption. For example, a fall in wage income will be associated with lower consumption, especially if there is serial correlation in wage income, so that a low outcome at one date forecasts low outcomes for several subsequent dates. Thus, uncertainty about wage income is a source of uncertainty about future consumption. With a concave utility function, uncertainty about future consumption reduces the expected utility from future consumption. The individual can increase the expected utility from future consumption if he/she is able to reduce the uncertainty – to smooth the possible consumption outcomes at future dates. This can be done, at least to some extent, by taking positions in assets with returns that are correlated with state variables. For example, the individual at date t could reduce the impact of uncertainty about his/her wage income in $t+1$ on his/her consumption in $t+1$ by short-selling the asset correlated with wage income. Since the state variables affect consumption and therefore utility, asset prices are affected by their covariances with state variables.

State variables that forecast future consumption can be thought of as being linked to changes in the probabilities attached to future contingent states. For example, a fall in the short-term interest rate arises in the consumption-based model because $E_t[\delta MU_{t+1}/MU_t]$ rises, suggesting that people are more pessimistic than they were about future consumption outcomes. In other words, people have increased the probabilities they attach to states in which consumption is relatively low. Assets that pay off relatively well in low consumption states will have increased in price relative to other assets.

Merton (1973) derives a consumption-based model with state variables in continuous time, which can be presented in approximate form in discrete time. The presentation below follows Huang and Litzenberger (1988, pp. 208–14). The equations are less opaque than they might seem at first. We start with the general expression for the expected premium on a risky asset, equation (4.4). This can be written using equation (4.5) as

$$E_t(R_{jt+1}) - R_{Ft+1} = -(1 - R_{Ft+1})\text{cov}_t[R_{jt+1}, U'(C_{t+1})/U'(C_t)] \tag{4.27}$$

where $U'(C_t) = dU(C_t)/dC_t = MU_t$, and we have incorporated the time-preference parameter δ in $U(C_{t+1})$. The individual's consumption is assumed to be a function of time (i.e. there is an unexplained element in the outcome at each date) and of realisations of the state variables. We assume for simplicity that there is only one state variable, θ, so $C_t = C(t, \theta_t)$. Using this expression, next date's consumption can be written approximately as

$$C_{t+1} \approx C_t + (\partial C_t/\partial t)dt + (\partial C_t/\partial \theta_t)d\theta \tag{4.28}$$

Next date's marginal utility can be written approximately as

$$U'(C_{t+1}) \approx U'(C_t) + U''(C_t)dC_t$$

This is simply an approximate expression for the slope of the utility function at the point $C_{t+1} = C_t + dC_t$. Using equation (4.28) and the fact that $dC_t = C_{t+1} - C_t$, the expression can be rewritten as

$$U'(C_{t+1}) \approx U'(C_t) + U''(C_t)[(\partial C_t/\partial t)dt + (\partial C_t/\partial \theta_t)d\theta]$$

Substituting for $U'(C_{t+1})$ in equation (4.27) gives

$$\begin{aligned} E_t(R_{jt+1}) - R_{Ft+1} &\approx -(1 - R_{Ft+1})\text{cov}_t\{R_{jt+1}, \{U'(C_t) + U''(C_t)[(\partial C_t/\partial t)dt \\ &\quad + (\partial C_t/\partial \theta_t)d\theta]\}/U'(C_t)\} \\ &\approx -[(1 - R_{Ft+1})U''(C_t)/U'(C_t)](\partial C_t/\partial \theta_t)\text{cov}_t(R_{jt+1}, d\theta) \end{aligned} \tag{4.29}$$

The second line follows because both $U'(C_t)/U'(C_t)$ and $U''(C_t)(\partial C_t/\partial t)dt/U'(C_t)$ are constants, and because $\text{cov}_t[R_{jt+1}, (\partial C_t/\partial \theta_t)d\theta] = (\partial C_t/\partial \theta_t)\text{cov}_t(R_{jt+1}, d\theta)$. The expected return and covariance are conditional on the observation of the state variable θ_t. Equation (4.29) says that the expected excess return on asset j is linearly related to the covariance of the return with the change in the state variable, $d\theta$.

Now suppose that there is a financial asset or mutual fund H_θ with returns that are correlated with changes in θ. Equation (4.29) holds for this mutual fund,

$$E_t(R_{H\theta t+1}) - R_{Ft+1} \approx -[(1 - R_{Ft+1})U''(C_t)/U'(C_t)](\partial C_t/\partial \theta_t)\text{cov}_t(R_{H\theta t+1}, d\theta)$$

which can be rearranged to give

$$-(1 - R_{Ft+1})U''(C_t)/U'(C_t) \approx [E_t(R_{H\theta t+1})$$
$$- R_{Ft+1}]/(\partial C_t/\partial \theta_t)\text{cov}_t(R_{H\theta t+1}, d\theta) \tag{4.30}$$

Substituting equation (4.30) in equation (4.29) gives

$$E_t(R_{jt+1}) - R_{Ft+1} \approx \frac{[E_t(R_{H\theta t+1}) - R_{Ft+1}]\text{cov}_t(R_{jt+1}, d\theta)}{\text{cov}_t(R_{H\theta t+1}, d\theta)}$$

Dividing top and bottom on the right by var$(d\theta)$ gives

$$E_t(R_{jt+1}) - R_{Ft+1} \approx (\beta_{j,\theta}/\beta_{H\theta,\theta})[E_t(R_{H\theta t+1}) - R_{Ft+1}]$$

where $\beta_{j,\theta}$ is the sensitivity of the returns on asset j to changes in the state variable θ, and $\beta_{H\theta,\theta}$ is the sensitivity of the returns on fund H_θ to changes in θ. If $\beta_{H\theta,\theta} \approx 1$, then

$$E_t(R_{jt+1}) - R_{Ft+1} \approx \beta_{j,\theta}[E_{t-1}(R_{H\theta t+1}) - R_{Ft+1}]$$

This says that the expected excess return on an asset is determined by the expected excess return on a fund H_θ correlated with the state variable, times the asset's sensitivity to the state variable. If there are n state variables, the model can be written as

$$E_t(R_{jt+1}) - R_{Ft+1} \approx \Sigma_{\theta=1}^n \beta_{j,H\theta}[E_t(R_{H\theta t+1}) - R_{Ft+1}] \tag{4.31}$$

The above model is known as the *intertemporal CAPM*. The expected return is not constant over time and is conditional on information available at the start of each period, unless it is assumed that the change in consumption has a constant expected value. In this case, information at date t means the observed outcomes of the state variables at date t, or of proxies for state variables.

The intertemporal CAPM is equivalent to the consumption CAPM; equations (4.27) and (4.30) give the same answer for the expected excess return. We can think of the covariances of an asset's returns with the state variables as explaining, together, the covariance of its returns with consumption. The intertemporal CAPM is not, in general, equivalent to the standard CAPM. The reason is that, if state variables other than wealth exist, the expected returns on assets are affected by their covariances with these state variables. For the standard CAPM to be correct in a multiperiod context requires that the maximisation of lifetime utility be equivalent to the maximisation of the expected utility from wealth at the next date, and that the utility from wealth be a function of its expected value and the variance of its value only. For this to hold, the utility from wealth in each possible state next date cannot be state-dependent, otherwise the utility from wealth as at the previous date will not depend only on the expected value and variance of wealth. It will also depend on the factors – the outcome for consumption, or for the state variables – that affect the state-contingent utility from wealth. The existence of the same utility from wealth across states implies that preferences, and consumption and investment opportunities, are fixed and known in advance (Fama, 1970; Cochrane, 2001, pp. 155–60). For investment opportunities to be constant, possible returns on risky assets each period must be identically and independently distributed, and the risk-free rate must be constant over time. The existence of state variables implies, in contrast, that consumption and investment opportunities are state-contingent.

4.4   Note on evidence

A major line of enquiry in testing the consumption-based model has been to see whether the size of the historic equity risk premium (about 6 per cent annually in the United States and United Kingdom) can be generated by variants of the model under plausible assumptions. The bottom line is that consumption per head, or in aggregate, is nowhere near variable enough for the standard versions of the model (Section 4.2.2 or 4.3.1) to generate a risk premium of the order of 6 per cent p.a. unless the investor is assumed to be implausibly risk averse. This is discussed further in the next chapter. Another approach is to examine the relation between consumption betas and cross-sectional differences in observed returns on shares (e.g. Mankiw and Shapiro, 1986). The standard CAPM performs at least as well as the consumption CAPM in cross-sectional tests. But there have been far fewer cross-sectional tests of the consumption CAPM than there have of the standard CAPM. This is probably because consumption-based models have not been used to estimate expected returns on assets either in empirical research or in practical business contexts.

4.5   Summary

To understand fully how a project's cost of capital is determined in theory, it is necessary to understand how risk premiums on assets are determined. In pursuit of that goal, this chapter has introduced the consumption-based approach to asset pricing, using the contingent-states framework. Consumption-based models are models of general equilibrium, unlike the CAPM and APT, and they provide explanations of the equity premium and the risk-free rate. The risk of an asset is measured by the covariance of its returns with the representative individual's consumption. Positive covariance with consumption implies that the asset should provide a positive expected premium over the risk-free rate, since the asset's pay-off tends to be small when consumption is relatively low and the marginal utility from the pay-off is relatively high. The chapter has considered briefly the difficult task of modelling expected returns in a dynamic multiperiod context, and has described the Mehra–Prescott and Merton models of expected returns. The next chapter includes discussion of quantitative predictions of the expected premium on equity made using consumption-based models.

   We have now completed our presentation of mainstream models of expected returns. It might be helpful to summarise in one place the main assumptions underlying the models, and the measure of an asset's risk in each case. The link with consumption in all the models stems from the assumption that utility derives from consumption.

Model	Key assumptions	Measure of an asset's risk
CAPM	Quadratic utility or returns are normally distributed. A single period. All consumption is from saving, or consumption not from saving is certain. Individuals have homogeneous beliefs.	Covariance with return on portfolio of all assets.
APT	Assets are priced so that gains from arbitrage are not possible. A few risk factors exist with which returns on assets are correlated.	Covariance with changes in risk factors, or with returns on funds correlated with risk factors.
Consumption CAPM	Quadratic utility function, or CRRA utility function and returns and consumption are lognormally distributed. Consumption not from wealth is given and can vary across contingent states. Homogeneous individuals.	Covariance with contingent change in consumption.
Intertemporal CAPM	An elaboration of consumption CAPM. There are state variables: factors that affect an individual's consumption plan.	Covariance with changes in state variables, or with returns on funds correlated with state variables.

Multifactor models can be interpreted either as examples of APT or of the intertemporal CAPM.
The Mehra–Prescott model is a multiperiod version of the consumption CAPM, with one risky asset.

5   The equity risk premium

The equity risk premium is the difference between the expected rate of return on the stock market and the risk-free rate. In recent years the size of the premium has been the premier question relating to the cost of capital, for theorists and practitioners alike. The reason is that the observed historic premium, measured over long periods and across many stock markets, is felt to be too large. From a theoretical perspective, it is too large because it has proved to be difficult to devise a plausible theory that predicts a premium of more than about 0.5 per cent p.a. Observed historic premiums are of the order of ten times bigger; this is the 'equity premium puzzle'. The (consumption-based) models that fail to predict observed premiums are not a minor curiosity. They 'have formed the backbone of our understanding of economic growth and dynamic micro, macro, and international economics for close to 25 years' (Cochrane, 1997, p. 12). From an investor's perspective, many observers doubt that equity will continue to provide a premium as large as the 6 per cent p.a. or more observed during much of the twentieth century, and they doubt that investors expected a premium of this size in the past.

A figure for the premium has to be included when the CAPM, or a multifactor model that includes the stock market return as a risk factor, is used to estimate the cost of equity. If a measure of the historic premium is not to be relied upon, what figure should be used? There is no definitive answer. Serious suggestions for the real premium to use are currently in a range between 1 per cent p.a. and 8 per cent p.a. (see, e.g., Ilmanen, 2003, for estimates at the low end; Brealey and Myers, 2003, for the high end). Given such a range, the choice made will often make more difference to a cost of capital estimate than will the choice regarding any other aspect, such as adjustment for tax or the method of estimating beta.

The contents of this chapter are somewhat heterogeneous, because the author believes it to be helpful to discuss issues related to the equity premium in one place. The first section concerns the role of the premium in estimating a project's cost of equity, and is linked with Chapter 6 on valuation and with Chapter 13 on applying the CAPM in practice. The next two sections are about evidence on the historic premium. The final section explains why the consumption-based model predicts a premium of 0.5 per cent p.a. or less, and reviews some of the modifications that have been made to the model so that it can predict a higher premium. This section can be viewed as a continuation of Chapter 4.

5.1   Use of a historic mean premium as a forecast

The historic premium is relevant to the cost of equity because it is – or, at least, was – widely used to forecast the expected equity premium, or excess rate of return on the stock market. The underlying assumptions that justify using the long-run historic premium as a forecast are that realised returns will tend to reflect *ex ante* expected returns, and that the *ex ante* expected return is constant over time. These assumptions imply, if they are true, that realised returns should fluctuate around a mean and that, as the number of *ex post* observations increases, the mean should become an increasingly accurate estimate of the constant expected return. So the historic mean return over many months or years is a more reliable estimate than the mean over fewer months or years in the more recent past.

If fluctuations around the mean are forecastable, the long-term mean will not provide the best forecast of premiums in the near future. For example, there is evidence that the variability of stock market returns changes over time, which could imply forecastability. Greater variability of returns might be thought to imply greater risk, and therefore a higher expected rate of return to compensate. But 'the relation between stock returns and the variability of returns is remarkably weak' (Cornell, 1999, p. 51). There is also evidence that expected excess returns are forecastable over a horizon of several years, from variables such as the dividend yield on the stock market (Section 3.4). This implies that one can produce a better forecast of expected excess returns in the near future than the historic arithmetic mean premium. It is an argument for using a multifactor model, which includes factors that predict changes in expected returns.

A point to note in passing is that the equity premium is, approximately, a real premium even if the returns are in nominal terms. Inflation *Inf* is part of the expected nominal return on equity $E(R_{Enom})$ and of the nominal risk-free rate R_{Fnom}, and if inflation is certain we have

$$
\begin{aligned}
E(R_{Enom}) - R_{Fnom} &= [1 + E(R_{Ereal})](1 + Inf) - (1 + R_{Freal})(1 + Inf) \\
&= E(R_{Ereal}) + E(R_{Ereal})\,Inf - R_{Freal} - R_{Freal}\,Inf \\
&\approx E(R_{Ereal}) - R_{Freal}
\end{aligned}
$$

However, the above conversion of an expected nominal premium into an expected real premium will tend slightly to overstate the expected real premium, if inflation is assumed to be uncertain (Section 10.1).

Arithmetic versus geometric mean
Assuming for now that a historic mean premium does provide a good forecast of the *ex ante* premium, a question that arises is whether the historic premium should be measured using the arithmetic or geometric mean excess return for the purpose of estimating the cost of equity. The historic equity premium in the United States or United Kingdom is around 2 per cent p.a. larger using the arithmetic mean, so the difference matters. Corporate finance texts are not unanimous on this question, although most recommend using the arithmetic

mean. The arithmetic mean premium for a sample of T observations, R_A^e, is

$$R_A^e = (1/T)\Sigma_{t=1}^T R_t^e - 1$$

where R_t^e is the premium or excess return for year t. The geometric mean premium, R_G^e, is

$$R_G^e = \left[\Pi_{t=1}^T (1 + R_t^e)\right]^{1/T} - 1$$

If premiums vary, the geometric mean is always smaller, and the difference between the two is positively related to the variance of the premiums. The difference is given approximately by $0.5\,\mathrm{var}(R_t^e)$.

For example, suppose the observed returns over three years are 20 per cent, −40 per cent and 50 per cent. The risk-free rate is zero, so these are also excess returns. The arithmetic mean return is 10 per cent p.a. and the geometric mean is 2.60 per cent p.a. The geometric mean is the correct *ex post* annual rate of return on an investment; an investment of £100 at the start of the three years would have been worth £100(1.026)^3 = £108 at the end.

However, we wish to use the historic premium to estimate the *ex ante* expected premium. A multiperiod project's cost of equity is the expected return on an asset of the same risk over a *one-period* horizon, not the expected geometric mean rate of return on the asset measured over many periods. This is discussed further in Section 6.1.1. The expected one-period return is the same as the expected arithmetic mean of a time-series sample of returns. This is larger than the expected geometric mean,

$$E(R_G) = E\left[\Pi_{t=1}^T (1 + R_t)\right]^{1/T} - 1$$

unless returns are certain and constant. Thus we are using the sample of historic returns to estimate the *ex ante* expected annual returns, not the *ex ante* expected geometric mean rate of return. Assuming a constant expected annual return over time, the arithmetic mean historic premium provides a better estimate of the expected annual return, because the geometric mean is a downward-biased estimator.

The arithmetic mean historic premium is only an estimate of the unknown expected premium. How does this affect the argument? Suppose for simplicity that the unknown expected excess return is a constant return R^e. Suppose in addition that the sample arithmetic mean is an unbiased estimator of R^e, $E(R_A^e) = R^e$, and R_A^e is normally distributed around R^e. The estimated discount factor using R_A^e is $1/(1 + R_A^e)$. Cooper (1996) points out that the estimated discount factor is biased upwards, because

$$E\left[1/(1 + R_A^e)\right] > 1/(1 + R^e)$$

and, *a fortiori*,

$$E\left[1/(1 + R_A^e)^T\right] > 1/(1 + R^e)^T$$

where T is a number of years into the future. This means that a *higher* premium should be used in the discount factor than the arithmetic mean R_A^e. Since the geometric mean is always below the arithmetic mean if returns vary, the upward bias in the discount factor is worse using the geometric mean. This point strengthens the argument for estimating the expected premium by the historic arithmetic mean premium. Cooper proposes a modified premium R^{e*} found from

$$1/(1 + R^{e*})^{\mathrm{T}} = b/(1 + R_{\mathrm{A}}^{\mathrm{e}})^{\mathrm{T}} + (1 - b)/(1 + R_{\mathrm{G}}^{\mathrm{e}})^{\mathrm{T}}$$

where $b = (T + N)/(N - 1)$ and N is the number of observations in the sample used to calculate $R_{\mathrm{A}}^{\mathrm{e}}$. The use of R^{e*} as the premium in the discount factor means that the discount factor is approximately unbiased. R^{e*} is not a constant, being positively related to N. However, using R_{A} of 9.0 per cent p.a. and R_{G} of 7.0 per cent p.a. (from real US equity returns during 1926–92), R^* varies only between 9.1 per cent p.a. for a future horizon of one year and 10.6 per cent p.a. for a horizon of thirty years (the corresponding premiums against treasury bills would be about 0.7 per cent p.a. lower).

The conclusion is that the equity premium should be estimated from the arithmetic mean of historic premiums, for the purpose of estimating the cost of equity. This tends to result in a slight upward bias in the resulting discount factor, which is probably not worth trying to correct. Using the geometric mean exacerbates the upward bias.

Which risk-free rate?

The equity premium is normally measured either in relation to the rates on three-month treasury bills or on twenty-year government bonds. As we are interested in the expected premium over a single period, the treasury bill is better matched with the concept of a risk-free return over a single period. An asset is risk free over a single period only if its pay-off or price is certain at the end of the period. An asset with a life of more than one period will have an uncertain price at each date before expiry, and its expected return may therefore incorporate a risk premium. However, it appears to be usual in practice to measure the risk-free rate by the rate on long-term government bonds, not by the rate on treasury bills (see Sections 10.3 and 13.1).

5.2   Evidence on historic premiums

Until recently, the evidence generally referred to on historic returns was derived from one source for the United Kingdom and one for the United States. The UK source is the *Equity-Gilt Study*, which has been published annually since 1956 and is now produced by Barclays Capital. It provides annual nominal and real returns on equity and UK government bonds (gilts) since 1900, before personal tax (except that income tax is subtracted from dividends from 1998, following a change in the tax regime in 1997). Nominal returns on gilts are calculated using undated gilts before 1962, and gilts with an average term to maturity of twenty years for 1962–89 and fifteen years for 1990 onwards. Nominal returns on equity are calculated using the FT-Actuaries All Share Index from 1963 and an index constructed by Barclays for preceding years. The index constituents during 1935–62 are the companies in the FT 30 Index.

The 2000 edition of the *Study* included two changes that reduce the 'bottom line' long-term historic premium it provides. First, the equity return estimates for the years up to 1935 were substantially revised; the Barclays index for those years now contains the thirty largest companies each year by market capitalisation, instead of an unchanging list of thirty large companies chosen to be similar to those in the FT 30 Index when it started in 1935. The effect was to reduce the estimated arithmetic mean real return on equity for 1919–35 from 17.3 per cent p.a. to 10.7 per cent p.a. Second, the series was extended back from a start date of 1919 to a start of 1900. The mean real premium for 1900–18 is lower (4.2 per cent p.a.) than the premium for 1919–1999 (6.0 per cent p.a.). The combined effects of these changes are that 'the historic real premium' is 5.6 per cent p.a. for 1900–99 in the 2000 edition, compared with 7.1 per cent p.a. for 1919–98 in the 1999 edition.

The primary source of historic data for the United States is the *Stocks, Bonds, Bills and Inflation (SBBI) Yearbook*, produced annually by Ibbotson Associates. The source of the SBBI data for equity returns is the Centre for Research in Securities Prices (CRSP), with data starting in 1926. For this reason, 'long-term returns on equity' for the United States have often been measured from 1926. However, daily stock index data are available from 1885, and a series of monthly returns starting in 1802 has been created for equity by Schwert (1990) and for bonds and bills by Siegel (1992) (though neither paper provides the annual figures themselves). Schwert's equity series is formed by splicing together nine indices. The constituents are six or seven bank stocks (1802–33), seven bank and twenty railroad stocks (1834–45), up to twenty-seven railroad stocks (1845–70), between twelve and fifty industrial and transportation stocks (1871–1925) and the CRSP value-weighted portfolio of NYSE stocks, including dividends (1926 onwards). For 1871–1938, the monthly dividend yields from Cowles (1939) are added to the monthly index values. Yields for 1802–70 are inferred from changes in index values, in the following way. The following regression is run using the Cowles monthly index and yield data for 1871–1938:

$$Yield_t = \Sigma_{m=1}^{12} D_m + \Sigma_{k=-3}^{3} \alpha_k R_{It+k} + e_t \tag{5.1}$$

where $Yield_t$ = total dividends paid during month $t \div$ index value at $t - 1$, D_m is one of twelve dummy variables, one for each month m in the year, and R_{It+k} = change in index value in month $t + k \div$ index value at $t + k - 1$. Monthly yields for 1802–70 are estimated using realised values of R_{It} and the values for D_m and α_k in equation (5.1) estimated during 1871–1938. The assumption is that yields were of similar magnitude before and after 1871, and Schwert refers to some evidence that supports this.

Redemption yields from 1790 are available on long-term US government and municipal bonds. Siegel (1992) notes that the credit standing of municipal bonds was superior to that of government bonds in the nineteenth century, and that government bond yields were biased downwards during 1865–1920. Demand for government bonds was boosted because banks could issue notes against these bonds held as reserves. He therefore favours a series constructed from the minimum of the yield of high-grade municipal and government bonds during 1800–61, from high-grade municipals during 1862–1920, and from government bonds thereafter.

Regarding short-term interest rates, US treasury bills were first issued in 1920. Rates on commercial paper are available before 1920, but they exhibit substantial premiums for default risk. To estimate a short rate without default risk for a given month t, Siegel assumes that the difference between the unknown risk-free short rate and the known risk-free long

Table 5.1. *Arithmetic mean real returns on US shares, government bonds (or proxies) and treasury bills (or proxies), 1802–1997*

Period	Equity % p.a.	Government bonds % p.a.	Treasury bills % p.a.	Premium against bonds % p.a.	Premium against bills % p.a.
1802–1997	8.5	3.8	3.1	4.7	5.4
Sub-periods					
1802–1870	8.3	5.1	5.4	3.2	2.9
1871–1925	7.9	3.9	3.3	4.0	4.6
1926–1997	9.2	2.6	0.7	6.6	8.5

Source: Siegel (1998, pp. 15 & 16).

rate is the same as the contemporaneous difference between the known short and long rates in the United Kingdom. He takes the US long bond yield for month t and adds the average UK short rate minus the average yield on UK Consols (government bonds with no redemption date). The UK short rate is the rate on East India Company bills for 1800–16 (minus seven basis points for default risk) and the Open Market Discount Rate for 1817–1919.

Siegel (1992; 1998; 1999) discusses the equity premium derived from the above data covering nearly two hundred years. The key findings are shown in Table 5.1. The premium in the nineteenth century was much lower than in the twentieth. The arithmetic mean real premium against long bonds during the whole period 1802–1997 was 4.7 per cent p.a.; it was 3.2 per cent p.a. during 1802–70, 4.0 per cent p.a. during 1871–1925 and 6.6 per cent p.a. during 1926–97. He attributes the higher premium in the latter period mainly to considerably lower real long and short interest rates; the real return on equity was less than one percentage point higher than in the previous period.

It should be noted that the estimate of the mean return on equity for 1802–70 in Siegel (1998, pp. 12 & 13) is 8.3 per cent p.a., compared with 6.9 per cent p.a. in his 1992 paper. The reason for the revision appears to be a departure from Schwert's method for estimating dividend yields during 1802–70: the revised dividend yields were estimated 'by statistically fitting the relation of long-term interest rate [rather than changes in equity index value] to dividend yields in the second subperiod, yielding results that are closer to other information we have about dividends during the period [presumably 1802–70]'.

A recent book by Dimson, Marsh and Staunton (2002) provides returns data on equity, government bonds and treasury bills across sixteen countries for 1900–2000, which are summarised in Table 5.2. They argue that previously available figures for equity returns are biased upwards in fifteen of the sixteen countries, the exception being Australia. The main reasons for the bias are, first, that returns were low in the first few decades of the century, and start dates for previous data series are two or more decades later than 1900, and, second, that the indices from which returns are calculated have not always included companies that were actually the largest hundred (or however many companies were in the index) in the year in question. Dimson et al. have sought to provide returns that an index tracker fund

Table 5.2. *Mean annual real returns on equity and government bonds in sixteen countries,*
1900–2000

Country	Equity		Government bonds		Equity premium	
	A	G	A	G	A	G
Australia	9.0	7.5	1.9	1.1	8.0	6.3
Belgium	4.8	2.5	0.3	−0.4	4.8	2.9
Canada	7.7	6.4	2.4	1.8	6.0	4.5
Denmark	6.2	4.6	3.3	2.5	3.3	2.0
France	6.3	3.8	0.1	−1.0	7.0	4.9
Germany (excl. 1922–23)	8.8	3.6	0.3	−2.2	9.9	6.7
Ireland	7.0	4.8	2.4	1.5	4.6	3.2
Italy	6.8	2.7	−0.8	−2.2	8.4	5.0
Japan	9.3	4.5	1.3	−1.6	10.3	6.2
Netherlands	7.7	5.8	1.5	1.1	6.7	4.7
South Africa	9.1	6.8	1.9	1.4	7.1	5.4
Spain	5.8	3.6	1.9	1.2	4.2	2.3
Sweden	9.9	7.6	3.1	2.4	7.4	5.2
Switzerland (from 1911)	6.9	5.0	3.1	2.8	4.2	2.7
UK	7.6	5.8	2.3	1.3	5.6	4.4
USA	8.7	6.7	2.1	1.6	7.0	5.0
Equally weighted mean	7.6	5.1	1.7	0.8	6.5	4.5

A = arithmetic mean
G = geometric mean
Source: Dimson, Marsh and Staunton (2002, tables 4.1, 4.2 & 12.2).

could replicate before costs, though they seem confident they have achieved this for all one hundred years only for the United Kingdom, the United States, Ireland and South Africa. They do not question the US CRSP data, but the (geometric) mean real return on equity is 0.7 percentage points smaller as a result of starting in 1900 instead of 1926. The average geometric mean real return across the sixteen countries using the start dates in previous studies is 3.0 percentage points higher than the mean return starting in 1900 (p. 42). They also report an overstatement of mean real returns of 2.3 per cent p.a. for 1919–54 compared with pre-2000 versions of Barclays Capital's *Equity-Gilt Study* for the United Kingdom (p. 37). However, the adjustments for the 2000 edition of the *Study* described above have resulted in figures that are close to those in Dimson et al.

Using arithmetic mean real returns, the largest equity premium is 10.3 per cent p.a. across the sample of countries, the smallest is 3.3 per cent p.a. and the equally weighted mean is 6.5 per cent p.a. Using geometric means, the largest is 6.7 per cent p.a., the smallest 2.0 per cent p.a. and the mean is 4.5 per cent p.a. Thus, although the premium is positive and substantial in every case, there are major differences across countries, and there is a difference of about two percentage points between the arithmetic and geometric means.

Jorion and Goetzmann (1999) study long-term returns on stock markets across thirty-nine countries. Their primary sources for index data are as follows: *International Financial Statistics*, published by the International Monetary Fund, for 1948–95; *Monthly Bulletin of Statistics*, United Nations, for 1945–48; *Statistical Yearbook*, League of Nations, for 1929–44; *International Abstract of Economic Statistics*, International Conference for Economic Services, for 1919–29. They do not attempt to remove bias caused by the choice of constituent companies in indices, but their series includes returns before as well as after temporary market closures, which alleviates potential bias resulting from the use of a series starting only after a market reopens.

Their main point is that the (geometric) mean annual real return on the US stock market during 1921–95 is the highest of the thirty-nine, regardless of whether dividends are included in returns (though they have long-term dividend data for only six countries). UK returns including dividends are almost as high as US returns. They therefore suggest that the *ex post* US (and UK) returns on equity could overstate the *ex ante* expected return; if the realised returns across the thirty-nine countries are viewed as a proxy for the distribution of *ex ante* possible returns, the United States and United Kingdom are at the extreme right of the distribution. However, the authors form a 'global' index from the thirty-nine countries, with the weights given by each country's share of the aggregate GDP, and note that the real rate of return on such an index would only be 0.3 per cent p.a. less than the rate for the United States. This is because the 'winning' US market starts with a weight of 46 per cent in 1921, and because, in general, the markets with relatively high returns have tended to be in countries with relatively large GDP. Thus, the idea that investors in the United States and United Kingdom have been lucky is undermined to some extent by the fact that the historic returns on an international equity portfolio would have been nearly as high as US or UK returns (Siegel, 1999, makes the same point). An additional observation is that the United States and United Kingdom are in the middle of the range of equity returns in the sample of Dimson et al. (2002), and not at the top as Jorion and Goetzmann find.

Twenty-five of the thirty-nine markets suffered periods of closure, but in most cases the market reopened and investors did not lose all their money. Investors did suffer 100 per cent loss in six of the cases of closure. If investors perceive that there is a positive probability of 100 per cent loss, the *ex post* mean return on a market that has survived with no episode of 100 per cent loss provides an upwardly biased estimate of the *ex ante* expected return, as highlighted and modelled initially by Brown, Goetzmann and Ross (1995). However, Li and Xu (2002) argue that models that estimate the size of this survival bias, including the model of Brown et al., imply that the bias is fairly small, if the market concerned is perceived *ex ante* to have a reasonable probability of surviving a hundred years. For example, if the *ex ante* probability of surviving a hundred years is 40 per cent, and the market has survived, the upward bias in the observed mean annual return as an estimate of the *ex ante* expected return is about 1 per cent p.a., according to Li and Xu. It should also be noted that there is in reality some risk of 100 per cent loss on 'risk-free' assets.

Several authors have emphasised that there is a great deal of variation in historic premiums in relation to their mean. This implies that, if an *ex post* mean is used as a proxy for an

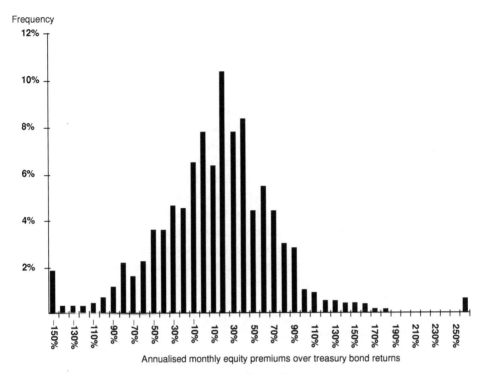

Figure 5.1   The distribution of US equity premiums, 1926–97
Source: Cornell (1999).

ex ante premium, the *ex ante* premium is estimated with a high degree of uncertainty, even using several decades of data. Figure 5.1 is a histogram taken from Cornell (1999) that shows the frequency with which the sizes of monthly US nominal premiums against bonds occur, in intervals of twenty percentage points. There are 864 observations in total from 1926–97. The premiums are multiplied by twelve to give an annualised figure, which means that a premium of less than −100 per cent is possible. The two bars representing premiums between 0 per cent p.a. and 20 per cent p.a. account for only about 14 per cent of the observations. The arithmetic mean of the annual premium is 7.4 per cent p.a. and the standard deviation of the premium is 21 per cent (the mean and standard deviation of the annualised monthly premium are almost the same). The standard error of the mean (standard deviation/$\sqrt{N}$, where N is the number of observations) is 2.4 per cent, so treating the historic mean as a forecast the expected premium lies between 2.6 per cent p.a. and 12.2 per cent p.a., using the conventional 95 per cent confidence interval given by the mean plus or minus two standard errors. Similarly, Fama and French (1997) report that the arithmetic mean monthly nominal annualised premium for 378 months during 1963–94 is 5.2 per cent p.a. with a standard error of 2.7 per cent p.a., implying a 95 per cent confidence interval for the expected premium of between −0.3 per cent p.a. and 10.6 per cent p.a. They find that uncertainty about risk premiums is quantitatively more important than whether the CAPM or their three-factor model is used, and more important than uncertainty about factor loadings (betas). Carleton and Lakonishok (1985), in their equally gloomy review of the problems of estimating the cost of equity, emphasise how sensitive estimates of the premium are to the estimation period chosen.

Summary

Until recently, the standard estimate of the arithmetic mean real premium found in textbooks was 8 per cent or 9 per cent p.a. This figure was based on the mean premiums in the United States from 1926 to the 1990s, and from mean premiums in the United Kingdom from 1919. In the last few years consideration of longer time periods, evidence from other countries and revisions to the pre-1936 estimates for the United Kingdom have all tended to push the number downwards; 5 per cent to 6 per cent p.a. now seems a reasonable 'ballpark figure' for the historic arithmetic mean premium, in the light of the recent evidence. But, given the volatility of observed premiums, any mean will be accompanied by a large standard error of at least 2 per cent. Thus, even if one believes that historic premiums have reflected past expectations, and that the *ex ante* expected premium is constant, the historic mean provides an unreliable estimate of the expected premium.

5.3   *Ex ante* expectations

We noted at the start that there are two reasons why the size of the historic premium is viewed as puzzling. One is the difficulty of creating a model that predicts such a large premium. The other is the pragmatic belief that the premium in the future cannot be as large as it has turned out to be in the past, and that it was never expected to be so large. Here we consider the second reason.

5.3.1   Inferring the expected premium

Suppose the corporate sector consists of a single company with constant leverage, and with a market value of £100. Its investments provide a return on equity of 10 per cent p.a. (after paying interest) and its cost of equity is also 10 per cent p.a. Each year the company has sufficient investment opportunities to absorb the increase in debt needed for constant leverage, plus 60 per cent of its surplus cash (its cash flow to equity). The remaining surplus cash is paid out as dividend, and it never needs to raise external capital. At the end of one year it will make a surplus of £10, of which £6 will be retained and £4 paid as dividend. At the end of two years it will make a surplus of £106 × 10% = £10.60, of which £6.36 will be retained and £4.24 paid out. And so on. It can be seen that the company provides a return on equity of 10 per cent p.a., in the form of a constant dividend yield of 4 per cent p.a. and a constant growth rate of 6 per cent p.a., given by the retention ratio times the return on capital. Since the company is the corporate sector, the value of the corporate sector is also growing by 6 per cent p.a.

   This stylised account of the link between the rate of return on capital and the growth of the corporate sector can be used to infer the future rate of return on capital from estimates of the growth of the corporate sector (or, approximately, of the whole economy) and from the yield on capital. This is what is done by rearranging the dividend discount model to give an expression for the expected rate of return on the stock market, R_M:

$$R_M = Div_{M1}/M_0 + g_M \tag{5.2}$$

where Div_{M1} is the aggregate dividend to be paid by listed companies during the next year, M_0 is the current value of the market and g_M is the long-term growth rate of aggregate dividends, which include all cash payments to shareholders, net of cash raised via share issues. If the aggregate dividend yield is constant, g_M is also the expected annual percentage capital gain. g_M cannot exceed the growth rate of the economy in the long run. If it did, the annual dividend payout would become increasingly large in relation to GDP, which is not a sensible prediction.

The estimated expected returns from the dividend discount model are much less volatile than the observed returns. A consequence of this is that the arithmetic mean of a sample of estimated expected returns from the dividend discount model will be an underestimate of the expected annual return or cost of equity (Fama and French, 2002). It is the case that, over a long horizon, the geometric mean rate of capital gain approaches the geometric mean rate of dividend growth, if dividend yield is constant over the long run. But, since capital values are more volatile than dividends, a given common geometric mean rate of capital gain and of dividend growth implies a higher arithmetic mean rate of capital gain than of dividend growth. That is,

if

$$\Pi_{t=1}^{T}(1 + \Delta M_t)^T = \Pi_{t=1}^{T}(1 + g_{Mt})^T$$

and

$$\mathrm{var}(\Delta M_t) > \mathrm{var}(g_{Mt})$$

then

$$(1/T)\Sigma_{t=1}^{T}\Delta M_t > (1/T)\Sigma_{t=1}^{T}g_{Mt}$$

where T is the number of periods, ΔM_t is the growth in market value in period t and g_{Mt} is the growth in market dividends.

For example, suppose the dividend growth rate is a constant 5.8 per cent p.a. (in practice, it would vary over time a little). Capital gains are either 40 per cent, or −20 per cent, with equal probability. So the geometric mean rate of capital gain is 5.8 per cent p.a., which matches the dividend growth rate. But the arithmetic mean capital gain is 10 per cent p.a. The expected dividend growth is 5.8 per cent p.a., whereas the expected capital gain would be 10 per cent p.a. If dividend yield were, say, 2 per cent p.a., the expected return from the dividend discount model would be 7.8 per cent p.a., compared with the true expected return of 12 per cent p.a. Fama and French estimate the actual downward bias at 1.3 per cent p.a. for 1951–2000.

The results of applying equation (5.2) vary somewhat over time, and there will always be scope for debate about any particular forecast of the expected rate of return on equity. At the time of writing (early 2004) the dividend yield on the UK stock market is around

3.0 per cent p.a. and the long-term growth rate for the United Kingdom's real GDP is forecast to be up to 2.5 per cent p.a. The US dividend yield is about 1.5 per cent, but nearly as much cash has been paid out via share repurchases in recent years as via dividends. Including repurchases adds perhaps another one percentage point to the yield (there is debate about exactly which repurchases to include). Real long-term growth in the United States is forecast to be up to 3.0 per cent p.a. Thus a reasonable forecast for the long-term rate of return on equity is 5.5 per cent p.a. at most for both countries. The real yield on long-term UK and US government bonds is around 2.0 per cent p.a. Let us take 1.3 per cent p.a. to be a suitable adjustment for the bias due to the variance in capital gains, although many studies do not include such an adjustment. These figures give an expected real equity premium for these two countries of up to 4.8 per cent p.a. A higher expected premium requires either a fall in the value of the stock market (which increases dividend yield), or higher forecast growth, or a lower risk-free rate.

An *ex ante* premium of up to 4.8 per cent p.a. for the United Kingdom and United States is somewhat below the historic arithmetic means of 5.6 per cent p.a. and 7.0 per cent p.a., respectively, for the twentieth century (Table 5.2). But it is fair to say that the recent downward revision of estimates of historic means has brought reasonable estimates of the historic premium and of the expected premium much closer than they were when the historic premium was taken to be 8 per cent to 9 per cent p.a. (for such a comparison, see Cornell, 1999, chap. 3). It was, apparently, not until the early 1990s that observers began to point out that the expected premium in the United States or United Kingdom implied by the dividend discount model – equation 5.2 – was much lower than 8 per cent p.a. (see, e.g., Gray, 1993; Scott, 1992).

5.3.2   *Ex ante* expectations in the past

One of the two assumptions underlying the use of the historic premium as a forecast is that realised returns are noisy, but unbiased, estimates of *ex ante* expected returns (the other is that the *ex ante* premium is constant). To check whether realised returns do provide an unbiased estimate, investors' past expectations about the premium can be reconstructed using data available at the time in question. Almost all researchers on this question agree that the premium in the twentieth century in the United States and United Kingdom has turned out to be larger than investors expected it to be. They agree that investors have been pleasantly surprised by the performance of equity in relation to government bonds or cash. But researchers have used somewhat differing methods and offered differing explanations for their findings.

UK evidence

Fitzgerald (2001) infers expected returns on equity using the dividend discount model and data from 1950–99. His assumptions regarding the expectations of investors in the past are as follows.

Expected nominal dividend growth $E_t(g) = (1 + g_{real}) [1 + E_t(Inf)] - 1$, where g_{real} is the geometric mean of annual real dividend growth over the previous ten years. These averages are modified, perhaps questionably, so that the maximum is 3 per cent p.a. and the minimum is −2 per cent p.a. This modification reduces the mean of the ten-year geometric means from 1.8 per cent to 0.8 per cent p.a.

Expected inflation $E_t(Inf) = 0.8(R_{Fnomt} - R_{Frealt})$, where R_{Fnomt} is the nominal long gilt yield at date t and R_{Frealt} is the yield on long index-linked gilts. The other 20 per cent of the difference in brackets is assumed to be a premium for bearing inflation risk rather than part of expected inflation. Index-linked gilts were introduced only in 1981, so $R_{Freal,t}$ for the years before 1981 is assumed to be the mean index-linked yield of 3.5 per cent p.a. observed during 1981–99.

Expected dividend yield $E_t(Div_{t+1}/M_t) = (Div_t/M_t)[1 + E_t(g)]$.

The above estimates produce an arithmetic mean expected nominal return on equity of 9.9 per cent p.a. during 1950–99, implying an expected premium against long gilts of only 1.4 per cent p.a. (though this ignores the downward bias in the estimates using the dividend discount model, explained in the previous section). The actual arithmetic mean return was 17.9 per cent p.a., eight percentage points larger than expected.

Fitzgerald goes on to suggest why investors were surprised by the performance of equity. If the actual return on shares matches the expected return, both dividends and market value will grow by $E_t(g)$, and the dividend yield will remain constant. He defines the return attributed to the unexpected change in dividend as the difference between actual and expected dividend, plus the difference between the market value necessary to maintain a constant dividend yield and the expected market value. He then defines a market 're-rating' as the difference between the actual market value and the value necessary to keep dividend yield constant, given the actual growth in dividends. Thus, we have

$$unexpected\ pay\text{-}off = re\text{-}rating + pay\text{-}off\ from\ unexpected\ change\ in\ dividend$$

$$(Div_{t+1} + M_{t+1}) - (Div_t + M_t)[1 + E_t(g)]$$
$$= \{M_{t+1} - Div_{t+1}/(Div_t/M_t)\} + \{[Div_{t+1} + Div_{t+1}/(Div_t/M_t)]$$
$$- (Div_t + M_t)[1 + E_t(g)]\}$$

For example, suppose the current market value M_t is 1000, the dividend for the year Div_t is 50 and the expected nominal growth in dividends $E_t(g)$ is 4 per cent p.a., so the expected pay-off is 1092. After one year, the dividend Div_{t+1} turns out to be 50 and the market value M_{t+1} is 1100. The total pay-off is 1150 and the unexpected pay-off is 58. The pay-off from the unexpected change in dividend is $1050 - 1092 = -42$. The pay-off from re-rating is $1100 - 1000 = 100$. Market value has increased despite the smaller dividend than was expected. Fitzgerald finds that, of the 8.0 per cent p.a. mean unexpected return on equity, 3.8 per cent p.a. is attributable to unexpectedly large dividend growth and 4.2 per cent p.a. to a tendency for dividend yield to fall – i.e. market value to grow more rapidly than dividends.

Wilkie (1995) has a different approach to estimating rates of return expected in the past. Whereas Fitzgerald argues that the historic premium was higher than expected because the rate of return on equity was surprisingly good, Wilkie argues that the historic premium was high because the risk-free rate was surprisingly bad. He studies returns in the period 1923–93, and suggests that inflation was higher than expected, especially during the Second

World War and from the mid-1950s onwards. He notes that retail price changes since 1600 do not show a long-term trend, and, indeed, that prices tended to fall during the nineteenth century after the Napoleonic Wars. He suggests that, on the basis of historic experience, and after allowing for the inflationary effects of the two world wars, investors would not have expected positive inflation until the 1950s. The geometric mean nominal rate of return on Consols was 3.7 per cent p.a. during 1756–1958, and the real rate was similar, given the record of inflation.

Wilkie then argues that the main reason for the healthy geometric mean real return on equity of 7.0 per cent p.a. during 1923–93 was the fact that nominal growth in dividends more than kept pace with inflation. Bond yields and interest on cash, on the other hand, did not keep pace, resulting in a mean real return on bonds of less than 2 per cent p.a., about 2 per cent less than might have been expected. If inflation *had* been zero, as was expected for many years, according to Wilkie, the return on bonds would presumably have been close to its long-term mean of 3.7 per cent p.a. and to the mean return on index-linked bonds during 1981–94 of 3.6 per cent p.a. So, with a real return on equity of 7.0 per cent p.a., the premium would have been 3.0 to 3.5 per cent p.a., instead of 5.5 per cent p.a.

Wilkie also cites an investment text by Whyte (1949, vol. 2, p. 96) as indicative of the views of investors fifty years ago: 'If the gilt-edged yield on irredeemable stocks happens to be 3.5 per cent, and if the [dividend] yield on an equity share is 5 per cent, the difference of 1.5 per cent will be viewed as the risk premium; a measure of what investors think is a fair reward for the extra risk incurred.' Whyte goes on to make clear that he regards a premium of 1.5 per cent p.a. as a plausible number.

US evidence

Fama and French (2002) proxy the expected one-year real return on equity by the actual dividend yield for the year, plus the actual real growth in dividend g_{div} or earnings g_{earn}. So the estimated expected premium for year t is

$$Estprem_t = Div_{Mt}/M_{t-1} + g_{divt} - R_{Ft} \qquad (5.3)$$

or

$$Estprem_t = Div_{Mt}/M_{t-1} + g_{earnt} - R_{Ft}$$

where the risk-free rate is proxied by the real rate on six-month commercial paper. The rationale for these estimates is that, although conditional expected returns vary over time, there is assumed to be a constant unconditional expected return around which the conditional expected returns fluctuate. Over a sufficiently long period the arithmetic mean of the observed premiums, or the mean of either estimate of the premiums, provides an estimate of the unconditional expected return. Unexpected inflation cannot be an explanation for a higher observed premium than the expected premium on this view of things, because the same real risk-free rate is subtracted from observed and expected returns on equity.

The authors contrast the results for two periods, 1872–1950 and 1951–2000. For 1872–1950 they find that the mean observed premium is 4.4 per cent p.a. and the mean estimated premium from equation (5.3) is 4.2 per cent p.a., so the two measures produce similar estimates of the unconditional expected return. But for 1951–2000 the mean observed premium is 7.4 per cent p.a. whereas the mean estimated premium is 2.6 per cent p.a. from dividend growth and 4.3 per cent p.a. from earnings growth. They argue that the latter two estimates are likely to be closer to the unconditional expected return than the estimate from the observed premium. The main reason is that the arithmetic mean accounting return on book equity during 1951–2000 is two percentage points p.a. below the mean return on equity at market values, so if the true expected premium had been as high as 7.4 per cent p.a. the typical corporate investment would have had negative net present value.

They note that the difference between the mean realised premium and the mean estimated premium cannot be explained by unexpected dividend or earnings growth during 1951–2000, since this would have caused both realised and estimated premiums to be higher by similar amounts. They also present evidence that forecast dividend and earnings growth in 2000 were not above the historical means of dividend and earnings growth. They therefore conclude that the large observed premium compared with the estimated premium is caused by growth in market value greater than the growth rate of dividend or earnings, and that these capital gains were due to a fall in the expected rate of return on equity (since they are not explained by an increase in expected growth rates). It is left an open question whether the conditional expected rate of return was temporarily low around 2000, or whether the unconditional expected rate has, in fact, fallen.

Claus and Thomas (2001) estimate that investors were expecting a similar premium, of 3.4 per cent p.a., using data from 1985–98. They use analysts' forecasts and the abnormal earnings method to estimate expected cash flows to equity each year for a large sample of listed firms. The abnormal earnings method of estimation is reviewed in Section 12.3; it is a way of arriving at reasonable forecasts of earnings. Analysts' forecasts of earnings growth are short term, for up to five years, and are used to estimate growth in abnormal earnings for this horizon. Thereafter abnormal earnings are assumed to grow at the expected rate of inflation – an assumption that the authors believe to be optimistic. The market-wide discount rate at a given date is inferred from the estimated total expected cash flows of the sample firms and from their prevailing total market capitalisation.

Gebhardt, Lee and Swaminathan (2001) also use the abnormal earnings method to calculate the cost of equity and the risk premium for forty-eight industry groups in each year during 1979–95. There is a wide variation across the industries in the average *ex ante* premium during this time, ranging from 8.4 per cent p.a. for toys to −2.8 per cent p.a. for real estate. The average is 2.5 per cent p.a. In contrast, the average premium observed *ex post* during 1979–95 is 7.2 per cent p.a.

Siegel's (1998) long-term figures (Table 5.1) also support the view that the premium in much of the twentieth century was untypically high. The equity premium measured against bonds was only 3.2 per cent p.a. during 1802–70 and 4.0 per cent p.a. during 1871–1925, compared with 6.6 per cent p.a. during 1926–97. Siegel emphasises that the real rates of return on equity vary less across the three periods than do the real rates on bonds and treasury bills, both of which were relatively low during 1926–97. He suggests that an explanation is that inflation was unexpectedly high after the Second World War and during the 1970s, so his diagnosis is similar to Wilkie's.

Blanchard (1993) reconstructs expected returns in the past by estimating time-varying forecasts using US annual data for 1927–93 from Ibbotson Associates. This study is akin to those of Fitzgerald, and Fama and French, but more elaborate.

Expected real risk-free rate. For any year t, the expected real risk-free rate over the next T years, $E_t[R_{Freal}(T)]$, is given by the prevailing redemption yield on government bonds maturing in T years, minus the expected rate of inflation over the same interval.

$$E_t[R_{Freal}(T)] = R_{Fnomt}(T) - E_t[Inf(T)]$$

Expected inflation is estimated as follows.

1. For each year, record realised (*ex post*) inflation over the next five years and next twenty years. Inflation in 1993 and beyond is assumed to be the same as inflation in 1992. Use these data to calculate perfect foresight inflation for each year as a weighted average of the realised inflation over the next five or twenty years.
2. Regress the perfect foresight five- and twenty-year inflation forecasts as at each year on four information variables that would be known as at year t. The signs of the coefficients for 1929–93 are given in brackets:

    real stock market dividend yield for year $t - 1$ (−);
    percentage real capital gain or loss on stock market for year $t - 1$ (+);
    nominal redemption yield on twenty-year government bonds (+);
    rate of inflation in years $t - 1$, $t - 2$ and $t - 3$ (+).

3. Use the actual figures for the above information variables as at year t, together with the regression coefficients, to estimate expected inflation for the next five and twenty years as at year t.

Expected real equity returns. The expected real return on equity in year t is the expected real dividend yield for the year plus the expected real long-term growth rate in dividends. The estimate is arrived at as follows.

1. Record the realised market dividend yield and growth rate of dividends for each year. Calculate the perfect foresight return as $Div_{realt}/M_{t-1} + av(g_{realt})$, where the second term is a weighted average of the realised real dividend growth rates over many future years. For years beyond 1992, g_{real} is assumed to be the sample average of 1.2 per cent p.a.
2. Regress $Div_{realt}/M_{t-1} + av(g_{realt})$ on the same four information variables as are used to predict inflation. The signs of the coefficients are the same in both regressions: lagged dividend yield (+); lagged change in stock market (−); nominal twenty-year bond yield (−); lagged inflation (+).
3. Use the actual figures for the four variables as at year t, together with the regression coefficients, to estimate the expected real return on equity as at year t.

The expected premium in any year is then the expected real return on equity minus the expected real five- or twenty-year bond yield. Blanchard also employs an alternative method, which is to use the four information variables to forecast directly the realised premium over the subsequent twenty years. The results are similar using this approach.

The headline result is that the mean real premium expected during 1927–93 was around 3 per cent p.a. Thus, investors were pleasantly surprised, if the above process captures their expectations. The time series of expected returns on bonds differs considerably from that on shares. The expected real return on bonds was negative or close to zero during the 1940s and 1950s, which raises the question of why investors were willing to buy them. The expected equity premium varied considerably; it was 10 per cent or more during the 1940s, but negative or close to zero in the mid-1960s and again in the 1980s. 'The two main conclusions . . . are that the [expected] equity premium has gone down steadily since the early 1950s, and that inflation contributed to the transitory increase above trend in the 1970s and the transitory decrease below trend in the 1980s' (p. 113).

Survey evidence

Another approach to estimating *ex ante* expected returns is to use survey data. One method is to ask investors directly what they think the expected rate of return on equity will be, although it appears that this type of evidence has started to be collected only in the last few years. Ilmanen (2003) discusses such evidence and notes a 95 per cent correlation between the past year's return and next year's expected return amongst private investors. One survey found that US private investors were expecting a long-term rate of return on equity of 19 per cent p.a. in 1999, a time when inflation was around 3 per cent p.a. By 2001–02 investors, chief financial officers and academics were forecasting an expected long-term equity premium of 2.5 per cent to 4.5 per cent p.a.

A second method is to use survey data to forecast the expected rate of return according to the dividend discount model. For example, Best and Byrne (2001) estimate expected dividend growth from *Blue Chip Economic Indicators* consensus forecasts for ten-year nominal US GDP growth, from March 1979 (when the forecasts first became available) to March 1999. They assume that long-term dividend growth is the same as ten-year GDP growth. Expected dividend yield is estimated from the twelve-month earnings forecasts on the S&P 500 from Institutional Brokers Estimation Service, with an assumed 40 per cent pay-out ratio. The expected risk-free rate is the prevailing redemption yield on ten-year government bonds. They perform the same exercise for the United Kingdom for the period April 1982 to April 1999, using GDP forecasts from Consensus Economics' *Consensus Forecasts*. The results are as follows.

> US expected premium 1979–99: 2.1 per cent (standard deviation 1.3 per cent) per half-year.
> Realised premium: 4.2 per cent (12.8 per cent) per half-year.
> UK expected premium 1982–99: 2.1 per cent (1.2 per cent) per half-year.
> Realised premium: 2.5 per cent (12.0 per cent) per half-year.

Once again, the results suggest that investors were pleasantly surprised, especially in the United States. The much greater volatility of the realised premium is also apparent.

Evidence from highly leveraged transactions

Kaplan and Ruback (1995) offer interesting indirect evidence about the size of premium assumed by companies and their advisers in the United States in the 1980s. They compare the actual 'transaction value' in a sample of fifty-one highly leveraged transactions (HLTs) during 1983–89 with, in each case, various estimates of the discounted value of the future cash flows. Most of the transactions are management buy-outs of listed companies. The transaction value is the market value of the equity and debt, plus fees for the transaction, minus the value of cash and marketable securities held by the bought-out firm. The cash flow forecasts are taken from prospectuses. The main 'capital cash flow' figure they use is the after-corporation-tax cash flow to equity, plus interest on debt. The forecast terminal value – the forecast market value of the equity and debt as at the end of the year of the most distant explicit cash flow forecast – is estimated by assuming that the forecast capital cash flow for the terminal year will grow at a nominal rate of 4 per cent p.a. in perpetuity.

It is possible to use the forecast cash flows to infer the actual discount rate used to arrive at the transaction value in each case, and the equity premium assumed can be inferred from the discount rate. The premium is for unlevered equity, since the cash flows discounted include interest. The authors divide each inferred premium by the estimated market-wide asset beta (the average beta of all shares as though they had no debt) to arrive at an estimated premium for a (levered) share with a beta of one – i.e. an estimated market premium. The median is 7.8 per cent p.a., close to the median historic premium from 1926 to the year of each transaction. So it looks as though the *ex ante* premiums used in valuing these HLTs were estimated by the historic arithmetic mean premium for the period after 1926. This evidence is not consistent with other studies, such as that by Claus and Thomas (2001), which find that the expected premium in the 1980s was around 3 per cent p.a.

The authors are concerned that the cash flow forecasts in the prospectus may be rigged, though they do not find evidence for this from various tests for bias in the forecasts. However, Cornell (1999, p. 117) notes that high discount rates may be used in HLTs to compensate for the illiquidity of the capital invested and that investors in HLTs during the boom years of the late 1980s may, in general, have been over-optimistic in their cash flow forecasts. Such optimism could imply that the inferred discount rates are biased upwards, though it could imply, instead, that the management buy-out (MBO) companies were overvalued.

Discussion

Most of the studies reviewed above indicate a range for historic *ex ante* expected premiums in the United Kingdom and United States of between 1.5 per cent and 4.5 per cent p.a. – considerably below the actual arithmetic mean premium since 1920, and especially since 1950, but in line with what one would expect from the dividend discount model. Three explanations have been offered for the discrepancy. The first is that unexpected inflation caused the real risk-free rate to be lower than expected (Siegel, 1998; Wilkie, 1995). Yet one would have expected the nominal yields on treasury bills to adjust upwards as inflation rose, to maintain a stable real rate. If this is accepted, an implicit part of the inflation explanation is the view that the US and UK governments managed to keep real rates lower at times than the real rates would have been in a free money market. The second explanation is that capital gains on equity exceeded the rate of dividend growth, which implies that the expected rate of return on equity must have been falling towards the end of the century (Blanchard, 1993; Fama and French, 2002). The third is that the growth rate of dividends and earnings was higher than expected (Fitzgerald, 2001; also Dimson et al., 2002, chap. 13).

5.4   Predictions from consumption-based theory

5.4.1   The standard model

The Mehra–Prescott experiment
From a theoretical perspective, the problem with a real equity premium of 6 per cent p.a. or more is that it is difficult to construct a plausible-seeming model that predicts such a premium. The first paper to demonstrate this was by Mehra and Prescott (1985). They estimate that the arithmetic mean real return on equity in the United States during 1889–78 was 7.0 per cent p.a. and the mean real risk-free rate was 0.8 per cent, so the equity premium was 6.2 per cent p.a. They investigate whether a consumption-based model of expected returns can predict a similar premium and risk-free rate using reasonable assumptions about risk aversion and time preference.

The Mehra–Prescott version of the consumption-based model has been presented in Section 4.3.2. They use the model to predict the expected rate of return on equity and the expected risk-free rate. They assume that the growth rate g in consumption evolves according to a two-state process, with $g_{up} = 1 + \mu + x$ and $g_{down} = 1 + \mu - x$. The value for μ is the arithmetic mean annual change in real consumption per head during 1889–78 (1.8 per cent p.a.), the value for x is the standard deviation of the annual change (3.6 per cent p.a.). There is negative serial correlation of -0.14 in consumption per head, which is matched by making the probability next period 0.43 of the same state and 0.57 of the other state. So consumption behaves in the model as it did in reality. The remaining variables are the representative individual's coefficient of relative risk aversion γ and the discount factor δ of future utility. The authors experiment with a range of values that they and others regard as plausible. They note that previous research on individuals' utility functions finds values for γ in the range zero to two, but they experiment with values of γ between zero and a generous upper limit of ten. δ is set between zero and one.

The now famous result is that none of the combinations of plausible values for γ and δ produces a predicted premium anywhere near the realised premium of 6 per cent p.a. The maximum predicted premium, with $\gamma = 10$, is 0.4 per cent p.a. This is the (theoretical) equity premium puzzle. The authors also note that, if the risk aversion parameter γ is set high enough to produce a premium of 0.4 per cent p.a. or more, the model predicts a risk-free rate that is a long way above the observed mean real risk-free rate of 0.8 per cent. For example, for $\gamma = 2$, the predicted risk-free rate is at least 3.7 per cent p.a. This has become known as the risk-free rate puzzle.

The reason that a γ of ten or more is regarded as unreasonable is that it implies implausible aversion to large gambles in relation to consumption. For example, if the amount x to be won or lost in a fifty-fifty gamble is equivalent to 20 per cent of consumption, an individual with $\gamma = 10$ and constant relative risk aversion (equation (4.8)) will pay 69 per cent of x to avoid the gamble, which seems much too high. But if x is only 0.2 per cent of consumption, the individual with $\gamma = 10$ will pay only 1 per cent of x to avoid the gamble, and even with $\gamma = 50$ the proportion paid would only be 5 per cent. Thus, if variations in the amount invested in equity are small in relation to the typical investor's total wealth, high γ does not seem so unreasonable (Cochrane, 1997). In the Mehra–Prescott experiment, pay-offs to equity are assumed to provide *all* of the individual's consumption, so the uncertain pay-offs are equivalent to large gambles in relation to consumption. High values of γ are more acceptable in a model in which pay-offs to equity are small in relation to consumption.

Of course, people realised before 1985 that the historic equity premium was 6 per cent p.a. or more, but it may not have been thought to imply unduly high risk aversion. In the context of the standard CAPM, Friend and Blume (1975) have shown that the value of γ can be inferred from the 'market price of risk', $[E(R_M - R_F)]/\text{var}(R_M)$, and from the proportion of individuals' wealth invested in equity. Their argument is in continuous time, and can be expressed in discrete time as follows (Huang and Litzenberger, 1988, pp. 100–02). The expected utility from wealth at date 1 can be written as

$$E[U(W_1)] = E\{U[W_0((1 + R_F) + \theta(R_M - R_F))]\}$$

where W_0 is the market value of wealth at date 0, θ is the proportion of wealth invested in equity, and R_M is normally distributed. This will have a maximum assuming that the utility function is concave. The representative individual maximises expected utility with respect to choice of θ by setting the first derivative equal to zero:

$$\partial E[U(W_1)]/\partial \theta = E[U'(W_1)(R_M - R_F)] = 0$$

where $U'(W_1) = dU(W_1)/dW_1$. Since $E(xy) = E(x)E(y) + \text{cov}(x, y)$, the right-hand equality can be written as

$$E[U'(W_1)]E(R_M - R_F) = -\text{cov}[U'(W_1), R_M]$$

If two variables x and y are bivariate normally distributed and if $E[f'(x)] < \infty$, it is the case that $\text{cov}[f(x), y] = E[f'(x)]\text{cov}(x, y)$ – a result known as Stein's lemma. Using this result,

$$E[U'(W_1)]E(R_M - R_F) = -E[U''(W_1)]\text{cov}(W_1, R_M) \tag{5.4}$$

Since $W_1 = W_0[(1 + R_F) + \theta(R_M - R_F)]$, and R_F is a constant, $\text{cov}(W_1, R_M) = W_0\theta\text{var}(R_M)$. Equation (5.4) can now be written as

$$-W_0 E[U''(W_1)]/E[U'(W_1)] = [E(R_M) - R_F]/\theta\text{var}(R_M) \tag{5.5}$$

The left-hand side is an expression for the individual's relative risk aversion, γ (see Section 4.2.2). Friend and Blume, and others, find that the market price of risk $[E(R_M) - R_F]/\text{var}(R_M)$ is in the region of two, using historic data. They offer various empirical estimates for the proportion of household wealth invested in equity, most of which are in the range 0.5 to 0.8. Thus they estimate γ from equation (5.5) to be greater than two but with an upper limit around four.

However, the above analysis in a multiperiod setting implies a variance of consumption over time similar to that of wealth (Cochrane, 1997). A change in wealth implies a similar change in consumption, in order to maintain the equality of marginal utility from consumption and from wealth each period. But wealth per head is several times more volatile than consumption per head. If consumption were more volatile than it has been, the equity premium puzzle would not arise, as we now see.

Predictions assuming lognormal distribution of consumption and returns

The Mehra–Prescott experiment predicts expected returns using a consumption-based model with a Markov process for consumption. Another consumption-based model is derived assuming constant relative risk aversion and a lognormal distribution of consumption and asset returns (Section 4.2.2). Abel (1990) finds that the results of the experiment are almost the same if consumption growth is calculated with the same mean and variance as in Mehra and Prescott (1985) but has a lognormal distribution. The risk premium predicted by this model is

$$E(R_s) - R_F \approx \gamma \text{cov}[\ln(1 + R_s), \ln(\Delta C)] \tag{4.21}$$

where R_s is the contingent return on equity and $\Delta C = C_s/C_0$ the contingent change in consumption per head. Equation (4.21) can be rewritten, using the definition of covariance, as

$$E(R_s) - R_F \approx \gamma \sigma[\ln(1 + R_s)]\sigma[(\Delta C)]\text{corr}[\ln(1 + R_s), \ln(\Delta C)]$$

or

$$[E(R_s) - R_F]/\sigma[\ln(1 + R_s)] \approx \gamma\sigma[(\Delta C)]\text{corr}[\ln(1 + R_s), \ln(\Delta C)] \tag{5.6}$$

The left-hand side, the equity premium divided by the standard deviation of returns on equity, is known as the Sharpe ratio (Sharpe, 1966, proposed this ratio as an *ex post* measure of a portfolio's performance, replacing the excess return and standard deviation for the market with those for the portfolio). The actual Sharpe ratio for 1889–78 is $6.2\%/16.5\% = 0.38$ (Mehra and Prescott, 1985, table 5.1); the ratio for 1947–96 is $8.3\%/16.7\% = 0.50$ (Cochrane, 1997, table 5.1). The standard deviation of real consumption growth, $\sigma(\Delta C)$, is about 1 per cent p.a. and the correlation of consumption growth with equity returns, $\text{corr}[\ln(1 + R_s), \ln(\Delta C)]$, is 0.2 at most. To give a predicted value for the Sharpe ratio of 0.3 using these values in equation (5.6) requires a value for the risk-aversion parameter γ of 150! This way of expressing the puzzle makes clear the nature of the problem for the consumption-based model: the variation in consumption per head is much too small, and the correlation between consumption and returns on equity too low, to justify the size of premium observed. The observed standard deviation of real returns on equity is about 17 per cent p.a. – much higher than the standard deviation of consumption growth. But the volatility of equity is not much of a concern for investors whose annual consumption, in aggregate, fluctuates very little, unless they are extremely risk averse.

The consumption-CAPM expression for the risk-free rate is

$$R_F \approx \rho + \gamma E(\ln \Delta C) - 0.5\gamma^2 \mathrm{var}(\ln\Delta C) \qquad (4.16)$$

where ρ is the marginal rate of time preference, normally assumed to be close to zero. Experimentation with this equation shows that the predicted interest rate is very sensitive to the value of γ, and first rises with γ and then falls, as the third term on the right overtakes the second. Growth of real consumption per head was 1.8 per cent p.a. during 1889–78 and variance of consumption growth was 0.13 per cent p.a. Let us assume that ρ is 2 per cent p.a. Then the predicted real risk-free rate is 5.3 per cent p.a. for $\gamma = 2$ (fairly similar to Mehra and Prescott's 3.7 per cent p.a.), 13.5 per cent p.a. for $\gamma = 10$, and turns negative above $\gamma = 29$. Another problem with high γ is that it implies high sensitivity of the risk-free rate to changes in consumption, via the term $\gamma E(\ln\Delta C)$. This causes the model to predict a much more volatile risk-free rate over time than is observed.

Long-term horizon

Suppose we take the view that investors are not 'myopic'; they are interested in their wealth after many years rather than after one year. It is sometimes said that equity is less risky considered over many years than it is considered over one year, because it is less likely that the rate of return will be negative over many years. On this view the high historic premium is even more puzzling.

But the risk of the total return on equity is probably a better measure of risk than the probability of a negative rate of return is, and the risk of the total return increases with the holding horizon. Suppose that future annual returns are drawn from a normal distribution with a positive arithmetic mean R_A and variance var(R). The central limit theorem (CLT) says that the variance of the mean of a sample is equal to the variance of the sample divided by the number of observations, so in this case var$(R_A) = $ var$(R)/T$, where T is the number of years. As the anticipated holding period increases the variance of the expected mean annual return reduces, and it becomes more likely that the mean annual excess return for the holding period will be positive. This appears to support the notion that the risk of equity declines as the holding period increases. However, the variance of wealth at the end of T years, or the variance of the expected *total* (compounded) return over a holding period of T years, increases with T at the rate var$(R)T$. Assuming that long-term investors are interested in the risk (variance) of end-of-horizon wealth, then equity becomes more, rather than less, risky as the holding period increases. In fact, there is mild negative serial correlation in annual returns on equity, which means that the variance of total return increases at a somewhat slower rate than var$(R)T$, but the variance of the total return does increase with the holding period (Cochrane, 1997). Whether a given expected annual premium is viewed as excessive expected compensation for the variance of the total return at date T depends on the investor's assumed utility function, just as it does if the horizon is a single period.

Is the test fair?

Any test that asks the consumption-based model to explain an observed historic mean premium assumes implicitly that the historic premium is a fair estimate of the *ex ante* expected premium. We have discussed, in Section 5.3, the suggestion that the expected premium was only about half the observed premium for much of the twentieth century. This reduces the problem for the consumption-based model, but even an expected premium of 3 per cent p.a. is too high.

It has also been suggested that historic consumption volatility is a defective proxy for investors' expectations of consumption volatility. Mehra and Prescott model annual consumption as changing by one plus the mean growth rate plus or minus the standard deviation of the growth rate. This precludes dramatic changes on a year-by-year basis. Rietz (1988) adds to the consumption process the possibility of a 'crash state' – that is, a severe though unlikely fall in consumption from one year to the next. The experiment is otherwise unchanged. He finds that the possibility of a crash state results in predictions for the risk premium and risk-free rate that match the data with more plausible values for risk aversion. For example, the predictions match the data if the crash is a 25 per cent fall in consumption (with normal growth thereafter), the probability of such a crash is 1.4 per cent p.a., $\gamma = 9.0$ and $\delta = 0.995$. $\gamma = 9$ is still very high; if the crash were a 50 per cent fall in consumption, with 0.3 per cent p.a. probability, the model matches the data with $\gamma = 5.3$ and $\delta = 0.980$. Rietz notes that, during the Great Depression in the United States, real per capita consumption fell by 22 per cent of its pre-1929 value and production fell by 48 per cent, although these falls happened over four years rather than one.

However, theorists have generally accepted Mehra and Prescott's historic premium of 6 per cent p.a. at face value as a fair estimate of the expected premium, and have suggested modifications to the consumption-based model that might enable it to predict such a premium and a real risk-free rate of 1 per cent p.a., given the historic consumption volatility and other relevant data. Some of the types of modification are outlined below. Fuller reviews include those by Campbell (2000), Campbell, Lo and McKinlay (1997, chap. 8), Cochrane (1997) and Kocherlakota (1996).

5.4.2   Modified utility functions

Non-expected utility

We have so far assumed that consumers maximise lifetime expected utility, and expected utility in a given period is $\Sigma_s \pi_s U_s$, where U_s is the utility in state s and π_s is the probability of state s. Risk aversion is modelled by diminishing marginal utility from consumption in each state, as with the CRRA utility function. Uncertainty about future pay-offs affects lifetime expected utility in two ways. First, in a timeless context, the rate at which marginal utility diminishes (the curvature of the utility function) determines the degree of risk aversion to a gamble. Second, with time introduced, lifetime utility is also affected by the distribution of pay-offs over time, and this is true regardless of whether there is uncertainty. Suppose that one hundred units of a perishable consumption good will be given to someone across two time periods, and that the instalments are certain. With diminishing marginal utility per period, the total utility from this sum will be higher if fifty is paid at each date than if ninety is paid in one period and ten in the other. A high value of γ implies a strong preference for similar consumption per period, and a reluctance to reduce consumption in one period in exchange for more in another (inelastic intertemporal substitution). Hence the rate at which marginal utility per period diminishes determines both the degree of risk aversion and the elasticity of intertemporal substitution. Expected utility from future consumption is also affected by the rate of time preference, which determines the discount factor δ.

It is possible to derive a non-expected (Epstein–Zin) utility function that includes separate parameters for the degree of risk aversion and for the elasticity of intertemporal substitution. This is an important innovation, but it does not appear to solve the premium puzzle. Weil (1989) shows that the risk aversion parameter affects the size of the predicted equity premium but does not affect the predicted risk-free rate, at least if consumption growth per period is identically and independently distributed. Thus, a two-parameter utility function does offer a way out of the problem identified by Mehra and Prescott that an increase in γ in the CRRA function increases both the premium and, up to a point, the risk-free rate. One can find values for the two parameters (for risk aversion and intertemporal substitution) that result in predictions of a high premium and low risk-free rate that approximately match reality. The value for the intertemporal elasticity parameter, 0.1, is considered to be realistic, but the required risk aversion parameter is implausibly high at around 45, using the same model and data for consumption growth as Mehra and Prescott. With a risk aversion parameter of 1 and the same intertemporal elasticity parameter, the predicted premium is 0.45 per cent p.a. and the predicted risk-free rate exceeds 20 per cent p.a. Weil concludes that the non-expected utility function he studies does not alleviate the risk premium puzzle, and that there is indeed a risk-free rate puzzle. The empirical estimates of an intertemporal elasticity of 0.1 suggest that consumers are very averse to intertemporal substitution, in which case the risk-free rate should be higher than observed. Average growth of consumption per head is 1.8 per cent p.a., so the marginal loss of utility from sacrificing current consumption is high in relation to the marginal gain from extra consumption in the future, and a high interest rate is needed for individuals to be indifferent between less consumption now and more risk-free saving.

A more radically different utility function is proposed by Benartzi and Thaler (1995). Their paper takes a behavioural finance approach. Investors maximise 'prospective utility' rather than expected utility, and their utility functions display 'myopic loss aversion'. Utility from investment is determined by unrealised gains or losses, rather than by consumption or wealth, and hence it is affected by the length of the evaluation period – i.e. the interval between assessments of gains or losses. The loss of utility from an x per cent loss in value from one evaluation date to the next exceeds the gain from an x per cent gain in value. The absolute value of the portfolio is irrelevant. For an asset such as equity with more variability of annual returns and a higher probability of loss measured over short than over long periods, the prospective utility increases with the assumed evaluation period.

To examine the implications of assuming a prospective utility function, the authors draw with replacement 100,000 actual returns on equity and bonds from 1926–90 measured over intervals of between one and eighteen months. These give simulated distributions of returns appropriate for evaluation periods of between one and eighteen months. The authors experiment with various specifications of the prospective utility function, and find for reasonable measures of aversion to loss that equity is preferred to bonds for evaluation periods in excess of about one year. In other words, a lower premium than has been observed would be expected if evaluation periods were longer than one year. For example, this result holds if the utility function is simply

$$U(x) = x \text{ for } x \geq 0; U(x) = 2.77x \text{ for } x < 0$$

where x is the percentage change in portfolio value from one evaluation date to the next and 2.77 is a loss aversion factor. They appeal to clinical experiments designed to ascertain preferences regarding gambles to defend a loss aversion factor between two and three. They argue that it is plausible that many investors, both individual and institutional, do assess their returns once a year, and that therefore the equity premium observed during 1926–90 is consistent with a market with prices set by investors with prospective utility. They also find that the prospective utility of an investor with an evaluation period of one year is at or close to the maximum with a portfolio invested between 30 per cent and 55 per cent in equity, with the rest in long-term government bonds. They note that this is the same range as the equity weighting of major US investing institutions.

Habit

Several authors have modified the utility function in such a way that a fall in consumption towards a certain level causes a massive loss of utility, so the individual is very averse to such a fall. The justification for this is the notion that utility from consumption in a given period is affected by the level of consumption that a person is used to, as well as by the amount consumed. A link can be made with the fact, noted earlier, that equity values are much more volatile than consumption per head. The observed size of the equity premium suggests that people are averse to the volatility of equity, even though, for most people, most of their income for consumption does not come from equity, and so the volatility of equity has only a minor impact on their consumption. The habit idea suggests that, if the impact, though minor, is severe enough to threaten or to exacerbate a threat to a person's lifestyle, that person may be very averse to the risk of equity.

An example of a model with habit is that of Campbell and Cochrane (1999). The representative individual has a modified utility function; the lifetime utility to be maximised is given by

$$U = E_0 \left[\Sigma_{t=0}^{\infty} \delta^t \frac{(C_t - X_t)^{1-\gamma} - 1}{1 - \gamma} \right] \tag{5.7}$$

where C_t is the agent's endowed consumption in period t, which is uncertain in advance, and X_t is consumption in period t given by habit. X_t is treated as external to the individual. We can read equation (5.7) as saying that the average standard of living enjoyed by others affects the individual's utility. The authors define the 'surplus consumption ratio' S_t as

$$S_t = (C_t - X_t)/C_t$$

The risk aversion parameter (curvature of the utility function) for period t is given by

$$\eta_t = -\frac{C_t U''(C_t, X_t)}{U'(C_t, X_t)} = \frac{\gamma}{S_t} \tag{5.8}$$

Hence the individual becomes more averse to risk as consumption approaches the habit level (S_t falls). The increase in risk aversion accelerates the increase in the expected return on equity as consumption falls. Marginal utility is given by

$$MU_t = dU_t(C_t, X_t)/dC_t$$
$$= (C_t - X_t)^{-\gamma}$$
$$= S_t^{-\gamma} C_t^{-\gamma}$$

Thus, the stochastic discount factor (Chapter 4) is

$$m_{t+1} = \delta \frac{U'(C_{t+1}, X_{t+1})}{U'(C_t, X_t)} = \delta \left(\frac{S_{t+1}}{S_t} \frac{C_{t+1}}{C_t} \right)^{-\gamma} \tag{5.9}$$

The distribution of the log of consumption growth is assumed to be normal around mean g:

$$\ln(C_{t+1}/C_t) = g + v_{t+1} \tag{5.10}$$

where v_{t+1} has a mean of zero and a constant variance for all t. Let $\ln(C_t) = c_t$ and $\ln(S_t) = s_t$. The process governing the evolution of the log of the surplus consumption ratio, s_t, is crucial because it determines how the log of X_t, the habit level, evolves in response to changes in consumption. The process is specified in such a way that the real risk-free rate is constant and that consumption never falls below the habit level (otherwise utility is not defined). The specified process for s_t is

$$s_{t+1} = (1 - \varphi)s + \varphi s_t + \lambda(s_t)(c_{t+1} - c_t - g) \tag{5.11}$$

where s is the steady-state value of the surplus consumption ratio, φ is a parameter that determines the autoregression of s_t, and $\lambda(s_t)$ is a 'sensitivity function'. Equation (5.9) can be rewritten, using equations (5.10) and (5.11), as

$$m_{t+1} = \delta(G)^{-\gamma} \exp[-\gamma(s_{t+1} - s_t + v_{t+1})]$$
$$= \delta(G)^{-\gamma} \exp\{-\gamma[(\varphi - 1)(s_t - s) + (1 + \lambda(s_t))v_{t+1}]\} \tag{5.12}$$

where $G = E(C_{t+1}/C_t)$. The fact that the distribution of s_{t+1} is affected by the outcome s_t means that the utility function (equation (5.7)) is not 'time separable'; the function differs at different dates, and depends on the surplus consumption ratio at the previous date.

The reason for wanting a constant risk-free rate is to avoid the risk-free rate puzzle: real rates have in practice been small and varied little compared with returns on equity. A constant risk-free rate is achieved by specifying the sensitivity function $\lambda(s_t)$ such that its value increases as s_t approaches zero. Thus, for a low consumption outcome at date t, and hence a low surplus consumption ratio, the surplus consumption ratio at date $t + 1$ becomes more sensitive to future deviations in consumption from the expected growth rate (see equation (5.11), last term in brackets). More volatile s_{t+1} implies smaller expected utility from consumption at $t + 1$, and higher marginal utility. This implies a larger marginal utility from risk-free saving, since risk-free saving increases future consumption by a fixed amount. In other words, the precautionary motive for saving is stronger.

We know from equation (4.3) that the risk-free interest rate is given by

$$1 + R_{Ft} = 1/E_t(m_{t+1})$$

It is possible for the risk-free rate to be constant because m_{t+1} is affected by two offsetting forces as consumption changes (see equation (4.17)). A fall in consumption at date t increases the marginal utility from consumption at date t, which acts to reduce m_{t+1}. But, as explained above, a fall in consumption is also associated with an increase in uncertainty about s_{t+1}, which increases the marginal utility from risk-free saving and acts to increase m_{t+1}. $\lambda(s_t)$ is specified such that the two effects offset each other exactly.

Equity is modelled as a claim on the consumption stream, so equity pay-offs are distributed in the same way as consumption. The variance of the surplus consumption term in equation (5.9) is much greater than the variance of the consumption term. This causes the variance of the stochastic discount factor, and hence the expected return on equity, to be much greater than in the standard consumption model without the habit term, for a given value of γ. Although the expected value of the stochastic discount factor, $E_t(m_{t+1})$, is constant by construction, the expected return on equity is higher and varies over time. For this reason, the model has the capacity to predict a high and variable premium alongside a low and constant risk-free rate. The expected return on equity varies because the greater sensitivity of the surplus consumption ratio to changes in consumption as consumption falls acts to increase the variance of m_{t+1} (equation (5.12)). This increases the expected return on equity, since (i) the pay-off on equity is consumption, (ii) consumption and the surplus consumption ratio are positively related, (iii) the surplus consumption ratio and marginal utility at $t + 1$ are negatively related, and so (iv) the pay-off is negatively related to the stochastic discount factor. Then a higher variance of the surplus consumption ratio implies a higher variance of the stochastic discount factor, a lower present value of a given set of contingent pay-offs and a higher expected return on equity.

For example, suppose the pay-off on equity (consumption at date 1) is 120 or 80 with equal probability. If $m_{t+1} = 0.95$ in both states, the present value of equity is 95 and the expected return is 5.3 per cent. Now suppose that $m_{t+1} = 0.70$ in the up state and 1.2 in the down state. $E_t(m_{t+1})$ remains at 0.95, but the present value of equity is 90 and the expected return is 11.1 per cent.

The model is used to produce simulated data for 500,000 months. The mean growth in real consumption per capita (g = 1.9% p.a.) and its standard deviation (σ_g = 1.2% p.a.) are set to replicate the historic US values for 1947–95. The arithmetic mean real risk-free rate of 0.9 per cent p.a. and the equity premium of 6.7 per cent p.a. during the period can, given the values of g and σ_g, be predicted almost exactly by setting $\gamma = 2.0$, $\delta = 0.89$ and $\varphi = 0.87$. The authors demonstrate that the simulated data display several features observed in the real data – for example, the positive relation between dividend yield and returns on equity measured over several subsequent years.

The reason for the high premium is very high risk aversion, which is measured in this model not by γ ($= 2.0$) but by η_t in equation (5.8). The parameter values result in a steady-state value for S of around 5.7 per cent, which gives a value for η_t of thirty-five at the steady state and which rises towards infinity as S_t falls towards its minimum of zero. With S of 5.7 per cent, habit levels (X_t) are quite close to actual consumption, so small-scale volatility in the equity pay-off (consumption) has a large effect on expected utility through the assumed collapse in an individual's welfare in possible states of the world with consumption at or just above the habit level. So the Campbell–Cochrane model does not solve the equity premium puzzle, in the sense of predicting a high premium without invoking very high risk aversion. It does offer a solution to the risk-free rate puzzle – it predicts a high premium combined with a constant and low risk-free rate – and the high premium does not require that the hypothesised variation in consumption be higher than the observed variation in consumption.

Habit and term premiums

Abel (1999) presents another complex habit-persistence model, in which the one-period real interest rate is allowed to vary. This allows some of the equity premium over the short term (treasury bill) rate to be explained as a term premium (the arithmetic mean excess return of long-term government bonds over treasury bills was 1.70 per cent p.a. in the Mehra–Prescott data). A second feature is that equity is modelled as a levered asset, so that the pay-off to equity is more volatile than consumption per head. This makes it possible for the model to predict a premium on levered equity of 6 per cent p.a. with a coefficient of relative risk aversion of eleven.

The habit level of consumption per head, X_t, is given by

$$X_t = C_t^{\gamma 0} C_{t-1}^{\gamma 1} (G^t)^{\gamma 2}$$

where $0 \leq \gamma_0, \gamma_1, \gamma_2 \leq 1$ and $G \geq 1$; G is a constant growth rate. If $\gamma_1 > 0$, X_t depends partly on consumption in the previous period. Abel derives expressions for the expected return on a 'canonical asset', which can make certain or uncertain payments over T periods. The payment on asset j in period t is represented by $a_{jt} y_{jt}^\lambda$, where $a_{jt} \geq 0$ is a constant and $y_{jt} > 0$ is a random variable. If $\lambda = 0$, the payments are certain. Unlevered equity is represented by $T = \infty$, $a_{jt} = 1$ for all t, and $\lambda = 1$. Levered equity has $\lambda > 1$. The term premium is the expected one-period return on an asset with $T > 1$, less the expected return on an asset with the same λ and with $T = 1$ (i.e. a one-period asset). A term premium will exist in the model if $\gamma_1 > 0$, so that utility is affected by the level of consumption per head in the previous period. The reason is that such an intertemporal link creates negative serial correlation between marginal utility in adjoining periods, and therefore between the stochastic discount factor and the interest rate in these periods. An increase in consumption in period t implies a relatively low marginal utility from consumption in that period but raises the habit level of consumption for period $t + 1$. The rise in the habit makes it more likely that the marginal utility from consumption at $t + 1$ will be relatively high. If there is no relation between utility from consumption across time periods, so that the stochastic discount factor varies independently from one period to the next, there is no term premium.

It may not be obvious why a term premium would ever arise in the case of an asset that provides certain real pay-offs, since there is no inflation risk. To help see why, let us consider a simple example.

Example

A one-period asset pays a real sum of £100 at date 1; a two-period asset pays £100 at date 2. Suppose first that the individual's consumption is equally likely to go up or down each period by 10 per cent (no serial correlation), and that the individual has CRRA utility with $\gamma = 2$ and $\delta = 0.9$. Then the value of the stochastic discount factor is $m_{up} = 0.9(C_{t+1}/C_t)^{-\gamma} = 0.9(1.1)^{-2} = 0.743$ in the up state and $m_{down} = 0.9(0.9)^{-2} = 1.112$ in the down state. The price of the one-period asset at date 0, $P_{one,0}$, is

$$P_{one,0} = E_0(m_1)£100$$
$$= [0.5(0.743) + 0.5(1.112)]£100$$
$$= £92.75$$

so the return is 7.82 per cent. The price of the two-period asset is

$$P_{two,0} = E_0(m_1)P_{two,1}$$

At date 1 the two-period asset has become a one-period asset, and its price will be £92.75 in each state. Thus the return on the two-period asset is 7.82 per cent each period; there is no term premium.

Now suppose instead that there is negative serial correlation between marginal utility in adjoining periods, as would arise in a habit-persistence model. There is now a 60 per cent probability that a rise in marginal utility will be followed by a fall, and a 40 per cent probability that a rise will be followed by a rise. In the first period a rise or fall remains equally likely, so the return on the one-period asset is 7.82 per cent, as before. The expected return on one-period assets in subsequent periods is also 7.82 per cent. Consider the two-period asset at date 1, when it is a one-period asset. If consumption rises in period 1, we have

$$P_{two,1}(up) = E_{1,up}(m_2)£100$$
$$= [0.4(0.743) + 0.6(1.112)]£100$$
$$= £96.44$$

where $E_{1,up}$ means the expected value at date 1, conditional on a rise in consumption. If consumption falls,

$$P_{two,1}(down) = E_{1,down}(m_2)£100$$
$$= [0.6(0.743) + 0.4(1.112)]£100$$
$$= £89.06$$

So the price at date 1 now differs across the states. But the expected price of the two-period asset at date 1 is £92.75, and the expected return in period 2 is 7.82 per cent.

The return on the two-period asset in period 1 is no longer certain, as it depends on the asset's price at date 1. The price of the two-period asset at date 0 is found from

$$P_{two,0} = E_0(P_{two,1}m_1)$$
$$= 0.5(£96.44)(0.743) + 0.5(£89.06)(1.112)$$
$$= £85.34$$

The expected return on the asset in period 1 is $0.5(£96.44/£85.34) + 0.5(£89.06/£85.34) - 1 = 8.68\%$. Hence there is a term premium on the two-period asset of 0.86 per cent in period 1. The reason is that its price at date 1 is negatively related to marginal utility; it is lower when the marginal utility is higher, when the asset is 'needed most'. To compensate for this loss of expected utility compared with the expected utility from a fixed payment at date 1, the expected return on the two-period asset has to be higher to provide the same expected utility as the one-period asset. If the changes in consumption were to exhibit positive serial correlation, the correlation between price and marginal utility would be positive and there would be a negative term premium. For a further discussion of term premiums, see Campbell, Lo and McKinlay (1997, section 11.1).

5.4.3   Market frictions

Disaggregated consumers
So far we have analysed aggregate demand for assets by considering a representative agent. But if the effect of economic shocks is not felt evenly across the population, data on changes in aggregate consumption will understate the volatility of consumption as experienced by individuals. This may help to reconcile the facts of a large equity premium with small fluctuations in aggregate consumption, as is demonstrated by Mankiw (1986) using a simple model. There are two periods, and consumption per capita in period 1 can take either of two equally probable values, C and $(1 - \varphi)C$, where $0 < \varphi < 1$. An asset's pay-offs are $1 + prem$ in the good state, in which C arises, and -1 in the bad state, in which $(1 - \varphi)C$ arises. $0.5prem$ can be thought of as the risk premium on the asset. To induce a consumer to hold the asset, the premium must be large enough for the utility gained in the good state to be equal to the utility lost in the bad state:

$$0 = (1 + prem)U'(C) - 1U'[(1 - \varphi)C]$$

where

$$U'(C) = dU(C)/dC.$$

This gives an equilibrium level for $prem$ of

$$prem = \{U'[(1 - \varphi)C] - U'(C)\}/U'(C)$$

which will be positive, since the marginal utility of consumption in the bad state exceeds the marginal utility in the good state.

So far this is a standard model with a representative agent. The modification introduced by Mankiw is to allow for the fall in aggregate consumption of φC in the bad state to be concentrated amongst a fraction λ of the population. This requires an assumption that the risk of a selective fall in consumption cannot be diversified away or insured against – i.e. it requires an implicit assumption of market frictions. Then the individual's consumption in the bad state is C with probability $1 - \lambda$ and $(1 - \varphi/\lambda)C$ with probability λ. If $\lambda = 1$, all individuals have the same consumption in the bad state and we are back with the representative-agent model. If $\lambda = \varphi$, the shock is so highly concentrated that the consumption of individuals affected by the negative shock falls to zero. Thus greater concentration of the shock implies a smaller value of λ. For example, if $\varphi = 0.05$ and $\lambda = 0.1$, a 5 per cent fall in aggregate consumption arises because 10 per cent of the population suffers a 50 per cent fall in per capita consumption. Each individual will now hold the asset only if

$$0 = (1 + prem)U'(C) - (1 - \lambda)U'(C) - \lambda U'[(1 - \phi/\lambda)C]$$

which implies that the premium is

$$prem = \lambda\{U'[(1 - \varphi/\lambda)C] - U'(C)\}/U'(C)$$

If utility is quadratic, λ has no effect on *prem*; but, otherwise, *prem* is negatively related to λ, because $\partial\, prem/\partial\lambda < 0$ (so long as the third derivative of the utility function is positive). So the premium rises if the fall in consumption is concentrated in a smaller proportion of the population. If $\lambda < 1$, the premium will be higher than would be inferred from a representative-agent model ($\lambda = 1$). Assuming a utility function with constant relative risk aversion and a coefficient $\gamma = 3$, *prem* would be 4.2 times higher than the value inferred with $\lambda = 1$.

A natural way to disaggregate consumers is to separate shareholders from non-shareholders. About one-quarter of individuals in the United States own shares. Their consumption may be more sensitive to stock market returns, and they form one of the major groups of traders in the market, directly involved in the setting of share prices. Mankiw and Zeldes (1991) use data on food consumption as a proxy for consumption of all goods and services. They have data for the years 1970–84. They find that the consumption of shareholders is both more variable and more correlated with returns on the stock market than is the consumption of non-shareholders. They use an equation similar to equation (5.5) to infer the coefficient of relative risk aversion γ for the shareholder group, and they find that $\text{cov}(R_{Mt} - R_{Ft}, \Delta C_t)$ is three times as large for shareholders as for all individuals. If this were true for the whole period 1890–1979 that Mehra and Prescott have studied, and if share prices were set by the shareholder group, a coefficient of relative risk aversion of 'only' six would be needed for the consumption-based model to predict a premium of 6 per cent p.a. However, it is not easy to measure the effects of the changes in stock market wealth on consumption, as is apparent from Poterba's (2000) review of the evidence.

Disaggregated consumers and transactions costs

Some papers introduce market frictions explicitly. Aiyagari (1993) and Heaton and Lucas (1996) explore two frictions that might help a consumption-based model to predict a larger premium. The first is to assume that markets for claims on labour income do not exist, so that individuals must self-insure against idiosyncratic shocks to labour income. This increases individual-specific uncertainty about future consumption (var($\ln \Delta C$) in equation (4.16)), which in turn increases precautionary saving, which in turn tends to lower the risk-free rate. However, with zero costs of trading financial assets, it is possible to eliminate the uncertainty caused by transitory shocks to labour income through appropriate saving and dis-saving. The second friction is to introduce costs of trading. Aiyagari assumes that trading in shares is costly whereas trading in risk-free assets is free. This increases the difference between the required rate of return on shares, measured before transactions costs, and the required rate on risk-free assets. But Heaton and Lucas find from simulations that 'imposing a cost in one market alone has a negligible impact on asset prices' because 'agents trade almost exclusively in the frictionless market' (p. 459). They explore a model that assumes the existence of labour income in the absence of employment insurance, and the existence of transactions costs for both equity and risk-free assets.

Individuals have CRRA utility. To model idiosyncratic shocks, Heaton and Lucas examine an economy with two (classes of) people. Both aggregate income (from labour and capital) and each person's share of aggregate income vary period by period. The process is determined by a Markov chain, with parameters set so that the characteristics of simulated aggregate labour income, income from capital and individual-level income match those of US household data for 1969–84.

The transactions cost function in the stock market says that trading costs per share increase with the number of shares traded; a justification of this is that more liquid assets will be traded first. The cost per £1 traded also falls with aggregate income. This keeps the cost per share approximately constant over time, since aggregate income and the share price both have an upward trend.

Transactions costs in the risk-free bond market are the spread between the lending and borrowing rates. Selling bonds represents borrowing, and only the person who borrows pays transaction costs. The spread is paid each period, so there is a transaction cost in having a loan outstanding, and it increases with the amount borrowed. The supply of bonds is zero, which means that, in any period, one of the people will be borrowing from the other. The upper limit on borrowing is set at 10 per cent of the income per person.

Heaton and Lucas explore the implications of a variety of parameter settings by means of numerical (Monte Carlo) simulations, with the economy allowed to evolve for 1000 years. They first establish that, if labour income is uninsurable and no trading in financial assets is allowed, individual consumption is much more volatile than aggregate consumption, and an equity premium of 8.2 per cent p.a. is predicted with $\gamma = 1.5$ and $\delta = 0.95$ in the CRRA utility function. But, with frictionless trading in financial assets, the volatility of individual and aggregate consumption are similar to one another, and the predicted premium is tiny. Transactions costs are associated with a higher volatility of individual consumption and with a higher premium. With the average trading cost for shares at 5.0 per cent of trade value, and the average spread on a loan at 4.2 per cent p.a., the simulated rate of return on equity is 7.9 per cent p.a. compared with a rate of return to lenders of 2.8 per cent p.a. So the simulated premium is 5.1 per cent p.a. gross of trading costs in shares (4.8 per cent p.a. net; only a minority of shares are traded each period). The simulations indicate that, using settings in the transactions cost functions that reflect real-world transactions costs, the equity premium is 3.0 per cent p.a. Hence the authors conclude that, if there is no insurance of labour income, reasonable estimates of transactions costs can explain about half the observed historic premium.

With risk aversion relatively low ($\gamma = 1.5$), the premium is due mainly to the direct effect of transactions costs rather than to risk aversion. The expected annualised cost of marginal trading in shares and the spread on borrowing are approximately equal. The premium is the difference between the expected rate of return on shares gross of costs and the risk-free rate for the lender, which is lower than the rate paid by the borrower. Most of this difference is due to the expected annualised cost for the saver of buying shares at the margin and then selling them at some point, when the individual has to dis-save.

Discussion

Attempts to reconcile consumption-based models with the historic premium are amongst the most challenging theories we examine. The papers considered in Section 5.4 are only a sample, and we have given only a flavour of them. The ideas that we have examined are that people are very averse to threats to their lifestyle or habit level of consumption; that some of the equity premium is a term premium; that individual consumption varies over time more than aggregate consumption per head; and that transactions costs in financial markets can account for some of the premium. A point that emerges is that consumption-based research appears, at this stage, to be some way from arriving at an *agreed* model that fits the data reasonably well, or that would help in practical estimation of the cost of equity. But, then, the expected equity premium is an elusive number; it is unobservable, it probably varies over time and across investors, and it appears that estimates of mean historic premiums are not a reliable guide to the (unconditional) mean expected premium.

5.5   Summary

This chapter has reviewed several topics related to the equity risk premium. It was first established that the *ex ante* premium in the cost of equity is an expected one-period excess return. If past premiums are used to estimate the expected premium, the correct estimator is the arithmetic mean premium rather than the geometric mean. We then reviewed evidence on the historic premium, which suggests that the realised premium has been around 5 to 6 per cent p.a. There is evidence that the historic premium has turned out to be larger than was expected, especially in the second half of the twentieth century.

The fourth section showed why standard consumption-based models do not predict a mean premium anywhere near as large as a historic mean of several per cent per annum, and then discussed the various modifications to the consumption-based model that have been made in an effort better to match predictions to the data. This continues to be an active area of research. The evidence that investors have been surprised by the degree of the outperformance of equity compared with government bonds is probably part of the answer to the difficulty that consumption-based models have in predicting an expected premium in the region of 6 per cent p.a.

Part II
A Project's Cost of Capital

6   Project valuation

The first part of the book has been concerned with the expected return on capital regarded as a financial asset, in the setting of a theoretical capital market. There is a shift in perspective at this point, from the pure theory of what determines the expected returns on assets in an artificial world, to more applied theory regarding the use and determination of discount rates in project valuation. The contingent-states abstraction provides a rich environment for analysis, which yields theories of how the expected returns on assets are determined. But it cannot be used directly for the purpose of estimating the cost of capital of a real project. The analyst could perhaps think of a project as providing different pay-offs in different future states, but he would have no means of estimating the state prices of the postulated states (the prices of elementary contingent claims). We need a way of thinking about discount rates that connects both with the theory of expected returns and with what is feasible in terms of estimation, of a project's cash flows and of expected returns on other assets. We are concerned now with the determination of the cost of capital of a particular project, not with the analysis of equilibrium, so the expected returns on existing assets are taken as given.

The main bridge between the world of theory and the real world has, to date, been the standard CAPM. The reason, presumably, is that the model offers the best available combination of theoretical grounding and ease of use in practice. It is not necessarily the 'best' model of asset pricing from either a theoretical or a practical perspective. One criterion for assessing a model is its generality. In the context of both consumption-based analysis and arbitrage pricing theory, the standard CAPM is a special case. Another criterion is the degree of empirical support. Multifactor models are much more successful at explaining cross-sectional and time-series features of observed returns. From the practical point of view, the CAPM is not the only way to estimate the expected rate of return on a share, and may not be the best way, as discussed in Part III.

The big selling point of the CAPM is that it offers a relatively user-friendly measure of risk. Theory and intuition say that the expected return on an asset is positively related to its risk (if investors dislike risk). An asset's beta in the standard CAPM is a measure of risk that is correct in a theoretical world, given certain assumptions, and that can be estimated in the real world. A large body of applied theory has developed that assumes that the CAPM is true, or, at least, that it is a satisfactory method of estimating the cost of equity. It may be that one of the multifactor models on offer will take over as the standard applied model of expected returns, but this does not seem to have happened yet (see Section 12.1).

The remainder of this chapter considers a variety of issues that arise in project valuation as we make the valuation problem more realistic. The chapter sets the scene for the subsequent five chapters, which introduce taxes, then inflation, and then multiple countries, as we continue the attempt to understand the cost of capital for real projects.

6.1   The valuation model

This section discusses the theoretical basis of the standard valuation model, before any complications such as taxes are introduced. Perhaps the most important point in this section is that the standard discounting procedure involves an implicit assumption that uncertainty regarding cash flows increases with the length of time into the future when a cash flow is predicted to materialise.

6.1.1   Multiperiod discounting

Most projects provide cash flows at different dates, so we need to consider discounting in a multiperiod setting. Chapter 2 established that, with one future period, the cost of capital $E(R_s)$ is the expected return that determines the project's market value V_0 for a given expected pay-off at date 1, $E(Y_s)$:

$$V_0 = E(Y_s)/[1 + E(R_s)] \qquad (2.2)$$

We now suppress the state subscripts s, and introduce dates for the cash flows, so equation (2.2) becomes

$$V_0 = E(Y_1)/[1 + E(R)]$$

The standard valuation model for a project with a life of T periods is

$$V_0 = \Sigma_{t=1}^{T} E(Y_t)/[1 + E(R)]^t \qquad (6.1)$$

assuming an identical cost of capital in each period. Equation (6.1) follows from the argument that the constant opportunity cost of capital is the expected one-period return on an asset of the same risk, $E(R)$. Consider a project that pays an uncertain cash flow Y_t at each date t. As at date $T - 1$ its market value is

$$V_{T-1} = Y_{T-1} + E(Y_T)/[1 + E(R)]$$

As at date $T - 2$ its value is

$$\begin{aligned} V_{T-2} &= Y_{T-2} + [E(Y_{T-1}) + E(V_{T-1})]/[1 + E(R)] \\ &= Y_{T-2} + E(Y_{T-1})/[1 + E(R)] + E(Y_T)/[1 + E(R)]^2 \\ &= Y_{T-2} + \Sigma_{t=1}^{T} E(Y_t)/[1 + E(R)]^t \end{aligned}$$

and so on back to date 0. So its value at date 0 is as given in equation (6.1). The value is such that, given the expected cash flow in each period $E(Y_t)$, the expected one-period return on capital at each date is equal to the cost of capital – namely the expected one-period return on an asset of the same risk. The project creates wealth if the initial value V_0 exceeds the initial cash cost of the project, I_0 – i.e. if net present value is positive. Equivalently, the project creates wealth if the internal rate of return exceeds $E(R)$, the hurdle rate. The internal rate of return is calculated using the expected values of the cash flows and is found from

$$I_0 = \Sigma_{t=1}^{T} E(Y_t)/(1 + IRR)^t \tag{6.2}$$

given I_0 and $E(Y_t)$ for each date t. If $V_0 = I_0$, then $E(R) = IRR$. But the use of IRR in capital budgeting is problematic if the expected cash flows to be discounted are not all positive, as was discussed in Section 1.2.

It is worth repeating that the expected one-period return $E(R)$ on an asset is the expected arithmetic mean return of the future returns over T periods. This is greater than the expected value of the geometric mean return, $E(R_G)$:

$$E(R_G) = E\big[\Pi_{t=1}^{T}(1 + R_t)\big]^{1/T} - 1$$

where R_t is the uncertain return on the asset in period t.

Example
Suppose a project costs £100 and will either increase in value by 75 per cent or decrease in value by 50 per cent each year, with equal probability. The project offers a single uncertain pay-off after three years. The possible pay-offs and their probabilities are determined by the possible sequences of increases and/or decreases in value over the three years:

£535.94	(12.5%)
£153.13	(37.5%)
£43.75	(37.5%)
£12.50	(12.5%)

The expected one-year return is $75\%(0.5) - 50\%(0.5) = 12.5\%$. This is the expected value of the arithmetic mean return observed over a number of years. It is also the rate of return that gives the expected value of the pay-off, £142.38:

$$E(R) = (£142.38/£100)^{0.33} - 1 = 12.5\% \text{ pa}$$

as in equation (6.1).

The expected geometric mean over three years is the weighted average of the rates of return that result in each possible pay-off. The highest possible rate of return, for example, is 75 per cent p.a.; there is a 12.5 per cent chance of receiving £535.94, in which case the investor will have received a rate of return of 75.0 per cent p.a. The weighted average of the rates of return is

$$E(R_G) = 0.125(75.0\%) + 0.375(15.3\%) + 0.375(-24.1\%) + 0.125(-50.0\%)$$
$$= -0.2\% \text{ pa}$$

which is lower – in this case much lower – than the expected one-year return.

The difference between the expected one-period return and the expected geometric mean raises the fundamental question of whether investors *should* be concerned with the expected one-period return. Should a project's cost of capital be the expected one-period return on an asset of the same risk, or the expected geometric mean on such an asset? How exactly should the risk of an asset be measured? Concern with the expected one-period return can be justified by the argument that investors maximise lifetime utility by making investment decisions with a one-period horizon. But this is the case only under certain restrictive assumptions (Section 4.3.1). Suppose an investor intends to keep the project for a large number of periods – for example, because selling it would be very costly. In this case it could be argued that the hurdle rate should be the expected geometric mean return on an asset of the same risk calculated over T periods, the life of the project, to compare with the project's expected geometric mean over T periods. A similar effect is achieved by working with log returns, and comparing the expected one-period return on the cash invested, expressed as $E[\log(1 + R_{inv})]$, with a hurdle rate expressed as $\log(1 + R)$. Markowitz (1977), from whom the above numerical example is adapted, recommends that long-term investors select a portfolio H that maximises $E[\log(1 + R_H)]$.

6.1.2   Application of the CAPM

Fama (1977) argues that the standard CAPM can be used as the model for the discount rate only under the assumption that the discount rates for future periods are certain. The discount rates need not necessarily be constant, but they must all be known in advance. The reason is as follows. For the CAPM to be a correct model of asset pricing in the multiperiod context, the expected returns across assets at the start of a period must be related to their period-specific market betas only, in line with the CAPM – equation (3.11). A requirement for equation (3.11) to hold is that investment opportunities at a given date must be independent of the returns realised during the period just ended; otherwise the risk of an asset relevant to its price will not be determined exactly by its period-specific market beta. The possible return on an asset can be uncertain, but only because of uncertainty about the cash flow next date and about the expected value of future cash flows as at the next date. If the discount rate (expected return) is uncertain, this implies an 'inadmissible' relation between the return realised during period t and the expected return during period $t + 1$, as in the intertemporal CAPM (Section 4.3.2). The relation would exist because the return during t depends on the realised value of the asset at the end of t, which depends partly on the discount rate for $t + 1$. Such a relation would be inadmissible in the sense that expected returns would not be given by the standard CAPM. One reason why is that, if the risk-free rate were allowed to be uncertain, the expected return on an asset would depend partly on its covariance with the risk-free rate (Bogue and Roll, 1974).

If the discount rate for project j is a constant rate $E(R_j)$ given by the CAPM, the risk-free rate, the market price of risk $[E(R_{Mt}) - R_{Ft}]/\text{var}(R_{Mt})$, and $\text{cov}(R_{jt}, R_{Mt})$ must all be certain. The argument also implies that there are conditions on the admissible evolution of uncertain project value, including any cash flow each period. Consider, for simplicity, a project that provides a single uncertain pay-off Y_{jT} to shareholders at date T. Its present value at any date t dates before T is given by

$$V_{jT-t} = E_{T-t}(Y_{jT})/[1 + E(R_j)]^t$$

where $E(R_j)$ is constant, for simplicity, as well as certain. V_{T-t} must evolve over time as an independent random variable, otherwise the realised value at one date could affect the expected return for the next period:

$$V_{jT-t+1} = E_{T-t}(Y_{jT})(1 + e_{jt+1})/[1 + E(R_j)]^{t-1}$$

where e_t is a random variable and $E_t(e_{t+1}) = 0$. In addition, $\text{cov}(e_{jt+1}, R_{Mt+1})$ must be known in advance, as this determines $\text{cov}(R_{jt}, R_{Mt})$, which must be constant if $E(R_j)$ is constant.

Fama (1996) adds a further twist concerning the implied distribution of future pay-offs. The argument from Fama (1977) is that admissible uncertainty about future pay-offs implies that the expected value of a single pay-off at date T evolves according to

$$E_{t+1}(Y_T) = E_t(Y_T)(1 + e_{t+1})$$

For $E_t(Y_T)$ to evolve in this way, each of the possible pay-offs at date T must be given by

$$Y_{aT} = E_t(Y_T)\Pi_{t=1}^{T}(1 + e_{at})$$

where the a subscript is a label for a possible payoff Y_{aT} and the time sequence of e terms that produces Y_{aT}. Y_{aT} is a convex function of the geometric mean of e_{at}; an x per cent increase in the geometric mean produces a larger increase in Y_{aT} than the fall produced by an x per cent decrease. The convexity means that the distribution of possible Y_T's must be skewed to the right, so median(Y_T) is below $E_t(Y_T)$, if $E_t(Y_T)$ is to be discounted using the CAPM. Thus, for a horizon more than one period ahead, the assumed distribution of possible net cash flows should *not* be symmetric; $E_t(Y_T)$ should exceed the median value of Y_T.

In the real world, the discount rate is not known for certain. In addition, someone forecasting possible future cash flows will probably not be thinking about the statistical properties of the distribution. It is not easy to establish the implications of the points in this section for discounting in practice. Fama (1996, p. 426) comments that 'in a world of uncertainty, the rigorous justification for estimating values by discounting expected pay-offs with CAPM . . . expected 1-period simple returns is fragile'. But he goes on to note that this is a relatively minor problem in the estimation of value in practice.

6.1.3   *Risk premium and time horizon*

The present value of a project is normally written as the expected cash flows discounted by the cost of capital (equation (6.1)). The discount rate has two components: the risk-free rate and a risk premium. It is, therefore, via the discount rate that the effects on present value are felt of both the time value of money and the expected premium to compensate for risk. For this reason, the cost of capital is sometimes referred to as a *risk-adjusted discount rate*, in contrast to the risk-free rate, which reflects the time value of money only.

The calculation in equation (6.1) involves an implicit assumption about the effect of the length of future time on the degree of present uncertainty about the project's future values and cash flows, as will now be explained. An alternative to equation (6.1) is to write present value as a series of *certainty-equivalent* cash flows discounted by the risk-free rate. Adjustment for risk is then made via the future value to be discounted rather than via the discount rate, which now reflects only the time value of money. The risk premium is represented as the difference between the expected value of an uncertain future cash flow, $E_0(Y_T)$, and its certainty-equivalent cash flow, $CE_0(Y_T)$. The certainty equivalent is the amount such that the individual is indifferent between a claim to receive the uncertain pay-off Y_T and a claim to receive the certain pay-off $CE_0(Y_T)$. Assuming that $E_0(Y_T)$ is discounted at a constant risk-adjusted rate R, the present value of $E_0(Y_t)$ can be written either as $E_0(Y_T)/(1 + R)^T$ or as $CE_0(Y_T)/(1 + R_F)^T$, where R_F is the risk-free rate. R_F is assumed to be constant, and so the risk premium $R - R_F$ is also assumed to be constant. So we can write

$$E_0(Y_T) = CE_0(Y_T)(1 + R)^T/(1 + R_F)^T \tag{6.3}$$

Equation (6.3) makes a crucial point about the normal practice of discounting cash flows, which was first noted by Robichek and Myers (1966) and emphasised later by Hodder and Riggs (1985). The assumption of a constant risk premium in the discount rate assumes implicitly that the expected compensation for risk measured in terms of the future cash flow – the difference between $E_0(Y_T)$ and $CE_0(Y_T)$ – grows at the rate $(1 + R_E)/(1 + R_F) - 1$ per period as one looks further into the future. For example, suppose R is 10 per cent p.a., R_F is 5 per cent p.a., and we are considering two pay-offs, one with an expected value of £100 after one year and the other with an expected value of £100 after five years. From equation (6.3), $CE(£100_1) = £95.5$ and $CE(£100_5) = £79.2$, so the present value of the compensation for risk increases from $£4.5/1.05 = £4.3$ for the year 1 payment to $£20.8/1.05^5 = £16.3$ for the year 5 payment. This is appropriate so long as it is in fact believed that the size of the payment becomes more uncertain the further into the future the payment is expected to be received, with uncertainty increasing at around the rate of $(1 + R)/(1 + R_F) - 1$ per period. Put another way, the belief is that uncertainty will be resolved at this rate as time elapses. If the resolution of uncertainty at approximately a constant rate is felt to be reasonable, at least roughly, then the normal discounting procedure in equation (6.1) is also reasonable. But if a project is such that cash flows 'further away' are viewed as becoming more uncertain at a diminishing rate, or not at all, then the normal procedure will bias the estimate of value downwards, possibly very seriously.

It follows that adjustments for risk should not be made to expected cash flows if a risk-adjusted discount rate is being used. In particular, it would be a mistake to reduce the expected value of a pay-off as the time horizon lengthens, merely because it will arise further into the future. The use of a risk-adjusted discount rate already builds in an assumption that uncertainty increases as the time horizon lengthens, as we have just seen.

6.1.4   *Valuation using certainty equivalents*

There is a circularity in using the CAPM as it is normally written as the discount rate to value a project. This is because the beta formula, $cov(R_j, R_M)/var(R_M)$, is written in terms of the possible returns on the project. But reference to returns assumes that the project's value is already known. The certainty-equivalent version of the valuation model avoids this circularity.

The CAPM can be written as

$$E(R_j) = R_F + \lambda \text{cov}(R_j, R_M)$$

or

$$V_{j0} = E(V_{j1})/[1 + R_F + \lambda \text{cov}(R_j, R_M)] \tag{6.4}$$

where R_j is the return on the market value of project j, $(V_{j1} - V_{j0})/V_{j0}$, and λ is the market price per unit of covariance risk, $[E(R_M) - R_F]/\text{var}(R_{Mt})$. The covariance term can be rewritten as

$$\text{cov}(R_j, R_M) = E\{[(V_{j1} - E(V_{j1}))/V_{j0}][R_M - E(R_M)]\}$$
$$= (1/V_{j0})\text{cov}(V_{j1}, R_M)$$

Substituting in equation (6.4),

$$V_{j0} = E(V_{j1})/[1 + R_F + \lambda(1/V_{j0})\text{cov}(V_{j1}, R_M)]$$
$$- [E(V_{j1}) - \lambda \text{cov}(V_{j1}, R_M)]/(1 + R_F) \tag{6.5}$$

which is the certainty-equivalent formula for V_{j0}, $E(V_{j1}) - \lambda \text{cov}(V_{j1}, R_M)$ being the certainty-equivalent value of $E(V_{j1})$.

Suppose that project j provides the single pay-off Y_{jT}. Its value on date $T - 1$ is

$$V_{jT-1} = [E_{T-1}(Y_{jT}) - \lambda \text{cov}(Y_{jT}, R_{MT})]/(1 + R_F)$$

from equation (6.5). Let us assume that the project's covariance risk is known in advance and constant, and let $\sigma_{jM}^* = \text{cov}(Y_{jT}, R_{MT})/E_{T-1}(Y_{jT}) = \text{cov}(V_{jt}, R_{Mt})/E_{T-1}(V_{jt}) = \text{a constant}$ for all t. This is not the same as $\text{cov}(R_j, R_M)$; it is the covariance of the value, per unit of its expected value, with the return on the market. The project's value on date $T - 2$ is then

$$V_{jT-2} = E_{T-2}(V_{jT-1})(1 - \lambda \sigma_{jM}^*)/(1 + R_F)$$
$$= E_{T-2}\{[E_{T-1}(Y_{jT})(1 - \lambda \sigma_{jM}^*)/(1 + R_F)](1 - \lambda \sigma_{jM}^*)/(1 + R_F)\}$$
$$= E_{T-2}(Y_{jT})[(1 - \lambda \sigma_{jM}^*)/(1 + R_F)]^2$$

and for any date $T - t$

$$V_{jT-t} = E_{T-t}(Y_{jT})[(1 - \lambda \sigma_{jM}^*)/(1 + R_F)]^t \tag{6.6}$$

This is the certainty-equivalent version of equation (6.1) (Fama, 1977).

We can now use the certainty-equivalent model to gain some insights into the determination, in theory, of a project's discount rate. The certainty-equivalent value of a cash flow T dates ahead is

$$CE_0(Y_{jT}) = E_0(Y_{jT})(1 - \lambda \sigma_{jM}^*)^T \tag{6.7}$$

from equation (6.6). The value of $1 - \lambda\sigma^*_{jM}$ can written using equation (6.3), substituting R_j for R:

$$CE_0(Y_{jT}) = E_0(Y_{jT})[(1 + R_F)/(1 + R_j)]^T$$

therefore

$$1 - \lambda\sigma^*_{jM} = (1 + R_F)/(1 + R_j)$$
$$R_j = (1 + R_F)/(1 - \lambda\sigma^*_{jM}) - 1 \tag{6.8}$$

Equation (6.8) shows that the relation between R_j and σ^*_{jM} is non-linear (Hull, 1986; equation (6.8) is the same as his equation 6). If σ^*_{jM} negative, $R_j < R_F$, and as the absolute value of the negative σ^*_{jM} rises R_j approaches -1, which means that value approaches infinity. If σ^*_{jM} is positive $R_j > R_F$, and R_j increases with σ^*_{jM} at an increasing rate. If σ^*_{jM} becomes large enough that $\lambda\sigma^*_{jM} > 1$, R_j changes from a huge positive value to a huge negative value; present value changes from just above zero to just below zero (for $T = 1$). The switch in sign appears counter-intuitive: one would expect the discount rate to tend towards infinity as risk increases. However, a negative discount rate is understandable; it arises because the project might produce negative cash flows – i.e. demands for payments from the owner. A negative discount rate arises when the certainty-equivalent value of the pay-off is negative, given a positive expected value and a positive risk-free rate, as can be seen from equations (6.7) and (6.8). A negative certainty-equivalent value means that the investor would, if necessary, be willing to pay to avoid undertaking the project despite the positive expected pay-off. He would pay to avoid a project if the possible demands for payments were sufficiently large and likely, just as he would pay to avoid a sufficiently risky gamble with a positive expected pay-off.

The non-linearity in the relation between R_j and σ^*_{jM} becomes pronounced when the expected value of the cash flows is small in relation to the possible future cash flows. Such a project is one with a significant likelihood of negative cash flows; Hull emphasises the case of a project with high fixed costs. In such cases, the possible percentage returns on the project are enormous in relation to the possible percentage returns on the market. A small percentage change in $\text{cov}(Y_{jt}, R_{Mt})/E_{t-1}(Y_{jt})$ can then induce a much larger percentage change in $\text{cov}(R_{jt}, R_{Mt})$. The project beta, and therefore the discount rate, will have a very large absolute value, which could run into hundreds of percent (for positive discount rates). This makes the valuation of such a project more than normally problematic. Present value is especially sensitive to changes in negative discount rates (Gallagher and Zumwalt, 1991). A negative rate between 0 per cent and -100 per cent means that present value exceeds expected future value, so if the expected cash flow is several periods in the future a small change in a negative rate will make a very large change in present value. Worse, a negative rate below -100 per cent means that the sign of the present value depends on the number of future periods.

The non-linearity of the relation between R_j and σ^*_{jM} seems odd in the light of the CAPM prediction of a linear relation between expected return and risk. The key to resolving this is the fact that the covariance between pay-off or value and market return,

$\sigma^*_{jM} = \text{cov}(Y_{jt}, R_{Mt})/E_{t-1}(Y_{jt})$ is not the same number as the covariance between project return and market return, $\text{cov}(R_{jt}, R_{Mt})$. The CAPM predicts a linear relation between R_j and $\text{cov}(R_{jt}, R_{Mt})$. As we have seen, the relation between $\text{cov}(Y_{jt}, R_{Mt})/E_{t-1}(Y_{jt})$ and $\text{cov}(R_{jt}, R_{Mt})$ is non-linear. So a non-linear relation between R_j and σ^*_{jM} is not inconsistent with the CAPM. The switch in sign of R_j at a sufficiently high risk also looks peculiar in the context of the CAPM. But what has happened is that the value of the asset has turned negative, so it would not be held (the project would not be undertaken). The derivation of the CAPM assumes an equilibrium in which all assets are held, so they all have a positive value.

6.1.5   Negative cash flows

The treatment of an expected negative cash flow – an expected payment to be made – requires care. If $E(Y_t)$ is negative, an increase in systematic risk measured by an increase in $\text{cov}(Y_t, R_{Mt})$ means that possible cash flows tend to be smaller (less negative) when market returns are high, and large (more negative) when market returns are low. An increase in $\text{cov}(Y_t, R_{Mt})$ appears to imply a higher discount rate. The problem is that discounting a negative expected value by a higher discount rate results in a less negative present value, which is the wrong way round. The higher $\text{cov}(Y_t, R_{Mt})$ is, the more the commitment to pay reduces expected utility, because the payments to be made are large when market returns are low. So the present value of the payment should become more negative as $\text{cov}(Y_t, R_{Mt})$ rises (the investor would pay more to avoid having to make the uncertain payment).

The answer to this is that, if $E(Y_t)$ is negative, the covariance risk is measured by $\text{cov}(-Y_t, R_{Mt})$, not by $\text{cov}(Y_t, R_{Mt})$ (Ariel, 1998; Patterson, 1995, pp. 202–04). $\text{Cov}(-Y_t, R_{Mt})$ is the covariance as though $E(Y_t)$ and the possible cash flows had the opposite sign and were positive. $\text{Cov}(-Y_t, R_{Mt})$ has the opposite sign to $\text{cov}(Y_t, R_{Mt})$, so if $\text{cov}(Y_t, R_{Mt})$ is positive a higher value for $\text{cov}(Y_t, R_{Mt})$ means a more negative value for $\text{cov}(-Y_t, R_{Mt})$. Since it is $\text{cov}(-Y_t, R_{Mt})$ that should be used in the CAPM, an increase in $\text{cov}(Y_t, R_{Mt})$ is associated with a *lower* discount rate.

The argument for using $\text{cov}(-Y_t, R_{Mt})$ in the CAPM if $E(Y_t)$ is negative is that this gives a consistent valuation of the expected cash flows from the point of view both of the payer and the recipient. A cash outflow from the payer is an inflow for the recipient. In equilibrium, the absolute present value of the outflow must be equal to the present value of the inflow, which implies that the discount rate is the same irrespective of the sign of $E(Y_t)$. The discount rate would not be the same if $\text{cov}(Y_t, R_{Mt})$ had one sign for the payer ($E(Y_t)$ negative) and the opposite sign for the recipient ($E(Y_t)$ positive). In the case of a project, the payer is the project's owner and the 'recipient' is the project.

Let us recap. If $\text{cov}(Y_t, R_{Mt})$ increases, $\text{cov}(-Y_t, R_{Mt})$ becomes more negative, as noted. The discount rate falls, and the present value of the negative expected cash flow becomes more negative. This makes sense from the owner's perspective. The possible negative cash flows will be relatively small (less negative) when market returns are high, and large if market returns are low. This is harmful for the owner. It makes sense from the recipient's perspective too. The fall in the discount rate makes the present value of the positive expected cash flow larger. The possible cash flows will be relatively large when market returns are low, which is beneficial for the recipient.

6.1.6   Bias caused by uncertainty about the discount rate

Uncertainty in estimates of value is caused by uncertainty about both future cash flows and the discount rate. Butler and Schachter (1989) and Cooper (1996) point out that uncertainty about the discount rate causes project value to be biased upwards, if the discount rate chosen is an unbiased estimate.

The point can be put like this. Suppose that projects all have the same discount rate R^*, which is estimated with error but without bias. Then the average project value over many projects will be higher than if the true discount rate R^* had been used. The reason is that $E[1/(1+R)] > 1/[1+E(R)] = 1/[1+R^*]$. For example, suppose that R^* is 10% and that R is estimated to be either 15% or 5%, with equal probability, so $E(R) = 10\%$. Then $E[1/(1+R)] = 0.911$, whereas $1/(1+R^*) = 0.909$. Thus uncertainty about the discount rate causes upward bias in estimates of value. The bias is positively related to the number of periods T, to the size of the discount rate and to uncertainty about the discount rate.

Butler and Schachter, and Cooper, provide estimates of discount factors that give unbiased estimates of value, based on realistic data on the size and uncertainty of discount rates. Their calculations suggest that the downward bias in values is not large. For example, Cooper finds that, for a discounting horizon of ten years, the cost of equity implied by a discount factor that gives an unbiased estimate is less than half a percentage point higher than the arithmetic mean historic return on equity. For a discount rate of 10.0 per cent p.a., an increase to 10.5 per cent p.a. reduces present value by less than 5 per cent p.a.

6.1.7   Note on real options

Part of the value of a firm in a dynamic setting, making investment and disinvestment decisions on an ongoing basis, is the value of its real options. A real option is an option on a project: the opportunity to undertake a new project, or to sell or suspend an existing project. Some projects may themselves have real options embedded in them. For example, suppose that undertaking project k in the future will not be possible unless project j is undertaken first. Part of the market value of j is the call option it provides on k. The discounted cash flow model of valuation is not the correct model to value real options. Their value can, in principle, be estimated by methods akin to the Black–Scholes or binomial methods used to value financial options. But these methods do not involve the cost of capital, so for this reason we do not consider the valuation of real options.

6.2   Capital: equity and debt

It is now time to say more about the arrangements under which projects are financed – i.e. provided with capital. Projects in the private sector are undertaken by companies or firms (we use the terms interchangeably, though in UK legal parlance a firm is a partnership).

A company does not normally have a single project; it can be seen as a collection of ongoing and potential projects. Each project has its own risk and therefore its own cost of capital, in principle. The parent's cost of capital is not applicable to a particular project, unless parent and project are of similar risk. We shall say more about this in Section 7.5.2 and in Part III, but elsewhere we shall leave to one side the distinction between a company and a project.

Companies raise two main types of capital, equity and debt, which differ because they are different types of financial asset; they differ in the rights they carry and in the nature of the claims they provide to future payments from the company. Companies sometimes raise capital by issuing securities that are neither ordinary shares nor debt, such as preference shares, shares with special voting rights, bonds convertible into shares, and equity warrants. The expected rates of return on such hybrid securities are not considered in this book (some are discussed in Copeland, Koller and Murrin, 2000, chap. 10).

6.2.1   Equity

The salient features of equity are that the shareholders are the owners of the company and that equity is the riskiest form of capital. The contract under which equity capital is provided is the constitution of the company, set out (in the United Kingdom) in the Memorandum and Articles of Association. These documents specify the rights of the shareholders and the powers of the directors. Some aspects of the constitution are common to all companies and are important in defining the nature of equity.

- The shareholders are the owners and collectively have control, ignoring agency problems for the moment, and assuming that the company is not in receivership. The feature of shares that gives the shareholders control is the entitlement to vote at general meetings of the company, for example, on appointments to the board of directors, matters of strategy and changes in the constitution. Ordinary shares carry one vote per share and are much the most common type of share, at least in the United Kingdom and United States, and we assume that all equity is in the form of ordinary shares.
- Shareholders enjoy the protection of limited liability. The most a shareholder can lose is the amount of cash he has paid for his shares; a company's creditors have no recourse to the shareholders if its assets are insufficient to pay in full what the company owes.
- Companies have a legal identity that is separate from the identity of the shareholders or staff. This greatly facilitates the transfer and trade of shares, amongst other things.
- The concept of default does not apply to equity. In particular, the payment of dividends is not a contractual obligation, unlike the payment of interest. Dividends are at the discretion of the board, which ultimately is controlled by the shareholders.
- Equity gives a claim to the company's residual cash flows – i.e. the cash inflows during a given year net of all the outflows. The net cash flow is a residual because it is what is left over after everyone else has been paid. Net cash flow is either retained or is paid out to shareholders. In the event of a liquidation, the shareholders rank behind all other claimants on the proceeds from the liquidation. The fact that the net cash flows to equity are a residual is the reason why equity is the most risky form of capital.

Return on equity

There are two measures of the return on equity: the market return, and the accounting return. The market return on equity in a given period t, denoted R_{Et}, is the return obtained as a percentage of the market value of the equity at the start of the period:

$$R_{Et} = (V_{Et} + Div_t)/V_{Et-1} - 1$$

where V_{Et} is the market value of the equity at date t (the end of period t) and Div_t is the total dividend or other cash payment to shareholders from the company, if any. The accounting return on equity in period t, denoted ROE_t, is

$$ROE_t = PAT_t/BV_{t-1}$$

where PAT_t is the profit after corporation tax and BV_t is the book value of equity, the shareholders' funds in the balance sheet. The market return is the return on equity viewed as a financial asset – the percentage return a shareholder actually receives in a given period. The accounting return is a measure of the company's operating performance.

Cost of equity

A project's cost of equity is defined analogously to the cost of capital. It is an opportunity cost: the expected rate of return that can be obtained from investing in another asset with the same risk as the project's shares. Neither the expected rate of return nor the risk of a risky asset can normally be observed, because they depend on unknown forecasts by investors of possible future returns. So they must be estimated; a project's cost of equity cannot be known precisely.

The expected rate of return on a financial asset is the expected market return. So a project's cost of equity is compared with the expected market rate of return on the cash invested, in assessing whether the project creates wealth. The expected market rate on the cash is the internal rate of return given the expected cash flows (from equation (6.2)). The cost of equity cannot be compared with the accounting return on equity.

The concept of the cost of equity as an opportunity cost is entirely consistent with the assumption that companies exist to maximise shareholder wealth. The board of directors does not pay the shareholders for the use of the shareholders' funds; rather, the board is the agent of the shareholders, investing in the business in the same way as a shareholder would if he/she had the knowledge and expertise of the board. We are meant to imagine the board ceaselessly scanning the horizon for real projects with positive net present value, exactly as shareholders would be presumed to do were they in the position of the board.

It is common to view dividend payments as part or all of the cost of equity, by analogy with interest on debt. There is some sense in this. Capital has a cost, and the cash flows or dividends from a project are the way in which this cost is paid over the project's life (there may be no cash flows in some periods, or negative cash flows – requirements for more investment). However, the 'cost of equity' does not mean 'dividends' or 'return on equity'. A company paying no dividends does not have a zero cost of equity, and neither does a company that provides a negative return on equity. The cost of equity is an *ex ante* concept; it is an opportunity cost estimated in advance of observing the project's pay-offs, and is independent of the observed cash flows, unless the risk changes over time. The pay-offs will generally turn out to be higher or lower than the expected values of the cash flows. That means that the pay-offs to shareholders, not the cost of equity, will turn out to be higher or lower than their expected values.

For example, a venture capitalist might say that he looks to invest in companies that, on average, provide a return on equity of 40 per cent p.a. over five years, if they survive. The pay-off comes from selling the stake in the company. The venture capitalist's hurdle rate for investment is not as high as 40 per cent p.a., because a large proportion of investee companies do not survive for five years. The *ex ante* expected rate of return on the cash invested in a typical investee company is less than 40 per cent p.a., allowing for the possibility that the company will fail before the venture capitalist can sell it. Surviving companies that provide a rate of return of 40 per cent p.a. or more produce a higher rate than the expected rate.

A second point is that, although dividends are the means by which the cost of equity is paid, it is misleading to view dividends themselves as a cost. If a company's aim is to maximise shareholder wealth, and it has undertaken all available projects with positive NPV, the payment of dividends is its *raison d'être*. All its other outgoings are costs from the perspective of the shareholders, but not the payments that the shareholders themselves receive.

6.2.2   Debt

The defining feature of a debt contract is that default by the borrower, a breach of the contract, gives the lender the right to demand repayment. If repayment is not forthcoming, the lender is empowered to take control of the borrower in order to obtain repayment. If the borrower does not default, the lender has no control and no votes in meetings of the company. The most obvious case of breach of contract is failure to pay interest or principal when it falls due, but breach of contract can arise in many other ways. The rights conferred by ordinary shares are the same across all companies, but the terms of bank loans and bond issues are negotiable and vary considerably. The terms affect the riskiness of the debt and hence the cost of debt. Some of the more important headings are as follows.

- Maturity of the loan. All corporate debt contracts specify a date or dates on which the borrower undertakes to make repayments of principal.
- Security. Several types of security for the lender are possible.
- Covenants. Debt contracts can contain financial or other covenants that serve to strengthen the position of the lender by specifying events of default. For example, the contract may require minimum interest cover (operating profit divided by interest) of, say, two times. If interest cover falls below two, it is an event of default.
- Information. The contract may give the lender access to certain private information, such as monthly management accounts.

There is now a large theoretical literature on why debt and the various features of debt exist (see, for example, Hart, 1995).

Cost of debt

For a lender, the cost of providing debt finance is an opportunity cost, as is the cost of providing equity for a shareholder. The cost of a loan is the expected rate of return that can be obtained from investing in another asset with the same risk as the loan in question. If there is no default, the actual rate of return to the lender will turn out, *ex post*, to have exceeded the expected rate, which allowed for the possibility of default. Since the risk of a loan is determined in part by the terms of the loan contract, the cost of debt is specific to the loan in question, as well as to the borrower. This contract specificity of risk for debt is an important difference from equity, for which the 'contract' is the same across all ordinary shares.

The cost of debt from the company perspective is normally viewed as the rate of return promised under the contract; the interest rate on a bank loan, or the redemption yield on a bond at the date of issue. This promised rate will be the same as the expected rate only if there is zero risk of default; otherwise the promised rate will exceed the expected rate. For example, suppose a company issues a two-year bond, with face value of £100 and coupon of 10 per cent, at a price of £103.57. The chance that the issuer will default is estimated to be 2 per cent in each year. The redemption yield on a two-year risk-free government bond is 5.00 per cent p.a. The promised rate of return on the corporate bond is the redemption yield R_{prom}, found from

$$£103.57 = £10/(1 + R_{prom}) + £110/(1 + R_{prom})^2$$
$$R_{prom} = 8.00\% \text{ pa}$$

However, the expected rate $E(R)$ is

$$£103.57 = £10(0.98)/[1 + E(R)] + £110(0.98)^2/[1 + E(R)]^2$$
$$E(R) = 5.84\% \text{ pa}$$

Of the 3 per cent p.a. 'spread' between the yield on the risky bond and the yield on a risk-free bond, 2.16 per cent p.a. is compensation for the expected loss from default and 0.84 per cent p.a. is a risk premium – the expected reward for bearing the risk.

The correct rate to use for the cost of debt is the expected rate of return rather than the promised rate. This may seem odd, from the company's perspective. After all, if the company does not default, it will make payments of interest and principal in full when due, and the interest payments are cash costs. The answer to this is that it is expected cash flows that are discounted by the cost of capital – the weighted average cost of equity and debt (to be discussed in Chapter 7). If there is some chance of default, the possible cash flows from which the expected cash flows are estimated should include some outcomes in which cash flows are insufficient to meet the debt obligations. If the expected cash flows reflect the possibility of outcomes that cause default, but the cost of debt is the promised rate of return, the cost of debt is biased upwards in relation to the expected cash flows.

The expected rate of return on risky debt can, in principle, be modelled by the CAPM, and we shall make use of this in Chapter 7. An alternative approach is to estimate the probability of default and use this to estimate the proportion of the observed promised rate on the debt that is compensation for the expected loss from default. If the credit rating is known or can be estimated, the probability of default can be estimated from data on default rates of bonds, ranked by credit rating. But, in practice, it is difficult to estimate the expected rate of return on a loan, and many texts do not recommend trying to adjust the promised interest rate or redemption yield. The size of the resulting upward bias in the cost of debt is positively related to the risk of default.

The following chapters discuss the cost of debt in the context of the weighted average cost of capital and the effects of leverage and taxes. There are other issues relating to the cost of debt that we do not discuss. There are many choices to make when arranging debt finance, which will affect the terms of the loan contract or bond. In addition, the nature of the company's exposure to changes in interest rates can be managed via interest rate derivative products. Discussion of these points would take us into the areas of financial contracting and risk management. We are effectively treating debt as though it were a homogeneous type of asset. Another topic not included is the term structure of interest rates. One reason for drawing a line here is that the term structure with no default risk is easy to observe, unlike the risk premium on equity. Also, we have concentrated in Part I on single-period models of expected returns.

6.3   Financing and taxes

There are a number of decisions concerning the financing of a company that affect its market value, and that could be viewed as affecting its cost of capital. In particular, the company's choice of internal or external finance, level of leverage and corporate governance arrangements can affect its value via the corporate and personal taxes paid, agency costs, information costs and costs of financial distress. *Agency costs* include market value lost because management fails to act in a way that maximises market value, the costs of monitoring and bonding mechanisms to curtail such non-value-maximising behaviour, and the costs of the efforts of lenders to protect their interests. *Information costs* arise from 'information asymmetry': parties external to the company have less information about it than does the management, and information is costly to provide and absorb. *Costs of financial distress* arise when a company is having difficulty finding the cash to meet its obligations. Being in this 'distressed' state might cause a number of problems: the company might be forced to sell assets that it would not otherwise have sold, or to forgo worthwhile investment opportunities, or to renegotiate its debt on less favourable terms; it might experience difficulty in obtaining credit from suppliers, in retaining staff or in selling its products.

6.3.1   Definition of cash flows to discount

In principle, the effects on project value of taxes, agency, information and distress costs could be captured either in the expected cash flows or in the discount rate. The choice depends on the view taken with regard to the concept of the cost of capital. The broadest view is that taxes and financing-related costs are part of the cost of capital; the narrowest view is that the cost of capital is the expected rate of return on a financial asset of the same risk as the project, measured after all taxes and costs.

A broad view is a natural view to take and perhaps matches better what people normally mean by the 'cost of capital'. For example, Keane (1978, p. 351) writes that the term 'has come to denote a composite of two distinct categories of cost, (a) the *transaction costs* including taxation effects associated with individual financial instruments (the effects of market imperfections) and (b) the *interest* cost (the price of time and risk)'. The broad view underpins several familiar arguments. One argument is that the (weighted average) cost of capital is U-shaped with respect to leverage; there is a tax advantage to debt, but the marginal expected costs of financial distress are increasing with leverage, so that the cost of capital starts to rise beyond a certain level of leverage. A second argument is that the cost of capital differs between external and internal funds. There is strong evidence that companies prefer to finance investment from retained profits rather than borrow or issue shares, and that the expected rate of return on investment is considerably higher at times when they do resort to external finance. The evidence comes both from surveys of company management and from quantitative tests of models of corporate investment expenditure. For example, Fazzari, Hubbard and Petersen (1988) find that investment is more sensitive to free cash flow and liquidity in firms that retain all or most of their profit, have relatively high leverage and are growing relatively quickly, controlling for other factors affecting investment. They argue that such firms are already investing all or most of their retained profit and are at or close to the limit of their capacity to borrow comfortably. Rather than borrow more or issue shares, they curtail investment. The implication is that further external funds would be too expensive or impossible to obtain.

However, the broad view does not conform with the concept of the cost of capital as an opportunity cost. A decision that changes, say, the agency costs in a company will presumably change its market value, but it will not change the expected rate of return on another asset of the same risk. A decision that changes the risk of a company *will* change its cost of capital. Policies affecting taxes and financing-related costs are presumed to affect value by affecting cash flows rather than risk. For example, the U-shaped cost of capital argument is a hypothesis concerning the trade-off between smaller tax payments and higher expected costs of financial distress as leverage rises. Risk does not come into it (leverage affects the risk of the project's equity and debt, but not the risk of the total pay-offs to capital). So the opportunity cost concept implies the narrow view: the cost of capital is a rate of return determined in the capital market. This is the view we have adopted. The narrow view implies that the U-shaped cost of capital and the greater cost of external funds should be understood as points about financing-related costs, not about the cost of capital.

Investors are interested in (derive utility from) the pay-offs they actually receive, after all taxes and costs. For this reason, rates of return on financial assets are measured after all company-level taxes and costs. Thus the narrow view implies that we treat agency, information and distress costs as cash flow items, associated with the raising and using of capital, but not incorporated in the discount rate. Similarly, 'flotation costs' – i.e. fees to intermediaries for services associated with the raising of external funds – should appear in cash flows. The argument that the foregoing financing-related costs should be captured in the cash flows rather than the discount rate obviously does not imply that financing policies have no effect on company value. Nor should it be taken to imply that financing policies are unimportant. The argument is just that financing-related costs do not affect the cost of capital. This position is consistent with most of the finance literature; standard expressions for the cost of capital, including the CAPM and the weighted average cost of capital, do not incorporate financing-related costs. The implicit assumption must therefore be that such costs are captured in cash flows. A partial exception to this principle in the literature is the treatment of flotation costs, since some texts recommend adjusting the cost of capital for flotation costs (see Ehrhardt, 1994, pp. 131–39, for a discussion).

The conventional treatment of taxes, however, involves two compromises. Investors are concerned with returns on assets after the subtraction of all tax, whether paid by the company or by the asset holder. Thus, to be consistent with the treatment of financing-related costs, all tax payments should be captured in cash flows rather than in the discount rate. But this is not how tax payments have been treated in the corporate finance literature. The first compromise is that cash flows are measured after the payment of corporation tax but *before* the payment of personal tax, and the cost of capital is measured accordingly – i.e. after corporation tax and before personal tax. So the impact of personal taxes on project value is captured in the discount rate, not in the cash flows. The reason for this is probably that different groups of shareholders or lenders to the same company can be paying different rates of personal tax on their investment returns, so that their returns differ after personal tax. More than one expected rate of return, after personal tax, can be inferred for a given financial asset. This difficulty is avoided – or, at least, it is ignored – by measuring returns before personal tax.

The second compromise is that the saving of corporation tax from interest payments is also captured in the discount rate, not in the cash flows. The reason seems to be that this was the way that Modigliani and Miller (1963) analysed the tax-induced impact of leverage on value, and it has stuck. Yet their treatment is not consistent with the opportunity cost concept. The tax-induced impact of leverage is an effect of financing on cash flows, not on project risk.

The treatment of taxes outlined above means that personal taxes and the tax saving from debt are treated as factors affecting the cost of capital. It implies that dividend policy – via personal tax – and leverage policy – via corporation tax – affect the cost of capital, but that other financing decisions have no effect. This is, arguably, a messy situation. For example, in the U-shaped cost of capital argument, we have now put one of the two factors that determine the U shape back into the cost of capital (the tax advantage of debt) but kept the other one out (the costs of financial distress). Nevertheless, the above set of assumptions explains why, in most of the corporate finance literature, tax is seen as affecting value partly via the cost of capital, whereas other financing-related costs are seen as affecting value via cash flows. The example below illustrates the treatment of financing-related costs assumed in this book.

Example: treatment of financing-related costs

Suppose a project costs £70, to be financed by a share issue, and will produce a single cash flow, after operating costs, in one year's time with an expected value of £100. This figure is net of some agency costs. For example, the staff could produce a higher cash flow were they more diligent in seeking to maximise shareholder wealth; the operating costs include the cost of producing the annual report, which is needed so that the shareholders can monitor the project. The expected value of taxable profit is £30 ($= £100 - £70$) and the corporation tax rate is 40 per cent, so the expected amount of tax to be paid is £12. The cost of capital – the expected rate of return after corporation tax on equity of the same risk – is 10 per cent p.a. Investors pay personal tax on returns on financial assets, but both the cash flows and the cost of capital are measured before personal tax. It costs £5 to organise the share issue and to provide investors with a one-off fee for investigating the project. This £5 'flotation cost' cannot be set against taxable profit (if it could, the expected tax to be paid would be lower). Net present value is calculated as follows.

Expected cash flows in one year

Cash flow after operating costs, net of agency costs	£100	
Corporation tax	(£12)	£88
Present value of expected cash flow after tax ($=£88/1.1$)		£80
Initial costs		
Investment required	£70	
Costs of issue and investigation	£5	£75
Net present value		£5

6.3.2   Further issues

Information costs and other financing-related costs can cause tricky problems of interpretation. It may be helpful to explore this area a little further.

Bias in expected cash flow

Information asymmetry between firms and investors may cause investors to form expectations about a firm's future cash flows that are biased in relation to the expectations they would form were they as well informed as the managers. Bias could also be a result of investor sentiment. The effects on value and on the firm's cost of equity are analysed by Stein (1996). The bias is assumed to take the simple form

$$Y^b = E(Y)(1 + \delta)$$

where Y^b is the biased expected value of a cash flow next date with an unbiased expected value of $E(Y)$, and the bias, δ, can be positive or negative. The biased market value of this cash flow is

$$V^b = E(Y)(1 + \delta)/(1 + R_E^b) \qquad (6.9)$$

where R_E^b is the biased discount rate from the CAPM:

$$R_E^b = R_F + [\text{cov}(Y/V^b, R_M)/\text{var}(R_M)][E(R_M) - R_F] \tag{6.10}$$

Rearranging equation (6.9) to provide the certainty-equivalent valuation of the cash flow gives

$$V^b = \{Y^b - [\text{cov}(Y, R_M)/\text{var}(R_M)][E(R_M) - R_F]\}/(1 + R_F) \tag{6.11}$$

The unbiased value V^* for the cash flow is

$$V^* = E(Y)/(1 + R_E^*)$$

where

$$R_E^* = R_F + [\text{cov}(Y/V^*, R_M)/\text{var}(R_M)][E(R_M) - R_F] \tag{6.12}$$

Rearranging gives

$$V^* = \{E(Y) - [\text{cov}(Y, R_M)/\text{var}(R_M)][E(R_M) - R_F]\}/(1 + R_F) \tag{6.13}$$

Comparison of equations (6.11) and (6.13), and of equations (6.10) and (6.12), shows, respectively, that $V^b - V^*$ has the same sign as δ and that $R_E^b - R_E^*$ has the opposite sign to δ. For example, if δ is positive (investors are too optimistic) $V^b > V^*$ and $R_E^b < R_E^*$, since in this case $\text{cov}(Y/V^b, R_M) < \text{cov}(Y/V^*, R_M)$.

In this situation, investors think that the expected return on V is R_E^b, but the managers know that the unbiased expected return on V^b is $E(Y)/V^b - 1$. From equation (6.9),

$$E(Y)/V^b = \left(1 + R_E^b\right)/(1 + \delta)$$

Thus, if δ is positive the unbiased expected return on the biased price V^b is below R_E^b. We have seen that R_E^*, the unbiased expected return on the unbiased price V^*, exceeds R_E^b.

Now suppose that the company is considering investing in a new project of the same risk as the firm, and assume that investors will have the same optimistic bias about the new cash flows. One question that arises is the rate at which a new cash flow should be discounted. Stein argues that, if the aim is to maximise market value in the near future, the hurdle rate for new projects should be $[(1 + R_E^b)/(1 + \delta)] - 1$, assuming that managers discount unbiased cash flows. But, if the aim is to maximise market value in the long term, managers should ignore investors' transient biases and discount by the unbiased, higher rate R_E^*.

Share issue under asymmetric information

Suppose that the managers succeed in exploiting their information advantage by selling shares to new investors at a price that they know to be too high. The existing shareholders gain the difference between the price at which the shares were sold and the fair price. In this case it seems clearer to treat the share issue as having provided a windfall gain in cash to the existing shareholders than to say that the company's cost of equity is temporarily reduced. If the proceeds are used to finance a new project, management's better-informed estimates of the cash flows and the cost of equity should be used to value the project. The windfall gain is a 'transaction' between new and old shareholders that is separate from the project and should not affect its value. In fact, there need be no new project for a windfall to arise, if the shares are overvalued.

Capital rationing

Outsiders' lack of information, together with transactions costs, can mean that it is very costly or impossible to raise external capital. The problem is much more severe for smaller companies. If the financing-related costs are so high that it is impossible to obtain external funds, even for a wonderful project, the situation is one of 'hard rationing', and a curious logical problem arises. The company's only source of funds for investment is retained profits. In this situation, the cost of capital for a given project would appear to be the expected return on the next-best project. But the next-best project can be identified if the future lasts for one period only, because projects can be ranked by expected return only in the one period. With a multiperiod future, there is, in theory, a problem of circularity: NPV is a function of the discount rate in each future period, which requires identification of the marginal project each period, which cannot be done without knowledge of the discount rate. As Burton and Dammon (1974) show, the problem of simultaneously finding marginal projects and discount rates cannot be solved in a multiperiod setting with hard rationing. The problem disappears if a constant discount rate is assumed and is used to value projects, but the rate chosen will be somewhat arbitrary.

Capital rationing is imposed artificially by some multidivisional groups on their divisions or subsidiaries. Taggart (1987) argues that imperfect information within a group may make it rational for HQ to impose divisional budgets, rather than setting divisional hurdle rates – i.e. rather than using the cost of capital to make investment decisions. The budget approach need not be caused by external capital rationing. Imperfect information can engender agency problems; for example, Taggart shows that unpredictable bias – over- or under-optimism at divisional level – weighs against the use of hurdle rates (predictable bias can be allowed for in setting the hurdle rate). Also, divisional managers may not appreciate externalities in their investment decisions at group level – for example, limited managerial capacity at group level to cope with growth.

Costs of intermediation

Another issue is how costs of intermediation affect the cost of capital. Banks spend money on attracting deposits, making lending decisions, monitoring borrowers and dealing with bad debts; investment banks organise issues of securities; and fund management businesses and other investors incur costs, including the transactions costs of trading securities. Some of the costs of intermediation are covered directly in fees paid by companies for loans and issues of securities, and by suppliers of funds – for example, fund management fees. The remaining costs appear as a spread between the returns provided by financial assets and the returns net of costs received by the depositing/investing public. In the case of tradable assets, it is perhaps possible to make a distinction between the costs of trading the assets – i.e. the bid-ask spread and broker's fees – and the costs of investment services – i.e. fees for fund management and advice. It might then be argued that the latter are fees for extra services, which the investor does not need to pay to obtain access to the capital market, and that the bottom-line rate of return on an asset received by the investor is the rate net of taxes and trading costs. This suggests that the required rate of return on an asset is set with the rate measured after expected trading costs. But normal practice is to treat the cost of equity and cost of debt as the expected returns on the company's equity and debt gross of trading costs. Since trading costs vary across assets, being higher for less liquid assets, the liquidity of the assets a company has issued is a factor that affects its cost of capital (see, e.g., Amihud and Mendelson, 1986). However, the distinction between trading/liquidity costs and other intermediation services is more difficult to make in the case of assets that are not normally traded – for example, unlisted shares and bank loans.

6.4   *Ex ante* determinants of project beta

6.4.1   *Decomposition of risk based on factors affecting profit*

A natural question to ask in the context of the CAPM is what determines a project's equity beta *ex ante*. This is distinct from the issue of how beta is estimated *ex post*, which is considered in Chapter 13. One approach is to apportion sensitivity to market returns to three sources: (i) sales sensitivity – the covariance of sales with returns on the market, or, alternatively, with economy-wide sales; (ii) the project's operating leverage – the sensitivity of its operating profit or cash flow to changes in sales; and (iii) its financial leverage. (i) and (ii) together explain the *business risk* of the project; the leverage constitutes the *financial risk*. Business risk in the CAPM is defined as the unlevered project's beta, its *asset beta*; financial risk is measured by the difference between the levered project's equity beta and its asset beta. Analysis of the effect of leverage on equity risk goes back to Modigliani and Miller (1958), and is discussed in the next chapter. The decomposition of business risk into sales sensitivity (or 'intrinsic business risk') and operating leverage originates with Lev (1974) and Rubinstein (1973). Callahan and Mohr (1989) and Myers (1977) review studies of the determinants of beta.

Several authors express the above three-way partition of risk in terms of accounting numbers. For example, Mandelker and Rhee (1984) posit that the return on a share can be proxied by the profit after tax, *PAT*, for the relevant period, in which case

$$\mathrm{cov}(R_t, R_{Mt}) \approx \mathrm{cov}(PAT_t / V_{Et-1}, R_{Mt})$$

where V_E is the market value of the firm's equity. Assuming no financial or operating leverage, and a constant margin over variable costs, the change in *PAT* depends on the change in sales:

$$PAT_t = PAT_{t-1}(Sales_t / Sales_{t-1})$$

An accounting measure of operating leverage, L_{op}, is the sensitivity of profit before interest and tax, *PBIT*, to sales:

$$L_{op} = (\Delta PBIT / PBIT) / (\Delta Sales / Sales)$$

Similarly, an accounting measure of financial leverage, L_{debt}, is the sensitivity of profit after tax to profit before interest and tax:

$$L_{debt} = (\Delta PAT/PAT)/(\Delta PBIT/PBIT)$$

L_{debt} and L_{op} are assumed to be constant. Thus profit after tax for period t can be written as

$$PAT_t = PAT_{t-1}L_{debt}L_{op}(Sales_t/Sales_{t-1})$$

and so

$$\text{cov}(PAT_t/V_{Et-1}, R_{Mt}) = L_{op}L_{debt}(PAT_{t-1}/V_{Et-1})\text{cov}(Sales_t/Sales_{t-1}, R_{Mt})$$

or

$$\beta \approx L_{op}L_{debt}\beta_{sales} \tag{6.14}$$

where β is the estimated market beta of the company's shares, and

$$\beta_{sales} = (PAT_{t-1}/V_{Et-1})\text{cov}(Sales_t/Sales_{t-1}, R_{Mt})/\text{var}(R_{Mt})$$

In empirical tests, Mandelker and Rhee (1984) and Chung (1989) report positive relations between share betas and the three variables on the right of equation (6.14) – i.e. the sensitivity of sales to market returns, operating leverage and financial leverage.

An alternative to the analysis of business risk in terms of sales sensitivity and operating leverage is analysis in terms of the choice between labour and capital in the firm's production process. Subrahmanyam and Thomadakis (1980) and Booth (1991) present a single-period contingent-states model in which the level of output and the amounts of capital and labour are chosen before the level of demand is known, and there are diminishing returns to both factors of production (via a Cobb–Douglas production function). The only uncertainty is the selling price. Operating profit is the value of sales less the fixed wage bill and the fixed amount of capital to be repaid. In this model, the business risk and the optimal capital/labour ratio chosen by the firm are negatively related, for a given technology or line of business. The more capital that is used in the production process, the less risky the return on capital. The reason is that an increase in capital makes little difference to total risk (= variance of operating profit), because it substitutes one fixed cost for another (labour), and it reduces the risk per unit of capital. But labour is supposed to be a more variable cost than capital, so Booth (1991) extends the model to allow the firm to vary its amount of labour and output, but not capital, in response to the demand it experiences. This may increase or decrease the variance of operating profit compared with the variance in the fixed-output case, depending on the nature of the uncertainty assumed to be faced by the firm. If risk increases, the cost of capital rises and the capital/labour ratio will be smaller, so the result is reinforced that the cost of capital is negatively related to the capital/labour ratio.

Other potential determinants of share betas have been studied. They include the existence of investment opportunities and other real options (the positive relation with beta predicted and found by Chung and Charoenwong, 1991), and the market power of the firm, proxied – for example – by the size of the firm, industry concentration and entry barriers (negative relation with beta predicted; mixed empirical findings in Sudarsanam, 1992). In addition, the beta of a multi-business company can be analysed as a value- or sales-weighted average of the constituent businesses.

Myers and Turnbull (1977) present an unusual model that uses the certainty-equivalent version of the CAPM (equation (6.5)). The observed cash flow each period affects the expectations of future cash flows, thereby affecting the project's value. The project's beta is a function of several features, and the sensitivity of value to returns on the market changes during the life of the project, which means that beta changes in a predictable way. This model is explained in the Appendix.

6.4.2   Decomposition of risk based on factors affecting value

The accounting-beta approach assumes that the observed return on a share is explained by the observed performance of the company; the share return in a given period reflects only the money the company has made for shareholders in that period. There is, therefore, an implicit assumption that expectations about the future do not change, since a change in expectations would be an additional factor affecting the share return. A rather different line of attack starts from the standard model for the value of a share P_0 as the present value of the future cash flows to shareholders, Div_t:

$$P_0 = \Sigma_{t=1}^{\infty} Div_t/(1 + R_{Et})^t \tag{6.15}$$

Suppose we consider this valuation over time, and allow investors' forecasts of future dividends and forecasts of future expected returns to change over time. Then changes in the share price are affected by changes in these forecasts, and beta is affected by the covariances of the changes in the forecasts with returns on the market.

Campbell and Mei (1993), building on Campbell and Shiller (1988) and Campbell (1991), assume that all of the change in share price from one date to the next is explained by the changes in the forecasts of future dividends and of expected returns. This ignores the money the company has made for shareholders in the period, or perhaps assumes that it is all paid out as dividend. So it is the other extreme from the accounting-beta approach, which ignores forecasts.

Ex ante, beta depends on the covariance of unexpected returns on the share and on the market, in the sense of the differences between possible returns and the expected value of the returns. Campbell and Mei show that the share valuation model, equation (6.15), implies that the unexpected excess log return on share j, r_{jt}^e, can be written approximately as

$$r_{jt}^e = r_{jt}^{div} - r_{Ft} - r_{jt}^{ertn} \tag{6.16}$$

where $r_{jt}^e = \ln(1 + R_{jt}) - E_{t-1}[\ln(1 + R_{jt})] - \ln(1 + R_{Ft})$, and r_{jt}^{div}, r_{Ft} and r_{jt}^{ertn} are unexpected log returns due, respectively, to a change in forecast dividends for j, a change in the forecast risk-free rate and a change in the forecast excess return (superscript ^{ertn}) on j. The idea is that an unexpected change in share price can be decomposed into the effects on price of revised forecasts of dividends and of the expected return, with the latter split into the risk-free rate and the risk premium (excess return). Given equation (6.16), the standard market beta $\beta_{j,M}$ can be decomposed as

$$\beta_{j,M} = \beta_{j,M}^{div} - \beta_{F,M} - \beta_{j,M}^{ertn} \tag{6.17}$$

where $\beta_{j,M}^{div}$, $\beta_{F,M}$ and $\beta_{j,M}^{ertn}$ are the betas against the market returns due, respectively, to changes in forecast dividends for j, changes in the forecast risk-free rate and changes in the forecast excess return on j. $\beta_{F,M}$ is the same for all shares.

The way that Campbell and Mei estimate the decomposition of betas in equation (6.17) is to use variables, such as dividend yield, that forecast the risk-free rate and excess return on the market. The returns of asset j due to changes in the forecast risk-free rate and changes in the forecast excess return on j can then be estimated, and hence $\beta_{F,M}$ and $\beta_{j,M}^{ertn}$ can be estimated. $\beta_{j,M}$ is estimated from past share prices in the normal way (Chapter 13), and $\beta_{j,M}^{div}$ is estimated as the residual from equation (6.17), given the other three betas. The authors find that 'excess return' betas ($\beta_{j,M}^{ertn}$) are negative, as expected, and much larger in absolute value than 'cash flow' betas ($\beta_{j,M}^{div}$), suggesting that changes in the forecast expected returns, or discount rates, on assets explain more of the movements in prices than changes in forecast cash flows do.

The decomposition in equation (6.17) is derived from the valuation model (equation (6.15)), without having specified a model of expected returns. So it follows without assuming that the CAPM holds. But if the CAPM does hold, it implies that

$$r_{jt}^{ertn} = \beta_{j,M} r_{Mt}^{ertn} \tag{6.18}$$

The return on j due to a revision of the forecast about the excess return on j is due to the return on the market due to a revision of the forecast about the excess return on the market (r_{Mt}^{ertn}), times the share's market beta $\beta_{j,M}$. This follows from the fact that the excess return on j is given by $\beta_{j,M}$ times the excess return on the market, under the CAPM. Using equation (6.18) and the definition of a beta, we can write

$$\begin{aligned} \beta_{j,M}^{ertn} &= cov\left(\beta_{j,M} r_{Mt}^{ertn}, r_{Mt}\right) / var(r_{Mt}) \\ &= \beta_{j,M} cov\left(r_{Mt}^{ertn}, r_{Mt}\right) / var(r_{Mt}) \\ &= \beta_{j,M} \beta_{M,M}^{ertn} \end{aligned} \tag{6.19}$$

where $\beta_{M,M}^{ertn}$ is the beta against the market returns due to changes in the forecast excess return on the market. Substituting this in equation (6.17) and solving for $\beta_{j,M}$ gives

$$\beta_{j,M} = \left(\beta_{j,M}^{div} - \beta_{F,M}\right) / \left(1 + \beta_{M,M}^{ertn}\right) \tag{6.20}$$

Equation (6.20) says that the standard beta is a linear function of $\beta_{j,M}^{div}$, the element of a share's beta due to changes in forecast dividends or cash flows. It implies that it is the differences across shares in $\beta_{j,M}^{div}$ that explain the differences in their standard betas. This specification is not supported by the evidence. We already know that there is little empirical support for the CAPM using observed returns (Section 3.4). The explanation offered by the Campbell–Mei analysis and evidence is that 'excess return' betas ($\beta_{j,M}^{ertn}$) are larger in absolute value than 'cash flow' betas ($\beta_{j,M}^{div}$) and that the two are uncorrelated.

6.5   Notes on the user cost of capital and investment

In this book investment is assumed to be carried out in discrete lumps known as projects, following the finance tradition. Investment is conceived of as expenditure to undertake a project, and the investment decision is based on project valuation: the project should be undertaken if it has a positive net present value. It would perhaps be remiss not to mention a slightly different approach to investment that has been taken in economics. According to this approach, investment is conceived of as the purchase of *capital goods* – i.e. real capital assets such as machines or know-how. The firm is assumed to have a production function – i.e. an expression that relates the firm's future output to the amount of capital goods it owns. It acquires capital goods until the benefit per period of another unit of capital goods is equal to the costs of owning and using the unit. These costs are known as the *user cost of capital*. The user cost is most naturally thought of as the cost per period of using a tangible capital good such as a machine. The concept is the cost of renting the good, even if the company actually owns it, and the cost of the owner's funds tied up is only one of the components of the rental cost; it is a 'broad view' of the cost of capital.

It is convenient to think in terms of an abstract 'unit of capital goods' k, which represents the capacity to produce one unit of output per period. Let a unit of capital goods have a market price at date t of P_{kt}. One component of the user cost is the opportunity cost of the funds tied up per unit of capital, RP_{kt}, where R is the opportunity cost of capital per period (i.e. *the* cost of capital in the rest of the book).

A second cost is the depreciation in the productive capacity of the capital goods during the period. One way to think of this is to assume that, as the machine ages, the amount it can produce per period diminishes. Depreciation reduces the value of capital in use by the rate of depreciation in period t. If the price per unit of new capital goods were constant, we would have $P_{kt+1} = (1 - Dep_{t+1})P_{kt}$ for capital in use. The depreciation of productive capacity is known as economic depreciation. Accounting depreciation is the rate at which a capital good is depreciated in a company's accounts, and may differ from economic depreciation.

A third component of the rental charge is the change in the market price per unit of new capital, $-\Delta_{t+1}P_{kt}$, where Δ_{t+1} is the percentage change and there is a minus sign because an increase in value is a negative cost. Thus the real user cost per unit of capital in period t is

$$R_{kt+1}P_{kt} = (R + Dep_{t+1} - \Delta_{t+1})P_{kt}$$

and $R_{kt+1} = R + Dep_{t+1} - \Delta_{t+1}$ is the real user cost of capital per £1 invested.

The firm invests until the marginal revenue product of capital, MRP_{kt+1}, is equal to the user cost R_{kt+1} (see Section 1.24). This assumes a single-period horizon, or, alternatively, a steady-state context with R_{kt} and MRP_{kt} constant over time. The marginal revenue product, or marginal cash flow from operations, is the increase in operating cash flow from owning an extra unit of capital good, holding constant the other factors of production. In a single-period context, we have $MRP_k = dY_1/dK_0$, where Y is the firm's operating cash flow and K is its stock of capital.

It is implicit in this view of investment, as it stands, that capital is highly malleable; the units of capital a company owns can be changed from period to period without cost or delay, to the amount at which $R_{kt} = MRP_{kt}$. As a step towards greater realism, a fourth component can be added to the user cost of capital, which represents the costs of changing the amount of capital a company owns. Examples of costs of investment are administration, installation, the recruitment of staff, retraining and the transactions costs of raising external funds. Costs of disinvestment could include redundancy and other costs of closure, and the transactions costs of the sales of tangible assets. Both investment and disinvestment could involve loss of value through the extinction of a real option. For example, a decision to withdraw from a line of business could effectively close off the option for the company to invest further in the business, were demand to increase unexpectedly.

The q-theory of investment

The q-theory follows from the concept of investment as the purchase of capital goods. We can derive the theory from a multiperiod model of the value of a firm with a production function and adjustment costs (Romer, 2002, chap. 8). The firm's objective is to maximise the present value of future cash flows to shareholders:

$$V_0 = \Sigma_{t=0}^{\infty}[Y(K_t) - I_t - A_K(I_t)]/(1 + R)^t$$

subject to the constraint

$$K_{t+1} = K_t + I_t$$

where $Y(K_t)$ is the production function – the operating cash flow in period t given the amount of capital K_t. The operating cash flow is before investment I_t ($= \Delta K_{t+1}$) and capital adjustment costs $A_K(I_t)$, which are written as a function of investment. There is no depreciation or change in the price of capital, which is assumed to be one per unit of capital. The Lagrangian equation to be maximised is

$$L = \Sigma_{t=0}^{\infty}[Y(K_t) - I_t - A_K(I_t) + \lambda_t(K_t + I_t - K_{t+1})]/(1 + R)^t \qquad (6.21)$$

The discounted sum of the Lagrangian multipliers, $\Sigma_{t=0}^{\infty} \lambda_t/(1 + R)^t$, gives the present value of a marginal relaxation of the constraints – i.e. the present value arising from a marginal increase in capital at each future date. A single multiplier λ_t represents the market value, as at date t, of a marginal unit of capital good at date $t + 1$. Differentiating equation (6.21) with respect to I_t and setting the result to zero gives the first-order condition for the optimum amount of investment in period t (all terms in the summations not involving I_t disappear):

$$\partial L/\partial I_t = [-1 - \partial A_K(I_t)/\partial I_t + \lambda_t]/(1 + R)^t = 0$$

or

$$\lambda_t = 1 + \partial A_K(I_t)/\partial I_t \qquad (6.22)$$

Equation (6.22) says that the optimum amount of investment is such that the cost of acquiring one more unit of capital good, which is one plus the marginal adjustment cost, is equal to λ_t, the market value at date t of an extra unit at $t + 1$. The firm does not need to know its cost of capital to decide how much to invest if it knows the market value of capital goods used in the firm. It simply compares the cost of a capital good with its market value in the firm. This is the q-theory of investment.

The ratio of the market value of a firm's capital to the cost of acquisition, or replacement cost, is known as Tobin's q, and it can be viewed as an indicator for the firm's investment policy. q in excess of one suggests that productive assets are worth more in the company than elsewhere, so the company can create shareholder wealth by investing. q less than one suggests that productive assets are worth more elsewhere, so the company should sell assets.

This theory has been used to try to explain changes in aggregate investment, and also in analysing the effects of tax on the cost of capital and investment (Chapter 8). It points towards a link between changes in stock market valuations and aggregate company investment – an issue that has been explored in several papers. If the q-theory is correct, a positive relation between q and investment might be expected, but the evidence for this to date is not very strong. For example, Blanchard et al (1993) report a positive relation over time between annual changes in corporate investment and annual changes in aggregate q. Corporate investment is given by the ratio of aggregate investment in capital goods by non-financial companies to the aggregate replacement cost of those goods. However, they find that both corporate profitability and the return on the stock market during the year explain changes in investment better than do changes in q.

6.6   Summary

Chapter 6 marks a turning point in the book, from models of expected returns on financial assets, in Part I, to factors that affect a project's cost of capital, in theory, in Part II. When an explicit model of the expected rate of return on a risky asset is needed, it is the CAPM that is used. The subject matter of Part II has a bearing on how to estimate a project's cost of capital, but we treat estimation in practice as a distinct topic, in Part III.

We have reviewed project valuation and the cost of capital, allowing for multiple future periods and for the fact that projects are carried out by companies, but without any further real-world complications. The first section considered various analytical issues that arise in discounting multiperiod expected cash flows. The distinction between equity and debt was then introduced, and the treatment of financing-related costs and taxes was explained. We argued that the notion of the cost of capital as an opportunity cost implies that financing-related costs should be treated as affecting cash flows rather than the discount rate. But taxes will affect the cost of capital, because of the conventions that cash flows and the discount rate are expressed before personal tax, and that the tax saving from interest is captured in the discount rate. We went on to review theories of how a project's systematic risk is determined *ex ante*. Finally, the chapter included a brief discussion of the concept of the user cost of capital, and of the q-theory of investment, according to which a firm can, in theory, decide whether to invest by comparing the cost of a capital good with the market value of the capital good in the firm. Having established the general framework for project valuation, we are now ready to introduce taxes.

Appendix 6.1: The Myers–Turnbull model

Project value in a given period is determined by the discount rate or rates in future periods, and by investor expectations about future cash flows. Myers and Turnbull (1977) present a model that explicitly links realised cash flows with project values over time, via changes in investor expectations. In this model the standard CAPM holds, R_F and λ are known in advance and constant, and project β_t is known in advance and can differ across dates. The authors note that realised cash flows can be viewed as expected cash flows plus an error:

$$Y_{t+1} = E_t(Y_{t+1})(1 + e_{t+1})$$

They assume that e_t has an element related to unanticipated changes in an economic index I_t (for example, GDP) and an idiosyncratic element ε_t uncorrelated with I_t:

$$e_t = \alpha I_t + \varepsilon_t \tag{A6.1}$$

where α measures the sensitivity of the error term to I_t and $E(\varepsilon_t) = 0$. Expectations are assumed to adapt as follows:

$$E_t(Y_{t+1}) = E_{t-1}(Y_t)(1 + \eta e_t) \tag{A6.2}$$

where η is the elasticity of expectations, $0 \le \eta \le 1$. The valuation of a project with future cash flows $Y_1, Y_2 \ldots Y_T$ is based on equation (6.5). At $T - 1$ the present value of Y_T is

$$V_{T-1} = \frac{E_{T-1}(Y_T) - \lambda \text{cov}(Y_T, R_{MT})}{1 + R_F} \tag{6.5}$$

$$= \frac{E_{T-1}(Y_T)(1 - \lambda \alpha \sigma_{IM})}{1 + R_F} \tag{A6.3}$$

where $\sigma_{IM} = \text{cov}(I_t, R_{Mt})$, which is assumed to be constant. The steps from equation (6.5) to equation (A6.3) are as follows:

$$\begin{aligned} \text{cov}(Y_T, R_{MT}) &= \text{cov}[E_{T-1}(Y_T)(1 + \alpha I_t + \varepsilon_t), R_{MT}] \\ &= \text{cov}[E_{T-1}(Y_T)\alpha I_t, R_{MT}] \\ &= E_{T-1}(Y_T)\alpha \text{cov}[I_t, R_{MT}] \end{aligned}$$

since $E_{T-1}(Y_T)$ is a constant as at period $T - 1$, α is a constant and ε_t is assumed to be uncorrelated with R_{MT}. At $T - 2$ the present value is

$$V_{T-2} = \frac{E_{T-2}(Y_{T-1})(1 - \lambda \alpha \sigma_{IM})}{1 + R_F} + \frac{E_{T-2}(Y_T)(1 - \lambda \alpha \sigma_{IM})(1 - \lambda \eta \alpha \sigma_{IM})}{(1 + R_F)^2} \tag{A6.4}$$

(see Section 6.1.3). The second term follows from equation (6.5) applied to the project value at date $T-1$:

$$\text{2nd term of equation (A6.3)} = \frac{E_{T-2}(V_{T-1}) - \lambda\text{cov}(V_{T-1}, R_{MT-1})}{1 + R_F}$$

Using equation (A6.3), $E_{T-2}(V_{T-1}) = E_{T-2}(Y_T)(1 - \lambda\alpha\sigma_{IM})/(1 + R_F)$, and from equations (A6.1) and (A6.2)

$$\text{cov}(V_{T-1}, R_{MT-1}) = \text{cov}[E_{T-2}(V_{T-1})(1 + \eta\alpha I_{T-1} + \eta\varepsilon_{T-1}), R_{MT-1}]$$
$$= E_{T-2}(V_{T-1})\eta\alpha\text{cov}[I_{T-1}, R_{MT-1}]$$

That is, the expectation about Y_T is revised according to equation (A6.2), once realised Y_{T-1} can be compared with $E_{T-2}(Y_{T-1})$. Project values at earlier dates are derived in analogous fashion.

The main purpose of the model is to enable an expression for period-by-period beta to be derived. The definition of beta is $\text{cov}(R_t, R_{Mt})/\sigma_{Mt}^2$, where R_t is the project return over period t. One plus the return on the project in period t is $(Y_t + V_t)/V_{t-1}$. Letting $Q_t = V_t/E_t(Y_{t+1})$, this can be written as

$$1 + R_t = \frac{Y_t + E_t(Y_{t+1})Q_t}{E_{t-1}(Y_t)Q_t}$$
$$= \frac{E_{t-1}(Y_t)(1 + e_t) + E_{t-1}(Y_t)(1 + \eta e_t)Q_t}{E_{t-1}(Y_t)Q_{t-1}} \tag{A6.5}$$

Using equations (A6.1) and (A6.5),

$$\text{cov}(R_t, R_{Mt}) = \text{cov}\{[(1 + \alpha I_t + \varepsilon_t) + (1 + \eta\alpha I_t + \eta\varepsilon_t)Q_t/Q_{t-1}], R_{Mt}\}$$
$$= \text{cov}\{[(\alpha I_t + \eta\alpha I_t Q_t)/Q_{t-1}], R_{Mt}\}$$
$$= [(1 + \eta Q_t)/Q_{t-1}]\alpha\sigma_{IM}$$

since α and η are constants and Q_{t-1} and Q_t are known at date t. So the beta of the project in period t is

$$\beta_t = [(1 + \eta Q_t)/Q_{t-1}]\alpha\sigma_{IM}/\sigma_M^2$$

It can be seen that beta is a function of η and $\alpha\sigma_{IM}$. Myers and Turnbull show that it is also a function of the length of the project and the growth rate of cash flows, via the ratio Q_t/Q_{t-1}.

In particular, beta will increase during the life of a project, if $\eta < 1$ in equation (A6.2). Project beta is a weighted average of the beta of the next cash flow and the beta of project value at the next date. With $\eta < 1$, forecast cash flows change by less than one for one with the deviation of the current cash payment from the previously expected payment. This makes the project value less sensitive to changes in market value than the current cash payment is. As the project progresses, its remaining value diminishes in relation to the cash flow at each date, so beta increases. With $\eta = 1$, forecast cash flows have the same sensitivity to the market as the current cash flow, so beta is constant and the discount rate is constant. If beta is forecast to change in the future, R_{Et} is forecast to change, and the current one-period discount rate is not the correct rate to apply to the cash flows for the whole project. However, Myers and Turnbull argue that the errors are small from assuming a constant beta and using the current estimate of R_{Et} for period 1. It is, in any case, hard to imagine how one would estimate future betas in practice.

The Myers–Turnbull paper articulates a case in which the way that expectations adapt, project length and the growth of cash flows all affect the risk. In addition, a project's cost of equity would be forecast to change (though the impact on value seems to be minor). The change is not ascribable to changing macroeconomic variables or investor tolerance to risk, but to the natural progression of the project as its value is realised in cash pay-outs.

7 Corporation tax, leverage and the weighted average cost of capital

Corporate and personal taxes affect a project's value because they affect the cash flows received by the providers of capital. It is conventional for some of the impact of taxes on cash flows to be reflected in the discount rate rather than in the cash flows to be discounted, as discussed in the previous chapter. In principle, it might be possible to prepare a cash flow forecast with bottom-line cash flows that were net of all the taxes expected to be paid. The project's cost of capital would then be a required rate net of all tax. In practice, cash flows and the cost of capital are never expressed net of all the taxes expected to be paid.

The current chapter is concerned with the combined effect of leverage and corporation tax on the cost of capital, ignoring personal tax. The reason why leverage has an impact is that it affects the amounts of corporation tax to be paid, because interest payments do not attract corporation tax. Before proceeding with this topic, we note some preliminary points about the effects of taxes on the cost of capital.

7.1 Preliminaries

7.1.1 Rates of return and levels of tax

One way of using the cost of capital in project appraisal is to compare it with the project's internal rate of return. There must, therefore, be consistency with respect to tax in the measurement of the internal rate of return and of the cost of capital. To clarify how taxes affect the rate of return on a project, consider a simple example. Suppose that projects A and B will each provide taxable payments of £20 p.a. in perpetuity, for certain. The £20 p.a. from project A is subject to corporation tax but not personal tax; the £20 p.a. from project B is subject to both types of tax. The corporation tax rate is 40 per cent, the personal tax rate on B is 25 per cent for all investors, and taxes are paid at the same time as the cash flow is received. The payments received by the owners will be £12 p.a. from A and £9 p.a. from B. Since both projects are risk-free, they should both be priced to provide the same rate of return, *measured after all tax*. This is because the utility of investors is determined by cash flows received after all tax, so it is the after-tax cash flows that are relevant in determining the prices of projects and financial assets. If the risk-free rate after all tax available in the economy is 5 per cent p.a., the price of A will be £12/.05 = £240 and the price of B will be £9/.05 = £180. A different price in either case would imply a risk-free rate higher or lower than 5 per cent p.a., and would therefore not be observed in equilibrium because it would present an opportunity for arbitrage (assuming that there are no transaction costs or constraints on trading). The rates of return on the projects can be expressed at three levels of tax: before all tax, after corporate tax but before personal tax, or after all tax. Both assets provide the same rate of return after all tax, 5 per cent p.a. The rates measured before personal tax but after corporation tax are £12/£240 = 5% pa on A and £12/£180 = 6.7% pa on B. The rates measured before all tax are £20/£240 = 8.3% pa on A and £20/£180 − 1 = 11.1% pa on B. Whichever level of tax is chosen to express a project's rate of return, or cash flows, the cost of capital must be expressed at the same level of tax.

If a tax rate changes, and the risk-free rate in the economy is unchanged, the market value of the project changes. For example, if the personal tax rate on B is increased from 25 per cent to 50 per cent, the after-tax cash flows from B fall to £6 p.a., and B's price of B falls to £120, at which price the rate of return after tax on B is 5 per cent p.a. The cost of capital for B expressed before personal tax increases from 6.7 per cent p.a. to 10.0 per cent p.a. If B were being valued using cash flows measured before personal tax, the cash flows to be discounted would not change, and the reduction in value from £180 to £120 would arise because of the increase in the discount rate from 6.7 per cent p.a. to 10.0 per cent p.a.

7.1.2   Financial assets compared with projects

If a project can issue more than one type of asset, the expected rate of return on a particular type of asset is no longer the same concept as the project's cost of capital. Each type of asset will have its own expected rate of return, none of which will constitute the project's cost of capital. The only financial assets we shall consider are ordinary shares and homogeneous bonds or loans, so all debt raised by a company is assumed to be the same in terms of security, maturity and other conditions. If we ignore personal tax, the expected rate of return on the project's shares at their (equilibrium) market price is the project's cost of equity, expressed after corporate tax if the cash flows are net of corporate tax. Similarly, the expected rate of return on the company's bonds at their market price is its cost of debt.

In a world with no taxes or other 'market imperfections', the distinction between equity and debt does not lead anywhere, because the financing of a project does not affect the present value of its cash flows (Section 7.2). For the purposes of valuation, a project can be thought of as a single financial asset, namely the unlevered equity, as in Part I of the book. The unlevered equity gives entitlement to all the cash flows. How the project is funded in reality can be put aside in calculating the cost of capital, because the value of the cash flows will always be the same.

In a world with taxes, a project can still be thought of as a financial asset, but as an asset providing entitlement to after-tax cash flows, the values of which are contingent on the management's financing policies. For a given stream of cash flows before tax, the financing policies affect the present value of the tax payments. One link between financing policy and value is the tax saving from interest, which means that debt policy affects the amounts of after-tax cash flows. If debt policy affects cash flows, the cash flows to which unlevered equity gives entitlement are not the same as the cash flows to which a debt and equity mix gives entitlement. So the internal rate of return measured after tax on a levered project cannot be compared with the cost of unlevered equity after tax to decide whether the project makes providers of capital better off. That is, the expected rate of return on the unlevered equity is no longer the project's cost of capital, unless the project is, in fact, unlevered.

A second link between financing policy and value is the fact that the taxation of dividends is different from the taxation of capital gains, which means that dividend policy may affect the cash flows after personal tax to levered or unlevered equity. Thus, with taxes, the financial asset that a levered project represents is a synthetic asset giving the same entitlement as the equity and debt combined, and the synthetic asset changes if there is a change in debt or dividend policy.

7.1.3   *Corporation tax, cash flows and investment*

A tax involves a definition of what is to be taxed, as well as a rate of taxation. In the case of corporation tax, there are a number of provisions that can make a large difference to the definition of taxable profit, and hence to a company's tax payments. However, we shall say relatively little about the provisions that define taxable profit, because the convention in corporate finance, which we follow, is to discount cash flows net of corporation tax. This means that the cost of capital must also be expressed after corporation tax, and the effects of the provisions that define taxable profit tax are captured in the cash flows, with the exception of the deductibility of interest.

The level of tax at which the cost of capital is expressed is the result of a choice regarding which tax effects are captured in the cash flows and which in the cost of capital. If it were possible to estimate a hurdle rate *after all tax* (which is difficult because personal tax rates vary across investors), all the effects on market value of the company's financing policies and of the government's tax policies would have to be captured in the future cash flows. A hurdle rate *before personal tax* puts the tax-related effects of the company's dividend policy into the discount rate. The standard tax-adjusted weighted average cost of capital (WACC) captures the tax effects of both dividend and debt policies, though doing so requires that cash flows overstate the amounts of corporation tax that a levered company will actually pay, as will become clear. Hence the tax-adjusted WACC puts the tax effects of financing policies, controlled by the company, into the cost of capital, but not the effects of provisions, which affect corporation tax. Finally, a hurdle rate *before all tax* captures both the company's policies and all the provisions that affect corporation tax. Some of these, such as investment tax credits and depreciation allowances, are explicitly intended to alter incentives to invest.

Our primary interest is in the cost of capital and valuation. It is probably easier to discount cash flows after corporation tax when valuing a project. This is because the present value from discounting before-tax cash flows at the discount rate before tax will not be equal to the correct present value from discounting after-tax cash flows at the discount rate after tax (unless we are dealing with perpetual cash flows, or with a marginal project in which the rate of return per period is equal to the cost of capital). For example, suppose a project costs £100 now and produces a single cash flow of £140 after one year. The taxable profit is £40, the corporation tax rate is 50 per cent and the required rate of return after tax is 10 per cent p.a. The correct present value is £109, found from discounting the after-tax cash flow of £120 by the after-tax cost of capital of 10 per cent p.a. The alternative of discounting £140 by 20 per cent p.a. gives an incorrect present value of £117. Also, the timing and amounts of the predicted actual tax payments will be incorporated explicitly in the cash flow forecast. These predicted payments will include the effects of depreciation allowances and investment credits. The after-tax approach enables the present value of the tax payments to be estimated more accurately than would be possible if cash flows were gross of tax, and if the impact of corporation tax were captured approximately via a before-tax discount rate.

It should be emphasised that the provisions relating to corporation tax and the statutory rate(s) of tax do affect project values and company investment decisions, and they would affect the cost of capital expressed before all tax. In fact, they also have a comparatively minor effect on the tax-adjusted WACC, via the assumed effective rate of corporation tax saved by interest on debt. Differences in the tax-related provisions across industries and across types of project can lead to large differences across projects in the effective rates of corporation tax they face, with the statutory rate being an upper limit. Under the before-tax approach, the variations mean that there are large differences in the cost of capital across projects of similar risk (see, e.g., King and Fullerton, 1984, for evidence). The availability of tax losses also reduces the effective rate of corporation tax on a project. If a company makes a loss, it pays no tax for that year and sets the loss against taxable profits in other years. In summary, the corporation tax rate a project faces, which appears below as T_C, should, realistically, be thought of as a project-specific effective tax rate rather than as the statutory rate. Under the after-corporate-tax approach to discounting adopted in this book, the variations in effective corporate tax rates do not show up as differences across projects in their costs of capital, except via the rate of tax saving due to interest.

As an aside, Stiglitz (1976) notes that it is possible to define taxable profit in such a way that, although corporation tax affects project value, it does not affect investment decisions. The same projects would be undertaken whatever the rate of corporation tax. This would be the case if immediate depreciation were allowed, so the entire cost of the project could be written off in one go against the taxable profit from existing projects. If there were no taxable profit available, the company would receive a payment equal to the cost times the rate of corporation tax. The subsequent operating profits would be taxed, with no deductions for depreciation. The effect of this scheme is that all that is taxed is the profit that is in excess of the profit required to cover the cost of capital before corporation tax. The reason is that the current tax saved by immediate depreciation can be shown to be equal to the present value of the tax on the profit required to cover the cost of capital. The same effect would be obtained by depreciating the project cost at the true economic rate of depreciation, and not taxing the profits necessary to cover the cost of capital. In both cases, only the value added is taxed. Any project with a positive net present value ignoring the tax will still have a positive, though lower, NPV after taking account of the tax. However, corporation tax as it is normally applied is a tax on the returns to equity capital, including the portion of returns that corresponds to the cost of equity. Corporation tax therefore normally affects company investment decisions.

7.2   The weighted average cost of capital

Notation

The following terms are used throughout the chapter. All the terms relate to a project with a given business risk, which can be either unlevered or levered.

Y_t = Operating cash flow before interest and tax in period t. This is the same as the operating profit in the case of a perpetual project, assuming there are no depreciation charges or other non-cash items affecting profit. Y_t is not the same as operating profit in the case of a finite project.

Int_t = Interest payable in period t.

V_U = Market value of the project unlevered.

V_L = Market value (equity + debt) of the project levered.

E_U − Market value of the equity with no debt ($= V_U$).

E_L = Market value of the equity given a leverage of L.

D = Market value of the debt.

L = $D/(E_L + D) = D/V_L$.

R_{EU} = Expected rate of return on the unlevered project's shares, or cost of unlevered equity, measured after corporation tax (if any). The expectation operator is now suppressed.

R_{EL} = Expected rate of return on the levered project's shares, or cost of levered equity, measured after corporation tax.

R_F = Risk-free rate of interest.

R_D = Expected rate of return on the levered project's debt, or cost of debt ($= R_F$ if the debt is assumed to be risk-free).

R_L = Cost of capital for the levered project.

$WACC$ = Weighted average cost of capital ($= R_L$).

T_C = Effective rate of corporation tax on the operating profit per period.

I = Cash investment at date 0 required to undertake the project.

7.2.1   *Without corporation tax*

In a world with no tax and a perfect capital market, Modigliani and Miller (1958) prove that the level of leverage or gearing makes no difference to a company's market value (their 'Proposition I') and, hence, no difference to its cost of capital, assuming that debt is part of a company's capital. Their proof is an arbitrage argument: if leverage did affect market value, there would be an opportunity for gain that is eliminated only if leverage does not affect value.

Consider two companies, j_U and j_L, that have the same constant annual expected cash flow before interest, $E(Y)$, in perpetuity. The risk attaching to the future cash flows before subtracting interest or tax – the *business risk* – is also the same. Company j_U is unlevered and has a market value of V_U. Company j_L is levered and has a market value $V_L = E_L + D$, where E_L is the value of the levered equity and D is the value of the perpetual bonds issued by j_L, on which interest is paid in cash. Capital does not depreciate and the debt is risk-free (we relax both these assumptions later). An investor owns a fraction α of the shares in j_L, so this shareholding is worth αE_L. The expected annual pay-off on this holding, denoted Y_1, is the investor's share of the expected cash flow before interest, less the interest on the debt:

$$Y_1 = \alpha[E(Y) - R_F D] \tag{7.1}$$

A course of action open to the investor would be to sell his/her shares in j_L, worth αE_L, borrow an amount αD, and buy shares in j_U worth $\alpha(E_L + D)$. It is assumed that he/she can borrow at the risk-free rate R_F (Modigliani and Miller remark that he/she could offer the shares in j_U as security). This alternative investment is specified in the way that it is because the expected cash flow from the shares in j_U, after interest on the personal loan, has the same risk as the expected cash flow from the former holding of the shares in j_L. The investor's expected return from his/her levered holding in j_U, denoted Y_2, is

$$Y_2 = \frac{\alpha(E_L + D)E(Y)}{E_U} - R_F \alpha D$$

$$= \frac{\alpha V_L E(Y)}{V_U} - R_F \alpha D \tag{7.2}$$

$\alpha(E_L + D)/E_U$ is the fraction of j_U the investor owns, and $R_F \alpha D$ is the cost of his/her personal loan. So the first line of equation (7.2) says that the expected return from his/her holding in j_U is his/her share of j_U's expected cash flow, $E(Y)$, less the cost of his/her personal loan. The second line merely substitutes V_L for $E_L + D$, the total value of j_L, and V_U for E_U. By comparing equations (7.1) and (7.2), it is clear that $Y_1 = Y_2$ only if $V_L = V_U$. But if $V_L \neq V_U$, the investor could increase his/her expected cash flow without increasing his/her risk. For example, if it is the case that a company can increase its total value by gearing up (whilst leaving its expected cash flows unaltered), we would have $V_L > V_U$, $Y_2 > Y_1$, and the investor would gain from a strategy of selling his/her shares in j_L, borrowing αD, and buying shares in j_U worth $\alpha(E_L + D)$. Such trading would reduce the price of j_L's shares and increase the price of j_U's shares until $V_L = V_U$. The gain available if $V_L > V_U$ is a pure, risk-free gain, if both companies have exactly the same cash flows in every future state of the world. Then, no matter which state arises, a higher rate of return will be obtained from the strategy involving investment in j_U.

Since the expected cash flow $E(Y)$ and the business risk are the same for both companies, and the above argument shows that both companies have the same market value, it follows that the capital of a company or project can be thought of as a financial asset – i.e. the unlevered equity. The expected rate of return on the asset at market value is the project's cost of capital, assuming a constant expected return each period (Section 6.1). This is also the cost of unlevered equity, which we denote R_{EU}. The cost of capital for a levered project of the same business risk, such as j_{L}, is the *weighted average cost of capital*, also sometimes referred to as the adjusted discount rate. The WACC is the expected rate of return from owning all the equity and debt, and the formula for the WACC follows from the fact that ownership of all the equity and debt gives entitlement to all the cash flow:

$$V_{\text{L}} WACC = \text{E}(Y)$$
$$WACC = \text{E}(Y)/V_{\text{L}}$$
$$= \left(\frac{\text{E}(Y) - R_{\text{F}}D}{E_{\text{L}}} \right) \left(\frac{E_{\text{L}}}{E_{\text{L}} + D} \right) + \frac{R_{\text{F}}D}{E_{\text{L}} + D}$$
$$= R_{\text{EL}} E_{\text{L}}/V_{\text{L}} + R_{\text{F}}D/V_{\text{L}}$$

or

$$= R_{\text{EL}}(1 - L) + R_{\text{F}}L \tag{7.3}$$

where R_{EL} is the expected rate of return on the levered equity, or cost of levered equity, and L is leverage, defined as D/V_{L}. Equation (7.3) says that a levered company's cost of capital is its levered cost of equity times the proportion of equity in the total market value of its capital, plus the cost of debt (here assumed to be risk-free) times the proportion of debt. We have just shown that, whatever the leverage, $WACC$ must be equal to R_{EU}. That is,

$$V_{\text{U}} = V_{\text{L}} = \text{E}(Y)/R_{\text{EU}}$$

and

$$R_{\text{EU}} = WACC = \text{E}(Y)/V_{\text{U}} = \text{E}(Y)/V_{\text{L}} \tag{7.4}$$

$WACC$ and R_{EU} vary with business risk only, and business risk is not affected by leverage.

It should be noted that, in theory, the market values of equity and debt are used in the WACC formula, not the accounting values. The cost of capital is given by the expected rate of return on the unlevered equity, valued at its market value. Similarly, because investors trade in shares and bonds at their market prices, the values of the companies' equity and debt are market values in the proof that $WACC$ is a constant equal to R_{EU}. If the accounting values of E_{L} and D differ from their market values, insertion of the accounting values in equation (7.3) will change the WACC number, in which case it will no longer be equal to the cost of capital – the expected rate of return on unlevered equity. It may be that managers define what they consider to be the optimum leverage in terms of book values, but market values should still be used in calculating the WACC (Brennan, 1973).

The expected rate of return on the equity of a levered company, or the cost of levered equity, is given by

$$R_{\text{EL}} = [\text{E}(Y) - R_{\text{F}}D]/E_{\text{L}}$$
$$= [R_{\text{EU}}(E_{\text{L}} + D) - R_{\text{F}}D]/E_{\text{L}}$$
$$= R_{\text{EU}} + (R_{\text{EU}} - R_{\text{F}})D/E_{\text{L}} \tag{7.5}$$

Equation (7.5) specifies a linear relation between the cost of equity and leverage (Modigliani and Miller's 'Proposition II'). The cost of equity rises because leverage adds financial risk, which is borne by the shareholders. Equation (7.5) is consistent with the WACC formula (equation (7.3)). Since $R_{EU} = WACC$,

$$R_{EL} = WACC + (WACC - R_F)D/E_L$$
$$= WACC(E_L + D)/E_L - R_F D/E_L$$
$$R_{EL}E_L = WACC V_L - R_F D$$
$$WACC = R_{EL}(1 - L) + R_F L$$
$$= R_{EU}, \text{ a constant with respect to } L$$

The above analysis has assumed that $E(Y)$ is a perpetuity. The conclusion stands that leverage does not affect value, whatever the nature of the forecast cash flows, if there are no taxes. This is because of the arbitrage argument; it is always possible for an investor to replicate a particular sequence of expected cash flows via 'home-made' leverage and suitable trades of the company's shares and bonds. However, the specification of the WACC, and of the cost of equity of a levered company, do depend on assumptions made about future cash flows, debt repayments and whether debt is risk-free. These matters are discussed in due course.

7.2.2   With corporation tax

Corporation tax is a tax on profit net of interest payments. Assuming for the moment that net cash flow is the same as taxable operating profit, the expected perpetual annual cash flow to equity after corporation tax is $[E(Y) - Int](1 - T_C)$, where T_C is the rate of corporation tax and Int is the interest payment in cash. One method of valuing a project would be to discount the cash flows to equity and the cash flows to debt separately, at their appropriate discount rates, and then to add the estimated values of the equity and debt. The market value of the equity would be $[E(Y) - Int](1 - T_C)/R_{EL}$, where R_{EL} is now the expected rate of return on a levered company's equity measured after corporation tax. The market value of the debt would be Int/R_F. The effect of corporation tax would be captured entirely in cash flows. This approach has, in fact, been advocated by Arditti (1973), on the grounds that the correct expected cash flows after corporation tax would be discounted. But Modigliani and Miller, in deriving the cost of capital, think it better to make no distinction between equity and debt in the project's capital, even though leverage affects market value once corporation tax is introduced (1963, p. 440): 'Since financing sources cannot in general be allocated to particular investments . . . , the after-tax or accounting concept [of cash flow net of interest and incorporating the tax saving] is not useful for capital budgeting purposes, although it can be extremely useful for valuation . . .' In consequence, they define expected cash flow after corporation tax as $E(Y)(1 - T_C)$, even for a levered company. Thus the Modigliani–Miller cash flow to be discounted ignores the saving in corporation tax of $Int T_C$ arising from interest payments.

The Modigliani–Miller view has determined the normal specification of the tax-adjusted WACC. If the cash flows to be discounted are $E(Y)(1 - T_C)$, in equilibrium we must have

$$WACC = \left(\frac{[E(Y) - R_F D](1 - T_C)}{E_L}\right)\left(\frac{E_L}{E_L + D}\right) + \frac{R_F(1 - T_C)D}{E_L + D}$$

$$= R_{EL}(1 - L) + R_F(1 - T_C)L \qquad (7.6)$$

This formula is the *tax-adjusted WACC* with risk-free debt. It takes leverage L as a given, so it does not establish the relation between the WACC and leverage.

By reasoning analogous to that presented in Section 7.2.1, Modigliani and Miller (1963) show that the relation between the values of a levered and unlevered company with the same expected cash flows and the same business risk must be

$$V_L = E(Y)(1 - T_C)/R_{EU} + Int T_C/R_F$$

$$= E(Y)(1 - T_C)/R_{EU} + R_F D T_C/R_F$$

$$= V_U + T_C D \qquad (7.7)$$

where R_{EU} is now the expected rate of return after corporation tax on an unlevered company. Hence the tax advantage of debt means that total value increases with leverage. The cost of capital is the expected rate of return after tax on marginal capital that gives net present value $= 0$, or $dV_L/dI = 1$, where I is cash invested. If a cash flow is defined as $E(Y)(1 - T_C)$ (as opposed to $E(Y - Int)(1 - T_C)$), the marginal expected rate of return is $dE(Y)(1 - T_C)/dI$, and the condition for $dV_L/dI = 1$ is

$$dV_L/dI = [dE(Y)(1 - T_C)/dI]/R_{EU} + T_C dD/dI = 1$$

or

$$dE(Y)(1 - T_C)/dI = R_{EU}(1 - T_C L) = R_L \qquad (7.8)$$

where R_L stands for the levered project's cost of capital, and $L = dD/dI$, the leverage of the marginal project. Equation (7.8) shows the relation between the cost of capital and leverage. Since R_{EU} is independent of L, equation (7.8) says that the cost of capital is a negative linear function of L. This implies that, in the absence of non-tax considerations, an all-debt financing policy is optimal.

The cost of equity after tax can be found from equation (7.7) as follows. The expected rates of return to equity and debt are, respectively, $[E(Y) - R_F D](1 - T_C)$ and $R_F D$. Their sum can be written as $E(Y)(1 - T_C) + T_C R_F D$. Thus, equation (7.7) can be rewritten as

$$V_L = E(Y)(1 - T_C)/R_{EU} + T_C D$$

$$= \{[E(Y) - R_F D](1 - T_C) + R_F D - T_C R_F D\}/R_{EU} + T_C D$$

Let $E(Y_E)$ stand for $[E(Y) - R_F D](1 - T_C)$, the cash flow to equity. The value of levered equity, E_L, is $V_L - D$, so we can write

$$E_L = V_L - D = \frac{E(Y_E) + R_F D - T_C R_F D + R_{EU} T_C D - R_{EU} D}{R_{EU}}$$

$$= \frac{E(Y_E)}{R_{EU}} - \frac{(R_{EU} - R_F)(1 - T_C)D}{R_{EU}}$$

Letting I_E be the cash invested as equity, and following the derivation of equation (7.8), the expected rate of return on equity at which $dE_L/dI_E = 1$ is

$$dE(Y_E)/dI_E = R_{EU} + (R_{EU} - R_F)(1 - T_C)dD/dI_E$$

so the company's cost of equity after corporation tax is

$$R_{EL} = R_{EU} + (R_{EU} - R_F)(1 - T_C)D/E_L \qquad (7.9)$$

This specifies a different relation between the cost of equity and leverage from equation (7.5).

The tax-adjusted WACC with risk-free debt is consistent with equations (7.8) and (7.9) (Copeland and Weston, 1988, p. 451). Using equation (7.8), we can write

$$WACC = R_{EU}(1 - T_C L) - R_F(1 - T_C)L + R_F(1 - T_C)L$$

$$= R_{EU}\left[\frac{E_L}{V_L} + \frac{E_L}{V_L}\frac{D}{E_L} - T_C\left(\frac{E_L}{V_L}\frac{D}{E_L}\right)\right]$$

$$- R_F(1 - T_C)\left(\frac{E_L}{V_L}\frac{D}{E_L}\right) + R_F(1 - T_C)L$$

$$= [R_{EU} + (R_{EU} - R_F)(1 - T_C)D/E_L]E_L/V_L + R_F(1 - T_C)L$$

$$= R_{EL}(1 - L) + R_F(1 - T_C)L$$

The step from the penultimate line uses equation (7.9).

The tax-adjusted WACC is potentially confusing. It might appear, from comparison with the no-tax version (equation (7.3)), as though allowance for corporation tax in the WACC means that tax is subtracted from the return to debt. Yet corporation tax is a tax on the returns to equity. What is going on is this. As noted, the expected cash flows to equity are $[E(Y) - R_F D](1 - T_C)$, measured net of corporation tax. The cost of equity, R_{EL}, is expressed net of corporation tax, and so is consistent with the cash flows. The reason for the tax adjustment to R_F is because the tax advantage of debt is not captured in the cash flows. It is therefore captured in the discount rate, by subtracting the corporation tax rate from the cost of debt.

The tax-adjusted WACC can be used to calculate a project's cost of capital, so long as its leverage is known, together with the expected rate of return on equity of the same risk as the project's levered equity, and the risk-free rate. The hardest part is estimating the relevant expected rate of return on equity (Chapters 12 and 13).

7.2.3   The WACC and the CAPM

The Modigliani–Miller theory does not specify any particular model of the expected rate of return on risky assets. It does say that, whatever model one cares to use, there is a linear relation between the expected rate of return on equity and leverage, given by equation (7.9) in the presence of corporation tax. If we are using the CAPM, the relation between a company's cost of equity and its leverage is

$$R_{EL} = R_F + \beta_L[E(R_M) - R_F] \tag{7.10}$$

where R_{EL} and $E(R_M)$ are measured after corporation tax, and β_L is the beta of the equity and is a function of the leverage ratio L. We have dropped the expectation operator from R_{EL} to be consistent with normal notation in the context of cost-of-capital formulas. The unlevered beta or asset beta is β_U. Substituting equation (7.10) into equation (7.9),

$$R_F + \beta_L[E(R_M) - R_F] = R_F + \beta_U[E(R_M) - R_F]$$
$$+ \{R_F + \beta_U[E(R_M) - R_F] - R_F\}(1 - T_C)D/E_L$$

which, after simplifying, gives

$$\beta_U = \beta_L[(1 - L)/(1 - T_C L)]$$

or

$$\beta_L = \beta_U + \beta_U(1 - T_C)D/E_L \tag{7.11}$$

In the absence of tax, the relation is simply

$$\beta_U = \beta_L(1 - L)$$

or

$$\beta_L = \beta_U(1 + D/E_L) \tag{7.12}$$

Thus, one effect of the tax is to make the risk of levered equity, and the cost of equity, less than they would have been in the absence of tax, as pointed out by Modigliani and Miller (1963).

The reason for the risk reduction is that there are tax savings from debt, *and* these savings are treated free of risk. The discount rate for tax savings implicit in the tax-adjusted WACC with risk-free debt is the risk-free rate, as can be seen from the derivation of equation (7.7). Without tax, the level of leverage has no effect on the (business) risk of the expected cash flows before interest, $E(Y)$. With tax, the cash flows before interest but after tax become $E(Y)(1 - T_C) + T_C R_F D$. The new element, $T_C R_F D$, is the tax saving, which is viewed as certain and is discounted at R_F; the remainder, which includes the interest on debt, is discounted at R_{EU}. So the business risk of $E(Y)(1 - T_C) + T_C R_F D$ is less than the risk of $E(Y)$. Hence the tax saving is valuable in this analysis not only because it saves tax but also because, implausibly, it reduces business risk. This is not explicit in the tax-adjusted WACC because the effect of the risk reduction is implicit, in the expression for the cost of levered equity, R_{EL}.

But tax savings are not risk-free. Corporate debt was assumed to be risk-free to simplify the analysis, not because this assumption can be justified. Even if the debt were risk-free it would not guarantee that the tax savings are risk-free. The effective rate of corporation tax, and therefore the rate at which tax is saved, can change over time for various reasons. Also, the project's future optimal level of leverage may be uncertain; if leverage falls, the tax savings will fall too. We allow for risky debt, and therefore risky tax savings, in the next section.

We arrived at equation (7.11) by inferring the relation between beta and leverage that must hold if the Modigliani–Miller theory adjusted for corporation tax is correct, and if the cost of equity is specified by the CAPM. It is noteworthy that the Modigliani–Miller predictions can be derived independently, from the CAPM (Hamada, 1969). The CAPM specifies a linear relation between a company's leverage and the expected rates of return on its debt and equity, via the linear relation between the expected rate of return and beta in equilibrium.

Consider again a company with expected net cash flow before interest of $E(Y)$ in perpetuity. We have specified that $R_{EU} = E(Y)(1 - T_C)/V_U$ and $R_{EL} = [E(Y) - R_F D](1 - T_C)/E_L$. The latter equation assumes that both interest and tax savings are risk-free, as in the Modigliani–Miller analysis. Since $E(Y)(1 - T_C)$ is given, we have

$$E(Y)(1 - T_C) = R_{EU} V_U = R_{EL} E_L + R_F(1 - T_C)D$$

Using the equality on the right-hand side, and substituting the CAPM expression for R_{EU} and R_{EL} (equation (7.10)), gives

$$\{R_F + \beta_U[E(R_M - R_F)]\}V_U = \{R_F + \beta_L[E(R_M - R_F)]\}E_L + R_F(1 - T_C)D$$

$$(7.13)$$

Letting $\lambda = [E(R_M) - R_F]/\sigma^2(R_M)$ and using the definition of beta,

$$V_U\{R_F + \text{cov}[Y(1 - T_C)/V_U, R_M]\lambda\}$$
$$= \{R_F + \text{cov}[Y(1 - T_C)/E_L, R_M]\lambda\}E_L + R_F(1 - T_C)D$$

The steps in arriving at the right-hand side are that the uncertain rate of return on the levered equity is $(Y - R_F D)(1 - T_C)/E_L$, and that $\text{cov}[(Y - R_F D)(1 - T_C)/E_L, R_M] = \text{cov}[Y(1 - T_C)/E_L, R_M]$, because $R_F D$ is certain. Since the covariance terms cancel out, the above equation simplifies to

$$V_U = E_L + (1 - T_C)D$$

This is the same result as equation (7.7). The Modigliani–Miller equations for the cost of equity and WACC follow from this equation, or, without tax, from $V_U = E_L + D$. Thus the argument in this paragraph shows that the Modigliani–Miller theory is implied by the CAPM.

The relation between beta and leverage, equation (7.11), has practical, as well as theoretical, interest. It enables the analyst to move from the observed beta for a given company j, estimated from its past share returns (Chapter 13), to a predicted beta for any company or project that is believed to have the same business risk as j, but has different leverage. The cost of equity using the predicted beta in the CAPM can then be inserted in the tax-adjusted WACC with risk-free debt. Such a procedure would be redundant if leverage had no effect on the WACC: in this case, all that would matter in determining the cost of capital would be the business risk. In equilibrium, all companies and projects of the same business risk would have the same WACC, whatever their levels of leverage. It is worth repeating that the *only* reason why leverage affects the WACC in the above analysis is that we have chosen not to capture the tax advantage of debt in the cash flows to be discounted.

7.2.4 *Risky debt*

The assumption of risk-free debt is a simplification. Corporate debt has default risk, so the future pay-offs are uncertain. Furthermore, the assumption of risk-free debt has the unfortunate implication that a project financed 100 per cent by debt has a cost of capital equal to the risk-free rate. Stiglitz (1969) shows that Modigliani and Miller's (1958) arbitrage argument without tax carries through with risky debt in the contingent-states framework, so long as both company and investor face the same costs of borrowing. The investor needs to be able to replicate exactly the distribution of state-contingent cash flows from holding the equity of a levered company. The investor can, in principle, replicate the cash flow distribution of a levered company by home-made leverage, as in the original Modigliani–Miller (1958) proof. He/she buys shares, partly with borrowed money, in an unlevered company that has the same future contingent cash flows before interest as the levered company, so that the ratio in each state of the cash flow from his/her shares to the interest on his/her personal loan is the same as the ratio of cash flow to interest for the levered company. To achieve replication, the pay-off to the lender in each state must be the same whether the lender has lent to the levered company or to the individual investor, in which case the expected return on the levered company's debt will be the same as the expected return on the loan to the investor, as required for the Modigliani–Miller argument. Bankruptcy for the levered company corresponds to a state in which the cash flow from the investor's shares in the unlevered company is less than the interest he/she owes. To achieve replication, the investor would have to pledge his/her shares as security, and his/her liability would have to be limited to the value of these shares. Fama (1978) calls this an assumption that individuals and firms have equal access to the capital market; the types of securities that can be issued by firms can also be issued by investors. Modigliani and Miller (1958) and Stiglitz (1969) also note that an investor who is a net lender can raise cash to buy the unlevered company's shares by selling bonds, instead of borrowing, in which case the opportunity cost of buying the shares is the loss of expected return on the bonds sold, not the investor's cost of borrowing.

The replication by an investor of a levered company's cash flows to equity would probably be impossible to achieve exactly. In particular, if an investor faces higher transactions costs of borrowing than a company, he/she cannot replicate the contingent cash flows. In any situation with potential for arbitrage, transactions costs set limits within which the price of the commodity can vary because would-be arbitrage is not profitable. In this case, the commodity is entitlement to contingent cash flows. Both the Modigliani–Miller arbitrage argument and the CAPM assume zero transactions costs, so neither will hold precisely in the presence of such costs. Corporate debt will add value by helping to complete the market; it provides packages of contingent claims that could otherwise be created only at greater cost, or not at all.

We may suspect that the costs of borrowing for a typical individual investor are so much greater than the costs for a typical listed company that, tax aside, corporate borrowing will add appreciable value for investors. But the differences in borrowing costs between investors and companies are less than they might seem, for various reasons. (i) Much investing in mature capital markets is done by large financial institutions rather than by individuals, and the borrowing costs of such institutions are similar to those of the companies they invest in. (ii) The cost of a personal loan secured by a mortgage is, in fact, similar to the cost of a large-scale corporate loan. (iii) If the default risk on a personal loan is high, the rate of interest charged will be correspondingly high. However, the expected losses from default should be subtracted from the promised rate of return to arrive at the expected rate of return, which is the correct measure of the individual's cost of debt. Ignoring transactions costs, an individual will face a higher cost of debt only to the extent that his/her loan has a higher systematic risk than the corporate loan.

Allowing for corporation tax, we can show that the Modigliani and Miller (1963) results obtain with risky debt in the world of the CAPM, except that the tax savings are discounted at the risky rate R_D rather than R_F (Stiglitz, 1969; Rubinstein, 1973). This means that R_D can be substituted for R_F in equation (7.9), the cost of levered equity given the cost of unlevered equity, the cost of debt and the leverage ratio, and in equation (7.6), the tax-adjusted WACC with risk-free debt. R_D is the expected rate of return on risky debt, not the promised rate. If expected rates of return on financial assets are specified by the CAPM, the expected rate on risky debt is given by

$$R_D = R_F + \beta_D[E(R_M) - R_F]$$

where β_D is the beta on risky debt. If the project is 100 per cent financed by debt, $\beta_D = \beta_U$. We know that

$$E(Y)(1 - T_C) = R_{EU}V_U = R_{EL}E_L + R_D(1 - T_C)D$$

Using the equality on the right-hand side, substituting the CAPM expressions for R_{EU}, R_{EL} and R_D, and using $\lambda = [E(R_M) - R_F]/\sigma^2(R_M)$ as before, gives

$$\{R_F + \beta_U[E(R_M) - R_F]\}V_U = \{R_F + \beta_L[E(R_M) - R_F]\}E_L$$
$$+ \{R_F + \beta_D[E(R_M) - R_F]\}(1 - T_C)D$$

or

$$\{R_F + \text{cov}[Y(1 - T_C)/V_U, R_M]\lambda\}V_U$$
$$= \{R_F + \text{cov}[(Y - R_DD)(1 - T_C)/E_L, R_M]\lambda\}E_L$$
$$+ [R_F + \text{cov}(R_D, R_M)\lambda](1 - T_C)D \qquad (7.14)$$

For any three variables, x, y and z, it can be shown that $\text{cov}[(x - y), z] = \text{cov}(x, z) - \text{cov}(y, z)$. Consider the term $\text{cov}[(Y - R_DD)(1 - T_C)/E_L, R_M]$, and think of $Y(1 - T_C)/E_L$ as x,

$R_D D(1 - T_C)/E_L$ as y and R_M as z. We can write

$$\text{cov}[(Y - R_D D)(1 - T_C)/E_L, R_M] = \text{cov}[(x - y), z] = \text{cov}(x, z) - \text{cov}(y, z)$$
$$= \text{cov}[Y(1 - T_C)/E_L, R_M] - \text{cov}[R_D D(1 - T_C)/E_L, R_M]$$
$$= \text{cov}(Y, R_M)(1 - T_C)/E_L - \text{cov}(R_D, R_M)D(1 - T_C)/E_L$$

Using this in equation (7.14) and simplifying gives

$$R_F V_U = R_F E_L - \text{cov}(R_D, R_M)D(1 - T_C)\lambda$$
$$+ [R_F + \text{cov}(R_D, R_M)\lambda](1 - T_C)D$$

therefore

$$V_U = E_L + D - T_C D$$

or

$$V_L = V_U + T_C D$$

which is the same as equation (7.7). The reason for this result is that, if the expected rate of return on risky debt is set by the CAPM, the (covariance) risk of the underlying cash flows is merely partitioned between equity and debt; it is not changed. If we again use the shorthand of x, y and z, as defined above, the risk of the company unlevered can be written as $\text{cov}(x, z)$ (with no debt, $E_L = V_U$). The risk of the company levered can be written as $[\text{cov}(x, z) - \text{cov}(y, z)] + \text{cov}(y, z) = \text{cov}(x, z)$. A change in leverage changes the positions of the company's shares and bonds on the securities market line, but does not offer the investor any opportunity for improved risk/return trade-off.

It can be seen that the present value of the tax savings from interest is the same, at $T_C D$, whether debt is assumed to be risk-free or risky. With risk-free debt, the tax saving is a perpetuity of $R_F T_C D$ that is discounted at R_F; with risky debt, the tax saving is a perpetuity of $R_D T_C D$ that is discounted at R_D. Having shown that $V_L = V_U + T_C D$ with risky debt, it is straightforward to show, following the steps in Section 7.2.2, that the tax-adjusted WACC with risky debt is given by

$$WACC = R_{EL}(1 - L) + R_D(1 - T_C)L \qquad (7.15)$$

and that the relation between the cost of equity and leverage is

$$R_{EL} = R_{EU} + (R_{EU} - R_D)(1 - T_C)D/E_L \qquad (7.16)$$

The relation between the beta of levered equity and leverage with risky debt can be found as follows (Conine, 1980). We know that

$$E(Y)(1 - T_C) = V_U[R_F + \lambda \text{cov}(R_U, R_M)]$$

and that

$$E[(Y - R_D D)(1 - T_C)] = E_L[R_F + \lambda \text{cov}(R_L, R_M)]$$

or

$$E(Y)(1 - T_C) = E_L[R_F + \lambda cov(R_L, R_M)] + D(1 - T_C)[R_F + \lambda cov(R_D, R_M)]$$

We combine these equations to eliminate $E(Y)(1 - T_C)$. Terms with R_F can be eliminated using the result established above that, with risky or risk-free debt, $(V_L =) E_L + D = V_U + T_C D$, to give

$$E_L[\lambda cov(R_L, R_M)] = V_U[\lambda cov(R_U, R_M)] - D(1 - T_C)[\lambda cov(R_D, R_M)]$$

Dividing through by $E_L \lambda var(R_M)$ gives

$$\beta_L = \beta_U(V_U/E_L) - \beta_D(1 - T_C)D/E_L$$

or

$$\beta_L = \beta_U + (\beta_U - \beta_D)(1 - T_C)D/E_L \tag{7.17}$$

Comparing equation (7.17) with the corresponding relation between the equity beta and leverage assuming risk-free debt,

$$\beta_L = \beta_U + \beta_U(1 - T_C)D/E_L \tag{7.11}$$

it can be seen that the relation between the equity beta and the debt/equity ratio is less steep if debt is risky. This is because β_D increases with leverage, so some of the greater financial risk is borne by lenders, whereas it is all borne by shareholders if debt is risk-free.

7.3   Expected cash flows that are not a constant perpetuity

7.3.1   Without corporation tax

So far we have assumed, for simplicity, that the project's expected cash flows before interest are the same each year for ever. 'Assets offering perpetual cash-flow streams are like abominable snowmen: often referred to but seldom seen' (Brealey and Myers, 1996, p. 535). Projects have a finite life, their operating cash flows are usually distinctly uneven, and their leverage may be expected to change. A policy of paying dividends and holding outstanding debt constant, for example, implies that expected leverage will rise during the life of a finite project. If leverage changes over time, then the costs of equity and debt will change. It would be incorrect to estimate the WACC using the costs of equity and debt estimated at the start of the project during its subsequent life, with changing leverage. In fact, even if it is assumed that the costs of equity and debt are constant, despite the changing leverage, their use in the WACC formula would not result in a valuation of the project that is consistent with the values of the equity and debt worked out separately (Ehrhardt, 1994, pp. 19–22).

The implication is that, for the WACC to be used correctly to value a project with a finite life, it is necessary to assume that the project's debt policy is to maintain constant leverage during its life (Linke and Kim, 1974, and others). The cash flows to equity and debt in period t are, respectively, Div_t and Y_{Dt}, where Div_t includes all cash payments to shareholders and Y_{Dt} stands for cash flows to debt (interest plus loan repayments). The total cash flow to providers of capital in period t is $Y_t = Div_t + Y_{Dt}$. The market values of the equity E_{Lt} and debt D_t are the present values of the expected flows to equity and debt discounted at the constant costs of equity and debt, respectively. We can write

$$E_{Lt} = E_{Lt-1}(1 + R_{EL}) - Div_t$$
$$D_t = D_{t-1}(1 + R_D) - Y_{Dt}$$

therefore

$$E_{Lt} + D_t = (E_{Lt-1} + D_{t-1})[1 + (E_{Lt-1}R_{EL} + D_{t-1}R_D)/$$
$$(E_{Lt-1} + D_{t-1})] - Div_t - Y_{Dt}$$

So, with leverage kept constant,

$$E_{Lt} + D_t = (E_{Lt-1} + D_{t-1})(1 + WACC) - Div_t - Y_{Dt}$$

for $t = 1, 2 \ldots T$, the terminal period. If $t = T - 1$, $V_{LT} = 0$ and

$$V_{LT-1} = (Div_T + Y_{DT})/(1 + WACC)$$
$$V_{LT-2} = (Div_{T-1} + Y_{DT-1})/(1 + WACC) + (Div_T + Y_{DT})/(1 + WACC)^2$$

and so on back to $t = 0$. Since $Y_t = Div_t + Y_{Dt}$, we have shown that

$$V_{L0} = \Sigma_{t=1}^{T} Y_t/(1 + WACC)^t$$

Leverage measured using market values could, in theory, be held constant by adjusting the amount of debt outstanding, but this would not be easy or cost-free in practice.

7.3.2   *With corporation tax*

With corporation tax, leverage affects the cost of capital; if leverage changes over time, so does the standard tax-adjusted WACC. The WACC can still be used as the discount rate if we assume that managers will adjust borrowing so as to maintain a constant market-value leverage ratio during the life of the project (Miles and Ezzell, 1980). But things are not quite the same as for perpetual cash flows, because the relation between the cost of equity and leverage is different from that given in equation (7.9). For a given level of leverage, risk-free rate and unlevered cost of equity, the numerical values of the levered cost of equity and of WACC will differ slightly from the numbers resulting from equations (7.9) and (7.6) respectively.

The Miles–Ezzell analysis starts with an equation that decomposes the value of a levered project into the present value of the cash flows as though there were no debt, plus the present value of the expected tax savings:

$$V_{L0} = \Sigma_{t=1}^{T} E(Y_{At})/(1 + R_{EU})^t + \Sigma_{t=1}^{T} T_C R_F L V_{Lt-1}/(1 + R_D^*)^t \qquad (7.18)$$

where $E(Y_{At})$ is the expected operating cash flow after corporation tax in period t, the expected life of the project is T periods and R_D^* is the discount rate for tax savings. The expected cash flows are discounted at the unlevered cost of equity. As the project is not a perpetuity, the cash flows include repayments of equity and debt, which are not subject to corporation tax, so $E(Y_{At}) \neq E(Y_t)(1 - T_C)$. Debt is assumed to be risk-free; managers are assumed to vary borrowing to keep market-value leverage L constant; and there is assumed to be sufficient tax payable before interest for all interest to relieve tax. But the tax savings vary with the project's market value V_{Lt}, which is no longer assumed to be constant. This is because the interest paid varies with the market value of the project, due to period-by-period adjustments in borrowing to keep L constant. So the amounts of the tax savings are uncertain, and the rate at which they are discounted, R_D^*, exceeds the risk-free rate. Equation (7.18) is a special case of the more general 'adjusted present value' formula (Section 7.5.4), which separates out the present value attributable to tax savings from the rest of the project's value, and does not require that future leverage remains constant.

The value of the project cannot be determined directly from equation (7.18) because there is a circularity: part of project value is the tax savings, but the tax savings depend on current and future project values. To escape, Miles and Ezzell use backward iteration to find future project values. They argue that the project value is known at the start of any period, and so the end-of-period tax saving is also known and can be discounted at the risk-free rate. For the period before the project ends, we have

$$V_{LT-1} = E(Y_T)/(1 + R_{EU}) + T_C R_F L V_{LT-1}/(1 + R_F)$$

Solving for V_{LT-1} gives

$$V_{LT-1} = E(Y_T)/\{(1 + R_{EU})[1 - T_C R_F L/(1 + R_F)]\} \tag{7.19}$$

Project value at $T - 2$ can now be found:

$$V_{LT-2} = E(Y_{T-1})/(1 + R_{EU}) + T_C R_F L V_{LT-2}/(1 + R_F) + V_{LT-1}/(1 + R_{EU}) \tag{7.20}$$

The unlevered cost of equity is the appropriate rate for discounting the project value at $T - 1$ because V_{LT-1} has the same risk as Y_T, which is discounted at R_{EU}. This follows because $Y_T = V_{UT-1}(1 + R_{EU})$ and because $V_{UT-1} = V_{LT-1}[1 - T_C R_F L/(1 + R_F)]$. Both $1 + R_{EU}$ and $1 - T_C R_F L/(1 + R_F)$ are constants, so Y_T, V_{UT-1} and V_{LT-1} have the same risk. Substituting equation (7.19) into equation (7.20) and solving for V_{LT-2} gives

$$V_{LT-2} = E(Y_{T-1})/(1 + R_L) + E(Y_T)/(1 + R_L)^2$$

where

$$1 + R_L = (1 + R_{EU})[1 - T_C R_F L/(1 + R_F)]$$

or

$$R_L = R_{EU} - T_C R_F L(1 + R_{EU})/(1 + R_F) \tag{7.21}$$

R_L is the project's cost of capital, given constant leverage of L, and can be used to discount $E(Y_t)$, $t = 1, 2 \ldots T$. If $L = 0$, $R_L = R_{EU}$. Equation (7.21) specifies a *different* relation between the project's discount rate and its leverage from the Modigliani–Miller relation allowing for corporation tax, equation (7.8). The discount rate that emerges for the tax shields, which we labelled R_D^*, can be shown to be given by $[(1 + R_{EU})^{T-1}(1 + R_F)]^{1/T} - 1$, where T is the number of periods ahead that a particular tax saving is obtained (Miles and Ezzell, 1985).

The project discount rate R_L can be written in the form of a WACC. The rate of return on equity in any period can be written

$$1 + R_{EL} = \frac{E(Y_{t+1}) + E(V_{t+1}) - [1 + R_F(1 - T_C)]LV_t}{(1 - L)V_t}$$

$$= \frac{1 + R_L - [1 + R_F(1 - T_C)]L}{(1 - L)}$$

Solving for R_L gives

$$R_L = (1 - L)R_{EL} + R_F(1 - T_C)L \tag{7.22}$$

This formula is the same as the tax-adjusted WACC with risk-free debt, but it does not give the same relation between the project's discount rate and leverage because the cost of equity is specified differently from equation (7.9), the expression for the cost of equity in the tax-adjusted WACC (equation (7.6)). The Miles–Ezzell relation between the cost of equity and leverage can be found by substituting the expression for R_L, equation (7.22), into equation (7.21). The very cumbersome expression for R_{EL} that results can be simplified easily to give the still cumbersome

$$R_{EL} = R_{EU} + \{R_{EU} - R_F[1 + T_C(R_{EU} - R_F)/(1 + R_F)]\}D/E_L \tag{7.23}$$

Miles and Ezzell (1985) also derive the relation between beta and leverage, under the same set of assumptions. The value of the tax saving in the next period is certain. The values of the subsequent tax savings are tied to the project values at the start of each period, and therefore have the same risk as the cash flows before interest. So the present value of the project can be written as

$$V_{L0} = [E(V_{U1}) + E(Y_1) + E(V_{TS1})]/(1 + R_{EU}) + T_C R_F L V_{L0}/(1 + R_F)$$

where $E(V_{TS1})$ is the expected value of tax savings as at date 1. The beta risk of the first element is β_U and the risk of the second element is zero. The second element is the value of the tax saving in the next period, and constitutes a fraction $T_C R_F L/(1 + R_F)$ of the total value. The beta of the project's capital (equity plus debt), β_{ED}, is the weighted average of the two: $\beta_{ED} = \beta_U[1 - T_C R_F L/(1 + R_F)]$. β_{ED} is also a weighted average of the betas of the equity (β_L) and debt, and as the debt is assumed to be risk-free we have $\beta_{ED} = \beta_L(1 - L)$. Using these two expressions for β_{ED}, we have

$$\beta_U = \beta_L(1 - L)/[1 - T_C R_F L/(1 + R_F)]$$

or

$$\beta_L = \beta_U(1 + D/E_L)[1 + R_F(1 - T_C L)]/(1 + R_F) \tag{7.24}$$

The relation between equity beta and leverage in equation (7.24) is steeper than the relation between beta and leverage for a perpetual project with risk-free debt, in equation (7.11). In deriving both equations (7.24) and (7.11), debt is assumed to be risk-free, so all the financial risk is borne by the shareholders. But in deriving (7.24) the tax savings beyond the first period have the risk of unlevered equity, whereas in deriving (7.11) the tax savings are assumed to be risk-free. There is more dampening of the impact of leverage on equity risk if the tax savings are assumed to be risk-free than there is if the tax savings have the risk of unlevered equity.

7.4   Use of the formulas

It is very easy to lose track of the meaning of the various formulas, and of the connections between them. The current section seeks to clarify matters by considering how the formulas can be used in estimating a project's cost of capital (there is further discussion of this in Chapter 14). We are treating the target optimum leverage for the company or project as given; it is determined by tax circumstances and by non-tax factors that are beyond our scope (Section 6.3). For non-perpetual projects, we are assuming that managers act to hold market-value leverage constant, so that the WACC will be constant. The cash flows to discount are after corporation tax, ignoring interest.

The most straightforward case is a project that has the same business risk and the same leverage as a listed company, which could be the parent or some other company, and which we shall label A. Since A is listed, the beta of its shares can be estimated from share price data and A's cost of equity can be estimated via the CAPM. In principle, the same could be done for A's debt, if it has listed bonds outstanding. The project's cost of capital can then be estimated without further ado by inserting the estimates for A's cost of equity and cost of debt into the WACC formula, together with its target leverage and the effective rate of corporation tax. No other formulas are needed.

Now suppose that we cannot find a perfectly matching company in terms of business risk and leverage. There is only a company B with similar business risk and substantially different leverage. B's costs of equity and debt can no longer be used directly as the project's cost of equity and debt. This is where the formulas that relate the cost of capital and leverage have a practical application. They can be used to estimate B's unlevered cost of equity, which will be our estimate of the project's unlevered cost of equity, since B and the project are assumed to have the same business risk. The unlevered cost of equity can then be used to estimate the project's actual WACC and (if desired) its cost of equity, given its target level of leverage. We have identified four sets of formulas that show the relation between leverage and the cost of capital, given a constant business risk. The formulas are presented in Table 7.1. There are four sets because we have considered four combinations of assumptions: (1) constant perpetual expected cash flows, risk-free debt and no tax; (2) perpetual cash flows, risk-free debt and corporation tax; (3) perpetual cash flows, risky debt and corporation tax; (4) non-perpetual cash flows, risk-free debt and corporation tax. A gap in the analysis is the case of non-perpetual cash flows, risky debt and corporation tax.

Table 7.1. *The cost of capital and leverage: formula summary*

1. Constant perpetual expected cash flows; risk-free debt; no tax

$$R_{EL} = R_{EU} + (R_{EU} - R_F)D/E_L \tag{7.5}$$

$$\beta_L = \beta_U/(1 - L)$$

$$= \beta_U(1 + D/E_L) \tag{7.12}$$

$$R_L = WACC = R_{EU} \tag{7.4}$$

$$= R_{EL}E_L/V_L + R_F D/V_L \tag{7.3}$$

2. Constant perpetual expected cash flows; risk-free debt; corporation tax

$$R_{EL} = R_{EU} + (R_{EU} - R_F)(1 - T_C)D/E_L \tag{7.9}$$

$$\beta_L = \beta_U + \beta_U(1 - T_C)D/E_L \tag{7.11}$$

$$R_L = WACC = R_{EU}(1 - T_C L) \tag{7.8}$$

$$= R_{EL}E_L/V_L + R_F(1 - T_C)D/V_L \tag{7.6}$$

3. Constant perpetual expected cash flows; risky debt; corporation tax

$$R_{EL} = R_{EU} + (R_{EU} - R_D)(1 - T_C)D/E_L \tag{7.16}$$

$$\beta_L = \beta_U + (\beta_U - \beta_D)(1 - T_C)D/E_L \tag{7.17}$$

$$R_L = WACC = R_{EU}(1 - T_C L) \tag{7.8}$$

$$= R_{EL}E_L/V_L + R_D(1 - T_C)D/V_L \tag{7.15}$$

4. Non-constant expected cash flows; risk-free debt; corporation tax

$$R_{EL} = R_{EU} + \{R_{EU} - R_F[1 + T_C(R_{EU} - R_F)/(1 + R_F)]\}D/E_L \tag{7.23}$$

$$\beta_L = \beta_U(1 + D/E_L)[1 + R_F(1 - T_C L)]/(1 + R_F) \tag{7.24}$$

$$R_L = WACC = R_{EU} - R_F L T_C(1 + R_{EU})/(1 + R_F) \tag{7.21}$$

$$= R_{EL}E_L/V_L + R_F(1 - T_C)D/V_L \tag{7.6}$$

The first formula in each set shows the relation between the cost of equity and leverage. It can be used to find the cost of unlevered equity from an estimate of the levered beta, or to find the cost of levered equity from an estimate of the unlevered beta. The second formula shows the relation between the equity beta and leverage, which can be used in the CAPM (equation (7.10)). This gives the same answers as the first formula. The third formula shows the relation between the project cost of capital and leverage. The fourth shows the WACC. The beauty of the WACC is that it is an easy formula to remember and gives the correct project cost of capital, for given values of R_{EL}, R_F or R_D, L and T_C. However, the WACC cannot be used to show the relation between the cost of capital and leverage. This is because, if L changes, R_{EL} and R_D also change, and the WACC formula does not itself tell us how they change. A change in L gives different numbers for the WACC across the four combinations of assumptions, with the exception of combinations (2) and (3).

Example

A project's managers estimate that it has the same business risk as a certain listed company that is unlevered and has a beta of 1. The risk-free rate is 4 per cent p.a. and the expected rate of return on the market is 10 per cent p.a., so the project's unlevered cost of equity is 10 per cent p.a. The project has a leverage ratio of 0.40; $D/E_L = 0.67$. The corporation tax rate is 30 per cent.

1. **Constant perpetual expected cash flows; risk-free debt; no tax**

$$R_{EL} = 10\% + 6\%(.67) = 14.0\% \text{ pa} \tag{7.5}$$

$$WACC = 14\%(.6) + 4\%(.4) = 10.0\% \text{ pa} \tag{7.3}$$

2. **Constant perpetual expected cash flows; risk-free debt; corporation tax**

$$R_{EL} = 10\% + 6\%(.7)(.67) = 12.8\% \text{ pa} \tag{7.9}$$

$$WACC = 12.8\%(.6) + 4\%(.7)(.4) = 8.8\% \text{ pa} \tag{7.6}$$

3. **Constant perpetual expected cash flows; risky debt; corporation tax**
   Assume debt has a beta of 0.1, so $R_D = 4.6$ per cent p.a.

$$R_{EL} = 10\% + 5.4\%(.7)(.67) = 12.5\% \text{ pa} \tag{7.16}$$

$$WACC = 12.5\%(.6) + 4.6\%(.7)(.4) = 8.8\% \text{ pa} \tag{7.15}$$

4. **Non-constant expected cash flows; risk-free debt; corporation tax**

$$R_{EL} = 10\% + \{10\% - 4\%[1 + .3(6\%)/(1.04)]\}(.67) \tag{7.23}$$
$$= 14.0\% \text{ pa}$$

$$WACC = 14.0\%(.6) + 4.0\%(.7)(.4) = 9.5\% \text{ pa} \tag{7.6}$$

The levered cost of equity R_{EL} could, in each case, be calculated using the CAPM and the applicable formula for levered beta β_L.

7.5   Issues concerning the WACC

7.5.1   *Circularity*

Use of a tax-adjusted WACC appears to involve circularity. If a project has positive NPV, the market value is greater than the initial cost. The WACC using market value will exceed the WACC using initial cost, because the tax-adjusted WACC is negatively related to leverage. It seems as though the project's market value is affecting its cost of capital, which is circular. If there is no debt, NPV > 0 does not present a problem; the cash flows are discounted at the appropriate unlevered cost of equity. The problem arises because of the tax adjustment in the WACC formula, which links the tax savings to leverage measured with market values.

The issue can be sidestepped by assuming that the project is marginal (NPV = 0). If NPV ≠ 0, one response is to assume that managers act to keep leverage measured with market values at a target level, in which case the Modigliani–Miller formula (equation (7.8)), or the tax-adjusted WACC formula using the target leverage, give the correct cost of capital (Myers, 1974, p. 18). An active debt management policy to maintain constant leverage is often contrasted with a passive policy of maintaining the same amount of debt, in which case the project's WACC changes during its life. Although the assumption of constant leverage enables the cost of capital to be found, there is still a problem when it comes to project valuation. The project NPV is estimated using the WACC with the target leverage. If NPV turns out to be positive, then the maintenance of market-value leverage at a set target involves borrowing more money, which is used to repurchase equity. The increase in borrowing means an increase in tax savings, which increases project value, and so on through iterations involving diminishing additions to value. Copeland and Weston (1988, p. 448) point out that such adjustments to debt and equity outstanding are easier said than done; the lender and the shareholders would have to agree to the transaction. As a pragmatic compromise, they argue that it is reasonable to assume that there is a long-run target leverage ratio, and they recommend ignoring the increase in borrowing and in project value implied by an attempt to reach the target market-value leverage at the outset. Positive NPV means that market-value leverage is temporarily below target. The project could support greater debt, which would result in more tax savings, but this is ignored, so project value will be understated slightly. In the spirit of Modigliani and Miller (1963), short-term fluctuations around the target are assumed not to have much effect on value.

The circularity problem can be avoided altogether by not using the WACC. Instead, a method of project valuation could be used in which the tax advantage of debt is captured in forecast cash flows rather than in the discount rate. Examples are the adjusted present value and cash-flows-to-equity methods, which are discussed below.

7.5.2   WACC and value additivity

The cash flows attributable to a project should be incremental – that is, flows that would not have arisen had the project not been undertaken. The incremental cash flows should include any changes to cash flows from the company's existing operations that result from the project. For example, if the project makes an existing production process cheaper, the savings should be included in the project's cash flows. On the other hand, overheads that the company would be paying anyway are not incremental. It may well be difficult to identify and estimate incremental cash flows in practice, but the principle is clear.

If a project's cash flows are truly incremental, the company's existing cash flows are unaffected by whether or not the project is undertaken; changes to the existing flows attributed to the project are assigned to the project. It is this point that underpins the principle of *value additivity*. This states that the total value of two or more projects, or of an existing company and a new project, is the sum of the present values of each project, if the total cash flow at each date is the sum of the cash flows of each project at that date. The condition is satisfied if project cash flows are incremental or independent of each other. The proof of value additivity is perhaps easiest to grasp in the contingent-states framework (Myers, 1968). Whatever state arises, the total cash flow is always the sum of the flows from the constituent projects. The present value of each state-contingent £1 is the discount factor appropriate to that state. This discount factor applies whether the source of a state-contingent £1 is a project j or a project k. Thus a project's value is determined only by its contingent cash flows and the applicable state-specific discount rates. Neither is affected by other projects. It follows that the total value of a combination of projects can only be the sum of each project's value estimated on its own. The Modigliani–Miller proposition that leverage does not affect value is an example of value additivity. Leverage partitions a project's contingent cash flows, and the sum of the parts is, by definition, the cash flows of the project with no debt.

Value additivity implies that any correlation between projects' cash flows makes no difference to the sum of their values. This is counter-intuitive at first sight, but it is quite consistent with the CAPM assumption that investors hold efficiently diversified portfolios. Suppose the incremental cash flows of two projects are negatively correlated, so that the combined cash flow of the two is less risky than the cash flow of either considered separately. No value is created by forming a company to undertake both the projects. Investors can achieve the same result by buying separate shares in the two projects.

Value additivity further implies that each project has its own cost of capital, which reflects its business risk and optimal leverage. A company can be seen as a collection of ongoing projects, and its WACC as a value-weighted average of the discount rates of the individual projects. It is wrong to think of this WACC as the correct cost of capital for these projects or for new ones, unless they all have the same risk (Keane, 1977). Departing from this principle will obscure the principle of value additivity. Suppose a company with one existing project undertakes a new project, and that the combined cash flows have less systematic risk than the existing cash flows. In the CAPM world, the new project must have a lower beta for the combined cash flows to have a lower beta. The company's WACC falls after acceptance of the new project. It may look as though the value of the existing project would rise, because its cash flows would be discounted at a lower rate, and that this would be a benefit attributable to the new project. But the cash flows attributable to the new project are defined correctly only if they do not affect the cash flows of the other project. The company's new, lower WACC is not the discount rate for the existing project or for the new one. The discount rate for each is the rate appropriate for the risk of the project's incremental cash flows considered on their own. The new project's value, estimated using the appropriate discount rate, can then be added to the value of the existing company without adjustment.

7.5.3   WACC and value maximisation

It is tempting to think that a company's managers can increase market value by reducing the company's cost of capital. However, we argue that this way of thinking is seriously misleading. To begin with, it is really projects that have a cost of capital rather than companies, at least if personal tax is ignored. A project's cost of capital depends on the prevailing risk-free rate of interest after tax, the risk of the project and the after-tax premium required in the capital market for bearing this risk. None of these things is under the managers' control. They might be able to reduce the project's risk, but in this case it would be clearer, conceptually, to think of the lower-risk version as a new project, with a new cost of capital.

A project's financing policies do affect the tax-adjusted WACC, because they affect the amounts of corporate and personal taxes paid. But it is implausible to think that a project's market value can be maximised by choosing the financing policies that minimise the tax-adjusted WACC. The reason is that the financing policies affect not only the taxes to be paid; they also affect the before-tax cash flows to be discounted, because they affect the expected cash flows related to agency and information factors, and to the costs of financial distress (Section 6.3). The company chooses its leverage and dividend pay-out policies to maximise its market value. The tax effects are captured in the tax-adjusted WACC; other effects are captured in the cash flows. The choices of leverage and dividend payout affect the WACC, but value is not necessarily maximised by minimising the WACC. Thus the WACC should not be interpreted as a way of expressing the relation between value and leverage. Rather, it specifies a discount rate, *given a level of leverage that has already been determined.*

Suppose, contrary to the above, that one views the concept of the cost of capital as encompassing all the costs and benefits associated with financing policy. It might be possible to specify a formula for this broadly defined cost of capital. The cash flows to be discounted would be invariant with respect to the various financing-related cash flows, which would all be captured in this 'broad' discount rate, and the maximisation of value would indeed be achieved by the minimisation of the broad discount rate. But the formula for the broad discount rate would not look the same as a tax-adjusted WACC, nor the same as any other cost-of-capital formula that failed to capture *all* the various financing-related cash flows. Furthermore, the maximisation of value would not be achieved by the minimisation of any discount rate that did not capture all financing-related costs, except by coincidence. A clear case in point is a tax-adjusted WACC, minimised with leverage of 100 per cent. Since most companies operate with leverage much lower than 100 per cent, it is reasonable to infer that value usually is not maximised by having very high leverage. These points were originally made by Keane (1977, 1978) and Haley and Schall (1978).

A separate point is that the maximisation of the market value of a firm's equity is not the same objective as the maximisation of the market value of its equity and debt (Fama, 1978; Fama and Miller, 1972, pp. 178–80; Jensen and Meckling, 1976, p. 335). A conflict of interest between shareholders and lenders is ruled out if debt is deemed to be risk-free (as Modigliani and Miller have assumed). But allowing for risky debt means recognising that shareholders may be able to increase their wealth at the expense of lenders, and vice versa. For example, the shareholders could increase the default risk of existing lenders by having the company issue new debt that is not subordinated to existing debt. The fall in value of the existing debt implies an increase in wealth for the shareholders. There can also be discrepancies between investment decisions that maximise the value of the equity on its own, the value of the debt on its own and the value of the equity plus debt.

The exploration of conflicts of interest in company financing is beyond our scope. We merely note that the standard valuation procedure, of discounting a project's expected cash flows to equity and debt combined by the project's WACC, abstracts from the shareholder/lender conflict.

7.5.4   Three alternative cash flow/cost-of-capital methods

Here we consider briefly three of the methods of valuation that have been proposed as alternatives to discounting $E(Y)(1 - T_C)$ by a tax-adjusted WACC. All three have the advantage that they disentangle the cost of capital from corporation tax. Both tax and financing-related costs are then fully captured in cash flows, and the discount rate becomes a pure opportunity cost, reflecting only the risk of the cash flows measured after corporation tax (but still before personal tax).

1. Adjusted present value (APV) (Myers, 1974; Brealey and Myers, 2003)
This method involves estimating the project value as though there were no debt, and adding the present value of the tax savings from interest. Cash flows after tax, $E(Y)(1 - T_C)$, are discounted at the company's unlevered cost of equity R_{EU}. The tax savings are forecast and discounted at a suitable discount rate, and their present value added. The thinking is that the only reason why the tax-adjusted WACC of a levered project is lower than its cost of equity if it were unlevered is the tax advantage of debt. With the value of the tax advantage estimated separately, the company's cash flows after tax (ignoring interest) can be discounted at R_{EU} whatever its level of leverage. The APV method makes explicit the question of the discount rate R_D^* for the tax savings. It gives the same valuation as the standard method, using a tax-adjusted WACC, if the tax savings are treated as certain and are forecast and discounted using R_F, or if the tax savings are treated as uncertain and are forecast and discounted using R_D.

APV calls for an estimate of the unlevered cost of equity. If there is no unlevered listed company with the same business risk as the project, then it will be necessary to unlever the cost of equity of a listed company of the same business risk. A second point is that, for projects of finite life, APV does not require the assumption that market-value leverage is held constant. In fact, it is not necessary to know the future leverage levels. The amounts of the tax savings have to be forecast period by period, and therefore the future amounts of debt outstanding have to be known, but it is not necessary to know the future market values of debt and equity. APV is a more transparent method than discounting using the WACC, but the WACC is simpler to use, especially if the WACC of an existing company (e.g. the parent) can be applied to the project in question.

2. Discount the correct cash flows after tax (Arditti, 1973; Ruback, 2002)
The actual expected cash flows after corporation tax for a perpetuity are $E(Y)(1 - T_C) + R_F D T_C$, not $E(Y)(1 - T_C)$. The cash flow to equity is $[E(Y) - R_F D](1 - T_C)$ and the flow to debt is $R_F D$. With cash flows measured in this way, the discount rate, which we shall label $WACC_1$, is

$$WACC_1 = \frac{[E(Y) - R_F D](1 - T_C)}{E_L} \frac{E_L}{E_L + D} + \frac{R_F D}{E_L + D}$$
$$= R_{EL} E_L / V_L + R_F D / V_L \tag{7.25}$$

The only difference between $WACC_1$ and the tax-adjusted WACC is that the tax advantage to debt is captured in the cash flows rather than the discount rate. This means that $WACC_1$ has to be constant with respect to leverage, and it leads to a relatively simple relation between the cost of equity and leverage, even if debt is assumed to be risky (Ruback, 2002). It is a bit puzzling why this approach has never caught on; it would save having to adjust the cost of capital for leverage. Why do people wish the tax advantage to debt to be captured in the cost of capital rather than in cash flows?

As an aside, Arditti (1973) and Haley and Schall (1978, 1979) assume that $WACC_1$ is U-shaped with respect to leverage, and note that the level of leverage at which $WACC_1$ is minimised is lower than the level at which value is maximised. The reason is that, as leverage is increased beyond the point at which $WACC_1$ is minimised, there is a stage during which the tax saving from more debt, captured in cash flows, outweighs the effect of the rising discount rate. Thus it appears that the minimisation of $WACC_1$ and the maximisation of value are not equivalent. But there is no reason why $WACC_1$ should be U-shaped, rather than flat, *unless* it captures some financing-related costs, such as agency costs. But then the formula must be different from that given by equation (7.25). (Haley and Schall, 1979, pp. 339–44, argue disconcertingly that $WACC_1$ is U-shaped even though $WACC_1$ does not capture any financing-related costs. It appears that this is due to an oversight on their part: they include the tax advantage to debt both in $WACC_1$, for leverage of less than 100 per cent, and in the cash flows.)

3. Discount cash flows to equity

This is a substantially different method from the previous methods considered, because discounting cash flows to equity by the cost of equity gives the value of equity, not the value of equity and debt. The cash flows relating to debt – expected loan drawdowns, interest payments and loan repayments – appear in the cash flow forecast, so the net cash flows after tax belong to the shareholders. The discount rate is the cost of levered equity. The tax savings from interest are captured in the cash flows, and are discounted at the cost of equity. If the same cost of equity is applied to every future period, there is an implicit assumption that leverage will remain constant. But in this case there is a problem with circularity (Taggart, 1991): the estimation of the cash flows to equity requires the estimation of the future amounts of debt, but with constant leverage we cannot estimate future amounts of debt without first estimating future values of equity. Perhaps for this reason, the cash-flows-to-equity method is absent or not prominent in textbooks. But it is widely used in practice to arrive at estimates of fundamental equity value; future borrowings are forecast, a constant cost of equity is used, and theoretical changes in the cost of equity due to changes in leverage are ignored or allowed for by making ad hoc adjustments to the cost of equity. To value a company that is a going concern, as opposed to a one-off project, the analyst has to subtract the estimates of future investment required in the company from the cash flows. The cash flows to be discounted are 'free' cash flows, available for distribution to the shareholders.

7.5.5   Changes in tax rates

We have assumed throughout the chapter that the rate of corporation tax is fixed. A natural question is how a change in the tax rate affects the cost of capital. If the corporation tax rate facing a particular company, but not others, were to rise unexpectedly, the higher tax presumably makes it harder to find positive NPV projects and reduces the firm's growth. We would assume that a single company or project can take the economy-wide expected rate of return after tax as fixed, for a given level of risk. There is no effect on the cost of equity expressed after tax, but the higher tax will reduce cash flows net of tax.

Suppose now that the tax increase is economy-wide, affecting all companies. The answer in this case is not so clear-cut. We would expect corporate investment to fall compared with what it would have been had the tax not been increased. The fall in the demand for equity capital may, in theory, cause the required rate of return on equity after tax to fall. The response of the equilibrium required rate to a shift in the demand for equity depends on the elasticity of supply of equity from savers with respect to the expected rate of return after tax. For example, an inelastic supply of equity implies that the expected rate after tax will fall by nearly the same percentage as the tax rate has risen. In this case, most investors are willing to accept a lower after-tax rate of return on equity; they do not decide to consume more instead, or to divert their savings from equity to another asset class, and the amount of new equity investment will not decline much. There are also the effects to consider of how the higher tax revenue is spent. Thus, an economy-wide change in the corporation tax rate may change the cost of equity expressed after corporation tax, and predicting the change calls for macroeconomic analysis.

7.6   Summary

This chapter has introduced corporation tax and the weighted average cost of capital, reviewed the relation between the WACC and leverage given the existence of corporation tax, discussed several issues in the application of the WACC in project valuation, and outlined three alternatives to the WACC. Under the assumptions we have made in Chapter 6 and in this chapter, the only reason why leverage affects the cost of capital is the tax savings from interest. The tax savings are one of the factors relevant to the question of how a company determines its capital structure, but certainly not the only one.

There is an intellectual satisfaction in establishing the relations between leverage and the cost of capital under various assumptions, and some of the analysis reviewed in this chapter will no doubt have been familiar to readers with a finance or accounting background. Yet its importance is limited, for two reasons. First, correct adjustment of the cost of capital for leverage – i.e. for the tax savings from interest – is of second-order importance in practical estimation of the cost of capital. The effect of adjustment for leverage is dwarfed by the uncertainty surrounding the appropriate risk premium; in CAPM terms, uncertainty regarding the equity risk premium and the project's unlevered beta. Second, the analysis has a serious limitation even on its own tax-driven terms, which is that it ignores personal tax. We turn to personal tax next.

8 Personal tax and the cost of equity: the old and the new views

Personal taxes do not appear either in conventional formulas for the cost of equity, such as the standard CAPM, or in the formulas for a project's cost of capital discussed in the last chapter. It is tempting to infer from this that personal taxes have no impact on the cost of capital, but such an inference is not warranted, at least not a priori. Personal taxes affect the cash flows that providers of capital receive from projects, and project cash flows are always measured before personal tax. Therefore, the cost of capital is always expressed before personal tax, and personal taxes affect the cost of capital.

Personal taxes are levied on the pay-offs from financial assets. The pay-offs are received by investors whose tax circumstances vary. This means that there is no single, market-wide rate of personal tax that applies to any particular financial asset, and there is no single after-tax rate of return on the asset. Given the market price and the future returns on the asset before personal tax, there are as many after-tax rates of return as the number of different personal tax rates facing the holders of the asset. This is probably the main reason why the cost of capital is never expressed after personal tax. The serious complication that there is no single rate of personal tax paid by all the holders of an asset is often ignored in analyses of the effect of personal tax on the cost of capital, and it is ignored in the current chapter. We assume that the tax rates on income T_I and on capital gains T_G apply to all investors.

In analysing the effects of tax on the cost of capital, it often helps to abstract from the impact of uncertainty or risk on required rates of return, although we did not need to do this in Chapter 7. In this chapter we shall assume a world of certainty, except where noted. An implication of this is that, with no transactions costs or constraints, all financial assets and projects will have the same, risk-free, rate of return after all tax. Any differences in rates of return before tax can thus be attributed to tax. An alternative assumption that has the same effect is that investors are risk-neutral. Under risk neutrality, the expected rate of return after tax on any asset is the risk-free rate. Another alternative is to assume that we discount certainty-equivalent, rather than actual, cash flows. The discount rate appropriate for certainty-equivalent cash flow is, again, the risk-free rate.

8.1   Extension of the Modigliani–Miller analysis

Notation

T_C = Corporation tax rate on company profits, as in Chapter 7.

T_I = Income tax rate on interest and dividends.

T_G = Capital gains tax (CGT) rate. Unless noted otherwise, this is assumed to be paid on an accruals basis, which means that the tax is paid on realised and unrealised gains at the end of each period. If there is a capital loss, the investor receives a rebate. In reality, CGT is paid only after a gain has been realised by selling the asset.

T_E^α = $\alpha T_I + (1 - \alpha)T_G$, where α is the constant pay-out ratio, $0 \le \alpha \le 1$. T_E^α is a weighted average personal tax rate on the return to equity.

R_A = Economy-wide rate of return after personal tax. If we assume certainty, all assets provide this rate.

R_C = A project's rate of return, or the rate of return on an extra unit of investment, before personal tax. This is not the same concept as the cost of capital, the hurdle rate for acceptance of the project. For a positive-NPV project, R_C exceeds the cost of capital.

R_E = Cost of equity before personal tax.

R_D = Cost of debt before personal tax, assumed to be paid in the form of interest that reduces taxable profit, as in Chapter 7.

In this section we extend the perpetual-projects framework of Modigliani and Miller to allow for personal tax. We assume that there are constant effective rates of corporation, income and capital gains tax which are common across all agents. Modigliani and Miller (1958; 1961; 1963) assume that a project's expected cash flow before taxes is perpetual and varies around a constant mean. They assume that profit is equal to net cash flow, and they ignore personal tax. Miller and Modigliani (1961) show that dividend policy – i.e. the proportion of profit paid out as dividend – does not affect project value or the cost of equity, given this framework. Modigliani and Miller (1963) show that leverage does increase value and leverage reduces the cost of capital, assuming that cash flows ignore interest and are net of corporation tax. The analysis can be amended to incorporate personal taxes (Farrar and Selwyn, 1967; Stapleton, 1972; Auerbach, 1983, pp. 919–21). Nothing hinges on the uncertainty of the cash flows from a tax perspective, so we assume certainty. The Modigliani–Miller valuation equation (7.7) under certainty is

$$V = Y(1 - T_C)/R_E + IntT_C/R_D \qquad (8.1)$$

Consider first an unlevered company, with perpetual certain cash flows that are paid out as dividends. Then $Y(1 - T_C) = Div$, $Int = 0$, and the valuation equation after personal tax becomes

$$V = Div(1 - T_I)/R_A \qquad (8.2)$$

The cost of capital is the rate of return a project must earn for its market value to be equal to the cash invested (NPV $= 0$). This can be found by differentiating equation (8.2) with respect to a marginal increase in investment I, and setting the result equal to 1:

$$dV/dI = [dDiv(1 - T_I)/dI]/R_A = 1$$

and therefore

$$dDiv(1 - T_I)/dI = R_A$$

So the cost of equity expressed before personal tax is

$$R_E = R_A/(1 - T_I) \qquad (8.3)$$

and this is used to discount dividends before personal tax.

Now suppose that a constant fraction α of cash flow after tax is paid out and $1 - \alpha$ is retained and invested at a constant rate of return before personal tax of R_C. In this case we have cash flow and dividend and capital gain all growing at a constant growth rate of $R_C(1 - \alpha)$. Retained cash flow in period 1 is $(1 - \alpha)Y(1 - T_C)$, which produces a perpetuity of $R_C(1 - \alpha)Y(1 - T_C)$. The perpetuity is after corporation tax and before personal tax, since R_C, the rate of return on an extra unit of investment, is defined in this way. Cash flow before personal tax is $Y(1 - T_C)[1 + R_C(1 - \alpha)]$ in period 2, $Y(1 - T_C)[1 + R_C(1 - \alpha)]^2$ in period 3, and so on. It can be seen that the growth rate is $R_C(1 - \alpha)$. The cash flow is allocated in constant proportions each period; α is paid as dividend, the income tax is αT_I, $1 - \alpha$ is retained and the CGT is $(1 - \alpha)T_G$. The value of the equity is the sum of the present values of the future cash flows to shareholders – i.e. the dividend net of income tax and CGT each period:

$$V = \Sigma_{t=1}^{\infty}\{Y(1 - T_C)[\alpha(1 - T_I) - (1 - \alpha)T_G]$$
$$\times [1 + R_C(1 - \alpha)]^{t-1}\}/(1 + R_A)^t \qquad (8.4)$$

We find the cost of equity before personal tax by substituting $1 \ (= dV/dI)$ for V and $R_C \ (= dY(1 - T_C)/dI)$ for $Y(1 - T_C)$ in equation (8.4), and solving for R_C. The right-hand side can be simplified to the same format as the dividend discount formula, $V = \Sigma_{t=1}^{\infty}Div_1(1 + g)^{t-1}/(1 + R)^t = Div_1/(R - g)$ (Section 12.2). Here we have $Div_1 = R_c[\alpha(1 - T_I) - (1 - \alpha)T_G]$, $R = R_A$ and $g = R_C(1 - \alpha)$, so we solve for R_C in

$$1 = R_C[\alpha(1 - T_I) - (1 - \alpha)T_G]/[R_A - R_C(1 - \alpha)]$$

therefore

$$R_C = R_A/[1 - \alpha T_I - (1 - \alpha)T_G]$$
$$= R_A/(1 - T_E^\alpha) = R_E \qquad (8.5)$$

where $T_E^\alpha = \alpha T_I + (1 - \alpha)T_G$. Equation (8.5) gives the cost of equity before personal tax, R_E, given that the proportion α of profit is retained. It is apparent that, if $T_I > T_G$, the cost of capital increases with the pay-out ratio α. This is also an implication of Brennan's (1970) analysis of the effect of dividend payments on the expected rate of return in the context of the CAPM, discussed in Appendix 8.1. If $\alpha = 0$,

$$R_E = R_A/(1 - T_G) \tag{8.6}$$

Suppose now that the project is all debt financed, and that all the interest can relieve corporation tax. Then we have $Y = Int$, and equation (8.1) after personal tax becomes

$$
\begin{aligned}
V &= Int(1 - T_C)(1 - T_I)/R_A + IntT_C(1 - T_I)/R_A \\
&= Int(1 - T_C)(1 - T_I)/R_A + T_C D \\
dV/dI &= [dInt(1 - T_C)(1 - T_I)/dI]/R_A + T_C dD/dI \\
&= [dInt(1 - T_C)(1 - T_I)/dI]/R_A + T_C
\end{aligned}
$$

since $dD/dI = 1$. The condition for $dV/dI = 1$ is $dInt(1 - T_C)(1 - T_I)/dI = R_A(1 - T_C)$, so the cost of debt before personal tax is

$$R_D = R_A(1 - T_C)/(1 - T_I) \tag{8.7}$$

Finally, suppose that the new investment is financed by debt and equity with a leverage ratio L. Substituting the expressions for R_E and R_D allowing for personal taxes into the tax-adjusted WACC formula gives

$$WACC = (1 - L)R_A/\left(1 - T_E^\alpha\right) + LR_A(1 - T_C)/(1 - T_I) \tag{8.8}$$

These substitutions are valid, because the WACC is expressed before personal tax. The effect of dividend pay-out on R_E is taken as given, like leverage.

Summarising these results shows that there are five possibilities for the cost of capital, and that which one applies depends on the company's financing policies.

Financing policy	Cost of capital	
1. All equity, all profits paid as dividends	$R_A/(1 - T_I)$	(8.3)
2. All equity, α paid out, $1 - \alpha$ retained	$R_A/[1 - \alpha T - (1 - \alpha)T_G] = R_A/\left(1 - T_E^\alpha\right)$	(8.5)
3. All equity, no dividends	$R_A/(1 - T_G)$	(8.6)
4. All debt	$R_A(1 - T_C)/(1 - T_I)$	(8.7)
5. Equity and debt	$(1 - L)R_A/\left(1 - T_E^\alpha\right) + LR_A(1 - T_C)/(1 - T_I)$	(8.8)

It is normal to assume that income is taxed more heavily than capital gains, so that $T_I > T_G$, in which case the cost of equity increases with the dividend pay-out ratio α. In the absence of non-tax considerations, the first, second and fifth of the above possibilities are hypothetical because, in the perpetual-projects framework, the firm will never choose all equity with dividends, nor a combination of equity and debt. With $T_I > T_G$, the firm will not pay dividends, and its cost of equity will be $R_A/(1 - T_G)$. It will choose all equity if the tax burden of debt is heavier – i.e. $1 - T_I < (1 - T_C)(1 - T_G)$ – or all debt if the reverse is true. Alternatively, if $T_I < T_G$, the firm will not retain any profits. Its notional cost of equity will be $R_A/(1 - T_I)$, but in this case it will always choose all debt, assuming $T_C > 0$, since the after-tax value of £1 paid as interest is $1 - T_I$, compared with $(1 - T_C)(1 - T_I)$ for dividend. An implication of the foregoing is that there will be a 'corner solution': the firm will choose either all debt, or all equity with no dividends; it will never choose to pay a dividend. This conclusion assumes that the firm can always reinvest cash at a rate of return before personal tax R_C of at least $R_A/(1 - T_G)$ for all equity, or $R_A(1 - T_C)/(1 - T_I)$ for all debt. Additional, non-tax, factors are called for to motivate the payment of dividends, just as non-tax factors are required to explain why a company would not choose 100 per cent debt if there is a tax advantage to debt.

Expressions (8.3) to (8.8) present costs of capital before personal tax given the cost of capital after personal tax, R_A. It should be mentioned that these relatively simple formulas can be derived only for the case of a perpetual project with level cash flows. They are not, in general, correct expressions of the cost of capital before personal tax, given R_A. This is the same point as we made about valuation before and after corporation tax, in Section 7.1.3. Dobbs and Miller (2003) show that, if we are starting from a fixed cost of capital after personal tax, the cost of capital before personal tax will not be fixed, in that it will – in general – be a function of the lifetime of the project. Also, the formula derived for the cost of capital before personal tax will depend on the assumptions made about the provisions regarding CGT. However, for the purpose of examining the effects of personal tax on the cost of capital, it is easier to work with simple expressions.

Related models

The accepted version of the CAPM allowing for personal tax was developed by Brennan (1970). In this version, the expected return on a share before personal tax is positively related to the dividend pay-out and yield, assuming that $T_I > T_G$. This is the same qualitative conclusion as is reached from the analysis based on a perpetual project, shown in expression (8.5). Brennan's amended CAPM is presented in Appendix 8.1.

Stiglitz (1973) develops a model under certainty under which the project has a finite, rather than perpetual, life. The analysis and conclusions are somewhat different. If the case of a tax advantage to external equity, $1 - T_I < (1 - T_C)(1 - T_G)$, is ruled out, the source of marginal capital is retained earnings or debt, and the cost of capital is the same for both. It is $R_A(1 - T_C)/(1 - T_I)$, expressed before personal tax. This model is outlined in Appendix 8.2.

8.2   The 'new view': the cost of equity and the source of equity

8.2.1   Introduction to the new view

At first glance, it is natural to think that a tax on dividends must increase the cost of equity, at least if the company is paying dividends. This is indeed the prediction of the 'traditional', or 'classical' or 'old' view of the impact of personal tax on the cost of equity. With perpetual projects and the payment of dividends, the cost of equity is given by equations (8.3) or (8.5); the CAPM allowing for personal tax is given by equation (8.6). In contrast, the 'tax capitalisation' or 'new' view (now thirty years old) maintains that the tax on dividends has no impact on the cost of equity. This may seem to be a bizarre proposition. But the argument behind it is as least as natural as the argument behind the old view, which is implicit in Section 8.1. We shall retain the 'old' and 'new' labels, as they are easy to work with.

The main distinctions between the two views can be brought out via the perpetual-projects model. Suppose that an unlevered firm pays a constant dividend of Div_t per period that incurs income tax at a constant rate T_I, and that CGT is zero. The market value of the equity is

$$E_0 = \Sigma_{t=1}^{\infty} Div_t(1 - T_I)/R_A \qquad (8.9)$$

The future tax payments are capitalised; that is, the value of the equity is net of the present value of the tax payments. An increase in the tax rate T_I reduces the current equity value E_0, assuming that the required rate of return after taxes, R_A, is fixed. Equation (8.9) expressed before personal tax is

$$E_0 = \Sigma_{t=1}^{\infty} Div_t/[R_A/(1 - T_I)]$$

The rate of return on equity before personal tax is $R_A/(1 - T_I)$. If the source of new equity is a share issue, $R_A/(1 - T_I)$ is also the cost of equity (before personal tax) R_E, as in equation (8.3), because this is what the cash can earn on the next-best alternative. With R_A fixed, if T_I increases so does the cost of equity. This is the old view of the cost of equity; it embodies the assumption that the marginal source of capital is a share issue.

But now suppose that the company's source of funds for new investment is retained earnings. The alternative to retention is payment as dividend. If the company retains £1, the shareholders gain a return of $R_C(1 - T_I)$. They forgo £1$(1 - T_I)$ now, on which they could earn the return R_A. They will be indifferent between pay-out and retention if

$$R_C(1 - T_I) = R_A(1 - T_I) \qquad (8.10)$$

So the cost of capital before personal tax for retained earnings, R_E, is equal to the required rate of return *after* personal tax on the shares, R_A, and is not affected by the tax rate on dividends, T_I. This is the new view of the cost of equity; it embodies the assumption that the marginal source of capital is retained earnings.

The above result may seem like a trick. How can a personal tax reduce market value and not increase the cost of capital expressed before personal tax? The tax reduces value because, other things being equal, it reduces the future cash flows received by shareholders, as can be seen clearly in equation (8.9). The required rate of return on the company's shares expressed before personal tax, $R_A/(1 - T_I)$, does indeed increase if T_I increases. But, now that we have introduced personal tax, the cost of capital is no longer the same concept as the required rate of return on a financial asset. The cost of capital is the rate that newly invested funds have to earn to leave shareholders as well off as they would have been if the funds had not been invested. If retained earnings are the source of the funds, the rate of return on the shares expressed before personal tax, $R_A/(1 - T_I)$, is not the same as the hurdle rate on new investment expressed before personal tax, the cost of equity R_E, which we have seen is equal to R_A. The reason for the difference is that, if retained earnings are the source of the funds, not investing them means paying them out, and the pay-out is taxed. So the presence of the tax on dividends has two effects, which balance each other. The tax reduces the cash payments to shareholders from the future dividends resulting from an investment – an effect that is in the valuation formula for the shares, equation (8.9). But the presence of the tax also means that retaining funds rather than distributing them saves the tax that would have resulted from distribution. This effect is not in the valuation formula, because an investor does not save any tax by buying the shares.

8.2.2   Cost of equity from retained earnings

We now develop the new view in a little more detail, simplifying a presentation in Auerbach (1979a; 1983), which includes CGT. The same results can be derived from the conditions for the maximisation of a multiperiod expression for the value of equity under certainty, subject to constraints (e.g. Edwards and Keen, 1984; Poterba and Summers, 1985). The model is an extension to the one introduced in Section 6.5.2, equation (6.20). As this route is more complicated and appears to provide little additional insight, we omit it.

Suppose a firm is unlevered, and future cash flows are certain and are net of corporation tax. The present value of the equity is E_0. In equilibrium, the gain at date 1 on the equity, $E_0(R_A)$, is the after-tax dividend at date 1, $Div_1(1 - T_I)$, plus the capital gain on the existing shares net of CGT, $(E_1 - E_0)(1 - T_G)$. CGT is assumed to be paid on an accruals basis.

If the CGT rate T_G exceeds the tax rate on dividends T_I, all profits are paid out, and new issues are the preferred marginal source of equity. In fact, it could be advantageous to issue shares and to pay out the proceeds as dividends, because this reduces the CGT liability on the existing shares. But, with $T_I > T_G$, dividends are a residual; cash is paid out once the firm has run out of investment opportunities offering a rate of return on capital of at least $R_A/(1 - T_G)$ per period, as explained below. The firm will use new issues only as a last resort, when the firm has projects with a rate of return that exceeds the cost of equity from new issues, and has insufficient retained profits available. New issues will never be used to fund dividends paid in excess of amounts available to distribute from operations. Auerbach assumes that $T_I > T_G$ and rules out both new share issues and share repurchases. If repurchases are allowed and are taxed as capital gains, then, effectively, the tax rate on distributions to shareholders becomes T_G rather than T_I, and there is no tax advantage to retention. He notes that repurchases used not to be quantitively important in the United States – but they have become important since the 1970s in both the United States and United Kingdom.

With no share issues or repurchases, we have in equilibrium

$$E_0(R_A) = Div_1(1 - T_I) + (E_1 - E_0)(1 - T_G)$$

or

$$E_0[1 + R_A/(1 - T_G)] = Div_1(1 - T_I)/(1 - T_G) + E_1 \qquad (8.11)$$

The value of E_1 is given by a similar expression, and so on into the future. If we assume that the firm's dividends grow at a slower rate than $R_A/(1 - T_G)$, the present value of $E_T \rightarrow 0$ as $T \rightarrow \infty$ and can be ignored, in which case equation (8.11) can be written as

$$E_0 = \Sigma_{t=1}^{\infty} \frac{Div_t(1 - T_I)/(1 - T_G)}{[1 + R_A/(1 - T_G)]^t} \tag{8.12}$$

Equation (8.12) is a version of the dividend discount model. The marginal source of capital is retained earnings, and the cost of equity before personal tax is $R_A/(1 - T_G)$. To confirm this, suppose an extra £1 is retained and invested. It provides a return per period before personal tax of R_C in perpetuity, which is paid out as dividend. The present value of this extra stream of dividend is $R_C(1 - T_I)/R_A$, and the amount forgone by retention now is the dividend after tax plus the extra capital gains tax: $1 - T_I + T_G R_C(1 - T_I)/R_A$. The cost of equity before personal tax is the value for R_C such that the present value of the £1 retained is equal to the amount forgone:

$$R_C(1 - T_I)/R_A = 1 - T_I + T_G R_C(1 - T_I)/R_A$$

therefore

$$R_C = R_A/(1 - T_G)$$

If $T_G = 0$, as assumed in Section 8.2.1, the cost of equity is R_A. The cost of equity is affected by the CGT rate but not by the rate of tax on dividends. The rate of tax on dividends does, however, affect the equity value E_0. Hence the new view prediction that an increase in the tax rate on dividends reduces the share price but does not increase the cost of capital or reduce investment.

8.2.3   Cost of equity and the q-ratio

A further implication of the foregoing analysis is that the market value of the firm will be less than the replacement value of its assets. The simplest way to show this is to think once more about the choice between paying £1 as dividend, and retaining it. A unit of dividend is worth $1 - T_I$ after personal tax. If the £1 is invested at a rate equal to the cost of equity, so that $R_C = R_A/(1 - T_G)$, the amount forgone by retention is

$$1 - T_I + T_G R_A(1 - T_I)/R_A(1 - T_G) = (1 - T_I)/(1 - T_G)$$

So, for shareholders to be indifferent between pay-out and retention, the unit retained must have a market value, and a q-value, of $(1 - T_I)/(1 - T_G)$, where q is the market value of the equity divided by the replacement value of the assets. q will be less than 1 if $T_I > T_G$.

We have noted that the firm's marginal source of capital, and thus its cost of capital, depends on whether retained earnings are sufficient to fund its worthwhile investment opportunities. This idea can be expressed in terms of the q-level at which a firm's equity trades (Auerbach, 1979b; 1983). We are assuming for simplicity that marginal q is equal to average q, the q at which the existing shares trade.

- If $q < (1 - T_I)/(1 - T_G)$, there will be no retention. Shareholder wealth is greater if all net cash flow is paid as dividend, in which case it is worth $1 - T_I$ per unit after tax, rather than retained, in which case it is worth $q(1 - T_G)$, which is less than $1 - T_I$. The firm has already invested 'too much', in the view of the stock market; further investment from retention would not cover the cost of equity.
- If $q = (1 - T_I)/(1 - T_G)$, the marginal investment would just cover the cost of equity; the firm is indifferent between pay-out and retention, so the pay-out policy affects neither the share price nor the cost of equity.
- If $q > (1 - T_I)/(1 - T_G)$, investment from retention adds value, compared with paying out, so all profits are retained.
- If $q \geq 1$, not only is investment from retention worthwhile, but so is investment from new issues.

From this analysis in terms of q it can be seen that the new-view assumption that the opportunity cost of £1 retained is £1 dividend forgone implies that the firm's equity is trading at a q-level of $(1 - T_I)/(1 - T_G)$, because only at that level is the firm both distributing and retaining some profit.

If $q > (1 - T_I)/(1 - T_G)$, the company will not be paying dividends, according to the new view. Retention is worthwhile because paying out imposes a cash loss on the shareholder; £1 paid out is worth £$1(1 - T_I)$, whereas £1 retained is worth £$1q(1 - T_G)$, which exceeds £$1(1 - T_I)$ if $q > (1 - T_I)/(1 - T_G)$. If q is constant, the cost of equity is $R_A/(1 - T_G)$, the same as it is if $q = (1 - T_I)/(1 - T_G)$ and the firm is paying dividends. The argument is that retention of £1, valued at £$1q$, will be worth £$1(1 + R_A)q$ after one period if the firm invests in a financial asset. So the return to the shareholder after all tax is R_A, the same as the shareholder can obtain by buying a financial asset. The return before personal tax is $R_A/(1 - T_G)$; the tax rate on dividends does not feature because the firm is not paying a dividend at either date. An odd implication of this analysis is that, whatever level of q the firm's shares happen to trade at, in the range $1 \geq q \geq (1 - T_I)/(1 - T_G)$ the cost of equity is the same. But constant q in this range implies no dividends. If the firm is to pay a dividend at some future time, q must have fallen by then to $(1 - T_I)/(1 - T_G)$. A change in q implies a change in the cost of equity; if q is going to fall next period, there will be a capital loss on the shares, and the cost of equity exceeds $R_A/(1 - T_G)$.

If $q \geq 1$, it is worthwhile for the firm to issue shares. The new-view cost of equity for a share issue depends on the lifetime of the project in relation to the length of time before the firm starts paying a dividend. Suppose that the firm has been issuing shares and then starts paying a dividend next period. This implies, according to the new view, that the firm's q-value falls from 1 to $(1 - T_I)/(1 - T_G)$ the next period, and that retained earnings become the marginal source of equity. There is a capital loss of $[(1 - T_I)/(1 - T_G) - 1]$ per £ over the first period. The rate of return on equity before personal tax, R_C, has to cover the capital loss as well as provide a return on the cash invested in the first period. Assuming that all the return is via the dividend, the requisite R_C is found from

$$R_A = R_C(1 - T_I) + (1 - T_G)[(1 - T_I)/(1 - T_G) - 1]$$

therefore

$$R_C = (R_A + T_I - T_G)/(1 - T_I)$$

With $T_I > T_G$, the cost of capital for new issues, $(R_A + T_I - T_G)/(1 - T_I)$, exceeds the cost of capital for retained profits, $R_A/(1 - T_G)$ (Auerbach, 1983; Edwards and Keen, 1984). This cost of equity for a new issue is for a one-period horizon, and, for a high income tax rate, it could be much higher than both the old-view cost of equity, $R_A/(1 - T_I)$ (assuming a perpetual project and 100 per cent pay-out), and the new-view cost of equity, $R_A/(1 - T_G)$. The cost of equity in subsequent periods is $R_A/(1 - T_G)$, since the marginal source of equity is retained earnings. To sum up, the firm's q matters in the new view because it affects the source of capital chosen by the firm, and because changes in q affect the cost of equity.

Example

To help see what is going on, consider a simple example. The firm buys a machine for £100, which provides a perpetuity of £10 p.a. before personal tax. The income tax rate is 50 per cent and there is no CGT. The equilibrium rate of return on assets after all tax, R_A, is 10 per cent p.a.

Suppose first that the firm buys the machine out of retained profit, which would otherwise have been paid as dividend. All the cash flows from the machine will be paid out as dividends. In this case q should be $(1 - T_I)/(1 - T_G)$, and the new-view cost of equity before personal tax for retained earnings is $R_A/(1 - T_G) = 10\%$ pa. The rate of return on the machine before personal tax is 10 per cent p.a., so it just covers the cost of capital. The cash flow is £5 p.a. net of income tax, so the market value of the machine is only £50 (£5/10%), not £100. Its q-value is 0.5 ($= 1 - T_I$). This is a marginal investment; if the firm had paid out the £100 as dividend, the shareholders would have received £50 after income tax, on which they could earn 10 per cent p.a. after tax, or £5 p.a.

Suppose next that the firm buys the machine out of retained profit, and is not paying a dividend. Its shares are trading at a q-value of, say, 0.6. The £100 retained is worth £60 in the firm. The value of the machine in the firm, assuming that all the future cash flows will be retained, is (£10/10%)0.6 = £60. Any project that provides a rate of return of at least 10 per cent p.a. will be worthwhile, if q is constant.

Now suppose that the firm buys the machine by issuing shares. When the firm makes the share issue, its shares must be trading at $q \geq 1$, or it would not issue. To justify the purchase, the cash flow after personal tax plus the value of the machine after one year must be at least £100(1 + R_A) = £110. But if the firm pays a dividend after one year, its share must be trading at $q = 1 - T_I$. The value of the machine will have dropped to only £50, a capital loss of £50. For the purchase to be worthwhile, the machine would have to provide a gross dividend of £120 after one year, or £60 after tax, and then £10 p.a. gross thereafter. Its after-tax cash flow plus value after one year would then be the £110 required; £60 net dividend plus £50 capital value. This is consistent with the one-period cost of equity before personal tax of $(R_A + T_I - T_G)/(1 - T_I)$ derived above. Substituting in the numbers gives (0.1 + 0.5 − 0.0)/0.5 = 120%, and 120 per cent of the initial investment of £100 is £120.

It can be seen that the new-view cost of equity for a new issue is a rather extreme case in which $q = 1$ at one date and suddenly drops to $1 - T_I$ at the next, when the firm starts paying a dividend. This maximises the contrast between the one-period cost of equity at date 1 and at date 2.

Why should q be $(1 - T_I)/(1 - T_G)$?

The mechanism or economic force that should prevent q from falling below $(1 - T_I)/(1 - T_G)$ is clear: firms should not invest in projects that do not cover their cost of capital. It is less clear why firms' equity will be valued at the critical q of $(1 - T_I)/(1 - T_G)$, as is required by the new view. If the rather contradictory supposition is made that a firm starts from scratch with retained profits, which will otherwise be paid as a dividend, then the firm will undertake all projects with positive NPV using $R_A/(1 - T_G)$ as the discount rate before personal tax, and the marginal project will have a q-value in the firm of $(1 - T_I)/(1 - T_G)$. But it seems that an ongoing firm simply waits until its q falls to the critical value, and then starts paying a dividend.

A situation in which new issues will be the marginal source of capital is when a firm has insufficient retained earnings to finance all its positive-NPV investments, and has exhausted its debt capacity. A firm in this position will not be paying a dividend, and its q-value should be one or more. At some stage its q-value will fall and it will start paying dividend, and the anticipated fall in its q-value pushes its cost of equity above the cost of equity for retained earnings when the firm is paying a dividend. Once the q-value has reached $(1 - T_I)/(1 - T_G)$, its cost of equity from retained earnings will be lower than its cost of equity used to be from new issues. Sinn (1991) emphasises this case, together with the consequent implication that immature companies face a relatively high cost of equity. It is noteworthy that this implication is derived entirely from tax considerations, not from the more familiar problems caused by information asymmetry and transactions costs.

Expressions for cost of capital

The new view implies modification to the CAPM and dividend discount formulas for the cost of equity, as discussed by Dempsey (1996). The one-period expected return on a firm's equity after all tax can be written as

$$E(R_A) = [E(E_{cum1}) - E_{ex0}](1 - T_G)/E_{ex0}$$
$$= \{E(Div_1)(1 - T_I) + [E(E_{ex1}) - E_{ex0}](1 - T_G)\}/E_{ex0} \qquad (8.13)$$

where E_{cum} is the value-cum-dividend, the day before the ex-dividend day, and E_{ex} is the value on the ex-dividend day. If the marginal source of equity is retained earnings and the new view is correct, $q = (1 - T_I)/(1 - T_G)$ and the cost of equity before personal tax for retentions is $E(R_A)/(1 - T_G)$. Equation (8.13) can be rewritten to give an expected rate of return on the shares that corresponds with this cost of equity:

$$E(R_A)/(1 - T_G) = [E(Div_1 q) + E(E_{ex1}) - E_{ex0}]/E_{ex0}$$

In principle, this can be estimated via a model of the expected rate of return on shares, such as the CAPM or the dividend discount model. If we assume that investors face single rates of income tax and of CGT, as we have throughout this chapter, the CAPM can be expressed after all tax as

$$E(R_A) = R_F(1 - T_I) + \beta[E(R_{MA}) - R_F(1 - T_I)]$$

where $E(R_{MA})$ is the expected rate of return on the market after all tax. Since we are assuming that $q = (1 - T_I)/(1 - T_G)$,

$$E(R_A)/(1 - T_G) = R_F q + \beta[E(R_{MA})/(1 - T_G) - R_F q]$$

The expression for $E(R_A)/(1 - T_G)$ using the rearranged dividend discount model is

$$E(R_A)/(1 - T_G) = [E(Div_1)q]/E_{ex0} + g$$

where g is the long-term growth rate of dividends, which is assumed to be constant. The trouble with these formulas, and with any that include personal tax, is that it is unrealistic to assume that investors face the same rates of personal tax.

Dempsey (1998) discusses the application of the new-view cost of equity $E(R_E^*) = E(R_A)/(1 - T_G)$ in discounting project cash flows by the WACC. Both the cash flows to be discounted and the WACC formula require modification. Rearranging equation (8.13) gives

$$E_{ex0} = [E(Div_1)q + E(E_{ex1})]/[1 + E(R_E^*)]$$

In the case of a perpetuity, the cash flow to equity is $E(Div)q$. We know that

$$E(Div)q = [E(Y) - Int](1 - T_C)q$$

where $E(Y)$ is the perpetual expected cash flow before interest Int, and $Int = R_D D$. The cash flow to be discounted by the WACC becomes $E(Y)(1 - T_C)q$, and the WACC formula becomes (see equation (7.6))

$$WACC = \frac{[E(Y) - R_D D](1 - T_C)q}{E_L} \times \frac{E_L}{E_L + D} + \frac{R_D(1 - T_C)q D}{E_L + D}$$
$$= R_E^*(1 - L) + R_D(1 - T_C)q L$$

Dempsey (1998) shows that the same WACC formula applies to projects with uneven and finite cash flows, assuming that managers act to hold leverage L constant, and that retained earnings are the source of equity. However, unless $q = 1$, $[E(Y)(1 - T_C)]q$ would be a strange cash flow to discount.

8.2.4   Comparison of old and new views

Until the current chapter we have been working with the standard approach to project valuation. Using this approach, a project is akin to a financial asset, which can be valued for a given leverage policy. The project's dividend policy is not considered explicitly; a project is just an operation that provides expected cash flows. The project's cost of equity is estimated by arguing that the next-best alternative is to buy shares in a company with the same risk as the project. Hence the cost of equity is the expected rate of return on shares of the same risk.

The introduction of personal tax forces us to think again about this analysis. There are two connected issues: dividend policy, and whether the cost of equity depends on the source of the equity capital. Let us consider dividend policy first.

Dividend policy matters under the old view because the cost of equity before personal tax is positively related to the proportion of cash flows paid out as dividends, assuming that the effective tax rate on dividends exceeds the effective tax rate on capital gains. A higher proportion of cash flows retained means a higher proportion that avoids the tax on dividends (equations (A8.5) and (A8.6)). The cost of equity expressed before personal tax is affected by the income tax rate.

Companies choose to pay out some cash as dividends because there are non-tax-related reasons for doing so. Companies arrive at their optimum pay-out policy by balancing, at least in theory, the agency and other benefits of higher pay-out (captured in the cash flows) against the higher personal tax payments (captured in the cost of equity). The process is analogous to the one by which firms are supposed to find their optimum leverage, assuming that there is a tax advantage to debt. If the optimal dividend payments tend to be in excess of the payments that would be made were dividends a residual, firms are expected to pay dividends and to make share issues from time to time.

Allowing for personal tax, a company can still be thought of as akin to a financial asset – an asset that now has a given dividend policy as well as a given leverage policy. However, the concept of a project with a dividend policy is less coherent than the concept of a project with a leverage policy. A project is something that starts at one date and finishes at a later date, so all the cash flow from a stand-alone project must eventually be paid out as dividends. Really, only a *company* can have a dividend policy – i.e. a policy regarding the proportion of the cash flows from its projects to pay as dividends. Because a company is an ongoing entity, it can, in principle, decide to defer any cash payment to shareholders to the indefinite future. Then all the cash flows from any particular finite project can be converted into capital gains, by not paying them as dividends. So the cost of equity for a project undertaken by a company reflects the business risk and leverage of the project, and the dividend policy of the company.

The new-view assumption that the alternative to retention is pay-out implies that dividends are the residual after all positive-NPV projects have been financed. There is no dividend policy beyond this. Agency and signalling factors are completely ignored. The new view regards payment of a dividend as indicating that retained earnings are the marginal source of equity, so firms should not be observed paying a dividend at the same time as issuing shares.

Now let us consider the cost of equity by the source of the equity capital. The old – and normal – view is that the cost of equity is the expected rate of return on shares of the same risk as the project, before personal tax. This is the expected rate for a market investor who buys shares in the project, if they exist – i.e. the cost of equity if the project is financed by a share issue to investors. Under the old view, the source of equity is either a share issue or retained cash, and the cost of equity is the same for both sources. The argument is that the amount of additional retained cash available for investment at a given date is assumed to be fixed by the cash flow from existing operations for the period just ended, and by the company's dividend policy. If the company has more retained cash at the given date than it needs to finance available positive-NPV projects, the next-best alternative to investing in a particular project is *not* the payment of more dividend, because the dividend payment is already fixed. The alternative is investment by the company in a share of the same risk, and the expected rate of return the company receives on such a share is the expected rate before personal tax – the same as the rate received by a market investor. If, on the other hand, the company has insufficient retained cash to finance all its positive-NPV opportunities, it will issue shares rather than withhold dividend. (Zodrow, 1991, argues that the marginal source of equity capital is a share issue under the old view. This is true for a company over time, but not for a project at a time when the parent happens to have surplus cash.)

If the income tax rate rises, the tax cost rises of paying dividends in excess of the amounts implied by treating dividends as a residual, and the pay-out ratio should fall. By assumption, the pay-out ratio is not perfectly elastic with respect to the tax disadvantage, because, if it were, dividends would be a residual. So an increase in the income tax rate faced by a firm's shareholders implies an increase in the firm's cost of equity before personal tax, possibly mitigated somewhat by a shift to smaller pay-outs. The value of equity is predicted to fall, assuming that the after-tax required rate on the shares (R_A) is constant. Some of the fall represents the present value of higher future tax payments, captured in the higher discount rate; some of it is a loss of value attributable to slower growth because the hurdle rate for new projects is higher; and some is a loss due to the lower pay-out ratio, which reduces the agency and other benefits of paying dividends.

Under the new view, the retained cash has a lower cost of equity than a share issue, as we have seen. This is because the next-best alternative to investing in a given project is assumed to be the payment of more dividend.

The tax rate on dividends has no effect on the cost of equity, nor on the 'pay-out policy' (i.e. dividends are the residual), so future gross dividend payments are unaffected by the tax rate. An increase in the tax rate reduces the dividends after personal tax, which are discounted at the after-tax required rate on the shares and will therefore be exactly 'capitalised' in equity value: value falls by the same percentage as the income tax rate rises, assuming a fixed R_A (King, 1974b).

A further point about the new view is that, because it implies a lower cost of equity than the old view (assuming that the income tax rate exceeds the CGT rate), it makes the existence of a 'Miller equilibrium' more plausible (Auerbach, 1983). In this equilibrium, discussed in Chapter 9, there is no tax advantage to debt; the total tax burden on equity and debt is the same. Conversely, under the old view the gain from leverage is positively related to the pay-out ratio. The effective tax rate on equity including personal tax is $1 - (1 - T_C)(1 - T_E^{\alpha})$, which increases with the pay-out ratio α. So the higher the pay-out ratio, the higher the tax saving from debt (Chang and Rhee, 1990).

It can be seen that the old- and new-view predictions about the cost of equity follow from their respective assumptions about dividend policy, which represent two extremes.

The pay-out ratio is set in stone under the old view; dividends are a pure residual under the new view. An in-between position, which is perhaps more realistic than either extreme, is that the proportion paid out is carefully managed and that it can be altered somewhat in response to changes in the company's investment opportunities in relation to its cash flows. But then the specification of the cost of equity is indeterminate.

One of the assumptions made in deriving the new view is that firms cannot repurchase their own shares, because repurchases are taxed as capital gains, not as income. This assumption is no longer realistic in the United States or United Kingdom, so the question arises as to whether the new view is relevant in present circumstances. Let us assume that repurchases have partially replaced dividends as means of distributing cash to shareholders, and that the CGT rate is lower than the income tax rate. (Even if capital gains are taxed at the same rate as dividends, there is a tax advantage to repurchases because they accelerate recognition of the purchase price of the shares as a deduction in computing CGT liabilities (Talmor and Titman, 1990).) It may be noted, first, that the use of repurchases reduces the cost of equity for a share issue under both views, because the effective tax rate on cash paid out is lower. One defence of the new view is that, although repurchases are possible, firms are constrained in how much they can repurchase. If so, it remains arguable that the marginal source of equity is withheld dividend rather than withheld repurchase. If repurchases reduce the effective tax rate on future, but not present, marginal pay-outs, then the cost of equity is actually lower than in the standard new view, because retention saves a higher tax rate now than will apply on future pay-outs (Sinn, 1991). Suppose, alternatively, that the marginal source of equity is a withheld pay-out composed of a mix of dividend and share repurchase, and that future pay-outs will be made with the same mix, which has an effective tax rate of, say, T_X, and $T_X > T_G$. Then the new-view argument could still be made, and the cost of equity before personal tax would remain $R_A/(1 - T_G)$. Hence the fact that repurchases happen does not in itself necessarily undermine the case for the new view.

As an aside, it may help readers on the trail of the new view to mention that the new-view results are not immediately obvious in the seminal works of King (1974a; 1977, chap. 8), though they are more so in King (1974b). The reason is that, in the analysis in King (1974a; 1977), the cost of capital R_F is expressed gross of personal tax. It is the risk-free rate because King assumes certainty, as we have done. For example, the table showing the cost of capital by the source of capital (1974a, p. 34; 1977, p. 238) states that the cost of equity is $R_F(1 - T_I)/(1 - T_G)(1 - T_C)$ for retentions and $R_F/(1 - T_C)$ for new issues (for a classical tax system). This looks, on the face of it, as though the cost of equity is affected by the income tax rate in the case of retentions but not in the case of new issues – the opposite of the new view! King's expressions are consistent with the new view if it is assumed that it is R_A, the required rate on financial assets after all tax, that is set in financial markets, not R_F, which in King is the required rate expressed before personal tax. That is, $R_F = R_A^{fixed}/(1 - T_I)$, where the 'fixed' superscript is for emphasis. Substituting this into King's expression for the cost of equity for retentions gives $R_A^{fixed}/(1 - T_G)(1 - T_C)$, or $R_A^{fixed}/(1 - T_G)$ expressed before personal tax, as in Auerbach (1979a). The cost of equity for new issues expressed before personal tax is $R_A^{fixed}/(1 - T_I)$.

King probably chooses to treat R_F as fixed before personal tax because different investors obtain different rates of return after personal tax on the same asset, since they face differing rates of personal tax. King and Fullerton (1984, pp. 11–12) argue that it is reasonable to assume that companies will invest in such a way that marginal projects earn the same rate of return measured before personal tax (under certainty), but not to assume that all investors earn the same rate after personal tax. In our notation, it means that it is R_F that is fixed, not R_A. With fixed R_F, the (new-view) cost of equity for retentions expressed before personal tax is $R_F(1 - T_I)/(1 - T_G)$, where both T_I and T_G are specific to the investor. So the cost of equity for retentions will vary across investors.

8.2.5   Tax irrelevance and dividend clienteles

So far we have assumed that the effective rates of tax are positive and are the same across investors. It has been argued by Miller and Scholes (1978) that the effective tax rate on dividends is zero. The argument is that an investor can avoid the tax by personal borrowing up to the level at which interest payments are equal to gross dividends from shares owned by the investor. Interest can be set against personal taxable investment income in the United States. As the dividends would be used to pay the interest, in effect the returns from the shares would be entirely in the form of capital gains. If the effective CGT rate is taken to be zero, the effective personal tax rate on equity is zero. The extra personal borrowing required increases risk, but this could be neutralised by using the proceeds of the loan to make an investment at the risk-free rate of interest. It may be possible to earn the risk-free rate gross of tax, by investing via a tax-exempt vehicle such as a pension fund, so that no personal tax at all is paid on the individual's investment returns. The same vehicle could be used to avoid income tax on corporate debt, in which case personal tax would be irrelevant, and the analysis of the previous chapter would apply, in which personal tax is ignored.

Although it is common to ignore personal tax, the motive is probably to keep things simple, not because authors believe that effective personal tax rates on returns to financial assets are zero. Empirical studies of investor behaviour and of personal tax receipts indicate that personal taxes on financial assets are far from entirely avoided. For example, Peterson, Peterson and Ang (1985) estimate that the effective tax rate on aggregate US dividends was 30 per cent in 1979; the calculation includes dividends received under the annual tax-exempt allowance and includes dividends not taxed by virtue of having interest payments set against them. At the same time, effective tax rates on dividends, capital gains and interest are difficult to estimate and are almost certainly lower than the statutory rates. One reason for this that has attracted much attention is the possibility that tax clienteles exist for dividends and debt. In the case of dividends, the idea is that a firm that has a high dividend yield or pay-out ratio attracts a clientele of shareholders facing relatively low marginal rates of income tax, whereas a firm with a low yield or that is not paying dividends attracts shareholders facing high marginal rates of income tax. Tax clientele arguments recognise that effective tax rates are not the same across investors, and they imply that effective tax rates differ across firms.

8.3   Evidence

Research testing the predictions of the old and new views is discussed in Dempsey (1998), Poterba and Summers (1985), Sinn (1991) and Zodrow (1991). On balance, the findings favour the old view. The new view assumes that dividends are a residual left over after positive-NPV investments have been financed, in which case we might expect them to fluctuate considerably. The old view assumes that dividend pay-outs are carefully managed, and the evidence on this point clearly supports the old view: companies aim to achieve a steady and predictable growth in dividends, and there is much evidence that dividend policy affects market value because of agency and signalling considerations (for a recent review, see Lease, John, Kalay, Loewenstein and Sarig, 2000). The fact that dividend-paying companies are observed to make seasoned equity offers is further support for the old view. In addition, there is a negative relation over time between the pay-out ratio and the tax rate on dividends. Companies tend to pay out more when dividends are relatively lightly taxed. This is consistent with the old-view assumption that companies seek to balance the agency and signalling benefits of dividend payments against the additional tax payments implied. If the tax disadvantage of dividends is reduced, higher pay-out ratios are predicted. However, a reduction in the tax disadvantage of dividends implies that shares will trade at a higher q-value. An increase in q in turn implies, under the new view, a temporary reduction in investment and increase in pay-out, until equilibrium at the higher q is reached. Thus a negative relation between the pay-out ratio and the tax rate on dividends is not necessarily inconsistent with the new view.

A simple point apparently in favour of the new view is that the bulk of corporate investment is funded from retained earnings, with very little being funded from the proceeds of share issues. This suggests that companies in aggregate do not pay out a lot more than they have left after financing worthwhile investment, and a possible explanation is that the cost of equity is lower for retained earnings. However, there are non-tax reasons why retained earnings are less costly. For example, retention avoids the transactions costs of a share issue. There is no hint from survey evidence that company executives regard the cost of equity as being lower for retained earnings for tax reasons, though recent surveys have not asked directly about this (Section 12.1).

Under both views, observed rates of return on shares measured before personal tax should be positively related to dividend yield and pay-out, assuming that the effective tax rate on dividends exceeds the effective CGT rate. There is a much-cited debate about this. Reviews by Lease et al. (2000) and Graham (2003) argue that US evidence should be viewed as showing no relation between the rate of return and dividend yield – a finding consistent with the tax irrelevance view. Morgan and Thomas (1998), using UK data, find a positive relation between the rate of return and yield. But there was probably a tax *advantage* to paying dividends during their estimation period, 1975 to 1993, due to the imputation system then in force in the United Kingdom. So the authors conclude that the personal tax argument cannot explain the positive relation between return and yield that they find.

8.4   Summary

Personal taxes affect the after-tax returns to providers of finance. Three taxes are relevant, namely the taxes on dividends, capital gains and interest. This chapter has concentrated on the implications arising from a higher effective tax rate on dividends than on capital gains.

Up to the current chapter, a project has been treated like a financial asset: as something that provides a claim to future pay-offs and can be bought and sold. It is true that, with the introduction of equity and debt, leverage becomes one of the many management decisions that affect value. But the project can still be thought of as a financial asset, with a given leverage. Similarly, the introduction of different rates of tax on dividends and on capital gains ushers in a further decision or sequence of decisions that can affect value – namely the amounts to pay out as dividends. According to the old view of the effects of personal taxes, the higher tax rate on dividends implies that the cost of equity expressed before personal tax is positively related to the amount of dividends the company chooses to pay. A project can be thought of as an asset with a given dividend policy (the parent company's), as well as a given leverage policy. The cost of equity is the same whether the source of the funds is a share issue or retained earnings.

The new view introduces a new ingredient to the valuation model, which is the source of the equity capital. It is argued that the cost of equity is less if the source is retained earnings than if the source is a share issue, assuming that the tax rate on dividends T_I is more than the CGT rate T_G. Underpinning the argument is the assumption that the alternative to investing funds in the project is paying them out as dividends, in which case they would incur income tax. The opportunity cost per £1 retained is the rate of return that would have been earned on the money paid out. With pay-out, the shareholder receives £1$(1 - T_I)$, on which he can earn R_A after tax, or $R_A/(1 - T_I)$ before personal tax. So the opportunity cost of retention before personal tax is $(1 - T_I)R_A/(1 - T_I) = R_A$, the rate of return on assets *after* income tax (and assuming CGT is zero). In contrast, the opportunity cost of buying an asset – i.e. the cost of capital for a share issue – is $R_A/(1 - T_I)$ before personal tax. The new-view argument is logical but is hard to 'fit in' to the standard valuation framework, because it implies that a project cannot be valued in the same way as a financial asset – i.e. without reference to the source of the funds.

The evidence indicates that companies manage their dividend policy carefully, which suggests that the alternative to investing in a particular project is usually not a higher dividend pay-out, but is either investing in a financial asset or raising less equity by a share issue. This supports the old view.

Appendix 8.1: Personal tax and the CAPM

Personal tax has been incorporated into the CAPM by Brennan (1970). The standard CAPM has two dates, and there is uncertainty about cash flows to equity at date 1. Investors $i, \ldots m$ maximise utility based on expected return and variance, which are now measured after personal tax. There is a risk-free asset that provides £1 at date 1 plus a certain taxable return R_F, and costs £1 per unit at date 0. There are n risky assets; a risky asset j is assumed to pay a certain dividend Div_{j1} and has an uncertain price P_{j1} at date 1. Investor i will adjust his holdings at date 0 until the marginal utility per £1 spent on the risk-free asset is equal to the marginal utility per £1 spent on each risky asset:

$$[\partial U_i/\partial E(V_{Hi})][1 + R_F(1 - T_{Ii})]$$
$$= \{[\partial U_i/\partial E(V_{Hi})][E(P_{j1}) - (E(P_{j1}) - P_{j0})T_{Gi} + Div_{j1}(1 - T_{Ii})]$$
$$- [\partial U_i/\partial var(H_i)][2\Sigma_k^n cov_{jk}(1 - T_{Gi})^2 x_{ki}]\} / P_{j0} \qquad (A8.1)$$

where $E(V_{Hi})$ is the expected value of the portfolio of investor i at date 1, T_{Ii} is the investor's personal tax rate on income, T_{Gi} is his/her personal tax rate on capital gains, $var(H_i)$ is the expected variance in the value of i's portfolio, $cov_{jk}(1 - T_G)^2$ is the after-tax covariance between the price changes of risky assets j and k, and x_{ki} is the number of units of k held by investor i. The left-hand side of equation (A8.1) is the marginal utility of an extra unit spent on the risk-free asset, and is given by the increase in utility from a marginal increase in expected portfolio value in date 1, times the after-tax rate of return on the risk-free asset. The right-hand side is the marginal utility of an extra unit spent on risky asset j, and is given by the difference between two terms. The first is the increase in utility from a marginal increase in expected portfolio value, times the expected after-tax rate of return on risky asset j. The second is the decrease in utility from a marginal increase in expected portfolio variance, times the expected rate of increase in variance from buying more of j, given by $2\Sigma_k^n cov_{jk}(1 - T_G)^2 x_{ki}$. This expression is the partial derivative of the portfolio variance $var(H_i)$ with respect to a marginal purchase of asset j:

$$var(H_i) = \Sigma_j^n \Sigma_k^n cov_{jk}(1 - T_{Gi})^2 x_{ji} x_{ki}$$
$$\partial var(H_i)/\partial x_{ji} = 2\Sigma_k^n cov_{jk}(1 - T_{Gi})^2 x_{ki}$$

Rearranging equation (A8.1) gives

$$\theta_i \Sigma_k^n cov_{jk}(1 - T_G)^2 w_{ki} = E(P_{j1})(1 - T_{Gi}) + P_{j0}T_G + Div_{ji}(1 - T_{Ii})$$
$$- P_{j0}[1 + R_F(1 - T_{Ii})]$$
$$= E(P_{j1}) + Div_{j1} - P_{j0}(1 + R_F) - [E(P_{j1} - P_{j0})]T_{Gi}$$
$$- (Div_{j1} - P_{j0}R_F)T_{Ii} \qquad (A8.2)$$

where $\theta_i = -2\partial U_i/\partial var(H_i) \div \partial U_i/\partial E(V_{Hi})$. θ_i is positive because $\partial U_i/\partial var(H_i)$ is negative. θ_i is positively related to investor i's degree of risk aversion.

To understand what is going on, it may help to suppose for a moment that there are no personal taxes. In this case, equation (A8.2) would be

$$\theta_i \Sigma_k^n cov_{jk} x_{ki} = E(P_{j1}) + Div_{j1} - P_{j0}(1 + R_F) \qquad (A8.3)$$

The individual's portfolio of risky assets is represented by $\Sigma_j^n x_{ji}$, and the contribution of asset j to the risk of this portfolio is $\Sigma_k^n cov_{jk} x_{ki}$, as explained above. So the left-hand side of equation (A8.3) shows the contribution to risk of asset j, multiplied by a measure of the risk aversion of investor i. The right-hand side shows the expected pay-off in excess of the risk-free pay-off per unit of asset j. In equilibrium, equation (A8.3) holds for all assets held by individual i; each asset provides the same expected excess pay-off per unit of risk. The standard CAPM derived in Section 3.1 ignores taxes, and we know from this derivation that investors will all hold a combination of the risk-free asset and the market portfolio of risky assets. This means that the composition of the portfolio of risky assets is the same for all investors. The level of risk is controlled entirely by the proportion of savings held in the risk-free asset, which varies across individuals. A relatively risk-averse individual will have high θ_i and low $\Sigma_j^n x_{ji}$. Thus all investors perceive the risk of asset j, $\Sigma_k^n \text{cov}_{jk} x_{ki}$, to be the same and demand the same expected excess pay-off, $[E(P_{j1}) + Div_{j1} - P_{j0}(1 + R_F)]$ per unit of risk. The individual's risk aversion, measured by θ_i, determines the proportion of the next £1 he/she saves that will be invested in risky assets. In equilibrium, equation (A8.3) holds for all investors and the asset market clears. Dividing equation (A8.3) by P_{j0} and summing across all m investors gives

$$\Theta\text{cov}(R_j, R_M) = E(R_j) - R_F \tag{A8.4}$$

where $\Theta = \Sigma_i^m \theta_i M_0$, which measures the collective risk aversion of investors, $R_j = (P_{j1} + Div_{j1})/P_{j0} - 1$, and $R_M = (M_1 + Div_{M1})/M_0$, where M is the total value of the market and Div_M is the total dividends. The left-hand side is derived as follows:

$$\Sigma_i^m \theta_i \Sigma_k^n \text{cov}_{jk} x_{ki}/P_{j0} = \Sigma_i^m \theta_i \Sigma_k^n \text{cov}[R_j, (P_{k1} + Div_{k1})/P_{k0}] x_k P_{k0}$$
$$= \Sigma_i^m \theta_i \Sigma_k^n \text{cov}[R_j, w_k R_k] M_0$$
$$= \Theta\text{cov}[R_j, R_M]$$

where $x_k = \Sigma_i^m x_{ki}$ and $w_k = x_k P_{k0}/M_0$. Summing over all assets, we have

$$\Theta\text{cov}(R_M, R_M) = \Theta\text{var}(R_M) = E(R_M) - R_F$$

or

$$\Theta = [E(R_M) - R_F]/\text{var}(R_M)$$

which means that equation (A8.4) is the same as the standard CAPM.

Returning to the after-tax version, Brennan sums equation (A8.2) across all investors in the same way that equation (A8.3), which ignores tax, is summed across investors in the previous paragraph. This, he writes, gives

$$\Sigma_i^m \theta_i \Sigma_k^n \text{cov}_{jk}(1 - T_G)^2 x_{ki} = E(P_{j1}) + Div_{j1} - P_{j0}(1 + R_F)$$
$$- [E(P_{j1}) - P_{j0}]T_{Gav} - (Div_{j1} - P_{j0}R_F)T_{Iav} \tag{A8.5}$$

where $T_{Gav} = \Sigma_i^m (T_{Gi}/\theta_i)\Sigma_i^m \theta_i$ and $T_{Iav} = \Sigma_i^m (T_{Ii}/\theta_i)\Sigma_i^m \theta_i$. T_{Gav} is the weighted average rate of personal tax on capital gains; T_{Iav} is the weighted average rate of income tax, and is applied to the difference between the dividend per £1 in a risky asset and the risk-free return per £1. The weights are given by $1/\theta_i$, which increases with tolerance to risk. The reason is that an investor who is relatively tolerant to risk will have a relatively large proportion of his/her savings in risky assets. Therefore, more of the capital gain and dividend income will be taxed at the rates payable by a more risk-tolerant investor than at the rates payable by a less risk-tolerant investor. Division of equation (A8.5) by P_{j0} and rearrangement eventually yields

$$E(R_j) - R_F = \Theta\text{cov}(R_j, R_M) + (Yld_{j1} - R_F)T$$

where $\Theta = \Sigma_i^m \theta_i (1 - T_G)^2 M_0$, Yld_{j1} is the prospective dividend yield on security j and $T = (T_{Iav} - T_{Gav})/(1 - T_{Gav})$. Summing over all assets and solving for Θ gives

$$\Theta = [E(R_M) - R_F - (Yld_{M1} - R_F)T]/\text{var}(R_M)$$

where Yld_{M1} is the prospective dividend yield on the market portfolio. So we have

$$E(R_j) = R_F + \beta_j[E(R_M) - R_F - (Yld_{M1} - R_F)T] + (Yld_{j1} - R_F)T \qquad \text{(A8.6)}$$

As might be expected, equation (A8.6) says that the expected return on an asset measured before personal tax is positively related to the amount of dividend to be paid at date 1, Div_{j1}, and thus to its dividend yield (since, for a given total pay-off at date 1, a larger dividend implies a higher rate of return and therefore a fall in the current price P_{j0}). This assumes that the weighted average rate of income tax exceeds the weighted average rate of capital gains tax.

The key step in the model is the process by which the after-tax equilibrium is arrived at, from which equation (A8.5) is supposed to result. Unfortunately, Brennan says nothing about this process. We have a situation in which variation across investors in T_{Ii} and T_{Gi} causes variation across investors in the expected returns on the same asset. As will be noted in Section 9.6, an equilibrium may not be possible in such a context, and, if it is, it is not clear why the effective tax rates on income and capital gains – the rates implicit in asset prices – will be cross-investor averages weighted by risk tolerance. The effective tax rate on a cash flow is normally considered to be the tax rate facing the price-setting marginal investor, rather than an average of the tax rates faced by all holders of the asset. However, the qualitative conclusion, that the expected return before personal tax is positively related to the proportion of profit after tax paid out as dividend, is intuitively plausible, and is the same as the conclusion under certainty assuming perpetual cash flows. (To those who consult Brennan's paper: the term $-T_G(Yld_{j1} - R_F)$ is omitted from his equation 2.18, and the right-hand side of the equation in note 16 should be divided by $\text{var}(R_M)$.)

A later version of the model presented by Litzenberger and Ramaswamy (1979) assumes that investors face progressive income tax schedules, and incorporates constraints on investor borrowing. These authors discuss aspects of the market-clearing process, but it is still not clear why the effective tax rate on dividends is a weighted average.

Appendix 8.2: The Stiglitz model

Stiglitz (1973) presents an analysis that shares most of the assumptions of the perpetual-projects case, with the major difference that the firm or project has a life cycle. It is a rich model, which is difficult to categorise. The firm starts when the owner has a wealth-creating idea that the firm implements. Investment requirements to exploit the idea exceed cash flows in the early life of the firm; later it starts making surplus cash flows, which can be distributed. The owner sells the firm after T periods. The owner seeks to maximise lifetime consumption, and can lend on personal account at the economy-wide rate $R_A = R(1 - T_I)$, where R is the interest rate before personal tax. He/she can also borrow at $R(1 - T_I)$, assuming that an individual's interest payments can be set against his/her taxable income. The initial market value of the firm is the initial investment it requires plus the NPV of the idea. The owner consumes at each date t an amount such that he/she is indifferent between consuming a further £1 at t and consuming £1$(1 + R_A)$ at $t + 1$. We assume certainty.

The firm, managed by the owner, chooses its financing policy so that the rate of return on the marginal unit invested is equal to R_A. The investment per period and resulting cash flows before tax have already been determined (the cost of capital before personal tax always turns out to be R, so there happens to be no circularity). If the firm retains cash flow that is in excess of any investment requirement, it invests in financial assets and earns the interest rate net of corporation tax, $R(1 - T_C)$ per period. The repayment of capital invested by the owner does not attract personal tax, so dividends to the owner that amount cumulatively to less than the cash he/she has invested do not incur personal tax. All further dividends are taxed at the rate T_{Div}, which can differ from the tax rate on debt interest, T_I. Capital gains are taxed on realisation, not accrual, at the same rate T_{Div} as dividends.

The cost of capital depends potentially on the source of finance, so the first step is to find the optimum financing policy. This is done by imagining a perturbation to the firm's financing policy over a consecutive pair of dates. The perturbation will add value if it results in an after-tax rate of return greater than R_A. Consider a decision to borrow an additional £1 at date t, pay it out as dividend at t, and repay the loan with interest at $t + 1$. The value added or lost from this extra borrowing depends on the tax rates and on the applicability each period of the tax on distributions, T_{Div}. There are three possible regimes.

Regime 1: T_{Div} is applicable in both periods, or is not applicable in either period
If T_{Div} is applicable, the firm must be paying a dividend in both periods. The gain to the owner from the extra dividend at t is £1$(1 - T_{Div})$, which the owner can invest outside the firm to provide £1$(1 - T_{Div})[1 + R(1 - T_I)]$ at $t + 1$. The firm has to repay £1$(1 + R)$ at $t + 1$, which reduces the dividend by £1$(1 - T_{Div})[1 + R(1 - T_C)]$. Hence, if

$$1 - T_I > 1 - T_C$$

the firm should borrow more; if $1 - T_I < 1 - T_C$ it should borrow less. The same result applies if $T_{Div} = 0$ in both periods. $T_{Div} = 0$ if, before the perturbation, new equity is being raised or capital previously invested by the owner has not been fully repaid.

Regime 2: T_{Div} does not apply at t but applies at t + 1
For this regime to exist, the pre-perturbation dividend must be positive at $t + 1$ and the cumulative dividend must by then have exceeded any cash invested by the owner. There is no tax on the extra dividend paid out at t, so we compare $1 + R(1 - T_I)$ at $t + 1$ with $(1 - T_{Div})[1 + R(1 - T_C)]$. Borrowing will be advantageous if

$$1 + R(1 - T_I) > (1 - T_{Div})[1 + R(1 - T_C)]$$

It is possible for borrowing to add value in this regime even if the income tax rate T_I exceeds the corporation tax rate T_C.

Regime 3: T_{Div} applies at t but not at t + 1
For this regime to exist, the owner must have put in nothing, or have been fully repaid by t, and the firm must be raising equity at $t + 1$. Here we compare $(1 - T_{Div})[1 + R(1 - T_I)]$ with $1 + R(1 - T_C)$. Borrowing will be advantageous only if

$$1 + R(1 - T_I) > [1 + R(1 - T_C)]/(1 - T_{Div})$$

It is possible for borrowing not to add value in this regime even if the income tax rate is less than the corporation tax rate.

The optimum financing policy depends on the tax rates, as well as on which regime applies. If there were a tax disadvantage to debt, with $1 - T_I < (1 - T_C)(1 - T_{Div})$, the firm would be a 'money machine'. The owner could borrow at $R(1 - T_I)$ and invest at the higher rate of $R(1 - T_C)(1 - T_{Div})$ via equity in the firm. If we ignore this case, it follows that debt or retained cash flow will be the marginal source of capital in every regime.

Suppose first that

$$1 - T_I < 1 - T_C$$

and

$$1 + R(1 - T_I) > (1 - T_{Div})[1 + R(1 - T_C)]$$

This might be called a mild tax advantage to debt. Extra borrowing is worthwhile in regime 2 but not in regime 1 (nor in 3). This combination of tax rates implies that the firm will not pay a dividend until the terminal date because the rate of return R on money retained is taxed less heavily in the firm than it would be if the money were paid out to the owner and lent by him/her. Stiglitz argues that the owner will not invest any equity; all the firm's external capital will be debt. In a one-period context, some investment by the owner would imply the existence of regime 2, in which borrowing is worthwhile. The firm can borrow £1 at date $T - 1$ and pay it out as untaxed dividend or investment forgone, so the owner has an extra $[1 + R(1 - T_I)]$ at date T. The dividend at T is reduced by $(1 - T_{Div})[1 + R(1 - T_C)]$, which we are assuming to be less than $[1 + R(1 - T_I)]$. Hence borrowing at $T - 1$ will be worthwhile until the dividend at $T - 1$ exceeds the amount invested by the owner, and becomes taxable (regime 1) – i.e. until the owner has invested nothing. However, it appears that investment by the owner could be worthwhile if there are many periods. The owner compares the total return over T periods, R_T, from investing outside the firm,

$$R_T^{out} = [1 + R(1 - T_I)]^T - 1$$

with the total return from investing in the firm with pay-out at date T,

$$R_T^{in} = \{[1 + R(1 - T_C)]^T - 1\}(1 - T_{Div})$$

If $1 - T_I < 1 - T_C$, it is possible to have $R_T^{in} > R_T^{out}$ for values of T above a certain number.

The owner could choose to realise the value of the NPV by having the firm borrow *more* than the initial investment required, and pay out the surplus. But the surplus would be taxable at T_{Div} and the firm would shift into regime 1, in which borrowing reduces value, given $1 - T_{\text{I}} < 1 - T_{\text{C}}$. So the owner will leave the NPV as the (unrealised) market value of the equity.

At least as much debt will be used if there is a stronger tax advantage to debt, such that $1 - T_{\text{I}} = 1 - T_{\text{C}}$, rather than $1 - T_{\text{I}} < 1 - T_{\text{C}}$. The owner is now indifferent between the retention of surplus cash flow and paying out in regime 1, and the firm might borrow to distribute some or all of the NPV. If the tax advantage of debt is stronger still, such that

$$1 - T_{\text{I}} > 1 - T_{\text{C}}$$

and

$$1 + R(1 - T_{\text{I}}) > [1 + R(1 - T_{\text{C}})]/(1 - T_{\text{Div}})$$

no surplus cash flow will be retained, and the firm will borrow to distribute all of the NPV, which represents the present value of the future surplus cash flows. The distribution of NPV will be taxable and the firm requires £NPV$[1 + R(1 - T_{\text{C}})]$ more capital at $t + 1$ to fulfil its pre-set investment schedule. This is regime 3.

In summary, for some combinations of tax rates a mixed capital structure with equity and debt is optimal; a corner solution is not inevitable. But no equity is raised externally; the source of marginal capital is always debt or retained cash flow (external equity does have a role in the extension of the model under uncertainty).

The final step is the argument that, if the marginal source of capital is debt or retained earnings, the cost of capital before corporate and personal tax is R, the interest rate before personal tax. Suppose the company changes its investment plan by investing an extra unit of real capital at date t for one period. This means borrowing for one period at the rate R, and repaying the loan at $t + 1$. Alternatively, if the source of the funds is retained earnings, it implies that the firm is lending; retained cash is invested in financial assets, which earn the interest rate R. Reducing lending means reducing surplus cash for one period, thereby forgoing a return before corporate tax of R. So R is the cost of capital before all tax, or $R(1 - T_{\text{C}}) = R_{\text{A}}(1 - T_{\text{C}})/(1 - T_{\text{I}})$ expressed after corporation tax and before personal tax.

9 Personal tax, leverage and multiple tax rates

The previous chapter concentrated on the specification of the cost of equity allowing for personal tax, assuming that the income tax rate on dividends exceeds the effective CGT rate. It questioned whether the cost of equity for retained earnings should be viewed as the expected rate of return on a company's shares at their equilibrium market price. The current chapter leaves this question aside. Here we consider further the effects of personal taxes on the expected rates of return on equity and debt viewed as financial assets. The analyses allow personal tax rates to differ across investors, in certain ways, as well as across types of asset. We revisit the effect of leverage on the weighted average cost of capital, this time allowing for personal tax, and we consider the effect of an imputation system. The chapter ends with an introduction to the general problem of price setting in a market in which investors are heterogeneous with respect to the tax rates they face.

The notation is the same as in Chapter 8, except for the following variations. The differences between dividends and capital gains, and between share issues and retained earnings, are ignored. So there is now assumed to be a rate of personal tax on equity, T_E, that is common across shareholders, and that could be zero (the α superscript for the pay-out ratio is dropped from T_E). The symbol T_I refers exclusively to the personal tax rate on interest in this chapter. There is no presumption that the tax rate on interest T_I and the tax rate on equity T_E are the same.

9.1 Leverage allowing for personal tax

9.1.1 The Miller model

The starting point for the analysis is the model presented by Miller (1977), which leads to a prediction that leverage has *no* effect on the cost of capital, as in the original Modigliani and Miller (1958) model, which ignores all tax. Allowing for personal tax, equilibrium in securities markets under certainty implies that $R_E(1 - T_E) = R_D(1 - T_I) = R_{Fexempt} = R_A$, where $R_{Fexempt}$ is the rate of return on a risk-free asset that is exempt from tax. Miller assumes that, although the personal tax rate on equity is zero across all investors, the personal tax rate on debt varies by category of investor. Tax-exempt investors pay no personal tax; taxpaying investors pay various rates of tax on interest, at least one of which is equal to or exceeds the corporation tax rate. Each category of investor has a limited demand for debt. Tax-exempt investors are willing to lend at the rate R_A. If the corporate sector wishes to borrow more than exempt investors are willing to lend, companies will have to offer more than R_A. Companies will cease to have a tax incentive to borrow once the marginal investor m is paying a rate of personal tax on interest, T_{Im}, such that

$$1 - T_{Im} = (1 - T_C)(1 - T_E) \tag{9.1}$$

If this equality obtains, the cost of equity and the cost of debt, measured before or after tax, are equal. The marginal investor is indifferent (from a tax perspective) between equity and debt, and the individual company is indifferent about how much it borrows. An investor i with a tax rate T_{Ii} below T_{Im} receives a 'bondholder surplus', a higher after-tax rate of return on corporate bonds than he/she requires.

The above argument presents a framework within which market forces, combined with specific provisions of the tax system, would result in there being an equal tax burden on returns to equity and to marginal debt. The existing Modigliani–Miller analysis did not explain how an equilibrium in which equality of the tax burden on equity and debt could arise. The 'Miller equilibrium' avoids the prediction of a tax-driven corner solution, though it then leaves unanswered the question why leverage appears to matter in practice. It also shows how the rates of personal tax might be determined that are reflected in the prices of equity and debt. These rates are the effective rates of tax by which the expected rates of return on equity and debt expressed after all tax should be grossed up, in order to obtain the costs of equity and debt expressed before personal tax.

However, the equilibrium is quite fragile, in that several conditions have to be met for it to exist. These conditions include the following.

- There must be regulations that prevent taxable investors from avoiding paying personal tax; otherwise no personal tax will be paid.
- There must be regulations that prevent tax-exempt investors from exploiting possibilities for tax arbitrage. For example, there needs to be something that prevents a tax-exempt investor from borrowing at the rate R_A and investing the proceeds in corporate bonds, pledging the bonds as security. Such a strategy will be profitable so long as R_D exceeds R_A. If there are tax-exempt investors but no restrictions on tax arbitrage, we would expect the expected rates on all assets to be driven down to R_A.
- There must be at least one category of investor that pays a high enough rate of tax on interest and a low enough tax rate on equity returns such that $1 - T_{Ii} \leq (1 - T_C)(1 - T_{Ei})$. If not, there will still be a tax advantage to debt.
- The supply of debt from the corporate sector must exceed the amount of debt demanded by investors who have personal tax rates such that $1 - T_{Ii} > (1 - T_C)(1 - T_{Ei})$. Otherwise, again, there will be a tax advantage to debt.
- Interest tax shields are not redundant (Section 9.1.3).
- Tax rates for investors are fixed; they are not related to the amount of the investor's income (Section 9.6).

In addition, if the assumption of certainty is dropped, the risk characteristics of assets affect their prices as well as the expected cash flows. For example, some investors i will wish to buy shares despite the fact that, for these investors, debt is less heavily taxed – i.e. $1 - T_{Ii} > (1 - T_C)(1 - T_{Ei})$. We would not expect investors' portfolios to be all equity or all debt. It is then no longer certain in theory that equilibrium prices of taxable debt and equity will be such that $1 - T_{Im} = (1 - T_C)(1 - T_E)$. We now discuss some of the extensions and modifications that have been made to the analysis.

9.1.2   Redundant tax shields

DeAngelo and Masulis (1980) study the Miller model under uncertainty, in the context of the contingent-states framework, but assuming risk-neutral investors. They allow for the possibility that interest may exceed taxable profit, which means that some or all of the tax saving may be lost in certain states. They also allow for the existence of non-debt tax shields, in the form of tax credits and depreciation allowances. These non-debt tax shields reduce the future taxable profits against which interest can be offset, and therefore they affect the state-contingent amounts of the tax savings from interest.

At the macro-level, the above modification implies that the aggregate tax savings from debt per period for the corporate sector are less than the statutory corporation tax rate T_C times the interest paid in that period. In addition, the marginal rate of tax saving diminishes as more debt is issued. Let us label the effective rate at which corporation tax is saved in aggregate on marginal interest to be paid in period t as T_{Ct}^E. This can be written as

$$T_{Ct}^E = \Sigma_{st} \pi_{st} T_{\text{shield}}(T_C, Profit_{st}, Int_{st})$$

where π_{st} is the probability that state s occurs in period t and T_{shield} stands for the rate at which corporation tax is saved. T_{shield} is written as a function of the corporation tax rate T_C, and of the taxable profit and interest paid that arise in state s on date t for the corporate sector. If debt is risk-free, Int_{st} is the same across all states; if debt is risky, Int_{st} varies across states. Let us assume for simplicity that T_{Ct}^E is constant over time, so that the t subscript can be dropped. Then a modified Miller equilibrium will arise if the corporate sector issues debt until $(1 - T_{Im}) = (1 - T_C^E)(1 - T_E)$. Since $T_C^E \leq T_C$, the personal tax rate on interest paid by the marginal investor, T_{Im}, will be smaller than in the original version of the equilibrium, equation (9.1).

At the micro-level, each firm will have its own tax credits and depreciation schedule, which means that it will have its own optimum leverage. The optimum is the level at which the marginal corporation tax advantage to debt is equal to the constant personal tax disadvantage to debt. The marginal corporation tax advantage diminishes with the amount borrowed according to a schedule that is specific to the firm. The personal tax disadvantage to debt is given by $T_I - T_E$; these personal tax rates are exogenous to the firm. Debt can be risk-free but some of the potential tax saving can still be lost in some states. This occurs if the state-contingent profit is insufficient for all the tax shields to be used. If there are provisions for carrying tax losses back or forward, the present value of the potential loss of tax saving is reduced but not eliminated.

The main conclusion of the DeAngelo–Masulis argument is that the optimum level of leverage will vary from firm to firm, depending on its schedule of non-debt tax shields. Estimating the optimum leverage would be quite difficult in practice; firms would have to know the marginal rates of personal tax applicable to returns on equity and on debt, amongst other things.

Talmor, Haugen and Barnea (1985) present a different analysis of leverage with non-debt tax shields. They present a two-date model with risky debt, assuming that only interest saves corporation tax and that personal tax on equity is zero. They find that the marginal value of the tax subsidy normally increases with the amount of debt, because the promised interest payment increases.

They consider two cases. In the first case, the amount of debt exceeds the amount of the non-debt tax shield – i.e. the amount (e.g. depreciation) that can be set against taxable profit at the future date. In this case an all-debt policy maximises value. The argument is as follows. A marginal increase in debt causes a marginal increase in the promised interest payment, $dInt$. If the firm is not bankrupt at the future date, the marginal tax saving is $dInt$ $(T_C - T_I)$. The increase in debt also causes an increase in the probability of bankruptcy. But there is no (tax-related) cost associated with this increased probability, because all the interest before the increase is assumed to continue to relieve corporation tax if the firm is bankrupt. Bankruptcy is more probable because there is a contingent state in which the cash flow is equal to the amount of the loan plus interest due without the marginal increase in debt. If the firm increases its debt, it will just be bankrupt in this state. But this will cost it nothing, and it will gain the marginal increase in the tax shield in non-bankruptcy states. Hence there is a gain in tax shield in some states from an increase in debt, at no cost, and an all-debt policy is optimal.

In the second case, the amount of debt is less than the amount of the non-debt tax shield. Again an increase in debt increases the probability of bankruptcy, and again there is no cost associated with this. But in this case debt increases total taxes paid in future states in which cash flow is less than the non-debt tax shield, and in which the firm is not bankrupt. In these states interest does not relieve corporation tax and attracts personal tax. In other states, in which cash flows are larger, debt does save tax. If the non-debt tax shield is sufficiently large in relation to the state-contingent cash flows, a small increase in debt reduces value and an all-equity policy is optimal. But a large increase in debt increases value: all debt is always optimal if debt exceeds the non-debt tax shield. The prediction of an all-debt or possibly all-equity solution contrasts with DeAngelo and Masulis (1980), who find that the tax subsidy declines as leverage increases, so that each firm has an optimum level of leverage. What explains the difference is that DeAngelo and Masulis assume that a loss-making firm survives but loses tax shields, whereas Talmor et al. assume that a loss means bankruptcy, with no loss of tax shield.

9.1.3   Firm-specific capital gains tax

Most models assume that the effective personal tax rate on equity, T_E, is either zero or is the same for all firms. However, Green and Hollifield (2003) develop a model in which T_E is firm-specific. They assume that all payments to shareholders are made by means of share repurchases by the firm, which attract capital gains tax. All shareholders pay tax on capital gains at the same rate. Green and Hollifield point out that the effective rate of CGT depends in part on the profile of gains to be realised through time. Only the portion of the value of a repurchased share that represents a capital gain is taxed; repayment of the initial market value of the share (the basis) is not taxed. The size of the benefit of not taxing the repayment of the initial value, reflected in a lower effective CGT rate, is a decreasing function of the growth rate of the firm's cash flows. 'Growth reduces the personal-tax advantage of repurchases because a larger fraction of the firm's present value is associated with more distant distributions, and a small[er] portion of the distribution is protected by the basis as one moves through time' (p. 186). Since firms have different growth rates, they will have different effective rates of CGT. An implication is that the cost of equity expressed before personal tax is relatively high for fast-growing firms facing relatively high effective CGT.

9.1.4   Leverage clienteles

An implication of the model under some assumptions is that there will be 'leverage clienteles'. The shares of firms that choose high leverage will be bought by investors with a tax position that differs from the position of investors who buy unlevered shares. This is demonstrated by Kim, Lewellen and McConnell (1979). Assuming for simplicity that there is no personal tax on equity, then, in Miller's equilibrium, $T_{\text{Im}} = T_{\text{C}}$. The rate of return on risk-free corporate bonds exceeds the rate on tax-exempt bonds by T_{C}, but interest saves the firm tax at a rate of T_{C}. So the cost of debt to (shareholders in) a levered firm is $R_{\text{D}}(1 - T_{\text{C}}) = R_{\text{A}}$, and it is also the case that $R_{\text{D}}(1 - T_{\text{Im}}) = R_{\text{A}}$. If investor i's rate of income tax, T_{Ii}, exceeds T_{C}, the investor prefers to borrow on personal account, and to hold unlevered shares, because personal borrowing saves more tax than corporate borrowing. This assumes that interest on personal borrowing can be offset against taxable income. Such an investor prefers to lend by buying tax-exempt bonds.

An investor with $T_{\text{Ii}} < T_{\text{C}}$ prefers the firm to borrow, and prefers to hold levered shares, because corporate borrowing saves more tax than personal borrowing. This investor will lend by buying taxable corporate bonds. If the firm has higher risk than the risk the investor wishes to bear, he will hold corporate bonds as well as leveraged equity. He will want the firm to take maximum advantage of the corporation tax saving from debt, because he can unlever his portfolio via holding bonds. Holding highly levered equity plus taxable bonds minimises the overall tax rate on his portfolio.

The prediction from the above is that a highly levered firm should be held by shareholders facing low rates of income tax, and an unlevered firm should be held by shareholders facing high rates of income tax. Also, firms should remain either highly levered or unlevered, assuming that there are transactions costs for investors to revise their portfolios following a change in leverage. But firm value is unaffected by leverage; the equilibrium effective tax rates on debt and equity are equal.

Taggart (1980) presents a somewhat different analysis, using a two-date model. Leverage clienteles are predicted under uncertainty but not under certainty. There is again no personal tax on equity, but a difference from Kim et al. (1979) is that no personal tax arbitrage is allowed, so that investors cannot, for example, borrow on personal account to buy shares, which are exempt from personal tax.

Under certainty, an investor i for whom $T_{\text{I}i} > T_\text{C}$ will hold exempt bonds or shares, but not taxable corporate bonds; an investor for whom $T_{\text{I}i} < T_\text{C}$ will hold taxable bonds but not exempt bonds or shares. Shareholders have different rates of personal tax, but they all agree that firms should not issue debt beyond the aggregate amount at which $T_{\text{I}m} = T_\text{C}$. The reason for this unanimity is that, if $T_{\text{I}m} = T_\text{C}$, all investors holding shares will have personal tax rates such that $T_{\text{I}i} \geq T_\text{C}$, and for all such investors the opportunity cost of holding shares is the rate on exempt bonds, which is R_A. The cost of debt to the firm before all tax is $R_\text{D} = R_\text{A}/(1 - T_{\text{I}m})$, and the cost of equity before all tax is $R_\text{A}/(1 - T_\text{C})$.

Under uncertainty, risky shares and risk-free tax-exempt bonds are no longer perfect substitutes. Corporate bonds are assumed to remain risk-free. It is also assumed that financial-markets are incomplete, in the sense that it is not possible to 'combine existing securities into a portfolio yielding any given pattern of contingent returns and at the same time any given tax treatment' (Taggart, 1980, p. 651). The only way to gain exposure to some patterns of contingent returns is to buy shares, and some investors may do so even though, for them, shares have a tax disadvantage.

Taggart argues that there will not be unanimity of shareholder preferences with respect to leverage, under uncertainty. A marginal increase in a firm's debt is paid out to shareholders now, and reduces the firm's cash flow next period by $1 + R_\text{D}(1 - T_\text{C})$. This reduction is certain, as corporate debt is assumed to be risk-free. Suppose that the corporate sector has issued debt to the point at which $R_\text{D}(1 - T_\text{C}) = R_\text{A}$, as in the certainty case. A shareholder who also invests in tax-exempt bonds would be indifferent to an increase in leverage; his/her shares provide $R_\text{D}(1 - T_\text{C})$ less next period, but he/she can invest the proceeds from the debt at the rate R_A. A shareholder who also invests in corporate bonds has $T_{\text{I}i} < T_\text{C}$, or he/she would be holding exempt bonds. He/she would prefer more leverage as he/she can invest the proceeds at the rate $R_\text{D}(1 - T_{\text{I}i})$, which is higher than $R_\text{D}(1 - T_\text{C})$. A shareholder who holds no bonds would also prefer more leverage. He/she has no bonds because he/she values risk-free exempt and corporate bonds at less than their price; his/her 'personal discount rate' on risk-free returns is greater than the higher of R_A and $R_\text{D}(1 - T_{\text{I}i})$. This means that the present value he/she assigns to a certain payment of $£1[1 + R_\text{D}(1 - T_\text{C})]$ is less than £1, so the £1 per share he/she would receive as a result of a marginal increase in the firm's debt is worth more to him/her than the resulting loss of $£1[1 + R_\text{D}(1 - T_\text{C})]$ per share next period. Thus, firms should issue more debt. But this will require an increase in R_D, to attract lenders in a higher tax bracket, in which case shareholders who also hold tax-exempt bonds will no longer be indifferent, but would prefer less leverage. So there will not be unanimity of preferences with respect to leverage. Taggart suggests that firms will have either of two clienteles of shareholder: one that prefers no leverage, and the other that prefers maximum leverage.

9.1.5   Dammon's analysis

Dammon (1988) examines the leverage decision in the context of the two-date contingent-states model of Dammon and Green (1987) (Section 9.6). Investors face a common personal tax schedule, which is progressive. They will hold mixed portfolios of equity and debt, depending on their risk aversion. Equity is assumed not to be taxed at the personal level, so taxable personal income is provided by debt only. Investors' state-contingent taxable incomes will differ across states, and since the personal tax schedule is progressive the variation in taxable incomes means that observed tax rates will differ across investors *ex post*. Suppose that the progressive schedule includes some rates that are lower than the rate of corporation tax, and some that are higher. Then there will be a tax advantage to debt in some states, and a tax disadvantage in others. It then follows that, if each project offers a unique distribution of unlevered cash flows, each project will have a specific level of leverage that maximises its market value.

Dammon suggests that the tax advantage to debt will be negatively related to 'per capita consumption and overall market returns' (p. 65). When market returns are high, personal incomes are high and marginal personal tax rates will also be high, which implies a low or negative tax advantage to debt. Projects with a low unlevered (asset) beta offer relatively high unlevered cash flows when market returns are low, and when the tax advantage to debt is high so value-maximising leverage is predicted to be negatively related to the project's unlevered beta. This is a familiar prediction, but in this model it is driven entirely by tax considerations.

The implications of the Dammon model clearly differ from those of Miller (1977). Leverage will affect the market values of individual projects and firms, and there will be no tax clienteles. These differences stem from the differing assumptions made about the personal tax rates that investors face. Miller assumes that each investor faces a single, fixed rate of personal tax that differs across investors. Dammon assumes that investors face the same personal tax schedule and that it is progressive, and so the tax rates payable by a given investor differ across contingent states.

9.1.6   Discussion

A number of other variants of the Miller model have been proposed, but we curtail the review at this point because the primary concern of this literature is the choice of leverage rather than the cost of capital (for other reviews of the effects of taxes on capital structure, see Graham, 2003, Haugen and Senbet, 1986, or Swoboda and Zechner, 1995). However, it should be noted that the choice of leverage is driven by tax minimisation in the above models. Leverage affects value via taxes, and if the cost of capital is taken to be the standard tax-adjusted WACC then the effect of leverage on value via taxes is captured in the cost of capital. In effect we have been discussing the determination of the costs of equity and debt before personal tax, and how leverage might affect a project's WACC. The models in this section can therefore be seen as an extension of the analysis in Chapter 7, allowing for personal tax and assuming that investors are interested in returns after all tax.

The main points that arise for our purposes are as follows. The prediction from the Miller model that leverage is irrelevant for an individual firm is not robust to changes in the assumptions made, for example about the availability of non-debt tax shields, or whether debt is risky. An individual firm or project may have a specific level of leverage that minimises the personal taxes paid by investors minus the corporation tax saving from interest. It may thus have a specific leverage that minimises its standard tax-adjusted WACC. Also, the supply of debt from the corporate sector can be less than the amount at which effective tax rates would be such that $(1 - T_{\text{Im}}) = (1 - T_{\text{C}})(1 - T_{\text{E}})$, at least if T_{C} is the statutory rate of corporation tax. The availability of non-debt tax shields is one reason why the effective rate at which debt saves corporation tax is likely to be less than the statutory rate of corporation tax.

These results can emerge, under certain assumptions, without bringing in non-tax factors such as costs of financial distress. If non-tax factors are introduced then there are further reasons why firms will not be indifferent to their choice of leverage. The tax advantage to debt, if it exists, becomes one of a number of factors that potentially affect the choice of leverage. However, Miller's general idea seems to have survived scrutiny: that the tax advantage to debt is less than it is if personal taxes are ignored, and may be non-existent. We now explore further the implications of this idea for expressions of the cost of capital.

9.2   The cost of capital under the before- and after-tax views

In this section we compare the WACC and CAPM under the assumption that there is no personal tax (the 'before-tax view') and under the assumption that the Miller equilibrium applies (the 'after-tax view') (Hamada and Scholes, 1985). Under both views, the firm gains the full value of tax savings from interest.

The before-tax view implies the analysis based on Modigliani and Miller in Chapter 7. Personal tax is ignored in estimating the cost of equity, the implicit assumption being that investors care about returns measured before personal tax. Thus the CAPM is

$$E(R_{\text{E}}) = R_{\text{F}} + \beta[E(R_{\text{M}}) - R_{\text{F}}] \tag{9.2}$$

where R_{F} and $E(R_{\text{M}})$ are measured before personal tax. If a tax-exempt risk-free asset exists, the only tax it can provide exemption from is corporation tax, so it will be held by companies and be priced to provide a return of $R_{\text{A}} = R_{\text{F}}(1 - T_{\text{C}})$, in which case equation (9.2) becomes

$$E(R_{\text{E}}) = R_{\text{A}}/(1 - T_{\text{C}}) + \beta[E(R_{\text{M}}) - R_{\text{A}}/(1 - T_{\text{C}})] \tag{9.3}$$

Alternatively, if the Miller equilibrium holds, we have the after-tax view, which implies

$$R_{\text{E}}(1 - T_{\text{E}}) = R_{\text{D}}(1 - T_{\text{I}}) = R_{\text{A}}$$

All types of asset will be priced to provide the same rate of return after personal tax R_{A}, under certainty. The CAPM holds for after-tax rates of return:

$$E(R_{\text{E}})(1 - T_{\text{E}}) = R_{\text{A}} + \beta[E(R_{\text{M}})(1 - T_{\text{E}}) - R_{\text{A}}]$$

But it is normal to measure the cost of equity before personal tax, which means dividing both sides by $1 - T_{\text{E}}$, to give

$$E(R_{\text{E}}) = R_{\text{A}}/(1 - T_{\text{E}}) + \beta[E(R_{\text{M}}) - R_{\text{A}}/(1 - T_{\text{E}})] \tag{9.4}$$

This is not the same as equation (9.2), because R_{F} – the yield gross of personal tax on taxable government bonds or treasury bills, as in the usual formulation – is not the same thing as

$R_A/(1 - T_E)$. R_A is the yield on tax-exempt risk-free bonds. Under the Miller equilibrium, we have $(1 - T_I) = (1 - T_C)(1 - T_E)$. Thus, if $T_C > 0$, we have $T_I > T_E$, and $R_F = R_A/(1 - T_I) > R_A/(1 - T_E)$. Equation (9.4) is correct only on the simplifying assumption that there is a single effective personal tax rate, T_E, across all shares and the market as a whole. This assumption implies that dividend policy does not affect the tax rate on equity.

The above reasoning implies that, if the before-tax view is true, $R_F = R_A/(1 - T_C)$, whereas, if the after-tax view is true, $R_F = R_A/(1 - T_I) = R_A/(1 - T_C)(1 - T_E)$. Unless $T_C = T_E$, the CAPM expressed before tax under the Miller equilibrium will have a different equity premium from the CAPM under the before-tax view, and expected rates of return will differ for $\beta \neq 1.0$. For example, suppose $R_A = 4\%$ pa, $E(R_M) = 10\%$ pa, $T_C = 50\%$, T_E 0%, and $\beta = 1.4$. Under the before-tax theory, from equation (9.3),

$$E(R_E) = 8\% + 1.4[10\% - 8\%]$$
$$= 10.8\% \text{ pa}$$

Under the Miller equilibrium, from equation (9.4),

$$E(R_E) = 4\% + 1.4[10\% - 4\%]$$
$$= 12.4\% \text{ pa}$$

As noted by Riener (1985), Strong and Appleyard (1992) and Taggart (1991), the tax-adjusted WACC can always be used, whether the before-tax view holds or the Miller equilibrium. The reason is that the impact of the differing views is captured in the rates R_E and R_D inserted in the formula. But the formula does not reveal what happens when leverage is changed, and the prediction will differ regarding the effect on the WACC of a change in leverage. Under the before-tax (Modigliani–Miller) view, leverage reduces the WACC (Chapter 7). Under the Miller equilibrium, leverage does not alter the WACC. This is easiest to show assuming certainty. Under the before-tax view,

$$R_F = R_{EL} = R_{EU}$$

where R_{EL} and R_{EU} are the rates of return on levered and unlevered equity before personal tax. Under certainty, both equity and debt provide the same rate of return to investors before personal tax. But the cost of debt to the company is $R_F(1 - T_C)$, because of the tax advantage. We have

$$WACC = R_{EL}(1 - L) + R_F(1 - T_C)L$$
$$= R_{EU}(1 - LT_C)$$

Under the Miller equilibrium,

$$R_F = R_A/(1 - T_E)(1 - T_C) = R_{EL}/(1 - T_C)$$

and we have

$$WACC = R_{EL}(1 - L) + R_F(1 - T_C)L$$
$$= R_{EU}$$

There is still a tax advantage to debt at the corporate level, as reflected in the formula. But it is exactly offset by the tax disadvantage at the personal level, and this is not apparent in the formula. The cost of debt before personal tax, R_F, is *higher* under certainty than the cost of equity before personal tax, R_{EL}. There is no tax advantage to debt after all taxes, so leverage does not reduce the cost of capital. We return to the position that applies if taxes are ignored, which is $WACC = R_{EL} = R_{EU}$ – the cost of unlevered equity.

Suppose that the Miller equilibrium does not hold exactly: there remains a tax advantage to debt that is less than the tax advantage would be were there no personal taxes. The tax advantage to debt allowing for personal tax (if any), or gain from leverage G_L, can be written

$$G_L = 1 - (1 - T_C)(1 - T_E)/(1 - T_I)$$

and

$$R_F = R_{EL}(1 - G_L)/(1 - T_C)$$

$G_L = T_C$ under the before-tax view, $G_L = 0$ under the after-tax view, and in between is $0 < G_L < T_C$, which means that $R_F(1 - T_C) < R_{EL}$. If we assume that the after-tax view is true but that for some reason there remains a positive tax advantage to debt, it can be shown that the equations listed in Table 7.1 apply, with $R_A/(1 - T_E)$ replacing R_F and with G_L replacing T_C (Taggart, 1991). The exception is the tax-adjusted WACC formula, which does not change. The cost of equity R_{EL} comes from the after-tax version of the CAPM (equation (9.4)) rather than the before-tax version (equation (9.2)), and the relation between β_L and β_U is affected by G_L.

An increase in leverage will reduce the WACC, though not as much as under the before-tax view. For example, with constant perpetual cash flows,

$$WACC = R_{EU}(1 - T_C L)$$

under the before-tax view becomes

$$WACC = R_{EU}(1 - G_L L)$$

Discounting a risk-free taxable cash flow

Just as a project's cash flows after corporation tax should always be discounted by the tax-adjusted WACC, a risk-free taxable cash flow should always be discounted by $R_F(1 - T_C)$, as demonstrated by Ruback (1986). He uses an arbitrage argument and assumes, as we have in this section, that the firm realises the full value of its interest tax shields. The starting point is to note that the present value of a risk-free cash flow after corporation tax received at date T, $PV[Y_T(1 - T_C)]$, is equal to D_{max0}, the maximum amount that the firm could borrow now, using the cash flow to repay principal and interest at date T. At $T - 1$, D_{maxT-1} is given by

$$D_{maxT-1}[1 + R_F(1 - T_C)] = Y_T(1 - T_C)$$

The reason is that, since the interest $R_F D_{maxT-1}$ provides a tax saving of $R_F D_{maxT-1} T_C$, this latter amount can be set against the principal and interest to be repaid from the cash flow. If this equation did not hold, there would be an opportunity for arbitrage. Assuming that the debt is refinanced every period, the same argument applies each time, so that the value of D_{max} in period 0 is given by

$$D_{max0}[1 + R_F(1 - T_C)]^T = Y_T(1 - T_C)$$

Since $D_{max0} = PV[Y_T(1 - T_C)]$, we have

$$PV[Y_T(1 - T_C)] = Y_T(1 - T_C)/[1 + R_F(1 - T_C)]^T \tag{9.5}$$

This proves that the correct discount rate is $R_F(1 - T_C)$. A similar argument applies if R_F is not assumed to be constant, or is uncertain, but the valuation procedure is slightly more complex. Ruback also shows that, using the adjusted present value method (Section 7.5.4), the discount rate for both the after-tax cash flow and the tax savings is R_F rather than $R_F(1 - T_C)$.

The argument applies regardless of whether there is any tax advantage to debt. For example, suppose that $T_E = 0$ and $T_I = T_C$, so there is no tax advantage. Equation (9.5) is still correct. There is still a corporation tax saving from interest, but it happens that the saving now exactly offsets the higher personal tax on debt.

9.3   Imputation systems

In the 'classical' tax system, profit is taxed via corporation tax, and dividend, paid out of profit net of corporation tax, is taxed separately via income tax. The tax rate on dividend is $1 - (1 - T_C)(1 - T_I)$ and the total tax rate on retained profit is $1 - (1 - T_C)(1 - T_G)$. The classical system exists in the United States, and it is the system we have been considering so far. But some version of the 'imputation' tax system exists in many other countries, so it is worth considering how this system affects the analysis.

Under an imputation system, the effective rate of personal tax on dividends is reduced in relation to the statutory rate, because some or all of the corporation tax on the profit paid out as dividend also counts as personal income tax. The total tax rate on retained profit is $1 - (1 - T_C)(1 - T_G)$, as in the classical system. The total tax rate on dividend is $1 - (1 - T_C)(1 - T_I)/(1 - T_S)$, where T_S is the 'rate of imputation' – the rate of income tax that also counts as corporate tax. Thus the effective personal tax rate on dividends allowing for imputation is $(1 - T_I)/(1 - T_S)$. With full imputation, $T_S = T_I$, so the effective personal tax rate on dividends is zero, and if it is also the case that $T_G > 0$ there is a tax advantage to paying dividends. In some versions of the system, tax-exempt shareholders are allowed to *reclaim* corporate tax paid by the company up to the rate of imputation, on the grounds that such corporate tax also counts as income tax, from which the shareholders are exempt. There is then a much larger tax advantage to paying dividends, from the perspective of exempt shareholders. This version of the imputation system existed in the United Kingdom from 1973 to 1997.

Since the motive for imputation systems is to reduce or eliminate the double taxation of dividends, it would seem reasonable to presume that the effective rate of personal tax on dividends is lower under imputation than it would be under a classical system, although the reverse could be possible. Thus the effect of an imputation system amounts to the effect of a lower effective tax rate on dividends. Under the old view of the cost of equity, a lower effective tax rate on dividends implies a lower cost of equity and higher dividend pay-out ratios. Under the new view, there is no effect on the cost of equity or on pay-out, but shares will trade at a higher q-value (Chapter 8).

To demonstrate the nature of the effect of an imputation system, suppose that the result of the system is that the effective tax rate on dividends is the same as the tax rate on capital gains, so there is a common tax rate on equity, which we label T_E. There would be no tax disadvantage to paying dividends at the margin, and the cost of equity would be the same under the old and new views. Let us also suppose that T_E is small enough in relation to the tax rate on interest that a Miller equilibrium applies, in which the tax advantage to debt is zero. We can then use the analysis of the previous section: $R_A/(1 - T_E)$ replaces R_F in the CAPM, and $G_L = 0$. Several writers have argued that the version of the imputation system that applied in the United Kingdom between 1973 and 1997 made it reasonable to assume that there was little or no tax advantage to debt, in which case the after-personal-tax analysis is more appropriate than the 'textbook' before-tax analysis.

Dimson and Marsh (1982), Dimson (1989) and Buckley (1995) argue that the UK system was such that cash flows after corporation tax should be discounted at a discount rate expressed after all tax. They argue that it was the case that, roughly speaking, $T_E \approx 0$, and $T_C \approx T_I$ (under the Miller equilibrium $T_C = T_I$, if $T_E = 0$). In this case the deduction of corporation tax from cash flows accounts for both corporation tax on equity and for personal tax on debt. Cash flows after corporation tax are equivalent to cash flows after all tax, so the discount rate should be after all tax:

$$E(R_{EA}) = R_F(1 - T_I) + \beta[E(R_M) - R_F(1 - T_I)]$$

and

$$WACC = E(R_{EA})(1 - L) + R_F(1 - T_I)L$$

where $E(R_{EA})$ is the expected rate of return on equity after all tax and $E(R_M)$ is measured after corporation tax, including advance corporation tax, the imputation tax credit on dividends. Ashton (1989; 1991) allows T_E to exceed zero, and his analysis is similar to that of Section 9.2 under the after-tax view.

Monkhouse (1993, 1996) analyses the cost of capital under the imputation system prevailing in Australia at the time. The CGT rate is assumed to be the same as the statutory income tax rate on dividends, but the effective tax rate on dividends is less than the statutory rate because 'imputation credits' accompanying dividends can be used to reduce the investor's income tax payable. Hence he assumes that dividend policy matters because the payment of dividends *reduces* the total tax burden on equity. This results in a CAPM with a negative relation between the cost of equity and dividend yield, which is the opposite of the relation derived under the classical tax system under the old view of the cost of equity (Appendix 8.1). Because the expression for the cost of equity includes the dividend yield, it is circular in a valuation context. We need the value of the equity to calculate the yield, and the value is what we are trying to find. To avoid the circularity, Monkhouse suggests putting the benefit of imputation credits in the cash flows to be discounted: the cash flows are to be net of corporation tax, with the value of the imputation credits added. The standard CAPM, without a dividend yield term, can then be used as the cost of equity in discounting these adjusted cash flows using the WACC.

A further point regarding imputation systems concerns the measurement of returns on equity. It is normal to measure returns on financial assets gross of personal tax; income tax and CGT are ignored. What this means is ambiguous under an imputation system. For example, suppose that $T_C = 40\%$, $T_I = 25\%$, the rate of imputation $T_S = 15\%$ and there is no CGT. A company pays out £100 of profit as dividend, gross of all tax. The total tax rate on the dividend is $1 - (1 - T_C)(1 - T_I)/(1 - T_S) = 47\%$, so the total amount of tax paid is £47. What is the dividend before personal tax? If the rate of imputation is viewed merely as reducing the effective rate of personal tax, the dividend gross of personal tax is £100 × $(1 - 0.4) = £60$, and the personal tax rate is 12 per cent $[= 1 - (1 - T_I)/(1 - T_S)]$. But, if the rate of imputation is viewed as reducing the effective rate of corporation tax, the dividend gross of personal tax is £60/0.85 = £71, and the personal tax rate is 25 per cent. Which approach is chosen will affect the rate of return on equity measured before personal tax. The latter approach is appropriate, arguably, if tax-exempt investors can reclaim corporation tax the company has paid on its dividends that is also counted as income tax. In the example, if the recipient of the £60 dividend net of corporation tax were exempt, he could reclaim £11 from the tax authority. This was the system in the United Kingdom until 1997, and UK data for returns on the stock market treat dividends as gross in the latter sense, in which corporation tax that also counts as income tax is reclaimed (Barclays Capital, 2000; Dimson, Marsh and Staunton 2002). Armitage (2004) discusses the measurement of past returns on UK equity and government bonds *after* personal tax.

9.4   A certainty-equivalent approach

Sick (1990) derives discount rates with risky debt and personal tax for certainty equivalent cash flows. He assumes a single tax rate on returns to equity of T_E and uses a two-date model. The present value of a cash flow to equity after corporation tax is

$$V_0 = \text{CE}(Y_1)/(1 + R_Z)$$

where $\text{CE}(Y_1)$ is the certainty equivalent of a cash flow after corporation tax at date 1, Y_1, and R_Z is the rate of return on risk-free (zero-beta) equity, expressed before personal tax. The certainty-equivalent interest rate on debt is the risk-free rate, R_F. The after-tax view is assumed, so $R_F(1 - T_I) = R_Z(1 - T_E)$. R_Z and R_F will differ if $T_E \neq T_I$: $R_Z = R_F(1 - T_I)/(1 - T_E) = R_F(1 - T_M)$. For a company financed by debt and equity, the value of the equity is

$$E_0 = [\text{CE}(Y_1) - (1 - T_C)R_F D_0 - D_0]/(1 + R_Z)$$

so the value of the company is

$$E_0 + D_0 = [\text{CE}(Y_1) - (1 - T_C)R_F D_0 - D_0 + D_0(1 + R_Z)]/(1 + R_Z)$$
$$= [\text{CE}(Y_1) - (1 - T_C)R_F D_0 + D_0 R_F(1 - T_M)]/(1 + R_Z)$$
$$= \frac{\text{CE}(Y_1)}{1 + R_Z} + \frac{R_F D_0 T^*}{1 + R_Z} \qquad (9.6)$$

where $T^* = T_C - T_M$. Equation (9.6) is an APV-type formula. The value of the project consists of two components. The first is the present value of the certainty equivalent of the future cash flow after corporation tax, calculated as though the project had no debt, discounted at the cost of risk-free equity. The second is the present value of the tax shield. Here the rate of tax saved by interest can be greater or less than the corporation tax rate, depending on the sign of T_M. If the personal tax rate on interest exceeds the personal tax rate on equity, T_M will be positive and T^* will be less than T_C. The value of the tax shield will be less than it would be with no personal tax, because, although interest saves corporation tax, it attracts personal tax at a higher rate than equity does. A second point about the value of the tax shield in equation (9.6) is that the certainty equivalent of the future tax saving is discounted at the cost of risk-free equity, not of debt. The reason is that the tax saving increases the cash flow to equity, and is therefore taxed at the rate applicable to equity.

This approach to valuation leads to slightly different formulas for the discount rate on expected cash flows from those considered so far. Let us assume that the firm maintains a constant leverage L, measured with market values. Then $D_0 = L(E_0 + D_0)$. Substituting this into equation (9.6) and solving for $E_0 + D_0$ gives

$$E_0 + D_0 = CE(Y_1)/(1 + R_Z - T^* R_F L)$$

If cash flow is to be received in T periods rather than one, we have

$$E_0 + D_0 = CE(Y_T)/(1 + R_Z - T^* R_F L)^T \tag{9.7}$$

Hence the discount rate for certainty equivalent cash flows after corporation tax is $R_Z - T^* R_F L$. Now let us assume that the familiar expected cash flows are to be discounted, rather than their certainty equivalents. For an all-equity project, we have

$$E_0 = CE(Y_T)/(1 + R_Z)^T = E_0(Y_T)/(1 + R_{EU})^T$$

or

$$CE(Y_T) = E_t(Y_T)(1 + R_Z)^T/(1 + R_{EU})^T$$

where R_{EU} is the cost of unlevered equity. Substituting for $CE(Y_T)$ in equation (9.7) gives

$$E_0 + D_0 = E(Y_T)(1 + R_Z)^T/(1 + R_{EU})^T(1 + R_Z - T^* R_F L)^T$$

So Sick's discount rate for expected cash flows, R^*, is given by

$$1 + R^* = (1 + R_{EU})(1 + R_Z - T^* R_F L)/(1 + R_Z)$$
$$R^* = R_{EU} - T^* R_F L(1 + R_{EU})/(1 + R_Z)$$

This can be compared with the Miles–Ezzell formula:

$$R_L = R_{EU} - T_C R_D L(1 + R_{EU})/(1 + R_D). \tag{7.19}$$

The formula for the relation between beta and gearing is also somewhat different using the certainty-equivalent approach. Although this form of analysis is coherent in the abstract, it is not the mainstream approach, possibly because of the difficulty of estimating certainty-equivalent cash flows in practice.

9.5   Evidence on leverage and tax

The large amount of evidence on the determinants of capital structure suggests that the availability or otherwise of corporate tax savings does affect a firm's choice between the use of debt or equity, but also that several non-tax factors are each at least as important in explaining this choice. Tax savings from debt may not be available because of non-debt tax shields or low profitability. But, if the savings are available, firms will seek to gain them to an extent, through increasing debt, so long as the non-tax context is favourable (for example, low probability of financial distress). Leaving non-tax factors aside, there is a gain from leverage if the tax savings from debt can be obtained with reasonable certainty.

The above summary is influenced by recent studies. The evidence from the 1980s and before on the tax gains from leverage is decidedly ambiguous. Several studies have found that leverage adds value, but that there appears to be no relation between a firm's non-debt tax shields and its level of leverage, or even to be a positive relation, suggesting that a firm's choice of leverage is not related to anticipated tax savings from interest. A fairly recent study in this vein is by Barclay, Smith and Watts (1995); reviews of earlier US evidence include those by Copeland and Weston (1988, pp. 516–23) and Haugen and Senbet (1986). Similarly, Lasfer (1995), using UK data, finds that leverage is unrelated to the effective rate of corporation tax, although there is a significant negative relation between leverage and a dummy variable, which equals one if the firm pays no corporate tax.

A problem for the foregoing studies is that a firm's anticipated effective rate of corporation tax varies over time, and hence the present value of future interest tax shields varies. The firm's leverage at a given time is partly the result of past financing decisions, so one may observe a firm with high leverage that is now at or close to 'tax exhaustion' – i.e. the firm's forecast profits and non-debt tax shields are such that it is not expecting to pay much corporation tax in the near future. This reduces the present value of tax savings from interest. If tax matters, the marginal or new source of funds for a tax-exhausted firm should be equity. MacKie-Mason (1990) notes that the impact of non-debt tax shields on a firm's choice between issuing debt or equity should be greatest in a firm that is close to tax exhaustion. He finds that the presence of tax losses or investment tax credits affects the debt/equity choice in firms close to tax exhaustion, but not in more profitable firms, controlling for several other factors, such as the likelihood of financial distress. Graham (1996) estimates an explicit marginal tax rate for each firm, defined as the present value of the current and expected future changes in the payments of corporation tax arising from an additional unit of profit earned today. Changes in tax payments can arise in the future due to the consequences of provisions for carrying tax losses backwards and forwards. He finds that the change in debt outstanding is positively related to the firm's marginal corporate tax rate, which supports the tax argument. But the tax variables add only 15 per cent to the explanatory power of a pooled cross-sectional regression the dependent variable of which is the change in a year in a measure of leverage. Graham (2000) presents evidence that many firms appear to leave money on the table, by not borrowing as much as might be expected, given estimates of the expected costs of financial distress.

A recent study by Kemsley and Nissim (2002) presents direct evidence from cross-sectional firm data that the use of debt contributes to a firm's present value via the tax shield, using a new method to estimate the contribution of the tax shield that, they argue, reduces bias in the estimate. Furthermore, there is no clear evidence for leverage clienteles, which are predicted in the Miller model. The weight of evidence from company behaviour suggests that there is a gain from leverage, which is a prediction of the before-tax (Modigliani–Miller) view. However, the gain from leverage is probably less than the statutory rate of corporation tax per unit of interest, especially in countries with imputation systems. The difference in yield between taxable and tax-exempt US bonds of similar risk indicates that the effective rate of personal tax on debt can be substantial, fluctuating between 16 per cent and 43 per cent from 1960 to 1999 (Van Horne, 2001, pp. 266–71). Swoboda and Zechner (1995) note that prevailing statutory corporate and personal tax rates are such that a Miller equilibrium is at least a possibility in most countries, though not in the United States at the time (assuming that firms pay corporation tax at the statutory rate).

9.6   Asset pricing with multiple personal tax rates

The existence of categories of investors and of financial assets that are liable to differing rates of personal tax raises questions regarding how asset prices are set. The problem is especially clear in a world of certainty, in which there is no diversification motive for investment decisions. Suppose an asset makes a single payment before personal tax of £100 in one year. There are two groups of investors: one group is exempt from tax, the other group pays tax at a rate of 50 per cent. All investors demand an after-tax return on the asset of 10 per cent. The price is set by the marginal investor. If the marginal investor is exempt, the asset price is £100/1.1 = £90.91. If the marginal investor pays tax at 50 per cent, the asset price is £50/1.1 = £45.45. But a price of less than £90.91 would be impossible to explain without more information about exempt investors. What limits their demand, preventing them from being the marginal buyers? In general, if tax arbitrage is possible, equilibrium prices do not exist. That is, a model of asset prices in which tax arbitrage is possible cannot explain how the prices are determined. Equilibrium prices can exist if limits to tax arbitrage are introduced, in which case the prices predicted will be affected by the nature of these limits.

Schaefer (1982) and Dammon and Green (1987) have studied the conditions necessary for equilibrium to exist in a financial market in the presence of differing personal taxes across investors and across assets. Equilibrium requires that arbitrage is not possible for any market participant, and we have to specify what this means. Schaefer studies assets that make risk-free payments. He concludes that a no-arbitrage position requires that investors face identical tax rates, in the absence of limits to tax arbitrage. If investors face differing tax schedules, but the schedules have at least one tax rate in common, a no-arbitrage position will also be reached. Dammon and Green employ a two-date contingent-states model to study the case of uncertainty. Assets provide state-contingent after-tax pay-offs at date 1 that are either zero or positive. Each individual i starts with an initial endowment of assets that provides a positive after-tax pay-off in every possible state, and he/she can trade these holdings at date 0 if he/she wishes. Individual i can gain from tax arbitrage if prices are such that he/she can obtain, via trading assets, an increased positive after-tax pay-off in some possible state(s) at zero or negative cost. More formally, tax arbitrage is possible if the individual can trade so as to satisfy the following system of inequalities:

$$\Sigma_j w_{ji} Y_{js} \geq 0 \text{ for all states } s$$
$$\Sigma_j w_{ji} P_j \leq 0 \tag{9.8}$$

where w_{ji} is the number of units of asset j traded by investor i, Y_{js} is the after-tax pay-off from asset j in state s and P_j is the price of asset j. w_{ji} can be positive, negative or zero; a negative value for asset j arises if the individual sells some of his/her initial holding of this asset. The definition of arbitrage here is genuine arbitrage. There is no risk involved because the individual is at least as well off in every state. If prices are such that there are no individuals for whom equations (9.8) can be fulfilled then tax arbitrage is not possible.

Another way of expressing the no-arbitrage condition, the 'dual' to equations (9.8), is that the prices of each asset must satisfy the following condition:

$$P_j = Dis_{si} \Sigma_s Y_{js}$$
$$Dis_{si} > 0 \text{ for all states } s \text{ and all individuals } i$$

where Dis_{si} is the discount factor applied by i to state s. This condition says that all investors assign the same values to assets. The discount factors need to be positive because each asset's expected cash flow (the sum of the cash flow in each state weighted by the state's probability) is assumed to be positive.

Under what conditions is tax arbitrage not possible? Consider first the case of assets that are perfect substitutes; they produce the same configuration of state-contingent cash flows before tax. Such assets can differ only in scale, not in risk. Suppose that all investors have linear tax schedules, which means that each individual's marginal tax rate is constant; it does not vary with his/her taxable income. In the case of perfect substitutes, it is clear that a no-arbitrage position requires all individuals to have the same personal tax rate. But, if assets are not perfect substitutes, Dammon and Green show that a no-arbitrage position need not require that all individuals have the same personal tax rates. In general, the more the configurations of state-contingent cash flows differ between two assets, the more tax rates across investors can differ without making arbitrage possible. The argument requires that the market for state-contingent claims be incomplete; it is not possible costlessly to replicate all configurations of cash flows. If it were, tax arbitrage would be possible unless personal tax rates were identical across individuals. The argument is essentially the same as the point that an investor may hold an asset for the diversification benefit it confers, even if the investor faces a higher tax rate on this asset than on others.

Now suppose that investors face progressive tax schedules, which means that the investor's marginal rate of personal tax increases with his/her taxable income, in practice in a stepwise fashion. Under certainty, and under uncertainty with assets that are perfect substitutes, equilibrium requires that investors have at least one tax rate in common in their tax schedules. Under uncertainty with assets that are not perfect substitutes, there is a range of variation of tax schedules within which equilibrium is possible. The mechanism that in theory ensures that prices are driven towards equilibrium is the effect of the tax-arbitrage trades possible under disequilibrium on investors' state-contingent taxable incomes. The arbitrage trades will reduce (or increase) the future *taxable* incomes of investors with pre-trade holdings of assets in whose hands the pay-offs would be subject to relatively high (or relatively low) tax rates. Thus trade will cause the contingent tax rates applying to pay-offs to fall if the pre-trade tax rates are high, and to rise if the pre-trade tax rates are low. This argument requires the existence of tax-exempt assets, or at least of assets with a proportion of their return that is non-taxable, in order that trade in assets can change investors' taxable incomes. Satisfaction of the no-arbitrage condition does not imply that investors will be observed to pay the same tax rates at date 1, unless it is assumed that there is certainty or that the assets are perfect substitutes. An example will help us to understand some of these results.

Example of asset pricing with investors who face differing tax rates

The capital market consists of two types of asset and two types of investor. Consider first assets that are perfect substitutes, before tax.

Asset A is tax-exempt and pays £1 in state s_1 and £2 in state s_2.
Asset B is taxable and pays £1 in s_1 and £2 in s_2.
The states are equally probable and the interest rate is zero.
Investor E (for exempt) pays no tax.
Investor T (for taxable) pays tax at a rate of 40 per cent.

Suppose the price of exempt asset A is worth £1.5. Then equations (9.8) can be fulfilled for both investors; E can give T up to £1.5 for each unit of B, and both will be better off. For example, suppose E were to give T £1.2 per unit of B. He raises the funds by selling asset A, receiving £1.5 per unit of A short-sold. As the pre-tax pay-offs per unit of B are exactly the same as those of A, the position in B exactly matches the sold position in A, and the pay-offs at date 1 are unchanged. E has gained £0.3 now per unit of A. T uses the £1.2 to buy 0.8 of a unit of A and receives £0.8 in state s_1 instead of £0.6, and £1.2 in s_2 instead of £0.9. So long as the price of asset B is below £1.5, gains to both investors are available. After trade, all tax will be avoided, because E will end up owning all of the taxable asset.

Now suppose that T faces a progressive tax schedule. As T sells units of the taxable asset B, his taxable income at the future date falls, and his marginal tax rate on income will be falling. If T's tax schedule is to overlap with E's, then T's schedule must include a marginal rate of zero. If it is assumed that T's taxable income comes from holding asset B, once T has sold enough of B that the rate on his remaining taxable income is zero no tax will be paid on either asset, and further tax arbitrage trades will not be possible.

Now assume that exempt asset A pays £1.0 in both states, so the assets are no longer perfect substitutes. T continues to face a single tax rate of 40 per cent.

A is now worth £1.0 to both investors, and, in this case, equations (9.8) cannot be fulfilled for both investors. No trades are possible as a result of which each investor gains or remains as well off in every state. E can not pay T more than £1.0 per unit of B, because to pay more would require selling more than one unit of A to buy each unit of B. E would then lose if s_1 were to arise, in which the pay-off on B is £1.0. If T receives £1.0 per unit of B, he can buy one unit of A. He gains if s_1 arises, because he receives £1.0 per unit of A instead of £0.6 per unit of B. But he loses if s_2 arises, because he would have received £1.2 after tax from B. T must face a tax rate of at least 50 per cent for one investor to gain and the other not to lose, or for both to gain, from trading the assets.

This example shows that, under uncertainty and with assets that are not perfect substitutes, it is not necessary for investors' tax rates to overlap to preclude tax arbitrage, but merely to be sufficiently close. The closeness required depends on the correlation between the assets' pay-offs. In this case a tax rate of 0 per cent for E and 40 per cent for T is close enough, but a rate of 50 per cent for T is not.

In practice, the market for contingent claims is surely far from complete, and financial assets are not close substitutes, though some sub-groups of them are (e.g. some government bonds). The implication of the above analysis is that there can be equilibrium in which investors hold units of the same asset and face differing rates of personal tax. The tax rate of the marginal, price-setting investor will vary across assets and over time, depending on who the marginal investor in each asset happens to be. A single equilibrium set of expected returns across assets will not exist.

The conclusion that there will be varying effective personal tax rates is reinforced when we allow for the presence of limits on tax avoidance, which we have so far ignored. Why do all investors not manage to achieve tax-exempt investment (in which case a single equilibrium set of prices would exist)? We can learn about the process of price determination by considering how differing categories of investor are constrained to pay differing rates of personal tax.

There are three types of method by which investors might reduce personal tax on financial assets. The first is postponement of the tax, for example by converting income into capital gain, which is taxed on the realisation of the gain. The second is tax arbitrage across agents facing different tax brackets, for example saving by a taxpayer via a tax-exempt vehicle. The third is tax arbitrage across income streams facing different tax treatment. For example, interest on personal loans can be set against an individual's taxable income in the United States. Thus the tax-adjusted interest rate on personal debt is the rate net of the marginal rate of income tax saved, in the same way as the cost of debt for a company adjusted for corporation tax is $R_D(1 - T_C)$. If an investor's tax-adjusted interest rate is less than the rate after personal tax available on an asset, the investor gains by borrowing and investing in this asset. The question, in each case, is what stops investors from exploiting the opportunity to reduce tax, and the general answer is legally binding constraints and market frictions. An example of a constraint is the limit on how much an individual can invest in a tax-exempt pension fund. An example of market frictions is the difficulties individuals face in reaching reliable agreements between themselves to exploit opportunities to reduce tax (such agreements would anyway be restricted if they became widespread). For discussions of tax avoidance tactics, and anti-avoidance measures, see Stiglitz (1985) or Scholes and Wolfson (1988).

The presence of different categories of investor with respect to tax circumstances raises the possibility that a particular asset will be owned by a particular category of investor, its 'tax clientele', as we have noted elsewhere. If there is no investor who is marginal across all assets, an asset's tax clientele sets its price, and the price would be different with a different clientele. Tax clienteles for shares have been proposed with respect to dividend yield and leverage. Researchers have also examined whether clienteles exist in government bond markets. For example, Schaefer (1982) studies the UK gilts market. He defines the effective tax rate on returns to gilts, if one exists, as the rate or bracket of rates at which no gilts are dominated. A gilt is dominated if it is possible to construct a portfolio of gilts with after-tax cash flows that provide a higher present value per £1 invested in the gilt concerned. The discount factors are required to be non-increasing with the time horizon (i.e. the discount rate is at least zero). He finds that there was no effective tax rate in the gilts market between 1968 and 1977; there was no single tax rate on gilt interest using which none of the gilts was dominated. This implies that there were clientele effects in the market; the prices of different gilts were determined by investors in different tax categories.

9.7   Summary

This chapter is the second on the effects of personal taxes on the cost of capital. The debate between old view and the new view in Chapter 8 was about how a company's cost of equity should be specified. In contrast, the discussion in the current chapter has been about the effects of personal taxes on the expected returns on financial assets before personal tax, especially the expected returns on equity and debt. This can be seen as an extension to the analysis in Part I, regarding the expected returns on assets ignoring taxes.

In some models the tax advantage to debt is zero, allowing for personal tax, which means that leverage has no effect on the weighted average cost of capital expressed before personal tax. This contrasts with the results derived in Chapter 7, in which personal tax was ignored. However, empirical evidence suggests that there is a tax advantage to debt. The chapter has outlined the effect of an imputation system on the cost of equity, which is to reduce the effective rate of personal tax on equity. It has also outlined an analysis with personal taxes using certainty-equivalent cash flows. Finally, the chapter has considered the analysis of asset pricing with investors who face heterogeneous rates of tax. No equilibrium is possible under certainty, but under uncertainty there can be an equilibrium in which investors hold units of the same asset and face different tax rates.

Whilst personal taxes have attracted a good deal of attention from researchers, little of the analysis in the last two chapters has found its way into texts, with the exception of the Miller equilibrium. No distinction is made between the cost of equity for retained earnings and for a share issue, and there is assumed to be a tax disadvantage to paying dividends. So, implicitly, the old view is assumed to be correct. It is also normal to assume that there is a tax advantage to debt.

10 Inflation and risk premiums

The analysis throughout the book is in real terms, because investors are assumed to be interested in real returns and payoffs. Behind this assumption is the view that utility derives from consumption, and that the amount of consumption into which a future payment can be converted is measured by the payment's real value rather than the nominal value. However, valuation in practice is often conducted in nominal terms. The question of whether to work in real or nominal terms depends primarily on whether it is easier to forecast cash flows in real or nominal terms. Our purpose here is to review the relationship between real and nominal analysis, taking the real or nominal cash flows as given. The introduction of inflation also enables a full description of the various types of risk premium to be presented.

The contents of this chapter are extensions to our earlier discussions of valuation, of the effects of taxes, and of risk premiums. It is felt to be helpful to consider issues concerning inflation in one place, as was done with the equity premium in Chapter 5.

10.1 Relations between real and nominal rates of return

10.1.1 Certain inflation

Inflation *Inf* is the percentage change in a price index during a given period. If inflation is treated as certain, the relation between a nominal rate of return R_{nom} on an asset and the corresponding real rate R_{real} is given by

$$1 + R_{\mathrm{nom}} = (1 + R_{\mathrm{real}})(1 + \mathit{Inf})$$

or

$$R_{\mathrm{nom}} = R_{\mathrm{real}} + \mathit{Inf} + R_{\mathrm{real}}\,\mathit{Inf}$$

or

$$R_{\mathrm{real}} = (R_{\mathrm{nom}} - \mathit{Inf})/(1 + \mathit{Inf}) \tag{10.1}$$

This is known as the *Fisher relation*. It applies whether the rate of return in question is certain or uncertain, and whether we are converting a given real rate to the corresponding nominal rate or vice versa. It is commonly written in approximate form as

$$R_{\mathrm{nom}} = R_{\mathrm{real}} + \mathit{Inf}$$

or

$$R_{real} = R_{nom} - Inf \qquad (10.2)$$

If inflation is treated as uncertain, as it is in reality, the Fisher relation is an approximation unless the asset is risk-free in real terms. This is explained below.

Discounting

To a first approximation, it makes no difference whether valuation is carried out in real or nominal terms. In the absence of taxation, and assuming that the same rate of inflation is applied both to the cash flows to be discounted and to the cost of capital, then discounting the nominal cash flows at the nominal cost of capital gives the same present value as discounting the real cash flows at the real cost of capital (see, e.g., Rappaport and Taggart, 1982). Probably the most important point about the cost of capital and inflation from a practical perspective is to be consistent – i.e. to discount nominal cash flows by a nominal discount rate and real cash flows by a real discount rate. A second very important point is that, if a nominal discount rate is used, it should incorporate expected inflation rather than past inflation; otherwise the cost of capital will be overstated in an era of falling inflation, and vice versa.

10.1.2   Uncertain inflation

Inflation risk premium

If inflation is uncertain, this raises the possibility that the *real* returns on an asset covary with inflation. If they do then inflation can be treated as a risk factor, or as a proxy for a risk factor, and the expected real return on the asset will, in theory, incorporate an 'inflation risk premium'. Some multifactor models of expected returns do include inflation as a risk factor (Section 13.5.1). Whether the premium is positive or negative depends on the sign of $cov(R_{real}, Inf)$ and on the relation between inflation and marginal utility. For example, if $cov(R_{real}, Inf)$ is negative and low inflation is associated with recession states (high marginal utility), the asset provides a relatively high real return when inflation is low and marginal utility is high. So, in this case, the inflation risk premium would be negative, in theory.

It should be noted that an inflation risk premium, if there is one, is a component of the expected real rate of return on an asset (and is therefore also a component of the expected nominal rate). An inflation risk premium is not part of the difference between the nominal rate and the real rate.

In the case of equity, it is debatable whether we would expect real returns to show positive or negative covariance with inflation, a priori. But, in the case of conventional debt, with promised cash flows fixed in nominal terms, we would expect $cov(R_{real}, Inf)$ to be negative and we would expect $cov(R_{real}, Inf)$ to be negatively related to the maturity of debt (i.e. the covariance becomes more negative as maturity lengthens). Changes in inflation should induce more volatility in the real rates of return over time on long-term debt than on short-term debt. If there is a positive inflation risk premium for assets with negative $cov(R_{real}, Inf)$, we would expect long-term debt to be priced to provide a higher inflation risk premium than short-term debt. There is evidence of an inflation risk premium on conventional bonds, in the region of 0.75 per cent to 1.00 per cent p.a., that is positively related to maturity (e.g. Van Horne, 2001, chap. 5).

Asset risk-free in real terms

An asset providing a risk-free real return, R_{Freal}, has a payoff that is fixed in real terms, and therefore has a nominal payoff that is indexed to inflation. If inflation is uncertain, the Fisher relation may not give the exact relation between the real and nominal rates of return on an asset. But the relation continues to hold in the case of an asset that is risk-free in real terms, since $\text{cov}(R_{\text{Freal}}, Inf) = 0$. The nominal rate changes with inflation in accordance with equation (10.1):

$$\begin{aligned} \text{E}(1 + R_{\text{nom}}) &= \text{E}[(1 + R_{\text{Freal}})(1 + Inf)] \\ &= (1 + R_{\text{Freal}})[1 + \text{E}(Inf)] \end{aligned}$$

Asset risk-free in nominal terms

The Fisher relation does not hold exactly in the case of an asset that provides a return that is risk-free in nominal terms, R_{Fnom}, and is therefore risky in real terms. In this case the real return on the asset is a function of the rate of inflation. If risk neutrality is assumed, the relation between a risk-free nominal rate and the corresponding expected real rate is found by taking expectations on the right-hand side of equation (10.1) to give

$$R_{\text{Fnom}} = \text{E}(R_{\text{real}}) + \text{E}(Inf) + \text{E}(R_{\text{real}} Inf)$$

Since, for any two variables x and y, $\text{E}(xy) = \text{E}(x)\text{E}(y) + \text{cov}(x, y)$, this can be rewritten as

$$R_{\text{Fnom}} = \text{E}(R_{\text{real}}) + \text{E}(Inf) + \text{E}(R_{\text{real}})\text{E}(Inf) + \text{cov}(R_{\text{real}}, Inf)$$

or

$$\text{E}(R_{\text{real}}) = [R_{\text{Fnom}} - \text{E}(Inf) - \text{cov}(R_{\text{real}}, Inf)]/[1 + \text{E}(Inf)] \tag{10.3}$$

Because R_{Fnom} is fixed, $\text{cov}(R_{\text{real}}, Inf)$ must be negative. Greater uncertainty about inflation implies a larger absolute value of $\text{cov}(R_{\text{real}}, Inf)$. If investors are risk-averse, $\text{cov}(R_{\text{real}}, Inf) < 0$ implies an effect on $\text{E}(R_{\text{real}})$ via the existence of an inflation risk premium, as discussed above. However, it is apparent from equation (10.3) that the covariance term has a separate effect on $\text{E}(R_{\text{real}})$, which applies if investors are assumed to be risk-neutral. A comparison of equations (10.1) and (10.3) shows that uncertainty about inflation increases the expected real rate from an asset with a given rate that is risk-free in nominal terms. This is because

$$\begin{aligned} \text{E}(R_{\text{real}}) &= \text{E}[(R_{\text{Fnom}} - Inf)/(1 + Inf)] \\ &> [R_{\text{Fnom}} - \text{E}(Inf)]/[1 + \text{E}(Inf)] \end{aligned}$$

To obtain an expected real rate equal to a given risk-free real rate, the required risk-free nominal rate is *less* if inflation is uncertain than if it is certain.

This is another Jensen's inequality effect. Suppose the risk-free asset pays out £1 nominal at the next date. The expected real value of the £1 nominal is $E[£1/(1 + Inf)]$. This exceeds the expected real value if inflation is fixed at its expected rate, $E(Inf)$:

$$1/[1 + E(Inf)] < E[1/(1 + Inf)]$$

As a result, the expected real return if inflation is uncertain exceeds the real return if inflation is fixed at its expected rate. For a given required real return, the price will be higher if inflation is uncertain.

For example, suppose an asset will provide £100 nominal at its terminal date in one year. Investors are risk-neutral and require an expected real return of 5 per cent. Inflation during the year is equally likely to be 0 per cent or 30 per cent; the expected value is 15 per cent. The price will be $0.5[£100/(1.05)] + 0.5[£100/(1.05)(1.30)] = £84.25$ and the nominal return will be 18.7 per cent. If inflation were guaranteed to be 15 per cent, the price would be £82.82 and the nominal return would be 20.8 per cent.

The normal method to convert a return that is risk-free in nominal terms to a corresponding real return is to assume that inflation is fixed at its expected value, and to use the Fisher-style formula $[R_{Fnom} - E(Inf)]/[1 + E(Inf)]$. The above argument implies that the resulting real return is a downward-biased estimate of the expected real return, if inflation is uncertain. In the example the expected real return is 5 per cent if the price is £84.25, but the real return from the Fisher formula is only 3.2 per cent.

Asset risky in real terms

In this case both R_{real} and R_{nom} will vary, and $cov(R_{real}, Inf)$ could be positive or negative. Equation (10.3) becomes

$$E(R_{nom}) = E(R_{real}) + E(Inf) + E(R_{real})E(Inf) + cov(R_{real}, Inf)$$

$$E(R_{real}) = [E(R_{nom}) - E(Inf) - cov(R_{real}, Inf)]/[1 + E(Inf)] \qquad (10.4)$$

Hence the relation between an expected real rate and the corresponding expected nominal rate depends partly on the sign and value of $cov(R_{real}, Inf)$, still assuming risk neutrality. In the case of the stock market, the relation between real returns on equity and inflation is uncertain a priori, so it is reasonable to assume that $cov(R_{Mreal}, Inf) = 0$, where R_{Mreal} is the real return on the market. Then equation (10.4) becomes

$$E(R_{Mreal}) = [E(R_{Mnom}) - E(Inf)]/[1 + E(Inf)]$$

or

$$1 + E(R_{Mnom}) = [1 + E(R_{Mreal})][1 + E(Inf)]$$

This is the same as the Fisher relation, since $E(R_{Enom})$ and $E(Inf)$ are fixed values. The relation between the expected nominal and expected real rates is the same as it would be if inflation were certain and equal to its expected value $E(Inf)$.

The above discussion is based on Lewellen and Ang (1982). It should be mentioned that Friend, Landskroner and Losq (1976), Adler and Dumas (1983) and others arrive at a slightly different result regarding the expected nominal return on a risky asset, assuming risk neutrality. They use continuous-time models, in which nominal returns on an asset and inflation evolve according to a Gaussian process. They conclude that the expected nominal rate of return on a risky asset is positively related to the covariance between the nominal rate and inflation, whereas in equation (10.4) the expected nominal rate is positively related to the covariance between the real rate and inflation.

To sum up, if inflation is uncertain, use of the Fisher relation with the expected value of inflation is incorrect in the case of estimating the expected real rate on an asset that is risk-free in nominal terms. In this case, use of the expression $[R_{\text{Fnom}} - \text{E}(Inf)]/[1 + \text{E}(Inf)]$ will produce an estimate of the expected real rate that is biased downwards. The bias exists regardless of whether the expected real rate incorporates an inflation risk premium. But the bias will be negligible for uncertainty about inflation amounting to a few percentage points. It seems reasonable to use the Fisher relation in the case of equity, assuming that $\text{cov}(R_{\text{Ereal}}, Inf) \approx 0$.

10.2   Inflation and effective rates of tax on real returns

In this section we assume for simplicity that inflation is treated as certain, so the issues in Section 10.1 do not arise. If we introduce taxes, it remains true that it makes no difference whether valuation is conducted in real or nominal terms, so long as the real and nominal cash flows after tax are calculated correctly. For example, suppose an asset provides a fixed real dividend of £100 p.a. before tax in perpetuity. The tax rate T is 50 per cent, the required real rate of return after tax is 10 per cent p.a. and inflation is 5 per cent p.a. The valuation in real terms is the present value of a perpetuity:

$$V = £100(1 - T)/R_{\text{real}} = £500$$

The valuation in nominal terms is the present value of a nominal stream growing at the rate of inflation, which can be found using the dividend discount formula. The nominal discount rate is $(1.1)(1.05) - 1 = 15.5\%$ p.a., from equation (10.1). So

$$V = £100(1 + Inf)(1 - T)/(R_{\text{nom}} - Inf) \qquad (10.5)$$
$$= £52.5/(0.155 - 0.05) = £500$$

Valuation in real and nominal terms would also give the same result if the real growth rate of the dividend were positive, or in general for any given sequence of future cash flows. But if the £100 p.a. were fixed in nominal terms then inflation would have a negative effect on the value, since the real value of the £100 would be declining over time.

Less obvious is the fact that inflation increases the effective tax rate on real returns. Most taxes are levied on nominal (money) amounts or values, and inflation affects the corresponding real rates of tax: for a given tax rate on a nominal cash flow or nominal capital gain, the resulting effective tax rate on the real interest or real gain is higher if there is inflation, and is positively related to the rate of inflation.

Let us examine this effect via an example. Consider a project that costs £100 and that provides a nominal payoff of £140 in one year. The tax rate on the nominal gain of £40 is 50 per cent, the rate of inflation is 10 per cent p.a., and the cost of capital after tax is 8 per cent p.a. (real) or 18.8 per cent p.a. (nominal). We note first that the market value of the project is £101, calculated using either real or nominal values. The before-tax nominal return on the £100 cost is 40 per cent, and the tax rate on this nominal return is 50 per cent. But the before-tax real return is $1.4/1.1 - 1 = 27\%$, and the after-tax real return is $1.2/1.1 - 1 = 9\%$, which is 67 per cent smaller. So a 50 per cent rate of tax on the nominal return has in this case translated into a tax of 67 per cent on the real return. The general formula is

$$T_{real} = [1 + Inf/(1 + Inf)R_{Breal}]T_{nom} \tag{10.6}$$

where R_{Breal} is the real rate of return on the asset before tax, T_{nom} is the nominal tax rate and T_{real} is the corresponding effective tax rate on the real income or gain (Schall, 1984, p. 112).

The reason for the positive relation between the effective tax on the real return and inflation is that, with positive inflation, some of the nominal return is compensation for inflation, so it is not part of the real return. With a tax on nominal returns, the component that compensates for inflation is taxed as well as the component that provides the real return. As inflation rises, the amount of the return that merely compensates for inflation also rises, and the tax paid on this adds to the tax on the real return.

One implication is that, for a given required real return after all tax, R_{Areal}, and a given rate of personal tax on nominal amounts, an increase in inflation causes the real cost of capital expressed before personal tax to increase. Hence this tax effect creates a positive theoretical relation between the rate of inflation and the real cost of capital as conventionally expressed – i.e. before personal tax.

It should be mentioned in addition that inflation can have a number of effects on the value of real taxable profit, and therefore on the real amounts of corporation tax to be paid. An important effect is that inflation causes the real value of depreciation allowances to decline, assuming that assets are valued at historic cost. The nominal profit for a given year t after corporation tax T_C is $Y_{realt}(1 + Inf_t)(1 - T_C) + Dep_t T_C$, where Y_{realt} is the real profit excluding depreciation, and the depreciation allowance Dep_t is fixed in nominal terms. The corresponding real profit after corporation tax is $Y_{realt}(1 - T_C) + Dep_t T_C/(1 + Inf)$, so the real amount of corporation tax is $T_C[Y_{realt} - Dep_t/(1 + Inf)]$. Thus the real amount of taxable profit for a given real profit Y_{realt} is positively related to the rate of inflation. However, if the normal method is followed of discounting cash flows after corporation tax by the standard tax-adjusted WACC, the effects of inflation on the amounts of real taxable profit are captured in the cash flows, and so do not affect the WACC.

Tax advantage to debt, and the Miller equilibrium
If personal tax is ignored, the tax advantage of debt is positively related to inflation, because the marginal effective rate of corporation tax saved, for a given real rate of interest, is positively related to inflation (Cohn and Modigliani, 1985). The relation is as shown in

equation (10.6), if T_{nom} is thought of as the corporation tax rate on nominal profit and T_{real} as the corresponding effective tax rate saved on real profit. It is therefore the case that the relation between the tax-adjusted WACC and inflation is not the simple Fisher relation, because the *real* tax-adjusted WACC is negatively related to inflation.

However, if we allow for personal tax, inflation has two opposing effects on the tax advantage of debt: it increases the effective rate of income tax on real interest, and increases the effective rate at which real interest saves corporation tax. Hochman and Palmon (1985) and Schall (1984) consider the Miller equilibrium (Chapter 9) under inflation, in which the effective rate of income tax on real interest is equal to the combined effective rate of corporation and personal tax on real returns to equity. They argue that an increase in inflation will cause a fall in the aggregate debt/equity ratio in the economy (ignoring the non-tax effects of leverage). Inflation increases nominal personal incomes, which puts more people in higher income tax brackets in that they have a tax incentive to invest in equity. In addition, an increase in inflation reduces the cut-off (equilibrium) rate of income tax on nominal interest that determines whether an investor prefers debt (if he/she faces a marginal rate of income tax below the cut-off rate) or equity. This also causes some investors to switch from debt to equity.

The argument why inflation reduces the equilibrium tax rate on nominal interest can be presented as follows (Schall, 1984). We consider a company with constant real profits, dividends, market value of equity and leverage. The nominal cost of equity before tax is assumed to be the same as the cost of debt, R_{Bnom}. Let one share provide entitlement to one unit of real dividend per period (so real growth is zero). Using the dividend discount formula already encountered (equation (10.5)), the market value of one share is

$$P = (1 + Inf)/[R_{Bnom}(1 - T_C) - Inf]$$

or

$$(1 + Inf)/P = R_{Bnom}(1 - T_C) - Inf$$

The next nominal dividend per share is $1 + Inf$ and the capital gain is $PInf$, so the nominal rate of return per share before personal taxes, using the above equation, is

$$(Div_{nom} + Cap\ gain)/P = [(1 + Inf) + P\ Inf)]/P$$
$$= [R_{Bnom}(1 - T_C) - Inf] + Inf$$

In this model there is a tax both on nominal dividends, T_{Div}, and on nominal capital gains on equity, T_G. The nominal rate of return per share after personal taxes is

$$[Div_{nom}(1 - T_{Div}) + Cap\ gain(1 - T_G)]/P$$
$$= [R_{Bnom}(1 - T_C) - Inf](1 - T_{Div}) + Inf(1 - T_G)$$
$$= R_{Bnom}(1 - T_C)(1 - T_{Div}) + Inf(T_{Div} - T_G)$$

The equilibrium nominal cost of debt after personal tax is $R_{\text{Bnom}}(1 - T_{\text{I}}^*)$. Indifference between debt and equity on the part of the firm requires that T_{I}^* be the rate such that

$$R_{\text{Bnom}}(1 - T_{\text{I}}^*) = R_{\text{Bnom}}(1 - T_{\text{C}})(1 - T_{\text{Div}}) + \mathit{Inf}(T_{\text{Div}} - T_{\text{G}})$$

So an increase in inflation requires a fall in T_{I}^* to maintain the equality, if $T_{\text{Div}} > T_{\text{G}}$, as is normally assumed to be the case. Put another way, an increase in inflation causes a larger increase in the tax burden on real interest than on real returns to equity, and therefore a fall in T_{I}^*, the equilibrium tax rate on debt, is required to restore the Miller equilibrium.

Discussion

We have seen that, ignoring personal tax, higher inflation *reduces* the real tax-adjusted WACC, for a given corporation tax rate on nominal profits. This is because higher inflation increases the corporation tax rate on real profits, and therefore increases the effective rate at which interest saves corporation tax. But, allowing for personal taxes, higher inflation increases the corresponding tax rates on real returns to debt and equity (equation (10.6)). Via this effect, higher inflation acts to *increase* the real tax-adjusted WACC before personal tax, for given personal tax rates on nominal returns and for given required real rates of return after all tax. These points imply that a project's optimal leverage, and the relations between leverage and the real tax-adjusted WACC and between leverage and the real cost of equity (expressed before personal tax), are conditional on the rate of inflation. By the same token, the relations between inflation and the real WACC and between inflation and the real cost of equity are conditional on the level of leverage. Whether inflation is seen as reducing or increasing the real cost of capital depends on the assumptions made about the interaction between taxes, inflation and expected returns on assets, and on the leverage of the relevant project. If required real rates of return after personal tax are viewed as fixed, and effective rates of personal tax are non-negligible, an increase in inflation may cause the real cost of capital before personal tax to rise.

This brings us to the question of the exact expressions – nominal and real – for the WACC, the cost of equity, and the relation between the WACC and leverage (all before personal tax) under the various sets of assumptions discussed in Chapter 7 – i.e. the nominal and real expressions in Table 7.1, allowing for inflation. Rashid and Amoako-Adu (1995) make a start with these derivations. The nominal expressions for the cost of capital and cost of equity are messy, even using simplifying assumptions (a perpetual project; risk-free debt; constant inflation). It should be said that the quantitative impacts of the tax effects of inflation are small if inflation is low – i.e. a few per cent per annum.

10.3   Risk premiums

The recognition of inflation potentially makes what is meant by 'risky' or 'risk-free' ambiguous, so it may be helpful at this point to set out a risk/return hierarchy, explaining the nature of the risk premium for different types of capital asset. We start with the safest type of asset, then build up the risks. The aim is to clarify the differences between several types of risk and risk premium that are commonly referred to.

A. Bond or bill with a payoff at date 1 certain in real terms

The return on the asset will need to be indexed to inflation, so that the nominal payoff at date 1, Y_{nom1}, is

$$Y_{nom1} = Y_{F1}(1 + Inf_1)$$

where Y_{F1} is the certain real payoff at date 1 – i.e. the same amount of consumption at date 1 as is obtainable from an amount of cash Y_0 at date 0, and Inf_1 is the *ex post* inflation rate during period 1. Y_{nom1} is uncertain *ex ante*. The single-period real return R_F on such an asset is

$$R_F = R(F1) = Y_{F1}/P_0 - 1$$

where P_0 is the price of the asset and $R(FT)$ denotes the one-period return on an asset that provides a certain real payoff at date T (this notation is useful below). R_F as given above is the only one-period real return that is certain. It is the only truly risk-free return.

B. Zero-coupon bond with a payoff at date T certain in real terms

A zero-coupon asset provides one cash payoff at a fixed date, and then expires. The nominal value of a payoff fixed in real terms is given by

$$Y_{nomT} = Y_{FT}\Pi_{t=1}^{T}(1 + Inf_t)$$

where Y_{nomT} is the nominal value of the payoff at the expiry date T periods from date 0. The real rate of return on such a bond over the T periods is $(Y_{FT}/P_0)^{1/T} - 1$ and is certain given the price. However, the real return over any one period is uncertain. It depends on the real percentage change in the bond's price, which is uncertain *ex ante*, unless it is assumed that the one-period risk-free real rate is constant over time. The expected real return during period 1 is

$$E[R(FT)] = E[(P_1)/(1 + Inf_1)]/P_0$$

The price during the asset's life matters because holders may want to sell the bond before maturity. This element of uncertainty could, in theory, cause the return on the bond to incorporate a risk premium, even though the real payoff at maturity is certain (see Section 5.4.2). The size of the premium is likely to be positively related to the length of time, or term, to expiry, because the sensitivity of the price to a change in forward real rates is positively related to the term (assuming that more than one forward rate changes and that each change has the same sign). Hence a premium of this type is often called a term premium, given by

$$\text{Term premium} = E[R(FT)] - R_F$$

A date $T - 1$ the bond becomes a single-period bond with a real value (the payoff) that is certain, so the return is R_F and there is no term premium.

C. Zero-coupon bond with a payoff certain in nominal terms

This type of asset has an additional element of uncertainty because the real value of the payoff depends in part on the rate of inflation between the issue date and expiry. The real rate of return is no longer certain even if the bond is held to maturity, and investors may require compensation for this extra risk via a real inflation risk premium, given by

$$\text{Inflation risk premium} = \text{E}[R(\text{nom}F1)] - R_{\text{F}} \qquad \text{(one-period bond)}$$

or

$$= \text{E}[R(\text{nom}FT)] - \text{E}[R(FT)] \qquad (T\text{-period bond})$$

where $R(\text{nom}FT)$ is the real return on an asset that provides a certain nominal payoff at date T. The expected real return on a T-period bond incorporates a term premium and an inflation risk premium.

D. Zero-coupon bond with an uncertain nominal payoff (i.e. a 'risky bond')

The payoff is no longer certain in nominal terms due to the presence of default risk. The borrower may pay nothing, or may pay an amount that is less than the promised nominal amount. The extra premium here is called a default risk premium, given by

$$\text{Default risk premium} = \text{E}[R(\text{nom}1)] - \text{E}[R(\text{nom}F1)] \qquad \text{(one-period bond)}$$

or

$$= \text{E}[R(\text{nom}T)] - \text{E}[R(\text{nom}FT)] \qquad (T\text{-period bond})$$

where $R(\text{nom}T)$ is the real return on an asset that provides an uncertain nominal pay-off at date T. The real default risk premium is the difference between the expected real return on the risky bond and the expected real return on a bond with a payoff certain in nominal terms. The expected real return incorporates a term premium, an inflation risk premium and a default risk premium.

For a given level of forecast inflation, the expected real rate of return on the risky bond will be less than the promised real rate, which is the rate that would be realised if there were no default. The difference between a promised rate and an expected rate is not a risk premium, but represents the expected loss from default.

Coupon-paying bonds provide a sequence of promised payments at fixed dates. So a coupon-paying bond is a combination of zero-coupon bonds, one for each payment, each with its own risk premium. If there were no costs of splitting the bond into its constituent zeros, the price of the bond would be the sum of the prices of the zeros; otherwise arbitrage gains would be possible.

E. Equity

With equity, the future cash flows to investors are uncertain, and there is no expiry date. Let us assume that the expected real return on equity, $\text{E}(R_{\text{E}})$, is constant over time. The exact definition of the risk premium on a share is debatable. Probably the normal notion is that it incorporates all the premiums that we have identified separately above, in which case the definition is

$$\text{Risk premium on equity} = E(R_E) - R_F$$

In practice, the premium is estimated against the rate on three-month Treasury bills or on long-term government bonds. If we assume that there is no default risk for government debt and that three-month bills have approximately zero inflation risk, then a Treasury bill is close to being an asset with a single payoff certain in real terms. In contrast, long-term government bonds that are safe in nominal terms may be priced to give both a term and an inflation risk premium.

Liquidity
If the market in an asset is illiquid, or the liquidity varies over time, then the expected rate of return on any asset will include a liquidity risk premium. This is the difference between the actual expected rate of return, ignoring costs due to illiquidity, and the notional expected rate on the same asset were it tradable in a liquid market. The liquidity premium may be substantial in the case of illiquid and unlisted shares. Most bank loans and corporate bonds are also illiquid. But debt has a maturity date and most lenders probably do not intend to sell before maturity, so the effect of illiquidity on the expected rate of return on debt is uncertain.

10.4   Summary

Inflation introduces some complications in comparison with analysis that implicitly assumes that inflation is zero. The relation between nominal and real returns is given by the Fisher relation (equation (10.1)) if inflation is treated as certain and there is no tax. But the existence of uncertain inflation implies that an asset with uncertain real returns will be priced to provide an inflation risk premium, which could in theory be negative. In addition, the Fisher relation is not quite correct for an asset that is either risky or risk-free in nominal terms, even if investors are assumed to be risk-neutral.

There are also interactions between inflation and taxes. A given rate of tax on nominal income or capital gain translates into a higher effective rate on the real income or real gain, if inflation is positive. So inflation is a variable that, in theory, affects the real, as well as the nominal, cost of capital. Ignoring personal tax, higher inflation implies a lower real WACC, as it increases the real rate of corporation tax saved by interest. Allowing for personal tax, higher inflation may imply a higher real WACC. The chapter ends with a round-up of the types of risk premium, allowing for inflation and for assets that exist for more than one period.

11 The international dimension

We have so far assumed implicitly that investors invest and companies operate entirely within a single country. We now consider some of the implications of the existence of more than one country. The chapter is concerned with two issues in particular: a project's cost of equity if more than one country exists, and the valuation of a foreign project – i.e. a project that is owned by a company with a head office in a different country.

11.1   The cost of equity

11.1.1   An integrated world capital market, and PPP holds

The cost of equity has been analysed in an international context under a variety of assumptions. One assumption that could be made is that there is an integrated world capital market. This means that there is no difference between domestic and foreign assets, for example in terms of transactions costs, tax treatment or the availability of information. The investment opportunity set is the same for all investors. A domestic asset can be defined as one that, from the perspective of a resident of the country concerned, is traded on a local financial market and has been issued by a local company or other body (e.g. the government). A local company is one with its head office in the country. An integrated market does not require the existence of a single worldwide currency, although concern about currency risk is no doubt one of the factors that, in practice, causes markets to be somewhat segmented.

Given an integrated market, it can be assumed either that purchasing power parity (PPP) holds or that it does not hold. Suppose that there are two countries, A and B, and that there is only one consumption good. Then PPP holds if the price of the good is the same in both countries. If A and B have different currencies, PPP requires that the price of the good in A be the same as the price in B, converted at the prevailing exchange rate:

$$P_A = SP_B$$

where P_A is the price per consumption unit in A's currency and S is the prevailing spot exchange rate, expressed as the cost in A's currency of a unit of B's currency. For example, if one consumption unit costs \$100 and the exchange rate is \$1.00 = £0.60, the cost in pounds is £60.

The notion of PPP is more involved if there are many goods. It is still necessary, for PPP to hold, for the price of each good to be the same in each country, at the spot exchange rate (commodity price parity). In addition, it is necessary for people in each country to spend the same proportions of their consumption budget on each good, otherwise the price index in country A will be calculated using weights that differ from the weights used in B, and PPP will not hold over time if percentage price changes differ across goods. For example, suppose there are two goods, x and y, and there is a single currency. Residents of A spend more of their budget on x than do residents of B. If the price of x rises more quickly than the price of y, then inflation is higher for A than for B, and PPP does not hold. The real value of one unit of currency – the amount of an individual's consumption package that one unit buys – falls by more for residents of A than for residents of B. Thus PPP requires the preferences of individuals to be the same across different countries (see Adler and Dumas, 1983, or Copeland and Weston, 1988, chap. 22, for a fuller discussion).

If there is an integrated world capital market, and PPP does hold, then the existence of different countries or national stock markets or currencies has no consequences for the analysis of asset pricing (see, e.g., Stulz, 1995a). Assets are priced as though there is a single capital market in a single country. PPP ensures that changes in exchange rates exactly reflect differences in inflation, via the relative PPP formula:

$$S_1 = S_0(1 + Inf_A)/(1 + Inf_B) \tag{11.1}$$

where S_t, is the spot exchange rate at date t and Inf_A is the rate of inflation in country A. Free trade in capital and money markets ensures that the real risk-free rate and real risk premiums will be the same for all investors.

Consider first an asset in country A that is risk-free in real terms and provides a real return at date 1 of $R_{Freal,A}$. An investment of S_0 in such an asset provides a nominal pay-off at date 1 of $S_0(1 + R_{Freal,A})(1 + Inf_A)$. An investment of S_0 in a risk-free asset in country B, exchanged back into currency A at the spot rate at date 1, provides $S_1 (1 + R_{Freal,B})(1 + Inf_B)$ (the amount S_0 of currency A buys one unit of currency B). If PPP holds (equation (11.1)), the investment of S_0 in country B provides a nominal pay-off at date 1 of

$$S_1(1 + R_{Freal,B})(1 + Inf_B) = S_0(1 + R_{Freal,B})(1 + Inf_A) \tag{11.2}$$

So any difference in pay-off between the two assets must be due to a difference in the real returns they provide. There would be no difference in a free market, or arbitrage would be possible, so the real risk-free rate will be the same in both countries.

For example, suppose the worldwide real risk-free rate is 5 per cent p.a. and inflation turns out to have been 10 per cent p.a. in the United Kingdom and 0 per cent p.a. in the United States. The nominal rate of return on an asset that is risk-free in real terms was $(1.05)(1.00) - 1 = 5\%$ pa in dollars and $(1.05)(1.10) - 1 = 15.5\%$ pa in sterling, and the UK pound will have fallen to 90.9 per cent of its dollar value at the start of the year. A UK investor would have received 5 per cent p.a. real whether he bought a sterling or a dollar asset that is risk-free in real terms.

It can be shown, further, that the location and nationality of a project make no difference to the real risk premium on its shares. Hence location and nationality make no difference to the cost of equity, since they affect neither the real risk-free rate nor the real risk premium. The shares of a company will be held by investors worldwide, with no 'home bias' on the part of investors in the country where the company is based. All investors will hold the same portfolio of risky assets, in theory. The standard CAPM can be derived, with the modification that the market portfolio is the value-weighted world market portfolio of risky assets:

$$E(R_j) = R_F + \beta_{j,\text{world}}[E(R_{\text{world}}) - R_F] \tag{11.3}$$

where $E(R_j)$ is the expected real return on asset j; R_F is the real risk-free rate, which is the same in every country; $\beta_{j,\text{world}}$ is the beta of asset j calculated with respect to the world market portfolio; and $E(R_{\text{world}})$ is the expected real return on the world portfolio. Equation (11.3) is often referred to as the *international CAPM*. In a practical context, the world portfolio means one of the global stock market indices; however, such indices differ considerably in their constituents and in their returns.

Harvey (1991) proposes an international version of the conditional CAPM, which is simply the conditional version of equation (11.3):

$$E\left(R_{jt}^e \middle| I_{t-1}\right) = (\lambda_t | I_{t-1})\text{cov}\left(R_{jt}^e, R_{\text{worldt}}^e \middle| I_{t-1}\right) \tag{11.4}$$

where the superscript ^{e} denotes an excess return; $E(R_{jt}^e | I_{t-1})$ is the expected excess return on asset j in period t, conditional on a set of information I available to investors at date $t-1$; $(\lambda_t | I_{t-1})$ is the conditional market price of risk $[\lambda_t = E(R_{\text{worldt}}^e)/\text{var}(R_{\text{worldt}}^e)]$; and cov $(R_{jt}^e, R_{\text{worldt}}^e | I_{t-1})$ is the conditional covariance of asset j with the world market. Equation (11.4) is a general form of the conditional model. To test the model, assumptions have to be made about the information that investors use to make predictions (Section 11.1.4).

It is also the case that interest rate parity will hold under an integrated money market. The interest rate parity relation states that the forward exchange rate between two currencies is determined by the current spot rate and the nominal risk-free rates according to

$$F_1 = S_0(1 + R_{\text{Fnom,A}})/(1 + R_{\text{Fnom,B}}) \tag{11.5}$$

where F_1 is the current forward foreign exchange rate for exchange at date 1 and R_{Fnom} is the return on an asset that is risk free in nominal terms. Interest rate parity is another no-arbitrage condition. Equation (11.5) says that the risk-free nominal return in a foreign currency B, exchanged into the domestic currency A at the forward exchange rate, is the same as the risk-free nominal return in the domestic currency.

11.1.2   *An integrated world capital market, and PPP does not hold*

If PPP does not hold, the real value of a unit of a given currency varies across countries. One pound spent in the United Kingdom by a representative UK resident does not buy the same amount of his/her consumption package as the dollar value of one pound spent by a US investor on *his/her* consumption package. Numerous studies have found that substantial divergences from PPP are the norm in practice. One reason is that there are transactions costs in attempting arbitrage through trade, and arbitrage is not possible at all for non-traded goods and services, so that commodity price parity is not expected to hold in the non-traded sector. In addition, differences in tastes across countries lead to differences in consumption packages.

Analysis of the determination of asset prices is awkward in this setting. If PPP does not hold, the location of the investor matters, because it affects the investor's assessment of the real returns on a given asset. So we are analysing prices in a market with agents with heterogeneous assessments of real returns. The problem is akin to that of specifying a project's cost of equity in a market with investors who face differing rates of personal tax (Chapter 9). The complication of differing personal taxes is caused by barriers that sustain the existence of tax clienteles, preventing highly taxed investors from avoiding tax. The complication of differing real returns on an asset across countries is caused by the factors that prevent PPP from holding, notably non-tradable goods and services.

It is perhaps easiest to think of departures from PPP that are caused by exchange rate changes. Consider two countries, the United Kingdom and United States, and suppose for simplicity that there is one consumption good and that inflation is zero in both countries. Then any change in the pound/dollar exchange rate causes a change in the real purchasing power of each currency in the other country. A US asset which is risk-free in real terms for a US resident is now a risky investment for a UK investor, who is exposed to currency risk. Equation (11.2) no longer holds. Interest rate parity will still hold (equation (11.5)), since we are still assuming an integrated money market. But interest rate parity ensures that a UK investor receives the same risk-free nominal (and real) return in pounds from a hedged position in any currency. It does not ensure that the *ex post* risk-free returns will be the same for residents across different countries.

For example, suppose that the real risk-free rate in the United States is substantially larger than it is in the United Kingdom. With zero inflation in both countries, the nominal risk-free rate is likewise higher in dollars, and so the dollar is at a discount in the forward foreign exchange market; $F_1 < S_0$, by interest rate parity. If PPP were expected to hold, the dollar would not be expected to depreciate (inflation is zero in both countries), and speculation would be expected approximately to equalise the two interest rates. But the rates can remain apart if the dollar is expected to become undervalued in relation to its PPP value.

The simple international CAPM of equation (11.3) is not correct, in theory, if PPP does not hold, and several authors have developed modified international asset pricing models in continuous time. These models are reviewed by Stulz (1995a) and Adler and Dumas (1983). For example, the conclusion of the Solnik–Sercu model, as summarised by Sercu and Uppal (1995, chap. 22), is that the expected return on a risky asset j, measured in a given currency, is given by an expression of the form

$$E(R_j) = R_F + \beta_{j,\text{world}}[E(R_{\text{world}}) - R_F] + \beta_{j,1}\, Currprem_1 + \beta_{j,2}\, Currprem_2 \ldots$$

$$(11.6)$$

where R_F is the risk-free rate in the currency of measurement, $\beta_{j,\text{world}} = \text{cov}(R_j, R_{\text{world}})/\text{var}(R_{\text{world}})$, $E(R_{\text{world}})$ is the expected return on the world market portfolio, $Currprem_n$ is the risk premium on holding foreign currency n, and $\beta_{j,n} = \text{cov}(R_j, S_n)/\text{var}(S_n)$ – the sensitivity of the asset's returns to the exchange rate with currency n. Equation (11.6) assumes that inflation is zero in all countries, so that nominal and real returns are the same. Sercu and Uppal (p. 607) remark that adjustment for inflation risk is 'not very important', because, empirically, covariances between real returns are almost the same as covariances between nominal returns.

A currency risk premium is the expected excess return (which could be negative) from holding a foreign currency invested at the risk-free rate. It is defined in nominal terms as

$$Currprem = \{E(S_1) - S_0[1/(1 + R_{Fnom,B})](1 + R_{Fnom,A})\}/S_0$$
$$= [E(S_1) - F_1)]/S_0 \tag{11.7}$$

The investor residing in country A gains pure exposure to currency B by buying a bill that provides a pay-off of one unit of currency B at date 1, free of risk in nominal terms, and exchanging the unit of B for A at the spot exchange rate at date 1. The expected pay-off in currency A from buying one B-bill is the expected spot exchange rate $E(S_1)$. So the first line of equation (11.7) shows the expected pay-off in currency A per B-bill, less the cost at date 0 in A, $S_0[1/(1 + R_{Fnom,B})]$, times one plus the nominal risk-free rate in A, $1 + R_{Fnom,A}$. This expected excess pay-off or risk premium in currency A per unit of B at date 1 is divided by S_0 to give the excess pay-off as a percentage of the amount of currency A invested in the B-bill. The second line of equation (11.7) substitutes the forward rate at date 0 for exchange at date 1, F_1, which is given by the interest rate parity relation (equation (11.5))

Let us now try to explain the equation for the expected return on asset j, (11.6). Consider an asset that is priced in dollars. A UK resident is interested in the returns converted into pounds. The variance of the returns in pounds depends partly on the covariance of the returns in dollars with exchange rate changes. With the exchange rate quoted in pounds per unit of foreign currency, positive covariance means that a positive dollar return tends to be associated with a rise in the value of the dollar, so that the variance of the returns converted to pounds is greater than the variance of the dollar returns. This positive covariance means that the risk of the asset is greater for a UK investor than for a US investor, assuming that risk is positively related to variance. A UK investor with a given level of risk aversion will demand a higher expected return on the asset than a US investor with the same level of risk aversion. The asset may therefore be priced to give an expected return that includes a risk premium for exposure to the exchange rate, and this premium will be positively related to the covariance of the dollar returns with the exchange rate.

It is worth repeating that the expected real rate of return on an asset will not be the same for investors based in different countries, if PPP is not expected to hold. That is, the real rates of return corresponding to a given nominal rate of return in a given currency will differ across investors in different countries. Thus the derivation of a model such as equation (11.6) has to contain a solution to the problem of arriving at an equilibrium expected rate of return in a market with agents who obtain heterogeneous real rates of return from a given asset.

Equation (11.6) would be very difficult to implement in practice. The betas called for could, in principle, be estimated for an asset with a price history, by regressing the asset's returns in a given currency A on the returns on a global market index expressed in A and on the exchange rates with other currencies. This still leaves the problem of estimating the currency risk premiums, measured in currency A. These are generally viewed as too small and too difficult to estimate to be worth trying to incorporate in a practical context. So most authors recommend the use of the simple international CAPM (equation (11.3)) as an approximation to a more correct model such as equation (11.6) (e.g. Stulz, 1995a, 1995b; Sercu and Uppal, 1995, p. 611; a dissenting author is Solnik, 2000, pp. 275–77).

A noteworthy implication of assuming an integrated capital market is that international diversification by a company, via the undertaking of a foreign project, does not reduce the project's cost of equity, whether or not PPP holds. In other words, a project's cost of equity is not affected by the nationality of the parent company. The reason is that a project is conceived of as a financial asset with a particular level of risk, as usual. The cost of equity is estimated as though the project were constituted as a separate company, with its own shares traded on the international capital market. Investors in all countries are assumed to have free access to all assets under an integrated market. A given project does not to create a new opportunity for diversification for investors in any country; it does not change the efficient frontier facing investors. Diversification across countries will reduce the systematic risk of a parent company's shares, in the same way that diversification by a company across industries within a single country reduces the risk of its shares. But it does not follow that either sort of diversification reduces the cost of equity for a given project.

11.1.3   Segmented capital markets

A different assumption that could be made is that national capital markets are segmented. Two markets are segmented from each other if there are costs or barriers to trade across the markets. It is customary to distinguish two types of barrier: direct and indirect. Direct barriers include rules in the foreign country that restrict investment by outsiders, rules in the domestic country that restrict foreign investment, and higher trading costs or higher taxes on foreign assets. Indirect barriers include problems regarding the quality of information and enforcement of shareholder rights, costs due to insider trading and lack of liquidity, and the presence of political risk and currency risk.

It is clear that two markets are segmented if exactly the same asset trades at a different price in the two markets. For example, if a share j is listed on the stock exchanges of countries A and B, we should observe $P_{jA} = SP_{jB}$, where P_{jA} is the price of j in currency A. If we do not, there must be some reason that prevents arbitrage. Segmentation is harder to detect in the case of assets that are not identical. Different shares with the same risk have the same expected return under an integrated market, so a difference in their expected returns indicates that the markets are segmented. But the measurement of both risk and expected rates of return is imprecise.

The degree to which stock markets are segmented is an empirical matter. The existence of segmented markets has several testable implications, which we now summarise.

(i) Differences in the cost of equity across countries
As a result of the barriers to foreign portfolio investment, the cost of equity for a given domestic project could differ depending on its location. Both the real risk-free rate and the real risk premium could differ. If money markets are segmented, then interest rate parity

may not hold; even nominal hedged risk-free rates may differ across currencies, from the perspective of an investor in a given currency. If money markets are integrated but capital markets are segmented then, arguably, real risk-free rates should be similar across countries but real risk premiums could differ. With integrated money markets interest rate parity will hold, and we might expect real risk-free rates to be approximately the same across countries. Suppose inflation is forecast to be 0 per cent p.a. in both the United Kingdom and the United States, but the risk-free nominal rate is 10 per cent p.a. in the United Kingdom and 5 per cent p.a. in the United States. The dollar must be worth 4.8 per cent more in pounds at the one-year forward rate compared with the spot rate, by interest rate parity. But the pound is not expected to depreciate according to PPP. One would expect investors to be selling dollars and buying pounds unhedged, since the expected real rate on nominal risk-free assets is 10 per cent in pounds and 5 per cent in dollars, and this trading would tend to close the gap between the nominal interest rates. However, such currency speculation is risky in nominal, as well as real, terms.

International CAPM under segmentation
The exact specification of the cost of equity under segmentation depends on the assumptions made about the nature of the segmentation and about the risk aversion of groups of investors. The extreme case of segmentation is a country that is completely closed to foreign investment, and in which domestic investors cannot invest abroad. In this case the expected rate of return on assets depends on the risk aversion of domestic investors, and the standard CAPM can be derived, as in Chapter 3, with the domestic market as the market portfolio. The case in which segmentation is a matter of degree is more realistic and more complicated. Several authors derive modified versions of the standard CAPM for the case of assets that are traded in a partially segmented market.

A good example is the paper by Errunza and Losq (1985). They assume that the world consists of country A, the assets of which can be freely traded, and country B, the assets & which can be traded only by residents of that country. Residents of A are blocked from trading in the assets of B, but not vice versa. They call this situation one of 'mild segmentation' of B's capital market. It is not fully segmented because the investors in B can also trade in A's assets. There is only one currency, so currency risk does not arise. In the model the risk premium on a segmented asset (traded in B) will exceed that on a free asset (traded in A) of the same covariance risk in relation to the world market. The argument is explained in Appendix 11.1.

Errunza and Losq's conclusion that the cost of equity is higher for segmented assets hinges on an assumption that the risk aversion of investors in aggregate is less than the risk aversion of investors in the segmented market, and on the nature of the partial segmentation. Alexander, Eun and Janakiramanan (1987) present a related model in which two markets are completely segmented, except for one share that is listed on both markets. In this setting, a listing on the second market does not necessarily reduce the expected rate of return, although the authors suggest that this is probable, at least if the aggregate risk version of investors in each market is similar. They also show that the presence of a dual listing affects the equilibrium expected returns on the other shares in both markets.

(ii) Fall in the cost of equity when barriers are reduced

An issue that has attracted much attention is the effect on the cost of equity when a company, or a whole country, takes steps to reduce the barriers that cause its assets to be segmented. One means by which a company's shares become more readily available to a wider pool of investors is by listing the shares on a foreign stock market, which should reduce the indirect barriers facing foreign investors. A similar step, for a country, is a decision by the government to 'liberalise' the stock market by reducing restrictions on foreign portfolio investment, which should reduce the direct barriers facing foreigners. It is natural to suppose that such actions will result in a lower cost of equity, and this is in fact what most authors would predict (e.g. Bekaert and Harvey, 2000). But this is not an inevitable prediction.

The question is considered in the context of the conditional CAPM by Bekaert and Harvey (1995, 2000). According to this model (equation (11.4)), the conditional expected excess return on a segmented market is equal to the conditional domestic market price of risk times the conditional variance of the domestic market:

$$E\left(R_{\text{domt}}^{\text{e*}}\middle|I_{t-1}\right) = \lambda_{\text{domt}-1}^{*}\text{var}\left(R_{\text{domt}}^{\text{e*}}\middle|I_{t-1}\right)$$

where $\lambda_{\text{domt}-1}^{*} = E(R_{\text{domt}}^{\text{e*}}|I_{t-1})/\text{var}(R_{\text{domt}}^{\text{e*}}|I_{t-1})$, the domestic market price of risk, determined by the risk aversion of domestic investors; the superscript ^{e} stands for excess; and the * is to mark that the domestic market concerned is fully segmented. Thus, with segmented markets, the expected returns on markets can vary across markets both because of variation in the local risk aversion and in the local market variance. The expected excess return on an integrated market is

$$E\left(R_{\text{domt}}^{\text{e}}\middle|I_{t-1}\right) = \frac{\text{cov}\left(R_{\text{domt}}^{\text{e}}, R_{\text{worldt}}^{\text{e}}\middle|I_{t-1}\right)E(R_{\text{worldt}}^{\text{e}}\middle|I_{t-1})}{\text{var}(R_{\text{worldt}}\middle|I_{t-1})}$$

$$= (\lambda_{\text{domt}-1}\middle|I_{t-1})\text{cov}\left(R_{\text{domt}}^{\text{e}}, R_{\text{worldt}}^{\text{e}}\middle|I_{t-1}\right) \tag{11.8}$$

where $\lambda_{\text{domt}-1} = E(R_{\text{domt}}^{\text{e}}|I_{t-1})/\text{var}(R_{\text{worldt}}^{\text{e}}|I_{t-1})$, the world market price of risk, determined by the risk aversion of unrestricted investors. Equation (11.8) says that the conditional expected return on an integrated market is equal to the conditional world market price of risk times the market's conditional covariance with the world market.

There is no theoretical necessity that $E(R_{\text{domt}}^{\text{e*}}|I_{t-1}) > E(R_{\text{domt}}^{\text{e}}|I_{t-1})$ – i.e. that the expected rate of return on a segmented market is more than the expected rate on a would-be integrated market. To make this prediction requires further assumptions. For example, Bekaert and Harvey (2000, p. 567) sketch how the prediction could be made that the cost of equity falls when an emerging market is liberalised (becomes integrated with the world market). They argue that the expected rate of return on the market will fall if its covariance with the world market is less than its own variance had been as a segmented market. This assumes implicitly that there is relatively little difference in risk aversion between investors in the segmented market and in the world market. They then suggest that, 'given that emerging economies have different industrial mixes and are less subject [than the world economy/market] to macroeconomic shocks originating from developed economies, covariances with world factors are low . . . Since local market volatilities tend to be large, the cost of capital should decrease after capital market liberalisations.'

(iii) Unexploitable opportunities for portfolio diversification

From the perspective of domestic investors, segmentation implies that there are opportunities for international diversification that they are unable to exploit. They therefore display home-country bias – i.e. their holdings are weighted towards their domestic market. Because international investment is restricted, correlations between national stock markets will be lower than they would be under an integrated capital market.

A related implication is that foreign direct investment (FDI) by a company in a country with a segmented capital market could provide the parent's shareholders with a diversification benefit that is unattainable via portfolio investment. This implies a lower cost of equity for the project compared with the cost of equity in the absence of barriers to foreign portfolio investment, assuming that all domestic investors face barriers. Errunza and Senbet (1981) discuss the implications of a setting in which domestic investors face differing barriers, including zero barriers for some investors. They argue that, with this assumption, a lower cost of equity for a foreign project requires the presence of barriers to foreign *direct* investment. With no barriers to FDI, the marginal investor in the equity of a foreign project could be a domestic investor facing zero barriers to foreign portfolio investment, in which case the cost of equity for the foreign project will be the same as if there were no barriers to portfolio investment abroad. But, if barriers to FDI exist, foreign projects will have lower expected rates of return than 'otherwise equivalent but purely domestic' projects. The cost of equity for a foreign project will be the cost for an equivalent domestic project, less an amount x per cent p.a. Equilibrium x per cent is given by the annualised expected gain from the portfolio diversification benefit, net of the annualised extra direct cost arising from the project's foreign location. If the extra directs costs of FDI differ across firms, x per cent is determined by the annualised direct costs applicable for the marginal firm investing in foreign projects.

11.1.4   Evidence on segmentation

In this section we review evidence on the three testable implications of market segmentation outlined in the previous section.

(i) Differences in cost of equity across countries?

The track record shows that real rates of interest are not always equal across countries. For example, Frankel (1991) supports the popular view that the real cost of capital was lower in Japan than in the United States between 1950 and 1989, and argues that this was largely because real interest rates were lower (because of high Japanese saving). There was a fixed exchange rate until 1973, and exchange controls until 1980. So money markets were segmented before 1980, and the real interest rate could be lower in Japan before 1980 because Japanese investors could not invest in dollars to obtain the higher real dollar rate.

The Japanese yen had been appreciating at an average *real* rate in excess of 3 per cent p.a. during the past thirty years (inflation was higher in Japan during the fixed exchange rate era). After 1980 Japanese investors could invest in the United States, but, Frankel suggests, real interest rates in Japan remained low in the 1980s because the appreciation of the yen was expected to continue.

The argument is this. Suppose that, in Japan, inflation after 1980 is, say, 0 per cent p.a. and the nominal interest rate is 0 per cent p.a.; in the United States inflation is 5 per cent p.a. and the nominal interest rate is 8 per cent p.a. So the real interest rate is 0 per cent p.a. in Japan and approximately 3 per cent p.a. in the United States. Money markets are integrated after 1980, so interest rate parity holds; Japanese residents investing in dollars and hedging the exchange risk will earn a nominal rate of 0 per cent in yen, as in Japan. If they leave their dollar deposits unhedged, and the real exchange rate stays the same (PPP holds), the yen will appreciate (the dollar weaken) by 5 per cent p.a. and they will obtain a real rate in yen of 3 per cent p.a. But the difference in nominal interest rates suggests an expectation that the yen will appreciate by 8 per cent p.a., or by 3 per cent p.a. in real terms (PPP does not hold). If this happens, Japanese holders of dollar deposits will obtain a real rate in yen of 0 per cent p.a. Given an expectation of yen appreciation of up to 8 per cent p.a., the real rate in Japan can be up to 3 per cent p.a. lower than in the United States without causing flows of money market funds from Japan that would tend to close the gap. Thus a difference in real rates of interest might persist even under integrated money markets, and the difference will probably cause the cost of equity to be lower for Japanese than for US companies.

The other part of the cost of equity is the risk premium. The national version of an asset pricing model ought to explain differences in observed excess returns across assets better than the international version, if a market is segmented. The reverse is true if a market is integrated. The evidence is muddy on this matter. Neither the national nor the international version of the standard CAPM (constant expected returns) is well supported at the level of individual shares, using realised returns. Harris, Marston, Mishra and O' Brien (2003) test the national CAPM against the simple international CAPM (equation (11.3)) for a large sample of US firms, using data from 1983 to 1998. They assume that the dividend discount model rearranged (Section 12.2) gives the correct value of the *ex ante* expected rate of return, using analysts' forecasts of earnings growth over the next five years to estimate the company's long-term growth rate. They find that the national CAPM gives estimates that are closer to the estimates from the dividend discount model, but that average 'error' is not much greater for the international CAPM.

There have been several tests of the international CAPM at the level of markets that have produced some support for the model. The (unconditional) world betas of mature stock markets are significantly and positively related to the cross-section of market returns (e.g. Harvey, 1995). In other words, differences in market betas do explain some of the cross-sectional differences in market returns, in the manner predicted by the CAPM. The same is not true for emerging markets, which mostly have world betas that are not significantly different from zero. A natural interpretation of these findings is that mature markets are more integrated than emerging markets.

The results of tests of the conditional international CAPM are similar. There is evidence for the predictability of market returns, which suggests that the conditional version is a better model. In fact, it is more accurate to say conditional *versions*, as many specifications have been tested. The nature of the tests is outlined in Appendix 11.2.

(ii) Fall in the cost of equity when barriers are reduced?

Lower barriers mean easier and cheaper access to an asset or market for foreign investors. If the result is a drop in the cost of equity, market value will rise, other things being equal. Several papers study share prices when companies list their shares on another market, or establish a depository receipt programme. An example of what can happen is the much-cited case of the Danish company Novo's listing on the New York Stock Exchange in 1981 (Eiteman, Stonehill and Moffett, 1998). The jump in the share price that occurred in the preceding months could not be explained by new information about the future growth of the company, so it has been ascribed to the effects of the listing. On the other hand, Jorion and Schwartz (1986) and others report that shares that are listed on a foreign stock exchange do not behave differently from shares with a domestic listing only. Rates of return on dual-listed shares are significantly related to their domestic betas, but not to their world or foreign-market betas. This suggests that a dual listing does not entirely remove the barriers to foreign investment.

Other evidence comes from the effect on aggregate market value of the liberalisation of a stock market, whereby some investment by foreigners is permitted. For example, Henry (2000) finds a positive average abnormal return around the date of the announcement of the liberalisation of a sample of emerging markets, after controlling for the effects of other contemporaneous reforms on equity value. He therefore argues that the upward revaluations are due to a fall in the cost of equity. Miller (1999) reports a positive average abnormal return around the date of the announcement of depository receipt programmes for foreign shares on US stock exchanges during 1985 to 1995. He argues that this is evidence that such programmes reduce indirect barriers to investment in the share concerned, such as poor information and low liquidity. The evidence of Foerster and Karolyi (1999) is less clear-cut. They examine a much longer event window of up to two years; most of the positive effect on the value of a depository receipt listing appears to be temporary.

(iii) Unexploitable opportunities for portfolio diversification?

Indirect evidence for segmentation comes from the evidence of weak correlations across stock exchanges, though correlations have been rising since the 1980s (e.g. Solnik, 2000, chap. 4). Stock markets are predicted to be highly correlated under an integrated world market. There is also strong evidence of home-country bias; investing institutions are nowhere near as well diversified internationally as would be expected were there no barriers to international investment. Cooper and Kaplanis (1995) offer a back-of-the-envelope estimate that, to account for the lack of international diversification, the barriers must equate to additional costs of around 2.7 per cent p.a. of asset value. An international portfolio has an average beta of 0.55 measured against the domestic market; the domestic equity risk premium is assumed to be 6 per cent p.a.; so the required premium on the international portfolio is

$(1 - 0.55) \times 6\%$, 2.7 percentage points lower than the premium on the domestic market. They argue that currency risk cannot account for additional costs of this size, which they ascribe mainly to information costs.

Low international diversification is presumed to be the reason why several studies report that shares are much more sensitive to their domestic market than to a world market proxy, or to an international index of the relevant industry for the share (Solnik, 2000, pp. 265–68). For example, Jorion and Schwartz (1986) test the relation between rates of return on Canadian shares and their betas measured against a world market index (proxied by a US index!) and against the domestic Canadian market, using data from 1968 to 1982. They remove the effect of multicollinearity between the returns on the world index R_{world} and the returns on the domestic index R_{dom} by running the regression

$$R_{\text{domt}} = \alpha + \beta R_{\text{worldt}} + e_{\text{domt}}$$

and they then estimate domestic betas against the error terms e_{domt} rather than R_{domt}. They find that rates of return across shares are significantly related to domestic betas but not world betas. However, Mittoo (1992), in a follow-up study, finds that the data from 1982 to 1986 supports integration between the Canadian and US markets, presumably because of reductions in the 1970s and early 1980s in the barriers that cause segmentation.

Several other studies have compared the shares of multinationals and the shares of domestic companies. The usual finding is that there is little difference between the two groups. For example, in regressions to explain changes in share price over time, international explanatory variables, such as a global stock index or international index for the relevant industry, do not explain more of the price changes of multinationals than of domestic companies. Again, the domestic betas of the shares of multinationals are nearly as large as the domestic betas of the shares of mainly domestic companies. This is a strange finding, because the value of a multinational, with much of its business abroad, ought – on average – to be less sensitive to the domestic stock market than the value of a company is with most of its business at home. This applies even in a segmented market. However, a study by Lombard, Roulet and Solnik (1999) reports that the shares of Swiss multinationals are more sensitive to returns on foreign shares grouped by region and by the relevant industry than are the shares of Swiss companies with mainly domestic sales. They use data from 1988 to 1997. For some reason, the finding for Swiss companies does not apply to a sample of US multinational and domestic companies.

Barriers to portfolio investment imply that foreign direct investment will add value, but the evidence on this is unclear. For example, Fatemi (1984) reports a positive stock market response to company announcements to diversify internationally. However, a recent study by Denis, Denis and Yost (2002) finds that single-business international firms are, on average, valued at a discount of 18 per cent in relation to a benchmark portfolio of single-business domestic firms in the same industry. In any case, the valuation of, or market reaction to, FDI is noisy evidence on the hypothesis that foreign projects have a lower cost of equity than equivalent domestic projects, because there are several other reasons why foreign investment might affect a company's value, positively and negatively.

11.2   The cost of equity for a foreign project

The context for the current section is the valuation of a foreign project – i.e. a project located in a country that differs from the country in which the head office of the parent company is situated. We are therefore considering foreign direct investment rather than portfolio investment. Compared with a domestic project, there can be added difficulties in managing a foreign project, forecasting its cash flows and payments to the parent company, and estimating its cost of capital. However, it is beyond our scope to consider the whole picture of the valuation and management of a foreign project; this is a major topic in texts on international corporate finance. Our discussion here is concerned mainly with the cost of capital.

11.2.1   Two methods of valuation

There is no agreed template for exactly how to value a foreign project; different authors make different recommendations. But, basically, there are two methods: to value the project from the perspective of the parent; or to value it from the perspective of an investor in the host country. For the most part, we assume for simplicity that the project is financed entirely by equity, and we ignore personal tax.

1. Present value from the perspective of the parent company

Present value is estimated by arriving at a forecast of the cash flows in the parent's currency, and discounting by the appropriate cost of equity as estimated in the country of the parent. The expected cash flows will have to be converted into the parent's home currency using forecast exchange rates; a pragmatic choice of forecast is the prevailing forward rate for each assumed remittance date. So the expression for present value from the parent's perspective is

$$V_{\text{dom}} = \Sigma_{t=1}^{T} Y_{\text{domt}}/(1 + R_{\text{Edom}})^t$$

where V_{dom} is the present value in the parent's domestic currency; Y_{domt} is the expected nominal cash flow for year t to be remitted to the parent, after corporation tax and possibly other tax, exchanged into the parent's domestic currency; R_{Edom} is the nominal cost of equity associated with the expected stream of cash flows in the parent's currency; and T is the number of years of the project's life.

If capital markets are segmented, the cost of equity for a foreign project is likely to differ, in theory, from the cost of equity for a similar project at home. In CAPM terms, risk is measured by beta against the domestic market. The beta of the returns on a given domestic industry in country A with respect to A's stock market is likely to differ from the beta of the returns on the same industry in country B with respect to A's stock market.

The cash flows expected by the parent are likely to differ from the flows that would be expected were the project owned by host-country residents. The factors that can cause differences in the two cash flows include arrangements between the parent and its foreign project (e.g. transfer pricing), host-country regulations and policies regarding foreign-owned operations, and the taxation of the project's earnings by both host and parent countries.

2. Present value using a host-country discount rate
The expression is

$$V_{\text{for}} = \Sigma_{t=1}^{T} Y_{\text{fort}}/(1 + R_{\text{Efor}})^t$$

where V_{for} is the present value expressed in the foreign (host) currency, Y_{fort} is the expected cash flow for year t to be remitted to the parent, expressed in the foreign currency, and R_{Efor} is the project's cost of equity estimated in the foreign currency. The present value in the parent's currency is simply $S_0 V_{\text{for}}$. Method 2 avoids the need to convert future cash flows to the parent's currency. The two methods will give the same valuation if the same future cash flows and discount rate are used, adjusted for expected exchange rate changes.

Example
Suppose a UK parent company is valuing a US project with one pay-off with an expected value of $100 in one year. The spot exchange rate is £0.7/$ and the one-year forward rate is £0.6/$. The estimated nominal cost of equity in pounds is 10 per cent p.a., so the project's value in pounds is (£0.6/$)$100/1.1 = £55. A return of 28.3 per cent in dollars (= 1.10(0.7/0.6) − 1) is required to give a return of 10 per cent in pounds. If the cost of equity in dollars is assumed to be 28.3 per cent p.a. then the value in dollars is $100/1.283 = $77.9 = £55 at the spot rate of £0.7/$. But this equivalence is justified only if an integrated capital market is assumed. If markets are segmented, it is not safe to assume that the project's cost of equity estimated in the host currency will be similar to the figure obtained by converting, in the above manner, the project's cost of equity estimated in the parent's country. It would not be not safe to assume, in the example, that a US investor would estimate the project's cost of equity at 28.3 per cent p.a. So method 2 will probably give a different estimate of value from method 1, if markets are segmented.

A majority of texts recommend method 1. The criterion for the acceptance of a foreign project is whether it increases the wealth of the shareholders of the parent company, and method 1 is more appropriate if capital markets are not fully integrated and most of the parent's shareholders are domestic investors. However, Sercu and Uppal (1995) recommend method 2, using the international CAPM to estimate the cost of equity (equation (11.3)), as they believe that most capital markets are integrated. Copeland, Koller and Murrin (2000) also recommend method 2, but using the standard national CAPM to estimate the cost of equity in the host country.

Method 2 discounts the parent's cash flows (before conversion to the parent's currency) by the host-country discount rate. A fully-fledged valuation from the foreign-country perspective would discount the expected cash flows as though the owner were a resident of the host country. Such cash flows could differ from the expected cash flows for a foreign parent. Eiteman, Stonehill and Moffett (1998, chap. 18) state that it is common practice for companies to value foreign projects in this way. Ang and Lai (1989) point out that the host-country value is of interest because it provides an estimate of the project's sale price if the sale were to a resident in the host country.

11.2.2   More on the cost of equity

The estimated cost of equity will generally differ, in practice, depending on whether the parent employs the standard (national) CAPM or the international CAPM. The risk-free real rates and equity risk premiums could be different, and the project's beta measured against a domestic index will be the same as its beta measured against a world index only by coincidence.

The decision regarding whether to use a national or international version of the CAPM is pertinent to any asset, not just to foreign assets or projects. It depends on one's judgement of the degree of market segmentation. There is no reason to presume that the national CAPM should be used for a domestic project and the international CAPM for a foreign project. If all or most of the parent company's shareholders are residents of the parent's country and face barriers to foreign portfolio investment, it is the domestic beta and domestic risk premium that are relevant for both domestic and foreign projects. Most texts assume that capital markets are segmented, so they recommend estimating the cost of equity for a foreign project from the parent's perspective (method 1), using the standard national CAPM or any other sensible method.

However, suppose we assume that capital markets are integrated and that the real rate of interest is the same across countries. If we assume that shares are sensitive to the world market only via the sensitivity of the domestic market to the world market, the share's world beta $\beta_{j,\,world}$ in equation (11.3) is given by

$$\beta_{j,world} = \beta_{j,dom}\beta_{dom,world} \tag{11.9}$$

where $\beta_{j,dom}$ is the beta of the share against the domestic stock market and $\beta_{dom,world}$ is the 'country beta', the beta of the domestic market against the world market (Solnik, 1974). So $\beta_{j,world}$ can be estimated indirectly from the domestic beta and the country beta.

In fact, Stulz (1995b) shows that, if equation (11.9) holds, the national CAPM is correct when the asset or market concerned is integrated in the world market, but that a mistake is made if the national CAPM is used under an integrated market and equation (11.9) does not hold. He first notes that, since the expected rate of return on the integrated national market is given by

$$E(R_{dom}) - R_F = \beta_{dom,world}[E(R_{world}) - R_F] \tag{11.10}$$

the risk premium on the national market (the left-hand side) is the correct market premium in the national CAPM if the market is integrated. It is also the correct premium if the market is segmented. But a mistake can arise if beta is estimated against the national market, and there is an integrated world market. The returns on asset j and the domestic market can be analysed via 'market model' regressions:

$$R_{jt} = \alpha_j + \beta_{j,dom}R_{domt} + e_{jt} \tag{11.11}$$

and

$$R_{domt} = \alpha_{dom} + \beta_{dom,world} R_{worldt} + e_{domt} \qquad (11.12)$$

where α is the intercept and e is the error term. By definition,

$$\beta_{j,world} = cov(R_{jt}, R_{worldt})/var(R_{worldt}) \qquad (11.13)$$

Substituting equation (11.12) into (11.11) and equation (11.11) into (11.13),

$$cov(R_{jt}, R_{worldt}) = cov[\alpha_j + \beta_{j,dom}(\alpha_{dom} + \beta_{dom,world} R_{worldt} + e_{domt}) + e_{jt}, R_{worldt}]$$
$$= \beta_{j,dom}\beta_{dom,world} var(R_{worldt}) + cov(e_{jt}, R_{worldt})$$

and therefore

$$cov(R_{jt}, R_{worldt})/var(R_{worldt}) = \beta_{j,dom}\beta_{dom,world} + cov(e_{jt}, R_{worldt})/var(R_{worldt})$$

If the idiosyncratic national risk of asset j is uncorrelated with returns on the world market, equation (11.9) holds, and we have

$$E(R_j) = R_F + \beta_{j,world}[E(R_{world}) - R_F]$$
$$= R_F + \beta_{j,dom}\beta_{dom,world}[E(R_{world}) - R_F]$$
$$= R_F + \beta_{j,dom}[E(R_{dom}) - R_F]$$

using equation (11.10). Thus the national CAPM is correct. But, if $cov(e_{jt}, R_{worldt}) > 0$, the beta of share j with respect to the world market is not explained only by $\beta_{j,dom}\beta_{dom,world}$. The national CAPM will understate the asset's expected return according to the international CAPM, which is the correct model under integrated markets. Stulz (1995b) also remarks on the difficulty of estimating the world equity premium from historic data, due to the changing degree of integration of markets over time.

Another possible specification is to assume that markets are mildly segmented, and hence to argue that shareholders will typically care about the covariance of a share with both the domestic market and the world market (e.g. Ehrhardt, 1994, chap. 7). In this case we could use an ad hoc two-factor model of the form

$$E(R_j) = R_F + \beta_{j,dom}Prem(R_{dom}) + \beta_{j,world}Prem(R_{world}) \qquad (11.14)$$

where $Prem(x)$ is the premium associated with variable x. The beta coefficients could be estimated from a bivariate regression:

$$R_{jt} = \beta_0 + \beta_{j,dom} R_{domt} + \beta_{j,world} R_{worldt} + e_{jt}$$

Since R_{domt} and R_{worldt} are likely to be collinear, more precise beta estimates can be obtained by removing the collinearity, for example by estimating

$$R_{jt} = \beta_0 + \beta_{j,dom}^* e_{domt} + \beta_{j,world}^* R_{worldt} + e_{jt} \qquad (11.15)$$

where $\beta^*_{j,dom}$ and $\beta^*_{j,world}$ are revised regression coefficients and e_{domt} is the error term in a regression of the domestic index on the world index:

$$R_{domt} = \gamma_0 + \gamma_1 R_{worldt} + e_{domt}$$

where γ_0 and γ_1 are regression coefficients. Thus e_{domt} can be thought of as the changes in the domestic index that are not explained by changes in the world index. Using equation (11.15), equation (11.14) becomes

$$E(R_j) = R_F + \beta^*_{j,dom}Prem(e_{dom}) + \beta^*_{j,world}Prem(R_{world})$$

The risk premiums in a given period can be estimated from a cross-sectional regression of observed returns on domestic shares against their betas $\beta^*_{j,dom}$ and $\beta^*_{j,dom}$:

$$R_j = \delta_0 + \delta_1 \beta^*_{j,dom} + \delta_2 \beta^*_{j,world} + e_j$$

for shares $j \ldots n$. The estimated premiums for domestic and world market risk are given by the averages over a number of periods of, respectively, δ_1 and δ_2.

11.2.3   Further issues

Currency risk
The currency risk of a project could mean two different things. The first is the effect of changes in exchange rates on the future cash flows of a project in the host country's currency. This is known as *economic exposure*. It could affect both the expected values of future cash flows and the assessment of their risk, in the host or parent currency. It is possible to reduce economic exposure by means of currency hedging, so the forecast cash flows should take account of any hedges that have been put in place. An important point is that an increase in economic exposure need not imply an increase in overall risk. For example, a decision to sell more of a project's output abroad could make a project's cash flows less risky, because of diversification across markets, although the project's exposure to exchange rates will probably have increased.

The second type of currency risk is the effect of the exchange rate on the cash flows of a project converted into a different currency from that of the host country. The possible cash flows in the host currency are now taken as given, so the effect of economic exposure is already recognised, in the host-currency cash flows. But the values of these cash flows in another currency will depend on the exchange rate with that currency. This is the risk we analysed in Section 11.1. The currency in which present value is estimated will matter, in theory, if purchasing power parity does not hold, and if capital markets are segmented.

Political risk
There could be various political risks to the remittable cash flows from a foreign project; for example, the foreign government might block transfers of funds to the parent at a given time, or might even take over the project. We have assumed earlier that project valuation is carried out by discounting the expected cash flows net of expected corporation tax, ignoring interest (Section 6.3). The governing principle of this method is that all factors

affecting the amounts of future cash flows are reflected in the expected values and associated probability distributions of the cash flows to be discounted, except personal taxes and savings in corporation tax from interest. To be consistent with the method, the uncertainties about cash flows arising from political risk should be captured in the forecast foreign-currency cash flows. This treatment is recommended in most texts and in Lessard's (1996) discussion of country risk. With this treatment, political risk does not affect the cost of capital unless it affects the estimated systematic risk of the cash flows.

However, it is, or at least used to be, common practice for companies to allow for political risk by adding a 'foreign risk premium' to the discount rate for foreign projects (Copeland et al., 2000, p. 347; Eiteman et al., 1998, p. 589). If the discount rate is adjusted for political risk then the expected cash flows should not be adjusted for political risk, to avoid double counting.

Foreign borrowing and corporation tax

It is usual to regard borrowing by a wholly owned foreign project as effectively forming part of the parent's total debt, regardless of whether the parent has contractually guaranteed the project's debt. The parent decides its optimal amount of debt, and, within this total, the amount of borrowing by any particular project is influenced by project- and country-specific agency and other factors. For example, the parent will seek to take advantage of host-country subsidies for local borrowing. Of course, the amount of external debt carried by the project will affect the cash flows available for the parent and will affect the project's cost of equity.

Ignoring non-tax factors and ignoring personal tax, the effect of leverage on the project's weighted average cost of capital is via the corporation tax saving of interest. But there is an extra twist to the analysis in the setting of a multinational company. Senbet (1979) analyses the effect of differences in corporation tax across countries for a multinational that has fixed its total level of investment (so total operating cash flows are fixed). The multinational is making decisions about how much and where to borrow. Senbet assumes for simplicity that the project's debt is risk-free and first shows that, ignoring tax, unsubsidised foreign borrowing will not affect the project's value. The Modigliani–Miller theory holds, unless real risk-free rates differ between the parent and host countries. He then supposes that real risk-free rates are the same, but that the corporation tax rate is higher in the foreign country, and that the higher foreign tax cannot be used to relieve domestic tax. The higher foreign tax has two opposing effects. It reduces the project's value relative to a situation in which the foreign tax rate is equal to the domestic tax rate. But it also means that there is a larger tax advantage to foreign debt. Senbet assumes that interest on debt is allowed to relieve local corporation tax only up to the interest on an amount of debt equal to the host-currency value of the project. Since he assumes that the parent's total investment is given, its choices are the location of its productive assets, and how much and where to borrow. All the assets have the same business risk. His model implies that the parent's choices regarding where to produce and where to borrow would be interdependent. The parent faces trade-offs: borrowing more in one country to obtain a tax saving at a high rate of corporation tax means producing more in that country, which means producing less in a country with a lower tax rate. The parent's capital structure now includes a new dimension of where the parent borrows, which affects where it produces and which affects the weighted average cost of capital of a project.

Risky governments

There is appreciable risk of default in lending to many governments, and this can cause a problem when it comes to estimating the cost of capital of a project within that country. Then government debt cannot be treated as a risk-free asset; in fact, it is conceivable – in some cases – that investment in a project's equity would be less risky than lending to the host government. Copeland et al. (2000, pp. 391–93) present three methods of estimating a nominal risk-free rate in the currency concerned – say, currency A. The simplest is to take the yield on US government bonds and to add the difference between inflation in country A and inflation in the USA. The same could be done using the bonds of any other country the government of which is assessed as having zero default risk. Alternatively, method 1 above, in which project value is estimated in the parent's domestic currency, bypasses the problem (if the parent's head office is in a country with a safe government).

WACC versus APV

In the case of a foreign project with debt, the adjusted present value method (Section 7.5.4) is probably recommended by a majority of authors over the weighted average cost of capital, including Brealey and Myers (2003), Eun and Resnick (2001), Levi (1990) and Sercu and Uppal (1995). Levi, for example, prefers APV because of 'the more explicit nature of allowance for complexities and the ability to use APV to see whether projects are profitable even before allowance is made for complexities' (p. 364). In Levi's presentation, the expression for the present value of a foreign project includes several separate cash flow items, with their own item-specific discount rates, in addition to the tax savings from interest. The separate cash flow items include depreciation allowances, savings from transfer pricing within the parent group and the illegal repatriation of income to the parent. APV can be estimated in either the host currency or the parent currency.

11.3   Summary

The existence of more than one country implies modification to the analysis of the cost of equity and to the analysis of project valuation. The first part of the chapter reviewed the determination of the expected return on equity under three sets of assumptions: an integrated capital market in the context of a world economy in which purchasing power parity holds; an integrated capital market and purchasing power parity does not hold; and segmented capital markets. Various types of evidence on integration were summarised, and the evidence indicates that markets are segmented to some extent. However, there are reasons for thinking that capital markets are becoming more integrated. These reasons include the rapid increase in international portfolio investment in the 1990s and the steps taken in many countries both to make their capital markets more open to foreign investors and to encourage international investment by investing institutions.

The second part of the chapter discussed the cost of equity for a foreign project. Valuation of the project can be carried out either from the perspective of the parent company, in the domestic currency of the parent, or in the currency of the project's host country using a host-country discount rate. The two approaches will give the same answer if capital markets are assumed to be integrated, but not if they are assumed to be segmented.

Appendix 11.1: Errunza and Losq's model

The argument starts with an assertion of the risk/return relations for restricted and unrestricted investors. The subset of restricted (country A) investors will hold quantities of freely traded assets such that the risk premiums on the vector of all free assets are given by

$$E(\underline{R}_{free}) - R_F = \alpha_{res} \operatorname{cov}\left(\underline{R}_{free}, \underline{V}_{res}^T \underline{R}_{free}\right) \tag{A11.1}$$

where $E(\underline{R}_{free})$ is the vector of expected returns on freely traded assets (country A's), R_F is the risk-free return, α_{res} is the coefficient of absolute risk aversion for the group of restricted investors (in country A), $\underline{V}_{res}^T$ is the transposed vector of the amounts of each asset held by restricted investors and $\underline{R}_{free}$ is the vector of the returns on each freely traded asset. In equation (A11.1), risk is measured by the covariance of the return on the asset with the pay-off on the total portfolio of the restricted investors. Equation (A11.1) states that, in equilibrium, the expected return on each asset is determined by the risk multiplied by a constant α_{res} that specifies the expected return required per unit of risk. Similarly, unrestricted investors (in country B) will hold quantities of all assets such that the risk premium on any asset is given by

$$E(R) - R_F = \alpha_{unres} \operatorname{cov}\left(R, \underline{V}_{unres}^T R\right) \tag{A11.2}$$

where $E(R)$ is the expected return on any asset, α_{unres} is the coefficient of risk aversion for unrestricted investors and $\underline{V}_{unres}^T$ is the transposed vector of the amounts of each asset held by unrestricted investors.

The authors prove that, in equilibrium, the risk premium on any freely traded asset will be

$$E(R_{free}) - R_F = \alpha M \operatorname{cov}(R_{free}, R_M) \tag{A11.3}$$

where α is the coefficient of absolute risk aversion for the aggregate population of investors, M is the value of the 'world market portfolio' of free and segmented assets and R_M is the uncertain return of the world market. The risk premium on a segmented asset – one that cannot be traded by restricted investors – will be

$$E(R_{seg}) - R_F = \alpha M \operatorname{cov}(R_{seg}, R_M) + (\alpha_{unres} - \alpha) M_{seg} \operatorname{cov}[(R_{seg}, R_{Mseg}) | \underline{R}_{free}] \tag{A11.4}$$

where R_{seg} is the expected return on a segmented asset, M_{seg} is the value of the segmented market portfolio, $\operatorname{cov}[(R_{seg}, R_{Mseg}) | R_{free}]$ means $\operatorname{cov}(R_{seg}, R_{Mseg})$ given the rates of return on freely traded assets and $\alpha_{unres} - \alpha \geq 0$. Comparing equations (A11.3) and (A11.4), it can be seen that the risk premium on a segmented asset will exceed that on a free asset of the same risk in relation to the world market, $\text{cov}(R_{\text{free}}, R_{\text{M}})$.

The proof works by showing that, if the two groups of investors hold portfolios that satisfy equations (A11.1) and (A11.2), and that satisfy the market-clearing condition that there is no excess supply of assets, then the assets must be priced so that equations (A11.3) and (A11.4) hold. The portfolios that satisfy the conditions are shown to be $(\alpha/\alpha_{\text{res}})(M_{\text{free}} + DP)$ for restricted investors and $(1 - \alpha/\alpha_{\text{res}})M + (\alpha/\alpha_{\text{res}})\,HP$ for unrestricted investors. M_{free} is the portfolio of all the freely traded assets. DP is the 'diversification portfolio' of free assets that is most highly correlated with the segmented market. It is defined by the vector

$$\underline{DP} = VAR_{\text{free}}^{-1} COV_{\text{free,seg}} \underline{V}_{\text{seg}}$$

where VAR_{free}^{-1} is the inverse of the variance-covariance matrix for free assets, $COV_{\text{free,seg}}$ is a matrix of the covariances between the free and the segmented assets and $\underline{V}_{\text{seg}}$ is the vector of values of the segmented assets ($= M_{\text{seg}}$). HP is the 'hedged portfolio' that has no correlation with any of the free assets. It is defined by the vector

$$\underline{HP} = \underline{V}_{\text{seg}} - \underline{DP}$$

Using $\underline{V}_{\text{seg}} = M_{\text{seg}}$, and $M = M_{\text{free}} + M_{\text{seg}}$, it is straightforward to verify that the sum of the portfolios held by restricted and unrestricted investors is equal to the world market portfolio M, and therefore that the market-clearing condition is satisfied.

The portfolio of restricted investors needs to be consistent with what might be called the CAPM for restricted investors, equation (A11.1), and with the CAPM for free assets, equation (A11.3). To check that it is, we substitute the portfolio of restricted investors $(\alpha/\alpha_{\text{res}})(M_{\text{free}} + DP)$ for $\underline{V}_{\text{res}}^T$ in the covariance term in equation (A11.1):

$$\begin{aligned}
\text{cov}(\underline{R}_{\text{free}}, \underline{V}_{\text{res}}^T \underline{R}_{\text{free}}) &= (\alpha/\alpha_{\text{res}})\left[\text{cov}\left(\underline{R}_{\text{free}}, \underline{M}_{\text{free}}^T \underline{R}_{\text{free}}\right) + \text{cov}\left(\underline{R}_{\text{free}}, \underline{DP}^T \underline{R}_{\text{free}}\right)\right] \\
&= (\alpha/\alpha_{\text{res}})\left[\text{cov}\left(\underline{R}_{\text{free}}, M_{\text{free}} R_{\text{Mfree}}\right) + VAR_{\text{free}} VAR_{\text{free}}^{-1} COV_{\text{free,seg}} \underline{V}_{\text{seg}}\right] \\
&= (\alpha/\alpha_{\text{res}})[\text{cov}\left(\underline{R}_{\text{free}}, M_{\text{free}} R_{\text{Mfree}}\right) + \text{cov}(\underline{R}_{\text{free}}, M_{\text{seg}} R_{\text{Mseg}})] \\
&= (\alpha/\alpha_{\text{res}})\text{cov}(\underline{R}_{\text{free}}, M_{\text{free}} R_{\text{Mfree}} + M_{\text{seg}} R_{\text{Mseg}}) \\
&= (\alpha/\alpha_{\text{res}})\text{cov}(\underline{R}_{\text{free}}, M R_{\text{M}}) \qquad\qquad\qquad\qquad\qquad (A11.5)
\end{aligned}$$

The first and fourth lines use the fact that $\text{cov}[x, (y + z)] = \text{cov}(x, y) + \text{cov}(x, z)$ and the second line uses the definition of the diversification portfolio $\underline{DP}$. Substituting equation (A11.5) for a given free asset into equation (A11.1) gives equation (A11.3). This shows that restricted investors will price free assets to give an expected risk premium given by equation (A11.3). It can be shown in a similar manner that unrestricted investors will require risk premiums on free and segmented assets given by equations (A11.3) and (A11.4).

Finally, the reason why $\alpha_{\text{unres}} - \alpha \geq 0$ is that α, the coefficient of risk aversion for the aggregate population of investors, is defined by

$$1/\alpha = 1/\alpha_{\text{unres}} + 1/\alpha_{\text{res}} \qquad\qquad\qquad\qquad\qquad (A11.6)$$

This specification means that the risk aversion of investors in aggregate will always be less than the risk aversion of either group. Equation (A11.6) can be rearranged to give

$$\alpha_{\text{unres}} = \alpha(1 + \alpha_{\text{unres}}/\alpha_{\text{res}})$$

It can be seen that, for $\alpha_{\text{unres}} \geq 0$ and $\alpha_{\text{res}} \geq 0$, $\alpha_{\text{unres}} \geq \alpha$. It will also be true that $\alpha_{\text{res}} \geq \alpha$. The definition of α is a key assumption in the model, which is made without comment.

Appendix 11.2: Testing the conditional CAPM

One way of testing the standard CAPM is first to calculate a series of prediction errors – i.e. actual returns less the returns predicted by the CAPM for each share j:

$$e_{jt} = R_{jt}^e - \beta_j R_{Mt}^e \tag{A11.7}$$

and then to test the relation across shares between the errors and the betas. The standard CAPM predicts that the errors should be independent of the betas; there should be no relation between them. To see this, suppose that there is in fact no support for the model; there is no relation between betas and observed returns. Then a significantly negative cross-sectional relation would be found between betas and the errors from equation (A11.7).

Tests of the conditional international CAPM are on similar lines but more complex. The prediction errors for the world and domestic markets are calculated from

$$
\begin{aligned}
e_{\text{worldt}} &= R_{\text{worldt}}^e - E\big(R_{\text{worldt}}^e \big| I_{t-1}\big) \\
e_{\text{dom1},t} &= R_{\text{dom1},t}^e - E\big(R_{\text{dom1},t}^e \big| I_{t-1}\big) \\
e_{\text{dom2},t} &= R_{\text{dom2},t}^e - E\big(R_{\text{dom2},t}^e \big| I_{t-1}\big) \\
&\quad \cdots \cdots \\
e_{\text{domn},t} &= R_{\text{domn},t}^e - E\big(R_{\text{domn},t}^e \big| I_{t-1}\big)
\end{aligned}
\tag{A11.8}
$$

for the world market and n domestic stock markets. To calculate these errors, it is necessary to specify a model of the conditional expected returns on the world market and on the domestic markets. This requires choosing the relevant information variables in the list I, and estimating the sensitivities between the expected returns and each information variable. This is normally done by first estimating a multifactor regression model of the form

$$R_{Mt}^e = \beta_{M0} + \beta_{M,F1} Factor_{1t-1} + \beta_{M,F2} Factor_{2t-1} + \cdots + e_{Mt}$$

where $Factor_{nt-1}$ is the value on date $t-1$ of the nth factor with which future returns on the market M are supposed to be correlated. Here M stands for the world market or for one of the domestic markets. Factors used in tests are similar to those used in other multifactor models of expected returns (Section 13.5) – for example, the market dividend yield and the lagged excess return on the market in question. Having estimated the sensitivity (beta) of a market's excess returns to each factor, the expected excess return for a given period t is estimated as

$$E\big(R_{Mt}^e \big| I_{t-1}\big) = \beta_{M,1} Factor_{1t-1} + \beta_{M,2} Factor_{2t-1} + \cdots \tag{A11.9}$$

Since the values of the factors change over time, so does $E(R^e_{M,t}|I_{t-1})$. The conditional means (over time) of the expected excess returns on the world and domestic markets can then be estimated, together with the conditional covariances of the domestic markets with the world market, and the conditional variance of the world market.

The conditional multifactor model is then tested by seeing whether the errors in equation (A11.8) are independent of the expected returns, as estimated by equations of the form of (A11.9). This in itself is a straightforward test of a time-varying multifactor model, as Bekaert (1995) notes. The conditional international CAPM is specifically tested for each domestic market by seeing whether, given the estimated conditional expected returns and conditional variance of the world market, and given the conditional covariance with the domestic market in question, the errors are independent of the expected returns as estimated by equation (11.8):

$$e_{domt} = R^e_{domt} - \frac{\text{cov}\left(R^e_{domt}, R^e_{worldt}\big|I_{t-1}\right)}{\text{var}(R_{worldt}|I_{t-1})} E\left(R^e_{worldt}|I_{t-1}\right)$$

(Harvey, 1991, pp. 112–15); see equation (A11.7) (the test of the standard CAPM). That is, does the general form of the conditional CAPM hold true using estimates of conditional expected returns rather than observed returns to estimates betas for domestic markets? The answer is a qualified 'yes' for developed markets, and 'no', as yet, for emerging markets.

Various other questions can also be examined. For example, although the conditional model allows the market price of risk λ_{dom} to vary over time (equation (11.4)), λ_{dom} should be the same across markets, if they are integrated. This is not the case, which is interpreted as a symptom of segmentation. Harvey (1995) provides a helpful overview of tests of the extent to which returns on emerging markets can be explained by international single- and multifactor asset pricing models.

Part III
Estimating the Cost of Capital

12 The cost of equity: inference from present value

The third part of the book turns to estimation of a project's cost of capital in practice. Parts I and II have been about understanding how the cost of capital is determined. Part III is about methods by which we can measure what the cost of capital is.

The first two chapters, 12 and 13, consider methods of estimating the cost of equity of a listed company. The current chapter starts with a brief review of evidence on the methods used in practice. Most of the remainder is concerned with the implementation of procedures whereby the expected return on a share is inferred from the combination of its price and of forecasts of future cash pay-offs from the share. A long-standing method is to rearrange the dividend discount model of share value, and we consider this approach in some detail. More recently a method has been developed whereby the discount rate is inferred from the combination of the book value of the equity and of estimates of the company's future 'abnormal earnings'.

Chapter 13, which follows, is also about methods of estimating the cost of equity of a listed company. It deals with the use of the standard CAPM for this purpose, and also with the implementation of three multifactor models of expected returns.

Chapter 14 is a guide to the estimation of the weighted average cost of capital of a project with no traded equity. The chapter goes through the choices to be made at each stage in the process, which will include the estimation of the cost of equity of a listed company. It also summarises evidence on the actual practices of company executives, and offers a ranking of the importance of various decisions to be made in arriving at an estimate of a project's WACC.

The final chapter considers the special and important case of the cost of equity of regulated utilities. A distinguishing feature of regulated utilities is that the actions of the regulator can affect the utility's cost of equity.

General discussions that focus on estimation in practice include, for the cost of equity, those by Davies, Unni, Draper and Paudyal (1999) and Cornell, Hirshleifer and James (1997) and, for the weighted average cost of capital, Copeland, Koller and Murrin (2000), Damodaran (1999, chap. 4), Ehrhardt (1994) and Water Services Association (1991). Texts that offer extensive practical discussion of the cost of capital in various places include those by Arnold (2002), Brealey and Myers (2003), Grinblatt and Titman (2002) and Patterson (1995).

12.1   Estimation of the cost of equity in practice

Evidence

Surveys are conducted from time to time into the methods of valuation and capital budgeting actually employed by companies and investment bankers. Further evidence comes from the deliberations of utility regulators (Chapter 15).

The most recent large-scale survey of company practice in the United States is that by Graham and Harvey (2001). Their findings come from questionnaire returns from the chief financial officers of 392 companies, 61 per cent of which are listed. Several methods to estimate the company's cost of equity are in use, before any adjustment for project-specific leverage or business risk. The methods used always or almost always are: CAPM (73 per cent of respondents); arithmetic average historic returns on the company's shares (39 per cent); CAPM with extra risk factors (34 per cent); dividend discount model (16 per cent); 'whatever our investors tell us they require' (14 per cent); and regulatory decisions (7 per cent, which is the proportion of the respondents that are regulated utilities). The main difference from earlier US surveys is that the standard CAPM has become more popular and the dividend discount model less popular.

Another recent US survey, by Bruner, Eades, Harris and Higgins (1998), is based on telephone interviews with executives in twenty-seven large companies noted by their peers for their financial sophistication, and with mergers and acquisitions (M&A) advisers in ten investment banks. The study reports that twenty-two of the companies and eight of the M&A advisers use the CAPM to estimate the cost of equity. The remaining methods used are multifactor models and the dividend discount model. 'A glaring result is that few respondents specifically cited use of any forward-looking method to supplement or replace reading the tea leaves of past returns' (p. 23), the only forward-looking method cited being the dividend discount model.

Survey evidence from the United Kingdom also suggests that the CAPM has become the most common method of estimating the cost of equity. McLaney, Pointon, Tucker and Thomas (2004) received questionnaire responses from finance executives at 193 UK listed companies: 47 per cent use the CAPM, 27 per cent use the dividend discount model and, perhaps surprisingly, 27 per cent use earnings yield. Rutterford (2000) obtained evidence from interviews with the finance directors of eighteen of the largest hundred UK companies: fourteen use the CAPM, five use the dividend discount model and four use 'the historic real rate of return on equity'; five companies use more than one method.

Cornell et al. (1997) discuss approaches to estimating the cost of equity that are used by regulatory bodies in the United States. The choice is either the dividend discount model or the CAPM; apparently, no other methods are seriously considered. The dividend discount model is given more weight as it is considered to be the more reliable method by regulators and courts.

Discussion

Let us reflect briefly on the methods mentioned in the above recent surveys. The methods infer the cost of equity from data of some sort, with the following two exceptions. The first is *seeking the views of shareholders*. There should be nothing wrong in principle with asking the views of a group of shareholders, assuming they are believed to be representative of the company's shareholders as a whole (or, better, the company's marginal shareholders). It is true that shareholders sometimes report that they are expecting rates of return that seem unreasonable, at least in hindsight (Ilmanen, 2003, reports some examples). Dimson, Marsh and Staunton (2002, p. 179) write that

we could in principle simply ask investors . . . but mostly [surveys] provide a source of amusement rather than useful information. Private investors' opinions appear to reflect what has happened in the recent past, or even sheer fantasy. Professional money managers seem (at best) to provide answers that reproduce, with some noise, the evidence from long-run historical studies. That approach is unlikely to inform us about the market's expectations.

Yet expected rates of return are set by the actual investment decisions of investors, and it is conceivable that their actual expectations may not be second-guessed accurately by academics or others. Suppose there were only one investor. He/she tells you, when asked, that he/she requires an expected rate of return on equity of 50 per cent p.a., and, furthermore, he/she buys shares at prices which imply that the expected rate is 50 per cent p.a. In that case this *is* the cost of equity, however irrationally high it may seem. And, yet, we might baulk at accepting a figure that seems too unreasonable (see Section 2.4.2).

The second exception to an estimate based on data is a *regulatory decision*. It should be noted that a regulatory decision results from the application of one or more of the other methods to estimate the cost of equity, usually the dividend discount model in the United States. In principle, regulators do not set the cost of equity themselves. Their role is to ensure that the companies they regulate do not make earnings that exceed the cost of equity determined by investors, and inferred via the dividend discount model.

The remaining methods infer the cost of equity from data. Use of the *arithmetic mean of a sample of past returns on the company's shares* is a simple method that relies on the assumptions that the mean return observed in the past is a good proxy for the rate of return expected by investors in the past, and that the expected rate of return on the share today is similar to the expected rate in the past. It would be better to work in real terms, unless inflation is believed to be and to have been constant. The trouble with this method is that it calls for an ad hoc adjustment if the assumptions are felt not to apply – for example, if the average share returns have been 'too large' or, alternatively, negative in the recent past.

The prospective *earning yield* is the predicted profit after tax per share divided by the current share price. The use of the earnings yield to estimate the cost of equity rests on the idea that the expected market return on a share (dividend plus change in share price as a percentage of the previous price) can be proxied by the expected accounting return on the share. The trouble here is that the expected accounting return is not a correct proxy for the expected market return, as will be explained in Section 12.2.2. Probably because company executives recognise this, earnings yield is a much less popular method of estimation than it used to be.

The remaining methods are the dividend discount model, the CAPM and multifactor models. We shall discuss these methods in detail, because they are generally felt to provide the best estimates of the cost of equity. The *dividend discount model* is used to infer a company's cost of equity from the share price and from forecast dividends and other cash flows to shareholders. The main difficulty lies in forecasting the future dividends and cash flows. The *CAPM* does not require forecasts of dividends but does require an estimate of the risk-free rate, the equity risk premium and the share's beta. If a *multifactor model* is used, the premium and beta are needed for each factor.

Neither the dividend discount model nor the CAPM/multifactor methods can be applied directly to a project or a company with no traded shares in issue. The dividend discount model requires the market value to be known, but it is the project's value that we are trying to estimate. The CAPM requires an estimate of the project's beta, but a project has no share price data from which to calculate beta. For now we put aside the problem of projects and companies without traded equity. We return to this problem in Chapter 15.

12.2   The dividend discount model

12.2.1   Method

The familiar dividend discount (or dividend growth or Gordon growth) model of share valuation is the general discounted cash flow model applied to equity. It says that the value of a share is equal to the present value of all future cash payments to which the share gives entitlement. Assuming that the company exists in perpetuity, we have

$$P_0 = \mathrm{E}(Div_1)/(1 + R_\mathrm{E}) + \mathrm{E}(Div_2)/(1 + R_\mathrm{E})^2 + \cdots$$
$$= \Sigma_{t=1}^{\infty}\mathrm{E}(Div_t)/(1 + R_\mathrm{E})^t \tag{12.1}$$

where P_0 is the current share price, Div_t is the dividend (or any other cash flow to shareholders) per share before personal tax at date t, and R_E is the company's cost of equity, assumed to be constant for now. For value to be finite, it must be that, as $t \to \infty$, $Div_t/(1 + R_\mathrm{E})^t \to 0$. We can think for simplicity of each period as being one year. Then equation (12.1) gives the value of a share that pays an annual dividend, with the next dividend being due in one year's time. If it is assumed that dividends grow at a constant annual rate g and that Div_1 is certain, equation (12.1) becomes

$$P_0 = Div_1/(1 + R_\mathrm{E}) + Div_1(1 + g)/(1 + R_\mathrm{E})^2 + \cdots$$
$$= \Sigma_{t=1}^{\infty}Div_1(1 + g)^{t-1}/(1 + R_\mathrm{E})^t \tag{12.2}$$

For value to be finite, we must have $g < R_\mathrm{E}$. Subtracting $P_0(1 + g)/(1 + R_\mathrm{E})$ from both sides gives

$$P_0 - P_0(1 + g)/(1 + R_\mathrm{E}) = Div_1/(1 + R_\mathrm{E}) - Div_1(1 + g)^t/(1 + R_\mathrm{E})^{t+1}$$

The subtraction of $P_0(1 + g)/(1 + R_\mathrm{E})$ on the right-hand side substitutes the right-hand side of equation (12.2) for P_0. The last term on the right-hand side approaches zero as t becomes large. Ignoring this term and solving for P_0,

$$P_0 = \frac{Div_1/(1 + R_E)}{1 - (1 + g)/(1 + R_E)}$$
$$= Div_1/(R_E - g)$$

This is the way the dividend discount model is usually written. Rearrangement gives an expression for the cost of equity,

$$R_E = Div_1/P_0 + g \tag{12.3}$$

Equation (12.3) says that a company's cost of equity is given by the prospective dividend yield on its shares plus the long-term growth rate g of dividend per share. The share price will also grow at rate g, so dividend yield will stay constant.

It is common to use a two- or three-stage model in which the growth rate is forecast to change at some future date. For example, the analyst might forecast actual dividends over a horizon of T years, after which growth is assumed to be the forecast long-term growth rate of the whole economy. In this case, equation (12.2) becomes

$$P_0 = \Sigma_{t=1}^{T} Div_t/(1 + R_E)^t + [Div_{T+1}/(R_E - g)][1/(1 + R_E)^T]$$

This and other multi-stage formulas cannot be simplifed, but R_E can be found by trial and error on a spreadsheet.

What equation (12.3) does is to infer the cost of equity from an assumed future stream of cash flows to a share, combined with the known market value of those cash flows, namely the share price. It infers the internal rate of return on the equity at market value, as is clear from equation (12.1). The procedure rests on the principle that, in equilibrium, the cost of equity is equal to the expected rate of return on the market value of the equity, and on any other asset of the same risk. This assumes that markets are efficient; P_0 is assumed to be a rational best guess of the share's true value – i.e. the estimated present value of the cash flows to the share. If market efficiency is not assumed, equation (12.1) cannot explain the value of the share and equation (12.3) cannot be used to infer the rate of return that investors require to hold the share.

The dividend discount model gives the correct expected rate of return on a share in theory under certainty, and under some characterisations of uncertainty (discussed below). It is also a simple model. The disadvantage from a theoretical perspective is that it does no more than 'back out' what the expected rate of return on a share must be, given its future dividends and market value. It provides no insight into why the share has the market price that it is observed to have. In particular, equation (12.3) includes no measure of risk. It also understates the one-period expected return, which is generally taken to be what the cost of equity means, in theory (Section 5.3.1). The disadvantage from a practical perspective is that the future dividends have to be estimated. The problem is likely to be worse if the firm is not paying a dividend.

Equation (12.3) is potentially confusing, because it makes it look as though the cost of equity is sensitive to the dividend yield and to the long-term growth rate. In fact, it is P_0 that is a function of the cost of equity, and of the expected cash flows captured by Div_1

and g (equation (12.2)). The cost of equity is not a function of the expected values of the cash flows (though it is a function of their risk). Equation (12.3) states what R_E must be, given the observed P_0 and given one's estimates of Div_1 and g. The problem is that we do not know the value of g used by 'the market' to value a share. The fact that the cost of equity inferred from equation (12.3) varies with one's estimate of g does not mean that, conceptually, the cost of equity is sensitive to the growth rate of future dividends. It means that the inference made via equation (12.3) about the estimated size of the cost of equity depends on the assumption made about the growth rate forecast by the market.

Equation (12.3) might also make it look as though dividend policy affects the cost of equity; a higher dividend pay-out implies a higher value of Div_1. However, a higher pay-out implies a lower growth rate of dividend per share, because more shares must be issued in the future to finance the firm's growth. The two effects must 'cancel out', given the firm's investment policy, which determines its underlying cash flows. So the value of Div_1 has no effect on R_E, ignoring personal taxes (Miller and Modigliani, 1961).

If the company does not pay a dividend, equation (12.1) still applies and it is still possible to infer the discount rate given the price and the forecast of dividends when they start to be paid (a company that will never pay a dividend has zero value). But the discount rate obviously cannot be inferred via the short cut of equation (12.3).

12.2.2   Elaboration

Uncertain dividends

To arrive at equation (12.3), we made an assumption that future dividends are known for certain. If dividends are assumed to be uncertain, equation (12.3) is correct under some, but not all, assumptions about the nature of the uncertainty (and continuing to assume a constant discount rate). Two possibilities are as follows. Suppose

$$Div_T = Div_1[1 + E_0(g)]^{T-1} + e_T$$

for each date T periods ahead, where e_T is a random error. Div_1 is certain and the expected value of g is constant. Then

$$E_0(Div_T) = E_0[Div_1(1 + g)^{T-1}] + E_0(e_T)$$
$$= Div_1(1 + g)^{T-1}$$

in which case equation (12.3) can be used. The assumption of constant growth is consistent with the underlying expected values of future dividends, and the expected dividend can be treated as a certain dividend. A second possibility is if

$$Div_T = Div_{T-1}(1 + g + e_T)$$

where e_T is a random error. In this case dividend realisations form a random walk with upward drift. Taking the expectations that

$$E_{T-1}(Div_T) = E_{T-1}[Div_{T-1}(1 + g + e_T)]$$
$$= Div_{T-1}(1 + g)$$

so

$$E_0(Div_T) = Div_1(1 + g)^{T-1}$$

assuming Div_1 is certain. Again, equation (12.3) can be used. But the equation will not be correct if future dividends are assumed to show serial correlation, nor if Div_1 is uncertain and correlated with $1 + g$ (Water Services Association, 1991, appendix 5).

Growth forecasts: analysts

The valuation model (equation (12.1)) takes forecast dividends as given; it is a further step to say where they come from. An obvious source is equity analysts. Forecasts of earnings and dividends per share by equity analysts will usually be available, at a price, for companies listed on a stock market. For example, the Institutional Brokers Estimate System (IBES) compiles investment analysts' consensus (average) forecasts of annual earnings for up to the next five years, for larger listed companies across the world. Analysts' forecasts do not extend beyond a horizon of a few years, so an estimate of the growth rate beyond the analysts' horizon will be needed. The estimate of g should be an estimate of the market's forecast of g that is implicit in the current share price. More precisely, it is the forecast of marginal (price-setting) investors that is needed. Analysts' forecasts are being used as a proxy for the forecasts of marginal investors. It may be that an individual investor disagrees with the analysts' forecasts, but, for the purpose of using equation (12.3) to estimate the cost of equity, he/she should use his/her best guess of what the market thinks g is, rather than what he/she him- herself thinks g is.

A common recommendation, at least in older books, is to use the growth rate of dividend per share measured over the last few years as the forecast of future g. But a suitable track record may not exist, and, even if it does, it may be hard to interpret – for example, if there has been a recent major change in dividend per share. More generally, the past growth rate should be seen as one of many pieces of information that go into investors' estimates of future g. If the growth rate seems likely to change in the future, then the forecast g, or gs in a multi-stage model, should certainly reflect this probable change. There is evidence that analysts' forecasts of growth rates are more accurate than extrapolations of historic growth rates and that changes in analysts' forecasts affect share prices, presumably because they affect investors' expectations about future cash flows (Patterson, 1995, chap. 4 reviews this evidence).

The cost of equity inferred is sensitive to the growth forecasts, especially if consensus earnings or dividend growth forecasts for the next few years are used as the long-term g in equation (12.3). There can be considerable variation in the inferred costs of equity of apparently similar companies – for example, regulated utilities in the same business with similar leverage (Myers and Borucki, 1994). There can also be considerable variation in the cost of equity for the same company over a period of a few years. For example, the cost of equity for British Petroleum plc jumped from 14 per cent p.a. in 1989 to 37 per cent p.a. in 1990, using equation (12.3) and the IBES consensus forecast growth rate in earnings for the next two years to estimate g (Davies et al., 1999, p. 96). In view of these unsettling variations in estimates over time and across companies, several authors recommend using an average of the estimated costs of equity of a sample of similar companies, including the company in question, rather than relying on the single estimate for that company (e.g. Cornell et al., 1997; Myers and Borucki, 1994). The sensitivity to short-term forecasts is also reduced by using a two-stage model, in which a long-term growth forecast is assumed after a date a few years into the future. Reasonable estimates of long-term growth rates will normally vary less across similar companies and over time than estimates of short-term growth rates. If the benchmark sample includes companies with appreciably different leverage, the costs of equity for such companies should be adjusted so as to provide estimates that would have applied had the companies had the same leverage as the company in question (see Chapter 14).

Growth forecasts: sustainable growth rate

An alternative approach to forecasting g is to specify a mechanical process that is assumed to generate future dividends. The sustainable growth rate formulation links the valuation model to a process representing a highly stylised vision of projects and corporate investment. It assumes a constant retention ratio and a constant return on equity:

$$g = (EPS_2 - EPS_1)/EPS_1$$
$$= (retEPS_1)ROE/EPS_1$$
$$= retROE \tag{12.4}$$

where EPS_1 is next year's earnings per share after corporation tax; ret is the retention ratio – the proportion of EPS retained; and ROE is the (accounting) return on equity, defined as the profit after tax for the year divided by the book value of the equity at the start of the year. Substituting equation (12.4) in (12.3) gives

$$R_E = (1 - ret)EPS_1/P_0 + retROE \tag{12.5}$$

An assumption of constant g implies constant ret and constant ROE. If the retention ratio is forecast to change, the growth rates of earnings and dividends will differ from each other; if the return on equity is forecast to change, the growth rate of earnings will change. A multi-stage model will be needed in either case.

Equation (12.5) assumes implicitly that all new investment is financed by retentions. If some future investment is forecast to come from share issues, and if forecast $ROE > R_E$, then $retROE$ underestimates g, the growth rate of dividends for existing shareholders. The reason is that existing shareholders gain some of the net present value created by the investment financed by issuing new shares. In this case equation (12.5) requires amendment (Miller and Modigliani, 1961).

Equation (12.2) sees a company as a financial asset providing a claim to a growing stream of cash flows. Equation (12.5) generates the growing cash flows by assuming that the company has a project that provides a level perpetuity, with provision for a proportion of the future level cash flows to be invested in identical projects in the future.

Example

Consider a project that requires an investment of £1,000 and that provides a payment after one year of £100, growing at 10 per cent p.a. in perpetuity. The dividend discount formulation treats this as a single investment in a financial asset:

	Year 0	Year 1	Year 2	Year 3	
Cash flow	−£1,000	£100	£110	£121	...
Asset value		£1,100	£1,210	£1,331	...

The internal rate of return (IRR) is 20 per cent p.a. Under the sustainable growth formulation, the same pay-offs are achieved from an initial investment of £1,000 in a project that provides a level perpetuity of 20 per cent p.a., together with provision to invest half the cash flow each year in identical new projects:

Year 0	Year 1	Year 2	Year 3	
−£1,000	£200	£200	£200	...
	£100 paid			
	£100 retained	£20	£20	...
		£110 paid		
		£110 retained	£22	...
			£121 paid	
			£121 retained	

The (one-period) return on equity is constant and equal to the IRR on the initial investment. We can see that a growth forecast based on the sustainable growth rate will be reasonable only to the extent that it is reasonable to assume that the return on equity on retained profit will remain constant. The trouble is that a constant return on equity implies that the percentage returns on existing and new investments are the same level in perpetuity. If the returns on an investment are not a level perpetuity – i.e. almost always – the forecast returns on equity will neither be constant nor equal to the forecast IRR on the investment (Fisher and McGowan, 1983). Over the life of a single project, the returns on equity per period will differ dramatically from the IRR. So a constant return on equity can be tenable only as an approximation. The sustainable growth formulation is useful for providing insight into where the value of a company's equity comes from (e.g. Brealey and Myers, 2003, chap. 4). But it will not always be the best approach to forecasting the growth of an actual company.

Earnings yield and cost of equity

A company's earnings yield is sometimes used as a rough guide to its cost of equity. The (prospective) earnings yield is EPS_1/P_0; next year's earnings per share after corporation tax divided by the current share price. However, the earnings yield does not, in theory, give the expected return on the share, because it is not a correct model of the expected return. We can demonstrate this by showing that earnings yield will generally give a different figure for the expected return from the figure provided by the dividend discount model, which is a correct model in theory. Writing the dividend discount model in terms of earnings, we have

$$P_0 = EPS_1(1 - ret)/(R_E - g)$$
$$EPS_1/P_0 = (R_E - g)/(1 - ret) \tag{12.6}$$

For most sets of values of R_E, g and ret, $EPS_1/P_0 \neq R_E$, and the difference can be substantial. In fact, earnings yield is a correct measure of the cost of equity only if either of two extremely unlikely circumstances apply (Kolbe, Read and Hall, 1984, p. 56). The first is that the company is not growing. The only investment is to maintain the scale of existing operations, and the cash invested is equal to the depreciation charge. The constant profit is the same as the net cash flow, and is all paid out as dividend. In this case $g = 0$ and $ret = 0$.

The second case is if the return on equity is constant and equal to the cost of equity. The relation between growth and retention is

$$g = (EPS_2 - EPS_1)/EPS_1$$
$$= ROE(retEPS_1)/EPS_1$$
$$retEPS_1 = g(EPS_1)/ROE$$

Substituting in equation (12.6),

$$P_0 = [EPS_1 - g(EPS_1)/ROE]/(R_E - g)$$
$$= [ROE(EPS_1) - g(EPS_1)]/ROE(R_E - g)$$
$$EPS_1/P_0 = ROE(R_E - g)/(ROE - g)$$

The equation shows how earnings yield is related to the return on equity, the cost of equity and the growth rate. It makes explicit that $EPS_1/P_0 \neq R_E$ if $ROE \neq R_E$. This is not obvious in equation (12.6) because the return on equity assumed is implicit in the values of g and ret; the relation is $g = retROE$. If some of the company's expected growth is from projects with positive net present value, $ROE > R_E$, and earnings yield underestimates the cost of equity. More importantly, it cannot be assumed that the return on equity will be equal to the cost of equity. A company's forecast return on equity in a given year will usually be materially different from the expected return on its shares.

Timing of dividends
Equation (12.3) assumes that the share has just gone ex-dividend and that the next dividend payment will be received in exactly one year (and it ignores the difference between the ex-date and the date when the dividend is actually paid). If dividends are paid semi-annually or quarterly, equation (12.3) will slightly understate the expected rate of return on the share. For quarterly dividends, for example, it would be more accurate first to convert equation (12.3) to a quarterly basis, with Div_{1q} being the dividend in three months, R_{Eq} the expected return per quarter and g_q the quarterly growth rate ($g_q = (1 + g_{annual})^{0.25} - 1$). The resulting annualised return assuming quarterly compounding is $R_E = (1 + R_{Eq})^4 - 1$.

There may still be complications. For example, it is common in the United States for the dividend to change once per year, rather than every quarter. If dividends are growing, and the annual rise is about to take effect, the next quarterly payment will be higher than the last and will then stay the same for three quarters. In this case, using the next payment in the quarterly version of equation (12.3) will overestimate the expected return. Siegel (1985) presents a simple approximate adjustment for the case in which quarterly dividends are changed annually:

$$Div^*_{1q} = Div_{1q}[1 + (N - 1.5)g_q]$$

where Div^*_{1q} is the adjusted dividend to use in the quarterly version of equation (12.3), Div_{1q} is the actual dividend next quarter and N is the number of quarters since the last change in the quarterly dividend; $N = 0$ if the next payment differs from the last. There is a different complication in the United Kingdom, where most dividend-paying companies pay an interim dividend halfway through their financial year that is smaller than the final dividend.

If the date at which one is estimating the cost of equity is part-way through a financial year/half-year/quarter, the prevailing share price at date t should be adjusted for the assumed growth rate g and the accrual of the next dividend:

$$P^*_0 = (P_t - Div_1\alpha)(1 - g\alpha)$$

where P^*_0 is the adjusted share price for use in equation (12.3), P_t is the actual price, Div_1 is the next dividend and α is the fraction of the time that has elapsed between the last ex-dividend date and the next. P^*_0 is an estimate of what the share price at the last ex-dividend date would have been given the prevailing price P_t.

It seems fair to say that the inaccuracies caused by the timing of dividends are very small compared with the general uncertainty about the cost of equity. An example will give a feel for this. Suppose that a company pays quarterly dividends that are growing (and changing) at 2.00 per cent per quarter. The first-quarter dividend last financial year was 10.00p, so the fourth was 10.61p and the total for the year was 41.22p. We are now at the start of the next financial year. The next dividend is forecast to be 10.82p and the total to be 44.61p. The share price is 541p. The correct estimate of the company's cost of equity uses quarterly figures in equation (12.3):

$$R_{Eq} = 10.82p/541p + 0.020 = 4.00\% \text{ per quarter}$$

or 16.99 per cent p.a. A reasonable way of arriving at an estimate using annual figures is to use the total dividend for the coming year and to estimate the growth rate of the total dividend each year by comparing it with last year's total: $44.61p/41.22p - 1 = 8.22\%$ p.a. Then

$$R_E = 44.61p/541p + 0.082 = 16.47\% \text{ pa}$$

The difference from the estimate using quarterly figures is 0.52 per cent p.a.

Changing discount rate
Equation (12.1) does not require the discount rate to be constant; the term structure of expected returns need not be flat. In a multiperiod setting, a change in share price can be

caused by a change in forecast discount rates, as well as by a change in forecast cash flows. If future dividends are taken as given, a fall in share price implies higher expected returns, but the increase in expected return need not be the same for every future period. For example, if returns are measured monthly and there is believed to be some short-term persistence (serial correlation) in monthly returns, a fall in price could imply an increase in expected returns for the next few months only.

If there is assumed to be some persistence in a change in expected returns, allowing expected returns to vary as well as forecast dividends makes the dividend discount model predict much more volatile share prices over time than it does if expected returns are assumed to be constant. This version of the model fits stock market data better; there is evidence of time-varying expected returns (Section 3.3), and share prices are much more volatile than can plausibly be explained by the model if expected returns are assumed to be constant (Shiller, 1981). Campbell and Shiller (1988) derive a version of the model in which expected returns and forecast dividends vary over time. Campbell (1991) rearranges this to explain the unexpected component of a single-period return in terms of a change in future expected returns and a change in the forecast growth rates of dividends. His aim is to explain observed monthly market returns on the New York Stock Exchange between 1927 and 1988. Each month t he uses a multifactor model to predict the returns on the stock exchange during subsequent months. This process gives an estimate of the future expected returns as at each month. From the actual monthly returns and the estimates of the expected returns, he is able to infer the proportions of the changes in actual monthly returns attributable to changes in expected returns (28 per cent), changes in forecast dividends (37 per cent) and negative correlation between the two (35 per cent). A negative correlation is a cause of market volatility; a rise in forecast dividends tends to be associated with a fall in expected return, both of which are associated with an increase in value. He finds some short-term persistence in changes in expected returns, such that a 1 per cent increase in next month's expected return is associated with a 5 per cent fall in market value.

This type of exercise is directed towards understanding changes in value over time, not to the estimation of the cost of equity. However, it provides additional perspective on the valuation model – equation (12.1). Short-term persistence in expected returns suggests that there are different discount rates for different future horizons or project lives. But the pragmatic short cut of equation (12.3) allows only one cost of equity to be forecast at a given date for all future periods.

12.3   The abnormal earnings method

The dividend discount approach infers the discount rate from cash flow data: the market value of a company's shares in conjunction with the cash flows forecast to be received by shareholders. An alternative is to use accounting data, namely the book value of equity and forecast earnings. Barker (2001) provides a clear review of recent accounting-based approaches to company valuation, which informs much of the discussion below.

Forecast earnings cannot be used without adjustment as a substitute for net cash flows in valuation. It is true that, over the lifetime of a project or company, the total earnings must be the same as the total of the cash flows to the shareholders net of inflows from them. In view of this, it might perhaps be thought that a project's present value could be estimated by adding the discounted value of earnings to the initial cost of the project. But such a method would introduce an upward bias to the estimate, because earnings are calculated net of a gradual subtraction of the initial cost of the project, via depreciation. The present value of earnings is net of the present value of the initial cost, as though it were incurred gradually in the future. So the present value of the depreciation charges will be less than the actual initial cost, incurred at date 0.

Example
Consider the following example of a project that lasts for three years and initially costs £90. The assets are depreciated on a straight-line basis. The cash flows to and from shareholders consist of the initial cost of £90 and a single dividend of £150 after three years, whereas earnings are −£30 in year 1, −£30 in year 2 and £120 in year 3. The total earnings of £60 are equal to the dividend net of the initial cost, but discounting the earnings and adding the initial cost gives a higher present value than discounting the single dividend, for any positive discount rate.

Year	0	1	2	3
Cash flow	(90)	0	0	150
Operating profit		0	0	150
Depreciation		(30)	(30)	(30)
Profit or earnings		(30)	(30)	120
Dividend		0	0	150
Investment	90	0	0	0
Book value	90	60	30	0

The upward bias is likely to be worse in the case of a profitable growing company, as opposed to a single project. Such a company will be retaining some or all of its profits, and may continue to do so for the foreseeable future. In this case, the convention that long-lived assets are depreciated means that earnings are being recognised much sooner than dividends will be paid. There are, in addition, other reasons why earnings can differ from cash flows, since earnings recognition depends on accounting policies and on judgement.

The problems with discounting earnings are avoided by discounting *abnormal earnings*, denoted *Abearn*, which are the earnings in excess of the earnings required to meet the cost of equity:

$$Abearn_{t+1} = (ROE_{book,t+1} - R_E)E_{book,t}$$
$$= Earn_{t+1} - R_E E_{book,t} \qquad (12.7)$$

where $ROE_{book,t}$ is the return on book equity for year t, R_E is the cost of equity, $E_{book,t}$ is the book value per share at the end of year t and $Earn_t$ is the earnings (profit after tax) per share. We shall see that the market value of the equity – the present value of the forecast dividends – can also be expressed as the current book value plus the present value of the forecast abnormal earnings. If normal earnings in a given year are positive but insufficient to cover the cost of capital, abnormal earnings will be negative.

Both normal and abnormal earnings depend in part on accounting policies. However, the present value of abnormal earnings is not affected by which accounting policies are employed, so long as the change in shareholders' funds in a given year is equal to the profit after tax less the dividend paid, if any. Accounting that satisfies this condition is often called clean surplus accounting. Then we have

$$Div_{t+1} = Earn_{t+1} - (E_{book,t} - E_{book,t+1}) \qquad (12.8)$$

This equation will not hold if the accounting policies allow there to be changes in asset value that do not pass through the profit and loss account – for example, an upward revaluation of the balance sheet value of an asset.

Using the definition of abnormal earnings in equation (12.7), equation (12.8) can be written as

$$Div_{t+1} = Abearn_{t+1} + R_E E_{book,t} + (E_{book,t} - E_{book,t+1})$$

Substituting this in the dividend discount model (equation (12.1)) gives

$$P_0 = \frac{Abearn_1 + E_{book,0}(1 + R_E) - E_{book,1}}{(1 + R_E)}$$
$$+ \frac{Abearn_2 + E_{book,1}(1 + R_E) - E_{book,2}}{(1 + R_E)^2} + \cdots$$
$$= E_{book,0} + \Sigma_{t=1}^{\infty} Abearn_t / (1 + R_E)^t \qquad (12.9)$$

Equation (12.9) says that the market value of the equity is equal to the current book value plus the present value of the forecast abnormal earnings. It can be rearranged to infer the discount rate R_E. Ohlson (1995) argues that abnormal earnings cannot be expected to last indefinitely, and presents a valuation model that includes a 'persistence parameter', which specifies the rate at which abnormal earnings will decline.

The reason why a change in accounting policy makes no difference to equity value is that it affects neither the underlying cash flows nor the dividends. This point can be explained as follows, in the context of the abnormal earnings model. The problem with discounting (normal) earnings is that, in any year, they might be either above or below the dividend, in which case the present value of the contribution to value for that year will either be overstated or understated. Obviously, the difference between profits after tax and dividends can be very substantial over a number of years.

Suppose we change the accounting policy in such a way that forecast profit for year 1 becomes higher by amount Y_1. For example, we capitalise some of the expected expenditures in year 1. Capitalised expenditure appears as an asset, the balance sheet value of which is reduced via depreciation in subsequent years, say by 50 per cent in year 2 and 50 per cent in year 3. The results of capitalising the expenditure are that the asset value in the balance sheet is greater and that profit recognition is brought forward, being higher than it would have been in the near future had the expenditure been treated as an operating cost. Cash of amount Y_1 will actually be spent in year 1, but will appear in the profit and loss account as depreciation of $0.5Y_1$ in year 2 and $0.5Y_1$ in year 3. As a result, abnormal earnings and normal earnings for year 1, and the capital at the end of year 1, will all be higher by amount Y_1. Normal earnings will be lower by $0.5Y_1$ in year 2 and $0.5Y_1$ in year 3. Abnormal earnings will be lower by $0.5Y_1 + Y_1R_E$ in year 2 and by $0.5Y_1 + 0.5Y_1R_E$ in year 3, from equation (12.7). The overstatement in present value from discounting the new normal earnings, after capitalising Y_1, would be equal to

$$\Delta PV_0 = Y_1/(1 + R_E) - 0.5Y_1/(1 + R_E)^2 - 0.5Y_1/(1 + R_E)^3$$

But there is no change to present value from discounting the new abnormal earnings:

$$\Delta PV_0 = Y_1/(1 + R_E) - Y_1(0.5 + R_E)/(1 + R_E)^2$$
$$- 0.5Y_1(1 + R_E)/(1 + R_E)^3$$
$$= 0$$

The distortion in discounting normal earnings arises because of timing differences between normal earnings and net cash flows. The use of abnormal earnings neutralises the effects of timing differences. In the example, an increase in present value from recognising more profit early is matched by an equal decrease in present value arising from the cost of the increase in capital that mirrors the increase in profit recognised early. The two effects cancel out because the difference between profit and cash is matched by an equal increase in capital, and because the discount rate – the rate at which the present value of future cash declines, which causes the value of normal earnings to be overstated – is equal to the cost of the extra capital.

It can be argued that the abnormal earnings method provides a more reliable estimate of the cost of equity than the dividend discount model (Claus and Thomas, 2001). It uses more of the information available about the company at a given date – i.e. the book value and explicit forecast earnings for the next few years. This means that the proportion of market value determined by the assumed long-term growth rate of earnings or dividends is less using the abnormal earnings method. The analyst may find it easier to work with forecasts of abnormal earnings than with forecasts of cash flows to shareholders. It is arguable that the plausibility of an assumed long-term growth rate is easier to assess for abnormal earnings than for dividends. But it should be remembered that the abnormal earnings model is the dividend discount model dressed up differently. The forecasting of future abnormal earnings requires the forecasting earnings and book values for each year, which is equivalent to forecasting future dividends (see equation (12.8)).

Measuring company performance

An application of the cost of equity, in conjuction with the abnormal earnings model, is in measuring company performance. The idea is that, if the aim of a company is to maximise shareholder wealth, the managers' performance over a given period t should be assessed in terms of shareholder wealth created during that period. The obvious measure of wealth created, at least if the company is listed on a stock exchange, is the percentage return on the shares during period t: $(P_t + Div_t - P_{t-1})/P_{t-1}$, which is also known as the market value added. (If there were a share split or a share consolidation, or a share issue that effectively involves one of these, such as a rights issue at a discount, P_{t-1} would need to be adjusted appropriately.) However, the change in share price reflects in part the change in investors' preceptions about the future growth of the company – i.e. about the future cash flows from ongoing operations, and future opportunities to create positive NPV. Future opportunities are, to some extent, beyond the control of managers, and it could be argued that their performance should be assessed by reference to the change in shareholder wealth that is most closely under their control. Abnormal earnings provide such a measure. The abnormal profit or loss in a given year is a measure of the wealth created or destroyed during that year by the company's ongoing operations. It is also known as economic value added and as shareholder value added. Abnormal profit is not the same as market value added, because abnormal profit does not reflect the change in investors' valuation of future cash flows and investment opportunities. Since accounting policies affect the measurement of abnormal profit, they affect the measurement of managers' performance, and much attention has been given to the definition of abnormal profit and its extraction in practice from company accounts (see, e.g., Stewart, 1991).

12.4   Inference from options prices

A radically different approach to estimating the cost of equity is to infer the expected rate of return on a share from the value of an option written on it. Hsia (1991) shows formally how this can be done, under certain assumptions, but it requires a knowledge of the Black–Scholes option pricing model, which is beyond our scope. McNulty, Yeh, Schulze and Lubatkin (2002) make a case for the option-based approach and suggest a pragmatic method of implementation. They argue that total volatility is a more relevant measure of risk than systematic risk, at least for corporate investors, who are not well diversified. They also argue that volatility increases at a decreasing rate with the time horizon rather than the constant rate implicitly assumed by discounting at a given rate per period that is invariant with respect to the time horizon (Section 6.1.3). They suggest that a company's cost of equity can be estimated by the prevailing yield on its corporate bonds plus the expected premium for 'equity returns risk', the additional risk borne by shareholder. This premium can be backed out of the prices of call options on its shares, and will decline with the assumed future time horizon, because the variance of the possible end-date share price implied in the prices of call option increases with the time horizon at a decreasing rate.

   The first step is to estimate the share's implied volatility from the price of a call option with maturity at a chosen date, using the Black–Scholes model. The next is to calculate the value of a notional put option maturing at the same future date, using the share's implied volatility, and the company's corporate bond rate as the risk-free rate. The exercise price of the notional put is set as the minimum price at the future date to give an investor in the shares at their current price the prevailing corporate bond rate net of expected dividends (estimated by the current dividend yield). The value of the notional put can be seen as the cost of the insurance that the shares will provide a rate of return at least equal to the yield on the company's bonds. The cost of the put can then be converted to an annualised rate, and this can be seen as an estimate of the premium above the yield on the company's bonds for holding the shares. The argument is that a package of the share and a put on the share has no downside risk and that, for the expected rate of return on £1 spent on the package to be the same as the expected rate on £1 spent on the bond, the difference between the expected rate on the shares and the expected rate on the bonds must be worth the same as the cost of the put.

McNulty et al. believe that the above options-based method gives more plausible estimates of the discount rates actually implicit in some market prices. They cite real-estate investment trusts, which pay out 90 per cent of their net cash flows as dividends. The price/dividend mutliple should be negatively related to the cost of equity, assuming similar growth rates across the trusts. There is a clear negative relation using the options-based estimates of the cost of equity, but no relation using CAPM estimates.

12.5   Summary

Survey evidence indicates that a handful of methods are used in practice to estimate the cost of equity. The most popular method in recent years has been the CAPM; other methods or proxies in use include the dividend discount model, the mean historic return on the company's shares, multifactor models, the company's earnings yield and asking the views of a sample of the shareholders. Here we have considered the dividend discount model. This works by inferring the cost of equity from the combination of the current value of a company's equity and from estimates of the future cash flows to shareholders. It is a correct way of representing the expected rate of return on equity, though it provides no insight into what determines the expected rate. We have shown en route that the prospective earnings yield is not a correct model of the expected rate of return.

The chapter has gone on to review the abnormal earnings method of estimation, which is a version of the dividend discount model. Arguably, it produces more reliable estimates of the cost of equity than the dividend discount model, because it uses more information about the company and because it is easier to forecast abnormal earnings than to forecast dividends.

The main practical problem with the forward-looking methods discussed in this chapter is that the inferred cost of equity is sensitive to the forecasts employed, whether the analyst is working with forecast dividends or with forecast abnormal earnings. The sensitivity to short-term forecasts for a particular company is reduced by using forecasts from a sample of similar companies, and also by using a two-stage model in which a long-term growth forecast is assumed after a date a few years into the future.

13 The cost of equity: applying the CAPM and multifactor models

This second chapter on estimating the cost of equity reviews the implementation of the standard CAPM and of multifactor models. The dividend discount and abnormal earnings methods infer the cost of equity from the present value of equity and from forecasts of the rewards to shareholders; the analyst solves the discounted cash flow equation for the discount rate. In contrast, the CAPM and multifactor models explain the cost of equity as the risk-free rate plus a risk premium or premiums. The CAPM requires the estimation of three numbers: the risk-free interest rate, the expected equity premium and the project's expected beta. The estimation of these numbers is discussed in turn. We have relatively little to say about the estimation of the risk-free rate, and we have considered the equity premium elsewhere, so much of the chapter is concerned with research on the estimation of beta.

The chapter goes on to consider the implementation of three multifactor models. One is a model in which the explanatory variables are several macroeconomic variables that are commonly used to explain the returns on financial assets. The second is the three-factor model of Fama and French, in which two of the variables are firm-specific characteristics. The third is also a model based on firm-specific variables, with the novel feature that the premiums on the variables are estimated using the abnormal earnings method.

13.1 Choice of risk-free rate

Consideration of the risk-free rate raises at least two questions. The first is whether to use a short- or long-term rate; the second is how to estimate a long-term risk-free rate. There is no consensus in the literature as to the correct answers to these questions. Regarding what is done in practice, several authors state that practitioners tend to use a yield on long-term government bonds as the risk-free rate. Rutterford's (2000) evidence supports this. She reports that, of fourteen large UK companies she interviewed that use the CAPM, twelve use the nominal yield on a UK government bond as the risk-free rate, choosing a maturity between seven and twenty years. The other two estimate a real yield. None uses a treasury bill rate. Bruner, Eades, Harris and Higgins (1998) report that, of the twenty-three US firms they interviewed that use the CAPM, nineteen use the nominal yield on Treasury bonds with a maturity of at least ten years. Many firms also said that they match the term of the risk-free rate to the term of the project.

Short or long rate?

Use of a short rate appears to fit with the concept of the cost of equity as a one-period expected return (Section 6.1.1). But the concept need not imply that the expected return is constant. In fact, unless the yield curve is approximately flat, we know that the expected returns in future periods are not identical. In principle, both the risk-free rate and the risk premium could differ in different future periods. In practice it is difficult or impossible to predict how the risk premium on a project will change over time, and so, doubtless, the assumption is normally made that the premium will remain the same. Cornell, Hirshleifer and James (1997, p. 19) write that 'regulators and practitioners rarely adopt or accept complex models designed to forecast future market-risk premiums'. In contrast, nominal risk-free rates of interest are known for each of many years ahead, and can be locked in by means of forward contracts. The real risk-free forward rate for each future year also can easily be estimated, given a forecast of the rate of inflation.

If we are discounting cash flows at different dates, the correct thing to do in theory is to discount cash flows at different dates by different discount rates. This is probably rarely done in practice, because it adds complexity and will normally make little difference to a valuation. Instead, as an approximation, a constant rate is used that is given by a prevailing long – rather than short – rate, as noted above. Ideally we should use a rate for a maturity that matches the forecast life of the project.

It might be argued that a short-term rate should be used because the CAPM is derived in a one-period context. But the implication of this point is that a robust and rigorous basis for using the CAPM to value a multiperiod project is lacking. In any case, we have seen in Section 6.1.2 that, if we assume that the CAPM can be used in a multiperiod context, the expected return need not be the same in every future period. So the arguments point in favour of using a long rate – or, better, a rate for a maturity that matches the life of the project.

Estimating a long-term risk-free rate

Let us assume that government bonds have no default risk. This does not mean that they have no risk, if we assume that investors are interested in real returns. The real yield on a conventional bond, with payments fixed in nominal terms, will depend on the future rates of inflation during its life. Much of the risk can be removed by investing in index-linked bonds, which provide nominal returns that vary with the observed rate of inflation. There will still be some uncertainty about the real rates on an index-linked bond in periods before maturity, but the term or risk premium on index-linked government bonds will be very small.

If index-linked government bonds exist, they should be used to estimate the nominal risk-free rate, rather than using the nominal yield on conventional government bonds. The formula is

$$1 + R_{\text{nom}} = (1 + R_{\text{real}})(1 + Inf) \tag{13.1}$$

where R_{nom} is the estimated nominal risk-free rate, R_{real} is the real yield on the index-linked bonds and *Inf* is the forecast rate of inflation, and all these rates are specific to a given maturity date.

Real risk-free bond yields will not exist unless the government has issued index-linked bonds. If only conventional government bonds exist, real yields have to be estimated by solving equation (13.1) for R_{real}, given the forecast rate of inflation. But nominal yields on conventional bonds, and real yields estimated by solving equation (13.1) for R_{real}, will probably include an inflation risk premium that is positively related to maturity (Section 10.3). That is, the nominal yield on a conventional bond can be broken down into the real yield assuming constant inflation plus expected inflation plus an inflation risk premium. Since the aim is to estimate the rate of return on an asset that is risk-free in nominal or real terms, the inflation risk premium should be estimated and subtracted from the estimated nominal or real yield on a conventional bond.

The inflation risk premium is ignored in many texts, and probably in many practical contexts. But Cornell et al. (1997) state that the following procedure is gaining acceptance amongst utility regulators: take the redemption yield on long-term bonds and subtract an estimate of the historic term premium, assumed to be mainly an inflation risk premium. For example, the average returns on twenty-year bonds less the average annualised returns on one-month US treasury bills was 1.37 per cent p.a. during 1926 to 1996. The result is an estimate of 'the expected long-run average of the short-run rate' (p. 14). Brealey and Myers (2003, p. 226) also recommend this approach. A problem is that the estimated inflation risk premium varies with the sample period and method of estimation; it was 1.80 per cent p.a. during 1926 to 2000 according to Brealey and Myers, compared to the estimate of 1.37 per cent p.a. by Cornell et al. for a very similar period. Patterson (1995, pp. 105–06) cites evidence that the inflation risk premium is less than 1 per cent p.a., and recommends a correction of the long-term yield of only 0.25 per cent p.a.

It should be noted that, if the above approach is used, the equity premium used in the CAPM should be a premium measured against the rate on treasury bills, since a long rate net of the inflation risk premium is effectively an estimate of expected short rates. For example, suppose the arithmetic mean historic premium is 9.1 per cent p.a. measured against one-month treasury bills, and 7.3 per cent p.a. measured against long-term bonds, so the inflation risk premium is estimated to be 1.8 per cent p.a. Current yields are, say, 2.0 per cent p.a. on treasury bills and 2.5 per cent p.a. on long-term bonds. These yields imply that, allowing for the inflation risk premium, short-term interest rates are expected to fall. Then the cost of equity for a company with a beta of one is $2\% + 9.1\% = 11.1\%$ pa if the yield on treasury bills is used as the risk-free rate, or $2.5\% - 1.8\%$ (inflation risk premium) $+ 9.1\% = 9.8\%$ pa if the yield on long-term bonds net of the inflation risk premium is used. On the other hand, if a long-term rate is used as the risk-free rate, and if the inflation risk premium is not subtracted, then the equity premium used should be measured against long-term rates. This would give a cost of equity of $2.5\% + 7.3\% = 9.8\%$.

Finally, if the relevant government's bonds are considered to have default risk, and certainly if they are given less than the top credit rating by rating agencies, then yields on such bonds should not be used as proxies for the risk-free rate. It would be better to use the yield on, say, US government bonds, converted into the local currency using prevailing spot and forward exchange rates.

13.2   Choice of equity premium

The choice of premium on the stock market is one of the most uncertain aspects of estimating the cost of capital. We have discussed the premium at length in Chapter 5; here we comment briefly on its estimation in practice.

The two approaches to estimation are to use a long-run historic average, or to estimate a forward-looking premium. Use of a historic average is based on the principle that the premium observed over many years in the past provides a good estimate for the premium to be expected over many years in the future. This had been the standard approach, found in all textbooks, until the late 1990s, although the considerable attendant uncertainties had been recognised (e.g. Carleton and Lakonishok, 1985). But many, perhaps most, academics and practitioners have come to doubt that the premium in the future will be as large as it has been in the past, at least if the historic premium is measured using an estimation period from the twentieth century. The arithmetic mean real premium between 1900 and 2000 was 5.6 per cent p.a. for the United Kingdom and 7.0 per cent p.a. for the United States, measured against the yield on long-term bonds (Dimson, Marsh and Staunton, 2002). But a simple forward-looking estimate based on applying the dividend discount model to the market suggests a premium of 3 per cent to 4 per cent p.a. This is why many people do not expect the premium in the future to be as large as it has been in the past, especially in the second half of the twentieth century. They place more faith in reasonable expectations about the future than in outcomes observed in recent decades. Futhermore, several researchers have argued recently that investors did not expect premiums as large they got in the twentieth century (Section 5.3.2).

Even if one accepts this point of view, and ignores the evidence from the twentieth century, reasonable forward-looking estimates of the premium in relation to a long-term interest rate would lie in a range between 1 per cent and 5 per cent p.a. or more for the United Kingdom and United States, at the time of writing (2004). The precise estimate chosen will be a matter of judgement. Forecasts of corporate earnings, which affect the cost of equity inferred via the dividend discount model, vary considerably over time. Claus and Thomas (2001) note that, in each year from 1985 to 1998, equity analysts forecast that US corporate earnings would grow at about 7 per cent p.a. in real terms, assuming forecast inflation of 5 per cent p.a. This compares with real growth of US GDP of 2.8 per cent p.a. since 1970. The average implied equity premium using the analysts' growth forecasts was 7.3 per cent p.a. Yet the premiums typically forecast by investors, chief financial officers and academics had fallen to the range 2.5 per cent to 4.5 per cent p.a. by 2001–02 (Ilmanen, 2003).

Not all researchers accept that the evidence from the past should be ignored. For example, Ibbotson and Chen (2003) and Mehra (2003) have recently defended the use of historic evidence to estimate the *ex ante* premium. Mehra's conclusion is that, 'before the [historic]

7

equity premium is dismissed, not only do researchers need to understand the observed phenomena, but they also need a plausible explanation for why the future is likely to be different from the past' (p. 67).

The response of many firms to uncertainty about the premium is simply to pick a reasonable-looking number. Thirteen of the UK firms Rutterford interviewed in 1996 estimated an equity premium. Eleven chose a 'gut feel' number between 4.5 per cent and 6.0 per cent p.a.; two chose a historic average, which was 7.5 per cent p.a. at the time using the Barclays Capital data (Section 5.2). Twenty-three of the US firms in the 1998 survey by Bruner et al. estimated an equity premium. Thirteen chose an ad hoc number between 4.0 per cent and 6.0 per cent p.a., two used an unspecified ad hoc number, three used a historic average, four used the estimate of an adviser, and one used a Value Line estimate. However, seven of the ten M&A advisers questioned by Bruner et al. used a historic average.

13.3   Estimating beta from historic data

In practice, a company's beta is estimated from its share returns in the fairly recent past, on the assumption that its past beta provides a good forecast of its future beta. That is, past observations of the excess returns on the share and on the market are treated as a sample of the distribution of possible excess returns in the future. There are a number of choices to be made to arrive at an estimation procedure, and a change in procedure will often result in a non-negligible change in the beta estimate. We discuss the main issues in turn.

13.3.1   OLS estimation

The most straightforward method to estimate the beta of a share j is to run an ordinary least squares (OLS) regression of the excess returns on j on the excess returns on the market:

$$R_{jt} - R_{Ft} = \alpha_j + \beta_j(R_{Mt} - R_{Ft}) + e_{jt} \tag{13.2}$$

for a sample of $t = 1, \ldots T$ observations, where the measurement interval could be a day or a month or some other interval (the choice of interval is discussed below). We shall refer to a beta estimated by equation (13.2) as an 'OLS beta'. The use of OLS assumes that returns are normally distributed and that the true betas are stable over time, in which case the forecast beta is presumed to be the same as the estimated historic beta. If these conditions hold, at least approximately, then uncertainty about the true beta is measured by the standard error of the estimated beta coefficient,

$$s^2(\beta_j) = \frac{\sum_{t=1}^{T} e_{jt}^2/(T-2)}{\sum_{t=1}^{T}[R_{Mt} - \mu(R_{Mt})]^2}$$

where μ stands for mean. For example, Fama (1976, p. 123) reports that the average standard error of the beta estimates across a random sample of thirty New York Stock Exchange shares is 0.22. The betas are estimated using sixty monthly returns from 1963 to 1968. Fama and French (1997) report that the average standard error of industry betas calculated from rolling sixty-month estimation periods during 1963 to 1994 is 0.12. So, with these figures, the average 95 per cent confidence interval is plus or minus 0.43 for a share and 0.24 for an industry (1.96 times the average standard error. For a given interval, we are 95 per cent certain that the true value of beta is within the interval.) Thus a typical beta estimate leaves the analyst with considerable uncertainty about the true beta, even if betas are presumed to be stable.

13.3.2   *Reversion to the mean*

It has been observed that betas are not stable; they have a tendency to revert over time towards their cross-sectional mean (Blume, 1971). This phenomenon is due in part to error in the estimation of true betas. The further above (or below) the mean an observed beta is the more likely it is that the estimation error is positive (or negative), and therefore, if the true beta is stationary over time, the next estimate is more likely to be nearer the mean than further away. But there is also evidence that true betas themselves regress towards the mean. It is possible to decompose a change in beta from one estimation period to the next into the change due to error in estimation and the change in true beta (Blume, 1975; Dimson and Marsh, 1983). Reversion to the mean implies that, for a given *ex post* OLS beta, the future beta will be closer to the mean, and that therefore an OLS beta does not provide an optimal forecast of beta in a future period.

Several adjustments to beta estimates have been proposed to allow for regression to the mean. Blume (1971) suggests estimating betas for a sample of shares over two adjacent non-overlapping periods and running the following cross-sectional regression:

$$\beta_{jt} = a + b\beta_{jt-1} + e_j$$

for shares $j = 1, \ldots n$ in the sample. The estimated coefficients a and b are then used to adjust the most recent estimate β_{jt} for the purpose of forecasting the share's beta in the subsequent period:

$$\text{est}\beta_{jt+1} = a + b\beta_{jt}$$

where $\text{est}\beta_{jt+1}$ is the estimated beta for date $t + 1$ as at date t.

Vasicek (1973, p. 1234) argues that a Bayesian adjustment is appropriate. We know that, the further away an OLS beta is from one (assuming the mean beta is equal to one), the more likely it is to be over- or underestimated.

Assume that there are 1,000 stocks under consideration, the betas of which are known to be distributed approximately normally around 1.0 with standard deviation of .5. Each of these true betas is equally likely to be underestimated or overestimated by [the OLS estimate of] β. Therefore, there are 500 stocks with true beta higher than the observed estimate, and 500 with true beta lower than the estimate. If an estimate of $\beta = .2$ is observed, the stock might be any of the approximately $500 \times .945 = 473$ stocks with true beta larger than .2 and underestimated, or any of the approximately $500 \times .055 = 27$ stocks with true beta smaller than .2 and overestimated. Apparently, given our sample and our prior knowledge of beta distribution, the former is much more likely, and thus, it is not correct to take .2 for an unbiased estimate.

This is why estimation error alone will cause the regression of estimated betas to the mean over time. Suppose our prior beliefs about beta are based on a sample with a cross-sectional mean of $\mu(\beta_{jt})$ and variance of $\sigma^2(\beta_{jt})$. Vasicek shows that the 'posterior' estimate of beta, $\text{est}\beta_{jt+1}$, to use as the forecast, is the following weighted average of the prior belief about its value, $\mu(\beta_{jt})$, and the observed OLS regression coefficient β_{jt} estimated as at period t:

$$\text{est}\beta_{jt+1} = \frac{\mu(\beta_{jt})/\sigma^2(\beta_{it}) + \beta_{jt}/s^2(\beta_{jt})}{1/\sigma^2(\beta_{jt}) + 1/s^2(\beta_{jt})}$$

where $s^2(\beta_{jt})$ is the variance of the regression coefficient β_{jt}. This estimate is constructed to minimise the expected error in the forecast, $E_t(\beta_{jt+1} - \text{est}\beta_{jt+1})$, given the prior beliefs of mean and variance, $\mu(\beta_{jt})$ and $\sigma^2(\beta_{jt})$.

The prior belief need not necessarily be that the mean beta is one. Some types of company are known to have relatively high or low betas. For example, Gombola and Kahl (1990) present evidence that the betas of most utility shares follow a mean-reverting process, but around a mean that is close to 0.5. They and others also discuss the problem of 'transient betas' that are temporarily much larger or smaller than usual, due to an episode of major fluctuation in the share price (see Section 15.3 for an example). A further point is that the mean beta across all shares can be well below one if a value-weighted index is used (see below).

The accuracy of forecast betas can be tested by means of the correlation between β_{jt+1}, the observed beta as at $t + 1$, and $\text{est}\beta_{jt+1}$, the forecast for $t + 1$, and by the mean squared error (MSE) of the forecast: MSE $= \Sigma_{j=1}^n (\beta_{jt+1} - \text{est}\beta_{jt+1})^2/n$, where n is the number of forecast betas. MSE can be decomposed as follows:

$$\Sigma_{j=1}^n (\beta_{jt+1} - \text{est}\beta_{jt+1})^2/n = [\mu(\beta_{jt+1}) - \mu(\text{est}\beta_{jt+1})]^2 + (1 - \beta_1)^2 \sigma^2(\text{est}\beta_{jt+1})$$
$$+ (1 - R^2)^2 \sigma^2(\beta_{jt})$$

where β_1 is the slope of the regression of β_{jt+1} on $\text{est}\beta_{jt+1}$, and R^2 is the R^2 of this regression; $\sigma^2(\text{est}\beta_{jt+1})$ is the variance of the estimated betas; and $\sigma^2(\beta_{jt})$ is the variance of the observed betas. The first term on the right-hand side, the squared difference between the mean observed beta and the mean forecast beta, is the bias in the forecast. The second term measures the inefficiency; if the slope of the regression of β_{jt+1} on $\text{est}\beta_{jt+1}$ were one (i.e. $\beta_1 = 1$), there would be no inefficiency. For an observed beta x per cent above or below the mean, the corresponding forecast beta would tend to be x per cent above or below the mean of the forecast. The third term measures the random error in the forecast, which can exist even if the forecast is unbiased and efficient.

Evidence on the MSE is presented by Klemkosky and Martin (1975) and Eubank and Zumwalt (1979) for US monthly returns, and by Dimson and Marsh (1983) for UK monthly returns. These studies find that both the Blume and the Vasicek methods of adjustment result in appreciably better forecasts, and that there is not much to choose between the two methods. OLS betas provide unbiased forecasts on average, but, since there is regression to the mean, low OLS betas are biased downwards and high betas biased upwards. The methods make little difference, on average, to the MSEs for OLS betas close to one; the reduction in both bias and inefficiency is greater the further away from one the beta in question is. The methods do not reduce the random error component of MSE.

The following figures from Eubank and Zumwalt (1979) give an idea of the degree of uncertainty about future beta and the improvement from the above adjustments. They report that, for estimation and prediction periods each of sixty months, the average MSE of the betas across all shares is 0.131. So the standard deviation of the error is $\sqrt{0.131} = 0.362$, giving a two-standard-deviation 'confidence interval' for estimated beta of plus or minus 0.724 (this is a different approach to the measurement of uncertainty about beta from the standard error of the OLS coefficient). There is, therefore, very considerable uncertainty about future beta, based on a typical historic estimate. The adjustment methods result in an MSE of about 0.115 – only a modest reduction from 0.131. However, the MSE is smallest for shares with beta close to one and largest for shares with high-betas, and the methods make more difference for larger MSEs. In other words, the OLS betas close to one provide the most reliable forecasts, and adjustment makes most difference for betas furthest away from one, especially high betas. For example, the average MSE across the quintile of shares with the highest OLS betas is 0.212, which reduces to about 0.162 using the Blume or Vasicek adjustments.

Dimson and Marsh (1983) estimate UK betas according to the trade-to-trade method (discussed below) and note that the average MSE is slightly greater for unadjusted trade-to-trade betas than it is if the forecast beta is simply a constant equal to the mean trade-to-trade beta across shares. The Blume and Vasicek adjustments reduce the average MSE across all shares from 0.17 to, respectively, 0.12 and 0.11, which is a much bigger improvement than is seen in US data.

13.3.3   Thin trading

Shares vary considerably in the frequency with which they are traded; 'thinner' trading means less frequent trading. It is probably the case that most listed shares on most markets trade less frequently than once a day. Dimson (1979) reports that about two-thirds of listed UK shares are traded less frequently than once a day, and one-third trade less than once a week. The examination of trading volumes of UK shares in the 1990s by this author suggests that Dimson's figures remain true for more recent years. A crude comparison across markets of annual turnover divided by number of listed shares suggests that thin trading will be at least as prevalent in most other markets, so the UK evidence summarised below will presumably be relevant internationally. The major exception is the New York Stock Exchange, where most stocks seem to trade a minimum of several times a day. This is indicated by evidence in McInish and Wood (1986), who allocate 963 New York stocks into quintiles by the frequency of trading (the data are from 1971 to 1972). For stocks in the least frequently traded quintile, the average time from the last trade to the market close is only forty-nine minutes.

Thin trading causes error in the variables, which biases beta estimates downwards. The bias arises because the share price does not change in the gaps between trades. The share price recorded at the end of a measurement interval is the price of the most recent trade, and, if there is a gap between the end of the interval and the most recent trade, the market index may have changed but the share price cannot have changed. The larger the gap, the more 'out of date' the share price will be. More infrequent trading implies larger gaps (less synchronicity with the market) and a smaller covariance between share and market returns, so the downward bias is more severe the less frequently the share is traded (Scholes and Williams, 1977, show this formally). Consistent with this bias, several studies report a strong positive relation between beta and the frequency of trading, even for New York shares. Furthermore, since it is smaller-cap shares that are less frequently traded (at least in the United Kingdom), the bias is worse for smaller companies; Dimson (1979) and Davies, Unni, Draper and Pavdyal (1999) find that smaller listed companies in the United Kingdom have smaller betas.

A further noteworthy feature of the UK evidence is that the mean betas of representative samples of shares, dominated by a number by smaller companies, are much less than one. Dimson (1979) reports a mean beta using monthly returns of 0.73, and Bartholdy and Riding (1994) report mean monthly-returns betas for New Zealand shares that are also substantially below one. The reason is that the market index employed in these studies is value-weighted, and the mean beta across the full population can differ from one unless the market index is equally weighted, or unless betas are value-weighted in calculating the mean. So bias caused by thin trading can pull the mean beta below one. However, if an equally weighted index is used, the mean beta must equal one. Then, if thin trading causes the betas of some shares to be biased downwards, the betas of frequently traded shares must be biased upwards, as Dimson demonstrates is the case via simulation. This upward bias may be small if a value-weighted index is used.

The explanation for the above statements about mean betas is as follows. The covariance of a share j with the market portfolio M can be written

$$\text{cov}(R_{jt}, R_{Mt}) = \Sigma_{k=1}^{N} w_k \text{cov}(R_{jt}, R_{kt})$$

where w_k is the proportion of M represented by share k and N is the number of shares in M (see, e.g., Fama, 1976, pp. 58–60). Using this expression, the variance of the market portfolio can be written as a value-weighted average of the covariances of the constituent shares:

$$\sigma^2(R_{Mt}) = \Sigma_{j=1}^{N} \Sigma_{k=1}^{N} w_j w_k \text{cov}(R_{jt}, R_{kt})$$
$$= \Sigma_{j=1}^{N} w_j \left[\Sigma_{k=1}^{N} w_k \text{cov}(R_{jt}, R_{kt}) \right]$$
$$= \Sigma_{j=1}^{N} w_j \text{cov}(R_{jt}, R_{Mt})$$

Thus β_j can be written as $\text{cov}(R_{jt}, R_{Mt})/\Sigma_{j=1}^{N} w_j \text{cov}(R_{jt}, R_{Mt})$. The equally weighted average beta is

$$(1/N)\Sigma_{j=1}^{N}\beta_j = (1/N)\Sigma_{j=1}^{N}\text{cov}(R_{jt}, R_{Mt})/\Sigma_{j=1}^{N} w_j \text{cov}(R_{jt}, R_{Mt}) \quad (13.3)$$

which will not, in general, equal one. If betas are calculated against an equally weighted index, then $w_j = 1/N$ for all j by construction, in which case the numerator and denominator are equal in equation (13.3), so the average beta must be equal to one. It can also be seen that the value-weighted average beta must equal one:

$$\Sigma_{j=1}^{N} w_j \beta_j = \Sigma_{j=1}^{N} w_j \text{cov}(R_{jt}, R_{Mt}) / \Sigma_{j=1}^{N} w_j \text{cov}(R_{jt}, R_{Mt})$$
$$= 1$$

We note in passing that the use of a value-weighted index conforms better with the CAPM theory, because the composition of the 'market portfolio' is given by assets in proportion to their respective market values. We can see that the statement sometimes encountered that 'the average beta is one by definition' is potentially misleading. The equally weighted average beta is certainly not one by definition if a value-weighted index is used (but the beta of the market portfolio is one by definition).

Several methods of estimating the beta of thinly traded shares have been proposed; the two most widely used by researchers are due to Scholes and Williams (1977) and Dimson (1979). The Scholes–Williams estimate, $\beta_j(\text{SW})$, is

$$\beta_j(\text{SW}) = (\beta_j^- + \beta_j + \beta_j^+)/(1 + 2\rho_M)$$

where ρ_M is the estimated first-order autocorrelation of market returns, β_j is estimated using equation (13.2), β_j^- is estimated from the OLS regression $R_{jt} = \alpha_j + \beta_j^- R_{Mt-1} + e_{jt}$, and β_j^+ is estimated from the regression $R_{jt} = \alpha_j + \beta_j^+ R_{Mt+1} + e_{jt}$. It is assumed that the gaps between the end of a period and the time within the period of the last trade in j are independently and identically distributed over time. The Scholes–Williams method is designed for use with daily returns, for shares that generally trade each trading day but do not necessarily trade at the close. If there is no trade in the share on a certain day, the resulting multiperiod return is ignored in calculating β_j, β_j^+ and β_j^-.

The Dimson 'aggregated coefficients' estimate, $\beta_j(\text{D})$, is

$$\beta_j(\text{D}) = \Sigma_{k=-n}^{n} \beta_{j,k}$$

where $\beta_{j,k}$ is a coefficient in a multiple regression of R_{jt} on R_{Mt+k}. For example, for $n = 1$, the multiple regression is

$$R_{jt} = \alpha_j + \beta_{j,k=-1} R_{Mt-1} + \beta_{j,k=0} R_{Mt} + \beta_{j,k=+1} R_{Mt+1} + e_{jt} \qquad (13.4)$$

The number of leads and lags is not prescribed, but it is common to use $n = 1$ or 2. The reasoning behind this method is as follows. The process generating observed returns is assumed to be

$$R_{jt} = \Sigma_{k=0}^{n} \pi_k R_{jt-k}^* + u_{jt}$$
$$= \Sigma_{k=0}^{n} \pi_k(a_j + b_j R_{Mt-k} + \varepsilon_{jt}) + u_{jt} \qquad (13.5)$$

Here, R_{jt} is the observed return on share j in period t, R_{jt-k}^* is the return that would have arisen in period $t - k$ if trading were continuous, and π_k is the probability of a trade in period $t - k$. It is assumed that shares trade at least once every n periods and hence that $\Sigma_{k=0}^{n} \pi_k = 1$. u_{jt} and ε_{jt} are error terms. Equation (13.5) incorporates the assumption that returns with continuous trading are generated by the market model: $R_{jt}^* = a_j + b_j R_{Mt} + \varepsilon_{jt}$, where a_j and b_j are the true values of the regression coefficients with continuous trading. The equation of a multiple regression of R_{jt} on R_{Mt+k} for $k = -n \cdots + n$ is

$$R_{jt} = \alpha_j + \Sigma_{k=-n}^{n} \beta_{jk} R_{Mt+k} + e_{jt} \tag{13.6}$$

For $n = 1$, this is the same as equation (13.4). Dimson argues that, since equations (13.5) and (13.6) both explain observed returns R_{jt}, the true beta with continuous trading, b_j, can be estimated by $\Sigma_{k=-n}^{n} \beta_{jk}$. This method is designed to cope with gaps in the period-by-period trading record, for example when daily data are used and some shares do not trade every day.

A third method of adjusting for thin trading is the trade-to-trade method (Dimson, 1979). Returns on the share and on the market are measured between days on which the share was traded. The returns for interval t are divided by $\sqrt{d_t}$, the square root of the number of days in the interval, which can vary from interval to interval. These weighted trade-to-trade returns are used as the observations in a market model regression to estimate the trade-to-trade beta. The weighting of each return by $1/\sqrt{d_t}$ is necessary to correct for the fact that larger intervals will tend to give rise to larger returns. The OLS regression model assumes that observations are drawn from the same population and therefore implicitly assumes that return intervals are of equal length, so the error terms with unweighted trade-to-trade returns are expected to be heteroscedastic.

Of the above three methods, the Dimson method is the easiest to estimate because it does not call for data on when trades occurred. The trade-to-trade method is awkward because the length of each interval is different, which may help explain why it is rarely used.

The methods do reduce bias, as can be seen by creating portfolios from shares ranked by frequency of trading, and calculating the mean betas of the constituents of each portfolio. The dispersion of the means of the betas after Scholes–Williams and Dimson adjustments is much smaller than the dispersion of the means of the unadjusted OLS betas (Scholes and Williams, 1977; Dimson, 1979; McInish and Wood, 1986). The trade-to-trade method provides the most efficient estimates in simulated data (Dimson, 1979). However, a puzzling finding is that the trade-to-trade adjustment does not appear to 'improve' estimated betas much in real data, in the sense of increasing the equally weighted average beta across samples that are representative of the population of listed shares. Results for the United Kingdom in Dimson and Marsh (1983, tables 1 and 7) indicate that the mean OLS beta from monthly returns is 0.74 and the mean trade-to-trade beta is 0.80. Armitage (2000) reports no difference between mean OLS and trade-to-trade betas from daily data for UK shares. Results for New Zealand in Bartholdy and Riding (1994, table 3) indicate that the mean OLS beta from monthly returns is 0.49 or 0.54, depending on the index. In this study none of the three adjustment methods increases the mean beta by more than 0.13.

A further point is that thin-trading bias causes OLS betas to have a spurious stability over time. Dimson and Marsh (1983) report that, in a sample of shares below the median trading frequency, the correlation between betas estimated using data from two adjoining estimation periods is higher for OLS than for trade-to-trade betas. Thus, although an *ex post* beta provides a more accurate forecast of the future beta using OLS, this evidence should not be viewed as a point in favour of the OLS method if, roughly speaking, shares are traded less frequently than once a day.

13.3.4   Measurement interval, company size and trading frequency

Betas are usually estimated using monthly or weekly returns for estimating the cost of equity, but daily returns are the norm in academic studies that use beta estimates. The return interval affects estimates of beta both in theory and in practice. Levhari and Levy (1977) and Handa, Kothari and Wasley (1989) show that the return interval affects beta in theory because, as the interval is changed, a share's covariance with the market (the top line of beta) changes at a different rate from the change in the variance of the market (the bottom line). The difference is such that, as the interval is lengthened, a beta below one becomes smaller and a beta above one becomes larger, so the distribution of betas widens. This analysis does not take account of the potential impact of thin trading. Handa et al. (1989) present beta estimates for twenty portfolios ranked by constituent company size, using various intervals between one day and one year, using data from 1926 to 1982. The companies are all listed on the New York Stock Exchange. The portfolio betas are related to the measurement interval in the manner predicted; the distribution is widest for the one-year interval. Whatever the interval, there is a negative relation between size and beta, which is also reported in several earlier US studies: the portfolio with the smallest companies has the largest beta. Handa et al. find that betas using annual returns have more explanatory power than betas using monthly returns in Fama–MacBeth-style cross-sectional regressions of portfolio returns on their betas. Indeed, in regressions that include a size variable (the market value of the portfolio), only size is significant if beta is estimated from monthly returns, but only beta is significant if beta is estimated from annual returns.

The negative relation between size and beta in the United States arises despite the effect of thin trading. It appears from Scholes and Williams (1977) and McInish and Wood (1986) that even the relatively small differences in trading frequency across US shares affect their beta estimates. McInish and Wood, for example, divide a large sample of New York shares into quintiles by frequency of trading, as noted above. The quintile portfolios are constructed such that each has approximately the same return over a six-month period in 1971/72, and therefore the same expected (daily-return) beta over this period. The mean OLS beta of shares in each quintile ranges from 0.744 for the most thinly traded to 1.494 for the most frequently, so thinly traded shares have smaller betas, as in other markets. A positive relation remains between estimated beta and the frequency of trading even using estimation methods that correct for thin trading. Despite this, it is the case that the smaller companies had *larger* betas in the United States up to the 1980s, although – presumably – smaller companies were traded less frequently. (Ehrhardt, 1994, reports that the relation between size and beta became positive in the 1980s).

The UK evidence is strikingly different. Trading frequency and company size are strongly positively related in the United Kingdom, and thin-trading bias is the probable reason why there is found to be a positive relation between size and beta (Davies et al., 1999; Dimson and Marsh, 1983). Furthermore, several authors have noted that the bias is most severe using daily returns. These phenomena can explain the finding that, when portfolios are formed according to the size of the constituent company, the distribution of portfolio mean betas narrows as the return interval is lengthened, whereas the distribution of betas widens with the interval in the United States. For example, Davies et al. (p. 42) present the average beta across samples of a hundred of the largest UK companies by market capitalisation, a hundred medium-sized companies and a hundred of the smallest, using various estimation periods. The results for the five-year period are representative:

Average beta calculated using	Full sample	Large company portfolio	Medium company portfolio	Small company portfolio
Daily returns	0.65	1.07	0.49	0.39
Monthly returns	1.01	1.08	1.04	0.88

Consistent with this is the finding that mean betas of representative samples of UK shares that are dominated by infrequently traded shares are a long way below one if daily returns are used. For example, Armitage (2000) notes that the mean daily-return OLS beta using the value-weighted Financial Times All-Share Index is only 0.39 across a sample of 580 UK companies, of all sizes, that have announced a seasoned equity offer. This compares with the mean monthly-return OLS beta of 0.73 in Dimson's (1979) sample of 421 shares or 0.76 in Bell and Jenkinson's (2002) sample of 1,434 dividend-paying shares (all of which were traded on the ex-dividend day). As mentioned, the mean beta does not increase much when betas are adjusted for thin trading. One conclusion from the UK evidence is that beta should be estimated, for cost-of-equity purposes, using monthly or longer-interval returns, since the downward bias caused by thin trading is most severe in daily data.

13.3.5   Length of estimation period

The estimation period has a major effect on the beta estimate. A priori, the choice regarding the length of the period potentially involves a trade-off. A longer estimation period gives a more reliable estimate of beta, assuming that beta is stable over time; the standard error of the beta coefficient falls as the number of return observations increases. On the other hand, given the evidence that betas are not stable over time, an unadjusted OLS beta becomes more 'out of date' the longer the estimation period is, so it may be that errors in forecast betas are positively related to the length of the estimation period.

Several studies present evidence on the effect on beta estimates of changing the estimation period. The overall finding is that forecast errors diminish with the use of longer estimation periods, though further improvement is small after about sixty months, or after about 400 days if daily returns are used. Forecast errors also diminish with the length of the prediction period. The prediction period is the length of time over which a beta is calculated *ex post*, to compare with a forecast beta. For example, Eubank and Zumwalt (1979), using monthly US returns, report average mean squared errors of 0.59 and 0.13 for a twelve- and

120-month estimation period, respectively, with a sixty-month prediction period. The average MSEs are 0.54 and 0.12 for a twelve- and 120-month prediction period, respectively, with a sixty-month estimation period. Dimson and Marsh (1983), using monthly UK trade-to-trade returns, find that beta stability increases as the estimation period is increased from one to twelve years, with more substantial improvements for periods longer than sixty months than are seen in the US data. Draper and Paudyal (1995) examine the stability of UK daily-return OLS betas. They recommend using at least 400 return observations and note that, for one-quarter of their sample, the betas change by more than 20 per cent with a change in estimation period from 100 to 400 days.

13.3.6   *Fat-tailed return distributions*

It has been known since the 1960s that distributions of observed stock returns have fatter tails than the normal distribution displays. This has not led to adjustment in the practice of beta estimation. However, Chan and Lakonishok (1992) argue in favour of using 'robust methods', given the fat-tailed distributions that describe cross-sections and time series of stock returns. A simple example of a robust method is to calculate the regression line so that it minimises the sum of absolute deviations, rather than the sum of squared deviations. This approach gives much less weight to outliers. The authors perform OLS and robust method regressions on simulated data for a sample of notional shares, from the following return-generating process:

$$R_{jt} - R_{Ft} = \alpha_j + \beta_j(R_{Mt} - R_{Ft}) + e_{jt}$$

with α_j set to zero, β_j to one and the error term set to various non-normal distributions that give distributions of simulated excess returns that approximate to distributions of observed excess returns. The cross-sectional variance of betas estimated by robust methods is smaller than the variance of the OLS betas, which implies that they estimate the true beta with less error (since the true betas are set at one).

13.3.7   *Commercial estimates*

The majority of companies use betas estimated by commercial services (Bruner et al., 1998; Rutterford, 2000), so it is of interest to see how some of them arrive at their estimates. Five examples are summarised below. All are US services except the first.

London Business School Risk Measurement Service
Estimation period: sixty months. Returns include dividends. Index: not stated.
Calculation method: trade-to-trade. 'We use Bayesian statistics to adjust our risk measures for estimate error' (Risk Measurement Service, 2002, p. 1).

Merrill Lynch
Estimation period: sixty months. Returns do not include dividends. Index: Standard & Poor's 500 (value-weighted). Calculation method: both unadjusted OLS beta and adjusted OLS beta reported. Adjusted beta = 2/3(unadjusted

beta) + 1/3(1), to reflect regression to mean (Blume adjustment). Source: Patterson (1995, p. 130).

Bloomberg

Estimation period: 104 weeks. Index: Standard & Poor's 500 (value-weighted). Other combinations of estimation period and index are possible. Calculation method: both unadjusted OLS beta and adjusted OLS beta reported. Adjusted beta = 2/3(unadjusted beta) + 1/3(1). Source: Bruner et al. (1998).

Value Line

Estimation period: 260 weeks. Index: New York Stock Exchange Composite Index (value-weighted). Calculation method: adjusted OLS beta is reported. Adjusted beta = 2/3(unadjusted beta) + 1/3(1). Source: Patterson (1995, p. 130).

Ibbotson Associates

Estimation period: sixty months. Index: New York Stock Exchange Composite Index (value-weighted). Four calculation methods: unadjusted OLS beta; OLS beta with Vasicek (Bayesian) adjustment; Dimson-style beta to allow for thin trading; Dimson-style beta with Vasicek adjustment. Source: Pratt (1998).

It can be seen that the services use monthly or weekly returns. All use a value-weighted index, except possibly London Business School. The use of a value-weighted index implies that, if thin trading is prevalent, the equally weighted average beta will be less than one, even after adjustment for thin trading. All the services make an adjustment for regression to the mean, and Merrill Lynch, Bloomberg and Value Line assume that the mean beta is one. London Business School adjusts for thin trading, and Ibbotson Associates offers betas adjusted and unadjusted for thin trading.

There can be substantial differences in estimates across methods of estimation and across commercial services. Differences across estimates for a given share of 0.4 or 0.5 are not unusual, and larger differences occur (Bruner et al., 1998, p. 21). In view of this, it seems sensible for a company to estimate its beta as an average of more than one estimate.

13.3.8   *Discussion*

This section has been about the use of betas estimated from past returns to forecast future betas. Three problems have been identified: betas tend to regress towards the mean; thin trading causes betas to be underestimated; and beta estimates change over time, which means that even betas adjusted for regression to the mean and for thin trading provide unreliable forecasts. Bias caused by regression to the mean is reduced by using a long estimation period of sixty months or more and applying the Blume or Vasicek adjustment. The standard error of a beta estimate is reduced by increasing the number of observations, which is an argument for using daily data. But thin trading bias is most pronounced in daily data, and it exists even in US data.

Thin trading bias is a serious problem in UK data, and presumably in data from most other stock markets. It is almost certainly the reason why the mean beta, using a value-weighted index, is at least 25 per cent below one with monthly returns and 60 per cent below one with daily returns. Adjustment for thin trading does not increase the mean beta. This presents a problem of interpretation. It may be that the adjustments for thin trading eliminate most of the bias, in which case the implication is that the majority of true betas of UK shares are well below one, and that large-cap shares tend to have betas above one (the value-weighted average beta must be one, using a value-weighted index). On the other hand, the adjustments may eliminate little of the bias, since the mean beta does not rise. So the question is whether large-cap shares really are riskier than small-cap shares, as measured by beta.

13.4   A Bayesian approach to estimating the CAPM

There is uncertainty about any particular estimate of the expected rate of return on a share. A new estimate, or any relevant new information, can be seen as an update of one's prior beliefs about the expected rate. This Bayesian approach to estimating the expected rate is developed by Pastor and Stambaugh (1999), and can be applied across different models of expected returns. They study the standard CAPM, the Fama–French three-factor model and an arbitrage pricing theory model with unknown risk factors inferred from the data. Consider the standard CAPM:

$$E(R_j) - R_F = \alpha_j + \beta_j[E(R_M) - R_F]$$

They argue that, if the user does not know anything about the company and believes or assumes that the CAPM is true, then his prior beliefs are that $\alpha_j = \mu(\alpha_j) = 0$, where $\mu(\alpha_j)$ is the cross-sectional mean of α_j, and that $\beta_j = \mu(\beta_j) = \Sigma_{j=1}^{n}$ estβ_j/n, the mean value of betas across the n shares in the sample, estimated by OLS regressions of $R_{jt} - R_{Ft}$ on $R_{Mt} - R_{Ft}$ using historic monthly data over a long period. Prior uncertainty about the error of the estimate of $E(R_j) - R_F$ is assumed to be given by $\mu(\sigma^2)$, the mean of the variances of the error terms in the n regressions used to estimate the betas. Prior uncertainty about α_j is represented by the assumed variance of α_j, σ_{α}^2. This is not estimated but is set artificially; it is the variable that represents prior uncertainty on the part of the user about the accuracy of the model for expected returns. Different values of σ_{α}^2 can be thought of as different degrees of confidence in the model across individuals. Prior uncertainty about β_j is more complicated to describe but is linked to the cross-sectional variance of the estimated betas. Finally, the user is assumed to have no prior idea about the equity premium $E(R_M) - R_F$.

The model user's prior beliefs are revised in the light of new information, to arrive at posterior beliefs. In this case, the new information is taken to be (i) knowledge of the particular OLS regression of $R_{jt} - R_{Ft}$ on $R_{Mt} - R_{Ft}$ for a given share j using historic monthly returns, and (ii) the arithmetic mean equity premium over a long period. The new information provides the user with stock-specific estimates of α_j, β_j and the regression error variance, σ_j^2, together with an estimate for $E(R_M) - R_F$. Exactly how the user updates his/her beliefs is determined by the prior probability density function for the expected returns, which is affected by the assumed prior belief about σ_{α}^2. The authors derive expressions for the posterior belief of the value of α_j and β_j. An approximate version of the expression for α_j is

$$\alpha_j = w_\alpha \mu(\alpha) + (1 - w_\alpha) \text{est} \alpha_j$$

where

$$w_\alpha = \mu(\sigma^2) / [\mu(\sigma^2) + T\sigma_\alpha^2]$$

where T is the number of observations used to estimate the OLS regression for share j.

They give the example of Bay State Gas, for which $\text{est}\alpha = 7.92\%$ pa and $\text{est}\beta = 0.42$, estimated from $T = 253$ monthly observations during 1975 to 1995. The prior beliefs are $\mu(\alpha) = 0$, $\mu(\beta) = 1.12$ and $\mu(\sigma^2) = 0.016$, the latter two means being estimated from 1994 stocks using monthly data from 1963 to 1995, conditional on $\mu(\alpha)$ being zero. If σ_α is assumed to be zero, the user has no uncertainty about alpha and the posterior belief is $\alpha = 0$. If, for example, $\sigma_\alpha = 5\%$ on an annualised basis, the monthly value of σ_α^2 to use in equation (13.6) is $(.05/12)^2 = 0.000017$ and $w_\alpha = 0.78$, giving an approximate value of $\alpha = 1.74\%$ from equation (13.6) (the figure using the exact formula is 0.73 per cent). Thus the posterior belief about alpha is shrunk from its regression estimate of 7.92 per cent towards the prior belief that alpha is zero. As $\sigma_\alpha \to \infty$, posterior $\alpha \to \text{est}\alpha$. The posterior belief about β, whilst shifted slightly towards the prior of 1.12, is 0.47 for $\sigma_\alpha = 5\%$, and within 10 per cent of the estimated value of 0.42 for all assumed values of σ_α, including $\sigma_\alpha = 0$. The mean equity premium was 8.1 per cent p.a. Thus we have a CAPM estimate for the excess return on Bay State Gas of $0.73\% + 0.47(8.1\%) = 4.54\%$ pa, using posterior beliefs. It can be seen that the updating process is such that, with many observations to estimate α and β (253 in this case), the estimated β dominates the prior belief about β, but even substantial uncertainty about α, such as $\sigma_\alpha = 5\%$, results in a posterior belief fairly close to the prior of zero. Pastor and Stambaugh (1999, p. 112) conclude that, whilst uncertainty about the accuracy of the model for expected returns – i.e. about α – increases the user's uncertainty about the expected excess return on the stock, the posterior estimate of the expected excess return 'is generally not affected greatly by uncertainty about α'. They also find that, assuming a prior belief that each of the three models studied is equally likely to be correct, uncertainty about which model is correct contributes less on average to the posterior standard deviation of an expected excess return than does uncertainty about parameter values within a model, even for $\sigma_\alpha = 0$ (there is still uncertainty regarding $\beta[E(R_M) - R_F]$).

13.5   Multifactor models

A multifactor model is one in which there is more than one risk factor that affects the expected return on an asset. The theoretical basis for multifactor models can lie either in arbitrage pricing theory (Section 3.3) or in the concept of state variables (Section 4.3). In the APT it is assumed that there are one or more variables (risk factors) with uncertain outcomes that affect returns across different assets. The APT shows that, to preclude arbitrage, there must be a linear relation between the expected return on an asset and the sensitivity of its returns to changes in a given risk factor. A state variable is a variable the realisation of which affects the price of an asset. In Merton's asset pricing model there is, in equilibrium, a linear relation between the expected return on an asset and its sensitivity to a given state variable.

For practical purposes there is no distinction between these theories. The procedure for developing a multifactor model is to find variables that explain the differences in returns across assets and over time, and to use these variables to predict expected returns. There is evidence that some firms are using multifactor models, at least in the United States (Graham and Harvey, 2001). However, Cornell et al. (1997) note that neither the Fama–French nor any other multifactor model is used in proceedings to estimate the cost of equity of regulated utilities.

In this section we review, first, the implementation of a macrofactor model, in which expected returns are predicted by several macroeconomic variables. We then review the implementation of the Fama–French three-factor model, in which the explanatory variables are the premiums on the market and on two firm-specific characteristics that are assumed to proxy for risk factors, since they help explain the differences in observed returns across assets.

13.5.1   A macrofactor model

Elton, Gruber and Mei (1994) provide a detailed account of how to estimate a macrofactor model to estimate the cost of equity, and our summary is based on their account. The search for explanatory variables uses (i) a mixture of economic intuition, to identify the economic variables that might be expected to affect the returns on shares; (ii) experimentation, to establish which of the variables identified do the best job of explaining observed returns; and (iii) the example of previous studies. Elton et al. end up including the following six variables in their model, using monthly data.

> *Change in yield on thirty-day treasury bills.*
> *Yield spread.* The yield on twenty-year government bonds less the yield on thirty-day treasury bills. These two variables are intended to capture changes in the component of discount rates accounted for by rates on default-free bonds.
> *Change in inflation forecast.* Professional forecasters' estimates of the GNP deflator for the current year during the first six months of the year and for the subsequent year during the second six months, reported by Blue Chip Indicators. A change in inflation could affect expected returns via a change in expectations both of future cash flows and of discount rates.
> *Change in real GNP forecast.* Any change in professional forecasters' estimates of real GNP for the current year during the first six momths and for the subsequent year during the second six months, reported by Blue Chip Indicators.
> *Change in a trade-value-weighted exchange rate.* This is taken from the Federal Reserve Bank of Dallas. (Changes in real GNP and in exchange rates could affect expectations of future cash flows.)
> *Residual market factor.* This is the return on the market not explained by the above five macroeconomic variables. Values for the residual market factor are given by the error terms e_t in the regression

$$R_{Mt} = \alpha + \Sigma_F \beta_{M,F} F_t + e_t$$

where α is the constant, R_{Mt} is the return on the market in month t, F_t is the value of macrovariable F and $\beta_{M,F}$ is the beta of the market with respect to variable F. The maximum estimation period used by Elton et al. is January 1978 to December 1990.

Having identified the six macrovariables or risk factors, the next task is to estimate the risk premiums on these variables. This involves several steps. First, the authors randomly select a hundred listed firms, and for each firm they regress the monthly returns on the shares against the monthly values of the six risk factors. This produces six betas per firm. Second, for each month they regress the returns of each of the hundred firms against the six betas for each firm. The coefficients on the six betas are estimates of the six risk premiums in the month in question. The premiums for the yield spread, change in forecast GNP and residual market factor are positive; the premiums for the change in interest rate, change in exchange rate and inflation are usually negative. Third, the monthly premiums are averaged over the months in the estimation period to produce a single premium for each risk factor. Finally, each premium is scaled so that it represents the premium for a share with average sensitivity to the factor in question. The scaled premium is the average beta for the factor times the average premium. For example, the average beta with respect to the change in forecast real GNP is 0.066 in 1990, and the average monthly premium for this risk factor is 0.621 per cent. So the scaled premium on the GNP variable for 1990 is $0.066 \times 0.621\% = 0.041\%$. This is the estimate of the amount of monthly return explained by the sensitivity of a share's returns to changes in forecast real GNP, for a share with average sensitivity to the GNP variable.

We now have estimates of the monthly risk premiums as at a given year. The annualised premiums are obtained by multiplying the monthly premiums by twelve. The cost of equity as at the end of the year for a share with average sensitivity to each of the factors would simply be the risk-free rate plus the sum of the six annualised risk premiums. To measure the cost of equity of a particular share j requires an estimate of the betas of j with respect to the six factors. The cost of equity is then given by

$$E(R_{jt}) = R_{Ft} + \Sigma_F(\beta_{j,F}/av\beta_F)Prem_F$$

where $E(R_{jt})$ is the expected return on j at date t, R_{Ft} is the prevailing risk-free rate, $\beta_{j,F}$ is the beta of j with respect to risk factor F, $av\beta_F$ is the average beta with respect to F across the sample of a hundred firms and $Prem_F$ is the estimated premium on F for a share with average sensitivity to F. Finally, the authors recommend that all the estimated premiums be multiplied by $1/1.18$, because the mean equity premium for the hundred firms during 1978 to 1990 was 18 per cent more than a historic mean equity premium.

It is, clearly, quite a business to apply a macrofactor model, but Elton et al. (1994) conclude that the model they apply produces 'useful and reasonable' estimates of the cost of equity. Davies et al. (1999) test the usefulness of a similar model using UK data, and come to the opposite conclusion. The reason is that none of the factors is significantly related to returns on the UK market as a whole, and only one – the difference between long- and short-term interest rates – is significantly related to the returns of more than a small proportion of the

562 shares in their sample. They find that their macrofactor model produces less accurate predictions of share returns than either the CAPM or the three-factor model.

13.5.2   *The three-factor model*

This multifactor model is easier to implement, because the three factors are given. We have discussed the model in Section 3.3. Here we review its implementation (see Fama and French, 1997, or Davies et al., 1999, for more detailed presentations). The first step is to estimate the risk premiums on the three factors, which can be done using historic data. The first factor is the return on the market less the risk-free rate; we have the seen that the equity premium can be estimated either via a historic average or via the dividend discount model applied to the market. The second factor is 'small minus big' (SMB). A large sample of firms is collected and the firms in the sample are ranked by market capitalisation at a given date each year. Those above the median are counted as big, those below as small. The premium on SMB in a given month or year is the return on a value-weighted portfolio of the small firms less the return on a value-weighted portfolio of the large firms. The third factor is 'high minus low' (HML). The firms are ranked by book-to-market ratio at a given date each year, and divided into two groups, one above and the other below the median. The premium on HML is the return on a value-weighted portfolio of the group above the median less the return on a value-weighted portfolio of the group below the median. The premiums on SMB and HML can be estimated by the arithmetic mean of the historic monthly or annual premiums over many years.

The second step is to estimate the firm's betas with respect to the three risk factors. The most straightforward approach is to extend the standard method of estimating the CAPM – i.e. to estimate the betas using monthly returns over the most recent five-year period:

$$R_{jt} - R_{Ft} = \alpha_j + \beta_{1j}(R_{Mt} - R_{Ft}) + \beta_{2j}(SMB_t) + \beta_{3j}(HML_t) + e_{jt}$$

where R_{jt} is the return on share j in month t and SMB_t and HML_t are the premiums for small size and a high book-to-market ratio, respectively, in month t. The third step is to use the estimated risk premiums, $Prem_M$, $Prem_{SMB}$ and $Prem_{HML}$, together with the estimated betas, β_{1j}, β_{2j} and β_{3j}, in the three-factor model of j's cost of equity:

$$E(R_{jt}) = R_{Ft} + \beta_{1j}(Prem_M) + \beta_{2j}(Prem_{SMB}) + \beta_{3j}(Prem_{HML})$$

The implementation of the three-factor model is fairly easy to understand, and it accounts for observed returns on shares much better than the CAPM. But it lacks a grounding in theory. A pragmatic drawback is that the data requirements are more onerous than for the CAPM, although estimates of the cost of equity from the model are available from Ibbotson Associates for over 5000 US companies.

13.5.3   *Use of the abnormal earnings method to estimate a multifactor model*

Gebhardt, Lee and Swaminathan (2001) propose using the abnormal earnings method (Section 12.3) to estimate the factor risk premiums and betas in a multifactor model. Using this method, risk premiums and betas are estimated from estimates of expected returns, instead of from observations of past returns. The first step is to infer the cost of equity across a large sample of firms, using equation (12.9):

$$P_0 = E_{\text{book},0} + \Sigma_{t=1}^{\infty} Abearn_t/(1 + R_E)^t$$

The authors suggest forecasting a firm's return on equity for the next three years using analysts' consensus forecasts. Beyond three years, they assume that the firm's return on equity reverts over the next nine years to the median return on equity for the industry it is in. Terminal value is estimated at the end of eleven years as a perpetuity of the abnormal earnings for year 12:

$$TV_{11} = E_{\text{book},11} + E(Abearn_{12})/R_E$$

This assumes that the net present value of new investments from year 12 is zero. The future book value is forecast by accumulating the current book value plus forecast earnings less dividends for each year:

$$E_{\text{book},t+1} = E_{\text{book},t} + Earn_{t+1} - Div_{t+1}$$

The cost of equity R_E for each firm is found from the discount rate at which the present value of the forecast abnormal earnings for the first eleven years plus the present value of the terminal value is equal to the current market value of the equity.

The second step is to relate the estimated firm-specific risk premiums to firm characteristics. Much of the cross-sectional differences in *ex ante* premiums for firms are explained by the following four firm characteristics: ln(book/market); ln(dispersion of analysts' forecasts for the firm); analysts' consensus long-term growth forecast for earnings; and last year's risk premium for the industry the firm is in, estimated using the abnormal earnings method. The authors report an adjusted R^2 of 0.58 in a cross-sectional multivariate regression using these variables to explain *ex ante* premiums. As expected, the book/market, growth and industry premium characteristics have positive coefficients, but the dispersion of analysts' forecasts has a negative coefficient, which seems odd. The book/market ratio is much the most significant variable. This step is equivalent to estimating an *ex ante* premium associated with each of the four characteristics.

The final step is to use the estimated coefficients or premiums on these characteristics together with the actual values of the variables for a given firm to estimate the firm's cost of equity:

$$E(R_{jt}) = R_{Ft} + B_{jt}/M_{jt}(Prem_{B/M,t}) + Disp_{jt}(Prem_{\text{disp},t})$$
$$+ g_{jt}(Prem_{g,t}) + Ind_{jt-1}(Prem_{\text{indt}-1,t})$$

B_{jt}/M_{jt} is the book-to-market ratio for firm j at date t and $Prem_{B/M,t}$ is the estimated premium on the ratio; *Disp* is the dispersion in analysts' forecasts for j; g_{jt} is the estimate of the long-term growth rate for j; and Ind_{jt-1} is the estimated risk premium for j's industry as at date $t - 1$. An advantage of the above method is that it avoids the need to estimate betas.

The method could be used to estimate any multifactor model in which the 'risk factors' are firm-specific variables.

13.6   Summary

The standard CAPM requires estimates of the risk-free rate, the equity risk premium and the firm's beta. The most common practice is to use the nominal yield on long-term government bonds to estimate the risk-free rate, although such a yield is not risk-free in real terms. Consensus is lacking at present on the best way of estimating the equity premium, and reasonable estimates lie in a range between 1 per cent and 5 per cent p.a., or wider. Much attention has been paid to the estimation of beta from past data, and the chapter has reviewed the main issues, including techniques to alleviate the biases in beta estimates caused by thin trading and by the tendency of betas to regress to the mean. The chapter has also outlined a Bayesian approach to the estimation of the CAPM, in which information from shares in general is combined with information about the particular share in question.

The application of multifactor models to estimate the cost of equity is more demanding and less well established than the application of the CAPM. The chapter has described how to apply three multifactor models. It remains to be seen if multifactor models become more popular with companies in the future, and if one particular type of model becomes established as the 'industry standard'.

14 Estimating a project's cost of capital

The subject of this chapter is how to estimate the cost of capital of an existing or potential investment project that has not issued traded financial assets and is not regulated. There is no existing market price of the project and no historic record of market prices. The remarkable fact is that the cost of capital of an untraded project cannot be estimated directly without using an estimate of the expected rate of return on another asset. All respectable procedures involve, as part of the process, identifying one or more listed companies that are thought to be similar to the project, and then estimating the expected rates of return on the shares of these similar companies. Thus we have already considered, in the preceding two chapters, an indispensable step. The current chapter fills in the other steps in arriving at a project's weighted average cost of capital. It also discusses evidence of company practice, and offers a ranking of the decisions to be made in order of their impact on the final estimate of the WACC. It is hoped that, by the end of the chapter, the reader will have a clear view of the whole estimation process, and of what matters and what does not matter in the process.

14.1   Estimating a project's cost of equity

14.1.1   Cost of equity from pure-play companies

The estimation of a project's cost of equity requires the identification of similar listed companies – i.e. companies with shares of similar risk to the shares that would be issued, at least hypothetically, by the project. There are no direct measures of the risk of the equity of an untraded project to compare with, say, the CAPM beta of the shares of a listed company. To estimate the beta of the project's equity would involve forecasting the possible returns on the equity, forecasting the possible returns on the stock market, and estimating the covariance between the two. In practice this simply cannot be done. The best that can be done is to use the cost of equity of a listed company in the same line of business and with similar leverage to the leverage of the project. There will inevitably be judgement about what counts as the same line of business, and about the project's risk in relation to the risk of the line of business in question.

The most straightforward case is that of a project to expand the capacity of an existing listed company with a single line of business. In this case it is reasonable to suppose that the project has a similar business risk and optimal leverage to that of the company's existing business, so that the parent's estimated cost of equity and WACC can be used for the project.

In the case of a company with several different lines of business, the company's cost of equity is not, in principle, the correct cost of equity of any of the individual business units, unless it is believed that each unit has a similar risk. It is more correct to try to find a listed company – or, preferably, several – with a single business as similar as possible to that of the project, and to use the average of the estimated costs of equity of these 'pure plays'. Ideally, the leverage across the pure plays should also be similar to that of the project, since the leverage affects the cost of equity. If the leverage is not similar, an adjustment should be made so that the estimated costs of equity of the pure plays are the costs that would apply were the pure plays to have the same leverage as the project (this is discussed below). The same technique can be used to find the cost of equity of an unlisted company, assuming it operates in a single business. In fact, even in the case of a listed company in a single business, it is a good idea to use the average of the estimates for several similar companies, including the company in question, assuming that any similar companies exist. The reason is that an average provides a more reliable estimate than a single observation. If no close matches by business can be found, then all one can do is resort to less close matches, or use an estimate of the cost of capital of the relevant industry.

A refinement of the pure-play method is to exploit the estimated cost of equity or WACC of firms with more than one business (Ehrhardt and Bhagwat, 1991; Harris, O'Brien and Wakeman, 1989). Firm j's cost of equity can be expressed as a value-weighted average of the costs of equity of its constituent projects or lines of business: $R_{Ej} = \Sigma_b w_{bj} R_{Eb}$, where w_{bj} is the proportion of the market value of firm j accounted for by a given line of business b. If the market values of a firm or its lines of business are not known, proportions of sales or earnings can be used as proxies for value. Assuming that there are more firms than lines of business, the cost of equity of each business can be estimated from a regression of each firm's cost of equity on its business weights:

$$R_{Ej} = \Sigma_b \alpha_b w_{bj} + e_j \tag{14.1}$$

for firms $j = 1, \ldots n$, where α_b are regression coefficients and e_j is an error term. If a firm is not active in a business, $w_{bj} = 0$. Each α_b coefficient is an estimate of the cost of equity for a line of business. If the firms' costs of equity are not unlevered, the estimated cost of equity for a given line of business reflects the weighted average leverage of firms operating in the business. Exactly the same procedure can be used to estimate the WACC directly for each business, by first calculating the WACC of each firm and then replacing R_{Ej} with $WACC_j$ in equation (14.1).

A second method is to estimate a project's beta using accounting information, and then to apply the CAPM using an 'accounting beta', β_{acc}. There are a number of possible measures, one being

$$\beta_{accj} = \text{cov}(ROE_j, ROE_M)/\text{var}(ROE_M)$$

where ROE_j is the accounting return on equity for project j and ROE_M is the accounting return on equity for all listed companies. This method works better for existing operations than for projects, since the analyst is not dependent on forecasts of accounting data if the operation has a track record. For example, Ezzamel (1979) suggests estimating a divisional 'earnings beta' β_{div} from a time-series regression of the changes in the division's profit after tax, PAT_{div}, on changes in aggregate profit after tax for all listed companies, PAT_M:

$$\Delta PAT_{divt} = \alpha_{div} + \beta_{div} \Delta PAT_{Mt} + e_t$$

However, accounting beta methods are, apparently, not much used in practice (Ehrhardt, 1994, p. 103).

One test of the efficacy of the pure-play technique is whether the risk of a multi-divisional firm is in fact related to the average risk of its constituent divisions. Fuller and Kerr (1981) collect a sample of multi-divisional firms with a pure-play match for each division. They find that the mean difference between the levered equity beta of a multi-divisional firm and the weighted average beta of the pure play for each division is 9 per cent, the weights being the divisional sales as a proportion of total sales. The mean difference is 18 per cent if the estimates of the divisional betas are all assumed to be 1.0. This suggests that the pure-play method does result in estimates of divisional costs of equity that are somewhat more accurate than an assumption that all divisions have the same cost of equity, with a beta equal to one. The authors find that a more elaborate procedure of unlevering the pure-play betas and then relevering the sales-weighted average according to the firm's leverage results in a poorer match between firm betas and sales-weighted average betas.

14.1.2   *Adjustment for difference in leverage*

Leverage affects the cost of equity, so the estimation of a project's cost of equity requires an assumption about the project's leverage. How a project's optimum leverage is chosen is discussed briefly in Section 14.2.1. The leverage assumed, however it is determined, may not be the same as the leverage of the parent or of other pure-play listed companies the costs of equity of which are being used to estimate the project's cost of equity. In addition, if there is more than one pure play, it is likely that the pure plays will differ in terms of their leverage.

Suppose we have estimated the cost of equity of a pure-play company. If we believe that the optimum leverage of the project in question is the same as the leverage of the pure play, then the cost of equity of the pure play can be used as the project's cost of equity without further ado. However, suppose we believe that the project's optimum leverage differs from the leverage of the pure play. The procedure recommended in texts is to find the unlevered cost of equity of the pure play, as though it had no debt, and then to find the cost of equity that the pure play would be estimated to have were its leverage the same as the optimum leverage of the project. This relevered cost of equity is the estimate of the project's cost of equity.

If we believe that the project's business risk differs from that of the parent or pure play, an (ad hoc) adjustment can be made to the parent's or pure play's unlevered cost of equity before relevering. Cornell, Hirshleifer and James (1997) report that, for some reason, US utility regulators adjust for a perceived difference in business risk between a utility and a pure play by changing the utility's assumed leverage. The utility's costs of equity and debt are estimated at its observed level of leverage, and then the same estimates are used in a WACC with a different leverage. Assuming, say, a higher leverage than the actual leverage is a way of reducing the WACC to reflect perceived lower business risk.

In Chapter 7 we derived four sets of formulas that show the relations between the cost of equity, WACC and leverage under four different sets of assumptions (all of which ignore personal tax). We shall now show, by means of an example, how the formulas can be used to adjust the cost of equity for leverage.

Example

A project is estimated to have an optimum level of leverage of 0.20 (debt divided by debt plus equity, measured at market values). So the debt-to-equity ratio is 0.25. The risk-free rate of interest is 4 per cent p.a., the equity risk premium is 5 per cent p.a. and the corporation tax rate is 30 per cent. The following relevant data have been estimated for a pure-play company that is believed to have the same business risk as the project.

Pure-play company	
Cost of equity	11% pa
CAPM beta of equity	1.4
Cost of debt	6% pa
CAPM beta of debt	0.4
Leverage (L)	0.80
Debt-to-equity ratio (D/E_L)	4.00

So there is quite a dramatic difference between the observed leverage of the pure play and the optimum leverage of the project, 0.20. We shall estimate the project's cost of equity using the formulas derived under the first three of the sets of assumptions considered in Chapter 7 (see Table 7.1). We omit the most complex of the formulas, derived under the assumption of non-constant expected cash flows (which gives answers similar to those under the first set of assumptions).

1. *Assumptions: constant perpetual expected cash flows; risk-free debt; no tax*
    The pure-play cost of unlevered equity can be found by rearranging equation (7.5) to give

$$R_{EU} = [R_{EL} + R_F(D/E_L)]/(1 + D/E_L) \qquad (14.2)$$

where R_{EL} is the cost of levered equity, R_{EU} is the cost of unlevered equity, R_F is the risk-free rate, D is the market value of debt and E_L is the market value of levered equity. Inserting the numbers from the above example,

$$R_{EU} = [11\% + 4\%(4.0)]/(1 + 4.0)$$
$$= 5.40\% \text{ pa}$$

The same answer can be found by unlevering beta:

$$\beta_U = \beta_L(1 - L) \qquad (14.3)$$

from equation (7.12), where β_L is the beta of equity in a firm with leverage of L, β_U is the unlevered or asset beta – the beta of equity in the same firm but with no debt – and $L = D/(D + E_L)$. Inserting the numbers from the example,

$$\beta_U = 1.4(0.2)$$
$$= 0.280$$

therefore

$$R_{EU} = R_F + \beta_U[E(R_M - R_F)]$$
$$= 4\% + 0.280(5\%)$$
$$= 5.40\% \text{ pa}$$

To find the project's cost of equity, the pure-play R_{EU} is relevered to the level of the project's optimum leverage using equation (7.5).

$$R_{EL}(\text{project}) = 5.4\% + 1.4\%(0.25)$$
$$= 5.75\% \text{ pa}$$

Or, via relevering beta (equation (7.12)),

$$\beta_L(\text{project}) = 0.280/(1 - 0.2) = 0.350$$

so

$$R_{EL}(\text{project}) = 4\% + 0.350(5\%)$$
$$= 5.75\% \text{ pa}$$

using the CAPM (equation (3.7)).

2. *Assumptions: constant perpetual expected cash flows; risk-free debt; corporation tax*
   The cost of unlevered equity can be found from equation (7.9):

$$R_{EU} = [R_{EL} + R_F(1 - T_C)(D/E_L)]/[1 + (1 - T_C)D/E_L] \qquad (14.4)$$
$$= [11\% + 4\%(0.7)(4.0)]/[1 + (0.7)(4.0)]$$
$$= 5.84\% \text{ pa}$$

where T_C is the corporation tax rate. The route via unlevering beta is, from equation (7.11),

$$\beta_U = \beta_L(1 - L)/(1 - T_C L) \qquad (14.5)$$
$$= 1.4(0.2)/0.76$$
$$= 0.368$$

Therefore

$$R_{EU} = 4\% + 0.368(5\%)$$
$$= 5.84\% \text{ pa}$$

The project's cost of equity is then

$$R_{EL}(\text{project}) = 5.84\% + 1.84\%(0.7)(0.25)$$
$$= 6.16\% \text{ pa}$$

using equation (7.9). Or, via relevering beta (equation (7.11)),

$$\beta_L(\text{project}) = 0.368 + 0.368(0.7)(0.25) = 0.433$$

so

$$R_{EL}(\text{project}) = 4\% + 0.433(5\%)$$
$$= 6.16\% \text{ pa}$$

3. *Assumptions: constant perpetual expected cash flows; risky debt; corporation tax*
   The cost of unlevered equity can be found from equation (7.16):

$$R_{EU} = [R_{EL} + R_D(1 - T_C)(D/E_L)]/[1 + (1 - T_C)D/E_L] \tag{14.6}$$
$$= [11\% + 6\%(0.7)(4.0)]/[1 + (0.7)(4.0)]$$
$$= 7.32\% \text{ pa}$$

where R_D is the cost of risky debt. Via unlevering beta, from equation (7.15),

$$\beta_U = [\beta_L + \beta_D(1 - T_C)D/E_L]/[1 + (1 - T_C)D/E_L] \tag{14.7}$$
$$= [1.4 + 0.4(0.7)(4.0)]/[1 + (0.7)(4.0)]$$
$$= 0.663$$

where β_D is the beta of the debt. Therefore

$$R_{EU} = 4\% + 0.663(5\%) = 7.32\% \text{ pa}$$

To find the project's cost of equity (and the WACC), we need to know the project's cost of debt. Let us suppose that this is 4.5 per cent p.a. The project's cost of equity is then

$$R_{EL}(\text{project}) = 7.32\% + (7.32\% - 4.50\%)(0.7)(0.25)$$
$$= 7.81\% \text{ pa}$$

using equation (7.16). For the CAPM route to give the same answer, the beta of the debt must be such that the risk premium on the debt, 0.5 per cent p.a., is equal to β_D times the market risk premium, 5 per cent p.a., which means that β_D must be 0.1. If we estimate R_D(project) to be 4.5 per cent p.a. and β_D (project) to be other than 0.1, it means that the CAPM is not providing the estimate of the cost of the risky debt, and, as a result, that the CAPM will provide a different estimate of the project's cost of equity. Using $\beta_D = 0.1$ (in equation (7.17)),

$$\beta_L(\text{project}) = 0.663 + (0.663 - 0.100)(0.7)(0.25)$$
$$= 0.762$$

therefore

$$R_{EL}(\text{project}) = 4\% + 0.762(5\%) = 7.81\% \, \text{pa}$$

Discussion

Two points stand out from the above example. The first is that large differences in leverage do have a large effect on the cost of equity. The pure-play company's cost of equity, with leverage of 80 per cent, is 11 per cent p.a., compared with an unlevered cost of equity that we have inferred to be between 5.75 per cent and 7.81 per cent p.a., depending on the assumptions.

Second, allowance for the riskiness of debt in the third set of calculations results in a project cost of equity that is either 1.7 or 2.1 percentage points higher than the costs of equity from the other two methods. This is a material difference, but the size and direction of the difference are specific to the example. The reasons for the difference are that the unlevered cost of equity is higher once the riskiness of debt is allowed for, and that the project's leverage is much lower than that of the pure play. In the pure-play company, the assumption that the beta of the debt is 0.4 is an assumption that a fair amount of the business risk is being borne by the lenders. When we reduce leverage to zero, the extra ('financial') risk to equity caused by the presence of debt is cut to zero, but, partly offsetting this, the portion of the business risk that was being borne by the lenders is taken on by the shareholders. Under the other two methods that assume that debt is risk-free, the lenders bear no business risk, so the only effect on equity of reducing leverage is to reduce the financial risk. The bias affecting the cost of equity from assuming risk-free debt would work the other way – the project's cost of equity would be overstated – if the project had a higher leverage than the pure play. The problem in practice with attempting to allow for the riskiness of debt is that it is often impossible to estimate.

Recommendations differ as to which method to use, or, indeed, whether it is worth making adjustments for differences in leverage at all. If there are only one or two pure plays, and they both have markedly higher or lower levels of leverage than that of the project, it seems clear that the costs of equity from the pure plays should not be used without adjustment. Most texts recommend making a relatively simple adjustment using formulas (14.2) or (14.3), which ignore corporation tax, or formulas (14.4) or (14.5), which allow for corporation tax. Both pairs of formulas assume that debt is risk-free.

Adjustment will probably make little difference if the levels of leverage of the pure plays are scattered around the leverage of the project. Ehrhardt (1994, p. 120) recommends against adjusting, 'unless you have some compelling reason to believe that your division is very different from the average division in that line of business with respect to debt capacity or tax liability'. He argues that operations in the same line of business will have similar optimum levels of leverage, and cites, in support of his recommendation, Fuller and Kerr's (1981) results, which suggest that divisional costs of equity are estimated more accurately without making leverage adjustments.

Measuring leverage

All the formulas assume that equity and debt are measured at market value, and the analysis abstracts from various practical issues regarding the measurement of leverage. For example, should short-term debt be included? Are preference shares debt or equity? Should holdings of cash be subtracted from debt? How do you estimate the market value of non-traded debt? Is volatility of the value of equity a problem?

Let us start by rehearsing what we are trying to do with the pure-play method. We estimate the pure play's cost of equity and its level of leverage, both at a particular time. We assume a linear relation between the cost of equity and leverage, holding other things constant, as in equations (14.2) to (14.7). The principle here is that debt entails fixed future commitments. As the pay-offs to equity are the residual cash flows, an increase in fixed commitments means an increase in the volatility (and beta) of the residual flows. That is what explains the relation between the cost of equity and leverage.

Some guidance can be suggested in the light of the above. Lease commitments are fixed and their present value should be included as debt. Preference shares with fixed dividend entitlements are more like debt than equity, in that their presence increases the risk to ordinary shareholders. Short-term debt should be included if the company normally operates with a similar amount of short-term debt, because having this debt outstanding entails ongoing fixed commitments. If in doubt, short-term debt should be included. Similarly, cash should not be subtracted if the company normally operates with a similar amount of cash, because having this cash is part of the normal modus operandi of the business, and will be reflected in its business risk. If in doubt, cash should not be subtracted.

Equity warrants in issue are call options written by the company. They are neither equity not debt, but their value should be counted as equity. With bonds convertible into equity, the value of the option to convert (a warrant) should be treated as equity and the remaining value should be treated as debt.

It is true that variation over time in the value of equity causes variation in the pure play's observed leverage. But the comparative stability of book value does not in itself make it a more suitable measure of the value of equity, for the purpose of estimating the cost of equity. What we wish to unlever is our estimate of the expected rate of return on the levered equity at market value, not at book value.

It is common to measure leverage using the market value of equity and the book value of debt, since there is no observable market price for untraded debt. The book value is the face value of the debt – i.e. the amount to be paid at maturity – and will usually be similar to the market value, unless the company is in difficulty. The market value of untraded debt can be estimated approximately if the analyst knows or can estimate the coupon – i.e. the promised interest rate as a percentage of the face value. The analyst can then estimate the credit rating on the debt, look up the redemption yield on bonds with the same credit rating and maturity, and discount the interest payments and principal on the untraded debt at the redemption yield.

In summary, unlevering and relevering can be a messy, approximate business in practice. Furthermore, the presence of securities with option features, such as callable bonds and equity warrants, means that the theoretical relation between the cost of equity and leverage will not be exactly linear. But, still, if there is a large difference in leverage between the project and a pure play, it is almost certainly better to adjust the pure play's estimated cost of equity for this difference, somehow.

14.1.3   Projects without a pure play

The type of project where the cost of equity is hardest to estimate is probably one for which there is no obvious pure play. This might be the case for a project to develop a new product or service, although there may be examples of other listed firms in the same industry that grew on the strength of a single new product where the cost of equity can be estimated. There is also a problem with projects that are not themselves business units – for example, the purchase of the proverbial new machine, or investment in staff training. A simple answer is to use the cost of capital of the company, or of the relevant business unit, in such cases. But it is plausible that some of the many sub-business-unit projects to be found within a given line of business will have levels of risk that differ from the risk of the business unit considered as a whole. For example, a project to reduce the unit's fixed costs, such as the installation of a more efficient heating system, is probably less risky than an increase in the capacity of the existing business.

There seems to be no alternative to making ad hoc adjustments to the estimated cost of capital of the most relevant business unit, in the cases of projects that have no pure plays and that are felt to have a different level of risk from that of the business unit. There has been theoretical analysis of the determinants of project betas (Section 6.4); the problem is in applying the theoretical insights in estimating project risk in practice. Some texts discuss this problem and offer some guidance. For example, Brealey and Myers (2003, p. 237) write that the analyst should 'consider whether *investors* would regard the project as more or less risky than typical . . . Here our advice is to search for characteristics of the asset that are associated with high or low betas.' They and others note that projects that increase the cyclicality of the business or that increase its operating leverage are likely to have higher systematic risk than the business itself, and vice versa. Operating leverage is measured by the elasticity of the operating cash flow with respect to sales per period. Operating leverage, and therefore systematic risk, increase if fixed costs increase.

14.1.4   Thoughts about total risk

It is plausible that many executives are concerned about total risk, as well as, or instead of, market-related (systematic) risk. Clements (1999, p. 250), for example, writes that a 'critical practitioner's response [to the claim that only market-related risk matters] is likely to be as follows. "Please give me the names of four or five major institutional fund managers who are prepared to forgive or overlook corporate downturns, and even disasters, on the simple grounds that firm-specific risk, rather than market risk, has caused them." Survey evidence (Section 14.3) indicates that the ad hoc adjustments made by company executives to the parent's estimated cost of capital are usually upwards, and can be very large.

It is worth repeating, first, that the assumption in estimating present value is that the future cash flows to discount are expected cash flows – i.e. possible cash flows at each date weighted by their probabilities. If there are possibilities of disaster – the project loses money (negative future cash flows), or is closed down early at substantial cost – these possibilities should appear as some of the possible cash flows used to estimate the expected cash flows.

Suppose that the analyst is trying to value a project with high total risk. There is a high probability of substantial loss and a high probability of substantial gain. But the project is not felt to be sensitive to the business cycle in the economy at large; it is not more likely to go wrong if there is a recession. The estimated beta would be below one. Clements' point is that many executives would feel uncomfortable about discounting the expected cash flows at a cost of capital that is lower than the cost of capital for a project with less total risk but more exposure to the business cycle. Nevertheless, the message from finance theory is that the cost of capital is a function of systematic risk, not total risk.

No doubt shareholders will want to know what has happened if the project proves a disaster. They will want to know, amongst other things, whether the project was as well designed and managed as it could have been. If it was, there is nothing to 'forgive or overlook'. However, it will doubtless be difficult to convince people who are less well informed than the managers that a project that was a failure was well managed. There are other issues involved as well, particularly for projects that are large in relation to the size of the parent.

If a large project goes wrong, it may threaten the survival of the parent. The 'costs of financial distress' may be large and will be difficult to estimate. For example, *if* the parent is forced into liquidation, and the shareholders receive nothing, the project's failure will arguably have destroyed the entire shareholder wealth of the parent (but here we enter the grey area of exactly what effects are attributable to the project). Furthermore, the unanticipated contraction or closure of operations damages the welfare of other stakeholders: staff, customers, suppliers and others. Thus taking high total risk can, in some cases, impose possible costs on other stakeholders, not just the shareholders. Opinions differ on how the interests of other stakeholders should be treated in corporate decision making. The costs of possible failure to other stakeholders will probably not be reflected explicitly in the forecasts of possible cash flows. But it would be natural for managers to worry about the effects of failure on others, for a mixture of altruistic and self-interested reasons. They know that they could be blamed by staff made redundant in the event of failure. So managers' unease about large downside risk could stem from a mixture of concern about their own jobs and professional reputations, from a suspicion that the costs of disaster to shareholders are larger than are shown even in the worst-case forecasts, and from an awareness of the knock-on costs of failure to other stakeholders.

It may be helpful to make a distinction between valuation and decision taking. To estimate the notional market value of a project objectively, the expected cash flows should be estimated as accurately and as fairly as possible. Similarly, reasonable and explicit decisions should be made about how to estimate the cost of capital, and the decisions should be adhered to. Neither the expected cash flows nor the cost of capital should be doctored to reflect total or downside risk. The theoretical implication from focusing on total or downside risk rather than systematic risk in assessing projects is that mistakes will be made; positive-NPV projects with high total risk are rejected, and negative-NPV projects with low total risk are undertaken. Also, the whole process is made less transparent and more arbitrary.

The objective market valuation arrived at then becomes an input in the decision-making process. For example, a project may be estimated to have a positive net present value, but also to have a non-negligible probability of jeopardising the survival of the parent. The managers may not be willing to live with this risk. This could be an agency problem; the shareholders may prefer the managers to take the risk. But shareholders themselves may not always wish to apply the rule of investing only in positive-NPV projects. Shareholders may wish to make some allowance for the knock-on costs of failure on other stakeholders, assuming that these costs are not in the forecast cash flows. Or, again, if the owners of a family firm have most of their wealth invested in the firm, they will probably be concerned about downside risk. What is happening in such examples is that the shareholder or manager perceives there to be costs or benefits from a project that are not reflected in the project's market value, estimated as though it were a traded financial asset. Having an undoctored valuation to hand, estimated in the conventional way, will help the decision makers be clear about their rationale for departing from the positive-NPV rule, if they choose to do so.

14.2   Estimating a project's WACC

14.2.1   The effect of leverage

We have discussed how to estimate a project's cost of equity, assuming a given optimum leverage. The final stage is to estimate the WACC. The assumptions underlying the use of the WACC were discussed at length in Chapters 6 and 7. We argued there that the only reason why the WACC differs from the unlevered cost of equity is the tax advantage of debt. This is not necessarily to say that a company's choice of leverage has little effect on the value of its equity plus debt. The point is that we have assumed that all the effects on value of the company's financing decisions are captured in the cash flows, except the tax advantage of debt and any effects of personal taxes. Likewise, transactions costs of issue and ongoing financing-related fees are assumed to be part of the cash costs of the project.

The standard recommendation in corporate finance texts is to assume that the parent operates with a target level of leverage, and that the target level applies to new projects. How a particular project is actually financed is then viewed as irrelevant. It affects neither the project's WACC nor its future cash flows (because cash flows relating to debt are ignored). The choice of target leverage is a matter of managerial judgement, and there has been much research on the factors that affect the choice. In fact, not all theories predict that the company will operate with a target leverage. The 'pecking order' theory predicts that debt will be used only if the company has insufficient internal cash (retained profits) to finance its expenditures in full. Therefore, the amount that the company borrows, if it borrows at all, is determined as a by-product of its other cash inflows and outflows.

It can be argued that the company's target leverage, if it has one, will not necessarily be appropriate for all projects. For example, a project to build new premises is likely to increase the company's debt capacity by more, per pound spent, than a project to invest in research and development, one reason being that a new loan could be secured on the property. Debt capacity means the optimum amount of debt for the company to borrow, assuming there is an optimum.

The effect of the tax advantage to debt on the WACC is fairly small – less than one percentage point – for typical levels of leverage, rates of corporation tax and rates of interest. The median levels of leverage of listed companies in the Group of Seven developed countries ranged between 19 per cent and 46 per cent for the period 1987 to 1991 (Rajan and Zingales, 1995, p. 1430). These estimates are gross of the companies' cash holdings, and they use the market value of equity and the book value of debt. Statutory rates of corporation tax were between 28 per cent and 50 per cent; these statutory rates represent the maximum rates of tax saving from interest. Suppose that the interest rate on corporate debt is 6 per cent p.a., and that the entire cost of debt is paid as cash interest. With this interest rate, the amount that the tax advantage reduces the median listed company's WACC, compared with its unlevered cost of equity, ranges from 0.40 percentage points for the United Kingdom ($6\% \times L$ of 0.19 $\times T_C$ of 35%) to 0.99 percentage points for Italy ($6\% \times L$ of 0.46 $\times T_C$ of 36%).

No tax advantage to debt

Suppose we believe that the tax advantage for the project is zero or is too small to worry about. Then there are three methods to estimate its WACC.

Method 1

The first and most direct method is to use the parent's WACC, given by the formula allowing for risky debt and with no adjustment for tax:

$$WACC = R_{EL}E_L/V_L + R_D D/V_L \qquad (14.8)$$

where debt and equity are measured at market value and $V_L = E_L + D$. The book value of debt can be used as an approximation. In using the parent's WACC, we implicitly assume that the project's business risk is similar to the business risk of the parent, and, to be correct, that the project's leverage will remain constant (Section 7.3.1). However, it need not be assumed that the project's optimal leverage is similar to the parent's current leverage. This is because leverage does not affect the WACC, if there is no tax advantage to debt.

There is a drawback to this method for companies with equity warrants or securities with option features in issue that account for a significant proportion of value. The drawback is the difficulty of estimating the expected rates of return on such hybrid securities. The cost of capital for warrants and convertibles is discussed in Copeland, Koller and Murrin (2000, chap. 10), Copeland and Weston (1988, chap. 13) and Patterson (1995, chap. 11).

Method 2

The project's WACC can be estimated by unlevering the cost of equity of a pure-play company, as discussed already, since the WACC and the unlevered cost of equity will be the same. With this method there is no need, for valuation purposes, to estimate the project's actual cost of equity, allowing for the project's assumed leverage, and there is no need to estimate its cost of debt.

On the other hand, the unlevering process introduces another layer of approximation. It may be that pure plays can be found with similar levels of leverage to the optimum leverage assumed for the project. In this case, a third method could be used.

Method 3

The pure-play cost of equity is a direct estimate of the project's (levered) cost of equity. Unlevering is unnecessary. But, if this route is taken, the pure-play cost of equity cannot be used as the project's cost of capital, unless leverage is close to zero. The cost of capital is given by the WACC – equation (14.8). It is debatable whether more approximation is involved in the unlevered cost of equity route (method 2) or in the WACC route (method 3).

Tax advantage to debt

Suppose, instead, that we believe there to be a material tax advantage to debt. Then the tax-adjusted WACC allowing for risky debt should be used:

$$WACC = R_{EL}E_L/V_L + R_D(1 - T_C)D/V_L \qquad (14.9)$$

The tax-adjusted WACC is the discount rate for expected net cash flows ignoring interest and debt repayments, net of corporation tax. The tax rate in equation (14.9) is the effective rate of corporation tax that is expected to apply to the project. This could be lower than the statutory rate if the company has tax losses to carry forward, or if the project benefits from tax allowances. Of course, if the project is expected to pay tax at a rate that is less than the statutory rate, this should show up in the expected tax payments in the cash flow forecasts, as well as in the T_C rate used in the WACC formula.

If there is a tax advantage to debt, the project's tax-adjusted WACC can be found from the parent's tax-adjusted WACC (method 1), assuming that the parent's leverage is roughly the same as the project's optimum leverage. It can also be found from the cost of equity of a pure play with the same leverage as the project, together with an estimate of the cost of debt (method 3). But method 2, the pure play's unlevered cost of equity, will overstate a levered project's WACC, as it ignores the tax advantage. The unlevered cost of equity should be relevered using equation (14.4) or (14.6).

14.2.2   *Estimating the cost of debt*

The approximate cost of debt is known, because the promised rate of return is always one of the terms of a debt contract. This is in contrast to equity (ordinary shares), for which there is no contractual rate of return. However, there are a few points to make regarding the estimation of the cost of debt.

The first is that, strictly speaking, companies and individuals borrow, but not projects, because a project is not an entity that is recognised in law as a party to a contract. Similarly, a project cannot issue shares. We are trying to estimate the costs of equity and debt, as though the project had issued these financial assets. It is easier, in a way, to sustain the fiction in the case of equity, because all (ordinary) shares have the same terms and conditions across issuers. This is emphatically not the case with debt. The terms and conditions of a loan contract or bond issue affect the riskiness of the debt and therefore affect the cost of debt. Unless the project is constituted as a separate company, a new loan supported by the project will be a loan to the parent, or to the parent's finance subsidiary.

The approximate cost of the debt is the interest rate offered by the would-be lending bank, or the estimated redemption yield on the new bonds at issue, on debt with a lifespan similar to that of the project, at the time the project is being valued. It is the cost of a new loan that is relevant, not the interest rate(s) on existing debt. So the cost of debt can be found by asking a banker. The cost will reflect the risk of lending to the parent, not the project, under the terms and conditions specific to the debt. It is probably normal practice to treat the interest rate on a new loan to the parent as the interest rate applicable to the project. This differs from the recommended practice in the case of equity, in which the parent's cost of equity need not be viewed as an acceptable proxy for the project's cost of equity, as we have seen.

We have noted that the promised rate of return on debt overstates the expected rate of return, because it ignores the possibility of default. The upward bias increases with the probability of default. This is why the promised rate is only an approximation to the true cost of debt. Many texts simply ignore this point, but some offer rules of thumb. Brealey and Myers (2003) and Copeland, Koller and Murrin (2000) suggest using the (promised) gross redemption yield as the cost of debt for bonds rated BBB ('investment grade') or higher, on the grounds that the probability of default is so small that the difference between the promised yield and the expected yield can be ignored. For bonds rated less than BBB, and for unrated debt thought to be riskier than BBB, they recommend using the prevailing yield on BBB-rated bonds as the cost of debt – i.e. the expected rate of return on the debt.

Another issue is the interest rate to use in the case of debt with a variable or floating rate of interest. The problem is that the interest rate is not known beyond the first interest period. There is an easy solution, now that interest rate swaps have become commonplace. This is to ask the lender, or to estimate from published swap rates, what the rate would be if the loan were swapped into a fixed rate.

14.2.3   Other issues

Personal taxes

Personal taxes have an impact on the cost of capital via a company's dividend and leverage policies, at least in theory. Chapter 8 discussed the 'old' and 'new' views of the cost of equity, which can imply different estimates of the cost of equity for the same company. For example, suppose that half of a company's returns comes from dividends, on which income tax is paid of 33 per cent, and half comes from capital gains, which are not taxed. The expected rate of return before personal tax is 12 per cent p.a., and this is the cost of equity before personal tax under the 'old' view. The expected rate net of personal tax is $6\%(1 - 0.33) + 6\% = 10\%$ pa, and this is the cost of equity before personal tax under the 'new' view.

Chapter 9 discussed the effect of personal taxes on the relation between the cost of equity and leverage. Under the standard analysis, which ignores personal tax, there is a tax advantage to debt. But under certain assumptions there is no tax advantage to debt allowing for personal tax, in which case leverage makes no difference to the WACC. The evidence suggests that there is a tax advantage, but the effective rate of corporation tax saved by interest is probably less than the statutory rate for many companies.

In practice, the cost of capital and cash flows to discount are estimated before personal tax, and in all probability the above debates about the impact of personal taxes are usually ignored. Several explanations can be suggested. The alternative views about the effects of dividend and leverage policies on the cost of capital will not usually make a large difference to one's actual estimate. The analysis is more complicated and less familiar with personal tax than without. The estimation of expected returns after personal taxes, or of the effective tax advantage to debt, is difficult. Companies do not pay personal taxes, so managers may feel that personal taxes are not their concern.

Inflation

The main practical question regarding inflation is whether to work with cash flows and a discount rate expressed in nominal or real terms. The Fisher relation between a nominal return R_{nom} and the corresponding real return R_{real} is

$$1 + R_{\text{nom}} = (1 + R_{\text{real}})(1 + Inf)$$

where *Inf* is inflation. Chapter 10 explained that this is an approximation, from a theoretical perspective, because it assumes implicitly that inflation is certain. In addition, a tax rate on a given nominal return corresponds to a higher tax rate on the real return. But there is no evidence that adjustments for inflation are made in practice to cost of capital estimates, other than the Fisher relation, and texts do not recommend attempting to make such adjustments.

International dimension

The international dimension raises two questions, as discussed in Chapter 11. The first is whether to use the national or international CAPM to estimate a company's cost of equity – assuming that a CAPM is being used in the first place. This question applies to any company, regardless of whether it operates abroad or competes with foreign companies, and the answer in principle depends on the view taken about how segmented the stock market is on which the company is listed. Explicit survey evidence is lacking on this point, but it seems likely, from a reading of several corporate finance texts, that the vast majority of companies currently use the national CAPM.

The second question is the method of valuing the equity of a foreign project. We reviewed two alternatives: to discount the expected net cash flows converted to the parent's currency at the cost of equity appropriate for the cash flows in the parent's currency; or to discount the cash flows in the host country's currency at a cost of equity appropriate for the cash flows in the host's currency. These methods will give different answers if the real costs of equity differ in the two countries. In addition, the project's net cash flows in the host country may differ from the expected cash flows to be remitted to the parent. Most companies probably value foreign projects both from the perspective of the parent and from the perspective of a host-country shareholder.

14.3   Evidence regarding practice

This section summarises evidence from recent UK and US surveys regarding the methods of estimating the cost of capital used by companies in practice. Evidence on estimating the cost of equity was reviewed in Section 12.1.

McLaney, Pointon, Thomas and Tucker (2004) report questionnaire responses from 193 UK listed companies. 53 per cent of respondents use the WACC as the discount rate in project appraisal, 11 per cent use the cost of equity and 28 per cent use a long-term borrowing rate (what the remainder do is not stated). 22 per cent adjust the cost of capital for the project's size, 18 per cent adjust for the division responsible for the project and 14 per cent adjust 'to recover the cost of non-economic projects'. 67 per cent take tax into account, mostly via the standard adjustment for corporation tax to the cost of debt.

Similar findings are reported by Arnold and Hatzopoulos (2000), based on ninety-six responses from listed UK companies. 54 per cent use the WACC, 10 per cent use the cost of equity, 11 per cent use the cost of debt (23 per cent of the smallest companies, 1 per cent of the largest), 6 per cent use 'an arbitrarily chosen figure', 10 per cent use other methods and 7 per cent left the question blank. In calculating the weights in the WACC, 30 per cent use a target debt/equity ratio, 44 per cent use the current market values of debt and equity, and 26 per cent use the current book values.

All eighteen of the large UK companies interviewed by Rutterford (2000) estimate the cost of capital as a WACC, though the WACC is a weighted average of the cost of equity and the cost of debt for only fifteen (it is not stated what the WACC means for the other three). Of the fifteen, ten use a target level of leverage, six use the company's current leverage and one uses both. All but one company make the standard adjustment to the cost of debt for the tax advantage, with the effective rate of corporation tax assumed to be at or close to the statutory rate. It may be mentioned that, allowing for personal tax, there was probably little tax advantage to debt for dividend-paying companies in the United Kingdom at the time of the interviews (1996), because tax-exempt investors could reclaim some of the corporation tax paid by the company (Section 9.3).

The average minimum hurdle rate – the rate actually used to discount project cash flows – is 0.93 percentage points above the average WACC. In addition, companies make very large upward adjustments to the minimum hurdle rate for many projects. 'There was no consensus . . . on how to adjust for differential project risk. 14 of the 18 firms made some adjustment for different levels of risk in projects, with 9 of those 14 making some adjustment for country risk or foreign exchange risk as well as for systematic risk . . . 15 firms had premiums of 0% to 8% over the base hurdle rate with the remaining three having maximum hurdle rates 10% or more above the base case' (p. 145).

Turning to US evidence, Graham and Harvey (2001) received questionnaire responses from 392 US firms, 61 per cent of which were listed. The most common methods of project appraisal are the internal rate of return (IRR), used always or almost always by 76 per cent of respondents, and net present value, used by 75 per cent. The adjusted present value technique is used always or almost always only by 10 per cent of respondents. Presumably some firms use one but not the other of these methods, so the proportion using discounted cash flow for appraisal – NPV, IRR or both – will be higher than 76 per cent. Yet only 64 per cent calculate their cost of equity. One wonders how the firms manage that use discounted cash flow without an estimate of the cost of equity. Are they using the cost of debt as the discount rate?

Regarding a project in a foreign country that is known to have a different risk from the company as a whole, 59 per cent of the respondents would use a discount rate not adjusted for the difference in risk, at least as one of the discount rates employed. However, many firms would also use an adjusted rate, with adjustment for: country and industry of the project (51 per cent); country only (35 per cent); or line of business only, if it matches that of a domestic division of the company (16 per cent).

Bruner, Eades, Harris and Higgins (1998) interviewed twenty-seven large US companies and ten advisers in mergers and acquisitions. Twenty-three of the twenty-four companies that use discounted cash flow techniques to evaluate investment opportunities do so using the WACC. Fourteen use a target leverage, four use their current leverage, and the response is listed as uncertain for the remainder. Fourteen estimate the cost of debt using the marginal cost (the cost of new debt); ten use the average cost of existing debt. Seven of the companies always adjust their estimate of the company's cost of capital to reflect the risk of individual investment opportunities, and a further nine sometimes do so. All ten of the M&A advisers use different WACCs to value different divisions in the same group, but only three use different discount rates or options-based valuation to value synergies and strategic opportunities. Several companies and advisers adjust project cash flows for differences in project risk, rather than adjusting discount rates. Bruner et al. suggest that 'risk-adjusted discount rates are more likely to be used when the analyst can establish relatively objective financial market benchmarks for what rate adjustments should be' (p. 25), for example the cost of equity of a pure-play company.

Cornell et al. (1997) discuss the estimation of the cost of equity by regulators of utility companies in the United States. They report that, if the dividend discount model is used, pure-play companies are found with similar leverage to the utility in question, and there is no unlevering and relevering. However, if the CAPM is used, pure-play betas are unlevered and relevered to the utility's leverage using equation (14.5). The authors state that the use of equation (14.5) is 'relatively standard' amongst regulators.

Poterba and Summers (1995) received questionnaire responses from 228 chief executive officers from amongst the largest 1000 US firms. They note that the average real hurdle rate, which was 12.2 per cent p.a. at the time of the survey (1990), is several percentage points above what they consider to be a reasonable WACC for a large firm, based on a long-term real rate of return of 7 per cent p.a. on equity with average leverage, and a real rate of less than 2 per cent p.a. on corporate bonds. 'Most' firms adjust their hurdle rates for different projects, and the adjustments are typically large; the average difference between a firm's highest and lowest hurdle rate is 11.2 percentage points. A further noteworthy, and rather odd, finding is that the reported hurdle rates are correlated neither with the industry the firm is in nor with the CAPM beta of the firm's shares.

Shao and Shao (1993) received questionnaire responses from ninety European affiliates of US multinationals. 41 per cent use the cost of debt as the discount rate, 30 per cent use the WACC, 10 per cent use a 'risk-free rate plus risk premium', 9 per cent use 'past experience' and 4 per cent use the cost of equity.

Discussion

Several points stand out from the above evidence. First, although the WACC appears to be the most commonly used method of estimating the cost of capital, other methods, especially the cost of debt, are also used. This is also reported in several earlier surveys that we have not summarised. Use of the cost of debt to estimate the cost of capital is a serious mistake, on the face of it. Second, it appears that many firms do adjust discount rates for project risk, and that these adjustments can be large. Third, there is evidence from Rutterford (2000) and Poterba and Summers (1995) that the discount rate actually used by a firm is, on average, substantially higher than a reasonable estimate of the firm's own cost of capital. It might be surmised that project-specific adjustments, when they are made, are usually upwards, so that the firm's estimated cost of capital is treated as a minimum discount rate rather than a mid-point rate.

This caution would have some justification in the case of a firm using the cost of debt as its cost of capital. But it seems unwarranted in the case of a firm that is using a realistic estimate of its WACC as its cost of capital, to discount realistic expected cash flows, as discussed in Section 14.1.4. Perhaps senior executives believe that cash flow forecasts for projects tend to be optimistic, or perhaps they reason that the cost of capital is a number that is estimated with such uncertainty that it is better to err on the side of prudence. There is a growing literature exploring the connections between capital budgeting procedures and internal politics and constraints within firms. For example, Jagannathan and Meier (2002) suggest that a firm will set a hurdle rate substantially above its estimated cost of capital if its managerial talent and organisational capacity are limited. Then it will undertake only the most worthwhile projects. They also argue, via numerical examples, that the exact hurdle rate chosen can vary within a range of several percentage points without resulting in capital budgeting decisions that make much difference to firm value. What matters for capital budgeting, according to their argument, is the ranking of projects in terms of NPV per pound invested, not the NPVs themselves.

14.4   Estimation: what matters and what does not matter

We have reviewed a range of issues in the estimation and application of the cost of capital. The issues correspond to decisions the analyst or executive has to take. In the light of the review, it may be helpful to offer a rough-and-ready ranking of the importance of these decisions, in terms of the likely impact of each decision on the cost of capital estimate. The impact depends both on how much reasonable variation there might be in the estimate of a particular variable – for example, leverage – and on how much difference a choice at either end of the reasonable range will make to the estimate of the WACC. We assume that the WACC is used to estimate the cost of capital and that the CAPM or the dividend discount model is used for the cost of equity.

Low-impact decisions
The decision taken will normally make a difference of less than two percentage points to an estimate of the cost of capital.

Estimate of effective corporation tax rate; project's assumed optimal leverage
These two variables have low impact because leverage affects the WACC only because of the tax advantage to debt, which has a small impact even for a large assumed tax rate and leverage.

Method of adjusting cost of equity of pure play for leverage – i.e. method of unlevering and relevering
The specifics of how the adjustment is done usually do not make much difference to the resulting cost of equity. But failure to adjust the cost of equity for leverage by some method will make a large difference, if there is a large difference between the leverage of the pure play and the project.

Measurement of leverage of parent or a pure play
The market value/book value ratio for the equity of most listed companies lies between 0.5 and 3.5 (Fama and French, 1993). For such companies, the choice of measuring leverage by book or market values will usually make less than two percentage points difference. For more extreme values of market/book, the choice of measurement makes more difference. For example, suppose a company has a market/book ratio of four. Leverage is, say, 50 per cent using book value, which means that it is 20 per cent using market value. The cost of equity is 15 per cent p.a. and the cost of debt is 7 per cent p.a. The WACC using book value is 11.0 per cent p.a.; the WACC using market value is 13.4 per cent p.a. – a difference of 2.4 per cent p.a.

Choice of risk-free rate in CAPM
The difference between short- and long-term rates of interest is rarely more than two percentage points. But the choice could conceivably have a greater impact, for the following reason. If a historic estimate of the equity premium is used, the choice of risk-free rate implies a matching choice for the premium over treasury bill rates or the premium over long bond rates. The difference between the premium over treasury bills and the premium over long bonds is up to two percentage points for some past periods. If current treasury

bill rates happen to be higher than long rates then the choice of a treasury bill rate for the risk-free rate, together with a historic premium over treasury bill rates, will give an estimate that is more than two percentage points higher than the choice of a long rate together with a premium over long rates.

Estimate of cost of debt

The promised rate of interest on new debt is known, or can be found out from potential lenders. If the promised rate is used as the cost of debt, which is probably standard practice, the resulting upward bias from ignoring the possibility of default is only likely to affect the WACC by more than two percentage points if the company is highly levered and new debt would be highly risky.

Medium-impact decisions

The decision could sometimes make a difference of more than two percentage points, but is unlikely to make a difference of more than four points.

Method of estimating beta

There can be substantial differences, of 0.5 or more, in estimates across methods of estimation or across estimation services (Bruner et al., 1998, p. 21). The impact of such differences is positively related to the size of the equity premium. If the equity premium is estimated to be, say, 5 per cent p.a., a difference in betas of 0.5 makes a difference to the cost of equity of 2.5 per cent p.a.

Choice of pure play

A company that estimates the cost of capital for its projects by its own estimated cost of capital is effectively using a pure-play sample of one. Another company in the same line of business could easily have an estimated cost of capital that differs by a few percentage points.

Choice of model of cost of equity

Certainly, the choice of model has the potential to make a large difference, but without conducting an empirical study it is difficult to assess how often the choice will make a difference of more than two percentage points. The differences calculated will depend on the assumptions made regarding the implementation of each model. Fama and French (1997) compare estimates of the costs of equity for forty-eight industries from the CAPM and the three-factor model. The estimates for twenty-five of the industries differ by more than two percentage points, using an estimation period of 1963 to 1994.

High-impact decisions

The decision is likely to make a difference of more than two percentage points, and could make a difference of more than four points.

Equity premium in CAPM
Both the range of respectable estimates and the uncertainty regarding the choice of method of estimation are large.

Growth rate in the dividend discount model
There are several reasons why this is a high-impact item for many companies. It is very difficult to forecast the long-term growth of a company's dividends. The average of analysts' forecast growth rates of earnings can be used, but analysts' forecasts extend to five years at most, so a guess has to be made about the growth rate beyond this horizon. Analysts' forecasts for a company can vary dramatically over a few years, and one may feel uncomfortable about inferring a similarly dramatic change in the company's cost of equity. There may be no forecast available for smaller listed companies, or only one or two, which increases the uncertainty of any estimate. The dividend discount model is more difficult to apply if the company does not pay a dividend at present.

Ad hoc adjustment to cost of capital for project risk
The impact of an ad hoc adjustment depends directly on the size of the adjustment. We count this decision as high-impact because of the evidence that some companies make very large ad hoc adjustments.

Certainty is not possible with the cost of capital. It involves estimating the expected rate of return on a project's equity, and this is not something that can be known for certain. But a good way of improving the reliability of an estimate of the cost of equity is to take the average estimate for several pure plays, including the parent company if appropriate, and/or to use an industry cost of capital. For the same reason, the analyst should consider using an average of the estimates from more than one method. It seems sensible, in addition, to regard the cost of capital as an uncertain input in the discounted cash flow, and to estimate the sensitivity of project values to the discount rate. These suggestions all involve more work, compared with using a single estimate of the cost of capital. The benefits of having more than one estimate are that the average is more reliable than any given single estimate, and that a sensitivity analysis will provide the analyst with a range of present values produced by the range of reasonable estimates. The analyst may feel uneasy about working with an average estimate, or with a range. But it is abundantly clear that the apparent precision of a single estimate is illusory.

14.5   The relation between theory and practice

In view of the uncertainties surrounding the estimation of the cost of capital, some readers may be wondering whether the theory in the first eleven chapters of the book has proved to be a failure, on the grounds that it cannot be implemented satisfactorily. The answer is that it probably should not be judged in this way. The main goal of most of the theory is to provide a better understanding of what determines the cost of capital, rather than to enable more accurate estimation of the cost of capital to be carried out.

The question of what the cost of capital is for a particular project – the question of estimation – is different from the question of why the cost of capital is the number that it is, or is estimated to be. The uncertainty associated with estimation stems not only from the fact that the future cash flows are uncertain, but also that it is uncertain what cash flows investors are expecting. Suppose that everyone were to agree, somehow, on the expected values of the dividends on a share. Then there would be no problem with estimation. The cost of equity would be the expected rate of return on the share at its market value, say 8 per cent p.a., and the shareholders would tell you that the expected rate of return on the share is 8 per cent p.a. But knowledge of the expected dividends that investors were forecasting would not, in itself, explain why the rate of return required by the (marginal) shareholder is 8 per cent p.a. Providing such an explanation is the purpose of a theory of expected returns.

At first glance, it seems reasonable to expect that a better theory will lead to better estimation. The CAPM was an advance in theoretical understanding that did appear to deliver a more accurate method of estimation, at least until the anti-CAPM evidence began to accumulate, and until people started to ask questions about the size of the equity premium. Yet, setting the anti-CAPM evidence aside, it is not obvious a priori that the CAPM, or any other theoretical model of expected returns, can deliver more accurate estimates than a method that merely infers what the expected return is, such as the dividend discount model, or asking the shareholders. This is because a theoretical model of expected returns cannot reduce uncertainty about the forecasts made by investors of the cash flows from a given asset or project. If investors' forecasts are not known for certain, it is misleading to think of a project's cost of capital as a precise number that is 'out there', like the height of a mountain, waiting to be measured more accurately. The best that can be done is to come up with a reasonable range of estimates, as suggested in the previous section.

The point can be put like this. We can find out from the dividend discount model, or from the abnormal earnings method, or from the shareholders, roughly what the expected rate of return is on a given share. Say it is 12 per cent p.a. for share j and 9 per cent p.a. for share k. We can also estimate these expected rates by applying the CAPM, or another asset pricing model. But it is doubtful whether the CAPM estimates should be viewed as superior. The primary contribution the CAPM offers is its explanation for why the expected rates differ between the two shares.

14.6   Summary

We have now considered all the stages in the process of estimating a project's cost of capital. It must be concluded that there is no method of estimation that can be described as accurate, even for a listed company. In any particular case, we are really working with a range of values that can be considered reasonable, and the range will probably be at least three percentage points. The uncertainty about the equity premium alone ensures that this is so. The current state of the art is that the analyst is faced with a number of choices in the estimation process, which we have examined in Part III. The process can be summarised as follows. We estimate a project's cost of capital by the WACC. The main problem lies with the cost of equity. To find the cost of equity, try to find listed companies in the same line of business as the project. Estimate the cost of equity of a listed company by one or more respectable methods, which include the dividend discount model, the CAPM, the abnormal earnings method or a multifactor model. An ad hoc adjustment to the resulting WACC may be justifiable, but it will be a guess. In principle, such an adjustment could be in either direction, not upwards only.

We have suggested that the uncertainty associated with estimation should not be seen as a failure of theory, nor of methods of estimation. It is due to uncertainty about investors' forecasts of future cash flows on assets and projects, and this uncertainty is unavoidable.

15 Regulated utilities

An important specific application of the cost of capital is in public sector regulation of certain companies that are in a monopolistic position, by virtue of what they do. The most important examples are utility companies, providing electricity, water, gas, rail and telephone services. For such companies, an estimate of the cost of capital is used to set the rate of return that the company is allowed to make on its capital. The cost of capital is one of the estimated costs that determine the price for the product that the regulator allows the company to charge. Thus regulators are obliged to provide and justify an explicit figure for the cost of capital, and this figure has a direct effect on the regulated company's income and on the prices paid by its customers. This differs from the situation in an unregulated company in a competitive market, in which the main impact of its estimated cost of capital is on internal investment decisions (capital budgeting); projects are valued automatically on the basis that the company pursues the pricing and other policies that maximise value. An issue that is distinctive to regulated companies is that the behaviour of the regulator affects the value of the company and can affect the risk of the returns to shareholders.

This chapter considers the role of the cost of capital in the price-setting process in the United States and United Kingdom, and discusses the effect of regulatory policy on risk. Good general discussions of the cost of capital for regulated utilities include those in Myers (1972), Robichek (1978), Kolbe, Read and Hall (1984), Patterson (1995, chap. 12) and, for the United Kingdom, Water Services Association (1991), Grout (1995) and Whittington (1998).

15.1 Price setting in the United States

Regulators exist to protect customers from the exercise of monopoly power and to ensure a satisfactory supply of the regulated companies' products. The principal method of protecting customers is the periodic fixing of a maximum price at which the company can sell its product. This limits the rate of return the company can make on its equity. In practice, the regulator may allow different prices to be charged to different types of customer, but we assume for simplicity that there is only one allowed price. The accepted aim to be sought in fixing the price was articulated by the US Supreme Court in 1944 (*Federal Power Commission v Hope Natural Gas Company*, 1944, quoted in Kolbe et al., 1984, p. 21).

The rate-making process under the act [the Natural Gas Act, 1938], i.e., the fixing of 'just and reasonable' rates, involves a balancing of the investor and the consumer interests . . . The return to the equity owner should be commensurate with returns on investments in other enterprises having corresponding risks. That return, moreover, should be sufficient to assure confidence in the financial integrity of the enterprise, so as to maintain its credit and to attract capital.

The statement in the penultimate sentence is known as the 'comparable earnings' standard, and implies that the company be allowed to make a rate of return equal to its cost of capital on its existing capital. This requires the estimation of the company's *rate base*, as well as its cost of capital. The rate base is the amount of capital tied up as equity and debt at a particular date. If the actual rate of return on the rate base is turning out to be persistently higher or lower than the estimated cost of capital, the product price should be adjusted. The statement in the last sentence is known as the 'capital attraction' standard, and implies that the company be allowed to make a rate of return on capital equal to its cost of capital on new capital invested. Put another way, positive-NPV investments are not allowed. For example, if a regulated company finds a more efficient way of providing its product, all the benefit should flow to customers via a lower product price.

The above aim of regulation implies that the market value of the company should be equal to the book value, at least immediately after a price-setting review. This can be shown using the sustainable growth version of the dividend discount model:

$$MV = R_{E,\text{allowed}} BV (1 - Ret)/(R_E - g)$$

where MV = market value, BV = book value, $R_{E,\text{allowed}}$ = allowed rate of return on book equity, R_E = cost of equity, Ret = proportion of the return on equity retained and g = growth rate of the returns to equity. In this model, $g = R_{E,\text{allowed}}Ret$ (Section 12.2.2). If the allowed rate of return on equity is set equal to the cost of equity, $R_{E,\text{allowed}} = R_E$, and

$$MV = R_{E,\text{allowed}} BV (1 - Ret)/R_{E,\text{allowed}}(1 - Ret) \qquad (15.1)$$
$$MV/BV = 1$$

If market value exceeds book value, it suggests that the actual rate of return exceeds the cost of capital, and vice versa. The way in which book value is measured does not affect the above result, as argued later in the current section. The view that the allowed rate should be set equal to the cost of equity assumes implicitly that a new review is as likely whether the actual rate is above or below the cost of capital. We assume for now that this is the case. If it is not the case, the allowed rate should not be equal to the cost of equity, as discussed in Section 15.3.

To try to set the product price at a level at which the company will earn its cost of capital, the regulator needs an estimate of the rate of return on capital at different price levels. This involves the estimation of the company's demand, cost and investment functions. For each potential product price, the regulator estimates the quantity demanded, the operating costs that will be incurred in providing that quantity, and the investment required to meet expected future demand. The operating costs and investment should be sufficient to ensure a satisfactory supply with respect to reliability, quality and environmental impact. Corporation tax is treated as a business expense, and the principle is that the customer should benefit from the corporation tax saving from debt rather than the shareholder. This implies that, if the tax advantage to debt allowing for personal tax is less than the estimated effective rate of corporation tax, there is a tax disadvantage to debt for the shareholders of a regulated utility (see Chapter 9).

The discussion so far implies that the aim of the regulator is to set the product price to provide an annual income Y_{allowed} given by

$$Y_{\text{allowed}} = Opcosts + (TaxableY - Int)T_C + R_{\text{allowed}}K$$

where $Opcosts$ = operating costs, $TaxableY$ = taxable income, T_C = effective corporation tax rate, R_{allowed} = allowed rate of return on the rate base and K = the rate base, the amount of capital as defined by the regulator (Patterson, 1995, p. 273). R_{allowed} is given by

$$R_{\text{allowed}} = R_{\text{E,allowed}} (1 - L_{\text{book}}) + R_{\text{D,embedded}} L_{\text{book}} \qquad (15.2)$$

Regulatory policy affects $R_{\text{E,allowed}}$ in two ways; it affects the cost of equity, R_E, and it affects the relation between R_E and $R_{\text{E,allowed}}$. We return to these points in Section 15.3. In the United States the cost of debt is proxied by $R_{\text{D,embedded}}$, the 'embedded' cost of debt. This is the interest expense for the year divided by the book value of debt outstanding at the start of the year. It is, therefore, the value-weighted average of the historic rates of interest on the company's outstanding debt, rather than the expected rate of return on the debt at its market price. L_{book} is leverage measured by book value. The variable $R_{\text{D,embedded}} L_{\text{book}}$ is not consistent conceptually with the cost of debt (see Chapter 7), but can be thought of as an approximation to the cost of debt.

The book value of debt in L_{book} is the amount of debt outstanding. The book value of equity is the rate base less the debt outstanding, and is therefore sensitive to the way the rate base is measured. The regulatory aim that investors in a utility be allowed to earn the utility's estimated cost of equity does not require any particular way of measuring the rate base, which determines the book value of equity (Greenwald, 1980; Whittington, 1998). So long as investors know that they will be allowed to earn the cost of equity on the book value of equity, however measured, the market value should be the same as the book value. An investor who buys shares with a market value equal to book value will then expect a rate of return equal to the cost of equity. This assumes that the method of measuring book value stays the same over time, and that profit is calculated in a way that is consistent with, or 'articulates' with, the method of measuring book value. A change in the method implies a windfall gain or loss to existing shareholders. But, ignoring the possibility of a change in method, the method chosen does have some impact. It affects the market value at any given time, the way in which the return on equity is measured, and the distribution over time of the income required from customers to provide the returns necessary for investors to obtain the cost of equity. The measurement of the rate base, and thus of book value, is therefore of some importance.

Example
Consider the following exaggerated example. A regulated project requires equity investment of £100. It will last for five years and the cost of equity is 10 per cent p.a. The regulator ensures that the achieved rate of return on equity is exactly 10 per cent p.a. The book value

of the equity during the project's life is measured by two alternative methods. The first is to subtract straight-line depreciation, which in this case is £20 p.a., from the initial cost of the asset. The second is to estimate book value by the cost of replacing the assets, in their partly used state. Suppose the replacement cost increases by 10 per cent p.a. during the first two years and then falls sharply. At the end of the five years the assets are worth nothing under either measure of book value.

The annual pay-off on equity that investors receive is the market-value capital gain or loss plus any dividend. As the rate of return on book equity is sure to be 10 per cent p.a., market value will always be the same as the book value. There is no reinvestment of cash, so the net cash flow required each year t to be paid as dividend is given by $0.1BV_{t-1}$, less the capital gain or loss. The project values and dividend payments under the two methods are as follows.

Year	0	1	2	3	4	5
Straight-line depreciation						
Book and market value	100	80	60	40	20	0
Dividend		30	28	26	24	22
Replacement cost						
Book and market value	100	110	121	81	41	0
Dividend		0	0	52	48	45

Note: allowed rate of return on book equity = 10% pa.

The rate of return on equity is 10 per cent p.a. under both cases, and it is easy to verify that the present values of the dividends are the same. But the project values and dividend payments differ year by year. The product price will be set lower under replacement cost than under straight-line depreciation during the first two years, because the project does not need to pay any dividends under replacement cost. Thereafter the position reverses.

Another example of how the measurement of book value can affect the evolution of the regulated price is the treatment of inflation (Patterson, 1995, pp. 274–77). One possibility is to depreciate assets at a straight-line x per cent p.a. without adjusting for inflation, and to set the nominal product price so that investors receive the nominal cost of capital times the unadjusted depreciated value of the assets (the 'original cost' approach). A second possibility is to depreciate assets by the same x per cent p.a., to adjust the historic costs of assets for inflation, and to set the product price so that investors receive the real cost of capital on the adjusted depreciated value of the assets (the 'trended original cost' approach). Under this second scheme, an asset that cost £100 when bought in year 0 would have a depreciation charge for year t of $x£100(1 + Inf)^t$, where Inf is the rate of inflation per period. It can be shown that the market value of the company is the same under both schemes, and so investors will be indifferent between them. But the time profiles of income required from customers will differ. The product price will be closer to the real cost of providing the product under the second approach of trended original cost.

Whatever way the book value of existing equity is measured, if new equity is invested in the company the book value has to increase by the amount of cash invested (Greenwald, 1980). This is because the allowed rate of return is allowed as a percentage of the book value. If book value differs initially from the actual cash invested, and the allowed rate on the book value is equal to the cost of equity, then the allowed rate on the cash will differ from the cost of equity.

The regulator seeks to fix the product price to ensure that the profit after tax as a percentage of the previous year's book value of equity will be equal to the cost of equity. As mentioned, this involves forecasting the company's operating costs and capital expenditure; the estimation of its cost of capital and measurement of its rate base are only part of the information required by the regulator in order to set the product price. In practice, profit as a percentage of book value will not turn out to be identical to the estimated cost of equity, which means there is some risk attaching to the returns to equity. Indeed, the allocation of business risk between customers and financiers is itself a policy issue.

A further point about equation (15.2) is that there is no tax adjustment to the cost of debt, because the tax saving from debt is passed on to the customers, and hence is captured in $Y_{allowed}$. If investors and the regulator agree precisely on the value of the tax saving, and personal tax and non-tax factors are ignored, leverage would then have no effect on value. With non-tax factors acknowledged, the relation between value and leverage is complicated and uncertain. There could be room for the company to increase its value through adjusting its leverage, if investors and the regulator do not agree precisely on the relation between value and leverage (Taggart, 1981; Oxera, 2002). For example, the company and its shareholders may believe that the regulator will feel obliged to rescue the company if it is in financial distress, perhaps through agreeing a product price increase or providing a guarantee to lenders. If so, gearing up by the company implies a transfer of some of the business risk to customers or taxpayers. If this transfer of risk is not fully reflected in a reduced cost of capital as estimated by the regulator, and as reflected in the regulated product price, shareholder wealth will increase with leverage.

15.2   Estimation of the cost of equity

Until the early 1980s the standard method by which regulators estimated the cost of equity was to use comparable earnings. This meant taking the average of the accounting rates of return on equity achieved recently by a sample of comparable utility companies (Kolbe et al., 1984, pp. 41–53). The utility was allowed to earn what it would have earned recently had its capital been invested in other firms of comparable risk. This was a natural way of applying the Hope Natural Gas judgement quoted above, but the comparable earnings method was criticised by Myers (1972) and others as being a poor proxy for the cost of equity. The cost of equity is set in the stock market, but the comparable earnings method does not look to market data. Further, the relation between risk and accounting rates of return is not well defined, and, in any case, it is problematic to compare accounting rates of return across firms. The comparable earnings method has been replaced by the dividend discount method (Section 12.2), generally referred to as *discounted cash flow* (DCF) in a regulatory context. However, the rate of return on equity achieved *ex post* continues to be measured by the profit after tax divided by book value. Consistency with the cost of equity measured via DCF (or via the CAPM) would suggest measurement of the rate of return on equity by the rate of return obtained on the shares, including dividends. The trouble is that the return on the shares is not a trustworthy measure of the return on the book value of equity, which is what the regulator is trying to control. Thus the return on book value is measured using profit after tax.

The CAPM and APT have often been contemplated and have sometimes been used as the primary method of estimation, but on the whole they have, apparently, been viewed with suspicion at regulatory hearings (Cornell, Hirshleifer and James, 1997). In addition to the problems with implementing the CAPM discussed in Chapter 13, market reaction to regulatory behaviour, or to news about such behaviour, may be an extra factor that induces instability of beta over time, as discussed in the next section.

There is circularity in the DCF method if the cost of equity is estimated using only data for the company being regulated. There is a positive relation between the growth rate assumed to be expected by investors and the cost of equity that emerges from DCF, but the growth rate $g = R_{E,allowed}Ret$, and $R_{E,allowed}$ is under the control of the regulator. Thus the cost of equity from DCF is affected by the growth rate that investors think the regulator will allow, whereas the regulator should be looking to an exogenous cost of equity estimate to determine what the allowed growth rate should be. The solution is to use DCF to estimate the cost of equity in a sample of companies believed to be of similar risk, and to take the average of the estimates as the cost of equity for the company in question. Myers and Borucki (1994, p. 20) recommend selecting a sample of matching utilities with approximately the same size, risk and market-to-book ratio.

However, there remains a second problem with DCF in the regulatory context, which is how to interpret the cost of equity estimate in the case of a company with a market value that differs appreciably from the book value. In this case, we must have $R_{E,allowed} \neq R_E$, from equation (15.1). Investors know that the aim of regulation is to ensure that $R_{E,allowed} = R_E$, so why should they assign a market value that differs from book value? For example, if market value exceeds book value, it implies that $R_{E,allowed} > R_E$. But investors know that the regulator will set $R_{E,allowed}$ equal to R_E, so they know that $R_{E,allowed}$ will be below the rate of return on book value implied in the price they are willing to pay for the shares. Myers and Borucki (1994) encountered this problem without resolving it. The share prices of US utilities that prevailed during the period they studied, the late 1980s and early 1990s, were much higher than the book values per share. They note (p. 25) that 'there is no way to square these numbers' with the assumption that the objective of regulators is to allow utilities to earn no more than their cost of capital in the long term.

15.3   Regulatory policy, risk and the allowed rate of return

The actions of the regulator affect the company's returns on capital and the risk of those returns, and so they affect the allowed rate of return on equity. There are two aspects to this. The first point is that regulatory policy affects the cost of equity. The regulator can decide how much risk is passed on to the customers. For example, if extra unforeseen costs arise, what proportion of these costs will the regulator allow the company to recoup from its customers? Thus the regulatory authority is itself in a position to influence the cost of equity, at least if it can make credible pre-commitments with respect to its future behaviour.

There is some evidence that regulatory policy can affect observed betas and thus the cost of equity as measured by the CAPM. There is a literature testing the relation between the tightness of regulation and beta. The findings are mixed. Binder and Norton (1999) find a negative relation between regulation and beta, controlling for other factors that affect beta, and suggest that this is the 'dominant result' from previous studies. A negative relation between regulation and beta is consistent with the idea that regulation transfers business risk from the shareholders to the customers. Buckland and Fraser (2001) examine the relation between betas and political and regulatory news using data for UK electricity companies during the 1990s. Most noteworthy is their finding of a sudden upward jump in betas on the day after the 1992 general election. There had been a strong possibility that the Labour Party would be elected, and Labour had promised tighter regulation of utilities. In the event the Conservative Party was re-elected, and the stock market and electricity shares both rose sharply, which presumably explains the jump in measured betas. Electricity betas remained above 1.0 for a few months, compared with their usual level of around 0.7. Buckland and Fraser speculate that the (transient) higher betas 'may indicate the market's acceptance that a further period of Conservative-led government would imply looser regulation and give investors access to greater, systematically varying returns in the electricity sector' (p. 14).

To the extent that there is uncertainty about future regulatory policy, this uncertainty will itself be a factor that increases the cost of equity, if the uncertainty augments the share's systematic risk. However, it appears to be normal to assume implicitly that the regulator maintains an unchanging policy over time with respect to the allocation of business risk between shareholder and customer. For example, Myers and Borucki (1994) and Elton, Gruber and Mei (1994) describe best practice in the use of DCF and APT, respectively, to estimate the cost of equity for utilities. Neither paper mentions the possible impact of the regulator on risk.

The second point is that the regulator's policy on intervention determines the relation between the allowed rate of return on equity and the cost of equity. A practical example of the making of this point can be found in a document published in 1991 by the UK Water Services Association and Water Companies Association (which have an incentive to 'talk up' the cost of capital). It is argued (pp. 54–62) that the regulatory, political and environmental risks faced by water companies are asymmetric; the potential shocks from these sources are mainly bad. For example, 'the most significant source of regulatory risk . . . [is that] the regulatory authorities may be more inclined to take a path that brings down the return if returns are higher than expected' (p. 59). Such negative shocks are also expected to be infrequent, and, for this reason, the achieved rate of return must exceed the expected rate in most years if the long-term rate achieved *ex post* is to equal the rate expected *ex ante*. Therefore, if water companies are restricted to earning the expected rate of return on equity in years without a negative shock, the achieved rate in the long run – including years with a shock – will be less than the expected rate. This is analogous to the 'rare disaster' explanation for the size of the historic equity premium in the United Kingdom and United States (Section 5.4.1); if there has been no disaster during the period in question, the observed rate of return will have exceeded the *ex ante* expected rate. The argument here is not that prospective regulatory interventions increase the water companies' cost of capital but that the companies should be allowed on average to earn more than their cost of capital in years with no regulatory shock.

Brennan and Schwartz (1982) provide rigorous derivations of the allowed rate of return on equity under various assumptions about the future behaviour of the regulator. They assume that the regulator wishes to pursue a consistent regulatory policy that enables an allowed rate to be estimated that 'is appropriate for the risk of the firm under that policy' (p. 507). They define a consistent policy as one that causes market value to be equal to book value at the time the allowed rate is being set. At one extreme is a policy of intensive intervention to ensure that the firm earns exactly a set rate of return on book equity. Since the allowed rate under this policy is risk-free, the cost of capital under this policy is the risk-free rate. Of more interest is a policy under which the rate that the firm can earn is reset to a predetermined allowed rate if the actual rate it has recently earned has hit a specified minimum or maximum. After having been reset, the earned rate can start to drift away again from the allowed rate, until it reaches the lower or upper limit. In this case there is some risk to shareholders, since the rate of return on equity is allowed to vary within the specified limits. The Brennan–Schwartz model itself is an adaptation of the Cox–Ingersoll–Ross model, which is set in continuous time. The price of a risky asset, or in this case the rate of return on equity, follows a random process; the drift, variance and covariance with aggregate economy-wide wealth are parameters set by the modeller. The asset's price can incorporate a risk premium for the same reason that risky assets provide an expected premium in the contingent-states model (Section 2.2). The premium will be positive if the price covaries positively with aggregate wealth.

In the model, the range within which the rate of return is allowed to vary affects the potential for gain and loss to shareholders. For example, if the risk-free rate is 8 per cent p.a. and the allowed range is between 8 per cent and 20 per cent p.a., the firm will be allowed to earn a lot more than the risk-free rate but will not be allowed to earn any less than the risk-free rate. The allowed rate itself is derived as the rate that ensures that market value equals book value at each regulatory intervention. In the setting described, the allowed rate depends on both the cost of equity and on the potential for upside in relation to downside. If we were comparing two allowed ranges, one between 8 per cent and 20 per cent p.a. and the other between 4 per cent and 16 per cent p.a., the allowed rate would need to be higher in the latter case, for a given estimate of the cost of equity. The allowed rate should *not* be set equal to the cost of equity, unless the potential for gain and loss is symmetric. A policy of resetting the rate to the estimated cost of equity would not, in general, be a consistent policy, because it would not ensure market value equal to book value. If the cost of equity is 12 per cent p.a. and the allowed range is between 8 per cent and 20 per cent p.a., the allowed rate would be set at less than the cost of equity, because there is more potential for upside than for downside.

The argument of the UK water companies was that the policy on intervention, as they perceived it, was such that the allowed rate should be greater than the cost of equity. This was because the allowed range was asymmetrical; it had an upside limit, albeit an uncertain one, but no downside limit.

A further point from the Brennan–Schwartz model is that beta estimated from past share returns is predicted to be even more unreliable for a regulated company than the beta for an unregulated company. This is because observed beta depends on how the regulated company's actual rate of return stands in relation to the upper and lower limits. Assuming that the relation between the company's actual rate and the rate of return on the market is positive, observed beta is predicted to be negative during periods when the company's actual rate of return is near the allowed lower or upper limit, and beta is expected to be positive when the actual rate is in the middle of the allowed range. Near the lower limit, an increase in the actual rate moves the rate away from the limit and makes an upward revision of product price less likely. So the share price is predicted to fall when the market rises (under the assumed positive relation between the actual rate and the market). Near the upper limit, an increase in the actual rate moves the rate towards the limit and makes a downward revision of product price more likely. So, again, the share price is predicted to fall when the market rises.

15.4   Price setting in the United Kingdom

The UK water, gas, electricity, telecommunications, airports and railway industries were privatised during the 1980s and 1990s via the flotation of a number of newly formed companies on the Stock Exchange. A separate regulatory body was created for each industry, and decisions of the regulators that have been contested by companies have been referred to the Monopolies and Mergers Commission (now known as the Competition Commission). The approach to price setting has been broadly similar across the regulators, and a few general points are noteworthy about regulatory practice in the United Kingdom.

Price cap system

The UK regime is designed to give companies some incentive to improve their performance. If a company manages to increase its profitability, shareholders are allowed to keep some of the gains. Price-setting reviews are held at fixed intervals, which range from four to ten years. In between, the maximum change in product price during a given year is determined by the observed inflation for the year plus a pre-set annual real change. So the price cap formula is summarised as $RPI + X$, for retail price index plus real percentage change in price. The X-factor was set at a negative number for most companies in the 1990s, in anticipation of efficiency gains. It was positive for water companies, because they were required to undertake substantial programmes of investment. A major amendment to the price cap formula is made for some companies, to the effect that they can pass on to customers changes in certain agreed costs of major inputs, via changes in their product price.

The regulated company is free to earn as much profit as it can between reviews, within the constraints of the price-setting formula and subject to the satisfaction of the regulator with respect to the quality of supply and investment for future provision. If the company earns more or less than its estimated cost of capital this is not supposed to trigger a revision of the price formula, and at a periodic price review regulators have discretion regarding how rapidly the company's actual rate of return should be forced down or up towards its estimated cost of capital. For example, Sir Bryan Carsberg, then the telecoms regulator, said in 1988 (quoted in Water Services Association, 1991, Vol. 2, p. 6),

> I do not think the benefits of efficiency should be taken away from the regulatee too quickly or the incentive effect can be lost. For example, if price-caps are set for successive periods of five years, and if the rate of return is always forced down to a barely acceptable level in the first year of each new five year period, the regulatee will have little incentive to become more efficient in the last year or two of the period. To avoid this danger, I believe that a price-cap should be set at a level such that any excess profits earned by the regulatee in one period can be carried forward to the next period and enjoyed to some extent for another two or three years.

A grey area is what happens if a company gets into difficulty. We would expect this to occur more often under price cap than under rate-of-return regulation. There have been two cases to date since the privatisations in which a regulated UK company has got into financial difficulty, in both of which the government has intervened. Railtrack, which maintains the rail infrastructure, was renationalised in 2002, and shareholders received almost nothing. British Energy, which operates nuclear power stations, was given financial support in 2002, but remains a listed company at the time of writing.

The essentials of the price cap system are presented by Myers (1972, pp. 82–84) under the heading 'conscious use of regulatory lag'. The system was advocated in the United Kingdom by Littlechild (1983); Armstrong, Cowan and Vickers (1994) provide a detailed discussion. Under the rate-of-return approach described in Section 15.1, the objective of regulation is that the company earns its cost of capital, within some margin of error. Efficiency gains are supposed to benefit the customer rather than the shareholder, and, arguably, there is insufficient incentive for regulated companies to be efficient. Probably for this reason, the price cap system has been adopted by numerous regulators in the United States and other countries in recent years. Another point of difference is that there should be somewhat less risk for shareholders under the rate-of-return system, which creates an incentive to substitute capital for labour. Consistent with this, betas of regulated companies tend to be lower in the United States than in the United Kingdom (Grout, 1995, p. 398).

Rate base
The initial value of the equity capital in UK regulated companies was taken to be the market value shortly after flotation, not some measure of the replacement cost of the assets. There were big differences between the two; in the case of water and gas, for example, market value was much lower than replacement cost. The use of market value after flotation involved circularity, since the market value depended on investor expectations regarding regulatory policy, including the initial measurement of the rate base. As explained in Section 15.1, shareholders are indifferent to how the rate base is measured, provided that new cash invested is added to the base and that the regulatory aim is that the actual rate of return on the base be equal to the cost of capital. But, under the price cap system, there

is more scope for the actual rate of return to diverge from the cost of capital, in which case the size of the base will matter to shareholders during the period of divergence. More importantly, the size of the base affects the evolution of the product price, and it affects the proceeds to the government at privatisation. For example, the government could have obtained a lot more for the water and gas companies than it did, had the regulator announced in advance that the companies would be allowed to earn the cost of capital on their assets valued at replacement cost. Such a policy would have required much higher prices for water than the actual post-privatisation prices, and this would have persisted for many years, since water and gas infrastructure has a long life.

There was considerable debate about, and variation in, exactly how the market value was measured. An extreme case was British Gas, the initial value of which was measured by the market value five years after flotation, to enable shareholders to capture the value of efficiency gains in the first few years after privatisation. The values of rate bases after the date of initial measurement were subsequently adjusted for inflation – i.e. a trended original cost method was used (Section 15.1).

Cost of capital

The models used for the cost of equity by UK regulators have been the CAPM and, to a lesser degree, DCF. From the early 1990s regulators have assumed an equity premium in the region of 4 per cent p.a., despite the evidence that the historic UK premium was 8 per cent p.a. A major justification for the lower premium was the views of many fund managers that the premium in the future would be much lower than it has been in the past. The cost of debt has been estimated by the prevailing risk-free rate over a suitable term plus an estimate of the company's default risk premium, not by the embedded cost. The company's weighted average cost of capital has usually been estimated in real terms and *before* corporation tax. So the cost of equity has been grossed up by an estimate of the company's effective rate of corporation tax. Arriving at the grossing-up factor has been awkward because of doubt about how to allow for the United Kingdom's imputation system (which was partially abolished in 1997), and about how to allow for investment incentives that reduced the corporation tax payable. This approach means that the tax saving from interest benefits customers, as in the United States. Grossing-up factors have been fairly small, usually less than 1.2 times the cost of capital after corporation tax. The real pre-tax WACC employed by all the regulators from the early 1990s was 7 per cent p.a., or close to that number.

15.5   A note on public/private projects

The alternative to a regulated private sector utility is public sector provision. A natural question is whether a utility's cost of capital differs according to whether it is in the public or the private sector. The same question arises about arrangements whereby private sector capital and companies are brought into public sector projects. Such public/private schemes have been implemented by governments in many countries in the last two decades.

In countries where the government can borrow at a lower rate than any other body, it is tempting to think that the cost of capital for government funds is the prevailing rate of interest at which the government can borrow, which will be less than the cost of private sector funds for governments considered to have a negligible risk of default. But the cost of capital for government projects is not, in theory, equivalent to the rate at which the government can borrow. The cost of capital for any project depends on the risk of the project, not on the source of the capital. It is true that the government may assess the risk somewhat differently from the way a private investor would assess it, and so arrive at a somewhat different cost of capital. It is also true that there has been inconclusive debate about whether and how a social rate of discount should be applied to public sector projects, which differs from the before-tax discount rate that would be applied were the project in the private sector. But these are second-order points. The first-order point is that the cost of capital will be roughly similar whether the money comes from the private or public sectors. As Brealey, Cooper and Habib (1996, p. 37) put it,

The notion that the government enjoys a lower cost of capital than private sector companies is misleading . . . The lower interest rate paid by the government simply reflects the guarantee provided by taxpayers . . . The risk presented by the projects does not disappear when the project is financed by the government. If cash flows from the project are unexpectedly low and do not suffice to service the debt raised by the government to finance the project, the shortfall is met by taxpayers, who play a similar role to that of equity-holders in a private sector company (but without the benefit of limited liability). Indeed, because it seems likely that the capital markets share risk better than does the tax system, the cost of capital for the government could well be *higher* than for corporations.

The risk does not disappear in a public/private venture, but the allocation of risks is a crucial issue that affects the value of the project and the whole way it is managed. The nature of the risks borne by each party to the project is intimately linked to the nature of the incentives they face to perform well. For example, a company that builds a structure bears more risk if it is obliged to maintain the structure in exchange for a pre-set fee than it does if it can pass on the actual maintenance costs to the government. The greater risk carries with it a greater incentive to build well and maintain efficiently. The allocation of risk also affects the cost of capital for the project as estimated by a private sector financier. As always, the cost of capital is positively related to the amount of (systematic) risk to which the financier will be exposed. This is partly up to the government in a public/private venture. The government can expect to reduce the cost it has to pay to a private company to finance and carry out a given project by reducing the risks to the company. But retaining risk for the taxpayer has a cost, albeit one that is hard to quantify.

15.6   Summary

The cost of capital is especially important for a regulated utility, since the regulator estimates its cost of capital from time to time, and the estimate is used in setting the prices the company is allowed to charge. This chapter has reviewed the rate-of-return approach to regulation, which was the norm for many years in the United States, and the more flexible price cap variant, which was pioneered in the United Kingdom in the late 1980s. In addition, we have noted that, to a first approximation, the cost of capital is the same whether a project is undertaken in the public sector or the private sector.

References

Abel, A. B., 1990, 'Asset prices under habit formation and catching up with the Joneses', *American Economic Review* 80, pp. 38–42.

—— 1999, 'Risk premia and term premia in general equilibrium', *Journal of Monetary Economics* 43, pp. 3–33.

Adler, M., and B. Dumas, 1983, 'International portfolio choice and corporation finance: a synthesis', *Journal of Finance* 38, pp. 925–84.

Aiyagari, S. R., 1993, 'Explaining financial market facts: the importance of incomplete markets and transactions costs', *Federal Reserve Bank of Minneapolis Quarterly Review* 17, pp. 17–31.

Alexander, G. J., C. S. Eun and S. Janakiramanan, 1987, 'Asset pricing and dual listing on foreign capital markets: a note', *Journal of Finance* 42, pp. 151–58.

Allsopp, C., and A. Glyn, 1999, 'The assessment: real interest rates', *Oxford Review of Economic Policy* 15, pp. 1–16.

Amihud, Y., and H. Mendelson, 1986, 'Asset pricing and the bid-ask spread', *Journal of Financial Economics* 17, pp. 223–49.

Ang, J. S., and T. Lai, 1989, 'A simple rule for multinational capital budgeting', *Global Finance Journal* 1, pp. 71–75.

Arditti, F. D., 1973, 'The weighted average cost of capital: some questions on its definition, interpretation and use', *Journal of Finance* 28, pp. 1001–07.

Ariel, R., 1998, 'Risk-adjusted discount rates and the present value of risky costs', *Financial Review* 33, pp. 17–30.

Armitage, S., 2000, 'The direct costs of UK rights issues and open offers', *European Financial Management* 6, pp. 57–68.

—— 2004, 'Returns after personal tax on UK equity and gilts, 1919–98', *European Journal of Finance* 10, pp. 23–43.

Armstrong, C. M., S. G. Cowan and S. J. Vickers, 1994, *Regulatory Reform: Economic Analysis and British Experience*, Cambridge, MA: MIT Press.

Arnold, G. C., 2002, *Corporate Financial Management*, 2nd edn., Harlow: Financial Times/Prentice Hall.

Arnold, G. C., and P. D. Hatzopoulous, 2000, 'The theory practice gap in capital budgeting: evidence from the United Kingdom', *Journal of Business Finance and Accounting* 27, pp. 603–26.

Ashton, D. J., 1989, 'Textbook formulae and UK taxation: Modigliani and Miller revisited', *Accounting and Business Research* 19, pp. 207–12.

—— 1991, 'Corporate financial policy: American analytics and UK taxation', *Journal of Business Finance and Accounting* 18, pp. 465–82.

Auerbach, A. J., 1979a, 'Wealth maximization and the cost of capital', *Quarterly Journal of Economics* 93, pp. 433–46.

1979b, 'Share valuation and corporate equity policy', *Journal of Public Economics* 11, pp. 291–305.

1983, 'Taxation, corporate financial policy and the cost of capital', *Journal of Economic Literature* 21, pp. 905–40.

Barclay, M. J., C. W. Smith and R. L. Watts, 1995, 'The determinants of corporate leverage and dividend policies', *Journal of Applied Corporate Finance* 7, pp. 4–19.

Barclays Capital, 2000, *Equity-Gilt Study*, London.

Barker, R., 2001, *Determining Value*, Harlow: Financial Times/Prentice Hall.

Bartholdy, J., and A. Riding, 1994, 'Thin trading and the estimation of betas: the efficacy of alternative techniques', *Journal of Financial Research* 17, pp. 241–54.

Bekaert, G., 1995, 'Market integration and investment barriers in emerging equity markets', *World Bank Economic Review* 9, pp. 75–107.

Bekaert, G., and C. R. Harvey, 1995, 'Time-varying world market integration', *Journal of Finance* 50, pp. 403–44.

2000, 'Foreign speculators and emerging equity markets', *Journal of Finance* 55, pp. 565–613.

Bell, L., and T. Jenkinson, 2002, 'New evidence on the impact of dividend taxation and on the identity of the marginal investor', *Journal of Finance* 57, pp. 1321–47.

Benartzi, S., and R. H. Thaler, 1995, 'Myopic loss aversion and the equity premium puzzle', *Quarterly Journal of Economics* 110, pp. 73–92.

Best, P., and A. Byrne, 2001, 'Measuring the equity risk premium', *Journal of Asset Management* 1, pp. 245–56.

Binder, J. J., and S. W. Norton, 1999, 'Regulation, profit variability and beta', *Journal of Regulatory Economics* 15, pp. 249–65.

Black, F., 1972, 'Capital market equilibrium with restricted borrowing', *Journal of Business* 45, pp. 444–55.

Black, F., M. C. Jensen, and M. S. Scholes, 1972, 'The capital asset pricing model: some empirical tests', in M. C. Jensen (ed.), *Studies in the Theory of Capital Markets*, New York: Praeger, pp. 79–121.

Blanchard, O. J., 1993, 'Movements in the equity premium', *Brookings Papers on Economic Activity* 2, pp. 75–138.

Blanchard, O. J., C. Rhee and L. H. Summers, 1993, 'The stock market, profit and investment', *Quarterly Journal of Economics* 108, pp. 115–36.

Blume, M. E., 1971, 'On the assessment of risk', *Journal of Finance* 26, pp. 1–10.

1975, 'Betas and their regression tendencies', *Journal of Finance* 30, pp. 785–95.

Bogue, M. C., and R. Roll, 1974, 'Capital budgeting of risky projects with imperfect markets for physical capital', *Journal of Finance* 29, pp. 601–13.

Booth, L., 1991, 'The influence of production technology on risk and the cost of capital', *Journal of Financial and Quantitative Analysis* 26, pp. 109–28.

Brealey, R. A., I. A. Cooper and M. A. Habib, 1996, 'Using project finance to fund infrastructure investments', *Journal of Applied Corporate Finance* 9, pp. 25–38.

Brealey, R. A., and S. C. Myers, 2003 and 1996, *Principles of Corporate Finance*, 7th edn. and 5th edn., New York: McGraw-Hill.

Brennan, M. J., 1970, 'Taxes, market valuation and corporate financial policy', *National Tax Journal* 23, pp. 417–27.

1973, 'A new look at the weighted average cost of capital', *Journal of Business Finance* 5, pp. 24–30.

Brennan, M. J., and E. S. Schwartz, 1982, 'Consistent regulatory policy under uncertainty', *Bell Journal of Economics* 13, pp. 506–21.

Brown, S. J., W. N. Goetzmann and S. A. Ross, 1995, 'Survival', *Journal of Finance* 50, pp. 853–73.

Bruner, R. F., K. M. Eades, R. S. Harris and R. C. Higgins, 1998, 'Best practices in estimating the cost of capital: survey and synthesis', *Financial Practice and Education* 8, pp. 13–28.

Buckland, R., and P. Fraser, 2001, 'Political and regulatory risk: beta sensitivity in UK electricity distribution', *Journal of Regulatory Economics* 19, pp. 5–25.

Buckley, A., 1995, 'The classical tax system, imputation tax and capital budgeting', *European Journal of Finance* 1, pp. 113–28.

Burton, R. M., and W. W. Dammon, 1974, 'On the existence of a cost of capital under pure capital rationing', *Journal of Finance* 29, pp. 1165–73.

Butler, J. S., and B. Schachter, 1989, 'The investment decision: estimation risk and risk-adjusted discount rates', *Financial Management* 18, pp. 13–22.

Callahan, C. M., and R. M. Mohr, 1989, 'The determinants of systematic risk: a synthesis', *Financial Review* 24, pp. 157–81.

Campbell, J. Y., 1991, 'A variance decomposition for stock returns', *Economic Journal* 101, pp. 157–79.

2000, 'Asset pricing at the millennium', *Journal of Finance* 55, pp. 1515–67.

Campbell, J. Y., and J. H. Cochrane, 1999, 'By force of habit: a consumption-based explanation of aggregate stock market behavior', *Journal of Political Economy* 107, pp. 205–52.

Campbell, J. Y., A. W. Lo and A. C. McKinlay, 1997, *The Econometrics of Financial Markets*, Princeton, NJ: Princeton University Press.

Campbell, J. Y., and J. Mei, 1993, 'Where do betas come from? Asset price dynamics and the sources of systematic risk', *Review of Financial Studies* 6, pp. 567–92.

Campbell, J. Y., and R. J. Shiller, 1988, 'The dividend-price ratio and expectations of future dividends and discount factors', *Review of Financial Studies* 1, pp. 195–228.

Carleton, W. T., and J. Lakonishok, 1985, 'Risk and return on equity: the use and misuse of historical estimates', *Financial Analysts Journal* 41, pp. 38–47.

Chan, L. K. C., and J. Lakonishok, 1992, 'Robust measurement of beta risk', *Journal of Financial and Quantitative Analysis* 27, pp. 265–82.

Chang, R. P., and S. G. Rhee, 1990, 'The impact of personal taxes on corporate dividend policy and capital structure decisions', *Financial Management* 19, pp. 21–31.

Chung, K. J., 1989, 'The impact of the demand volatility and leverages on the systematic risk of common stocks', *Journal of Business Finance and Accounting* 16, pp. 343–60.

Chung, K. J., and C. Charoenwong, 1991, 'Investment options, assets in place, and the risks of stock', *Financial Management* 20, pp. 21–33.

Claus, J., and J. Thomas, 2001, 'Equity premia as low as three percent? Evidence from analysts' earnings forecasts and domestic and international stock markets', *Journal of Finance* 46, pp. 1629–66.

Clements, A. W., 1999, 'The cost of capital – the practitioners' view', *European Journal of Finance* 5, pp. 247–55.

Cochrane, J. H., 1997, 'Where is the market going? Uncertain facts and novel theories', *Economic Perspectives, Federal Reserve Bank of Chicago* 21, pp. 3–37.

1999, 'New facts in finance', *Economic Perspectives, Federal Reserve Bank of Chicago* 23, pp. 36–58.

2001, *Asset Pricing*, Princeton, NJ: Princeton University Press.

Cohn, R. A., and F. Modigliani, 1985, 'Inflation and corporate financial management', in E. I. Altman and M. Subrahmanyam (eds.), *Recent Advances in Corporate Finance*, Homewood, IL: Irwin, pp. 341–70.

Conine, T. E., 1980 'Corporate debt and corporate taxes', *Journal of Finance* 35, pp. 1033–37.

Connor, G., and R. A. Korajczyk, 1995, 'The arbitrage pricing theory and multifactor models of asset returns', in R. A. Jarrow, V. Maksimovic and W. T. Ziemba (eds.), *Handbooks in Operations Research and Management Science*, Vol. IX, Amsterdam: Elsevier, pp. 87–144.

Cooper, I., 1996, 'Arithmetic versus geometric mean estimators: setting discount rates for capital budgeting', *European Financial Management* 2, pp. 157–67.

Cooper, I., and E. Kaplanis, 1995, 'Home bias in equity portfolios and the cost of capital for multi-national firms', *Journal of Applied Corporate Finance* 8, pp. 95–102.

Copeland, T. E., T. Koller and J. Murrin, 2000, *Valuation: Measuring and Managing the Value of Companies*, 3rd edn., New York: Wiley.

Copeland, T. E., and J. F. Weston, 1988, *Financial Theory and Corporate Policy*, 3rd edn., Reading, MA: Addison-Wesley.

Cornell, B., 1999, *The Equity Risk Premium*, New York: Wiley.

Cornell, B., J. I. Hirshleifer and E. P. James, 1997, 'Estimating the cost of equity capital', *Contemporary Finance Digest* 1, pp. 5–26.

Cowles, A., 1939, *Common Stock Indexes 1871–1937*, Bloomington, IN: Principia Press.

Dammon, R. M., 1988, 'A security market and capital structure equilibrium under uncertainty with progressive personal taxes', *Research in Finance* 7, pp. 53–74.

Dammon, R. M., and R. C. Green, 1987, 'Tax arbitrage and the existence of equilibrium prices for financial assets', *Journal of Finance* 42, pp. 1143–66.

Damodaran, A., 1999, *Applied Corporate Finance*, New York: Wiley.

Danthine, J.-P., and J. B. Donaldson, 2002, *Intermediate Financial Theory*, Upper Saddle River, NJ: Prentice Hall.

Davies, R., S. Unni, P. Draper and K. Paudyal, 1999, *The Cost of Equity Capital*, London: Chartered Institute of Management Accountants.

DeAngelo, H., and R. Masulis, 1980, 'Optimal capital structure under corporate and personal taxation', *Journal of Financial Economics* 8, pp. 3–27.

Dempsey, M., 1996, 'The cost of equity capital at the corporate and investor levels allowing a rational expectations model with personal taxations', *Journal of Business Finance and Accounting* 23, pp. 1319–31.

    1998, 'The impact of personal taxes on the firm's weighted average cost of capital and investment behaviour: a simplified approach using the Dempsey discounted dividends model', *Journal of Business Finance and Accounting* 25, pp. 747–63.

Denis, D. J., D. K. Denis and K. Yost, 2002, 'Global diversification, industrial diversification, and firm value', *Journal of Finance* 57, pp. 1951–63.

Dimson, E., 1979, 'Risk measurement when shares are subject to infrequent trading', *Journal of Financial Economics* 7, pp. 197–226.

    1989, 'The discount rate for a power station', *Energy Economics*, July, pp. 175–80.

Dimson, E., and P. Marsh, 1982, 'Calculating the cost of capital', *Long Range Planning* 15, pp. 112–20.

    1983, 'The stability of UK risk measures and the problem of thin trading', *Journal of Finance* 38, pp. 753–83.

Dimson, E., P. Marsh and M. Staunton, 2002, *Triumph of the Optimists: 101 Years of Global Investment Returns*, Princeton, NJ: Princeton University Press.

Dobbs, I. M., and A. D. Miller, 2003, 'Capital budgeting, valuation and personal taxes', *Accounting and Business Research* 32, pp. 227–43.

Draper, P., and K. Paudyal, 1995, 'Empirical irregularities in the estimation of beta: the impact of alternative estimation assumptions and procedures', *Journal of Business Finance and Accounting* 22, pp. 157–77.

Edwards, J. S. S., and M. J. Keen, 1984, 'Wealth maximization and the cost of capital: a comment', *Quarterly Journal of Economics* 99, pp. 211–14.

Ehrhardt, M. C., 1994, *The Search for Value: Measuring the Company's Cost of Capital*, Boston: Harvard Business School Press.

Ehrhardt, M. C., and Y. N. Bhagwat, 1991, 'A full-information approach for estimating divisional betas', *Financial Management* 20, 60–69.

Eiteman, D. K., A. I. Stonehill and M. H. Moffett, 1998, *Multinational Business Finance*, 8th edn., Reading, MA: Addison-Wesley.

Elton, E. J., M. J. Gruber and J. Mei, 1994, 'Cost of capital using arbitrage pricing theory: a case study of nine New York utilities', *Financial Markets, Institutions, and Instruments* 3, pp. 46–73.

Errunza, V. R., and E. Losq, 1985, 'International asset pricing under mild segmentation: theory and test', *Journal of Finance* 41, pp. 897–914.

Errunza, V. R., and L. W. Senbet, 1981, 'The effects of international operations on the market value of the firm: theory and evidence', *Journal of Finance* 36, pp. 401–17.

Eubank, A. A., and J. K. Zumwalt, 1979, 'An analysis of the forecast error impact of alternative beta adjustment techniques and risk classes', *Journal of Finance* 34, pp. 761–76.

Eun, C. S., and B. G. Resnick, 2001, *International Financial Management*, 2nd edn., Boston: McGraw-Hill.

Ezzamel, M. A., 1979, 'Divisional cost of capital and the measurement of divisional performance', *Journal of Business Finance and Accounting* 6, pp. 307–19.

Fama, E. F., 1970, 'Multiperiod consumption-investment decisions', *American Economic Review* 60, pp. 163–74.

1976, *Foundations of Finance*, Oxford: Basil Blackwell.

1977, 'Risk-adjusted discount rates and capital budgeting under uncertainty', *Journal of Financial Economics* 5, pp. 3–24.

1978, 'The effects of a firm's investment and financing decisions on the welfare of its security holders' *American Economic Review* 68, pp. 272–84.

1991, 'Efficient capital markets II', *Journal of Finance* 46, pp. 1575–1617.

1996, 'Discounting under uncertainty', *Journal of Business* 69, pp. 415–28.

Fama, E. F., and K. R. French, 1989, 'Business conditions and expected returns on stocks and bonds', *Journal of Financial Economics* 25, pp. 23–50.

1992, 'The cross-section of expected stock returns', *Journal of Finance* 47, pp. 427–66.

1993, 'Common risk factors in the returns on stocks and bonds', *Journal of Financial Economics* 33, pp. 3–56.

1996, 'Multifactor explanations of asset pricing anomalies', *Journal of Finance* 51, pp. 55–84.

1997, 'Industry costs of equity', *Journal of Financial Economics* 43, pp. 153–93.

2002, 'The equity premium', *Journal of Finance* 57, pp. 637–59.

Fama, E. F., and J. MacBeth, 1973, 'Risk, return and equilibrium: empirical tests', *Journal of Political Economy* 81, pp. 607–36.

Fama, E. F., and M. H. Miller, 1972, *The Theory of Finance*, New York: Holt, Rinehart and Winston.

Farrar, D. E., and L. L. Selwyn, 1967, 'Taxes, corporate financial policy and return to investors', *National Tax Journal* 20, pp. 444–62.

Fatemi, A. M., 1984, 'Shareholder benefits from corporate international diversification', *Journal of Finance* 39, pp. 1325–44.

Fazzari, S. M., R. G. Hubbard and B. C. Petersen, 1988, 'Financing constraints and corporate investment', *Brookings Papers on Economic Activity* 1, pp. 141–95.

Ferson, W. E., and C. R. Harvey, 1991, 'The variation of economic risk premiums', *Journal of Political Economy* 99, pp. 385–415.

Fisher, F. M., and J. I. McGowan, 1983, 'On the misuse of accounting rates of return to infer monopoly profits', *American Economic Review* 73, pp. 82–97.

Fisher, I., 1930, *The Theory of Interest*, New York: Macmillan.

Fitzgerald, A., 2001, *Still Puzzling over the Risk Premium*, working paper, Napier University, Edinburgh.

Foerster, S. R., and G. A. Karolyi, 1999, 'The effects of market segmentation and investor recognition on asset prices: evidence from foreign stocks listing in the United States', *Journal of Finance* 54, pp. 981–1013.

Frankel, J. A., 1991, 'The Japanese cost of finance: a survey', *Financial Management* 20, pp. 95–127.

Friend, I., and M. E. Blume, 1975, 'The demand for risky assets', *American Economic Review* 65, pp. 900–22.

Friend, I., Y. Landskroner and E. Losq, 1976, 'The demand for risky assets under uncertain inflation', *Journal of Finance* 31, pp. 1287–97.

Fuller, R. J., and H. S. Kerr, 1981, 'Estimating the divisional cost of capital: an analysis of the pure-play technique', *Journal of Finance* 36, pp. 997–1009.

Gallagher, T. J., and J. K. Zumwalt, 1991, 'Risk-adjusted discount rates revisited', *Financial Review* 26, pp. 115–25.

Gebhardt, W. R., C. M. C. Lee and B. Swaminathan, 2001, 'Toward an implied cost of capital', *Journal of Accounting Research* 39, pp. 135–76.

Gollier, C., 2001, *The Economics of Risk and Time*, Cambridge, MA: MIT Press.

Gombola, M. J., and D. R. Kahl, 1990, 'Time-series processes of utility betas: implications for forecasting systematic risk', *Financial Management* 19, pp. 84–93.

Graham, J. R., 1996, 'Debt and the marginal tax rate', *Journal of Financial Economics* 41, pp. 41–73.
2000, 'How big are the tax benefits of debt?', *Journal of Finance* 55, pp. 1901–40.
2003, 'Taxes and corporate finance: a review', *Review of Financial Studies* 16, pp. 1075–1129.

Graham, J. R., and C. R. Harvey, 2001, 'The theory and practice of corporate finance: evidence from the field', *Journal of Financial Economics* 60, pp. 187–243.

Gray, W., 1993, 'Historical returns, inflation and future return expectations', *Financial Analysts Journal* 49, pp. 35–45.

Green, R. C., and B. Hollifield, 2003, 'The personal-tax advantages of equity', *Journal of Financial Economics* 67, pp. 175–216.

Greenwald, B. C., 1980, 'Admissible rate bases, fair rates of return and the structure of regulation', *Journal of Finance* 35, pp. 359–68.

Grinblatt, M., and S. Titman, 2002, *Financial Markets and Corporate Strategy*, 2nd edn., New York: McGraw-Hill.

Grout, P., 1995, 'The cost of capital in regulated industries', in M. Bishop, J. Kay and C. Mayer (eds.), *The Regulatory Challenge*, Oxford: Oxford University Press, pp. 386–407.

Haley, C. W., and L. D. Schall, 1978, 'Problems with the concept of the cost of capital', *Journal of Financial and Quantitative Analysis* 13, pp. 847–70.
1979, *The Theory of Financial Decisions*, 2nd edn., New York: McGraw-Hill.

Hamada, R. S., 1969, 'Portfolio analysis, market equilibrium and corporation finance', *Journal of Finance* 24, pp. 13–31.

Hamada, R. S., and M. S. Scholes, 1985, 'Taxes and corporate financial management', in E. I. Altman and M. Subrahmanyam (eds.), *Recent Advances in Corporate Finance*, Homewood, IL: Irwin, pp. 187–226.

Handa, P., S. P. Kothari and C. Wasley, 1989 'The relation between the return interval and betas: implications for the size effect', *Journal of Financial Economics* 23, pp. 79–100.

Harris, R. S., F. C. Marston, D. R. Mishra and T. J. O'Brien, 2003, 'Ex ante cost of equity estimates of S&P 500 firms: the choice between global and domestic CAPM', *Financial Management* 32, pp. 51–67.

Harris, R. S., T. J. O'Brien and D. Wakeman, 1989, 'Divisional cost-of-capital estimation for multi-industry firms', *Financial Management* 18, pp. 74–84.

Hart, O., 1995, *Firms, Contracts and Financial Structure*, Oxford: Oxford University Press.

Harvey, C. R., 1991, 'The world price of covariance risk', *Journal of Finance* 46, pp. 111–57.
1995, 'The risk exposure of emerging equity markets', *World Bank Economic Review* 9, pp. 19–50.

Haugen, R. A., and L. W. Senbet, 1986, 'Corporate finance and taxes: a review', *Financial Management* 15, pp. 5–12.

Heaton, J., and D. J. Lucas, 1996, 'Evaluating the effects of incomplete markets on risk sharing and asset pricing', *Journal of Political Economy* 104, pp. 443–87.

Henry, P. B., 2000, 'Stock market liberalization, economic reform, and emerging market equity prices', *Journal of Finance* 55, pp. 529–64.

Hirshleifer, J. I., 1970, *Investment, Interest and Capital*, Englewood Cliffs, NJ: Prentice Hall.

Hirshleifer, J. I., and J. G. Riley, 1992, *The Analytics of Uncertainty and Information*, Cambridge: Cambridge University Press.

Hochman, S., and O. Palmon, 1985, 'The impact of inflation on the aggregate debt-asset ratio', *Journal of Finance* 40, pp. 1115–25.

Hodder, J. E., and H. E. Riggs, 1985, 'Pitfalls in evaluating risky projects', *Harvard Business Review* 63, pp. 128–35.

Hoy, M., J. Livernois, C. McKenna, R. Rees and T. Stengos, 1996, *Mathematics for Economics*, Don Mills, Ont.: Addison-Wesley.

Hsia, C., 1991, 'Estimating a firm's cost of capital: an option pricing approach', *Journal of Business Finance and Accounting* 18, pp. 281–87.

Huang, C., and R. H. Litzenberger, 1988, *Foundations for Financial Economics*, New York: North Holland.

Hull, J. C., 1986, 'A note on the risk-adjusted discount rate method', *Journal of Business Finance and Accounting* 13, pp. 445–50.

Ibbotson Associates, annual *Stocks, Bonds, Bills and Inflation*, Chicago: Ibbotson Associates.

Ibbotson, R. G., and P. Chen, 2003, 'Long-run stock returns: participating in the real economy', *Financial Analysts Journal* 59, pp. 88–98.

Ilmanen, A., 2003, 'Expected returns on stocks and bonds', *Journal of Portfolio Management*, Winter, pp. 7–27.

Jagannathan, R., and I. Meier, 2002, 'Do we need CAPM for capital budgeting?', *Financial Management* 31, pp. 56–77.

Jagannathan, R., and Z. Wang, 1996, 'The conditional CAPM and the cross-section of expected returns', *Journal of Finance* 51, pp. 3–53.

Jensen, M. C., and W. H. Meckling, 1976, 'Theory of the firm: managerial behavior, agency costs and ownership structure', *Journal of Financial Economics* 3, pp. 305–60.

Jorion, P., and W. N. Goetzmann, 1999, 'Global stock markets in the twentieth century', *Journal of Finance* 54, pp. 953–80.

Jorion, P., and E. Schwartz, 1986, 'Integration v segmentation in the Canadian Stock Market', *Journal of Finance* 41, pp. 603–13.

Kaplan, S. N., and R. S. Ruback, 1995, 'The valuation of cash flow forecasts: an empirical analysis', *Journal of Finance* 50, pp. 1059–93.

Keane, S. M., 1977, 'The irrelevance of the firm's cost of capital as an investment tool', *Journal of Business Finance and Accounting* 4, pp. 201–16.

1978, 'The cost of capital as a financial decision tool', *Journal of Business Finance and Accounting* 5, pp. 339–53.

Kemsley, D., and D. Nissim, 2002, 'Valuation of the debt tax shield', *Journal of Finance* 57, pp. 2045–73.

Kim, E. H., W. G. Lewellen and J. J. McConnell, 1979, 'Financial leverage clienteles', *Journal of Financial Economics* 7, pp. 83–109.

King, M. A., 1974a, 'Taxation and the cost of capital', *Review of Economic Studies* 41, pp. 21–36.

1974b, 'Dividend behaviour and the theory of the firm', *Economica* 41, pp. 25–34.

1977, *Public Policy and the Corporation*, London: Chapman & Hall.

King, M. A., and D. Fullerton (eds.), 1984, *The Taxation of Income from Capital*, Chicago: University of Chicago Press.

Klemkosky, R. C., and J. D. Martin, 1975, 'The adjustment of beta forecasts', *Journal of Finance* 30, pp. 1123–28.

Kocherlakota, N. R., 1996, 'The equity premium: it's still a puzzle', *Journal of Economic Literature* 34, pp. 42–71.

Kolbe, J. L., J. A. Read and G. R. Hall, 1984, *The Cost of Capital: Estimating the Rate of Return for Public Utilities*, Cambridge, MA: MIT Press.

Lasfer, M. A., 1995, 'Agency costs, taxes and debt: the UK evidence', *European Financial Management* 1, pp. 265–85.

Lease, R. C., K. John, A. Kalay, U. Loewenstein and O. H. Sarig, 2000, *Dividend Policy: Its Impact on Firm Value*, Boston: Harvard Business School Press.

Lessard, D. R., 1996, 'Incorporating country risk in the valuation of offshore projects', *Journal of Applied Corporate Finance* 9, pp. 52–63.

Lev, B., 1974, 'On the association between leverage and risk', *Journal of Financial and Quantitative Analysis* 9, pp. 627–42.

Levhari, D., and H. Levy, 1977, 'The capital asset pricing model and the investment horizon', *Review of Economics and Statistics* 59, pp. 92–104.

Levi, M. D., 1990, *International Finance*, 2nd edn., New York: McGraw-Hill.

Lewellen, W. G., and J. S. Ang, 1982, 'Inflation, security values and risk premia', *Journal of Financial Research* 5, pp. 105–23.

Li, H., and Y. Xu, 2002, 'Survival bias and the equity premium', *Journal of Finance* 57, pp. 1981–95.

Linke, C. M., and M. K. Kim, 1974, 'More on the weighted average cost of capital: a comment and analysis', *Journal of Financial and Quantitative Analysis* 9, pp. 1069–80.

Littlechild, S., 1983, *Regulation of British Telecommunications Profitability*, London: Her Majesty's Stationery Office.

Litzenberger, R., and K. Ramaswamy, 1979, 'The effect of personal taxes and dividends on capital asset prices: theory and empirical evidence', *Journal of Financial Economics* 7, pp. 163–96.

Lombard, T., J. Roulet and B. H. Solnik, 1999, 'Pricing of domestic versus multinational companies', *Financial Analysts Journal* 55, pp. 35–49.

Lucas, R. E., 1978, 'Asset prices in an exchange economy', *Econometrica* 46, pp. 1429–45.

Machina, M. J., 1987, 'Choice under uncertainty: problems solved and unsolved', *Journal of Economic Perspectives* 1, pp. 121–54.

McInish, T. H., and R. A. Wood, 1986, 'Adjusting for beta bias: an assessment of alternative techniques', *Journal of Finance* 41, pp. 277–86.

MacKie-Mason, J. K., 1990, 'Do taxes affect corporate financing decisions?', *Journal of Finance* 45, pp. 1471–93.

McLaney, E., J. Pointon, M. Thomas and J. Tucker, 2004, 'Practitioners' perspectives on the UK cost of capital', *European Journal of Finance* 10, pp. 123–38.

McNulty, J. J., T. D. Yeh, W. S. Schulze and M. H. Lubatkin, 2002, 'What's your real cost of capital?', *Harvard Business Review* 80, pp. 114–21.

Mandelker, G., and S. G. Rhee, 1984, 'The impact of the degree of operating and financial leverage on the systematic risk of common stock', *Journal of Financial and Quantitative Analysis* 19, pp. 45–57.

Mankiw, N. G., 1986, 'The equity premium and the concentration of aggregate shocks', *Journal of Financial Economics* 17, pp. 211–19.

Mankiw, N. G., and M. D. Shapiro, 1986, 'Risk and return: consumption beta versus market beta', *Review of Economics and Statistics* 68, pp. 452–59.

Mankiw, N. G., and S. P. Zeldes, 1991, 'The consumption of stockholders and nonstockholders', *Journal of Financial Economics* 29, pp. 97–112.

Markowitz, H. M., 1959, *Portfolio Selection*, New Haven, CT: Yale University Press.

1977, 'Investment for the long run', in I. Friend and J. L. Bicksler (eds.), *Risk and Return in Finance*, Vol. I, Cambridge, MA: Ballinger Publishing, pp. 219–44.

Mehra, R., 2003, 'The equity premium: why is it a puzzle?', *Financial Analysts Journal* 59, pp. 54–69.

Mehra, R., and E. C. Prescott, 1985, 'The equity premium: a puzzle', *Journal of Monetary Economics* 15, pp. 145–61.

Merton, R. C., 1972, 'An analytical derivation of the efficient portfolio frontier', *Journal of Financial and Quantitative Analysis* 7, pp. 1851–72.

1973, 'An intertemporal capital asset pricing model', *Econometrica* 41, pp. 867–87.

1977, 'A re-examination of the capital asset pricing model', in I. Friend and J. L. Bicksler (eds.), *Risk and Return in Finance*, Vol. I, Cambridge, MA: Ballinger Publishing, pp. 141–59.

Miles, J. A., and J. R. Ezzell, 1980, 'The weighted average cost of capital, perfect capital markets and project life: a clarification', *Journal of Financial and Quantitative Analysis* 15, pp. 719–30.

1985, 'Reformulating tax shield valuation: a note', *Journal of Finance* 40, pp. 1485–92.

Miller, D. P., 1999, 'The market reaction to international cross-listings: evidence from Depositary Receipts', *Journal of Financial Economics* 51, pp. 103–23.

Miller, M. H., 1977, 'Debt and taxes', *Journal of Finance* 32, pp. 261–75.

Miller, M. H., and F. Modigliani, 1961, 'Dividend policy, growth and the valuation of shares', *Journal of Business* 34, pp. 411–33.

Miller, M. H., and M. S. Scholes, 1978, 'Dividends and taxes', *Journal of Financial Economics* 6, pp. 333–64.

Mittoo, U. R., 1992, 'Additional evidence on integration in the Canadian stock market', *Journal of Finance* 47, pp. 2035–54.

Modigliani, F., and M. H. Miller, 1958, 'The cost of capital, corporation finance, and the theory of investment', *American Economic Review* 48, pp. 261–97.

1963, 'Corporate income taxes and the cost of capital: a correction', *American Economic Review* 53, pp. 433–43.

Monkhouse, P. H. L., 1993, 'The cost of equity under the Australian dividend imputation tax system', *Accounting and Finance* 33, pp. 1–18.

1996, 'The valuation of projects under the dividend imputation tax system', *Accounting and Finance* 36, pp. 185–212.

Morgan, G., and S. Thomas, 1998, 'Taxes, dividend yields and returns in the UK equity market', *Journal of Banking and Finance* 22, pp. 405–23.

Myers, S. C., 1968, 'A time-state-preference model of security valuation', *Journal of Financial and Quantitative Analysis* 3, pp. 1–34.

1972, 'The application of finance theory to public utility rate cases', *Bell Journal of Economics and Management Science* 3, pp. 58–97.

1974, 'Interactions of corporate financing and investment decisions – implications for capital budgeting', *Journal of Finance* 29, pp. 1–25.

1977, 'The relation between real and financial measures of risk and return', in I. Friend and J. L. Bicksler (eds.), *Risk and Return in Finance*, Vol. I, Cambridge, MA: Ballinger Publishing, pp. 49–80.

Myers, S. C., and L. S. Borucki, 1994, 'Discounted cash flow estimates of the cost of equity capital – a case study', *Financial Markets, Institutions and Instruments* 3, pp. 9–45.

Myers, S. C., and S. M. Turnbull, 1977, 'Capital budgeting and the capital asset pricing model: good news and bad news', *Journal of Finance* 32, pp. 321–33.

Ohlson, J. A., 1995, 'Earnings, book values, and dividends in valuation', *Contemporary Accounting Research* 11, pp. 661–87.

Oxera, 2002, *The Capital Structure of Water Companies*, Oxford: Oxera Consulting.

Parker, R. H., and G. C. Harcourt, 1969, *Readings in the Concept and Measurement of Income*, Cambridge: Cambridge University Press.

Pastor, L., and R. F. Stambaugh, 1999, 'Cost of equity capital and model mispricing', *Journal of Finance* 54, pp. 67–121.

Patterson, C. S., 1995, *The Cost of Capital: Theory and Estimation*, Westport, CT: Quorum Books.

Peterson, P. P., D. R. Peterson and J. S. Ang, 1985, 'Direct evidence on the marginal rate of taxation on dividend income', *Journal of Financial Economics* 14, pp. 267–82.

Poterba, J. M., 2000, 'Stock market wealth and consumption', *Journal of Economic Perspectives* 14, pp. 99–118.

Poterba, J. M., and L. H. Summers, 1985, 'The economic effects of dividend taxation', in E. I. Altman and M. Subrahmanyam (eds.), *Recent Advances in Corporate Finance*, Homewood, IL: Irwin, pp. 227–84.

1995, 'A CEO survey of U.S. companies' time horizons and hurdle rates', *Sloan Management Review*, Fall, pp. 43–53.

Pratt, S. P., 1998, *Cost of Capital: Estimation and Applications*, New York: John Wiley.

Rabin, M., and R. H. Thaler, 2001, 'Anomalies: risk aversion', *Journal of Economic Perspectives* 15, pp. 219–32.

Rajan, R. G., and L. Zingales, 1995, 'What do we know about capital structure? Some evidence from international data', *Journal of Finance* 50, pp. 1421–60.

Rappaport, A., and R. A. Taggart, 1982, 'Evaluation of capital expenditure proposals under inflation', *Financial Management* 11, pp. 5–13.

Rashid, M., and B. Amoako-Adu, 1995, 'The cost of capital under conditions of personal taxes and inflation', *Journal of Business Finance and Accounting* 22, pp. 1049–62.

Riener, K. D., 1985, 'A pedagogic note on the cost of capital with personal taxes and risky debt', *Financial Review* 20, pp. 229–35.

Rietz, T. A., 1988, 'The equity premium: a solution', *Journal of Monetary Economics* 22, pp. 117–31.

Risk Measurement Service, 2002, *Introduction to Risk Measurement*, London Business School.

Robichek, A. A., 1978, 'Regulation and modern finance theory', *Journal of Finance* 33, pp. 693–705.

Robichek, A. A., and S. C. Myers, 1966, 'Conceptual problems in the use of risk-adjusted discount rates', *Journal of Finance* 21, pp. 727–30.

Roll, R., 1977, 'A critique of the asset pricing theory's tests', *Journal of Financial Economics* 4, pp. 129–76.

Roll, R., and S. A. Ross, 1980, 'An empirical investigation of the arbitrage pricing theory', *Journal of Finance* 35, pp. 1073–103.

1994, 'On the cross-sectional relationship between expected returns and betas', *Journal of Finance* 49, pp. 101–21.

Romer, D., 2002, *Advanced Macroeconomics*, Boston: McGraw-Hill.

Ross, S. A., 1976, 'The arbitrage theory of capital asset pricing', *Journal of Economic Theory* 13, pp. 341–60.

1977, 'Return, risk and arbitrage', in I. Friend and J. L. Bicksler (eds.), *Risk and Return in Finance*, Vol. I, Cambridge, MA: Ballinger Publishing, pp. 189–218.

Ruback, R. S., 1986, 'Calculating the market value of riskless cash flows', *Journal of Financial Economics* 15, pp. 323–39.

2002, 'Capital cash flows: a simple approach to valuing risky cash flows', *Financial Management* 31, pp. 85–103.

Rubinstein, M. E., 1973, 'A mean-variance synthesis of corporate financial theory', *Journal of Finance* 28, pp. 167–81.

1976, 'The valuation of uncertain income streams and the pricing of options', *Bell Journal of Economics* 7, pp. 407–25.

Rutterford, J., 2000, 'The cost of capital and shareholder value', in G. Arnold, and M. Davies (eds.), *Value-based Management: Context and Application*, Chichester: Wiley, pp. 135–50.

Samuelson, P. A., 1969, 'Lifetime portfolio selection by dynamic stochastic programming', *Review of Economics and Statistics* 51, pp. 239–46.

Schaefer, S. M., 1982, 'Tax-induced clientele effects in the market for British government securities', *Journal of Financial Economics* 10, pp. 121–59.

Schall, L. D., 1984, 'Taxes, inflation and corporate financial policy', *Journal of Finance* 39, pp. 105–26.

Scholes, M. S., and J. Williams, 1977 'Estimating betas from non-synchronous data', *Journal of Financial Economics* 5, pp. 309–27.

Scholes, M. S., and M. A. Wolfson, 1988, 'The cost of capital and changes in tax regimes', in H. J. Aaron, H. Galper and J. A. Pechman (eds.), *Uneasy Compromise: Problems of a Hybrid Income-Consumption Tax*, Washington, DC: Brookings Institution.

Schwert, G. W., 1990, 'Indexes of US stock prices from 1802 to 1987', *Journal of Business* 63, pp. 399–426.

Scott, M. F., 1992, 'The cost of equity capital and the risk premium on equities', *Applied Financial Economics* 2, pp. 21–32.

Senbet, L. W., 1979, 'International capital market equilibrium and the multinational firm financing and investment policies', *Journal of Financial and Quantitative Analysis* 14, pp. 455–80.

Sercu, P., and R. Uppal, 1995, *International Financial Markets and the Firm*, Cincinnati, OH: South Western College Publishing.

Shao, L. P., and A. T. Shao, 1993, 'Capital budgeting practices employed by European affiliates of U.S. transnational companies', *Journal of Multinational Financial Management* 3, pp. 95–109.

Sharpe, W. F., 1964, 'Capital asset prices: a theory of market equilibrium under conditions of risk', *Journal of Finance* 19, pp. 425–42.

1966, 'Mutual fund performance', *Journal of Business* 39, pp. 119–38.

1977, 'The capital asset pricing model: a multi-beta interpretation', in H. Levy and M. Sarnat (eds.), *Financial Decision Making under Uncertainty*, New York: Academic Press, pp. 127–36.

Shiller, R. J., 1981, 'Do stock prices move too much to be justified by subsequent changes in dividends?', *American Economic Review* 71, pp. 421–36.

Sick, G. A., 1990, 'Tax-adjusted discount rates', *Management Science* 36, pp. 1432–50.

Siegel, J. J., 1985, 'The application of DCF methodology for determining the cost of equity capital', *Financial Management* 14, pp. 46–53.

1992, 'The real rate of interest from 1800–1990', *Journal of Monetary Economics* 29, pp. 227–52.

1998, *Stocks for the Long Run*, New York: McGraw-Hill.

1999, 'The shrinking equity premium', *Journal of Portfolio Management*, fall, pp. 10–17.

Sinn, H.-W., 1991, 'Taxation and the cost of capital: the "old" view, the "new" view and another view', *Tax Policy and the Economy* 5, pp. 25–54.

Solnik, B. H., 1974, 'The international pricing of risk: an empirical investigation of the world capital market structure', *Journal of Finance* 29, pp. 365–78.

2000, *International Investments*, 4th edn., Reading, MA: Addison-Wesley.

Stapleton, R. C., 1972, 'Taxes, the cost of capital and the theory of investment', *Economic Journal* 82, pp. 1273–92.

Stein, J. C., 1996, 'Rational capital budgeting in an irrational world', *Journal of Business* 69, pp. 429–55.

Stewart, G. B., 1991, *The Quest for Value*, New York: HarperCollins.

Stiglitz, J. E., 1969, 'A re-examination of the Modigliani–Miller theorem', *American Economic Review* 59, pp. 784–93.

1973, 'Taxation, corporate financial policy and the cost of capital', *Journal of Public Economics* 2, pp. 1–34.

1976, 'The corporation tax', *Journal of Public Economics* 5, pp. 303–11.

1985, 'The general theory of tax avoidance', *National Tax Journal* 38, pp. 325–37.

Strong, N. C., and T. R. Appleyard, 1992, 'Investment appraisal, taxes and the security market line', *Journal of Business Finance and Accounting* 19, pp. 1–24.

Stulz, R. M., 1995a, 'International portfolio choice and asset pricing: an integrative survey', in R. A. Jarrow, V. Maksimovic and W. T. Ziemba (eds.), *Handbooks in Operations Research and Management Science*, Vol. IX, Amsterdam: Elsevier, pp. 201–23.

   1995b, 'The cost of capital in internationally integrated markets: the case of Nestlé', *European Financial Management* 1, pp. 11–22.

Subrahmanyam, M., and S. Thomadakis, 1980, 'Systematic risk and the theory of the firm', *Quarterly Journal of Economics* 94, pp. 437–51.

Sudarsanam, P. S., 1992, 'Market and industrial structure and corporate cost of capital', *Journal of Industrial Economics* 40, pp. 189–99.

Swoboda, P., and J. Zechner, 1995, 'Financial structure and the tax system', in R. A. Jarrow, V. Maksimovic and W. T. Ziemba (eds.), *Handbooks in Operations Research and Management Science*, Vol. IX, Amsterdam: Elsevier, pp. 767–92.

Taggart, R. A., 1980, 'Taxes and corporate capital structure in an incomplete market', *Journal of Finance* 35, pp. 645–59.

   1981, 'Rate-of-return regulation and utility capital structure decisions', *Journal of Finance* 36, pp. 383–93.

   1987, 'Allocating capital among a firm's divisions: hurdle rates vs budgets', *Journal of Financial Research* 10, pp. 177–90.

   1991, 'Consistent valuation and cost of capital expressions with corporate and personal taxes', *Financial Management* 20, pp. 8–20.

Talmor, E., R. Haugen and A. Barnea, 1985, 'The value of the tax subsidy on risky debt', *Journal of Business* 58, pp. 191–202.

Talmor, E., and S. Titman, 1990, 'Taxes and dividend policy', *Financial Management* 19, pp. 32–35.

Tobin, J., 1958, 'Liquidity preference as behavior towards risk', *Review of Economic Studies* 25, pp. 65–86.

Van Horne, J. C., 2001, *Financial Market Rates and Flows*, 6th edn., Upper Saddle River, NJ: Prentice Hall.

Vasicek, O. A., 1973, 'A note on using cross-sectional information in Bayesian estimation of security betas', *Journal of Finance* 28, pp. 1233–39.

von Neumann, J., and O. Morgenstern, 1947, *Theory of Games and Economic Behavior*, Princeton, NJ: Princeton University Press.

Water Services Association, 1991, *The Cost of Capital in the Water Industry*, Water Services Association and Water Companies Association, United Kingdom.

Weil, P., 1989, 'The equity premium puzzle and the risk-free rate puzzle', *Journal of Monetary Economics* 24, pp. 401–21.

Wilkie, A. D., 1995, 'The risk premium on ordinary shares', *Journal of the Institute of Actuaries* 119, pp. 1–43.

Whittington, G., 1998, 'Regulatory asset value and the cost of capital', in M. E. Beesley (ed.), *Regulating Utilities: Understanding the Issues*, London: Institute of Economic Affairs.

Whyte, L. G., 1949, *Principles of Finance and Investment*, Cambridge: Cambridge University Press.

Zodrow, G. R., 1991, 'On the "traditional" and "new" views of dividend taxation', *National Tax Journal* 44, pp. 497–509.

Index

Abel, A. B. 107, 114–15
abnormal earnings method *see* cost of equity
Adler, M. 228, 237, 239
adjusted discount rate 159, *see also* weighted average
    cost of capital
adjusted present value 170, 171–74, 178, 215, 254
agency costs 137
Aiyagari, S. R. 75, 118
Alexander, G. J. 242
Allsopp, C. 36
Amihud, Y. 143
Amoako-Adu, B. 232
Ang, J. S. 228, 249
Appleyard, T. R. 213
arbitrage portfolio 54
arbitrage pricing theory (APT) 53–57, 86, 294
    CAPM and 57
    evidence 62–63
Arditti, F. D. 160, 178–79
Ariel, R. 131–32
Armitage, S. 217, 288, 290
Armstrong, C. M. 332
Arnold, G. 261, 315
Arrow–Debreu security *see* elementary claim
Ashton, D. J. 216
asset
    beta 143
    market value 5
    valuation 24–31, 32–33, 68–72
asset market *see* capital market
asset pricing models, brief comparison 86
Auerbach, A. J. 182, 187, 188, 190, 194, 195

Barclay, M. J. 219
Barclays Capital 90–91, 217
Barker, R. 272
Barnea, A. 208
Bartholdy, J. 286, 288
Bayesian estimates 283–84, 293–94
behavioural finance 34, 59, 110–11
Bekaert, G. 243–44, 258
Bell, L. 290
Benartzi, S. 110
Best, P. 103

beta estimates 282–83
    accounting beta 301–02
    Blume adjustment 283
    commercial estimates 291–92, 319
    company size 289
    estimation period 290–91
    evidence 284, 286, 288–91
    fat-tailed returns 291
    market indices 286–87
    measurement interval 289
    regulated utilities 329, 331, 332
    reversion to mean 283–85, 292
    thin trading 285, 288–89, 292–93
        Dimson adjustment 287–88
        Scholes–Williams adjustment 287, 288
        trade-to-trade adjustment 288–89
    Vasicek adjustment 283–84
    see also capital asset pricing model, multifactor
        models
Bhagwat, Y. N. 301
Binder, J. J. 329
Black, F. 47, 49, 61
Blanchard, O. J. 101–03, 105
Bloomberg 292
Blume, M. E. 90, 106–07, 283
Bogue, M. C. 126
bond
    coupon-paying (conventional) 234, 279–80
    index-linked 279–80
    zero-coupon 233–34
Booth, L. 144
Borucki, L. S. 267, 268, 328, 329
Brealey, R. A. 87, 168, 178, 254, 261, 269, 280, 307,
    308, 313, 334
Brennan, M. J. 159, 184, 185, 198–201, 330
Brown, S. J. 94
Bruner, R. F. 262, 278, 282, 291, 292, 316, 319
Buckland, R. 329
Buckley, A. 216
budget constraint 10–13, 14–15, 16, 25, 42
Burton, R. M. 142
business risk 143, 158
Butler, J. S. 131, 132
Byrne, A. 103

Callahan, C. M. 143
Campbell, J. Y. 34, 60, 75, 109, 111, 116, 145–47,
    272
capital 3–4
    book value 4
    expected return on 21
    marginal rate of return on 14
    marginal revenue product of 147–48
    market value 4
    see also equity, debt
capital asset pricing model (CAPM) 86
    Black (zero-beta) version 47–49, 66–67
    certainty-equivalent version 128–31, 150–52
    conditional version 59–60, 238, 243–44, 246,
        257–58
    consumption CAPM and 73
    discounting and 123–24, 126–27, 128–31
    estimation 264, 321–22
        Bayesian 293–94
        beta 282–93
        equity premium 281–82, 320
        risk-free rate 278–81, 318–19
    ex ante determinants of project beta 143–47,
        150–52
    evidence 60–62, 245–46, 247
    international version 238, 239–41, 242, 245–46,
        247, 250–52
    leverage and 163–65, 166–68, 170, 171–74, 304–07
    Merton's intertemporal CAPM and 84–85, 126
    multifactor models and 52–53
    multiple periods 52, 123–24
    personal tax 185, 191–92, 198–201, 212–13, 216,
        217
    Roll's critique 49–52, 61
    standard version 38–47, 63–66, 257
capital budgeting 5–7, 19, 309–10, 317
capital goods 147–49
capital market 15, 21, 39, 44
    complete 26, 28
    incomplete 33, 34–36
    integrated 236–41, 250–51
    segmented 241–47, 251–52
capital market line 44
capital rationing 142
Carleton, W. T. 96, 281
Carsberg, B. 332
choice, axioms of 7–8, 22–23
certainty-equivalent value 22, 73, 128–31, 217–20
Chan, L. K. C. 291
Chang, R. P. 194
Charoenwong, C. 144
Chen, P. 281
Chung, K. J. 144
Claus, J. 101, 104, 275, 281
clean surplus accounting 274
Clements, A. W. 308, 309
Cohn, R. A. 230
company 13, 31–32
    performance measurement 275–76
    private 35–36
    project and 132–33, 176, 193–95

stakeholders 309–10
    see also debt, equity
Cochrane, J. H. 52, 60, 62, 79, 84, 87, 106, 107, 108,
    109, 111
conditional models of expected returns 59–60, 238,
    243–44, 246, 257–58
Conine, T. E. 167
Connor, G. 62
consumption-based models of expected returns
    consumption CAPM 72–73, 75–77, 84, 86, 107–09
    evidence 85, 106
    Campbell–Cochrane model 111–14
    market frictions 116–19
    Mehra–Prescott model 79–82, 106
    Merton's intertemporal CAPM 82–85, 86, 126, 294
    modified utility functions 109–16
    multiple periods 78–85
contingent states
    asset valuation 24–31, 32–33, 36–37, 68–72
    CAPM and 38–41, 47
    meaning 20
    personal tax 207–08, 210–11, 220–24
    project valuation 20–22, 31, 33, 34–36, 123, 165,
        176
    see also consumption-based models of expected
        returns
Cooper, I. 89, 132, 246
Copeland, T. 133, 162, 175, 219, 237, 249, 253, 254,
    261, 311, 313
Cornell, B. 88, 95, 98, 104, 261, 262, 268, 279, 280,
    295, 302, 316, 328
cost of capital 4–5, 21, 35–36, 186–87
    cash flows and 137–40, 176–77
    ex ante determination for a project 129–31
    financing-related costs and 137–43
    multiple periods 124–32
    negative cash flows 131–32
    public sector 333–34
    relation between theory and practice 320–21
    risk-free taxable cash flow 214
    separation theorem and 19
    taxes and 155–56, 179, 181–85
    Stiglitz model 185, 201–04
    see also cost of debt, cost of equity, inflation,
        interest rate, regulated utilities, user cost of
        capital, weighted average cost of capital
cost of debt 136
    CAPM 166
    estimation 136–52, 312–13, 319
    issues not covered 137
    personal tax 184
    risky governments 254, 280–81
    see also regulated utilities
cost of equity 89, 134–35, 186–87
    bias in expected cash flow and 140–41
    dividend policy and 139, 183–85, 193–95, 266
    estimation for a listed company
        abnormal earnings 101, 272–76, 297–99
        discussion of methods 262–64, 321–22
        earnings yield 263, 269–70
        evidence 262

from options prices 276–77
mean of past returns 263
regulatory decision 263
views of shareholders 262–63
estimation for an untraded project 317–20
adjustment for business risk 302–03
adjustment for leverage 302–08, 318
choice of model 319
from pure-play companies 300–02, 318, 319
projects with no pure play 306, 308
leverage and 159–60, 161–62, 163–65, 166–68,
171–74, 314
personal tax
dividend clienteles 196
evidence 197
extension of Modigliani–Miller analysis 182–85
imputation systems 215–17
new or tax capitalisation view 185–96, 197–98,
216
old or classical or traditional view 185–86, 190,
192–96, 197–98, 216
q-theory 188–92, 197
share repurchases 195
source of equity capital 187–91, 193–94
total risk and 308–10
integrated capital markets 236–41
Solnik–Sercu model 239–41
segmented capital markets 241–44, 248–55
choice of CAPM 250–52, 314
Errunza and Losq's model 255–57
evidence 244–47
see also capital asset pricing model, dividend
discount model, equity risk premium,
multifactor models, regulated utilities
Cowles, A. 91
currency risk 252
currency risk premium 239–41

Dammon, R. M. 210–11, 223
Dammon, W. W. 142
Damodaran, A. 261
Danthine, J.-P. 20, 34, 47, 72
Davies, R. 261, 267, 286, 289–90, 296, 297
DeAngelo, H. 207–08
debt 3
features 135
tax *see* Miller equilibrium, weighted average cost of
capital
see also cost of debt
debt capacity 311
default risk premium 234
demand, theory of 7–9
demand curve 13, 15–16
Dempsey, M. 191, 192, 197
Denis, D. J. 247
depreciation 147
derivation of a result 38
Dimson, E. 92–93, 94, 216, 217, 263, 281, 283, 284,
285, 286, 287–88, 289, 291
discount rate *see* cost of capital, interest rate
diversification, international 241, 244, 246–47

dividend discount model 324
abnormal earnings and 275
analysts' growth forecasts 267–68, 320
changing discount rate 271–72
decomposition of risk and 145–47
dividend policy and 266
earnings yield and 269–70
inferring equity premium 99, 100–01, 281
inferring cost of equity 191–92, 264–66
sustainable growth rate 268
timing of dividends 270
uncertain dividends 266–67
see also regulated utilities
Dobbs, I. M. 185
Donaldson, J. B. 20, 34, 47, 72
Draper, P. 291
Dumas, B. 228, 237, 239

economic exposure 252
Edwards, J. S. S. 187, 190
efficient portfolio 42–52, 65–67
Ehrhardt, M. C. 139, 168, 251, 261, 289, 301, 302,
306, 308
Eiteman, D. K. 246, 249, 253
elementary claim
meaning 25
Elton, E. J. 63, 64, 295–96, 329
equity 3
features of 133
market value 21
return on 134, 217, 268–70
see also cost of equity
equity risk premium 47, 87, 234–35, 333
arithmetic v geometric mean 88–90
consumption-based models and 107–19
historic *ex ante* premiums 96
historic *ex post* premiums 90–96
international evidence 92–94
Mehra–Prescott model and 79–82, 106
methods of forecasting 88–90, 99, 281–82, 320
risk-free rate and 280
Equity-Gilt Study 90–91, 93
Errunza, V. 242, 244, 255
Eubank, A. A. 284–85, 290
Eun, C. S. 242, 254
expected value 20
expected return 21
Ezzamel, M. A. 302
Ezzell, J. R. 169–72

Fama–French three-factor model 57–59
application 297
Fama, E. F. 7, 49, 57–59, 60, 61, 62, 63, 64, 66, 84,
95, 97, 100–01, 105, 126–27, 129, 165, 177,
282, 286, 297, 318, 319
Farrar, D. E. 182
Fatemi, A. M. 247
Fazzari, S. M. 137–43
Ferson, W. E. 60
financial distress, costs of 137
financial risk 143

Fisher, F. M. 269
Fisher, I. 7
Fisher relation 225, 226, 227, 228, 229, 231, 235, 314
Fitzgerald, A. 98–99
flotation costs 138–39
Foerster, S. R. 246
foreign direct investment (FDI) 244, 247–48
foreign risk premium 253
Frankel, J. A. 244–45
Fraser, P. 329
French, K. R. 57–59, 62, 95, 97, 100–01, 105, 282, 297, 317–18, 319
Friend, I. 106–07, 228
Fuller, R. J. 302, 307, 308
Fullerton, D. 156, 196

Gallagher, T. J. 130
Gebhardt, W. R. 101, 297
Glyn, A. 36
Goetzmann, W. N. 94
Gollier, C.
Gombola, M. J. 284
Gordon growth model *see* dividend discount model
Graham, J. R. 197, 219, 262, 295, 316
Gray, W. 98
Green, R. C. 208–09, 210, 220–23
Greenwald, B. C. 325, 327
Grinblatt, M. 261
Grout, P. 323, 332
Gruber, M. J. 62

Haley, C. W. 34, 177, 179
Hall, G. R. 323
Hamada, R. S. 164, 212
Handa, P. 289
Harcourt, G. C. 3
Harris, R. S. 61, 245, 301
Hart, O. 135
Harvey, C. R. 60, 238, 243–44, 245, 258, 262, 295, 316
Hatzopoulos, P. D. 315
Haugen, R. 208, 211, 215–19
Heaton, J. 118–19
Henry, P. B. 246
heterogeneous investors 33, 34–36, 116–17
    personal taxes 220–24, 239
    multiple countries 238–40
Hirshleifer, J. 3, 7, 20
Hochman, S. 231
Hodder, J. E. 128
Hollifield, B. 208–09
Hope case (*Federal Power Commission v Hope Natural Gas*) 324, 327
Huang, C. 44, 83, 96–106
Hubbard, R. G. 138
Hull, J. C. 130
hybrid securities 133, 311

Ibbotson Associates 91, 292, 297
Ibbotson, R. G. 281
Ilmanen, A. 87, 103, 263, 281

income effect 11, 13
indifference curve 7–8, 10–13, 41
Indro, D. C. 90
inflation
    discounting/valuation and 226, 229, 314
    effective tax rates and 229–32
    equity risk premium and 88, 98
    real and nominal returns 225–32
    taxable profit and 230
inflation risk premium 226–27, 234
    choice of risk-free rate and 280
information costs 137
Institutional Brokers Estimate System (IBES) 267
interest rate 5, 36
    under certainty 7–19
    see also risk-free rate
interest rate parity 238, 239
intermediation, costs of 142–43
internal rate of return (IRR) 6–7, 125, 134, 265, 269
investment 4
    aim of 5
    capital goods and 147–49
    corporation tax and 156–57
    external funds and 138
    policy regarding 14, 31–32, 34–35
    q-theory of 148–49, 188–92
    return on 6, 19, 21

Jagannathan, R. 60, 317
Janakiramanan, S. 242
Jenkinson, T. 290
Jensen, M. C. 61, 177
Jensen's inequality 26, 28, 76, 228
Jorion, P. 93, 246, 247

Kahl, D. R. 284
Kaplan, S. N. 104
Kaplanis, E. 246
Karolyi, G. A. 246
Keane, S. M. 138, 172–76, 177
Keen, M. J. 187, 190
Kemsley, D. 220
Kerr, H. S. 302, 307, 308
King, M. A. 35, 156, 194, 195–96
Kim, E. H. 209
Kim, M. K. 168
Klemkosky, R. C. 284
Kocherlakota, N. R. 109
Kolbe, J. L. 270, 323, 324, 327
Korajczyk, R. A. 62

Lagrange multiplier 11, 25, 64, 65, 148
Lakonishok, J. 96, 281, 291
Lai, T. 249
Lasfer, M. A. 219
Lease, R. C. 197
Lee, C. M. C. 297
Lee, W. Y. 90
Lessard, D. R. 253
Lev, B. 143

leverage
  measurement of 307–08, 318
  operating 308
  target level of 310–11
  see also cost of equity, Miller equilibrium,
    weighted average cost of capital
Levhari, D. 289
Levi, M. D. 254
Levy, H. 289
Lewellen, W. G. 209, 228
liberalisation of a stock market 243–44, 246
Li, H. 94
Linke, C. M. 168
liquidity risk premium 235
listing on a second stock market 242–43, 246
Littlechild, S. 332
Litzenberger, R. H. 44, 83, 106, 201
Lo, A. W. 60, 116
lognormal distribution 76
Lombard, T. 247
London Business School Risk Measurement Service
  291
Losq, E. 242, 255
Lucas, D. J. 118–19
Lucas, R. E. 79

MacBeth, J. 61
McConnell, J. J. 209
McGowan, J. I. 269
Machina, M. J. 33
McInish, T. H. 285, 288, 289
MacKie-Mason, J. K. 219
McKinlay, A. C. 60, 116
McLaney, E. 262, 315
McNulty, J. J. 276–77
Mandelker, G. 143–44
Mankiw, N. G. 85, 116–17
market risk premium *see* equity risk premium
Markov process 79
Markowitz, H. M. 38, 39, 41, 126
Marsh, P. 92–93, 216, 283, 284, 285, 288, 289, 291
Martin, J. D. 284
Masulis, R. 207–08
Meckling, W. H. 177
Mehra, R. 79, 107, 281–82
Mei, J. 62, 145–47
Meier, I. 317
Memorandum and Articles of Association 133
Mendelson, H. 143
Merrill Lynch 291
Merton, R. C. 43, 82
Miles, J. A. 169–72
Miller, A. D. 185
Miller, D. P. 246
Miller equilibrium (set after personal tax) 194, 211,
  220
  basic model 205–07
  capital gains tax 208–09
  CAPM and 212–13
  Dammon's analysis 210–11
  inflation and 231–32

  leverage clienteles 209–10, 216–20
  redundant tax shields 207
  WACC and 211–14
Miller, M. H. 7, 64, 139, 157–61, 163, 165, 175, 177,
  182, 196, 205, 211, 266, 268
minimum-variance frontier 43, 48–52
Mittoo, U. R. 247
Modigliani, F. 139, 157–61, 163, 165, 175, 182, 205,
  230, 266, 268
Modigliani–Miller theory 34, 157–60, 163, 165
  CAPM and 164
Mohr, R. M. 143
monetary policy 36
Monkhouse, P. H. L. 217
Morgan, G. 197
Morgenstern, O. 23
multifactor models of expected returns 52–59, 257–58
  abnormal earnings method and 297–99
  application 294–99
  estimation 264
  evidence 61–63
  macroeconomic variables 295–97
  see also Fama–French three-factor model
mutual fund theorem 44
Myers, S. C. 20, 87, 128, 143, 145, 150, 168, 175,
  176, 178–79, 254, 261, 267, 268, 269, 280,
  307, 308, 313, 323, 327, 328, 329, 332

Nissim, D. 220
no-arbitrage condition 18, 26, 28, 53–57, 69, 157,
  214, 220–23, 234, 238
Norton, S. W. 329

Ohlson, J. A. 274
Oxera 327

Palmon, O. 231
Parker, R. H. 3
Pastor, L. 293–94
Patterson, C. S. 131, 132, 261, 267, 280, 292, 311,
  323, 325, 326
Paudyal, K. 291
Petersen, B. C. 138
Peterson, P. P. 196
political risk 252–53
portfolio theory 38–44
Poterba, J. M. 117, 187, 197, 316
Pratt, S. P. 292
Prescott, E. C. 79, 107
production 13–18, 31–32, 144
production function 14, 15, 16–18, 147
production possibility curve *see* production function
project 4
  company and 132–33
  cost of capital and 176
  cost of debt and 313
  financial assets and 154–55
  valuation
    cash flows to discount 137–40, 175–76
    cash flows and taxes 154–57, 160, 178–79,
      193–95

project (*cont.*)
    corporate decision making and 309–10
    equity valuation 179
    financing-related costs and 137–43
    foreign project 248–50, 252–54, 314–15
    Myers–Turnbull model 145, 150–52
    Stiglitz model 185, 201–04
    uncertainty about discount rate 131–32
    under certainty 5–7
    under uncertainty 20–22, 31, 33, 34–36, 124–32
    see also cost of equity, weighted average cost of
        capital
purchasing power parity 236–37, 238–39

Rabin, M. 33
Rajan, R. G. 311
Ramaswamy, K. 201
Rappaport, A. 226
Rashid, M. 232
Read, J. A. 323
real options 132
regulated utilities
    role of cost of capital 323–24, 331–32
    cost of debt 325, 333
    cost of equity
        Brennan–Schwartz model of allowed rate of
            return 330–31
        CAPM 328, 329
        comparable earnings 327
        estimation 327–28, 333
        discounted cash flow (dividend discount model)
            327–28
        effect of regulation 328
    inflation 326
    leverage 327, 333
    rate base 324, 325–27, 332–33
    role of regulator (US) 323–27
    role of regulator (UK) 331–33
    weighted average cost of capital 333
representative individual 16, 29, 69, 70–71
Resnick, B. G. 254
return 5
    rate of 5
    real and nominal 225–32
    taxes and 153, 229–32
Rhee, S. G. 143–44, 194
Riding, A. 286, 288
Riener, K. D. 213
Rietz, T. A. 109
Riggs, H. E. 128
Riley, J. G. 20
risk aversion 26–27, 33, 34–36, 106–08, *see also*
    utility functions
risk-adjusted discount rate 127, *see also* cost of capital
risk-free rate or risk-free return 29, 36, 43, 233
    applying CAPM and 278–81
    consumption-based models and 76, 105, 108, 113
    equity risk premium and 90
    inflation and 228
    multiple countries 237, 239, 241–42, 246–47
risk neutrality 26, 75

risk premium 26, 28, 29–31, 55, 70, 73–74, 76–77
    currency 239–41
    default 234
    definitions 232
    inflation 226–27, 234, 280
    foreign 253
    liquidity 235
    term 114–16, 233
    time horizon and 127–28
    see also equity risk premium, multifactor models
Robichek, A. A. 128, 323
Roll, R. 49–52, 53, 61, 126
Romer, D. 148
Ross, S. A. 52, 53, 55
Ruback, R. S. 104, 178–79, 214–15
Rubinstein, M. E. 69, 70, 143, 166
Rutterford, J. 262, 278, 282, 291, 315

Samuelson, P. A. 78
Schachter, B. 132
Schaefer, S. M. 220, 224
Schall, L. D. 34, 177, 179, 230, 231
Scholes, M. 61, 196, 212, 224, 286, 287, 288, 289
Schwartz, E. 246, 247, 330
Schwert, G. W. 91
Scott, M. F. 98
Selwyn, L. L. 182
Senbet, L. W. 211, 219, 244, 253–54
Sercu, P. 239–40, 241, 249, 254
separation theorem 14, 19, 32–33
Shao, A. T. 316, 317
Shao, L. P. 316, 317
Shapiro, M. D. 85
shareholder/lender conflict 177
Sharpe ratio 107
Sharpe, W. F. 45, 53
Shiller, R. J. 145, 272
Sick, G. A. 217–20
Siegel, J. J. 91–92, 94, 101, 104, 271
Sinn, H.-W. 191, 195, 197
small companies effect 60
Solnik, B. 241, 246, 247, 250
Stambaugh, R. F. 293–94
Stapleton, R. C. 182
state claim *see* elementary claim
state variable 59, 82–83, 294
states of the world *see* contingent states
Staunton, M. 92–93
Stein, J. C. 140–41
Stein's lemma 106
Stewart, G. B. 276
Stiglitz, J. E. 156, 165, 166, 185, 201–04, 224
stochastic discount factor 32–33, 68–72, 75, 76–77
    conventional discounting and 69
Stocks, Bonds, Bills and Inflation Yearbook 91
Strong, N. C. 213
Stulz, R. M. 237, 239, 241, 250–51
substitution
    intertemporal 110
    marginal rate of 8, 12, 69
substitution effect 11, 13

Sudarsanam, P. S. 145
Summers, L. H. 187, 197, 316, 317
supply curve 13, 15–16
Swaminathan, B. 297
Swoboda, P. 211, 220

Taggart, R. A. 142, 179, 209–10, 213, 214, 226, 327
Talmor, E. 195, 208
Taylor's expansion 74
tax avoidance 223–24
tax clienteles 224
tax shields *see* Miller equilibrium
term premium 114–16, 233
Thaler, R. H. 33, 110–11
Thomas, J. 101, 104, 275, 281
Thomas, S. 197
time preference 10, 15
  marginal rate of 12, 70, 71, 76
  subjective discount rate 24
Titman, S. 195, 261
Tobin, J. 44
Turnbull, S. M. 145, 150–52
two-fund separation 49

Uppal, R. 239–40, 241, 249, 254
user cost of capital 147–48
utility
  expected utility theory 22–24, 33–34
  lifetime 10, 18, 25, 71, 78, 126
  mean-variance 39–41
utility functions 16
  constant relative risk aversion (CRRA) 73–75, 78
  habit and 111–16
  non-expected utility 109–11
  quadratic 40–41, 72, 73

valuation *see* asset, project
value additivity 175–76
Value Line 292
Van Horne, J. C. 220, 227
Vasicek, O. A. 283–84
von Neumann, J. 23

Wang, Z. 60
Water Services Association 261, 267, 323, 329, 332
wealth, maximisation of 14, 31–32, 35, 134, 176–77
weighted average cost of capital (WACC) 155
  ad hoc adjustment for project risk 315–16, 317, 320
  certainty-equivalent approach 217–20
  circularity 174–75
  comments on 180
  corporation tax only 160–62, 312, 318
  corporation and personal taxes 138–39, 182–85, 192, 212–13, 313–14
  estimation 310–15, 317–20
  evidence on how estimated 315
  evidence on tax gain from leverage 219–20, 311
  foreign borrowing and 253–54
  foreign project and 254, 316
  formulas compared 172–74
  inflation and 230–31, 232
  Miller (after-tax) equilibrium and 211–14
  no tax 159–60, 311
  non-perpetual cash flows 168, 185
  risky debt 165–67
  value additivity and 176
  value maximisation and 176–77
Weil, P. 110
Weston, J. F. 162, 175, 219, 237, 311
Whittington, G. 323, 325
Whyte, L. G. 100
Wilkie, A. D. 99–100, 104
Williams, J. 286, 287, 288, 289
Wolfson, M. A. 224
Wood, R. A. 285, 288, 289

Xu, Y. 94

Zechner, J. 211, 220
Zeldes, S. P. 117
Zingales, L. 311
Zodrow, G. R. 194, 197
Zumwalt, J. K. 130, 284–85, 290

For EU product safety concerns, contact us at Calle de José Abascal, 56–1°, 28003 Madrid, Spain or eugpsr@cambridge.org.